The Camera Assistant's Manual

FOURTH EDITION

The Camera Assistant's Manual

FOURTH EDITION

David E. Elkins, S.O.C.

ELSEVIER

AMSTERDAM • BOSTON • HEIDELBERG • LONDON
NEW YORK • OXFORD • PARIS • SAN DIEGO
SAN FRANCISCO • SINGAPORE • SYDNEY • TOKYO
Focal Press is an imprint of Elsevier

Focal Press

Focal Press is an imprint of Elsevier
30 Corporate Drive, Suite 400, Burlington, MA 01803, USA
Linacre House, Jordan Hill, Oxford OX2 8DP, UK

Library of Congress Cataloging-in-Publication Data
Elkins, David E.
The camera assistant's manual / David E. Elkins.—4th ed.
p. cm.
Includes index.
ISBN 0-240-80558-5
1. Cinematography—Handbooks, manuals, etc. I. Title.
TR850.E37 2005
778.5′3—dc22

2004018939

British Library Cataloguing-in-Publication Data
A catalogue record for this book is available from the British Library.

For information on all Focal Press publications
visit our website at www.books.elsevier.com

05 06 07 08 09 10 9 8 7 6 5 4 3 2 1

Printed in the United States of America

To my father,
who always believed in me

Contents

Preface

The fourth edition of this book includes all of the information from the previous three editions along with expanded sections and new information. Chapter 3, Second Camera Assistant, contains new sections, including one that discusses dealing with the film lab, one about the effects of x-rays on motion picture film and transporting exposed film on airplanes in this time of heightened security along with some basic information about working in video. Chapter 4, First Camera Assistant, has an expanded camera prep section, focusing tips for the 1st AC and basic information about working in video. Chapter 5, Problems and Troubleshooting contains additional problems you may encounter and how to deal with them. Chapter 6, Cameras, contains many new illustrations of cameras and magazine threading diagrams. Appendix B, Equipment, includes names of some of the most commonly used video cameras and some new items in the section on Specialized Camera Equipment. Appendix C, Camera Department Checklists, Production Forms, and Labels, has been expanded to include many new forms and labels that may be needed by the camera department during the course of a production. All of the forms from the third edition have been revised and improved for this edition. Also included in this appendix is a newly designed camera report especially for use on video productions. All of the forms and labels in Appendix C are available for download on the companion website for this book. Added to Appendix D, Tools and Accessories, is a list of special tools for the working camera assistant and Appendix E, Tables and Formulas, contains many updated and useful tables and formulas you may need. In addition, there is a companion website for this edition that contains much of the information from the book. The web address is www.cameraassistantmanual.com. For those of you that buy this new edition, you should have all the information you need in order to start your career as an assistant cameraman.

In a recent review of the third edition, a reviewer wrote, "I find it highly unlikely that someone who has never been on a film set would buy this book." I found that statement quite amusing, because in the many years since the first edition came out I have had many people thank me for writing the book and telling me how much it helped them when they first stepped onto a film set. Many beginners as well as professional camera assistants have this book in their ditty bag.

As you read this edition, you may notice that some items are repeated from one chapter to another. One of the most important aspects of the job is clear communication between crew members. Part of this communication involves repetition of orders and requests. When a Director of Photography (D.P.) requests a specific lens, filter, or other accessory to be placed on the camera, the assistant always repeats it back to him. When the D.P. announces the t-stop to be set on the lens for a specific shot, it is always repeated back. The repetition of the orders and requests is important to ensure smooth operation of the film set and communication among the camera crew. In light of this, I have chosen to repeat some things from one chapter to the next to stress the importance of repetition of orders.

As a motion picture camera assistant, you must be constantly aware of many things happening around you during the performance of your job. There are many responsibilities and duties that a camera assistant should know about. This book is intended to be a guide for the beginner who would like to learn to become a camera assistant. Because of all of the information, including tables and charts, the book is also meant to be used by working professionals. When I first started in the film industry, there was no book that explained how to do the job of a camera assistant. Even while I was in film school, there was no course dealing with this specific area of production. All my training came from on-the-job work experience. I hope that with this book any student or beginning filmmaker who wishes to become a camera assistant will find it a little easier to learn the job duties and responsibilities. And for those working professional camera assistants, I hope that this new edition will be a valuable reference source that will always be kept in your ditty bag. With the knowledge obtained from this book, it should be easier to obtain your first job because you will at least know the basics and should have no trouble applying them to actual shooting situations. While this book will provide the basic information needed to do the job, nothing beats on-the-job training. Actually being on set and doing or observing is the best way to learn.

I begin with a description of the basics of cinematography in Chapter 1, because many readers of this book may have no previous photography or cinematography experience. This introduction will help beginners to understand much of the terminology used throughout the book. In Chapter 2 there is a description of the chain of command within the camera department and how each member works with and relates to the others. I chose to cover the job responsibilities of a Second Camera Assistant in Chapter 3, and then move on to the First Camera Assistant in Chapter 4. My reason for this is that when most people first start in the camera department, they start as a Second Camera Assistant or Loader. Once they have worked at that position for some time, they move up to First Camera Assistant. The length of time spent at each position depends on each person's situation or preference. Chapter 5 discusses problems that may arise, and what you should do to either correct or prevent them. This is an important part of the job of a camera assistant. Despite careful checking of the equipment prior to production, something inevitably goes wrong at the worst possible time. If you know how to troubleshoot many of the most common problems, you will show that you are a professional and will most likely be hired on many more productions. Chapter 6 contains illustrations of most of the currently used cameras and magazines, and Chapter 7 contains some tips and guidelines on what to do before you have the job, once you are working, and after the job is over. Chapter 7 also contains information on the camera union including how to join, examples of the fees for joining, and examples of rates of pay. All of the information in these chapters is based on my experience as a camera assistant and from tips or advice other members of the camera department have given me.

The appendices cover five areas: film stock, equipment, checklists, tools and accessories, and tables. Appendix A is a complete listing of all film stocks available from the various manufacturers at the time of publication. It lists the recommended exposure index (EI) ratings for each stock for different lighting conditions. Appendix B lists the names of the most common pieces of equipment that you will be working with and should know about. Appendix C contains checklists for camera rental items, filters, and expendables that are usually needed on each production. In addition I have included some typical production forms and labels that the camera assistant may need in the day-to-day performance of the job. Some of these forms and labels are my design based on industry standards, and some I have specially designed based on my experience. Appendix D lists the basic tools and accessories that a camera assistant needs to do the job. Appendix E contains many useful tables and formulas that you may need to refer to in the day-to-day course of your job.

Following the appendices is a list of recommended books for the camera assistant who would like to learn more about the film industry. The Glossary lists many of the key terms used in the book and their meanings. Included in the Glossary are the items on the expendable list, camera rental items, and various filters mentioned in the book.

Acknowledgments

In preparing this book I have used the knowledge and information received from many friends and colleagues. I would like to extend my deepest thanks to all who have contributed their ideas and helped me in the preparation of this book and throughout my career. Special thanks go to many people who have been especially helpful.

Thanks so much to Arri, Panavision, and Filmtools for providing the images used in the cover design of this edition. To the many Directors of Photography with whom I have worked, including Eric Anderson, Ken Arlidge, Arledge Armenaki, Richard Clabaugh, Robert Collins, Steve Confer, Greg Easterbrook, Robert Ebinger, Paul Elliott, David Fang Yuen, Tom Fraser, Victor Goss, Kim Haun, Gerry Lively, Paul McIlvaine, D.A. Oldis, Tony Palmieri, Marvin Rush, Aaron Schneider, Stephen Sealy, John Schwartzman, Randy Sellars, Tom Spalding, Joe Urbanczyk, Richard Walden, and Mark Woods, thanks for all your help and understanding. To my fellow camera assistants who have shared many of their ideas, Chip Bailey, Bobby Broome, Michael Cardone, Gina DeGirolamo, Buddy Fries, Chris Goss, Beth Horton, David Huey, Duane Manwiller, Michael Martino, Kelly McGowan, Michael Millikan, Steve Monroe, Chris Mosely, Haywood Nelson, Chris Poncin, Maricella Ramirez, Brian Sorenson, Scott Ressler, Tim Roarke, Pat Swovelin, Ray Wilbar, and all the others whose names I cannot remember, thanks for the many enjoyable hours of working together. To all the other crew members on the various productions on which I have worked, thanks for making each workday a little more interesting and enjoyable.

I would like to extend a very special thanks to cinematographer David W. Samuelson for his help and encouragement. Thank you so much for allowing me to reproduce many of the illustrations from your books, *The Panaflex Users Manual* and *Hands-On Manual for Cinematographers*. Without your support this book would not be complete. Thank you so much.

I would also like to thank Jon Fauer, the author of many great books including the *Arriflex 16SR Book* and the *Arriflex 35 Book*. Thanks so much for allowing me to reproduce some of the illustrations from those excellent books. Your support is greatly appreciated.

To the employees at the various camera rental houses, Birns & Sawyer, Clairmont Camera, Keslow Camera, Otto Nemenz, Int., Panavision, Inc., Panavision Hollywood, and Ultravision, thanks for all the help before and during the many productions we have done together. To Brian Lataille, thanks for the information about the Steadicam. To Larry Barton of Cinematography Electronics, thanks for providing me with much needed information. To Bill Russell and Franz Wieser at ARRI Inc.; Frank Kay, Dan Hammond, Phil Radin, and Jim Roudebush at Panavision; Matt Leonetti at Leonetti Camera; Conrad Kiel and Philip Kiel at Photosonics; Gary Woods at Aaton; and Grant Loucks at Alan Gordon Enterprises, thanks for letting me use the various illustrations included in the book. Thanks to Sandra Kurotobi at Fuji Film for providing copies of Fuji film can labels. Thanks to John Mason, Mike Brown, Kerry Driscoll, and Lori Hannigan from Eastman Kodak for their support and for providing the illustrations of the Kodak film can labels. Thank you to Donald Burghardt for allowing me to reproduce pages from his Camera Log Book. Thanks to Walt Rose of Foto Kem for granting permission to reproduce the Foto Kem camera reports and purchase order form. To David Eubank, thanks for providing the many screen shots from your excellent software programs, pCam, pCine, and Eubank's Log. Thanks to 2nd AC Leon Sanginiti, Jr. for his excellent contributions to the chapter dealing with the Second Camera Assistant. To Mike Denecke, thanks for letting me use the illustration of the Time Code Slate. To Rudy at the Paramount Studios Camera Department, thanks for your help. Thank you to B. Sean Fairburn, Victor Goss, Steve Heuer, Ryan Sheridan, and David Speck for providing information on working in video and HD. Special thanks to John Ames for proofreading the material on working in video or HD, and making suggestions and contributions to that information. Thanks to Jeremy Boon for drawing some of the illustrations that I could not find anywhere else. Special thanks to my colleague Joe Lopina for drawing many of the illustrations of the tools and equipment used by an assistant cameraman. Thanks to Matthew A. Petrosky and Steve Pedulla for their ideas and insight and special thanks to Matt for his contributions to the forms and his knowledge of new equipment and technology. To Nicole Conn for allowing me to use the names "Demi Monde Productions" and "Claire of the Moon" in the various examples and illustrations in the book, thanks for letting me have so much fun on your film. Thanks to Pat Swovelin for his 2nd A. C. Pointers. To Tim Roarke, thanks for being a great friend and colleague.

To the former staff of Columbia College-Hollywood, especially Allan Rossman and Dianne McDonald, thank you for your help and guidance. Thanks to the students for keeping me inspired and excited about this business. To Mike Hanly for giving me some insight on dealing with a camera rental house, thanks for your help. To Richard Clabaugh, who spent many hours reading the final manuscript of the first edition and offering his suggestions, thanks for your time and effort.

Thanks to the current and former faculty and staff at The North Carolina School of the Arts School of Filmmaking for their help, support, and encouragement. Special thanks go to Arledge Armenaki, Richard Clabaugh, Robert E. Collins, David Fang Yuen, Cindy Baggish, William Buck, Steven Jones, Gerald Paonessa, Sam Grogg, Dale Pollock, Eleanor Cowen, Drew Detweiler, Brandon Johnson, Tiger Poston, Joc Lopina, Eric Self, Robert Hackney, Brian O'Connell, Kim Tafoya, Alice Thompson, and Janice Wellerstein. And thanks to all the students for their enthusiasm and spirit that reminds me every day of why I got into this business.

To everyone that I have worked with at Focal Press since the first edition was published, including Karen Speerstra, Sharon Falter, Marie Lee, Valerie Cimino, Tammy Harvey, Terri Jadick, Elinor Actipis, Theron Shreve, and Cara Anderson, thanks for making the writing of this book a little easier because of your help and guidance.

Thanks to my family and friends for being understanding and supportive. To Peter, Janet, Fred, Doreen, Paul, Karen, and Candy, thanks for always being there.

And finally to my wife Jan, thank you for your love, support, and understanding. You have filled my life with much joy and happiness, and you make each day so special. With love always.

Introduction

The process of motion picture photography started when George Eastman introduced the first 35 mm film in 1889, and Thomas Edison, along with his assistant W.K.L. Dickson, designed the Kinetograph and Kinetoscope, also around 1889. The Kinetograph was used to photograph motion pictures and the Kinetoscope was used to view them. These early pieces of equipment were very basic in their design and use. As film cameras became more complex, a need developed for specially trained individuals to work with this new technology and equipment. Two of these individuals became known as the First Assistant Cameraman (1st A.C.) and the Second Assistant Cameraman (2nd A.C.).

One of the most well known of the early cinematographers was Billy Bitzer, who shot most of the films of director D.W. Griffith. As a cameraman he did all of the jobs himself: carrying the equipment, setting it up, loading film, and so on. In 1914 D.W. Griffith hired an assistant to work with the cameraman. This assistant was called a camera boy, and his job was only to carry the equipment for the cameraman. Each morning, the camera boy would move all of the equipment from the camera room to wherever the scenes were being shot for the day. There was a lot of equipment, and many trips back and forth were required to get everything in place. In addition, the camera boy was required to take notes of what was being shot. There were no script supervisors at that time.

Around 1916, cameraman Edwin S. Porter asked for an assistant, after returning from a long location shoot. This camera assistant had some additional duties that the camera boy did not have. Because all of the early cameras were hand-cranked, the assistant had to count the number of turns of the crank and keep a log of the number of frames shot. Other duties included slating the scene, keeping track of footage, loading and unloading film, carrying and setting up the equipment, and anything else that the assistant may have been asked to do.

Because these two early cameramen had an assistant, a new position was created within the camera department. Many of the techniques of these early cameramen and assistants were probably passed on to others, and they developed into the very specific job duties performed today by the 1st A.C. and 2nd A.C. Some of those early job duties are still part of the camera assistant's job requirements. Because this was such a new technology, the early camera assistants had no one to learn from, so they probably set most of the guidelines for performing their specific jobs. Each had specific responsibilities but was also capable of doing the other's job if necessary.

Today, a beginning filmmaker has a wide choice of places to get the training to work as a camera assistant. There are many colleges and universities that offer a complete curriculum dealing with motion picture production. In addition to the larger institutions, many smaller colleges and trade and technical schools offer film classes. There are also many schools and training facilities that now specialize in training filmmakers in the many crafts associated with filmmaking. In addition, there are many specialized workshops that teach very specific aspects of film production. There are workshops for camera operating, camera assisting, editing, and much more. These workshops may be 1 or 2 days long or possibly even 1 or 2 weeks long. They are usually very intense and teach a great deal of information in a very short period of time.

Instead of attending one of these schools, a beginning filmmaker may know someone in the film industry who is willing to train him or her, and give that important first break. I know many film professionals who have never attended film school but obtained their training and experience by starting out working on various productions. There is no right or wrong way to gain the experience. It is a matter of which way is best for you.

If you choose to attend film school, the best way to gain actual production experience is to work on as many student film productions as possible. Even though these productions are done on a much smaller scale than most professional productions, the basics will be the same, and you can apply what you have learned in your film classes. When you start looking for that first professional job, any experience, even if it is on a student production, increases your chance of getting a job. For those who do not wish to go to film school, or perhaps cannot afford the cost, it may be a little more difficult to obtain that first job. If you have an acquaintance or relative in the film industry, it may be a little easier. For me, film school was a valuable and rewarding experience. I was hired on my first production as a production assistant only 1 month after completing film school. That position led to my first job as a 2nd A.C. on the same film. The film crew was going to do some second unit shooting and needed a 2nd A.C. to load magazines and keep camera reports. The production manager had been a classmate of mine in film school, and he recommended to the Director of Photography (D.P.) that I be given the chance to work as the 2nd A.C. on the second unit. The D.P. gave me the opportunity to prove that I could do the job, and this led to my first job on a feature film as 2nd A.C.

You must be willing to work hard, not only at getting the job but also once you have the job, to prove that you are capable of handling it. If you have been in film school recently, an excellent way to learn about available jobs is to talk to your instructors. Ask them if they know about any productions that you may be able to work on. You also should stay in contact with other film students who were in your classes. There are also a few publications that come out daily or weekly that deal strictly with the film industry. Two of the most popular of these are *The Hollywood Reporter* and *Daily Variety.* Both publications have a listing of productions being done now or sometime in the future. The list often contains phone numbers or addresses to obtain more information about each production. These two publications also have web sites that contain listings of upcoming productions, but you must become a subscriber to access much of the web information. Unfortunately often by the time you obtain the listing and call or send a resumé the position has been filled. In addition, many of the listings are specifically for union jobs, which can be filled only by members of the specific guild or union. There is more discussion on union versus non-union work in Chapter 7. In addition to the various publications, there are many great web sites devoted entirely to the film industry, some specifically for listing jobs and crew positions available.

When you first try to get a job on a film, you may be asked to work for little or no money. The production company may be just starting out and have only enough money for the basic expenses. Or they may expect you to prove you can do the job before they offer you any pay. If you can afford to take such a job, it is an excellent way to get some experience. Three of my first jobs as a camera assistant were without pay, but they helped me to get paying jobs later because I had proved that I could do the job and was not afraid to work long, hard hours. Not everyone will find it necessary to work for free. I mention it only so that you know what you might encounter when you first start looking for work. The important thing to remember is not to get discouraged and give up. The film industry is a very competitive business; breaking into it may take awhile. If you don't get the first few jobs you apply for, keep trying. If you want a job bad enough and are willing to work, you will eventually find one.

Once you do start working in the industry, always stay in contact with people with whom you have worked in the past. Call them periodically just to say hello and find out what they are doing. They may be working on a production that needs additional crew members. Also, if you are working on a production that needs additional people, be sure to let other film professionals know about it. This process of keeping in touch with other film crew people is called *networking* and is probably one of the best ways to get jobs. Many of my jobs came from recommendations from people with whom I have worked on other productions. Also, many D.P.s will call me back to work with them on other productions.

Another good way to break in to the business is to get a job at a camera rental company. This is a good way to learn about the wide variety of camera equipment and accessories that an assistant cameraman uses in the day-to-day performance of the job. Working at a rental house will enable you to meet a lot of camera assistants and D.P.s. Developing a good relationship with the assistants and D.P.s will most likely help you get that first job as an assistant. One problem associated with working at a rental house is the fact that you are removed from actual production work for an extended period. This may be acceptable for some people because it provides an opportunity to learn the equipment, but for others it may not work. You must decide what is the best route for you to take and then give it all you've got.

No matter what route you take to break into the film industry, keep in mind that nothing beats on-the-job training. You can learn so much from just being on set and observing how things are done or actually doing the job yourself. Reading books and sitting in a classroom can give you some basics, but until you are actually on set doing the job, you will not fully understand the joy of being a filmmaker.

Good luck to all the aspiring camera assistants who read this book. I hope that you find the motion picture industry to be as exciting and rewarding as I have. And don't forget, work hard but have fun, too.

1

Basics of Cinematography

The motion picture industry uses many terms and principles that are not used anywhere else. To perform your duties as a Camera Assistant, you need to be aware of these terms and the basics of cinematography along with the names of specific pieces of equipment. You will hear many of these terms in the day-to-day performance of your job. By introducing and explaining them here, I hope to make it easier for you as you read the book, as well as the first time you step onto a film set. To my knowledge all of this information is true and accurate and is based on my experience as well as research done in the compilation of this text. If you would like a more in-depth discussion about any of this information, you may consult any of the books listed in the recommended reading at the end of the book.

FILM FORMATS

The term *format* may be used to indicate a few different things in the motion picture industry. When I say film format, I am referring to the size of the film stock being used for shooting. The two primary film formats used for shooting most filmed productions, and the formats that you will most often be working with, are 16 mm and 35 mm. Almost all professional cinematography is shot using one of these two formats. The 65 mm/70 mm format is a popular release print format but is used very infrequently for production primarily because of cost.

The film contains perforations so that it can move through the camera. The perforations may also be referred to as *perfs* or *sprocket holes*. These are equally spaced holes that are punched into the edges of the film so that it can be transported through the camera at a constant speed. Standard 16 mm film contains two perforations per frame on each side of the film. There are 40 frames per foot of 16 mm film. The standard 35 mm format contains four perforations per frame on each side of the film, and there are 16 frames per foot (Figures 1.1 through 1.3).

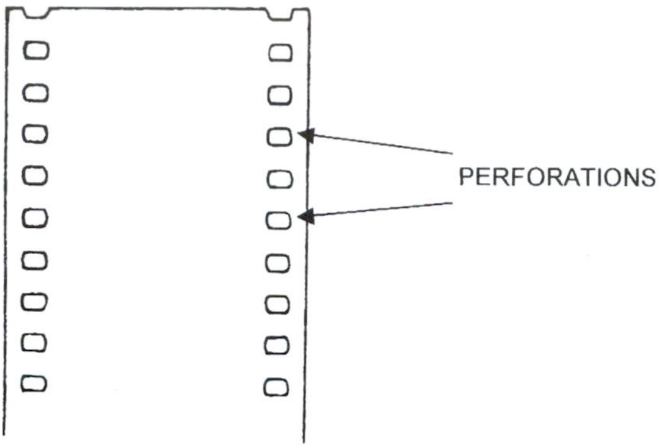

Figure 1.1 A piece of film showing perforations.

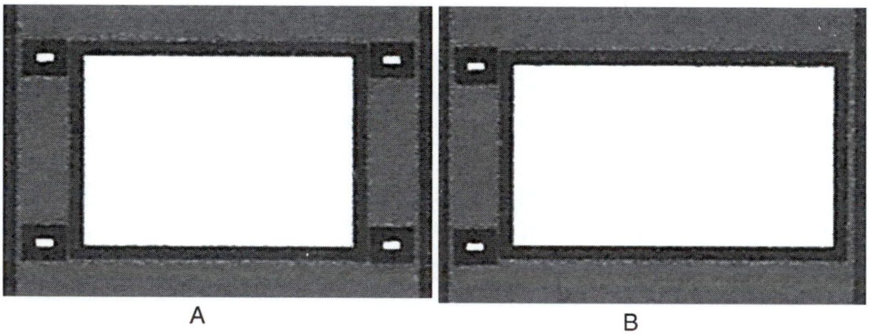

Figure 1.2 **A,** Regular 16 mm film frame. **B,** Super 16 mm film frame.

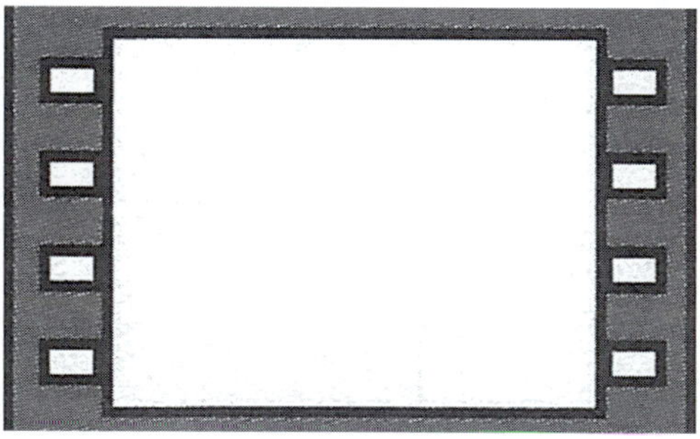

Figure 1.3 35 mm film frame.

The 65 mm/70 mm format is a popular release print format. Many films that are photographed on 35 mm film are enlarged to 65 mm/70 mm for release to theaters. A larger negative will result in a sharper, clearer picture when projected on the big screen. Figure 1.4 shows the 65 mm/70 mm film frame.

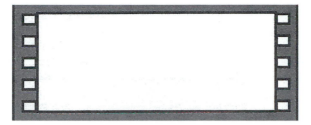

Figure 1.4 The 65 mm full frame.

SYNC SPEED

The term *sync speed* refers to the speed at which the film moves through the camera in order to create the illusion of normal motion when viewed. In the United States, normal sync speed is 24 frames per second (24 f.p.s.). This means that 24 frames of film travel through the camera each second during filming and projection. In Britain and Europe, sync speed is 25 frames per second (25 f.p.s.). Anything filmed at a frame rate less than sync speed will have the illusion of high speed when projected. Anything filmed at a frame rate more than sync speed will have the illusion of slow motion when projected. For the purposes of the examples in this book, I will assume we are shooting at a sync speed of 24 f.p.s. For 16 mm cinematography, at sync speed the film will travel through the camera at the rate of 36 feet per minute. For standard 35 mm cinematography, at sync speed the film will travel through the camera at the rate of 90 feet per minute. For 3-perf, 35 mm cinematography, at sync speed the film will travel through the camera at the rate of 67.5 feet per minute. The 3-perf format is explained later in this chapter.

SYNC AND MOS

The two types of motion picture filming are sync and MOS (pronounced "em-oh-es"). During filming, recording synchronous sound, such as dialogue, along with the picture is referred to as *sync* filming. When we are filming without recording synchronous sound, this is referred to as *MOS* filming. The Hollywood legend says that the term *MOS* came from a German director who could not say "Without Sound." Instead he would say "Mit Out Sound," which gives us the term MOS. The literal translation of the term is Minus Optical Sound. MOS filming is used whenever there is no sound involved or the sound will be added at a later date during post-production.

FILM STOCK

Any piece of motion picture film stock is made up of three main components. Looking at a cross-section of a piece of film shows the three components: emulsion, base, and anti-halation backing (Figure 1.5).

Emulsion

Emulsion is the part of the film that is sensitive to light. It may be light brown (color film) or light gray (black and white film). It uses silver halide crystals suspended in a gelatin substance. Exposure to light causes a change in the silver halide crystals and forms what is called a *latent image*, which means an image that is not yet visible. When the film is developed and processed at the laboratory, it is exposed to various chemicals, forming a visible image. The emulsion layer of a piece of color film is made up of many layers so that it can record all of the colors in the scene. These layers include filter layers, and separate layers each sensitive to one of the three primary colors. Figure 1.6 shows the many layers that make up the emulsion layer of color motion picture film stock.

Base

The base is the flexible, transparent support for the emulsion. In the early days of filmmaking, it was made up of highly flammable cellulose

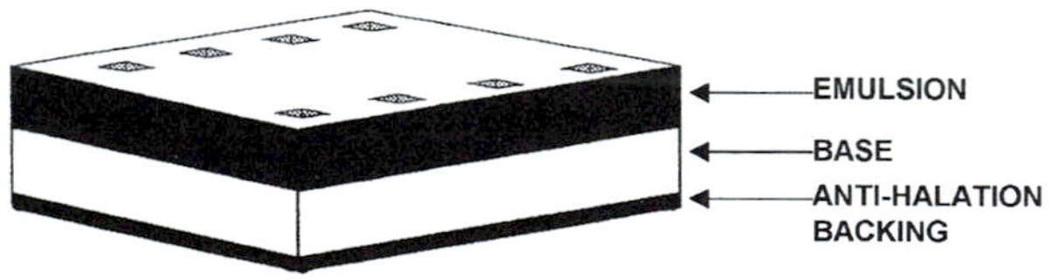

Figure 1.5 Enlarged cross-section of a piece of film (not drawn to scale).

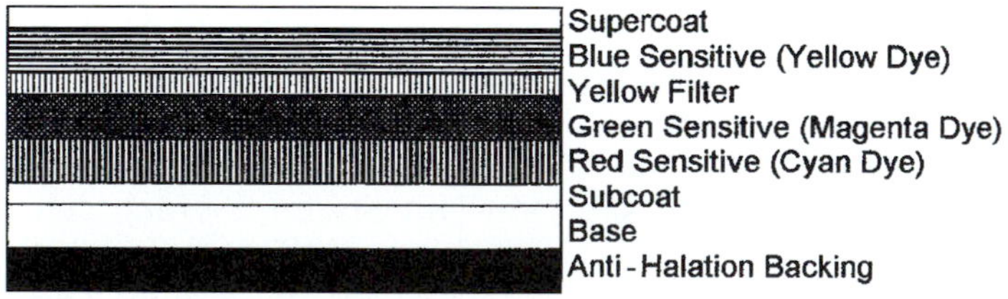

Figure 1.6 The various emulsion layers of color motion picture film.

nitrate. Today the base is made up of a more stable cellulose acetate, which is not flammable and is much more durable and long lasting. The base does not play a part in forming the image on the film, but acts only as a support for the emulsion.

Anti-Halation Backing

The anti-halation backing is the dark coating applied to the back of the base. It is there to prevent light from passing through the film, bouncing off the back of the camera, and then passing through the film again, causing a flare or flash in the image.

TYPES OF FILM

Two main types of film are available for shooting: negative and reversal.

Negative Film

Negative film produces a negative image when developed, in which blacks are white, whites are black, and each color is its opposite or complementary color. A positive print must be made from the negative so that you have something that is suitable for projection and viewing. Recently it has become very common to directly transfer the negative to videotape for editing and projecting. During the transfer process, the colors are switched back to their positive image electronically.

One of the primary advantages of using negative film is the ability to make any exposure corrections during the laboratory printing process. Negative film is also better suited to making a large number of copies, as is done for feature films that are being shown in many different theaters at the same time. For all professional cinematography, negative film is the most commonly used.

Reversal Film

Reversal film produces a positive image when developed, and the camera original can be projected without making a print. A good example of reversal film is Super 8 mm home movie film. Most slide film is also reversal-type film. It is possible to make a print from reversal, but it is not as well suited as negative film for making multiple copies.

FILM STOCK MANUFACTURERS

The two companies that manufacture film stock for professional motion picture productions are Eastman Kodak and Fuji. Since the most widely used film in the motion picture industry is manufactured by Eastman Kodak, most of the examples in this book will use Eastman Kodak Color Negative Film. I am not saying that Eastman Kodak is better than Fuji, but most of the productions that I have worked on have used Eastman Kodak motion picture film. (See Figures 3.3 through 3.6 in Chapter 3 for illustrations of Eastman Kodak and Fuji film can labels.)

Eastman Kodak uses a series of numbers to designate each specific film stock, and they are commonly written in the following manner: 5218-039-051 or 7218-999-8877. The numbers 5218 and 7218 refer to the type of film, 039 and 999 are the emulsion numbers, and 051 and 8877 are the roll numbers of that particular emulsion. It is customary to include both the emulsion number and roll number when asking for the film's emulsion number. To distinguish between 16 mm and 35 mm film stock, Eastman Kodak designates any film stock that begins with the number 72 as 16 mm and any film stock that begins with the number 52 as 35 mm. So, for the example given, 7218-999-8877 is 16 mm film stock and 5218-039-051 is 35 mm film stock.

Fuji designates its film stocks using the prefix 85 for 35 mm film stock and 86 for 16 mm film stock. For example, 8592-301-001 is 35 mm film and 8632-701-01 is 16 mm film. See Appendix A for a complete listing of all current motion picture film stocks available at the time of publication of this edition.

FILM STOCK PACKAGING SIZES

In addition to knowing which film stock to use for your production, you must know what sizes are available for the rolls of film. The size of the roll is based on what camera system you are using. Certain cameras only accept specific size rolls of film. For example, 16 mm film is available on rolls ranging in length from 100 to 1200 feet, and 35 mm film is available on rolls ranging from 100 to 2000 feet. See Figure A.2 in Appendix A for a complete listing of all currently available motion picture film stock packaging sizes.

Film stock may be packaged on a daylight spool or on a plastic core. Daylight spools, sometimes called camera spools, allow you to load or unload the film in daylight or subdued light, while film wound onto a plastic core must be loaded or unloaded in complete darkness. See Figure 1.7 for an illustration of 16 mm and 35 mm daylight spools.

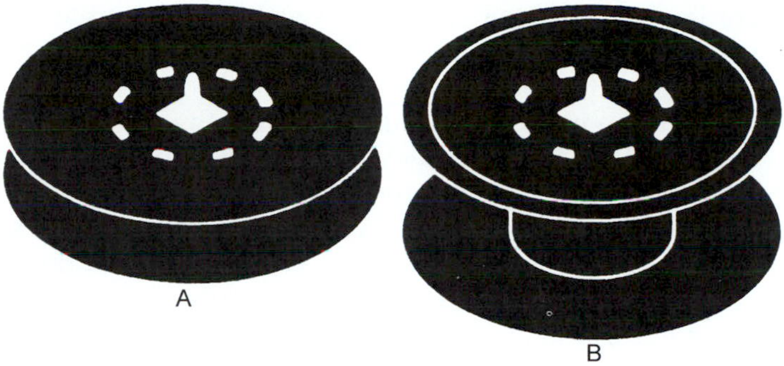

Figure 1.7 **A,** 16 mm daylight spool. **B,** 35 mm daylight spool.

See Figure 1.8 for an illustration of 16 mm and 35 mm plastic film cores.

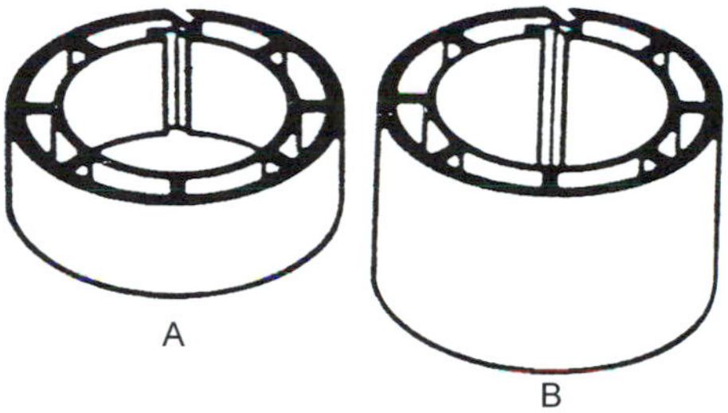

Figure 1.8 **A,** 16 mm 2-inch plastic core. **B,** 35 mm 2-inch plastic core.

EXPOSURE INDEX OR ASA

All motion picture film is sensitive to light in varying intensities. The measurement of how sensitive a particular film stock is to light is called the film speed and is expressed by an *exposure index* (EI) or *ASA number*. Today most motion picture film can labels list the film speed as an EI number.

The larger the EI or ASA number, the more sensitive the film is to light, and the less light it needs for a proper exposure. The smaller the EI or ASA number, the less sensitive the film is to light and the more light it needs for a proper exposure. In other words, a film stock with an EI of 500 is more sensitive to light than a film stock with an EI of 200. This means that to obtain an exposure, you need less light with EI 500 film than with EI 200 film.

There is a standard series of EI numbers used to rate the film's light sensitivity: 12, 16, 20, 25, 32, 40, 50, 64, 80, 100, 125, 160, 200, 250, 320, 400, 500, 650, 800, 1000, etc.

In theory these numbers go infinitely in both directions. By looking closely at this list you will see that the values double every three numbers. What this means is that every three numbers equals a change of one full f-stop, or each ASA or EI value is equal to 1/3 of a stop.

In the upcoming section on f-stops, you will see that there is also a standard series of f-stop numbers, which in theory also go infinitely in both directions. As stated in that section, each f-stop number admits half as much light through the lens as the f-stop number before it. This means that a change of one full f-stop either doubles the amount of light or cuts it in half. So doubling or dividing in half the ASA or EI number is the same as doubling or dividing in half the amount of light. As an example, the same amount of light that gives you an exposure of f/4 at ASA 200 will require an f/5.6 at ASA 400 or an f/2.8 at ASA 100.

The EI or ASA is determined by the film's manufacturer based on extensive testing of the film. This number is what the manufacturer feels will give the "best" or "ideal" exposure of the film. Each film can label should show the recommended EI rating for the film stock, for both daylight and tungsten light. The ultimate decision on what speed to rate the film is up to the Director of Photography, and is usually based on his or her experience in using the particular film stock.

COLOR TEMPERATURE AND COLOR BALANCE

For professional cinematography, each light source is considered to be a different color and therefore has what is referred to as a different *color temperature.* The human eye cannot accurately distinguish between the different colors of light, but motion picture film stock is much more sensitive.

Scientists take what they refer to as an ideal substance, or "black body", and heat it. They then measure its temperature as it emits different colors of light. Think of this black body as a piece of coal being heated up. As this substance gets hotter it begins to glow different colors, first yellowish-orange, then red, then blue, and so on. The color of the light is then identified by the temperature at which it became that color. This temperature is called color temperature. Reddish color light has a lower color temperature and bluish color light has a higher color temperature. Color temperature is measured in degrees Kelvin (K), which is a temperature scale used in physics.

The two main types of light sources for professional cinematography are referred to as daylight and tungsten light. Daylight has a color temperature of approximately 5600 degrees Kelvin, written as 5600° K, and is bluish in color. Daylight is obviously the light source outside during the day, which is actually a combination of sunlight and skylight, while tungsten light refers to professional motion picture lighting fixtures used to create artificial light. Tungsten light has a color temperature of approximately 3200 degrees Kelvin, written as 3200° K, and has a reddish-orange color. All film stocks have a particular color balance, and when we refer to any certain film stock, we say that it is either daylight balanced or tungsten balanced.

When filming in a particular light source it is usually common to use a film stock that is color balanced for filming in that type of light. Daylight-balanced film can be shot in daylight without making any adjustments to the light or adding any filters to the camera or light source to correct the color temperature. Tungsten-balanced film can be shot in tungsten light without making any adjustments to the light or adding any special filters to the camera or light source to correct the color temperature. You may use either film in the opposite type of light, but you must place a specific filter on the camera or light source in order to correct for the difference in color temperature. These specific filters are discussed later in this chapter in the section on filters.

ASPECT RATIOS

The shape of the image frame is expressed as a ratio of its width to its height. This is referred to as the *aspect ratio* of the image. The three most commonly used aspect ratios for filmed productions are 1.33:1, read as "one three three to one"; 1.85:1, read as "one eight five to one"; and 2.40:1, read as "two four oh to one." The 1.33:1 aspect ratio may also be referred to as *academy aperture*. It is 1.33 times as wide as it is high. Many of the early motion pictures were shot using this aspect ratio. Academy aperture is also often said to have an aspect ratio of 1.37:1. Present-day television still uses the academy aperture, and any films shot strictly for television are usually shot using the academy aspect ratio (Figure 1.9).

The standard aspect ratio for most theatrical motion pictures is 1.85:1. This format is usually referred to simply as "one eight five." This wider format is obtained by chopping off the top and bottom portions of the academy aperture to give an image that is exactly 1.85 times as wide as it is high (Figure 1.9).

The 2.40:1 aspect ratio is also called *anamorphic,* and the image is 2.40 times as wide as it is high. To obtain this aspect ratio, a special anamorphic lens is used that squeezes the wider image onto a standard 35 mm frame of film. When the image is projected, it is unsqueezed to

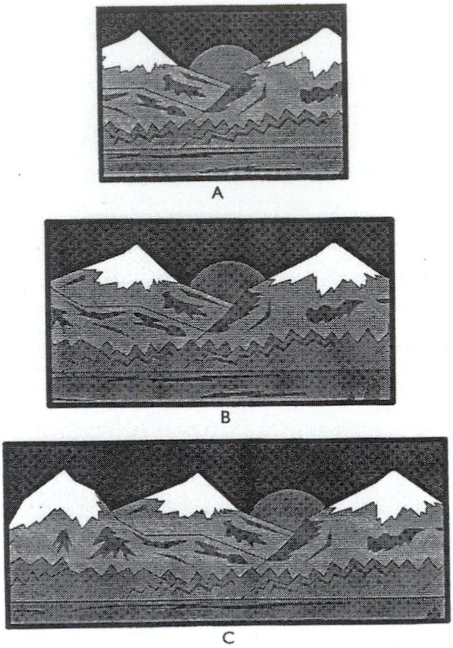

Figure 1.9 Comparison of 1.33, 1.85, and 2.40 aspect ratios: **A,** 1.33:1. **B,** 1.85:1. **C,** 2.40:1. (Courtesy of Panavision, Inc.)

produce the wide screen image. Depending on whom you speak with or what reference material you use, the anamorphic aspect ratio may also be listed as 2.35:1 or 2.36:1 (Figure 1.9).

In addition to the aspect ratios previously named, two others that are commonly used are 1.66:1 and 1.78:1. The 1.66:1 aspect ratio is also the aspect ratio used when shooting Super 16 mm film format. The 1.78:1 aspect ratio may also be referred to as 16 × 9 format and is often referred to as HDTV (high definition television). The new HDTV televisions have a screen that is almost the same aspect ratio as the standard 1.85:1 movie screen (Figure 1.10).

When shooting 35 mm film, Super 35 is a common way to go. Super 35 is essentially 1.33:1 aspect ratio, and it is the largest frame area you can have on a 35 mm film frame. By having this larger frame area, Super 35 allows you to use a combination ground glass in the camera and a common top frame line for the shot, thereby allowing multiple print formats to be struck from a single original negative. By using the proper ground glass or viewing screen in the camera and framing properly, you would be able to obtain an anamorphic (2.40:1) print from a Super 35 frame, as well as a standard theatrical print

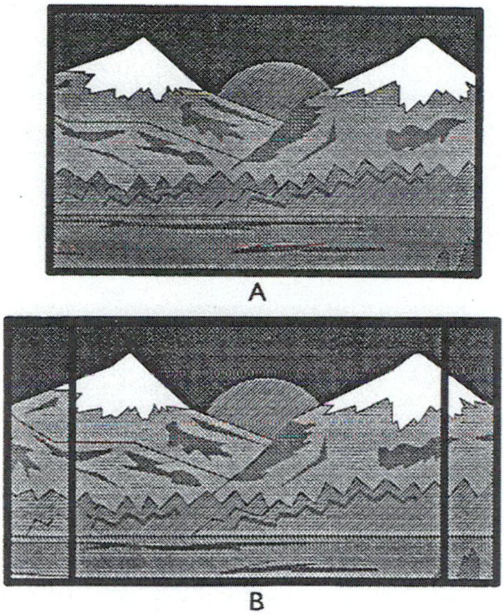

Figure 1.10 **A,** 1.66:1 aspect ratio. **B,** 1.78:1 aspect ratio (HDTV). (Courtesy of Panavision, Inc.)

(1.85:1) and an image size appropriate for video or television presentation. To obtain a wide screen image from the Super 35 frame, an optical print is required, which adds to the total cost.

It is not uncommon, when shooting, to frame for two different formats at the same time. You may be shooting a feature film, but we all know that most films eventually end up on television. By having a combination ground glass such as a TV/1.85, you can frame the shots accordingly so that they will look correct on a movie screen, as well as when formatted for television. The 35 mm full camera aperture illustrated in Figure 1.11 shows the Super 35 mm film frame. As indicated, this frame can be used for multiple aspect ratios.

There are many different formats for shooting, and which one to use is often the decision of the Director of Photography, Director, and sometimes even the Producer. This decision determines which ground glass is going to be ordered for the camera. See Figures 4.36 through 4.38 in Chapter 4 for illustrations of the many ground glasses available for both Arriflex and Panavision 16 mm and 35 mm cameras. Many of these the ground glasses are marked for multiple formats.

Some camera manufacturers have recently developed camera systems that are designed to reduce film waste. Instead of the standard four perforations per frame, these systems use three perforations per frame of 35 mm film, resulting in a 25% savings in film use. When

INTENDED ASPECT RATIO	SIZE	DESCRIPTION
16 x 9	.3775 X .2123	Digital CCD Area
16 x 9 (2.40:1)	.3775 X .1579	Digital CCD Extended Area for Anamorphic
1.37 : 1	.404 X .295	Regular 16mm Camera Aperture
VARIOUS	.486 X .295	Super 16mm Camera Aperture
VARIOUS	.980 X .735	35mm Full Camera Aperture
2.40 : 1	.825 X .690	Anamorphic Projection Aperture
1.85 : 1	.825 X .446	35mm 1.85 : 1 Projection Aperture
2.40 : 1	.945 X .394	Super Panavision 35mm Extracted Area for Anamorphic Projection
1.33 : 1	.792 X .594	35mm TV Transmitted Area *(SMPTE recommended practice)*
	.713 X .535	35mm TV Safe Action
1.78 : 1	.945 X .531 (16 x 9)	4-Perf Transmitted Area
VARIOUS	.980 X .546	Panavision 3-Perf 35mm Camera Aperture
1.78 : 1	.910 X .511 (16 X 9)	3-Perf Transmitted Area
2.20 : 1	2.072 X .906	65mm Camera Aperture
2.20 : 1	1.912 X .870	70mm Projection Aperture *(Panavision Super 70mm)*
2.40 : 1	1.912 X .797	Extracted for 2x Projection

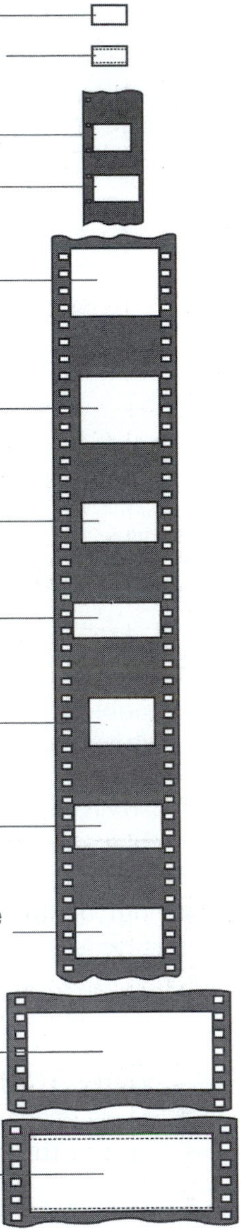

Figure 1.11 Examples of Panavision aspect ratios. (Courtesy of Panavision, Inc.)

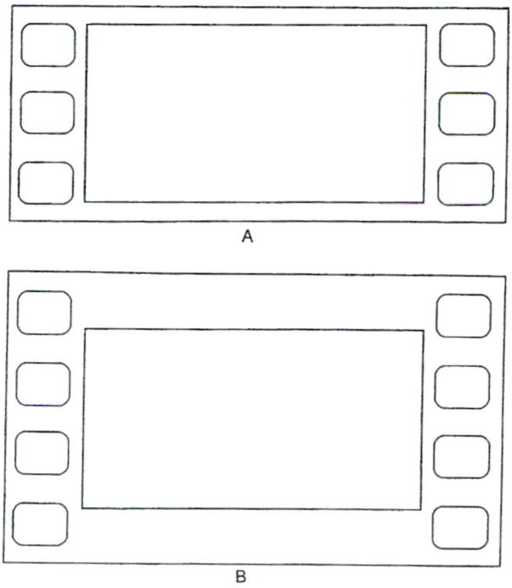

Figure 1.12 **A,** 1.85 film frame when using 3-perf cameras. **B,** 1.85 film frame when using 4-perf cameras. (Courtesy of Panavision, Inc.)

shooting 1.85:1 aspect ratio and even 1.78:1 aspect ratio, and using 4-perf 35 mm film cameras, the top and bottom part of the film frame are wasted. By using 3-perf cameras there is almost no wasted film. Check with the camera rental company for the availability of 3-perf pull down cameras (Figure 1.12).

There are also two additional aspect ratios that are used primarily for special effects or other special applications: Imax and Vistavision. With both of these the film is transported sideways or horizontally through the camera. They both require the use of special cameras, with Vistavision using standard 35 mm film, and Imax using 65 mm film.

EXPOSURE TIME

The length of time that each frame of film is exposed to light is called the exposure time. At sync speed, film is traveling through the camera at the speed of 24 frames per second. This means that each frame is traveling through the camera at a speed of 1/24th of a second. For half the time, the film is being moved in and out of position in an area of the camera known as the gate, and for half the time it is being held steady in the gate so that it can be exposed to the light entering the lens. Half of 1/24th of a second is equal to 1/48th of a second. For convenience this is rounded to the nearest tenth, making it 1/50th of a second. Most light meters are calibrated with a setting for 1/50th of a second. This is the actual amount of time that each frame of film is being exposed to the light. Therefore, at sync speed we say the standard exposure time for all motion picture photography is 1/48th or 1/50th of a second.

F-STOPS AND T-STOPS

All motion picture lenses contain some type of adjustable iris or diaphragm to control the amount of light that enters the lens and strikes the film. A wide opening allows more light to strike the film than a small or narrow opening. The measurement of the width of this opening is called an *f-stop*. The standard series of f-stop numbers is 1, 1.4, 2, 2.8, 4, 5.6, 8, 11, 16, 22, 32, 45, and so on.

It is important to remember that the f-stop numbers go infinitely in both directions. All lenses are marked along the barrel of the lens with these f-stop numbers. By turning the diaphragm or iris adjustment ring on the lens barrel to a specific number, you are adjusting the size of the iris diaphragm within the lens and controlling how much light gets through to the film. Each f-stop admits half as much light through the lens as the f-stop before it. In other words, an f-stop of 4 admits through the lens half as much light as an f-stop of 2.8. Conversely, each f-stop admits twice as much light through the lens as the f-stop after it. In other words, an f-stop of 5.6 admits through the lens twice as much light as an f-stop of 8. It is also important to remember that as the f-stop numbers get larger, the opening of the iris diaphragm gets smaller.

In addition to f-stops, there is a more precise representative of the amount of light reaching the film through the lens. This is called a *t-stop*. While an f-stop is a mathematical calculation based on the actual size of the opening of the diaphragm, a t-stop is a measurement of the true amount of light transmitted through the lens at a particular diaphragm opening. The t-stop takes into account any light that is lost due to absorption through the many optical elements of the lens. The t-stop is more accurate and should always be used when setting the exposure on the lens. F-stops and t-stops are discussed further in Chapter 4.

EXPOSURE METERS

To determine the correct exposure setting for the particular shot, we measure the intensity of the light with an *exposure meter* or *light meter.* The two basic types of light meters used for measuring the exposure of an object are incident meters and reflected meters.

Any light that is falling on an object is called *incident light* and is measured with an *incident light meter.* The meter contains a white, translucent dome called a *photosphere,* which is mounted over a light sensor. The photosphere simulates a three-dimensional object, such as the human face, and averages the light falling on an object from all angles. The recommended and standard way to use an incident light meter is to stand at the position of the subject being photographed and point the photosphere toward the camera when taking the light reading (Figures 1.13 and 1.14).

Any light that bounces off or is reflected by an object is called *reflected light* and is measured with a *reflected meter.* The light that is reflected by an object is based on the color and texture of the object.

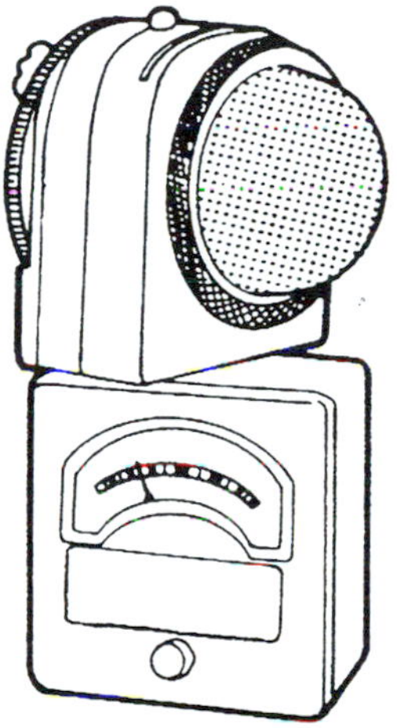

Figure 1.13
Spectra incident light meter.

Incident Meter
is pointed at camera
from subject position

Figure 1.14 Using the incident light meter.

A white object reflects more light than a black object. A smooth object reflects more light than a textured object of the same color. The area in which a reflected meter actually reads the light is called the *angle of acceptance*. The most commonly used reflected light meters are called spot meters and have a very narrow angle of acceptance, usually around 1 degree. The recommended and standard way to use a spot meter is to stand at the position of the camera and point the meter toward the subject being photographed (Figures 1.15 and 1.16).

In recent years a new type of light meter has been introduced that is becoming quite popular among cinematographers. It is a combination meter that combines an incident and reflected light meter into one compact light meter. These combination meters are a bit more expensive than purchasing either an incident or reflected meter separately. The good news is that they are usually a bit less expensive than if you

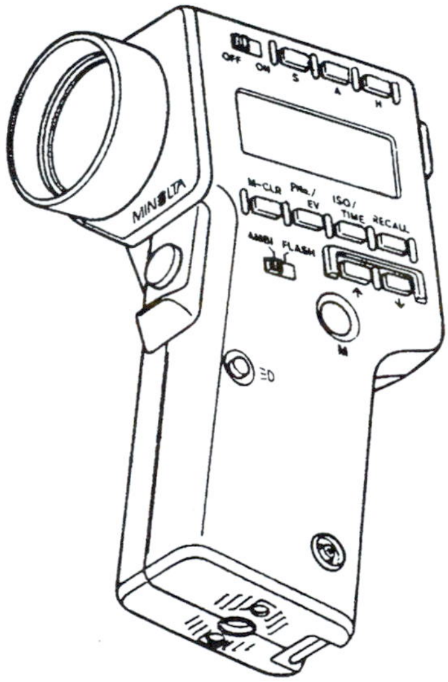
MINOLTA

Figure 1.15
Minolta reflected (spot) meter.

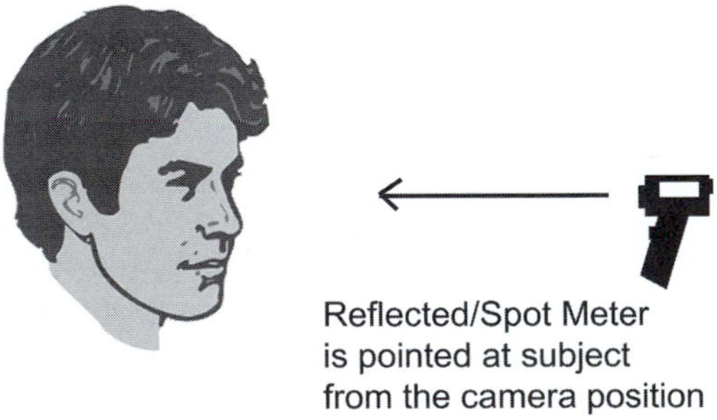
Reflected/Spot Meter
is pointed at subject
from the camera position

Figure 1.16 Using the reflected (spot) light meter.

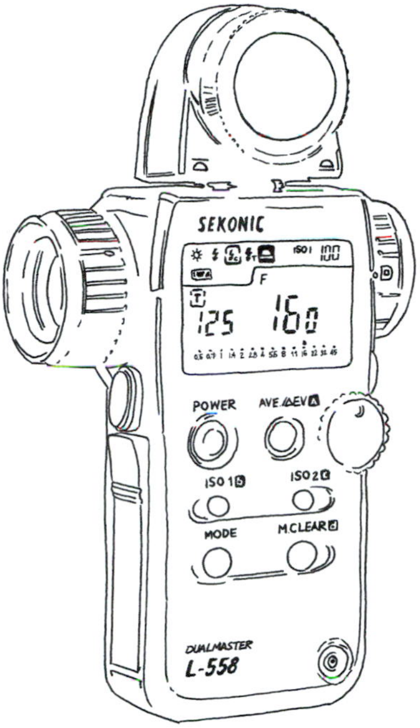

Figure 1.17
Sekonic combination light meter.

were to purchase both an incident meter and a reflected meter. One advantage of the combination meter is that you don't need to have two separate meters to measure the light (Figure 1.17).

THE CAMERA

All motion picture cameras are made up of many different components and accessories. Each camera manufacturer has its own specific design for the various parts, and these parts are usually not interchangeable from one make of camera to another. A basic motion picture camera may be made up of the following components: gate, shutter, inching knob, viewing system, lens, magazine, and motor. There are many more specific components that are used on all motion picture cameras that you will learn about as you work as a camera assistant. For now I will discuss only these basic parts.

Gate

The gate may be described as the opening in the camera that allows light passing through the lens to strike the film. It may also be referred to as the *aperture*. We sometimes refer to the entire area within the camera where the film is exposed as the gate. As the film moves through the gate, it moves by a process known as intermittent movement.

Intermittent Movement

To the human eye, it appears that the film is constantly moving as it travels through the camera. Actually, as the film moves through the camera, each frame is held in place in the gate for a fraction of a second before it moves on and is replaced by another frame. While the film is held in the gate for this fraction of a second, it is being exposed to light. The process of holding one frame of film in the gate, and then moving it, so that the next frame is brought into position, is called *intermittent movement.* This process of starting and stopping the film happens at the rate of 24 frames per second, which we learned earlier is called sync speed.

As the film travels through the camera, it will most likely pass through one or more sprocket wheels or rollers, in either the magazine, the camera, or both. These rollers or sprocket wheels help move the film into and out of the gate area. To relieve some of the tension on the film between its continuous movement as it passes through the rollers, and the intermittent movement in the gate area, you will often thread the film with a loop before it enters the gate and another loop after it exits the gate. This loop is nothing more than a slack length of film between the rollers or sprocket wheels and the gate, which acts as a buffer between the intermittent movement and the continuous movement of the film (Figures 1.18 and 1.19).

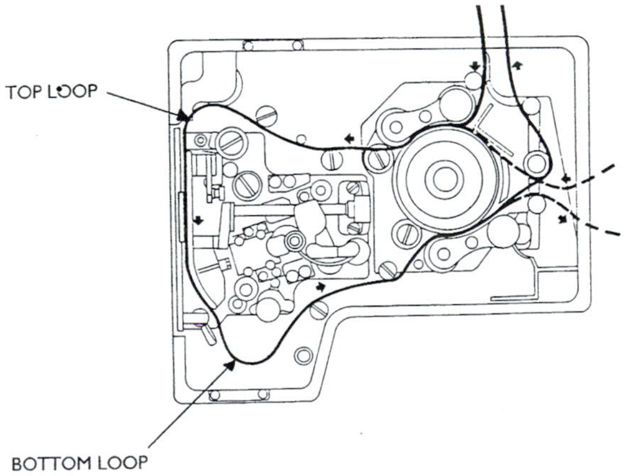

Figure 1.18 Threading diagram showing the loops in the Panavision camera. (Reprinted from the *Panaflex Users Manual* with permission of David Samuelson and Panavision, Inc.)

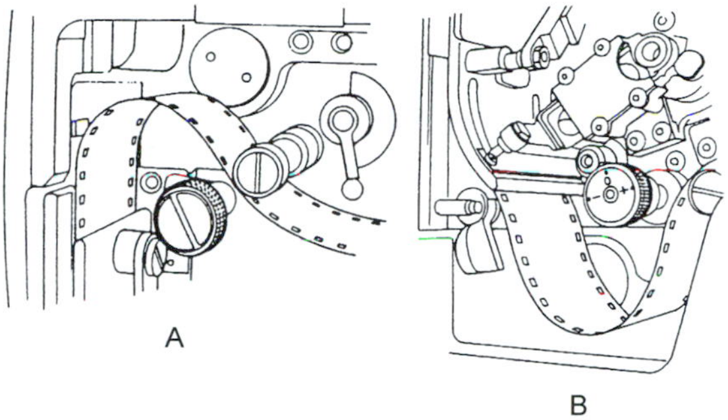

Figure 1.19 Close-up detail of top and bottom loops in the Panavision camera. **A,** Top loop. **B,** Bottom loop. (Reprinted from the *Panaflex Users Manual* with permission of David Samuelson and Panavision, Inc.)

There are four components to the gate area that work together to make this intermittent movement happen.

Pull Down Claw To move the film, a small hook or claw engages into a perforation in the film and pulls it through the gate. This small hook or claw is called the pull down claw. Each camera contains some type of pull down claw to move the film. Some of the more advanced cameras, especially those used for special effects cinematography, contain two pull down claws (Figures 1.20 and 1.21).

Registration Pin Once the pull down claw pulls the film into the gate so that it may be exposed, it must be held perfectly still during this exposure process. A small metal pin engages into the film's perforation and holds it in place so that it may be exposed. This small pin is called the *registration pin*. Some 16 mm cameras do not have the registration pin, but because of their design, the film is held securely in the gate area to ensure a steady image. As with the pull down claw, some of the more advanced cameras, especially those used for special effects cinematography, contain two registration pins (Figures 1.20 and 1.21).

Aperture Plate The metal plate that contains the opening or aperture through which light passes to the film is called the *aperture plate*. The opening may be called the *gate* or the *aperture* (not the same as the lens aperture or f-stop) and is usually the same size as the aspect ratio being used. The term *aperture* means "an opening," and we usually speak separately of lens apertures and camera apertures (Figures 1.20 and 1.21).

Pressure Plate The area where the film is being held in the gate during exposure is called the *film plane* or *focal plane*. To keep the

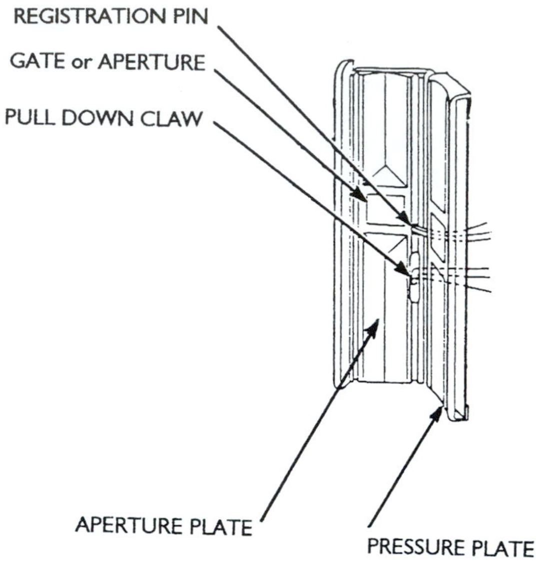

Figure 1.20 Gate area of Arriflex 16S camera showing various components. (Courtesy of ARRI Inc.)

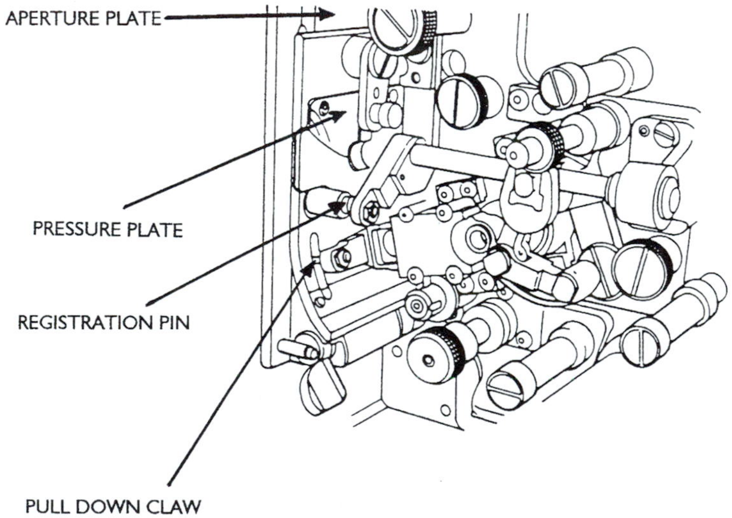

Figure 1.21 Panavision 35 mm gate area showing various components. (Reprinted from the *Panaflex Users Manual* with permission of David Samuelson and Panavision, Inc.)

film flat against the aperture plate during exposure, the camera contains a small metal plate located behind the film that pushes it against the aperture plate and keeps it flat and steady in the gate area. This small metal plate is called the *pressure plate* because it puts pressure against the film (Figures 1.20 and 1.21).

When referring to the gate, most camera personnel usually are referring to the entire area in the camera that contains the pull down claw, registration pin, aperture plate, and pressure plate.

Shutter

A basic definition of the shutter is that it is an on/off switch for the light striking the film. The shutter is mechanically linked to the other parts of the intermittent movement so that its timing is synchronized with the movement of the pull down claw and registration pin. The shutter spins and alternately allows the light to either expose the film or allows the light to go to the viewfinder eyepiece so that the camera operator may see the image. As the pull down claw moves the film into position, the shutter is in the closed position so that no light strikes the film. Once the frame of film is in place and being held by the registration pin, the shutter is then in the open position so that the light may strike the film and create an exposure.

Shutter Angle

The opening in the shutter that allows the light to strike the film and create an exposure is called the *shutter angle*. A typical shutter is circular in design and the standard shutter angle for motion picture production is 180 degrees. On all professional motion picture cameras, you will have either a fixed 180-degree shutter or a variable shutter that can be adjusted to different shutter angles. Changing the shutter angle affects how long the film is exposed to light. Reducing the shutter angle reduces the amount of time that the film is being exposed to light, and increasing the shutter angle increases the amount of time that the film is being exposed to light. A variable shutter is sometimes used to achieve some type of exposure effect or visual effect. It sometimes helps to have a variable shutter when filming sports or any other fast-action scene. A cinematographer may want to change the exposure of a shot without affecting depth of field; this can be achieved by changing the shutter angle.

Depending on the model of the camera, the shutter may be adjusted during the shot, or only while the camera is not running. Check with the rental house if you are not sure if the camera has an adjustable shutter or how the adjustable shutter operates. In most cases the shutter will be one of two types, a standard solid 180 degree shutter, sometimes referred to as a half-moon shutter, or a double-bladed 180 degree shutter, sometimes referred to as a butterfly shutter (Figures 1.22 and 1.23).

In addition to the rotating mirror shutter, some cameras, such as those from Panavision, contain a focal plane shutter. The focal plane shutter is located at the film plane or focal plane, and it is what controls the light striking the film, while the mirror shutter is only for the reflex viewing system (Figure 1.24).

Inching Knob

Most professional motion picture cameras contain an *inching knob.* This is usually a small knob, located either inside the camera body or on the outside of the camera. By turning this knob you are able to slowly advance or "inch" the film through the camera movement to check that it is moving smoothly. Whenever you thread the film into the camera, you should turn the inching knob a few turns to check that the film is traveling smoothly and not binding or catching anywhere.

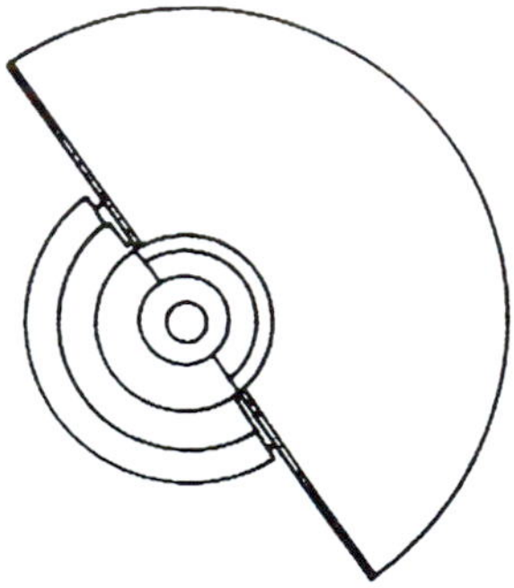

Figure 1.22
Standard or half-moon shutter. (Reprinted from the *Hands-On Manual for Cinematographers* with permission of David Samuelson.)

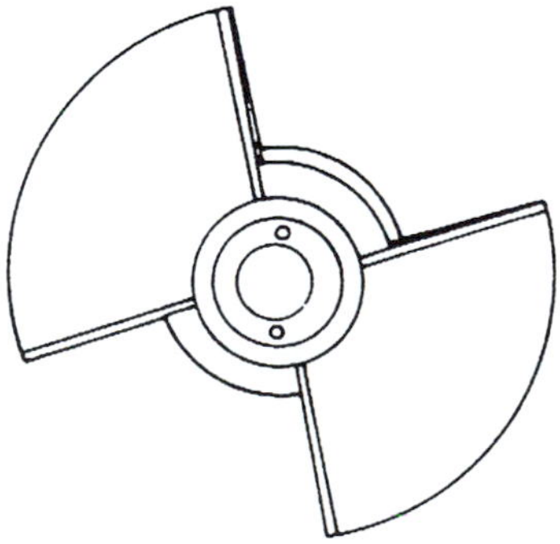

Figure 1.23
Double-bladed or butterfly shutter. (Reprinted from the *Panaflex Users Manual* with permission of David Samuelson and Panavision, Inc.)

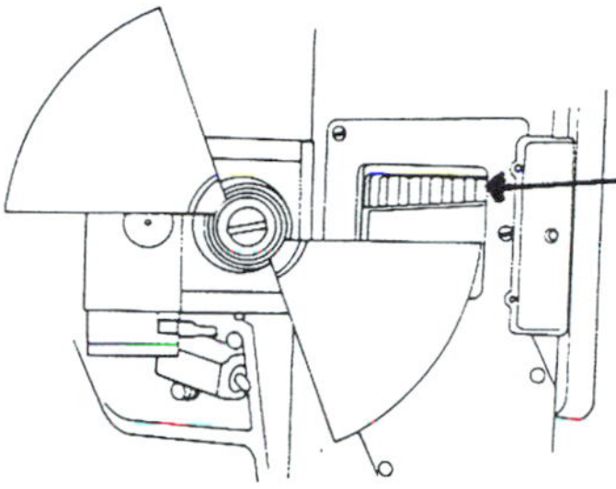

Figure 1.24 Panavision focal plane shutter. (Reprinted from the *Panaflex Users Manual* with permission of David Samuelson and Panavision, Inc.)

Failure to turn the inching knob before turning on the camera could result in torn film (Figure 1.25).

Viewing System

The viewing system or viewfinder allows the camera operator to view the scene. There are three basic types of viewing systems that have been used on motion picture cameras over the years. The rack over viewing system and direct viewfinder are older viewing systems that are not used today for most professional motion picture productions and are not discussed here. The current standard viewing system for professional motion picture cameras is the mirrored-shutter reflex viewfinder system. A reflex viewfinder is one that allows you to view the image directly through the lens, even during filming. The mirrored-shutter reflex system means that the rotating shutter is actually a spinning mirror. As the shutter spins and is in the open position, all of the light entering the lens strikes the film and creates an exposure. When the shutter is closed, all of the light is reflected off the mirror and

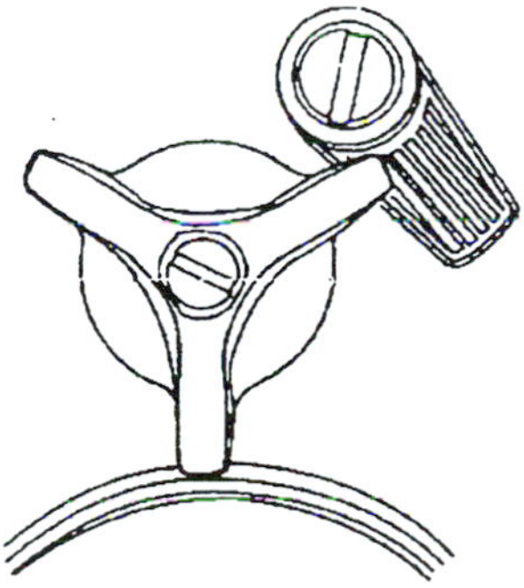

Figure 1.25
Inching knob on Panavision camera. (Reprinted from the *Panaflex Users Manual* with permission of David Samuelson and Panavision, Inc.)

directed to the eyepiece for the camera operator to view the shot (Figure 1.26).

Diopter Adjustment

Because of the differences in each person's vision, the viewfinder of most cameras has an adjustable diopter. By setting the diopter according to your particular vision, the image will appear in focus when you look through the eyepiece, providing the lens focus is set correctly. To adjust the diopter, it is best to remove the lens, but it can be done with the lens in place. You then point the camera at a bright light source or white surface. While looking through the eyepiece, turn the diopter adjustment ring until the crosshair or grains of the ground glass in the viewfinder are sharp and in focus. A further discussion of the viewfinder adjustment is located in Chapter 4.

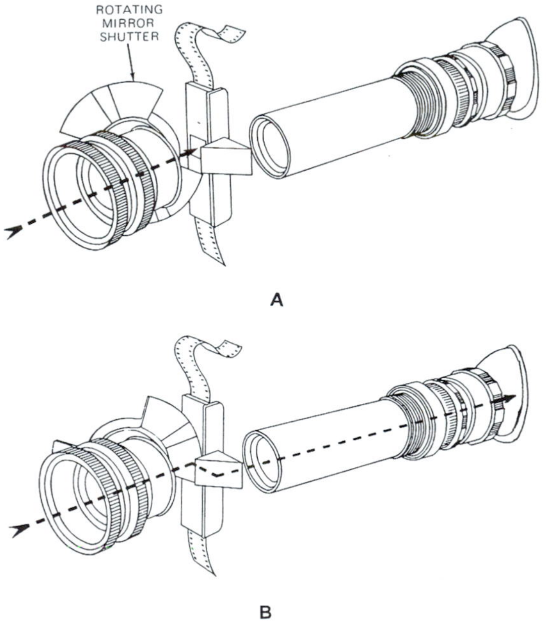

Figure 1.26 Simple mirror reflex viewfinder system. **A,** With mirror shutter open, all light is directed to the film. **B,** With mirror shutter closed, all light is directed to the eyepiece. (Courtesy of ARRI Inc.)

Lens

A technical definition of a lens is a device containing one or more pieces of optically transparent material, such as glass, which bends the rays of light passing through it, causing them to focus at a point. This point is called the *film plane* or *focal plane*, and the light causes an exposure on the film's emulsion at this point. All lenses are referred to by their focal length, and it is the focal length that determines the size of the image. The technical definition of *focal length* is the distance from the optical center of the lens to the film plane when the lens is focused at infinity. The *optical center* is a mathematical point within the lens that is determined by the lens manufacturer. The focal length of the lens is always measured in millimeters (mm).

There are three general categories of lens focal lengths: telephoto, normal, and wide-angle. When filming in the 35 mm film format, it is generally accepted that a lens with a focal length of 50 mm is considered a normal lens because it approximates an image size that is the same as that seen by the human eye. In the 35 mm film format, as a general rule, any lens that has a focal length less than 50 mm may be called *wide-angle*, and any lens that has a focal length more than 50 mm may be called *telephoto*. When filming in the 16 mm film format, it is generally accepted that a lens with a focal length of 25 mm is considered a normal lens. In 16 mm, as a general rule any lens that has a focal length less than 25 mm may be called wide-angle, and any lens that has a focal length more than 25 mm may be called telephoto. A wide-angle lens will distort the image because it exaggerates distances and makes small rooms seem larger than they actually are. A telephoto lens compresses objects together and makes them appear closer than they actually are.

Primes and Zooms

While wide-angle, normal, and telephoto are categories of focal lengths, when we speak of the physical lens itself we refer to two basic types. *Prime lenses* have a single, fixed focal length that cannot be changed. Some examples of prime lenses are 18 mm, 25 mm, 32 mm, 75 mm, and so on. *Zoom lenses* have variable or adjustable focal lengths that can be changed during shooting. By turning the barrel of the zoom lens, you are able to change the focal length. Zoom lenses are most often referred to by their range of focal lengths, such as 12 mm to 120 mm, or 12 to 120, 25 mm to 250 mm, or 25 to 250, etc. (Figures 1.27 and 1.28). A further discussion of lenses can be found in Chapter 4.

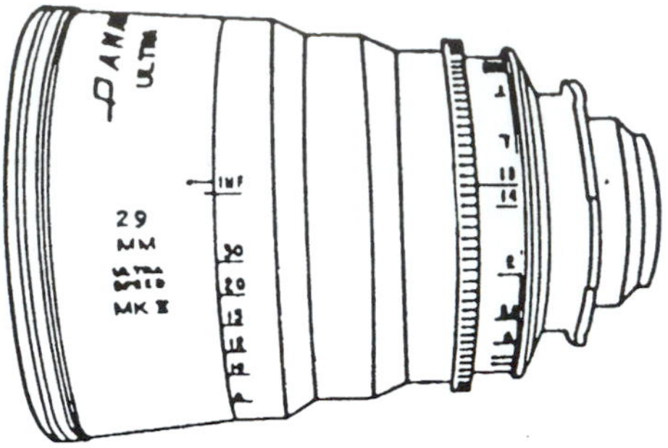

Figure 1.27
Prime lens. (Reprinted from the *Panaflex Users Manual* with permission of David Samuelson and Panavision, Inc.)

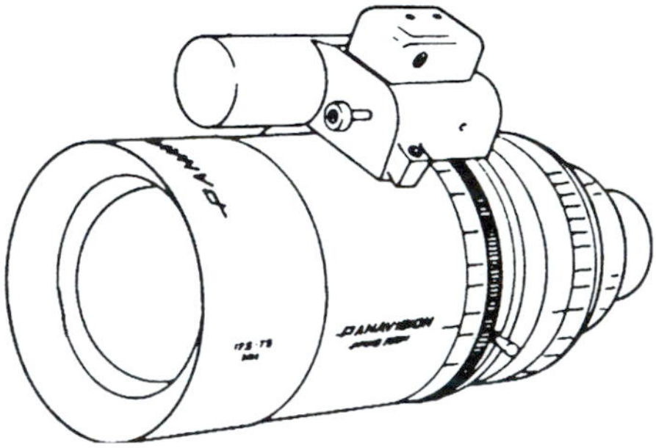

Figure 1.28
Zoom lens with zoom motor attached. (Reprinted from the *Panaflex Users Manual* with permission of David Samuelson and Panavision, Inc.)

Magazines

A *magazine* may be described as a removable, lightproof container that is used to hold the film before and after exposure. Each camera uses a different type of film magazine. In any film magazine, the area that holds the fresh, unexposed raw stock is called the *feed side.* The area that holds the exposed film stock is called the *take-up* side. A further and more complete discussion of types of magazines and the procedure for loading and unloading them can be found in Chapter 3.

Motor

The three main types of camera motors are variable, constant, and crystal. Almost all professional motion picture cameras today use a crystal motor. The camera motor contains a crystal that is similar to the crystal found in a quartz watch. The sound recorder also contains a similar crystal. This crystal vibrates at a precise, constant frequency, ensuring that during shooting the camera and sound recorder are running in sync so that the picture and sound will match. Most crystal motors have the ability to run at variable speeds for slow motion or high speed filming, either by use of a built-in adjustable speed control or by using some type of optional speed control device.

When using any professional motion picture camera, it is important to remember that they all contain DC motors and must be powered from a battery source. Depending on the camera you are using, these batteries may be 8, 12, or 24 volts. Batteries come in different sizes and types depending on the shooting situation. The three most common types of batteries are the belt, block, and on-board. Belt batteries are often used for hand-held camera work or in a situation where the block battery is not practical such as when the camera is mounted to a car mount or remote crane. Block batteries are the most common and are used for most studio and location work when the camera is mounted to a tripod or dolly. On-board batteries are batteries that attach directly to the camera and make a very compact package, especially for hand-holding the camera. Be sure that you obtain the proper type and voltage battery for your shooting situation. If unsure about the voltage needed for a particular camera, you should always check with the rental company from where you are renting the camera equipment. Chapter 4 contains illustrations of the various types of batteries.

Additional Camera Components

Depending on the model and age of the camera you are using, it may have some additional components that are worth mentioning briefly. The *footage counter* may either be analog or digital, and it counts off how many feet of film pass through the camera when it is running.

The analog footage counter usually contains a numbered dial that moves whenever the camera is turned on. This dial must first be set to "zero" when loading a fresh roll of film onto the camera. As the film travels through the camera, the numbers on the dial register the approximate amount of film footage exposed. The analog type of footage counter is not very accurate.

The digital footage counter works in a similar way but is much more accurate. Whenever a new roll of film is placed on the camera, the footage counter is reset to "zero." As the film travels through the camera, the footage counter indicates precisely how much film has been used. All of the currently used professional motion picture cameras contain a digital footage counter.

Some older cameras have a *lens turret* on the front of the camera. This allows you to have two or three lenses mounted on the camera at one time. When it comes time to change lenses, you simply rotate the turret until the new lens is in line with the film plane. It is important to remember that you cannot and should not move the lens turret while the camera is running. Some cameras also contain a *buckle switch* or *buckle trip switch*. This switch serves as a safety mechanism within the camera. If the film loop becomes too large or too small, or if the camera runs out of film during shooting, the buckle switch will turn off the camera.

FILTERS

One of the most frequently used pieces of equipment in cinematography is the filter. It is a device that modifies the light reaching the film in order to achieve a specific effect. Filters may change the overall look of the image, change or enhance the color of the image, or simply adjust for the correct color temperature. They may be placed in front of the lens, behind it, or even on the light source.

Most behind-the-lens filters are made of a plastic gel-type material and must be handled carefully. Some cameras contain a small filter slot in the aperture plate or directly behind the lens for the placement of behind-the-lens filters. The types of filters that can be used behind the lens are very limited. Many Directors of Photography use behind-the-lens filters if they need to place more filters in the matte box or in front of the lens, or it may simply be a matter of not wanting to see the filter when looking through the viewfinder. It is important to remember that when using behind-the-lens filters you are not able to see the effect of the filter through the lens. Because of this, you should always place a label on the camera whenever a behind-the-lens filter is being used. This label should indicate what type of filter it is and also that it is behind the lens. This label is a reminder that you have a behind-the-lens filter in place. Without this label, you may forget that the filter is behind the lens.

While working on a feature film as First Assistant Cameraman, I had a problem with a behind-the-lens filter. During one day of filming the Director of Photography asked me to place an 85 gel filter behind the lens. We were using the Panavision GII camera system, so I placed an optically correct 85 gel in one of the gel holders and inserted it in the filter slot on the camera. I then placed a small piece of tape over the filter slot on which I wrote the number 85. At the end of the shooting day, I packed the camera away and forgot to remove the 85 gel behind the lens. The next morning the Director of Photography asked for an 85 glass filter to be placed in the matte box. I put the 85 filter in the matte box and we proceeded to shoot. At the conclusion of shooting the first scene, I suddenly remembered that the 85 gel was still in the camera. I immediately went to the D.P. and told him that the last scene was shot with two 85 filters on the camera, one behind the lens and one in front of the lens. He was very understanding and told me not to worry about it because it was only two thirds of an f-stop difference and it could be corrected in post-production. I removed the behind-the-lens filter and we continued to shoot. Needless to say I was quite embarrassed and vowed to never let that happen again. That night when I packed the camera away I found my reminder tape stuck to the inside of the camera case.

For our purposes, we will deal only with filters that are placed on the camera in front of the lens. Many filters require an exposure compensation based on the color and the density of the filter. Keep in mind that if there is an exposure compensation, you would always open the f-stop the appropriate amount. In other words, if your exposure was an f 5.6 without the filter and your filter requires a compensation of 1 f-stop, your exposure with the filter would be an f 4. If you are not sure about the exposure compensation of a particular filter, check with the rental company where you rented the camera equipment. A quick way to determine the exposure for a particular filter is to take a light reading with an exposure meter in the light you are shooting under. Then hold the filter over the photosphere of the light meter and take another reading. Compare the difference and you will have determined your exposure compensation for that filter. The most common filters, their effect, and any exposure compensation are covered briefly.

Conversion Filters

The most frequently used filters are called *conversion* filters. They are also sometimes referred to as color-correction filters. These are filters that are used to convert one color temperature to another. Because there are two different types of color balance for film (daylight or tungsten), there are two basic types of conversion filters.

85 Filter

When using tungsten-balanced film in daylight, it is usually standard practice to use a number 85 filter to correct the color temperature. This filter converts the daylight color temperature to the color temperature of tungsten light. When using this filter, an exposure compensation of two thirds of a stop is required. The 85 filter is orange or amber.

80A Filter

When using daylight-balanced film in tungsten light, a number 80A filter is used to correct for the difference in color temperature. This filter converts the tungsten color temperature to the color temperature of daylight. When using this filter, an exposure compensation of two stops is required. The 80A filter is blue.

Neutral Density Filters

Many times when filming outdoors in daylight, the Director of Photography may wish to reduce the amount of light entering the lens, or reduce the depth of field for the shot. A neutral density filter would be used to do this. One reason for wanting to reduce depth of field is when filming a close-up of an actor or actress. By reducing depth of field, the background will be out of focus, thereby drawing the viewer's attention to the subject being photographed.

Neutral density filters are usually abbreviated ND filter. The most commonly used neutral density or ND filters are ND3, ND6, and ND9. When using these, you must remember to adjust your exposure accordingly. The ND3 requires an exposure compensation of one stop, the ND6 2 stops, and the ND9 3 stops. For a complete discussion of depth of field, see Chapter 4.

Polarizing Filters

A polarizing filter reduces glare or reflections from shiny, nonmetallic surfaces such as glass and water. To remove the reflections in a shot, you would place the polarizer in front of the lens and rotate it while looking through the viewfinder until you either remove or minimize the reflections. Once the correct position of the polarizer has been determined, be sure to lock it in place so that it doesn't move during the shot. Polarizers are also used quite often to saturate colors when filming outdoors in daylight. It can darken a blue sky and help clouds appear whiter and puffier in the sky. When using a polarizer filter, you must adjust your exposure by 2 stops.

Combination Filters

Any filter that combines two or more filters into one filter is called a *combination filter.* The most common combination filters are those that combine an 85 with the series of neutral density filters to get 85ND3, 85ND6, and 85ND9. Another common combination filter is the 85 plus Polarizer, which is usually called an 85Pola. When using a combination filter, to obtain the correct exposure compensation, add together the exposure compensation for each filter. For example, when using an 85ND6, your exposure compensation would be 2 2/3 stops—2 stops for the ND6 plus 2/3 of a stop for the 85.

Diffusion Filters

When talking about diffusion filters, we may be referring to many types and styles of filters that will give a similar effect. A general definition of a diffusion filter is a filter that is used to soften the image or look of the picture. A diffusion filter is usually made of glass containing a rippled surface, which prevents the light from focusing sharply. It will produce an image in which fine details are not clearly visible. It may also give the appearance that the image is out of focus. One of the most common uses of diffusion filters is to minimize or soften any facial blemishes or wrinkles on an actor or actress. Some names of the most commonly used diffusion filters are Tiffen Diffusion, Harrison & Harrison Diffusion, Black Dot Texture Screen, Black Pro-Mist, White Pro-Mist, Soft Net, Net, Supa-Frost, and Classic Soft.

Two popular types of diffusion filters being used are the Tiffen Black Pro-Mist and the White Pro-Mist. The White Pro-Mist softens the image without causing it to appear out of focus. It also spreads light slightly by creating a small amount of flare from light sources, and it will slightly reduce the contrast. The Black Pro-Mist softens the image with a more subtle flare from light sources and slightly reduces contrast by lightening shadows and darkening highlights. The White and Black Pro-Mist filters require no exposure compensation. Tiffen has recently introduced two new diffusion filters, Warm Pro-Mist and Warm Black Pro-Mist. These filters combine the 812 Warming Filter with the Pro-Mist and Black Pro Mist. With the addition of the 812, the Warm Pro-Mist and Warm Black Pro-Mist require an exposure compensation of 1/3 of a stop.

Soft Nets and Nets actually are in a separate category called *nets*. A net may be any fine mesh type material that is placed on the camera and acts as a diffuser. The Tiffen White Soft Net and Black Soft Net require an exposure compensation depending on the density of the filter. In the early days of filmmaking, many Directors of Photography would stretch a stocking material over the front of the lens to create the diffusion effect. Some filter manufacturers currently offer net filters that have the net sandwiched between two pieces of optically correct clear glass. The Black Dot Texture Screen is a glass filter with a series of random black spots spread across the filter. Light striking this filter spreads out over a wider area, thereby diffusing or softening the image. Black Dot Texture Screens require an exposure compensation of 1 stop. All diffusion filters are available in sets ranging in density from light to heavy diffusion, usually number 1/8, 1/4, 1/2, 1, 2.

Fog Filters and Double Fog Filters

To simulate the effects of fog, we may use a fog filter or double fog filter. In a real fog situation, the fog causes lights to flare, and using a double fog filter best produces this effect. The fog filters are also available in sets ranging in density from very light to very heavy. No exposure compensation is needed when using these filters.

Low Contrast Filters

To lighten the shadow areas of a scene, a Director of Photography may use a low contrast filter. This causes the light from the highlight areas of the scene to bleed into the shadow areas, which produces a lower contrast. In other words, it lightens the shadows without affecting the highlight areas. They do not soften the image or make it appear out of focus as diffusion filters do. As with diffusion and fog filters, they are available in varying densities. No exposure compensation is required for these filters.

Soft Contrast Filters

A soft contrast filter may be used to lower the contrast in a slightly different manner than a low contrast filter. It is different from the low contrast filter because it darkens highlights without affecting the shadow areas. They are also available in varying densities. No exposure compensation is required for these filters.

Ultra Contrast Filters

Another way to lower the overall contrast of a scene is to use the ultra contrast filter. This filter lowers the contrast evenly throughout the scene by equally lightening the shadow areas and darkening the highlight areas. They are available in varying densities and require no exposure compensation.

Coral Filters

To make a scene appear warmer, a Director of Photography may use a coral filter. The coral filter may be used when filming a sunset or a fireside scene to give the scene a warmer look. Another use of the coral filter is when filming outside in daylight. Because the color temperature of daylight changes from early morning to late afternoon, the Director of Photography may use a coral filter along with, or in place of, the 85 filter to give the scene a slightly warmer look. Coral filters come in varying densities, and an exposure compensation is required based on the density of the filter.

Enhancing Filters

To create brighter reds, oranges, and rust browns when filming outdoors, a Director of Photography may use the enhancing filter. While creating spectacular effects on the reds and oranges in the shot, it has very little effect on other colors. This filter is especially useful when filming fall foliage. The enhancing filter requires an exposure compensation of 1 stop.

Graduated Filters

Sometimes we only want to alter a portion of the frame with a specific filter. To do this, the Director of Photography would use a graduated or grad filter. Only half of the filter contains the specific filter, while the remaining half is clear. For example, we may use a Neutral Density Grad or a Coral Grad for certain effects. Some graduated filters also come in varying densities (Figure 1.29).

Diopters

When doing extreme close-up work, we may need to use a special type of filter called a *diopter* on the lens. The diopter is actually a type of lens, but because it is mounted in front of a standard lens, similar to a filter, it is being mentioned here. The diopter acts like a magnifying

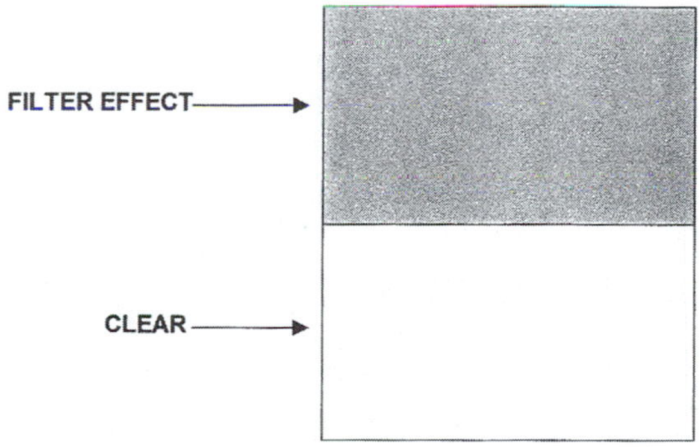

Figure 1.29
Graduated filter.

glass and allows the lens to focus closer than the lens's normal focusing range allows. Diopters come in varying strengths as follows: +1/4, +1/2, +1, +1 1/2, +2, +3, and so on. The higher the number, the closer the lens will focus. The glass of the diopter is curved on one side and, when placing the diopter on the lens, this curved side must face away from the lens. When using a diopter, no exposure compensation is required.

Optical Flat

A special filter that should be included in every camera package is the optical flat. It is an optically correct, clear piece of glass that has many uses. It may be placed in front of the lens to protect the lens for a shot in which something is being projected toward the camera. You also may be shooting in windy situations, where dust and dirt may be blown toward the lens, or on a beach where water may be blown toward the lens. The optical flat will protect the front element of the lens from these items. In addition, it can be used to cut down on the noise level of the camera. Much of the noise from the camera comes out through the lens. By placing an optical flat in front of the lens, you can reduce this noise and achieve a quiet sync sound take during shooting. So, if the Sound Mixer asks you to place an optical flat on the camera, it usually means that he or she is hearing some camera noise through the microphone.

Currently more than 200 types of filters are available. The previously named filters are only a sampling of what is available to the cinematographer. This small listing is intended to give you a basic understanding of the most commonly used filters. Through experimentation and use of the filters, a Director of Photography usually knows which filter to use for a specific application or effect. For a listing of more filters and the common filter sizes, see Appendix B.

Filter Manufacturers

There are many different manufacturers of filters, including Tiffen, Harrison & Harrison, Mitchell, Schneider Optics, Formatt Filters, Ltd., Wilson Film Services, and Fries Engineering.

CAMERA MOUNTS

Many different devices and tools are available for mounting the camera, moving it, and keeping it smooth and steady when following the action within a scene.

Tripod and Spreader

One of the most common supports for the camera is a three-legged device called a *tripod*. Each of the three legs of the tripod can be adjusted in height according to the shot needed. The feet of the tripod are usually placed into an adjustable brace called a *spreader*. The spreader holds the legs in position and keeps them from collapsing when the legs are extended or spread out (Figure 1.30).

If a spreader is not available, many assistants use a piece of carpet measuring approximately 4 feet × 4 feet. The points of the tripod feet will grip the carpet and prevent the tripod legs from moving or spreading apart. The two most commonly used tripods are the standard tripod and the baby tripod. The two names most commonly used to refer to the tripod are "sticks" and "legs" (Figure 1.31).

All tripods have one of two types of top castings for the head to attach to: either the Mitchell flat base or bowl shaped, or ball base (Figure 1.32).

High Hat/Low Hat

For doing extreme low angle shots where a tripod will not work, a mounting device called a *high hat* or *low hat* is used. The high hat or low hat consists of a camera-mounting platform similar to the top casting of the tripod, which is most often mounted to a square piece of plywood. The mounting platform of the high hat or low hat may either be a Mitchell flat base or bowl shaped. By using the high hat or low hat, you are able to get the camera lens just a few inches above the floor (Figure 1.33).

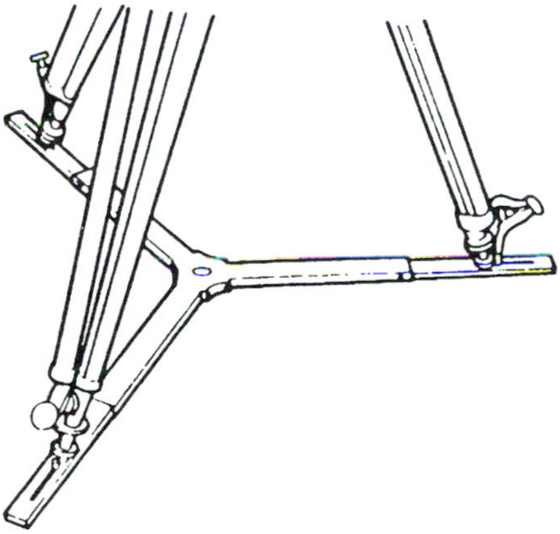

Figure 1.30
Tripod legs locked onto the spreader. (Reprinted from *Motion Picture Camera and Lighting Equipment* with permission of David Samuelson.)

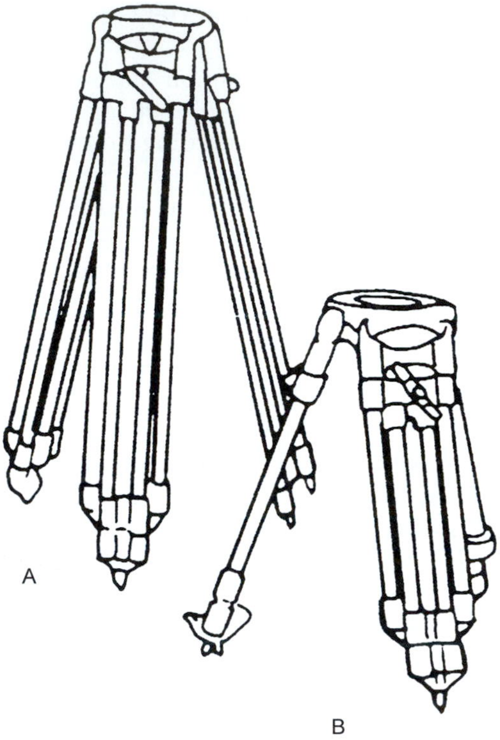

Figure 1.31
A, Standard tripod. **B,** Baby tripod. (Reprinted from the *Panaflex Users Manual* with permission of David Samuelson and Panavision, Inc.)

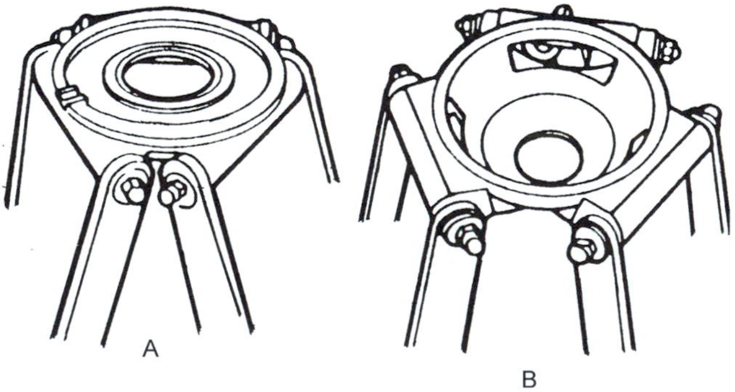

Figure 1.32 Tripod top castings. **A,** Mitchell flat base. **B,** Bowl shaped. (Reprinted from *Motion Picture Camera and Lighting Equipment* with permission of David Samuelson.)

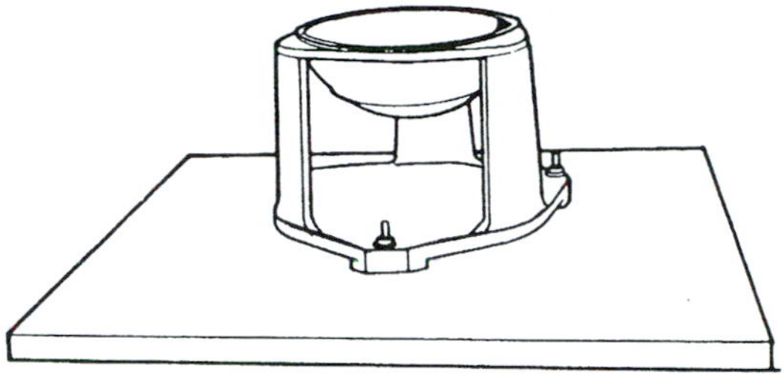

Figure 1.33 High hat with bowl-shaped top casting. (Reprinted from *Motion Picture Camera and Lighting Equipment* with permission of David Samuelson.)

Tripod Heads

To make smooth moves with the camera so that you can follow the action within a scene, the camera must be mounted onto some type of tripod head. This head will allow the Camera Operator to make smooth pan and tilt moves when following the action. Any horizontal movement of the camera to follow the action is called a *pan* or *panning,* and any vertical movement of the head is called a *tilt* or *tilting*. The two most common types of heads are the fluid head and gear head.

Fluid Head

Because of its ability to make smooth pan and tilt moves, the fluid head is the most commonly used tripod head. The internal elements of the head contain some type of viscous fluid, which provides a slight resistance against the movements. There is usually an adjustment on the outside of the head to increase or decrease the amount of resistance. Depending on the type of shot, the Camera Operator may want more or less resistance to make a smooth pan or tilt move. The pan and tilt movements are controlled by a pan handle, which is usually mounted to the right side of the head. By moving the handle left and right, or up and down, you are able to make smooth pan and tilt moves. Some of the most common fluid heads are manufactured by O'Connor, Sachtler, Vinten, Cartoni, Ronford Baker, and Weaver Steadman. When ordering a fluid head, be sure that it contains the same style base as the tripod top casting, either a Mitchell flat base or a ball leveling base (Figure 1.34).

Gear Head

For very precise and smooth movements, you might choose to use a gear head. The pan and tilt movements are controlled by two wheels

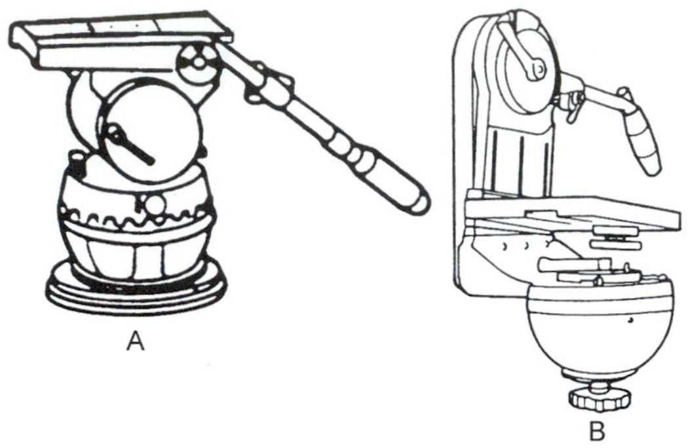

Figure 1.34 Two types of fluid heads.
A, Sachtler head. (Reprinted from the *Panaflex Users Manual* with permission of David Samuelson and Panavision, Inc.)
B, Ronford-7 head. (Reprinted from *Motion Picture Camera and Lighting Equipment* with permission of David Samuelson.)

that are connected to gears or belts within the head. One of the wheels is located to the back of the head and controls the tilt; the other wheel is located on the left side and controls the pan. It takes much practice to be able to operate the gear head correctly, but once you learn it, you will most likely not want to use any other type of tripod head. On most productions, when ordering equipment you would always obtain a fluid head along with the gear head because there are certain shots that just cannot be accomplished with the gear head. Some of the most common gear heads are the Arriflex Arrihead, Panavision Panahead, Worral, and Mini Worral (Figure 1.35).

Steadicam

A highly specialized mounting device for the camera is the Steadicam, a body-mounted harness that is worn by a specialized Camera Operator. It consists of a vest, a special support arm, and the basic Steadicam unit onto which the camera is mounted. The arm consists of six springs that absorb the up-and-down movement of the camera, allowing it to give a steady image. The Steadicam allows the operator to do traveling shots where a dolly or crane is not practical, or to bring an actor from one location to another within the scene, without an edit. With the

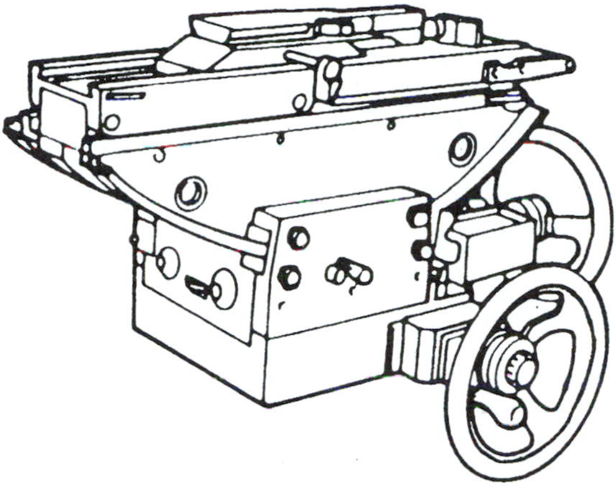

Figure 1.35
Panavision Panahead gear head. (Reprinted from the *Panaflex Users Manual* with permission of David Samuelson and Panavision, Inc.)

Steadicam, the operator can follow an actor while running, up or down stairs or an incline, through a building, in wheelchair-mounted shots, car mount, and many other types of special shots. To be able to use the Steadicam properly, many Camera Operators attend special classes to be certified to use the system. Since the Steadicam was first introduced to the film industry, it has gone through many changes. There have been many different models of the system, including Model I, Model II, Model III, Model III-A, EFP, Master, and Pro (Figures 1.36 through 1.39).

Dolly

A wheeled platform onto which the head and camera may be mounted is called a *dolly*. The dolly often contains seats for the Camera Operator and Camera Assistant. Not all shots in a film are stationary. Some require the camera to move in order to follow the action within a scene. By mounting the camera to the dolly, you are able to do traveling or moving shots very smoothly. The dolly is usually placed on some type

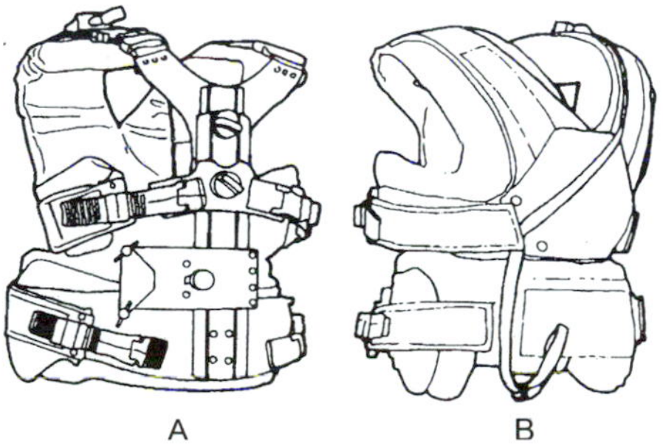

Figure 1.36
Steadicam vest. **A,** Front view. **B,** Back view. (Reprinted from the *Hands-On Manual for Cinematographers* with permission of David Samuelson.)

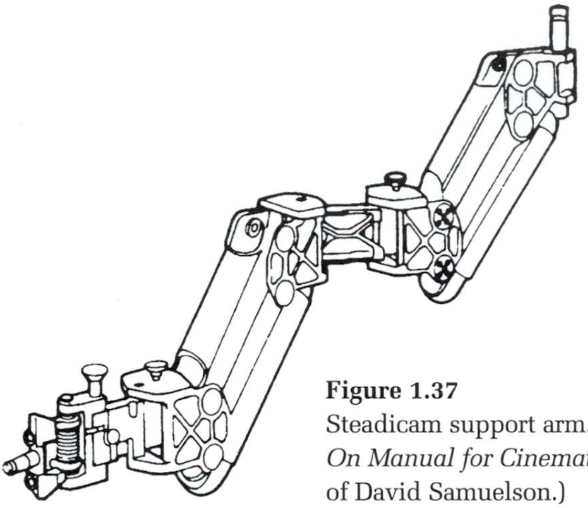

Figure 1.37
Steadicam support arm. (Reprinted from the *Hands-On Manual for Cinematographers* with permission of David Samuelson.)

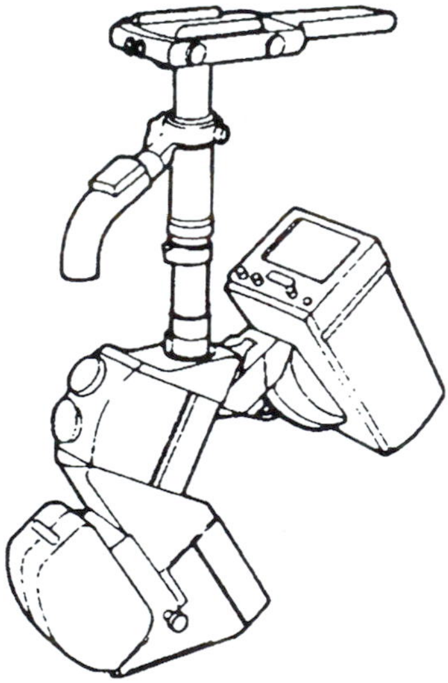

Figure 1.38
Main Steadicam unit. (Reprinted from the *Hands-On Manual for Cinematographers* with permission of David Samuelson.)

of track so that the movement will be free of vibrations. Most dollies contain some type of boom arm, which is operated hydraulically or by air pressure to raise or lower the height of the camera during a shot. When using a dolly, the same head that was mounted to the tripod may also be mounted to the dolly. The dolly contains a mounting platform similar to the top piece of the tripod, so that the head may be locked firmly in place (Figure 1.40).

Figure 1.39
Steadicam operator using the system with an Arriflex 35BL camera. (From a photo of Ted Churchill.) (Reprinted from the *Arriflex 35 Book,* 3rd ed., by Jon Fauer with permission of the author and ARRI Inc.)

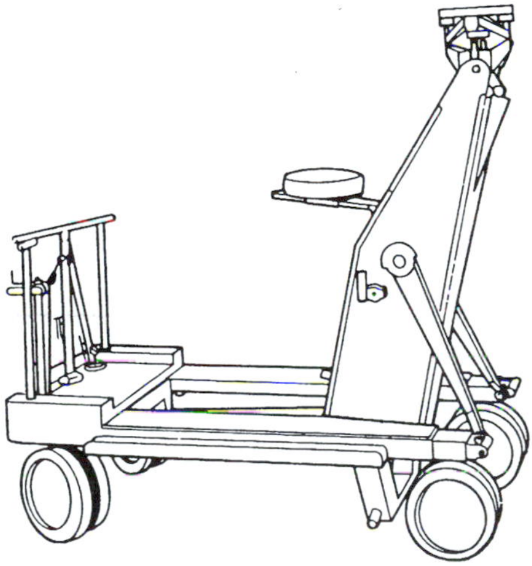

Figure 1.40
Camera dolly. (Courtesy of J.L. Fisher, Inc.)

Crane

For many of the high angle shots that you have seen in films, a piece of equipment known as a *crane* is usually used. The crane allows you to start a shot from a very high angle, and then boom down and move in to a very close shot. Or you may do the opposite, by starting low and then booming or craning up to a high angle shot. A crane should be used only when necessary. It is very important to have qualified grips who thoroughly know how to operate the crane safely. Chapman manufactures the most commonly used crane for motion pictures.

The previously mentioned pieces of equipment are only a small sampling of the wide variety of equipment used by a camera department. As you work more frequently on different types of productions, you will learn about and use many other specialized pieces of equipment. Whenever you come across a piece of equipment that you are not familiar with, ask the rental house to explain it to you so that you feel comfortable using it. Never try to use a piece of equipment that you are not familiar with.

2

The Camera Department

FILM PRODUCTIONS

The number of members in the film camera department depends on the kind of film being shot. Big-budget feature films usually have a larger crew than a low-budget film, TV commercial, or music video. It also depends on whether the production is union or non-union. In the United States the typical camera department usually consists of the following crew members:

Director of Photography (D.P.)

Camera Operator

First Assistant Cameraman (1st A.C.) (Focus Puller)

Second Assistant Cameraman (2nd A.C.) (Clapper/Loader)

Loader (optional position on larger multicamera productions)

This list is based on a union, big-budget feature film and includes only the basic crew positions. All of the following lists of camera department personnel responsibilities are based on a union, big-budget feature film. Each job is different, so not all of these jobs will be done on every show. Some of the similarities or differences between union and non-union work are discussed in Chapter 7.

Often when multiple cameras are being used there will be additional Camera Operators and assistants. The responsibilities of these additional crew members are exactly the same as the key members of the camera crew. These additional crew positions are hired on an as-needed basis. Additional crew members hired on a daily basis are often referred to as day players.

Smaller non-union productions most likely will not have the loader position, and often on non-union productions the D.P. also serves as the Camera Operator. Each member of the camera department has specific duties and responsibilities, and each position is related to all the others. While the following lists include the basic responsibilities, each production will be a bit different; therefore what each person does on the production may vary slightly. You must be able to make adjustments based on the type of production you are working on. The important thing to remember is to be flexible and willing to help out in any way, providing you don't step on anybody's toes or cross over into another department where your help may not be wanted or welcome.

The D.P. is the head of the camera department, and he or she is directly responsible to the Director. This chapter lists the D.P. and the Camera Operator responsibilities. Since this book is primarily about the jobs of Assistant Camera Operators, Chapter 3 covers in detail the responsibilities of the 2nd A.C., and Chapter 4 the responsibilities of the 1st A.C.

Director of Photography

The D.P. is the head of all technical departments on a film crew and is responsible for establishing how the script is translated into visual images based on the director's request. The D.P. decides which camera, lenses, and film stock will be used for the production. The D.P. hires or recommends the Camera Operator and often also hires or recommends the 1st A.C. In many cases, mostly on non-union productions, the D.P. acts as Camera Operator, so that position will not be a part of the film crew. In hiring the 1st A.C., the D.P. usually bases the decision on past work experience and chooses someone he or she is comfortable working with. If that person is not available, the D.P. may ask for a recommendation from his or her usual 1st A.C. or a recommendation from another D.P. The position of 1st A.C. is very important, and the D.P. wants to have someone who can be trusted and is good at the job. Because the 1st A.C. works closest with the 2nd A.C., the 1st A.C. usually hires or recommends the 2nd A.C. Again, this is usually based on past working experiences, or on a recommendation of another trusted Camera Assistant.

During shooting, all members of the camera department must work closely together as a team to get the job done. The D.P. decides where the camera is placed for each shot and which lens is to be used. It is up to the Camera Assistants to get the camera set up each time and place all appropriate accessories on the camera for shooting. The D.P. decides how the lights are to be placed for each shot, and once the lights are set, he or she gives the 1st A.C. the correct exposure to be set on the lens for shooting. In addition to working closely with the Camera Assistants, the D.P. works closely with the Camera Operator to decide the composition for the shot. The D.P. along with the Director, may also decide if there are to be any dolly moves for the shot and when they will take place.

Many D.P.s started their film careers as Camera Assistants, so they should know and understand the requirements of the job. They probably worked a few years each as 2nd A.C. and 1st A.C. Then they may have been a Camera Operator for a few years before finally becoming a D.P. The length of time that is spent at each position is based on each person's individual circumstances.

There are also many D.P.s who arrived at the position without ever having been a camera assistant. They may have been a Lighting Technician or Gaffer before becoming a D.P. They also could have started their career as a documentary filmmaker or television news cameraperson. If the D.P. has never been a camera assistant, he or she may not be fully aware of all the duties of the job. In any case you must be able to work closely with the DP to get the job done.

Many D.P.s started out working on small, low-budget films, or even some student film projects. These small projects enabled them to gain valuable experience that later helped them get their first big break on a major, big-budget production. Some D.P.s started out as apprentices to well-known D.P.s. By working with these professionals, they learned many valuable skills that helped them when it came time to start out on their own.

The following are many of the responsibilities of the D.P. They are listed in no particular order.

- Reads the script so that he/she understands the story and has an idea of what may be involved in the shooting of the film
- Works with the director, production designer, and set construction supervisor to determine the "look" of the film and how the sets will be designed and constructed
- Assists the Director in translating the screenplay into visual images
- Attends production meetings to discuss the script and make any suggestions to help the production run smoothly
- Goes on location scouts with the Director and any other production personnel to help determine their suitability for filming, both aesthetically and from a practical production standpoint
- Chooses camera, lenses, filters, film stock, and any other camera equipment that may be needed
- Consults with 1st A.C. on any camera equipment or accessories that may be needed
- Recommends the camera rental house to use for renting equipment
- Recommends the grip and lighting equipment rental companies to use for renting equipment

- Recommends the laboratory that will process the film
- Supervises any camera tests that may be necessary or arranges for them to be done
- Supervises any film tests that may be necessary or arranges for them to be done
- Supervises any lighting, costume, and makeup tests or arranges for them to be done
- Hires or recommends the members of the camera crew, the gaffer, and the key grip
- Works closely with the Production Manager or Production Coordinator to determine the size of the camera, grip, and lighting crews
- Works with the grip and electric crews to determine the type and quantity of equipment needed for each department
- Maintains the photographic quality and continuity of the production
- Sets the camera position, camera angle, and any camera movement for each shot based on the Director's request
- Selects the lens and filter required for each shot
- Determines the correct exposure (t-stop) for each shot
- Works with the Director when lining up and matching action and screen direction from shot to shot
- Works with the Camera Operator to set the composition for each shot based on the Director's request
- Determines if the shot will require a dolly or crane move
- Plans and supervises the lighting of all scenes, working closely with the Gaffer and the electrical crew
- Maintains the continuity of lighting from scene to scene
- Supervises the crews for all cameras in use on the production
- Supervises each technical crew while on stage or location
- Specifies the laboratory instructions for developing and processing of exposed film
- Views dailies with the Director and other production personnel
- Supervises the color timing of the final print of the film
- Supervises the transfer from film to videotape
- Provides exposure meters and other necessary tools associated with performing the job

Camera Operator

The next person in line in the camera department is the Camera Operator. In the United States, the Camera Operator works closely with the D.P. to determine the composition for each shot as instructed by the director. In Britain, the Director and the Camera Operator work together to determine the placement of the camera and the composition of the shots. In Britain, the D.P., or Lighting Cameraman as he or she is sometimes called, deals primarily with the lighting of the set.

The primary job of the Camera Operator is to make smooth pan and tilt moves in order to maintain the composition of the subject. The Camera Operator keeps the action within the frame lines in order to tell the story.

Sometimes the Camera Operator decides the placement of the camera and also chooses the lens for each shot. The 1st A.C. works most closely with the Camera Operator during rehearsals and actual shooting. There may be a complicated camera move that requires zoom lens moves and many focus changes during the shot. The Camera Operator rehearses these moves with the 1st A.C. before shooting them to be sure they are done at the correct time during the shot. If a problem arises with any of these moves during the shot, the Camera Operator is often the only one who can detect it and must let the 1st A.C. know where the problem occurred so that it can be corrected for the next shot.

The Camera Operator rehearses any dolly moves that may have been determined by the D.P. The Camera Operator will sometimes let the dolly grip know when it is the right time to move the dolly during the shot. The Camera Operator also works with the sound department and boom operator to set the placement of the boom microphone during the shot. He or she may let the boom operator look through the camera to see the frame size, or may just tell the boom operator where the edge of frame is so that the microphone is placed where it is not in the shot. The Camera Operator should tell the 2nd A.C. if any actor's marks are visible in the frame and if they should be made smaller for the shot. When actual shooting starts, the Camera Operator sometimes instructs the 2nd A.C. where to place the slate so that it is visible in the frame.

The following are many of the responsibilities of the Camera Operator, which are listed in no particular order:

- Reads the script so that he/she understands the story and has an idea of what may be involved in the shooting of the film
- Adjusts the viewfinder diopter for his or her vision
- Adjusts the seat of the dolly for comfort and proper positioning prior to each shot
- Maintains the composition as instructed by the Director or the D.P.
- Watches to make sure the proper eye lines and screen directions are maintained
- Makes smooth pan and tilt moves during each shot to maintain the proper composition

- Approves or disapproves each take after it is shot: certifies that no microphones, lights, stands, or other unwanted items were in the frame
- Works closely with the 1st A.C. to ensure proper focus, zoom moves, and t-stop settings for each shot
- Works closely with the 2nd A.C. regarding the proper size and placement of actors' marks; if the marks are seen in the shot, the Camera Operator informs the 2nd A.C. to make them smaller or to remove them
- Notifies the 2nd A.C. when the camera has reached sync speed so that he or she may slate the shot
- Works closely with the dolly grip during rehearsals and takes to ensure smooth dolly or crane moves
- Works closely with the sound department to ensure proper placement of microphones during each take by telling them where the edges of the frame are located
- May act as D.P. on any second unit shooting during the production
- Views dailies with the Director and other production personnel

The responsibilities of the First Assistant Cameraman and Second Assistant Cameraman are covered in detail in Chapters 3 and 4. Following is a checklist of many of the responsibilities of each of these positions. They are listed in no particular order.

First Assistant Cameraman (1st A.C. or Focus Puller)

- Knows and understands all professional motion picture camera equipment and accessories currently used in the industry
- Reads the script so that he/she is aware of the story and recommends any special equipment that he/she feels may be needed to carry out specific shots
- Works with the D.P. and/or Camera Operator to choose the camera equipment that will be used on the production
- Recommends the 2nd A.C. and Loader/Trainee to the D.P. and/or Production Manager
- Works with the 2nd A.C. to prepare a list of expendables, which is then given to the production office or Production Manager so that the items may be purchased
- Preps the camera package alone or along with the 2nd A.C.; ensures that all equipment is in proper working order
- Responsible for the overall care and maintenance of all camera equipment during production
- Mounts the camera head onto the tripod, dolly, or other support piece and ensures that it is working properly

- Unpacks, assembles, and warms up the camera and all of its components at the start of each shooting day
- Does not leave the camera unattended
- Loads and unloads proper film into the camera for the shots and setups
- Resets the footage counter to zero after each reload
- Resets the buckle switch in the camera if necessary
- Keeps all parts of the camera clean and free from dirt and dust, including camera body, lenses, filters, magazines, and so on
- Oils and lubes the camera as needed
- Sets the viewfinder eyepiece for each key person looking through the camera
- Before each shot, ensures that the camera is level and balanced
- If the camera is mounted on a tripod, ensures that it is securely positioned and leveled
- Checks to be sure that no lights are kicking into the lens, causing a flare, when the camera is in its proper position
- Places proper lens, filter, and any other accessory on the camera as instructed by the D.P. or Camera Operator
- Checks that lenses and filters are clean before filming
- Sets the t-stop on the lens before each take as instructed by the D.P.
- Measures the distances to subjects during rehearsals and marks the lens or focus marking disk
- Checks the depth of field for each shot as needed
- Follows focus and makes zoom lens moves during takes
- Adjusts the shutter angle, t-stop, or camera speed during a take, as needed and as instructed by the D.P.
- Checks that camera is running at correct speed during filming
- Gives the 2nd A.C. footage readings from the camera after each take
- After each printed take or when instructed by the D.P., checks the gate for hairs or emulsion buildup and requests another take if necessary
- Supervises the transportation and moving of all camera equipment between filming locations
- Works with the 2nd A.C. to move the camera to each new position
- Works with the 2nd A.C. to be sure that all camera batteries are kept fully charged and ready for use
- If there is no 2nd A.C. on the production, then also performs those duties
- Orders additional or special camera equipment as needed
- Checks call sheet daily to be sure any additional camera equipment and crew members are requested if needed

- Arranges for the return of any camera equipment no longer needed
- Arranges for the return and replacement of any damaged camera equipment
- Oversees all aspects of the camera department
- Disassembles the camera and its components at the completion of the shooting day and packs them away into the appropriate cases
- At the completion of filming, wraps and cleans all camera equipment for returning to the rental house
- Provides all the necessary tools and accessories associated with performing the job

Second Assistant Cameraman (2nd A.C. or Clapper/Loader)

- Before production, obtains a supply of empty cans, black bags, camera reports, and cores from the lab or asks the Production Manager to arrange this
- Prepares a list of expendables with the 1st A.C.
- Preps the camera package along with the 1st A.C.
- Cleans the camera truck and/or darkroom for use during the production, and ensures that each is loaded with the proper supplies and equipment
- Loads and unloads film in the magazines, and places proper identification on each if there is no loader
- Checks with loader (if there is one) to be sure that all film magazines are loaded and properly labeled
- Checks darkroom to be sure that it is light proof on a daily basis if necessary
- Communicates with the Script Supervisor in order to obtain the scene and take number for each shot, and also which takes are to be printed
- Records all information on the slate
- Records all information on the camera reports
- Checks with Script Supervisor as to what takes are to be printed for each scene
- Helps to set up the camera at the start of each shooting day
- Marks the position of actors during the rehearsals
- Slates each scene, whether sound (sync) or silent (MOS)
- Assists in changing lenses, filters, magazines, and so on, and in moving the camera to each new position
- Sets up and moves video monitor for each new camera setup and makes sure the cable is connected to the film camera

- Prepares exposed film for delivery to the lab and delivers it to the production company representative at the end of each shooting day
- Cans and labels any film recans or short ends
- Serves as camera department contact with production office, film laboratory, and camera equipment rental house
- Maintains a record of all film received, film shot, short ends created, and film on hand at the end of each shooting day during the production
- Maintains an inventory of film stock and expendables on hand and requests additional supplies from the production office as needed
- Maintains an inventory of camera equipment on hand, additional equipment ordered, and any equipment damaged or returned
- Distributes copies of the camera reports and film inventory forms to the appropriate departments
- Keeps a file of all paperwork relating to the camera department during the production: camera reports, daily film inventory forms, processing reports from the lab, equipment packing lists, expendable requests, etc.
- Keeps a record of all hours worked by the camera department and prepares time cards at the end of each day
- Performs the job of 1st A.C., if necessary, in the absence of the 1st A.C. or when additional cameras are used
- Works with the 1st A.C. to move the camera to each new position
- Works with the 1st A.C. to ensure that all camera batteries are kept fully charged and ready for use
- At the end of each shooting day, helps the 1st A.C. pack away all camera equipment in a safe place
- At the completion of filming, helps the 1st A.C. wrap and clean all camera equipment for returning to the rental house
- At the completion of filming, cleans and wraps the camera truck
- Provides all the necessary tools and accessories associated with performing the job

Loader

- Maintains an inventory of all film stock initially received from the production company
- Maintains a record of all film received, film shot, short ends created, and film on hand at the end of each shooting day during the production
- Loads and unloads all film magazines during the course of filming

- Properly labels all loaded film magazines, cans of exposed film and short ends, and recans of unexposed film
- Prepares exposed film for delivery to the lab and delivers it to the production company representative at the end of each shooting day
- Provides all the necessary tools and accessories associated with performing the job

VIDEO OR HD PRODUCTIONS

In addition to these positions, there are additional positions that may be found on a production that is shooting video or HD digital video format. Those positions are as follows:

Digital Imaging Technician (D.I.T.)

Video Controller

Camera Utility

Digital Utility

Although all of my experience has been on film productions, I wanted to include these classifications, which are currently listed under the International Cinematographers Guild classifications. This information is by no means complete; it has been provided to me by a number of sources, and I apologize for any errors or omissions.

Digital Imaging Technician (D.I.T.)

- Creates the equipment package for the production based on stage or location, how the show will be presented, and who will be using the equipment (film or video oriented)
- Should know each piece of equipment, how it works, and how to troubleshoot each part of the system
- Sets up, operates, troubleshoots, and maintains digital cameras, monitors, cables, recording devices, and other related equipment
- Should know the production's entire post-production path and how it will be finally delivered once completed
- Make recommendations on post-production facilities and other technical issues to keep the post-production path as smooth and uneventful as possible

- Should know how to match the color on two or more cameras and maintain the look of the cameras if a Video Controller is not on the production
- Should establish a creative relationship with the D.P. so that he/she can set the color of the cameras, often before the D.P. asks for a specific change.

Video Controller

- Matches or shades multiple cameras to each other so that a consistent look is maintained throughout the production
- Should be knowledgeable on every master control/shading system in use for video and HD production, including video trucks, control room installations, and hand-held camera control devices
- Should be knowledgeable on the NTSC system so that changes to cameras are broadcast legal
- Should be up-to-date on all waveform monitors and vectorscopes and be able to read and calibrate each
- Should attend the setup and prep session for the equipment that will be used
- Should be able to match a minimum of four cameras without the use of charts after the initial setup of the cameras, including but not limited to Gamma, Gain, Iris, RGB white balance, RGB black balance
- Will listen to the Director or Technical Director and match or shade a camera before it is switched for live broadcast or live recording
- For sitcoms, should match all cameras during rehearsals and will make only fine changes during shooting
- Should know what the broadcasters and production companies are expecting in the look of their shows
- In many cases the D.I.T. performs the duties of the Video Controller

Camera Utility

The Camera Utility is primarily found on television shows, sitcoms, and multicamera feature films. He or She has various responsibilities depending on the type of production. Some of those responsibilities are listed here in no particular order.

- Assists D.I.T. or Video Controller in the setup of the camera
- Wrangles the many cables connecting the camera to the sound equipment, video recorders, and monitors
- Assembles each camera system and knows how to maintain proper pressure of the pneumatic camera pedestals
- On sitcoms, places marks for actors if no second assistant is on the production
- Switches camera tapes as needed if no second assistant is on the production
- Keeps camera reports and inventory sheets if no second assistant is on the production
- Records bars and tone on a few tapes before the day's shooting begins
- Assists the D.I.T. in any manner needed including the setup and connection of all equipment
- Should be knowledgeable on the setup of each piece of gear being used and how each piece is connected and integrates with other pieces of equipment

Digital Utility

The Digital Utility is often an additional position not found on all productions. Many of the duties are the same as those of the Camera Utility. Some of those responsibilities are listed here in no particular order.

- Wrangles the many cables connecting the camera to the sound equipment, video recorders, and monitors
- Assembles each camera system and knows how to maintain proper pressure of the pneumatic camera pedestals
- On sitcoms, places marks for actors if no second assistant is on the production
- Switches camera tapes as needed if no second assistant is on the production
- Keeps camera reports and inventory sheets if no second assistant is on the production
- Records bars and tone on a few tapes before the day's shooting begins
- Assists the D.I.T. in any manner needed including the setup and connection of all equipment
- Should be knowledgeable on the setup of each piece of gear being used and how each piece is connected and integrates with other pieces of equipment

3

Second Camera Assistant

In most cases, when you first join the camera department, you will be starting as a Second Camera Assistant (2nd A.C.). In Britain, Europe, and Australia, the 2nd A.C. may be called the Clapper/Loader. Sometimes you may start as a Loader, which is very similar to the 2nd A.C. The Loader is primarily responsible for loading and unloading film into the magazines, and filling in all of the paperwork relating to the film stock shot during the production. The Loader rarely leaves the camera truck or loading area. On some occasions, the Loader works alongside the 2nd A.C. on the set to gain further experience. The union entry-level position is that of the Loader.

Many of the job duties of the Loader are the same as for a 2nd A.C., so if you are working as a Loader, some of this chapter also applies to you. The main difference between the Loader and 2nd A.C. is that the 2nd A.C. has more responsibilities. The 2nd A.C. works directly with the First Camera Assistant (1st A.C.) during the production and performs many different job duties each shooting day. This chapter discusses in detail each of the 2nd A.C.'s duties and responsibilities. Since there are three different stages of production, these duties are separated into three categories: pre-production, production, and post-production.

PRE-PRODUCTION

Depending on the type of production, the 2nd A.C. may or may not be involved in most pre-production activities. Pre-production is the period before actual shooting when most of the planning and preparation for the production take place. It has been said that the best pre-production leads to the best production. On many smaller productions, the 2nd A.C. will most likely not start work until filming actually begins. But on large productions such as TV shows or feature films, the 2nd A.C. may play a small part in the pre-production process. The 2nd

A.C. may have to contact the laboratory that will be processing the film to work out any details and also to obtain any of the necessary lab supplies required for the production. The 2nd A.C. may meet with the 1st A.C. to prepare the list of expendables and possibly offer ideas for the camera equipment package. And finally, the 2nd A.C. may work closely with the 1st A.C. to perform the camera prep where all of the equipment is checked to be sure it is in proper working order before shooting begins. Each job will be a bit different and the responsibilities of the 2nd A.C. during pre-production will differ accordingly.

Working with the Laboratory

As the 2nd A.C. you will most likely be the one person dealing with the lab on a regular basis. You will serve as the liaison between the Director of Photography (D.P.) and the lab personnel. In most cases your production will be assigned one individual at the lab who will be working on your film. This will be the person you speak to each day to discuss the previous day's footage. It is very important to work out any specific details and procedures with the lab before production begins. The D.P. may have very specific guidelines as to how the film should be handled during processing. Often during pre-production, film tests will be shot so that the D.P. and lab can establish these guidelines and requirements as quickly as possible. The lab may have specific requirements as to how the film should be packaged and labeled, as well as what information is required on the camera reports. Much of this information is covered in detail in the section on camera reports later in this chapter. Working all of this out during pre-production saves time and, it is hoped, will help to eliminate most problems during production.

The lab should know whom to contact if it finds any problems with the film. It is important to be made aware of any problems as soon as possible so that any reshoots can be scheduled if necessary. If the problem is camera or magazine related, you may need to obtain a different camera or magazine. You don't want to use a particular magazine if it is repeatedly scratching the film. If the problem is film related, it may be necessary to contact the company that supplied the film to work out any of these problems. If the production company purchased short ends from one of the many companies that sell short ends, you may need to contact them about the film problem. I know of a situation in which the 2nd A.C. loaded film stock that was thought to be EI 500 film but that actually was EI 250 film because of an error in labeling by the film supplier. I was on a feature film production in which we had a problem with the film stock. We were using fresh factory sealed cans of film. There was a problem with the developed image, which was eventually traced back to a manufacturing error. Working with the lab and the film manufacturer, the problem was figured out very quickly, and we were provided with new film stock so that we could reshoot. Although we did fall behind schedule briefly, it didn't affect the overall production. Please note that due to the very high quality control standards at Kodak and Fuji, this type of event happens very infrequently.

Obtaining Laboratory Supplies

Part of establishing the relationship with the lab includes obtaining all of the lab supplies you will need to keep your production running smoothly. You should either go to the lab and pick up a supply of empty film cans, black bags, camera reports, spare cores, and daylight spools, or ask the production company to arrange to have these items picked up. Remember to obtain various sized cans and bags. These items are necessary so that you can do the job properly, and you must have them available to you during production. The black bag is usually made out of paper or some type of plastic material. It is used to protect the roll of film from light and also from scratches when it is placed in the film can. You should never place a roll of film into a film can without first placing it in a black bag. Many assistants may also refer to the changing bag as a "black bag." It is not the same as the black bags used for wrapping exposed and unexposed film in a film can. The cans and bags are used to can out, which means to wrap and store any short ends and any exposed film during the production. A short end may be described as any roll of film left over from a full size roll, which is still large enough for shooting purposes. For example, you may load 1000 feet of 35 mm film into the camera and only shoot 275 feet of it. The remaining 725 feet would be referred to as a short end because it is less than a standard full size roll. Short ends are explained in more detail later in this chapter in the section on camera reports.

The spare cores or daylight spools are needed to wind the film on the take-up side of the magazines, if the magazine does not have a collapsible core. The camera reports will be filled out during shooting. Many times the production company will have already picked up these supplies for you, but it is a good idea to have a supply of your own in case of emergency. Keep a constant inventory of these items, as you should not run out of any of them during shooting. As shooting progresses you may ask the production office to have someone pick up additional supplies as needed. Never wait until you have run out before ordering additional supplies. It is better to have extra supplies on hand than to run out at a critical time during shooting.

Remember: Never run out of film cans, black bags, cores, or daylight spools.

Choosing and Ordering Expendables

During pre-production the 2nd A.C. and 1st A.C. should prepare a list of expendables. This list is given to the production office so that it may purchase these items for the camera department. Expendables are items that will be needed daily in the performance of your job such as camera tape, permanent felt tip markers, ballpoint pens, compressed air, lens tissue, lens cleaning solution, and so on. They are referred to as expendables because they are items that are used up or expended during the course of the production. It is usually a good idea for both assistants to prepare the list because each may need specialty items that should be included with the basic supplies. In addition, you should check with the D.P. and Camera Operator to see if there are any special items that they may need. The first order should give you enough supplies to start filming, and as the shooting progresses, check the expendable supply regularly to see if anything is getting low and if you need to order more. When you see that additional items are needed, prepare a list and present it to the production office so that it may purchase the items for you. As with lab supplies, do not wait until you run out to order expendables. It can be quite embarrassing for the 2nd A.C. to unload the exposed film, place it in a black bag and film can, and then discover that there is no tape to seal the can. For a complete list of the standard items on a camera department expendables list see Figure C-3 in Appendix C.

Remember: Never run out of expendables that you may need to do the job.

Preparation of Camera Equipment

Camera preparation, or prep, is usually done by the 1st A.C., but many times on larger productions the 2nd A.C. also works on the camera prep. The camera prep is important because it gives the camera assistants a chance to check each piece of equipment before shooting. By doing this you know if you have everything necessary and also that everything works properly. Please see the section on camera prep in Chapter 4 for the procedures to follow. In addition you should also look at the camera prep checklist, Figure C-4 in Appendix C.

Preparation of Camera Truck

When the camera prep has been completed, and if you are using a camera truck, the equipment should be loaded onto the truck. Before loading the truck, be sure that it has been cleaned out. Sweep the floor and clean off the shelves. If the truck is kept clean, there is less chance that the camera and equipment will get dirty.

Once the truck has been cleaned, load the equipment on the shelves. The shelves should then be labeled as to what is on each of them. The labels are important to help you locate items in a hurry and are especially useful when using additional camera crew members who may not be familiar with the setup of the truck. In addition to labeling the shelves, each equipment case should be labeled with a brief description of what is inside. When loading the camera truck, common sense is the key. Do not place camera, lenses, or filters on high shelves, because they may fall while the truck is moving. These items should be kept on middle or lower shelves for ease of accessibility and safety. Most camera trucks have a workbench where you will perform the daily camera setup and maintenance. The workbench is also a good area to work on the various paperwork associated with the camera department. The camera case and accessory (AKS) case is usually kept under the workbench so that it may be accessed easily each shooting day.

Most camera trucks contain shelves that have a lip along the front edge to help prevent the cases from sliding off during transport. In addition all shelves should have a provision for attaching some type of straps across them to prevent cases from sliding off during moving. By using a logical system and order as to how the truck is loaded, you will be able to quickly set up at the start of each day and locate any item in a hurry.

One of the key items that is often included in the camera truck is a nitrogen tank with a regulator, hose, and nozzle. This tank is used for blowing dirt and dust off the camera equipment and especially for cleaning out the film magazines before loading and after unloading film. Many assistants use some type of small compressed air can on set, but the nitrogen tank is the best thing to have when working out of a camera truck. If the truck is equipped with a darkroom, it should be cleaned and stocked with all necessary supplies. Figure 3.1 shows a typical camera truck setup.

Preparation of Darkroom

When using a darkroom, whether it is on a stage or on a camera truck, you should first ensure that it is lightproof. The best way to do this is to

Figure 3.1 Typical camera truck setup. (Reprinted from the *Arriflex 35 Book* by Jon Fauer with permission of the author and ARRI Inc.)

go into the darkroom, close the door, turn off the light, and stay in for at least 5 minutes to allow your eyes to adjust to the dark. After approximately 5 minutes, hold your hand 12 inches from your face with your fingers spread apart. If you are able to see your hand, then light is leaking in. Find the leaks and plug them or cover them with tape. Check along the floor, walls, and ceiling, and along the doorframe where it closes. Never use a darkroom until you are sure that it is completely lightproof. Also, be sure that the door has a lock on the inside to prevent anyone from opening it while you are loading or unloading film. The controls for the darkroom light should be located inside the darkroom so that there is no chance of someone turning on the light while you are loading or unloading film. The darkroom should be checked daily to ensure that no light is leaking in. It should especially be checked daily if it is located on a camera truck that has been driven from location to location. The shifting and swaying of the truck during driving can cause the seams of the walls, floor, and door of the darkroom to separate.

Once you are sure that the darkroom is lightproof, clean and stock it with all necessary supplies and equipment. Only the items that are needed for the loading and unloading process should be kept in the darkroom. Any additional items may be stored on other shelves in the camera truck so they do not clutter the darkroom.

Set up the darkroom in a neat and orderly manner, with each item having an assigned location. This will help you do the job much faster so you do not have to search for something each time you load or unload. It is very important to keep the darkroom clean. Dirt and dust from a dirty darkroom can get inside the magazines and cause scratches on the film. Take the few extra minutes each day to be sure that your darkroom is clean and orderly and ready for use.

Camera tape, pens, permanent felt tip markers, compressed air cans, empty cans, and camera reports should all be kept within easy

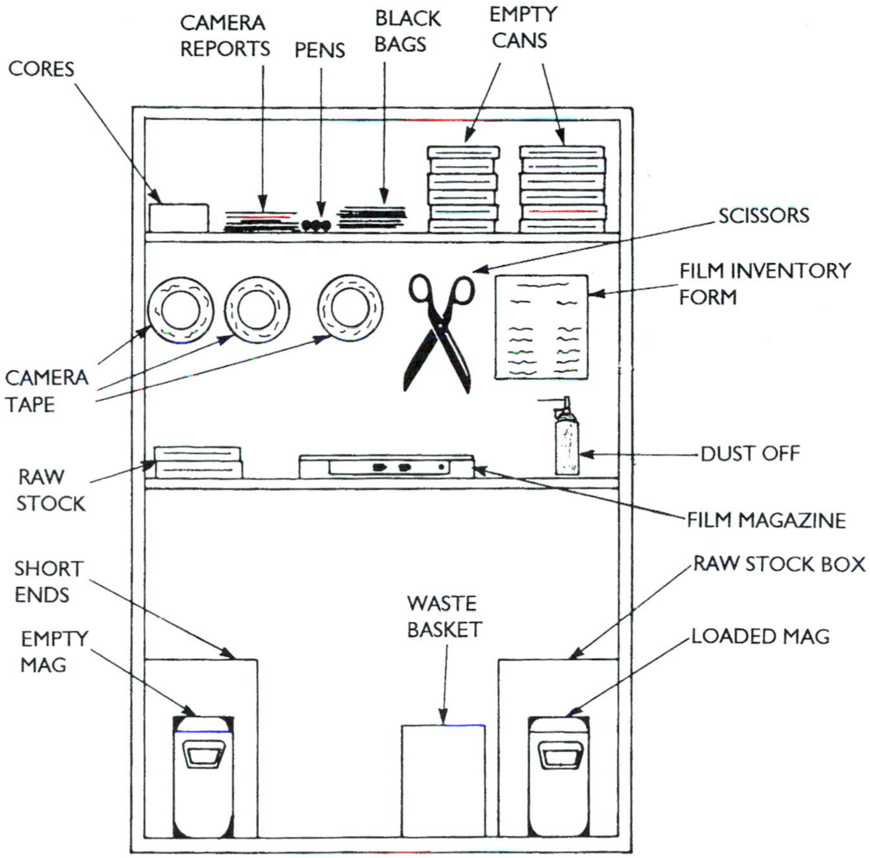

Figure 3.2 Typical darkroom setup.

reach. Before using the darkroom, be sure that you have everything you need to load or unload the film. You don't want to discover after you have opened the film magazine that all the film cans are in a box outside the darkroom. Always be sure to separate the raw stock and short ends from the exposed film. Raw stock is any fresh, unexposed film, and short ends are short, unexposed rolls of film left over from a full roll. Figure 3.2 shows a typical darkroom setup.

PRODUCTION

Once you have completed all of the pre-production procedures, it is time for filming to start. Putting a large production together is a complex and consuming operation that requires both dedication and endurance from everyone involved. The production phase of shooting is a complex operation that requires a great deal of dedication, hard work, and attention to detail on the part of all involved, especially the 2nd A.C. Proper performance of the duties and responsibilities of the 2nd A.C. is vital to the smooth operation of the production. You must keep track of how much film is shot, how many rolls are used, which scenes and how many takes of each are shot, along with many other aspects of the job. You should be very organized and able to jump in at a moment's notice with any information or equipment needed during shooting. An average feature film may shoot over 100,000 feet of film, using over 100 rolls of film. Each day will require many shots and setups to get the day's work completed. All of this information must be accurately kept track of by the 2nd A.C.

Start of the Day Procedures

The first thing you should do each day is check with the D.P. to see what film stock is needed for the day and load up all of the magazines if they are not loaded. If you were able to get all of the magazines loaded the night before, then you should help the 1st A.C. set up the camera. Have all of the cases open and hand things to the 1st A.C. as they are needed. Once the camera is set up you should prepare all of the equipment carts.

Check that all filters and lenses are clean. If you haven't already done so, prepare a supply of camera reports for the day's shooting. Also prepare marks for the actors. Double check your film inventory, expendables supply, and film cans and bags. If you establish a daily routine, the job will go much more smoothly, and you should have fewer problems on set.

Camera Reports

Each roll of film shot during the production must have a camera report that shows which scenes were shot and how much film was used for each shot. Each lab has its own style of camera report, and each one contains the same or similar basic information. It is usually a good idea to use the report from the lab that will be processing the film, but if this is not possible, then any camera report will suffice. I have designed a generic camera report that can be used when you don't have specific lab reports available (Figure C.9 in Appendix C). The report is also available for download on the companion web site for this book.

No matter what style of camera report you use, most of the basic information on it is the same. I separate all camera reports into two sections, the heading section and the shooting section. The heading of the report should contain most of the following information: production company, production title, production number, Director, D.P., magazine number, roll number, camera number, footage, film type, emulsion number, date, and developing instructions. The basic heading information, such as the production company, production title, Director, and D.P., should be self-explanatory. The production number is a number assigned to that particular production by the company that is filming it. The company may have many different productions going on at the same time, and one way to keep track of them is to assign a different number to each one. When filming a television series, it is customary to assign a new production number to each new episode being filmed. Check with the production office to see if the production you are working on has been assigned a specific production number.

The magazine number is most often the serial number of the magazine as assigned by the manufacturer. Many assistants assign numbers to the magazine, such as 1, 2, 3, and so on. If you choose to number the magazines in this manner, keep a written record showing which magazine serial number corresponds to your numbering system. During the camera prep, label the magazines with camera tape and place the corresponding number on this piece of tape. The magazine number is useful if there is a problem with a particular roll of film. If there is a problem with a magazine (or “mag”), you can check the camera report to see which magazine was used and have it repaired or replaced if necessary. I prefer to use the serial number of the mag so that there is less confusion. I often place a small piece of tape on the outside of the magazine with the magazine serial number written on it so that I don’t have to search for it when things get rushed.

The roll number is assigned each time the camera is loaded with a new roll of film. The common practice is that the first roll of film placed on the camera on the first day of shooting is roll number one (1), the next one is roll number two (2), then roll number three (3), and so on. Each time a new roll is placed on the camera, it is assigned a new number, whether it is a full roll of film or a short end. On each new shooting day, the roll number that you start with will usually be the next higher number from the one you ended with on the previous day. For example, on day number ten (10) of shooting, you ended with roll number forty-seven (47). When you start day number eleven (11), the first roll placed on the camera will be roll number forty-eight (48). The exception to this practice is if you do not remove the last roll of film from the camera on the previous day, and continue with it on the next day; or, if you remove a roll from the camera without breaking it, with the intention of using it again later in the day, when you later place this roll back on the camera, it will retain its original roll number. If more than one camera is being used, it is standard to make the roll number a combination of the camera letter and the roll number, such as A-1, A-2, B-1, B-2, and so on. It is a good idea to check with the Editor or the production company to see how it would like the roll numbers labeled each day. I have been on some productions in which we started with roll number one (1) each day. I find this confusing but it is what the production company or Editor wanted so I did not question it.

The camera number is actually a letter assigned to the camera during camera prep. If only one camera is being used, then no number is assigned, but if more than one camera is being used, the primary camera would be "A," the second camera would be "B," then "C," and so on. The footage refers to the amount of footage loaded into the magazine (400′, 1000′, 250′, etc.) corresponding to the camera report. Remember that it is not always the same as the size of the magazine. Many times a short end will be loaded into a magazine instead of a full roll of film. The film type refers to what film stock you are using, for example, Kodak 7229, 7274, 5218, 5246, 5284; Fuji 8622, 8652, 8562, 8592; and so on. The emulsion number is the emulsion number and roll number listed on the film can label. For example, if you are using Eastman Kodak Color Negative 7229-032-1902, the film type is 7229 and the emulsion number is 032-1902. For Eastman Kodak Color Negative 5218-197-1102, the film type is 5218 and the emulsion number is 197-1102. See Figures 3.3, 3.4, 3.5, and 3.6 for examples of Eastman Kodak and Fuji 16 mm and 35 mm film can labels.

Figure 3.3 Eastman Kodak 16 mm film can label. (Courtesy of Eastman Kodak Company.)

Figure 3.4 Eastman Kodak 35 mm film can label. (Courtesy of Eastman Kodak Company.)

Figure 3.5 Fuji Film 16 mm film can label. (Courtesy of Fuji Photo Film U.S.A., Inc.)

Figure 3.6 Fuji Film 35 mm film can label. (Courtesy of Fuji Photo Film U.S.A., Inc.)

When film is manufactured it is made in very large rolls, approximately 54 inches wide. These rolls are then sliced into 16 mm or 35 mm wide rolls. From these large 16 mm or 35 mm rolls, smaller rolls are cut, which is what you receive when you order a 400-foot, 1000-foot, or other size roll from the manufacturer. For example, using the film number 5218-197-1102, 5218 is the film type, 197 is the emulsion number and 1102 would be the roll number cut from the larger roll. When filling in the camera report, you should always include all of the numbers following the film type in the space labeled *emulsion number.*

The date on the camera report corresponds to the date that the roll of film is exposed. The developing instructions are usually given to you by the D.P. Some of the most common developing instructions include, "Develop Normal," "One-Light Work Print," "Prep for Video Transfer," "Time to Gray Card or Gray Scale," "Print All," "Print Circle Takes Only."

Because much of the heading information, such as Production Company, Production Title, Director, and Director of Photography, will remain the same during the production, it may be filled in before production to save time. I recommend filling out a batch of camera reports beforehand so that when you are in the midst of shooting and get rushed, at least you will have some reports ready to use. Many times, the film type, emulsion number, and footage amount may also be filled in before production if you are using only one or two film stocks and one or two roll sizes for the entire production. Prepare a stack of camera reports for each film stock and roll size so that you will be prepared when things start getting a bit crazy on the set. Anything you can do to save time will help you in the long run.

During shooting you will fill in the shooting portion of the camera report with the following information: scene number, take number, dial reading, footage, remarks, G (Good), NG (No Good), W (Waste), T (Total), and SE (Short End). Figures 3.7 through 3.9 illustrate examples of the different styles of camera reports. Each one of these different styles is discussed separately.

During shooting you will receive the scene number and take number from the Script Supervisor. Write these numbers in the appropriate space on the report. At the end of each take, check the footage counter on the camera to obtain the dial reading. If you cannot see the footage counter, ask the 1st A.C. to give you the information. Many times the 1st A.C. calls out the reading to you at the end of each take or gives you a hand signal to indicate the number on the camera footage counter. (See Chapter 4 for more information on the hand signals.) Round the footage amount from the camera and write the rounded amount on the camera report. Most professional motion picture cameras have a digital footage counter. When a new roll is placed on the camera, the footage counter should be reset to zero. Each time the camera is turned on, the numbers on the footage counter get progressively higher. To make the addition and subtraction on the camera report easier, round all dial readings to the nearest ten (10). As we all should have learned in elementary arithmetic, if the number ends in 0, 1, 2, 3, or 4, round it down, and if it ends in 5, 6, 7, 8, or 9, round it up. For example, if the camera footage counter shows a reading of 247, round it to 250. On the camera report, next to the appropriate scene and take number, write the number 250 in the dial column.

To determine the footage amount for each take, subtract the previous dial reading from the one just recorded. For example, if the previous dial reading on the camera report is 210 and the present dial reading is 250, the footage for the present take is 40 (250 – 210). Table 3.1 shows an example of camera footage counter amounts and the corresponding dial reading and footage amounts for each. The information in Table 3.1 is used in each of the three different styles of camera reports so that you can compare the differences between each report.

The first camera report style is shown in Figure 3.7. The SD column may be used to indicate whether the scene was shot sync or MOS. If the shot was done with sync sound, write S in the column for sync,

Table 3.1 Corresponding Camera Report Dial and Footage Amounts

Camera Footage Counter	Camera Report Dial	Camera Report Footage
66	70	70
121	120	50
162	160	40
205	210	50
247	250	40
279	280	30
364	360	80
433	430	70
498	500	70
550	550	50
607	610	60
649	650	40
703	700	50
754	750	50
802	800	50
836	840	40
885	890	50
942	940	50
968	970	30

and if it was done without sound, write M in the column for MOS. Most assistants do not use this column on the camera report. In the Remarks column of the report, you may record a variety of information, including filters used, f-stop or t-stop, focal length of lens, camera to subject distance, MOS, if the shot was done without sound, tail slate or second slate, depending on the situation. You also may note whether the shot was interior (int), exterior (ext), day (day), or night (nite). There is no set rule as to what information should go in the Remarks column. Check with the D.P. and 1st A.C. to see if they want anything written in this space. Each production is different.

For the type of camera report shown in Figure 3.8, write the scene and take numbers as you did in the previous style of report. Round the

CAMERA REPORT

Co. Submitted By: Demi Monde Productions P.O.#:

Bill To: Demi Monde Productions Date Exposed: Phone Contact

Picture Title: Claire of the Moon Loader:

Director: N. Conn D.P.: R. Sellars

Sheet of

ROLL # 5 ☐ BLACK & WHITE ☑ COLOR
EMUL.# 5218 – 237 4862 MAG # 10146
DEVELOP FOOTAGE 1000
☑ NORMAL ☐ PUSH ___ STOP(S) ☐ PULL ___ STOP(S)
FILM WORKPRINT ☐ PRINT ALL ☑ PRINT CIRCLED TAKES
VIDEO PREP & TRANSFER ☐ TRANSFER ALL ☐ TRANSFER CIRCLED TAKES
TRANSFER AT ___ fps ☐ EDGE # PUNCH

FOTOKEM FILM AND VIDEO
FOTO-KEM INDUSTRIES, INC.
2801 W. Alameda Ave. • Burbank CA 91505
818 846 3101 Voice Mail
Production Services Fax 818 841 7532
Customer Services Fax 818 841 0630

SCENE NO.	TAKE	DIAL	FEET	SD.	REMARKS	SCENE NO.	TAKE	DIAL	FEET	SD.	REMARKS
54	1	70	70			82 A	2	700	50		
	2	120	50				3	750	50		
	3	160	40			82 B	1	800	50		
	4	210	50				2	840	40		
54 A	1	250	40			36	1	890	50		
	2	280	30				2	940	50		
82	1	360	80				3	970	30		
	2	430	70			OUT AT 970'					
	3	500	70							G	600
	4	550	50			DEVELOP NORMAL				NG	370
	5	610	60			ONE LIGHT WORKPRINT				W	30
82 A	1	650	40							T	1000

2050-60 (9/00) THIS CAMERA REPORT SUBJECT TO PROVISIONS ON THE REVERSE SIDE
OPEN 24 HOURS A DAY, 7 DAYS A WEEK

Figure 3.7 Example of one camera report style. (Courtesy of Foto-Kem Industries, Inc.)

dial reading and put it in the Dial or Counter column, depending on which type of report you are using. In the Print column, write the footage only for the takes that are to be printed. The information in the Remarks column is the same as in the previous example.

As you can tell from looking at the third type of camera report shown in Figure 3.9, the only sections that are the same in the shooting portion of the report are the Scene number and the Remarks column. Instead of writing down the dial readings in one column and the footage amounts in another column, only the footage amount is written in the space for the particular take number. Column 1 6 is for take 1 and for take 6, column 2 7 is for take 2 and take 7, and so on. Because there is no space for the dial readings, you should make your own column and write them along the left or right edge of the report, just as a reference. As shown in the example, the dial readings are written along the right edge of the Remarks column. So, for this camera report style, scene 54, take 1, was 70 feet, take 2 was 50 feet, take 3 was 40 feet, and so on.

color by deluxe® **deluxe laboratories**
1377 North Serrano Ave., Hollywood, CA 90027 (213) 462-6171

CAMERA REPORT
SOUND REPORT No. 179450

DATE ______ CUSTOMER ORDER NUMBER ______
COMPANY Demi Monde Productions
DIRECTOR N. Conn CAMERAMAN / RECORDIST R. Sellars
PRODUCTION NUMBER OR TITLE Clairie of the Moon
MAGAZINE NUMBER 10146 ROLL NUMBER 5
TYPE OF FILM / EMULSION 5218 237 4862
PRINT CIRCLED TAKES ONLY: [✔] ONE LITE [ ] TIMED

SCENE NO.	TAKE	DIAL	PRINT	REMARKS
54	1	70		
	(2)	120	50	
	3	160		
	(4)	210	50	
54 A	(1)	250	40	
	2	280		
82	(1)	360	80	
	2	430		
	(3)	500	70	
	4	550		
	(5)	610	60	
82 A	1	650		
	(2)	700	50	
	(3)	750	50	
82 B	(1)	800	50	
	2	840		
36	(1)	890	50	
	(2)	940	50	
	3	970		
				G 600
OUT AT 970'				NG 370
	DEVELOP NORMAL			W 30
TOTAL	ONE LIGHT WORKPRINT			T 1000

All contracts with this company are accepted with the understanding that all film delivered to it is covered by the owner against loss. This company takes every necessary precaution for the safekeeping of the film, but assumes no responsibility for its loss.

DEL-82 (10/90)

Figure 3.8 Example of a second camera report style. (Courtesy of Deluxe Laboratories.)

You will notice on each of these styles of camera reports, certain take numbers and footage amounts have circles drawn around them. After each setup, the Script Supervisor will tell you which takes are to be circled. These are the takes that the Director likes and wants to con-

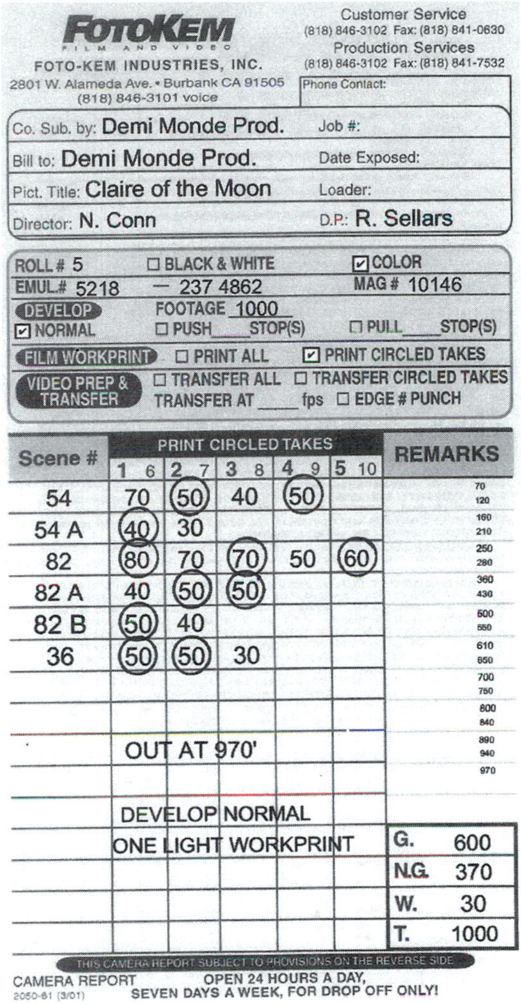

FOTOKEM FILM AND VIDEO
FOTO-KEM INDUSTRIES, INC.
2801 W. Alameda Ave. • Burbank CA 91505
(818) 846-3101 voice

Customer Service
(818) 846-3102 Fax: (818) 841-0630
Production Services
(818) 846-3102 Fax: (818) 841-7532
Phone Contact:

Co. Sub. by: Demi Monde Prod. Job #:
Bill to: Demi Monde Prod. Date Exposed:
Pict. Title: Claire of the Moon Loader:
Director: N. Conn D.P.: R. Sellars

ROLL # 5 ☐ BLACK & WHITE ☑ COLOR
EMUL.# 5218 — 237 4862 MAG # 10146
DEVELOP FOOTAGE 1000
☑ NORMAL ☐ PUSH____STOP(S) ☐ PULL____STOP(S)
FILM WORKPRINT ☐ PRINT ALL ☑ PRINT CIRCLED TAKES
VIDEO PREP & TRANSFER ☐ TRANSFER ALL ☐ TRANSFER CIRCLED TAKES
TRANSFER AT ____ fps ☐ EDGE # PUNCH

Scene #	PRINT CIRCLED TAKES 1 6	2 7	3 8	4 9	5 10	REMARKS
54	70	(50)	40	(50)		70 120
54 A	(40)	30				160 210
82	(80)	70	(70)	50	(60)	250 280
82 A	40	(50)	(50)			360 430
82 B	(50)	40				500 550
36	(50)	(50)	30			610 650
						700 750
						800 840
	OUT AT 970'					890 940 970
	DEVELOP NORMAL					
	ONE LIGHT WORKPRINT					G. 600
						N.G. 370
						W. 30
						T. 1000

THIS CAMERA REPORT SUBJECT TO PROVISIONS ON THE REVERSE SIDE
CAMERA REPORT OPEN 24 HOURS A DAY, SEVEN DAYS A WEEK, FOR DROP OFF ONLY!
2050-61 (3/01)

Figure 3.9 Example of a third camera report style. (Courtesy of Foto-Kem Industries, Inc.)

sider for use in the editing of the film, and they are called the good or printed takes. Circling lets the lab know which takes are to be printed during processing. If the film is being transferred to videotape, the circled takes are the takes that will be transferred to videotape. Most labs will not print circled takes in 16 mm because it is cheaper to print the entire roll, but for a video transfer, circled takes are used in 16 mm. When circling particular takes, you should also circle the corresponding footage amounts to make it easier to add up the footage. No matter what format you are shooting, 16 mm, 35 mm, or video, I recommend always circling the good takes. The camera report serves as a record for the Editor and Director to know which takes were the best and are to be considered for use in the finished film. During editing, they can refer to the report and know immediately which takes the director liked during shooting.

The circled takes are called good (G) takes. The takes on the report that have not been circled are called no good (NG). If for some reason you circled a take and then the Director decided not to print it, draw slashes through the edges of the circle and write "Do Not Print" in the Remarks column. An example of a circled take that is not to be printed is shown on the camera report in Figure 3.10.

At the bottom right of most camera reports, there are usually spaces labeled G, NG, W, SE, and T. If the camera report does not have any of these spaces on it, write them in yourself. "G" stands for GOOD and will be the total amount of footage for all circled takes. Write the total footage for all circled takes on the report in the section marked G. "NG" stands for NO GOOD and is the total amount of footage for all takes not circled. Mark the total footage for all noncircled takes in the section marked NG. "W" stands for WASTE and may be the amount of film left over after the good and no good totals are added together. "T" stands for TOTAL and is the total amount of film loaded into the magazine for the particular roll of film. "SE" stands for SHORT END and may be the amount of film left over after all the good, no good, and waste totals are added together. You should add up the totals for G and NG, and subtract this amount from the total amount of film loaded into the camera. This remaining amount of film, if any, may either be called waste or a short end depending on the amount. If it is waste, write it in the section marked W. If it is a short end, mark it in the section marked SE. A short end is a roll of film that is available for shooting that is left over from a full size roll. In other words, let's assume you loaded a 1000-foot roll of film into the camera and only shot 370 feet. The 370 feet of exposed film would be sent to the lab for developing with all other film shot during the day's shooting. The remaining 630 feet (1000 – 370) is left over and is called a short end. As a general rule, for 35 mm format, anything that is more than 100 feet is called a short end, and anything that is less than 100 feet is called waste. When I worked at one of the major Hollywood studios, the camera department said that

SCENE NO.	TAKE	DIAL	FEET	SD	REMARKS
54	1	70	70		
	2	120	50		
	3	160	40		
	4	210	50		DO NOT PRINT
54 A	1	250	40		
	2	280	30		

Figure 3.10
Marking a circled take to indicate that it is not to be printed.

anything less than 200 feet was waste and anything more than 200 feet was a short end. As a general rule, for 16 mm format, anything more than 40 feet is a short end, and anything less than 40 feet is waste. The waste footage may either be thrown away or saved as a "dummy load" to use when scratch testing the magazines during the camera prep. It is a good idea to save these dummy loads for use in the camera prep or for practicing loading a new magazine. Unless told otherwise by the production company, use the figures shown in Table 3.2 for short end and waste values.

The combined total of G, NG, W, and SE should equal the total amount of footage loaded in the magazine. This total amount is written in the section marked T.

Before removing the magazine from the camera, the 1st A.C. often places a hand over the lens and runs the camera for approximately 10 feet so that there will be a blank area of film at the end of the roll for safety reasons. If you remove the magazine immediately after the last take, you may fog the last few frames of the shot. This 10 feet of film can be included in the good or no good totals depending on what the last shot was. At the bottom of the report, after the last take, write the amount of footage that the roll ended at. For example, if the last dial reading on the camera report is 970 feet, write "OUT AT 970." If the roll of film rolled out during the last take, write the amount of footage that the roll ended at or write "ROLLOUT." Whenever possible, it is better to reload the camera than to risk having a rollout, because when the film rolls out it is not good for the camera or the film. If you are in doubt as to whether you should reload or risk rolling out, check with the D.P. or Director and let one of them make the decision. For example, I have been in the situation where after shooting a take that was 90 feet long, I had 100 feet of film left in the magazine, and the Director said he wanted to shoot another take of the scene. I have learned not to fully trust the footage counter or the film manufacturer when it comes to the size of the film roll. Rather than make the decision myself to take the chance and shoot with the remaining 100 feet of film, I usually check with the D.P. or Director. If either one chooses to take the risk and shoot another take, and the film rolls out, it is his or her responsibility. Whenever the film does roll out, write at the bottom of the

Table 3.2 Recommended Footage Amounts for Short End and Waste Rolls

Film Format	Waste	Short End
16 mm	Less than 40 feet	More than 40 feet
35 mm	Less than 100 feet	More than 100 feet

report "SAVE TAILS" as an indication to the lab to print the roll to the very end.

In addition, at the bottom of the report, write any developing instructions to the lab as given to you by the D.P. The instructions may include the following: develop normal, one-light print, time to gray scale, time to color chart, push one stop, print circle takes only, prep for video transfer, transfer circle takes only, and so on. Figures 3.7, 3.8, and 3.9 show the G, NG, W, SE, and T at the bottom of each camera report, as well as the developing instructions.

Often the magazine may be loaded with a short end of film. Looking at the camera report you may assume that it is for a full roll of film. The camera report should be marked in some way to indicate that it is a short end. This eliminates confusion and you don't risk running out of film in the middle of a shot because you forgot that it was a short end. The standard procedure for marking a camera report for a short end is to draw a diagonal line across the shooting part of the report to indicate it is a short end. This should be done before filling in the information on the report so that each time you look at the report, this diagonal line will remind you that it is a short end. The assistant will also write the footage in the lower left corner. A typical camera report for a short end is shown in Figure 3.11.

Each time you load a magazine with a fresh roll of film, a camera report should be attached to it. As stated earlier in this chapter, to save time, many 2nd A.C.s prepare a supply of camera reports with most of the heading information filled in ahead of time. Fill out as much information as possible in the heading so that the report is ready for shooting. This includes the Production Company, Production Title, Director, and Director of Photography. When you load the magazine, any additional heading information such as film type, emulsion number, and magazine number can be filled in on the report before attaching it to the magazine.

Some labs preprint the heading information on the report for you. This saves time during the loading process. If you have some of the heading information filled in ahead of time, each time a magazine is loaded only a small amount of information needs to be added to the report. This is discussed further in the section on loading magazines.

Sometimes it may be necessary to remove a partially shot roll of film from the camera, knowing that it will be used again later the same day. When doing this, remember not to break the film when removing the magazine. If possible you should mark the frame in the gate with an "X" before removing it from the camera, so that when placing the magazine back on the camera you can line up the film exactly as it was before removing it. Attach the camera report to the magazine and place the magazine back in its case for later use. When the partially shot roll

color by deluxe® **deluxe laboratories**
1377 North Serrano Ave., Hollywood, CA 90027 (213) 462-6171

CAMERA REPORT
SOUND REPORT No. 179450

DATE ______ CUSTOMER ORDER NUMBER ______
COMPANY Demi Monde Productions
DIRECTOR N. Conn CAMERAMAN RECORDIST R. Sellars
PRODUCTION NUMBER OR TITLE Clairie of the Moon
MAGAZINE NUMBER 10149 ROLL NUMBER 8
TYPE OF FILM / EMULSION 5218 237 4862

PRINT CIRCLED TAKES ONLY: [✓] ONE LITE [ ] TIMED

SCENE NO.	TAKE	DIAL	PRINT	REMARKS
17	(1)	130	130	
	2	220		
	(3)	290	70	
17 A	(1)	360	70	
	(2)	470	110	
42	1	530		
	(2)	580	50	
	3	630		
	(4)	680	50	
	(5)	720	40	
OUT AT 720'				
DEVELOP NORMAL				
ONE LIGHT WORKPRINT				
				G 520
				NG 200
740				W 20
TOTAL				T 740

All contracts with this company are accepted with the understanding that all film delivered to it is covered by the owner against loss. This company takes every necessary precaution for the safekeeping of the film, but assumes no responsibility for its loss.

DEL-82 (10/90)

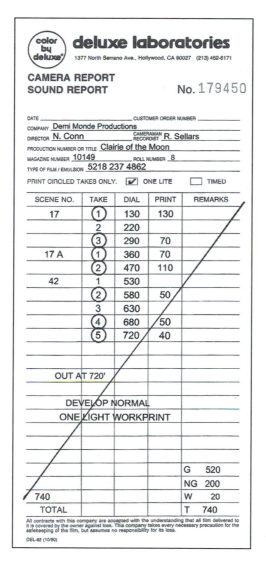

Figure 3.11 Example of a completed camera report for a short end.

is placed back on the camera, the roll number remains the same as mentioned earlier. Be sure to inform the Script Supervisor that you are using a roll from previously in the day, and that it is not a different roll number but rather the same roll number as before.

Each time a new magazine is placed on the camera, the 2nd A.C. takes the camera report from the magazine and usually places it on the back of the slate, on a clipboard, or some other type of hard surface.

This gives a smooth writing surface to write out the report during shooting. Some assistants prefer to use a clipboard for the report; some use the back of the slate. You may use whichever system is more convenient for you. Be sure to write clearly and legibly on the camera report so that the people at the lab, the Editor, and any other people reading it will be able to read the report without any difficulty.

Recording Shot Information

Throughout the course of filming it is often the responsibility of the 2nd A.C. to keep track of detailed information for each shot including a basic description of the scene, lens used, t-stop, focus, filters, lens height, film stock, and other information that is pertinent to the shot. Appendix C contains a Camera Department Log Sheet that you may use for this record keeping. I have also used an item called *The Camera Log*, which is a 4 × 6 inch spiral bound book available at most expendables supply stores. This pocket-size book contains pages to record all of the pertinent information for each shot. It also contains pages for recording your hours worked along with basic equipment information. See Figures 3.12 and 3.13 for examples of pages from *The Camera Log*.

Many assistants have a PDA (Personal Digital Assistant), with the most common ones using the Palm operating system. A program for the Palm operating system called HanDBase is currently available. First Assistant Cameraman David Eubank has designed a database called Eubank's Log, which works with the HanDBase software. Eubank's Log allows you to enter all of the information for a particular shot into your Palm operating device. Later when you sync your PDA with your desktop computer, all of the information goes to the desktop version of HanDBase, and you may then print out reports for particular shots or scenes. Some screen shots from Eubank's Log can be seen in Figures 3.14 and 3.15.

Magazines

A magazine may be described as a removable lightproof container that is used to hold the film before and after exposure. Two basic types of magazines are in use today: coaxial and displacement. When we speak about the areas within the magazine, the feed side contains the fresh unexposed raw stock, while the take-up side contains the exposed film.

The coaxial magazine has two distinct compartments, one for the feed side and one for the take-up side. These two compartments share

THE CAMERA LOG™

Week Ending:

Date	Call	Meals 1st	Meals 2nd	Camera Wrap	Wrap

Date						
Re-Rates						

Date	Equipment
	Received Returned
	Received Returned
	Received Returned
	Received Returned
	Received Returned
	Received Returned

Figure 3.12 *The Camera Log* page for recording hours worked and equipment information. (Courtesy of Donald Burghardt.)

a common dividing wall between them. The magazine is called coaxial because the feed and take-up rolls share the same axis of rotation. Because there are two separate compartments, it is much easier to do the loading and unloading of the magazine. During the loading process, only the feed side needs to be loaded in the dark; the take-up side can be loaded in the light. During the unloading process, the take-up side must be unloaded in the dark, and the feed side may be unloaded in the light, unless there is a short end. If there is any short end left in the magazine, then the feed side also must be unloaded in the dark.

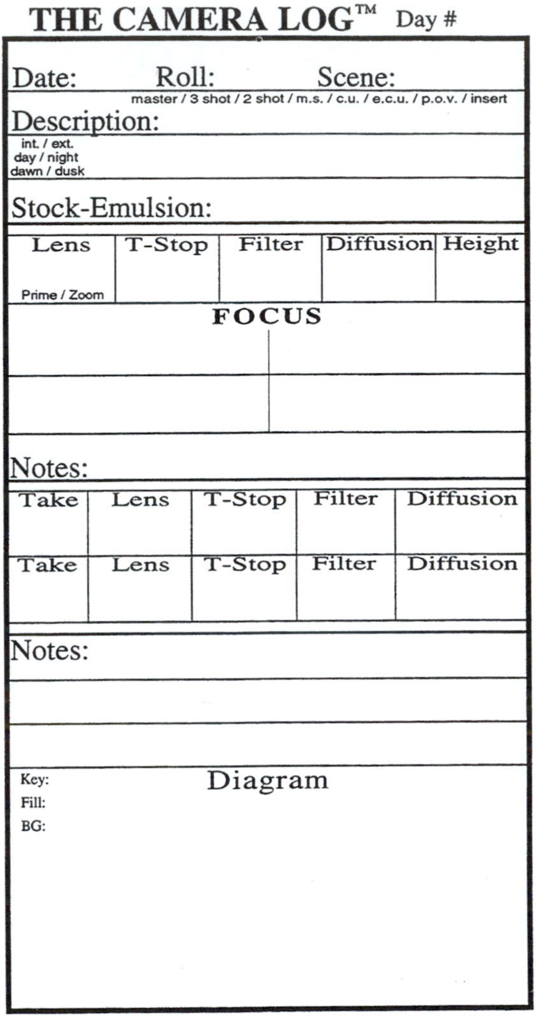

THE CAMERA LOG™ Day #

Date: Roll: Scene:

master / 3 shot / 2 shot / m.s. / c.u. / e.c.u. / p.o.v. / insert

Description:

int. / ext.
day / night
dawn / dusk

Stock-Emulsion:

Lens (Prime / Zoom)	T-Stop	Filter	Diffusion	Height

FOCUS

Notes:

Take	Lens	T-Stop	Filter	Diffusion
Take	Lens	T-Stop	Filter	Diffusion

Notes:

Key:
Fill:
BG:

Diagram

Figure 3.13 *The Camera Log* page for recording shot information. (Courtesy of Donald Burghardt.)

A displacement magazine is so named because, as the film goes from the feed side to the take-up side, it is displaced from one side to the other. There are two different types of displacement magazines: the single-chamber displacement magazine and the double-chamber displacement magazine. On a displacement magazine the feed side is usually toward the front of the camera and the take-up side is toward the back of the camera when the magazine is in place. During shooting, as

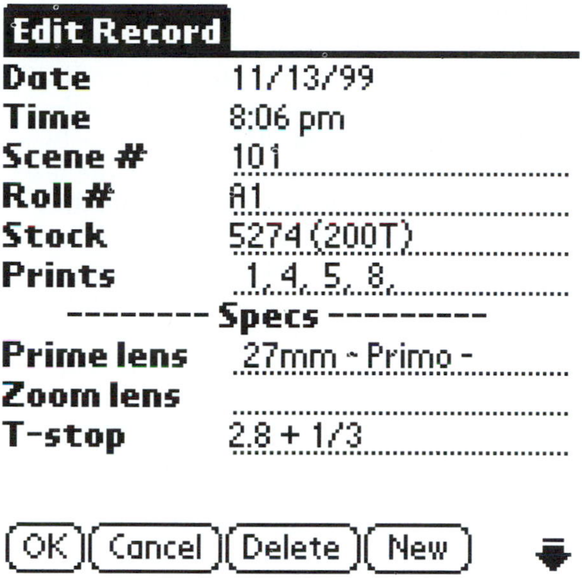

Figure 3.14 Screen shot #1 from Eubank's Log. (Courtesy of David Eubank.)

Figure 3.15 Screen shot #2 from Eubank's Log. (Courtesy of David Eubank.)

the film is displaced from the feed side to the take-up side, the film moves from the front of the camera to the back. This will cause a shift in weight on the camera, so the camera must be periodically rebalanced.

The double-chamber displacement magazine has two distinct compartments that share a common dividing wall between them. One side is for the feed roll of film and one side for the take-up roll, and may be handled the same as the coaxial magazine during the loading and unloading process. In other words, the feed side must be loaded in the dark and the take-up side loaded in the light during loading, and the take-up side unloaded in the dark during unloading.

The single-chamber displacement magazine contains both the feed and the take-up sides of the magazine in the same compartment. Because of this, the entire loading and unloading process must be done in the dark. Most single-chamber displacement magazines are not able to hold a full roll of film on both the feed side and the take-up side at the same time. This means that during shooting, as the feed roll gets progressively smaller and the take-up roll gets progressively larger, the film is displaced from the feed side of the magazine to the take-up side.

A variation of the displacement magazine is called an active displacement. During operation of the camera, the feed and take-up rolls actually shift position during filming to compensate for the transfer of the film from the feed roll to the take-up roll. This allows the magazine and therefore the overall camera to be smaller in size and much more compact. Many newer 35 mm film cameras use an active displacement type of magazine. It is a good idea to be familiar with the loading and unloading procedure for as many different magazines as possible. Figure 3.16 shows two sides of a coaxial magazine. Figures 3.17 and 3.18 show the single-chamber and double-chamber displacement magazines. Figure 3.19 shows the Aaton 35 active displacement magazine.

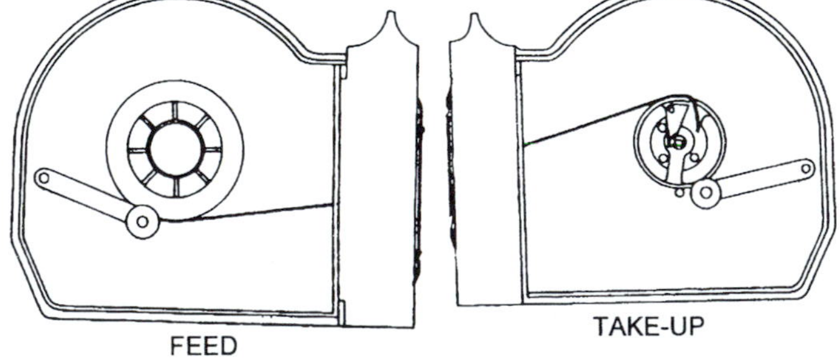

Figure 3.16 Arriflex 16SR coaxial magazine. (Courtesy of ARRI Inc.)

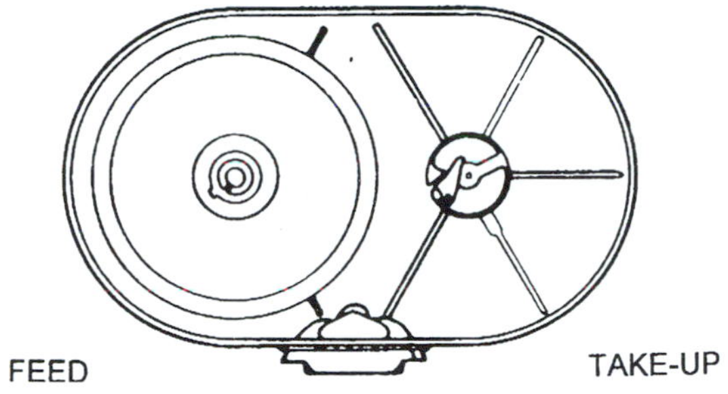

Figure 3.17
Single-chamber displacement magazine. (Courtesy of ARRI Inc.)

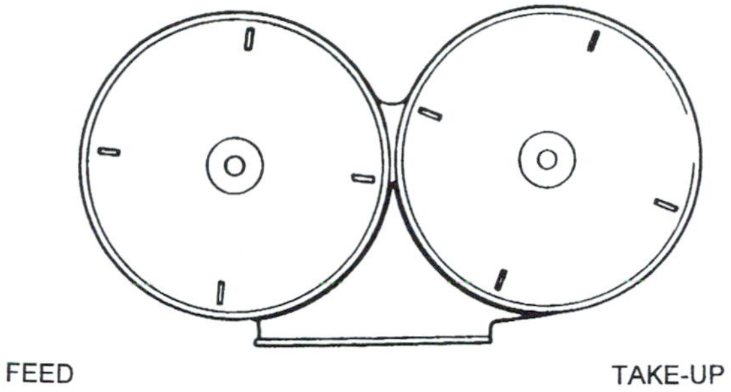

Figure 3.18
Double-chamber displacement magazine. (Reprinted from *Motion Picture Camera & Lighting Equipment* with permission of David Samuelson.)

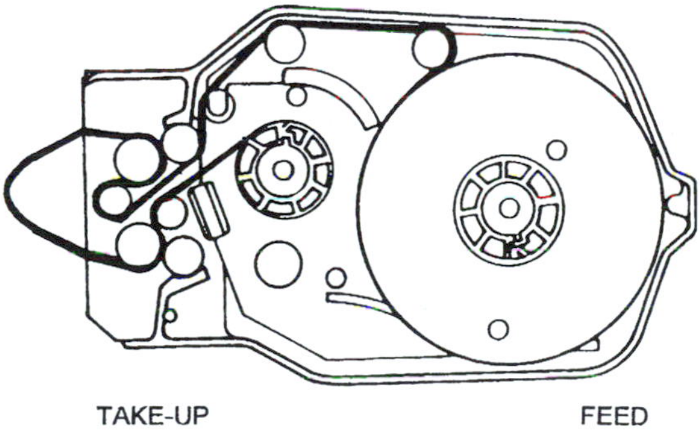

Figure 3.19
Active displacement magazine. (Courtesy of Aaton, Inc.)

Loading Magazines

Before loading any magazine, clean it thoroughly to remove any dirt, dust, or film chips. Blow out the magazine using some type of compressed air or nitrogen tank. Also check the magazine to see if it contains any electrical contacts where it attaches to the camera. It is important to keep these contacts clean. Otherwise the film will not travel properly through the magazine. Be sure that the darkroom, changing bag, or changing tent is clean and that you have all the necessary items before you start to load any magazines. You should have camera tape, permanent felt tip markers, camera reports, extra cores, film cans, and so on. Most important, be sure that you have the correct film stock to load into the magazine.

When a fresh roll of raw stock is removed from the black bag, it will have a small piece of tape on the end to hold the roll together. I remove this tape and recommend placing it inside the bottom of the film can. Be sure to remove all of the tape from the end of the roll. Many camera or magazine jams have occurred because of a small amount of tape left on the roll. Once you have removed the film from the black bag, place the bag back in the film can and put the lid on the can to reduce the chance of the piece of tape or the black bag getting stuck in the magazine during the loading process.

Some magazines require a plastic core on the take-up spindle or core adapter to wind the exposed film around. You should have extra cores available in this case. The best way to secure the film to the plastic core is to fold approximately 1 to 1 1/2 inches of the film against itself, keeping the edges of the film straight against each other. Position the core so that the slot is facing in such a way that as it rotates, the film is pulled tight against the core. You want to be sure that as the core rotates, the film does not pull loose from the slot in the core. By positioning the slot correctly, the film will be pulled tight as the core rotates and eliminate any chance of the film coming off the core (Figure 3.20).

Certain magazines have a collapsible core on the take-up side. When the film is first placed on the collapsible core, it is inserted into a slot and locked in place. When placing the film on the collapsible core, place it so that the end of the film is approximately half the way into the slot. Do not place it in the slot in such a way that the end of the film touches the edge of the core. During shooting, while the core is spinning, the film may rub against the inside edge of the core and

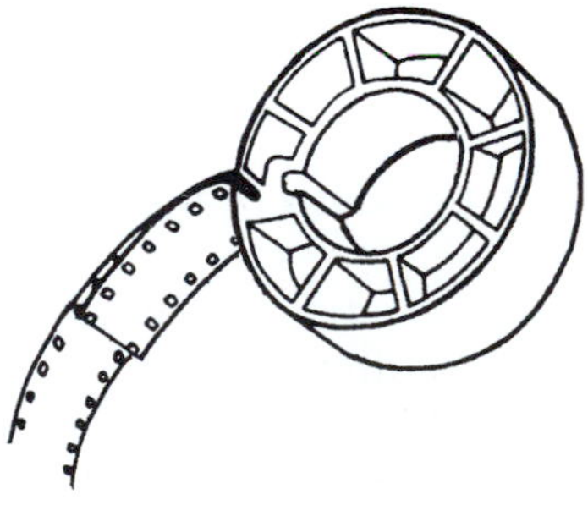

Figure 3.20
Securing the end of the film to a plastic core.

cause unnecessary noise in the camera. When you are ready to remove the exposed film from the take-up side, release the lock and the core will collapse, which allows you to easily remove the roll of film from the magazine. Some cameras have the ability to accept internal loads, commonly referred to as daylight spools, without the use of a magazine. In this case, you should have extra daylight spools available onto which the exposed film may be taken up. See Figures 1.7 and 1.8 for illustrations of daylight spools and plastic cores. Figure 3.21 shows a collapsible core. Many magazines will accept a daylight spool, but it is not recommended because as the spool rotates, the flanges of the spool rub against the interior of the magazine, causing unnecessary noise during shooting.

For ease of loading and threading the film, the end of it should have a straight edge, and it should be cut so that the cut bisects the perforations. Before loading a roll of film into a magazine, you may need to cut the film so that you bisect a perforation. This makes it easier to thread the film into a magazine that contains geared teeth or sprocket wheels. Remember, you will need to do this in the dark so that you do not expose the film stock. Be very careful if you need to cut the film in a darkroom, and especially if you are using a changing bag or changing tent, so that you do not cut the bag or tent (Figure 3.22).

Once you have loaded the magazine, an identification label must be placed on the lid to identify what is loaded in it. On a coaxial magazine, the identification label should be placed on the take-up side of the magazine. The identification label should contain the following information: production company, production title, date, footage, film type, emulsion number, roll number, and magazine number. If more than one person is loading magazines on the production, the Loader's initials also should be written on this piece of tape. The roll number space is left blank and filled in when the magazine is placed on the camera.

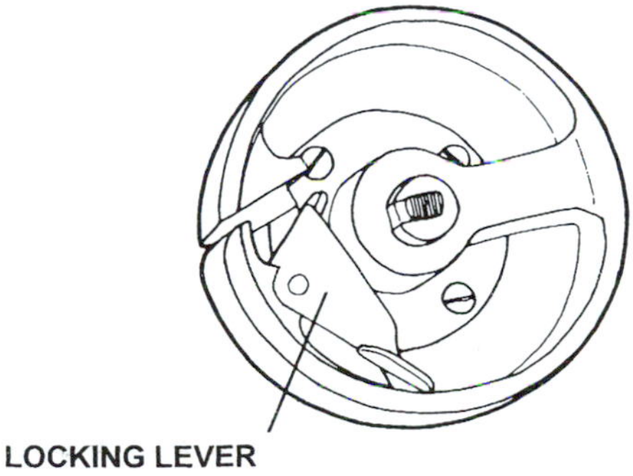

Figure 3.21
Collapsible core. (Reprinted from the *Arriflex 16SR Book* by Jon Fauer with permission of the author and ARRI Inc.)

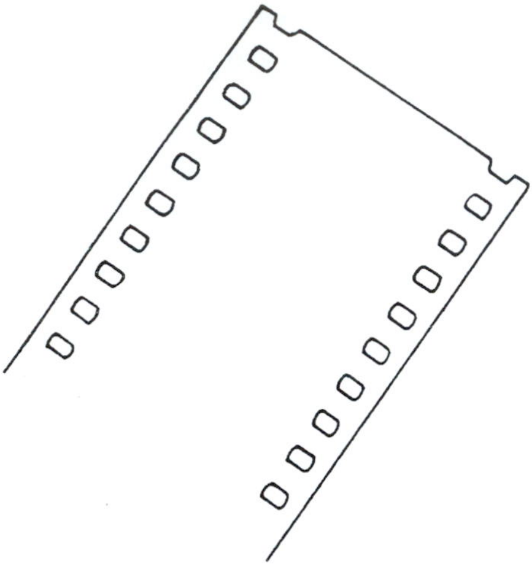

Figure 3.22
End of film cut straight, showing bisected perforations.

On many productions the identification label is usually made from a piece of 1-inch-wide white camera tape and a black permanent felt tip marker. Quite often many assistants will use a color-coding system for labeling the magazines when they are using more than one type of film stock. For example, use white tape for slow-speed film, yellow tape for medium-speed film, and red tape for high-speed film. This is especially useful when you are in a hurry because you don't have to take time to read the label to know what type of film is loaded in the magazine. The color of the tape indicates the type of film being loaded. Table 3.3 is a suggestion of what color tape to use based on some of the currently available Eastman Kodak Color Negative and Fuji Color Negative films. Keep in mind that not all film stocks are listed in the table; the system shown is based on the color-coding system I have used successfully for many years. You may adjust this to suit your particular shooting needs,

Table 3.3 Camera Tape Color Coding System When Using Various Films

Kodak	EI	Fuji	EI	Tape Color	Ink Color
7245/5245	50 D	8622/8522	64 D	White	Black
7212/5212	100 T	8632/8532	125 T	White	Red
7217/5217	200 T			Yellow	Red
7274/5274	200 T	8652/8552	250 T	Yellow	Black
7246/5246	250 D	8662/8562	250 D	Blue	Black
7218/5218	500 T	8672/8572	500 T	Red	Black

D = daylight; T = tungsten

depending on how many different film stocks you are using on your production. If you are unable to use a tape color-coding system, you can still color-code the film by using 1-inch-wide white camera tape with a different color marking pen for each film stock. This will work just as well as the tape color-coding system. The important thing to remember is that if you develop a system, you should stick with it; don't change it from production to production. The magazine label is usually 6 to 8 inches long and may look like the ones shown in Figures 3.23 and 3.24. Some expendables supply stores offer a special 2-inch-wide tape that is imprinted with spaces to write in the film information for the mag label. An example of this type of tape label is shown in Figure 3.25.

Once the magazine has been loaded, place a piece of tape over the magazine lid as a safety measure. On many magazines it is recommended that you wrap tape around the edges where the lid attaches to the magazine, to prevent light leaks and as a safety measure to keep the lid from coming off. This is especially important when filming outside in bright sunlight since the intensity of direct, bright sunlight for an

Date	Production Company Production Title		Roll # Mag #	
Footage	Film Type	Emulsion Number		Loader Initials

A

10/29/91	Demi Monde Productions "Claire of the Moon"	Roll #7 Mag # 10143	
1000'	5218 - 237 - 4862		DEE

B

Figure 3.23 **A,** Information to be included on a magazine ID label. **B,** Completed magazine ID label.

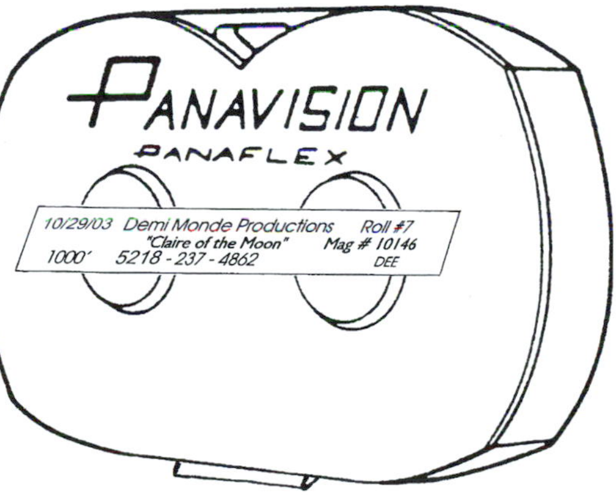

Figure 3.24 Magazine identification label in place on the magazine. (Reprinted from the *Panaflex Users Manual* with permission of David Samuelson and Panavision, Inc.)

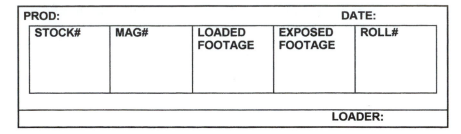

PROD:			DATE:	
STOCK#	MAG#	LOADED FOOTAGE	EXPOSED FOOTAGE	ROLL#
			LOADER:	

Figure 3.25 Preprinted 2-inch tape magazine label.

extended period on a magazine can cause fogging of the film even from a very small light leak. If you are using the color code system for the magazine identification labels, the tape used for sealing the lid should be the same color as that used for the identification label.

Once the magazine has been loaded and an identification label attached, you should attach a camera report to it. You should have filled in the heading portion previously, so now you only have to fill in the footage, film type, emulsion number, magazine number, and so on. Tape the camera report to the magazine so that it is ready for use when the magazine is loaded onto the camera. When the magazine is then removed from its case for use, the camera report is already attached and you do not have to search to find a report. The report is removed from the magazine and placed on the back of the slate or clipboard for use during filming. When you hand a new magazine to the 1st A.C., be sure to write in the proper roll number on the identification label. Once you have finished using a particular magazine and roll of film, the camera report is reattached to it and the magazine is placed back in the case. When you take the mag to the darkroom to unload and reload, the report is there so you can complete the unloading process without having to locate the report for that roll of film.

If the magazine is loaded with a short end, the footage amount on the identification label should be circled in a contrasting color so that it stands out. In addition, you should make an additional, smaller identification label with only the footage marked on it, which is placed alongside the larger identification label. When the magazine is loaded onto the camera, place this smaller piece of tape next to the footage counter of the camera. Each time you or the 1st A.C. looks at the footage counter to obtain the dial readings, you will be reminded that there is a short end in the magazine. The short end identification label and smaller reminder label are shown in Figures 3.26 and 3.27.

When using short ends for filming be aware that the labels on the cans may not always be completely accurate. This is often true for short ends purchased from an outside supplier and not usually the case with

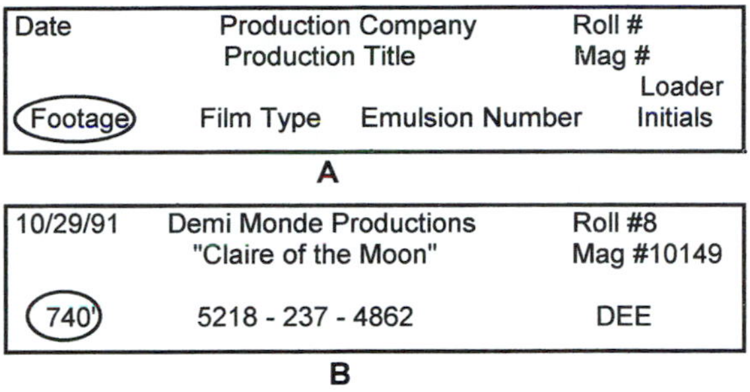
Date
Production Company
Production Title
Roll #
Mag #
Footage
Film Type
Emulsion Number
Loader Initials
A
10/29/91
Demi Monde Productions
"Claire of the Moon"
Roll #8
Mag #10149
740'
5218 - 237 - 4862
DEE
B

Figure 3.26
A, Information to be included on a short end ID label. **B,** Completed short end ID label.

740'

Figure 3.27
Example of a short end reminder label.

short ends that you have created during the course of production. You may load a magazine with what you think is a 370-foot short end only to discover that the film rolled out after 325 feet had traveled through the camera. Whenever this happens you should keep a record listing the amounts indicated on the can labels versus the actual amount that ran through the camera. In some cases the production company may be able to obtain additional film stock at no charge to make up for this discrepancy.

After the magazines have been loaded, place them in their case and attach another identification tape to the lid for each magazine inside. This is just a small piece of tape with the footage amount written on it. Many assistants may also place a small identification tape on the sides and front of the case. If you are using the color-coding system, use the same color tape used on the magazine identification label. Using the color-coding system saves time because you do not have to pick up the magazine or open the case to know what type of film is loaded. An illustration of a properly labeled magazine case is shown in Figure 3.28.

During the day's shooting, there will be many times when you will be required to unload and load magazines. When is the right time to go to the darkroom and reload any used magazines? It depends on the individual circumstances of the particular production that you are working on. In most cases, when there is a new lighting setup being done, the 2nd A.C. will usually have enough time to complete the reloading process. Always check with the 1st A.C. to see if it is all right to leave the set and do this job. The 1st A.C. usually has a lot on his or

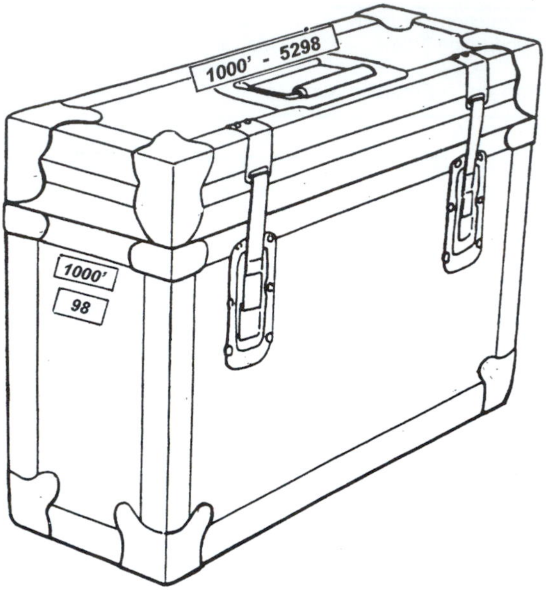

Figure 3.28 Magazine case showing identification tape on top and side.

her mind, and may not realize that you have two or three magazines that need to be reloaded. Let the 1st A.C. know the situation, and if it is convenient, you will be allowed to reload. If you are shooting a lot of film, you may have to leave the set during shooting; just be sure to work it out with the first assistant so your on-set duties can be covered for the brief time you will be away from the set. You should never wait until all of the magazines have been shot before reloading. This could result in the production having to stop shooting until you have time to load more film. If you keep ahead of this throughout the day, the filmmaking process will go much smoother, and there should be no delays because a magazine is not ready. Try to find out ahead of time from the D.P. what film stock you will be using the next day and load the magazines before you go home for the night.

During the loading process, mistakes can happen, and there may be an instance when you accidentally expose a fresh roll of film to the light. In a rush you may open the magazine or the film can in the light, or possibly the lid of the magazine was not locked properly and unexpectedly opened in the light. You should immediately place this exposed roll of film in a black bag and put it back into the film can. Wrap the can with 1-inch white camera tape and place a warning label on the can that reads, "FILM EXPOSED TO LIGHT—DO NOT USE."

This warning should be written on the top of the can and also along the edge on the sealing tape. Place this can in a safe place away from all fresh raw stock, short ends, and exposed film that has been shot. You do not want to risk loading this film by accident and trying to shoot with it.

Finally, if film is accidentally exposed, do not try to hide it. Notify the 1st A.C. immediately so that it can be brought to the attention of the D.P. and then to the production manager. By telling the appropriate people about this as soon as possible, you will show that you are a professional, and they should understand that it was probably only an accident and you did not do it intentionally. By trying to hide it you will only cause yourself problems, including losing your job and possibly not getting other jobs.

I remember the first time that I accidentally flashed a fresh roll of film. I was in the darkroom at a rental house, and someone knocked on the door to ask me a question. Because of this I became distracted and accidentally opened the feed side of the coaxial magazine that I had just finished loading. I immediately informed the D.P. and fortunately he was extremely understanding about it. We got another roll of film and the good thing was that I didn't loose the job and continued to work with the D.P. after that.

Unloading Magazines

Before unloading or downloading magazines check that you have everything needed to can out the film. You should have empty cans, black bags, black and white camera tape, and so on. Always remove the exposed film and place it in a black bag and can before removing any short end or waste. When unloading a roll of film that is on a plastic core, place the thumb of one hand on the inside edge of the core, and, using your other hand on the outside edge of the roll, gently lift the roll of film with the core off the take-up spindle. As the roll starts to come up and off the spindle, slide your hand under the roll to keep the film from spooling off. When using a collapsible core, release the lock on the core, place your thumbs inside the core, and gently pull the roll of film up so that your thumbs are inside the center of the roll to prevent the film from coming out from the center. Many assistants will place a plastic core in the center of the roll that has been removed from a collapsible core in order to stabilize it. Check with the lab processing the film to see if they require a core placed in the center of the roll.

Always place the exposed film in a black bag and film can. Do not tape the end of the film to the roll. The standard industry rule for wrapping a can of exposed film is to use 1-inch black camera tape. Some assistants use special red tape that is imprinted with the words "EXPOSED FILM—OPEN IN DARKROOM ONLY." Place the identification label from the magazine on the film can, along with the top copy of the camera report. Be sure that the camera report is completely filled out with all the proper takes circled; that the footage amounts are totaled for G, NG, W, SE, and T; and that the lab instructions are written on it. Have the Script Supervisor double-check the report and initial it so that you are sure that the correct takes are circled. Once the can of exposed film is ready, keep it in a safe place away from any raw stock so that it does not get reloaded by mistake. See the section, Preparing Exposed Film for Delivery to the Lab later in this chapter for a more detailed discussion of paperwork and preparing exposed film for delivery to the lab.

If there is any film left in the feed side of the magazine, remove it now. If it is a short end, it must be unloaded in the dark. You will know if it is a short end or waste based on the totals on the camera report. If it is a short end, place it in a black bag and in a film can, and wrap it with tape. A general rule is to wrap all cans of unexposed film in 1-inch white camera tape unless you are using the color-coding system. As I have mentioned before, however, if you have been using the color-coding system, wrap the film can in the appropriate color tape. Place a label on the can containing the short end so that you know how much and what type of film is in the can. Using the appropriate color tape, place an identification label on the can with the following information: date, footage, film type, emulsion number, and the words "SHORT END." Put the initials of the assistant unloading the magazine on this label. In addition, write along the edge of the can, on the piece of sealing tape, the amount of footage in the can. The label for a can containing a short end is shown in Figure 3.29. See Appendix C for a custom Short End label that you may use for labeling short end film cans. This label may be downloaded from the companion web site of the book for your personal use.

There may be times when you have to can up a roll of raw stock that was loaded but not used. It may be the end of production and filming is completed. When this happens, place the film in a black bag and into a film can. If possible, use the original film can that the film came in. Seal the can with the appropriate color tape, and place an identification label on the can. This label should contain the following information: date, footage, film type, emulsion number, and the word "RECAN." The assistant's initials should also be placed on this label. Write the footage on the piece of sealing tape on the edge of the can. The label for a recan roll of film is shown in Figure 3.30. See Appendix C for a custom Recan label that you may use for labeling recan film cans. This label may be downloaded from the companion web site of the book for your personal use.

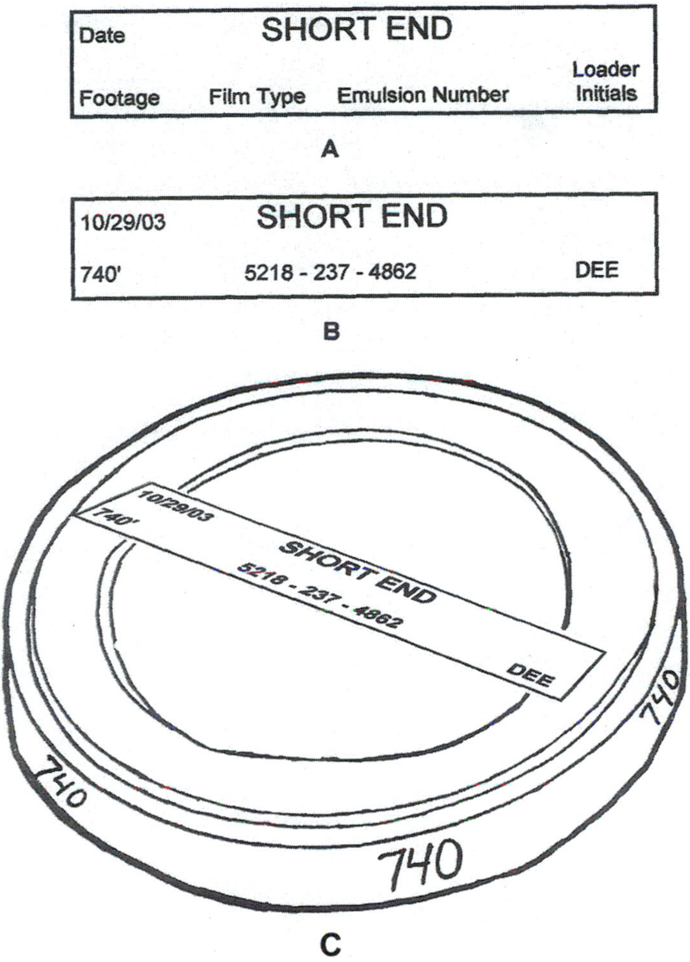

Figure 3.29 **A,** Information to be included on a short end can label. **B,** Completed short end can label. **C,** Proper labeling of a film can containing a short end.

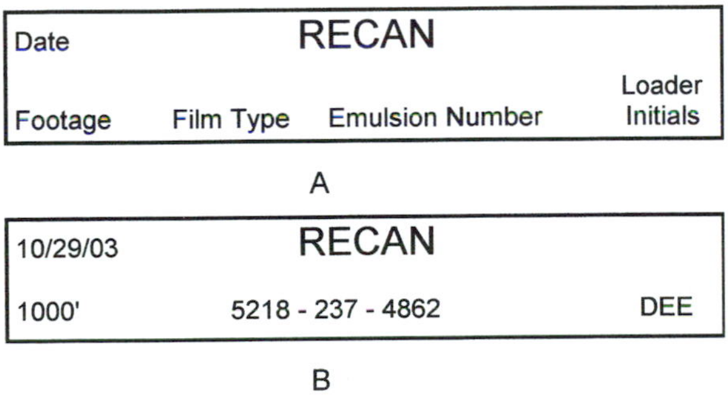

Figure 3.30
A, Information to be included on a recan label. **B,** Completed label for a recan roll of film.

As when loading a magazine, accidents can also happen when unloading. If you should accidentally expose to light a roll that has been shot, you should tell the 1st A.C. and D.P. immediately. This situation is more serious than exposing a fresh roll of film. By exposing a roll that has already been shot, you are now requiring the production company to reshoot everything that was on that particular roll. Hopefully the footage on the roll can be easily reshot that day or on another day. This will most likely cost the production company a lot of unexpected money and may result in your losing your job, even if it was only an accident. The important thing to remember when loading and especially when unloading film is not to be rushed and to take your time. Rushing can only cause costly mistakes, not only to the production company but also to you if you lose the job. Don't let anybody rush you during the loading or unloading of any film magazine.

Using a Changing Bag or Changing Tent

If a darkroom is not available, you should have a changing bag or changing tent available for loading and unloading magazines. Most 2nd A.C.s have their own changing bag or changing tent. It should be a standard part of your kit or ditty bag. If you don't have one of your own, they are available for rental at most camera rental houses. Ask the production company to rent one along with the camera equipment. An assistant will often rent a changing bag or tent just to have an extra in case of emergencies. The changing bag is actually two bags, one within another. They are sewn together along the edges and along the sides of the two sleeves, which have elastic cuffs. At the top of each bag is a zipper so that you have access to the inside of the bag. With the zippers closed and your arms in the sleeves, you have a completely lightproof compartment for loading and unloading magazines.

The important thing to remember when using a changing bag or tent is not to panic if something goes wrong. The area inside the bag is very small and confined, and you should take your time when working in the bag. One of the most common problems encountered when unloading film is that the core will come out of the center and the film will start to spool off the roll from the center. When working in a small changing bag with a 35 mm film magazine, this can be especially frustrating because of the lack of space to work in the bag. If this happens with the exposed roll of film, do not try to force the core back into the center of the roll. Carefully place the film back into the center of the roll without the core, and continue the unloading process normally. Most labs that I have worked with have told me that it is not necessary for a core to be placed in the center of the roll to develop and process the film. If the core comes out of a roll of unexposed raw stock or a short end, do not try to force the core back into the center of the roll. Place this roll into a black bag and can, and start over with a new roll of film. If something does go wrong while you are working in a changing bag, remember, never open the bag or remove your arms until all film, whether exposed or unexposed, is in a black bag and in a film can.

Before using the bag or tent, always turn it inside out and shake it to remove any loose film chips or material that may have become stuck in the bag. To check the bag for light leaks, place it over your head; once your eyes have adjusted to the darkness, see if any light is leaking in. It is best to do this outside in bright sunlight so that you can better see any light leaking in. This may sound pretty silly and you will look foolish doing this, so I recommend doing it when nobody else is around. If any holes are found, they may be covered with black camera tape or gaffer tape if they are not too large. When loading a magazine, place it in the inner bag with the can of unexposed raw stock. If necessary be sure to place an empty core on the take-up side of the magazine before placing it in the bag. Close both zippers of the bag or tent and then insert your arms into the elastic sleeves so that the elastic is past your elbows. When the magazine lid is removed, some assistants place it under the magazine to conserve space in the bag. Load the film in the usual manner and then place the lid back on the magazine, being careful not to catch the black bag between the magazine and the lid. Be sure that the lid is securely locked on the magazine before removing your arms from the bag and opening the zippers. Place the proper label on the magazine and tape the lid around the edges. Place the black bag back in the can, replace the lid on the can, and put it aside so that it is ready when it is time to unload the magazine.

The unloading process is the reverse of the loading process, as described earlier. Be sure that the bag is clean and free from dirt, dust, and film chips. Place the magazine in the inner bag along with the appropriate number of black bags and cans to can out any exposed film or any short ends. Again, remember to not remove your arms or open the bag until all film is placed in black bags and film cans.

A variation of the changing bag is the film-changing tent. I wish that the changing tent was available when I first started out as an assistant because it is a great item to have in your ditty bag or kit. It is similar in size and shape to a changing bag, but instead of lying flat, it forms a lightproof tent in which you load and unload magazines. Creating a tent over the working surface makes it so much easier for the assistant to load and unload film in comfort. You don't have the bag resting on top of your arms, on top of the film, or on top of the magazines while trying to load or unload film. This helps to eliminate the possibility of the tent becoming caught in the magazine when closing and attaching the lid. Figure 3.31 shows a changing bag and a changing tent.

When you are finished using the changing bag or changing tent, always shake it out to remove any film chips or other foreign matter. See Figure 3.32 and follow these instructions for folding the changing bag:

1. Lay bag flat and close both zippers.
2. Fold arms in toward center of bag.
3. Fold bag one-third up from the bottom.
4. Fold bag one-third down from the top.
5. Fold bag once more from either top or bottom.
6. Fold bag one-third from the right to the left.
7. Fold bag once more from the left. Keep the bag in a secure place so that it remains clean and cannot become ripped or torn.

The changing tent is folded in a similar manner. See Figure 3.33 and follow these instructions for folding the changing tent.

1. Remove support rods, lay tent flat, and close both zippers.
2. Fold arms in toward center of bag.
3. Fold bag in half from the bottom.
4. Fold support rods and lay them on the tent.
5. Carefully roll tent up tightly and place it in its carry bag so that it remains clean and cannot become ripped or torn.

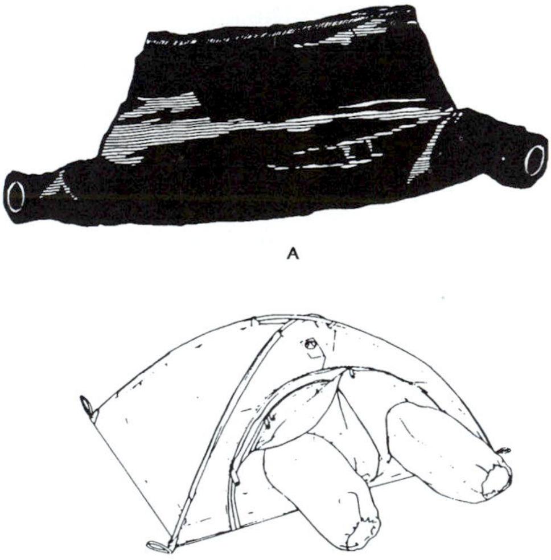

A

B

Figure 3.31
A, Changing bag. (Reprinted from the *Arriflex 16SR Book* by Jon Fauer with permission of the author and ARRI Inc.) **B,** Changing tent. (Reprinted from the *Arriflex 35 Book* by Jon Fauer with permission of the author and ARRI Inc.)

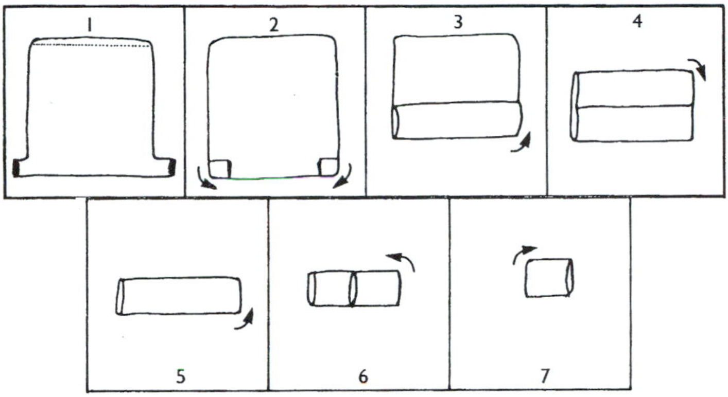

Figure 3.32 Properly folding the changing bag.

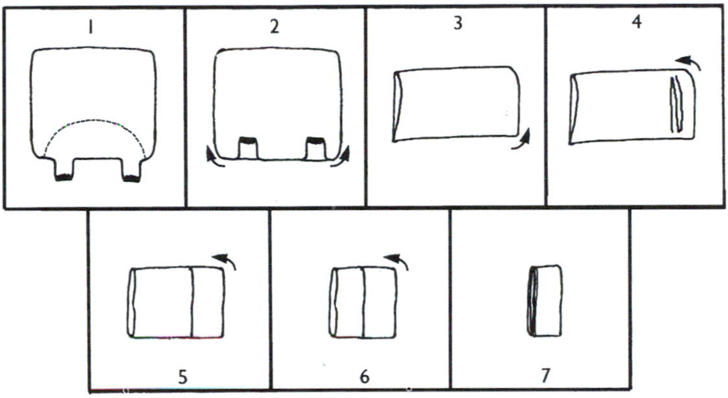

Figure 3.33 Properly folding the changing tent.

Whenever working as a 2nd A.C., you should never wear any type of clothing, such as loose sweaters, that have fibers or threads that could get into the magazines. These small fibers or threads could scratch the film and create additional shooting time if scenes need to be reshot. This is especially important when working in a changing bag or changing tent. The process of placing your arms in the bag or tent could cause fibers or threads to become loose and fall into the magazine. In addition, if you wear a watch that has an illuminated dial, it should be removed before going into the darkroom or placing your hands in the changing bag or changing tent. The light from the dial could cause a slight fogging on the edges of the film. It is always better to take that extra step and be safe.

Setting Up the Camera

At the start of each shooting day the camera must be set up and made ready to shoot as quickly as possible. The actual setting up of the camera is usually handled by the 1st A.C. The 2nd A.C. stands nearby and hands pieces of equipment to the 1st A.C. as they are asked for. It is important for the 2nd A.C. to know and understand the proper setup of the camera system in case he or she must step in and serve as 1st A.C. in an emergency or when additional cameras are used. The procedure for setting up the camera is discussed in detail in the section, Setting Up the Camera, in Chapter 4.

Marking Actors

During rehearsals the 2nd A.C. places marks on the floor for each actor, for each position he or she takes during the scene. Any time an actor stops and does something or speaks a line, a mark must be placed for him or her. These marks are often referred to as action points. For example, if an actor walks in the door and stops, then walks over to a table and stops, and then goes to the window for the remainder of the scene, there will be one mark at the door, one at the table, and a final mark at the window. Actors use these marks so that they know where to stand, the 1st A.C. uses them for focus measurements, and the D.P. uses them for lighting purposes. The marks are usually made with the colored paper tape that was included in the expendables list. It is important to use only colored paper tape for actor's marks. The adhesive on the paper tape is not as strong as the adhesive on the cloth camera tape, so there is less chance of damage when removing the paper tape from the floor or carpet of a private home or business. When placing marks, be sure to make a small tab on the end of the tape to make it easier to remove later on. If the floor or ground is seen in the shot, place tape marks for the rehearsal and then remove them or make them very small for the actual shot. You may be able to use a color of tape that is close to the color of the floor surface. If the mark is made small enough the camera may not pick it up in the shot, but the actor should still be able to see it if necessary. If you are working outside or on a surface where you cannot place tape marks, use anything that is handy, such as leaves, sticks, twigs, rocks, and so on. Ideally, when working outside, you would use something that would blend in with the surroundings and not look like an actor's mark. When working on pavement or concrete, many assistants use a piece of chalk to make the marks for the actor. Just remember to remove any marks before shooting so that they are not visible on film. I once worked on a television series, and in one episode a scene required two characters to meet up with each other on the street. The 2nd A.C. placed a large chalk mark on the pavement for each actor. Unfortunately when it came time to film the shot, nobody said anything about the marks; they were not removed before shooting and were clearly visible in the finished show.

If more than one actor is in the scene, each actor's marks should be a different color. This makes it easier and less confusing for each actor. When ordering the expendables you would order different colors of paper tape for this purpose. The most common type of mark used is the "T" mark, shaped like the letter "T" and measuring 3 to 5 inches wide by 3 to 5 inches high. A "T" mark is placed with the top portion of the "T" just in front of the actor's toes and the center portion extending between the actor's feet (Figure 3.34). Often when the actor has to stop at a very precise spot, a sandbag will be placed on the ground at the spot so that when the actor touches the sandbag he or she is in the correct place.

Another type of mark is the toe mark. These are usually 3- or 4-inch-long strips of tape placed at the end of each actor's foot (Figure 3.35).

A variation of the toe mark is the "V" mark. It consists of two strips of tape placed at each actor's foot in the shape of the letter "V" (Figure 3.36).

One other and more precise form of mark is a box created with tape, placed completely around the actor's feet (Figure 3.37).

Slates

The slate is used to identify the pertinent information for each scene shot during the production. There are two basic types of slates: sync

Figure 3.34
Example of a "T" mark.

Figure 3.35
Example of toe marks.

Figure 3.36
Example of a "V" mark.

Figure 3.37
Example of a box mark.

and insert. The sync slate is used anytime you are recording sound. The top part of the slate contains two pieces of wood painted with diagonal black and white lines. The top piece of wood is hinged to the bottom piece of wood, which is attached to the slate. These pieces of wood, along with the slate, are sometimes referred to as the clapper. Some assistants use a sync slate that has the clapper part that is painted with different color stripes that often correspond to the colors of a typical color chart on most film sets. The type of slate and clapper is up to the individual camera assistant. An example of a sync slate is shown in Figure 3.38.

Another type of sync slate is the time code or electronic slate. These types of slates are becoming more common because so much that we film these days is being edited on videotape. When using the time code slate there is a very precise electronic clock installed in the sound recorder and often in the camera, although it is not necessary in the camera. These clocks produce a signal that is recorded on the edge of the sound magnetic tape and on the film. The slate contains a digital readout display showing hours, minutes, seconds, and frames. When the sticks of the slate are clapped together, the display freezes momentarily and the image is recorded on film. This precise time information is recorded on the sound track and, in the editing process, it is a simple matter of matching up the sound with the picture that has the same time code information. These time code slates have been used quite extensively on music videos over the years but are becoming more and more prevalent on features, television shows, and commercials as well (Figure 3.39).

The insert slate is usually a much smaller version of the sync slate, and it does not contain the wooden clappers. It is often used when shooting MOS shots or, as the name implies, when shooting

Figure 3.38
Sync slate.

Figure 3.39
Time code slate. (Courtesy of Denecke, Inc.)

inserts. The sync slate may be used for inserts or MOS shots without clapping the sticks together. An example of an insert slate is shown in Figure 3.40.

The information written on the sync and insert slate is usually as follows: production title, Director, Cameraman (D.P.), roll number, scene number, take number, int/ext, day/nite, and the date. Often when using more than one camera, a separate slate is designated for each camera. In this case, the slate would also have the camera letter written on it so that the Editor can easily distinguish which camera photographed the particular shot. When using the insert slate, the unit number and the production number may also be placed on the slate. The production title is the working title of the film during shooting. The Director is the name of the person who is directing the film. On the slate, place the first initial and last name of the Director. Place the first initial and the last name of the D.P. on the slate in the space labeled CAMERA. The roll number refers to the camera roll number that is

DATE	UNIT	CAMERA
SCENE	TAKE	ROLL
CAMERAMAN		PROD. NO.

Figure 3.40
Insert slate.

being shot at the time. Get the scene and take numbers, which correspond to the scene in the script that is being filmed, from the Script Supervisor. "INT" means that you are filming on an interior set and "EXT" refers to an exterior set. "DAY/NITE" refers to the time of day that the scene takes place. The date is the month, day, and year that you are filming. Much of this basic information may be placed on the slate using stick-on vinyl lettering or a label made with a laminated label maker that can be purchased from any office supply store. If you don't have the stick-on letters or label maker, you may simply write this information on a piece of 1-inch-wide white camera tape and place it on the slate. The information that is continually changing, such as the roll, scene, and take numbers, would usually be written on the slate by using some type of erasable marker. The most commonly used slates are made of a material that allows you to use a dry erase marker to record the information.

Before each shot, check with the Script Supervisor for the scene number and take number. Always write the numbers clearly on the slate to make it easier for the Editor to read. When shooting a portion of a scene or a pick-up of action within a scene, a letter is usually added to the scene number. For example, if you are shooting scene number 15 and are doing only a small part of the scene, the scene number may be written as 15A, 15B, 15C, and so on. The Script Supervisor will tell you when to add a letter to the scene number and when to change scene numbers. Some letters that are not usually used for slating scene numbers are I, O, Q, S, and Z, which can resemble numbers when written hurriedly. The letter I resembles the number one (1), O and Q resemble the number zero (0), S resembles the number five (5), and Z resembles the number two (2). Check with the Script Supervisor to find out which letters not to use when slating scenes.

In Britain it is common practice to not use scene numbers on the slate as is done in the United States. Instead, they are written as shot numbers, and the first shot on the first day of filming is shot number 1. The next is shot 2, then shot 3, and so on. Each shot would still be broken down into different takes if a particular shot is done more than once.

When using more than one camera, the roll number would be a combination of the camera letter and the number of the roll of film, for example, roll number A-1, A-2, A-3, B-1, B-2, and so on. If only one camera is used, the assistant may still use the A prefix for all roll numbers to avoid any confusion by the editors. If more than one camera is used, it is recommended that you have a separate slate for each camera, and mark the lettering on each slate in a different color to distinguish one slate and camera from the other. For example, when using two cameras, the "A" camera slate may be labeled in red letters and the "B" camera slate in blue letters.

Slating Procedures

During shooting, the 2nd A.C. is responsible for slating each shot, whether it is sound (sync) or silent (MOS). Remember to obtain the correct scene and take number from the Script Supervisor. The Sound Mixer also needs to know the scene and take number, and usually preslates the shot, which means that the Sound Mixer starts the sound recorder and speaks into the microphone, calling out the scene and take number before rolling for the shot. When it is time to roll the shot, the recorder is ready to go.

The standard procedure for rolling the shot and slating a sound take is as follows. The Director or Assistant Director calls for quiet on the set and then for sound to roll. When the recorder is turned on and has reached the proper speed, the Sound Mixer calls out "SPEED." At this time the Camera Operator or 1st A.C. turns on the camera. When the camera reaches the proper speed, the operator or assistant calls out "SPEED," or "MARKER," or some other similar command to indicate that the camera is running. Now the 2nd A.C., who has been waiting patiently in front of the camera, usually calls out "MARKER," and claps the sticks together. While waiting for the camera to be turned on and to reach speed, the 2nd A.C. should be holding the slate in the shot with the clapper sticks held open at approximately a 45° angle to each other. After "MARKER" is called, the 2nd A.C. claps the sticks together, holds them still for a brief moment, and then quickly exits the frame.

With the time code slate, holding the sticks open allows the time code to run freely. Once the sticks are clapped together, the time code freezes on the display for a brief moment. It is important to hold the slate still for a couple of seconds after slating so that the numbers on the display can be read clearly. After the time code numbers appear, the date appears before the slate goes blank. This additional information on the slate also helps to keep the shots better organized in post-production.

It is quite common for the Sound Mixer to wait about 5 seconds after rolling with time code, before calling out "Speed." This is called prerolling and is important for syncing the dailies in post-production, because it often takes around 5 seconds for the time code equipment, both sound recorder and time code cameras, to lock once they are rolling. Without allowing the preroll, the Editor may be unable to sync the footage because the camera and sound device were not running in sync.

It is the responsibility of the Camera Operator to frame the slate properly, but the 2nd A.C. should know approximately where to place it so that the Camera Operator does not have to move the camera to photograph the slate. Position the slate in such a way that it is not too big or too small in the frame. A general rule for positioning the slate in front of the camera so that it can clearly be seen is as follows: For 35 mm film, hold the slate 1 foot from the camera for every 10 millimeters in focal length. For example, with a 50 mm lens the slate should be held 5 feet away; for 25 mm, 2 1/2 feet; for 100 mm, 10 feet; and so on. For 16 mm film, hold the slate 2 feet from the camera for every 10 millimeters in focal length. For example, with a 50 mm lens the slate should be held 10 feet away. It is not necessary to measure this distance, only to approximate it so the slate fills up the frame. The slate should also be well lit so that the information on it can be read clearly. When filming in a dark set, use your small flashlight to illuminate the slate or possibly have an electrician set up a small light that is turned on for the slate and then turned off before the action of the scene begins. The 1st A.C. should adjust the focus for the slate so that it is easy to read and not blurry and out of focus, and may also briefly open the f-stop if necessary to photograph the slate properly. Once the slate has been photographed, the focus and f-stop will be shifted back to the correct position for the scene. It is quite common for the Operator and 1st A.C. to call out "SET" after slating to indicate that they are ready for the Director to call "ACTION."

When clapping the sticks together, remember to hold the slate perfectly still. Many assistants who are new at slating will move the slate in a downward motion when clapping the sticks. This causes a blurred image, making it difficult for the editor to read the slate. Another good practice to follow is to never cross the frame after slating, if possible. If you slate from the right, then exit to the right; if you slate from the left, then exit to the left. This is a courtesy to the actors as well as the Camera Operator. Sometimes it may not be possible to do this because of lights, C-stands, set walls, furnishings, or actors preparing to enter the shot. Be sure to watch where you go after a shot. Many times a shot is ruined because the 2nd A.C. does not watch where he or she moves after slating the shot, and ends up standing in front of a light, causing a shadow on the actor, or moves in the way of the dolly.

When slating a close-up shot of the actor, it is usually necessary to hold the slate very close to the actor's face. Don't clap the sticks so loudly that you startle the actor and ruin his or her concentration. The sound microphones are very sensitive, so a light clap is sufficient.

Often the slate will not be framed properly, or it may be missed completely by the Camera Operator, and the Camera Operator will call for second sticks or second marker. When this happens, insert the slate quickly into the shot, and when the Camera Operator tells you that it is framed properly, call out "SECOND STICKS" or "SECOND MARKER" before clapping the sticks together. Whenever you do second sticks, be sure to note it in the Remarks column of the camera report.

There are also situations in which it is not possible or practical to clap the slate at the beginning of the scene. When this happens you do what is called a tail slate. The tail slate is clapped the same way as a head slate, the only difference being that the slate is held upside down in the frame and is photographed at the end of the scene. If you know before the shot that you will be doing a tail slate, hold the slate closed with all of the proper information written on it, and photograph the slate at the beginning of the shot simply for identification of the roll, scene, and take numbers. Tell the Sound Mixer whenever you are doing a tail slate. The sound and camera will roll normally, but when the director calls "CUT," the camera and sound recorder should be kept running. As soon as the director calls "CUT" the 2nd A.C. calls out "TAIL SLATE" and inserts the slate into the frame before clapping the sticks together. Always make note of a tail slate in the Remarks column of the camera report (Figure 3.41).

If you use two cameras on a production and they will be rolling together, there are two ways that you may slate the scene: separate slates or a common slate. When doing separate slates, each camera is slated individually, using the correct slate for each camera. When sound and cameras are rolling, the cameras are slated in order. Each slate is held in front of its respective camera. The 2nd A.C. slates the A camera first, then the B camera, then the C camera, and so on. When doing separate slates the 2nd A.C. calls out the camera letter before clapping the sticks. For example, when using two cameras labeled "A" and "B," the 2nd A.C. calls "A camera marker" before slating the A camera, and then "B camera marker" before slating the B camera. When doing a common slate, photograph an identification slate before the shot, showing the correct roll, scene, and take numbers for each camera. When sound and cameras are rolling, only one slate is used, and it is held so that the back of the slate is facing both cameras. The 2nd A.C. calls out "A and B

Figure 3.41
A tail slate is always held upside down at the end of the shot.

cameras, common marker," before clapping the sticks together. Many 2nd A.C.s have a large set of clapper sticks that are used when doing common slates. These larger sticks are easier to see and tell the Editor that it is a common slate for more than one camera.

There are a number of ways that you may slate an MOS shot. Since there is no sound for an MOS shot, you want to be sure that the Editor knows that the sticks have not been clapped. The most obvious way to do this is to hold the slate with the sticks closed and your hand over them. Many assistants hold the sticks in an open position with their hand in between the two sticks to indicate that they have not or cannot be clapped together. In any case, when slating an MOS shot, be sure to indicate it clearly on the slate and also on the camera report.

Properly slating a shot is important and many beginners don't realize the importance of doing it correctly or even doing it at all. During post-production the Assistant Editor is responsible for syncing up the film dailies, and he or she must be able to read the slate so that it can be placed within the film in the proper place. If the information on the slates, including the scene and take information, cannot be read, the Assistant Editor's job becomes much more difficult and time consuming.

Changing Lenses, Filters, and Magazines

Change or add any piece of equipment on the camera as quickly as possible. The usual procedure for changing anything on the camera is as follows. When the D.P. or Camera Operator requests a piece of equipment, the 1st A.C. tells the 2nd A.C. While the 2nd A.C. obtains the new item from the case, the 1st A.C. removes the old item from the camera and prepares the camera to accept the new item. When the 2nd A.C. brings the new item to the camera, it is exchanged for the old item with the 1st A.C. While the 1st A.C. places the new item on the camera, the 2nd A.C. places the old item back in the case. Whenever the D.P. or 1st A.C. calls out a piece of equipment to you, it should always be repeated back so that he or she is sure that you heard it and heard it correctly.

Before handing a new lens to the 1st A.C., set the aperture to its widest opening. If it is a zoom lens, set it to the widest angle focal length. Whenever handing off any piece of equipment to each other, it is a good idea to call out "GOT IT" or some other verbal signal as an indication to the other assistant that it is all right to let go of the item. This is especially important when exchanging lenses. Many times lenses or filters are dropped and damaged because one assistant released his or her grip on the item before the other assistant had a firm hold on it.

Also, remember never to leave an equipment case opened when you are away from it. If a case is in use you should lock at least one of the latches. This makes it easier to open when you have to go back into the case. Any case that is not in use should have both latches secured. This is a good safety habit to get into because if you leave the case unlatched and someone tries to pick it up and move it while you are away from it, the contents could spill out and become damaged. If this did happen, it would be blamed on the person who left the case unlatched and not the person who tried to pick it up and move it. You never know when the gaffer or key grip suddenly decides to place a light or C-stand exactly where your cases are. If you close and secure at least one of the latches of the cases, you can be confident that even if somebody else moves the case, the contents will be safe.

Always check lenses and filters for scratches and dirt or dust before handing them to the 1st A.C. Tell the 1st A.C. if the lens or filter needs to be cleaned when handing it to him or her. Once the D.P. or Camera Operator has approved the new item, it then may be removed and cleaned by either assistant. When changing from a prime lens to a zoom lens or from a zoom lens to a prime lens, you should bring both lens cases to the camera to make the change quicker and easier. Once the change has been completed, you may then return both cases to the cart or storage area. Also, when changing lenses you may have to change the lens support rods and support brackets because of the physical size or weight of the lens. When bringing the lens from the case, the 2nd A.C. should remember to bring the appropriate lens support rods and support brackets when required.

When changing magazines and before handing the new magazine to the 1st A.C., write the new roll number on the identification label, remove the camera report from the magazine, and place it on the back of the slate or on the clipboard. If the magazine contains a short end, remind the 1st A.C. of this and tell him or her to place the small reminder tape next to the footage counter. Whenever possible never hand a new magazine to the 1st A.C. without first writing the new roll number on the identification label.

Using a Video Tap and Monitor

Today most productions are using a video tap incorporated into the film camera so that the Director can view the shot on a monitor while it is being filmed. During the camera prep all of the needed accessories and cables should have been obtained for the video system. During each shooting day, the camera is moved to many different locations and sets for the various shots. Whenever the camera is to be moved, the 1st A.C. usually disconnects the video cable from the camera. It is the responsibility of the 2nd A.C. to be sure that the monitor is moved along with the camera, set up, and connected for each shot. On some productions, a separate person, such as a Production Assistant or possibly a Camera Trainee, may be responsible for moving and setting up the monitor for each shot. Just be sure that whenever the camera moves, the monitor moves along with it as quickly as possible and is connected to the camera for the Director and other production personnel to view the shot.

Preparing Exposed Film for Delivery to the Lab

At the end of each shooting day, all the film shot must be sent to the lab for processing. As I mentioned in the section on unloading magazines, all exposed cans of film should have the proper identification label on them, along with the top copy of the camera report. This assists the lab so that it knows which shots to print and what if any special instructions need to be followed during the developing process. Check with the Script Supervisor regarding the circled or printed takes. The best time to check with the Script Supervisor is at the time you place a new magazine on the camera. When you take the old magazine off the camera, give the camera report for that roll to the Script Supervisor who will check to ensure that the correct takes are circled, and then return it to you. Total up the amounts and write the G, NG, W, SE, and T on the camera report.

You should also place an additional piece of tape on the can, with the developing instructions to the lab printed on it. Some examples of specific developing instructions include: "DEVELOP NORMAL—PREP FOR VIDEO TRANSFER," "DEVELOP NORMAL—ONE-LIGHT PRINT," "PUSH ONE STOP," "DEVELOP ONLY—NO WORK PRINT." There are many other types of developing instructions that may be used. Be sure to check with the D.P. before sending any film to the lab (Figures 3.42 and 3.43).

In place of the magazine identification label and developing instructions label, some assistants may use a preprinted label that is filled in with the appropriate information and placed on the exposed film can. This label may look like the one shown in Figure 3.44. See Appendix C for a custom Film Can Label that you may use for labeling exposed cans of film. This label may be downloaded from the companion web site of the book for your personal use.

When sending the film to the lab, it is common for the 2nd A.C. to prepare a purchase order form that details the specific developing

DEVELOP NORMAL
PREP FOR VIDEO TRANSFER

A

DEVELOP NORMAL
ONE-LIGHT PRINT

B

PUSH ONE STOP

C

DEVELOP ONLY
NO PRINT

D

Figure 3.42 Examples of developing instruction labels. **A,** Develop and prepare for video transfer. **B,** Develop and make a one-light work print. **C,** Push the developing by one stop. **D,** Develop only and do not make a work print.

Figure 3.43 Magazine identification label and developing instructions label on exposed film can.

Laboratory ______
Date ______ Prod # ______
Prod. Co. ______
Prod. Title ______

Exposed Footage ______
Film Type ______

Camera ______ Mag # ______ Roll # ______

☐ Process Normal ☐ One Light Print ☐ Best Light Print
☐ Prep for Transfer ☐ Time to Gray Scale ☐ Timed Work Print
☐ Time to These Lights ______ — ______ — ______
☐ Other ______

Figure 3.44 Example of a blank film can label.

instructions for that day's filming. Some production companies use their own purchase order form, and some laboratories have their own form that they require you to use. An example of a standard laboratory purchase order can be seen in Figure 3.45. In addition, I have created a general all-purpose purchase order form that can be seen in

FOTOKEM
FILM AND VIDEO
FOTO-KEM INDUSTRIES, INC.

2801 W. ALAMEDA AVE., BURBANK, CA 91505
(818) 846-3101

(LAB USE ONLY)
TOTAL FILM ROLLS
TOTAL SOUND REELS
NOTES: __________
RECEIVED BY __________
TIME RECEIVED __________

Laboratory Purchase Order
FILM DAILIES ONLY

Date: Customer P.O. # * Customer Code:

Company: Open Acc. COD MOA

Address: City: State: Zip:

Phone Number: Contact For Negative Report:

IF THIS ORDER IS TO BE SHIPPED PLEASE FILL IN THE SHIPPING INFORMATION AT BOTTOM OF THE PAGE

TITLE:

PROCESSING	FILM WORKPRINT/FILM DAILY	VIDEO TRANSFER
☐ Color Size: ☐ 16 mm	NOTE: THIS SECTION IS FOR FILM PRINTING ONLY!	VIDEO DAILIES
☐ B + W ☐ 35 mm ☐ Super 16	INSTRUCTIONS	Please Contact Video Scheduling to arrange for video tape Dailies
☐ Process Normal Roll #		VIDEO PREP.
☐ Special Processing Roll #		☐ Normal Video Prep for Telecine
PICTURE ORIGINAL		☐ Special Video Prep for Edge No. Encoding
VAULT ☐ RETURN ☐		☐ Film Transfer At FotoKem
		☐ Outside Transfer

Note: Unless circled takes are requested, all dailies print orders will be "print all." No circled takes available in 16mm.

NOTES:

Work Authorized By: Order Written By:

* FOTOKEM'S TERMS CONTROL

ALL WORK IS ACCEPTED SUBJECT TO FOTOKEM'S TERMS. SEE SELECTED TERMS ON THE REVERSE SIDE.

SHIPPING & DELIVERY INSTRUCTIONS

Deliver to:

Address: City: State: Zip:

Phone Number: Attention:

VIA: ☐ COD ☐ Prepaid

PLEASE FILL OUT THIS ORDER AS COMPLETELY AS POSSIBLE. IT WILL HELP US DO A BETTER JOB FOR YOU.

2051-38 (5/00) THERE IS A MINIMUM CHARGE OF $45.00 PER ITEM (UNLESS OTHERWISE INDICATED)

Figure 3.45 Example of a film laboratory purchase order. (Courtesy of Foto-Kem Industries, Inc.)

Appendix C that is also available for downloading on the companion web site to the book.

The information on the purchase order should include complete contact information for the production company. This includes name, address, telephone, and contact person. The title of the production and production number should be clearly indicated on the purchase order (P.O.). The P.O. should list the total number of cans being sent to the lab, total footage, roll numbers and the film type, format (16 mm or 35 mm), and whether it is color or black and white film. The type of processing (Normal, Prep for Video Transfer, One-Light Workprint, etc.) and any special instructions should be listed on the purchase order as well. Many assistants will prepare a separate purchase order for any special or unusual developing instructions such as Pushing, Pulling, Skip Bleach, or Forced Processing a roll or rolls of film. One copy of the purchase order is sent to the lab with the film. Each film can should have a copy of the camera report for that roll attached to the can. A copy of the P.O. should be given to the production office and the camera department should always keep a copy.

Send the exposed film to the lab as soon as possible. Each lab usually has a specific cutoff time each day for when the film must be delivered in order for it to be ready the following day. As a 2nd A.C. you should know the cutoff times for the lab you are using. Until the exposed film is ready to be sent, keep it in a cool, dry place away from any direct sunlight and away from any raw stock so that it does not get loaded by mistake. See the section in this chapter, Ordering Additional Film Stock, for information on the proper care and storage of film stock.

Once you are ready to send the film, it is common for the assistant to stack the cans four or five high, and tape them together. You should invert the top can so that you do not tape over the attached camera report. If the film is to be shipped, place it in a sturdy cardboard box, and fill any unused space with crumpled newspaper or other packing material to prevent the cans from moving around during shipping. If film is to be shipped, label the box on all sides "EXPOSED FILM—KEEP FROM RADIATION" or "EXPOSED FILM—DO NOT X-RAY." See Appendix C for a custom shipping label that you may use for labeling shipping cartons of exposed cans of film. This label may be downloaded from the companion web site of the book for your personal use.

Film Inventory and Record of Film Shot

Throughout the production you will be receiving shipments of film stock. You should have a supply of daily film inventory sheets so that you may keep an inventory of all film stock received. In most cases the production company needs an inventory of each different film stock, as well as a grand total for all film stocks combined. For example, if you are using Eastman Kodak Color Negative 5218 and 5274 on your production, you may have three separate totals for the film inventory, one for 5218, one for 5274, and one for the combined total of both. When keeping the inventory, you may use a standard inventory form or make up one of your own. A large part of the production's budget is spent on film stock, and it is important to keep accurate records in case there are any questions during the production. I was once hired on a show and was told that the previous camera assistants had been caught stealing film stock, so it was important to keep proper records that would be periodically reviewed for accuracy. Examples of different types of daily film inventory forms can be found in Figures 3.46, 3.47, and 3.48. These are only three examples of some of the inventory forms I have used most often during my career. There are other styles out there and you may design your own based on what works best for you. Two of these commonly used forms can also be seen in Appendix C and are also available for downloading on the companion web site to the book.

At the end of each shooting day, after the equipment has been packed up and the film sent to the lab, the 2nd A.C. prepares a daily film inventory form that contains the following information: film received; each roll number shot; a breakdown of G, NG, W, SE, and T for each roll; film on hand at the end of the day; totals for each day; and a running total for the entire production. Be careful when totaling up these numbers, because it is important to the production office to account for every foot of film used on the production. It is easy at the end of a long shooting day to make a mistake in calculations, so be sure to use a calculator. If you have time I recommend checking your figures from the previous day's shoot each morning. You will be more awake and refreshed after a good night's sleep and better able to catch any small errors in arithmetic.

Once these reports have been filled out, give a copy to the production office along with copies of the camera reports for each roll. You should also keep a copy of any reports for the camera department in case there are any questions later. I recommend taking all of the camera reports for a particular day and stapling them to the inventory form for that day. This way if there is ever any question later on, you will have everything for that day all together and will not have to search for it. When using more than one camera, keep separate totals for each camera, as well as combined totals for all cameras.

Completing Film Inventory Forms

The following example shows how to fill out the daily film inventory forms and how each day's totals relate to the next day's daily film inventory form.

Example: You have been hired as the 2nd A.C. on a feature film. The film is called "Claire of the Moon" and is being produced by Demi Monde Productions. The Director is Nicole Conn and the Director of Photography is Randy Sellars. The D.P. has decided to use two film stocks for this shoot, Eastman Kodak 5218 and 5274. He will be doing some hand-held shots, so he will need 400-foot rolls in addition to 1000-foot rolls.

On the first day of production the following film stock is received:

Eastman Kodak 5274-148-0739	5200 feet	4–1000-foot rolls, 3–400-foot rolls
Eastman Kodak 5218-237-4862	5400 feet	3–1000-foot rolls, 6–400-foot rolls

On the second day of production, the following film stock is received:

Eastman Kodak 5274-148-0739	7000 feet	5–1000-foot rolls, 5–400-foot rolls
Eastman Kodak 5218-237-4862	5000 feet	3–1000-foot rolls, 5–400-foot rolls

Figures 3.49 through 3.61 show the completed camera reports and completed daily film inventory forms for day 1 and day 2. So that you

(Text continues on p.129.)

PRODUCTION ______________________________ DATE ____________

DAY # ____________

FILM TYPE

LOADED	ROLL #	GOOD	NG	WASTE	TOTAL	SE	FILM ON HAND	
							PREVIOUS	
							TODAY (+)	
							TODAY (-)	
							TOTAL	
							400' ROLLS	
							1000' ROLLS	
							SHORT ENDS	
							OTHER	
							COMMENTS:	

TOTALS	GOOD	NG	WASTE	TOTAL	
TODAY					
PREVIOUS (+)					
TOTAL TO DATE					

FILM TYPE

LOADED	ROLL #	GOOD	NG	WASTE	TOTAL	SE	FILM ON HAND	
							PREVIOUS	
							TODAY (+)	
							TODAY (-)	
							TOTAL	
							400' ROLLS	
							1000' ROLLS	
							SHORT ENDS	
							OTHER	
							COMMENTS:	

TOTALS	GOOD	NG	WASTE	TOTAL	
TODAY					
PREVIOUS (+)					
TOTAL TO DATE					

TOTALS	GOOD	NG	WASTE	TOTAL
TODAY				
PREVIOUS (+)				
TOTAL TO DATE				

TOTAL FILM ON HAND	
PREVIOUS	
TODAY (+)	
TODAY (-)	
TOTAL	

Figure 3.46 Daily film inventory form #1.

PRODUCTION ______________________________ DATE ______________

DAY # __________

FILM TYPE	LOAD TYPE	ROLL #	GOOD	NO GOOD	WASTE	TOTAL	SE
			GOOD	NO GOOD	WASTE	TOTAL	SE
		PREVIOUS					
		TODAY (+)					
		TO DATE					

UN-EXPOSED FILM ON HAND											
	FILM TYPE				FILM TYPE						TOTAL
	1000' LOADS	400' LOADS	SE		1000' LOADS	400' LOADS	SE		ON HAND	ON HAND	ON HAND
PREVIOUS											
TODAY (+)											
TODAY (-)											
TO DATE											

Figure 3.47 Daily film inventory form #2.

PRODUCTION ______________________________ DATE______________

DAY # ___________

FILM TYPE	ROLL #	LOADED	GOOD	NO GOOD	WASTE	TOTAL	SE

TOTALS	LOADED	GOOD	NO GOOD	WASTE	TOTAL	SE
TODAY						
PREVIOUS (+)						
TOTAL TO DATE						

FILM ON HAND / FILM TYPE						TOTALS
PREVIOUS BALANCE						
(+) REC'D TODAY						
(–) USED TODAY						
TOTAL TO DATE						

Figure 3.48 Daily film inventory form #3.

Co. Submitted By: Demi Monde Productions	P.O. #
Bill To: Demi Monde Productions	Date Exposed:
Picture Title: "Claire of the Moon"	Loader:
Director: N. Conn	D.P.: R. Sellars

ROLL # **1**	☐ BLACK & WHITE	☒ COLOR
EMUL. # 5274 — 148 0739	MAG # 10161	
DEVELOP FOOTAGE 400 ☒ NORMAL	☐ PUSH ____ STOP(S)	☐ PULL ____ STOP(S)
FILM WORKPRINT	☐ PRINT ALL	☒ PRINT CIRCLED TAKES
VIDEO PREP & TRANSFER	☐ TRANSFER ALL TRANSFER AT ____ fps	☐ TRANSFER CIRCLED TAKES ☐ EDGE # PUNCH

SCENE NO.	*TAKE*	*DIAL*	*FEET*	*SD*	*REMARKS*	*SCENE NO.*	*TAKE*	*DIAL*	*FEET*	*SD*	*REMARKS*
32	1	80	80								
	(2)	120	(40)								
	(3)	160	(40)								
32 A	1	210	50								
	(2)	270	(60)								
32 B	(1)	300	(30)								
32 C	1	320	20								
	(2)	360	(40)								
						DEVELOP NORMAL				*G*	210
						1 - LITE PRINT				*NG*	150
										W	40
	OUT AT 360									*T*	400

Figure 3.49 Completed camera report for roll #1.

DATE CUSTOMER ORDER NUMBER

COMPANY Demi Monde Productions

DIRECTOR N. Conn CAMERAMAN R. Sellars

PRODUCTION NO. OR TITLE "Claire of the Moon"

MAGAZINE NUMBER 10109 ROLL NUMBER **2**

TYPE OF FILM / EMULSION 5274-148-0739 400'

PRINT CIRCLED TAKES ONLY: ☒ ONE LITE ☐ TIMED

SCENE NO.	TAKE	DIAL	PRINT	REMARKS
32 C	①	40	40	
	②	80	40	
32 D	①	150	70	
36	1	170		
	②	190	20	
	3	200		
36 A	1	220		
	②	240	20	
	3	260		
	④	280	20	
36 B	①	350	70	
	2	390		
	OUT AT 390'			
	DEVELOP NORMAL			
	ONE LITE PRINT			
				G 280
				NG 110
				W 10
				T 400

Figure 3.50 Completed camera report for roll #2.

Co. Sub. by: Demi Monde Productions	Job #:
Bill to: Demi Monde Productions	Date Exposed:
Pict. Title: "Claire of the Moon"	Loader:
Director: N. Conn	D.P.: R. Sellars
ROLL # **3** ☐ BLACK & WHITE	☒ COLOR
EMUL. # 5218 — 237 4862	MAG # 10146
DEVELOP FOOTAGE 1000 ☒ NORMAL ☐ PUSH ____ STOP(S)	☐ PULL ____ STOP(S)
FILM WORKPRINT ☐ PRINT ALL	☒ PRINT CIRCLED TAKES
VIDEO PREP & TRANSFER ☐ TRANSFER ALL TRANSFER AT ____ fps	☐ TRANSFER CIRCLED TAKES ☐ EDGE # PUNCH

SCENE #	PRINT CIRCLED TAKES 1 / 6	2 / 7	3 / 8	4 / 9	5 / 10	REMARKS
79	30	(40)	(40)	30		30 70
79 A	(20)					110 140
79 B	0	(30)				160 160
79 C	20	(20)				190 210
79 D	30	(30)				230 260
79 E	(10)	(10)				290 300
79 F	(20)					310 330
94	(20)	20	(40)			350 370
99	60	(80)	50	(70)		410 470
						550 600
						670
			OUT AT 670			
			DEVELOP NORMAL			
			1 - LITE PRINT			
						G. 430
						N.G. 240
						W. 0
						T. 670
						SE 330

Figure 3.51 Completed camera report for roll #3.

PRODUCTION Claire of the Moon DATE

DAY # 1

FILM TYPE 5218

LOADED	ROLL #	GOOD	NG	WASTE	TOTAL	SE	FILM ON HAND	
1000	3	430	240	0	670	330	PREVIOUS	0
							TODAY (+)	5,400
							TODAY (-)	670
							TOTAL	4,730
							400' ROLLS	2,400
							1000' ROLLS	2,000
							SHORT ENDS	330
							OTHER	0
							COMMENTS:	

TOTALS	GOOD	NG	WASTE	TOTAL
TODAY	430	240	0	670
PREVIOUS (+)	0	0	0	0
TOTAL TO DATE	430	240	0	670

FILM TYPE 5274

LOADED	ROLL #	GOOD	NG	WASTE	TOTAL	SE	FILM ON HAND	
400	1	210	150	40	400	0	PREVIOUS	0
400	2	280	110	10	400	0	TODAY (+)	5,200
							TODAY (-)	800
							TOTAL	4,400
							400' ROLLS	400
							1000' ROLLS	4,000
							SHORT ENDS	0
							OTHER	0
							COMMENTS:	

TOTALS	GOOD	NG	WASTE	TOTAL
TODAY	490	260	50	800
PREVIOUS (+)	0	0	0	0
TOTAL TO DATE	490	260	50	800

TOTALS	GOOD	NG	WASTE	TOTAL	TOTAL FILM ON HAND	
TODAY	920	500	50	1,470	PREVIOUS	0
PREVIOUS (+)	0	0	0	0	TODAY (+)	10,600
TOTAL TO DATE	920	500	50	1,470	TODAY (-)	1,470
					TOTAL	9,130

Figure 3.52 Completed daily film inventory form #1 for day 1.

PRODUCTION Claire of the Moon DATE ____________

DAY # 1

FILM TYPE	LOAD TYPE	ROLL #	GOOD	NO GOOD	WASTE	TOTAL	SE
5274	400	1	210	150	40	400	0
5274	400	2	280	110	10	400	0
5218	1000	3	430	240	0	670	330
			GOOD	NO GOOD	WASTE	TOTAL	SE
		PREVIOUS	0	0	0	0	0
		TODAY (+)	920	500	50	1,470	330
		TO DATE	920	500	50	1,470	330

UN-EXPOSED FILM ON HAND												
	FILM TYPE 5218				FILM TYPE 5274				5218	5274	TOTAL
	1000' LOADS	400' LOADS	SE		1000' LOADS	400' LOADS	SE		ON HAND	ON HAND	ON HAND
PREVIOUS	0	0	0		0	0	0		0	0	0
TODAY (+)	3,000	2,400	330		4,000	1,200	0		5,730	5,200	10,930
TODAY (-)	1,000	0	0		0	800	0		1,000	800	1,800
TO DATE	2,000	2,400	330		4,000	400	0		4,730	4,400	9,130

Figure 3.53 Completed daily film inventory form #2 for day 1.

PRODUCTION Claire of the Moon DATE

DAY # 1

FILM TYPE	ROLL #	LOADED	GOOD	NO GOOD	WASTE	TOTAL	SE
5274	1	400	210	150	40	400	0
5274	2	400	280	110	10	400	0
5218	3	1000	430	240	0	670	330

TOTALS	LOADED	GOOD	NO GOOD	WASTE	TOTAL	SE
TODAY	1,800	920	500	50	1,470	330
PREVIOUS (+)	0	0	0	0	0	0
TOTAL TO DATE	1,800	920	500	50	1,470	330

FILM ON HAND / FILM TYPE	5218	5274				TOTALS
PREVIOUS BALANCE	0	0				0
(+) REC'D TODAY	5,400	5,200				10,600
(–) USED TODAY	670	800				1,470
TOTAL TO DATE	4,730	4,400				9,130

Figure 3.54 Completed daily film inventory form #3 for day 1.

Co. Submitted By: Demi Monde Productions	P.O. #
Bill To: Demi Monde Productions	Date Exposed:
Picture Title: "Claire of the Moon"	Loader:
Director: N. Conn	D.P.: R. Sellars

ROLL # **4**	☐ BLACK & WHITE	☒ COLOR
EMUL. # 5274 — 148 0739	MAG # 10149	
DEVELOP FOOTAGE 1000 ☒ NORMAL	☐ PUSH ____ STOP(S)	☐ PULL ____ STOP(S)
FILM WORKPRINT	☐ PRINT ALL	☒ PRINT CIRCLED TAKES
VIDEO PREP & TRANSFER	☐ TRANSFER ALL TRANSFER AT _____ fps	☐ TRANSFER CIRCLED TAKES ☐ EDGE # PUNCH

SCENE NO.	*TAKE*	*DIAL*	*FEET*	*SD*	*REMARKS*	*SCENE NO.*	*TAKE*	*DIAL*	*FEET*	*SD*	*REMARKS*
24	1	70	70				3	670	40		
	(2)	160	(90)			97	(1)	690	(20)		
	3	200	40				2	720	30		
	(4)	240	(40)			135	(1)	780	(60)		
24 A	(1)	290	(50)				(2)	830	(50)		
	2	340	50				3	870	40		
	(3)	400	(60)			146	1	910	40		
10	1	430	30				(2)	940	(30)		
	2	450	20								
	3	470	20				OUT AT 940			*G*	490
	(4)	500	(30)							*NG*	450
	5	530	30							*W*	60
	(6)	560	(30)			DEVELOP NORMAL				*T*	1000
10 A	1	600	40			ONE LITE PRINT					
	(2)	630	(30)								

Figure 3.55 Completed camera report for roll #4.

Co. Sub. by: Demi Monde Productions	Job #:
Bill to: Demi Monde Productions	Date Exposed:
Pict. Title: "Claire of the Moon"	Loader:
Director: N. Conn	D.P.: R. Sellars

ROLL # **5** ☐ BLACK & WHITE ☒ COLOR

EMUL. # 5274 — 148 0739 MAG # 10161

DEVELOP FOOTAGE 400
☒ NORMAL ☐ PUSH ____ STOP(S) ☐ PULL ____ STOP(S)

FILM WORKPRINT ☐ PRINT ALL ☒ PRINT CIRCLED TAKES

VIDEO PREP & TRANSFER ☐ TRANSFER ALL ☐ TRANSFER CIRCLED TAKES
TRANSFER AT ____ fps ☐ EDGE # PUNCH

SCENE #	PRINT CIRCLED TAKES 1 / 6	2 / 7	3 / 8	4 / 9	5 / 10	REMARKS
7	(60)	20	(70)	40		60 80
7 A	40	(30)	(30)	10	20	150 190
7 B	(30)	(20)	20			230 260
						290 300
						320 350
		OUT AT 390				370 390
		DEVELOP NORMAL				
		1 - LITE PRINT				

G.	240
N.G.	150
W.	10
T.	400

Figure 3.56 Completed camera report for roll #5.

Co. Submitted By: Demi Monde Productions	P.O. #
Bill To: Demi Monde Productions	Date Exposed:
Picture Title: "Claire of the Moon"	Loader:
Director: N. Conn	D.P.: R. Sellars

ROLL # **6** ☐ BLACK & WHITE	☒ COLOR
EMUL. # 5218 — 237 4862	MAG # 10014
DEVELOP FOOTAGE 1000 ☒ NORMAL ☐ PUSH ____ STOP(S)	☐ PULL ____ STOP(S)
FILM WORKPRINT ☐ PRINT ALL	☒ PRINT CIRCLED TAKES
VIDEO PREP & TRANSFER ☐ TRANSFER ALL TRANSFER AT ____ fps	☐ TRANSFER CIRCLED TAKES ☐ EDGE # PUNCH

SCENE NO.	*TAKE*	*DIAL*	*FEET*	*SD*	*REMARKS*	*SCENE NO.*	*TAKE*	*DIAL*	*FEET*	*SD*	*REMARKS*
5	1	20	20			57	(2)	810	(40)		
	2	40	20				3	850	40		
	(3)	130	(90)				(4)	920	(70)		
	(4)	200	(70)								
	(5)	280	(80)								
5 A	1	300	20				OUT AT 920'				
	(2)	400	(100)								
5 B	(1)	440	(40)								
	2	520	80								
	(3)	550	(30)								
12	1	590	40			DEVELOP NORMAL					
	(2)	660	(70)			1 - LITE PRINT				*G*	680
	(3)	730	(70)							*NG*	240
	4	750	20							*W*	80
57	(1)	770	(20)							*T*	1000

Figure 3.57 Completed camera report for roll #6.

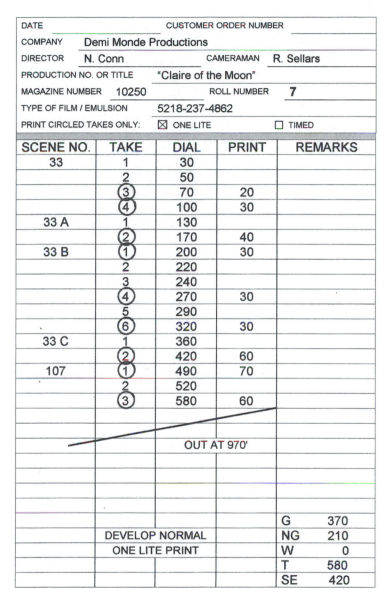

DATE ________ CUSTOMER ORDER NUMBER ________

COMPANY Demi Monde Productions

DIRECTOR N. Conn CAMERAMAN R. Sellars

PRODUCTION NO. OR TITLE "Claire of the Moon"

MAGAZINE NUMBER 10250 ROLL NUMBER 7

TYPE OF FILM / EMULSION 5218-237-4862

PRINT CIRCLED TAKES ONLY: ☒ ONE LITE ☐ TIMED

SCENE NO.	TAKE	DIAL	PRINT	REMARKS
33	1	30		
	2	50		
	③	70	20	
	④	100	30	
33 A	1	130		
	②	170	40	
33 B	①	200	30	
	2	220		
	3	240		
	④	270	30	
	5	290		
	⑥	320	30	
33 C	1	360		
	②	420	60	
107	①	490	70	
	2	520		
	③	580	60	
		OUT AT 970'		
				G 370
	DEVELOP NORMAL			NG 210
	ONE LITE PRINT			W 0
				T 580
				SE 420

Figure 3.58 Completed camera report for roll #7.

PRODUCTION Claire of the Moon DATE ______

DAY # 2

FILM TYPE 5218

LOADED	ROLL #	GOOD	NG	WASTE	TOTAL	SE	FILM ON HAND	
1000	6	680	240	80	1,000	0	PREVIOUS	4,730
1000	7	370	210	0	580	420	TODAY (+)	5,000
							TODAY (-)	1,580
							TOTAL	8,150
							400' ROLLS	4,400
							1000' ROLLS	3,000
							SHORT ENDS	750
							OTHER	0
							COMMENTS:	

TOTALS	GOOD	NG	WASTE	TOTAL
TODAY	1,050	450	80	1,580
PREVIOUS (+)	430	240	0	670
TOTAL TO DATE	1,480	690	80	2,250

FILM TYPE 5274

LOADED	ROLL #	GOOD	NG	WASTE	TOTAL	SE	FILM ON HAND	
1000	4	490	450	60	1,000	0	PREVIOUS	4,400
400	5	240	150	10	400	0	TODAY (+)	7,000
							TODAY (-)	1,400
							TOTAL	10,000
							400' ROLLS	2,000
							1000' ROLLS	8,000
							SHORT ENDS	0
							OTHER	0
							COMMENTS:	

TOTALS	GOOD	NG	WASTE	TOTAL
TODAY	730	600	70	1,400
PREVIOUS (+)	490	260	50	800
TOTAL TO DATE	1,220	860	120	2,200

TOTALS	GOOD	NG	WASTE	TOTAL	TOTAL FILM ON HAND	
TODAY	1,780	1,050	150	2,980	PREVIOUS	9,130
PREVIOUS (+)	920	500	50	1,470	TODAY (+)	12,000
TOTAL TO DATE	2,700	1,550	200	4,450	TODAY (-)	2,980
					TOTAL	18,150

Figure 3.59 Completed daily film inventory form #1 for day 2.

PRODUCTION Claire of the Moon DATE ______

DAY # 2

FILM TYPE	LOAD TYPE	ROLL #	GOOD	NO GOOD	WASTE	TOTAL	SE
5274	1000	4	490	450	60	1000	0
5274	400	5	240	150	10	400	0
5218	1000	6	680	240	80	1000	0
5218	1000	7	370	210	0	580	420

	GOOD	NO GOOD	WASTE	TOTAL	SE
PREVIOUS	920	500	50	1,470	330
TODAY (+)	1,780	1,050	150	2,980	420
TO DATE	2,700	1,550	200	4,450	750

UN-EXPOSED FILM ON HAND

	FILM TYPE 5218				FILM TYPE 5274				5218	5274	TOTAL
	1000' LOADS	400' LOADS	SE		1000' LOADS	400' LOADS	SE		ON HAND	ON HAND	ON HAND
PREVIOUS	2,000	2,400	330		4,000	400	0		4,730	4,400	9,130
TODAY (+)	3,000	2,000	420		5,000	2,000	0		5,420	7,000	12,420
TODAY (-)	2,000	0	0		1,000	400	0		2,000	1,400	3,400
TO DATE	3,000	4,400	750		8,000	2,000	0		8,150	10,000	18,150

Figure 3.60 Completed daily film inventory form #2 for day 2.

PRODUCTION Claire of the Moon DATE

DAY # 2

FILM TYPE	ROLL #	LOADED	GOOD	NO GOOD	WASTE	TOTAL	SE
5274	4	1,000	490	450	60	1,000	0
5274	5	400	240	150	10	400	0
5218	6	1,000	680	240	80	1,000	0
5218	7	1,000	370	210	0	850	420

TOTALS	LOADED	GOOD	NO GOOD	WASTE	TOTAL	SE
TODAY	3,400	1,780	1,050	150	2,980	420
PREVIOUS (+)	1,800	920	500	50	1,470	330
TOTAL TO DATE	5,200	2,700	1,550	200	4,450	750

FILM ON HAND / FILM TYPE	5218	5274				TOTALS
PREVIOUS BALANCE	4,730	4,400				9,130
(+) REC'D TODAY	5,000	7,000				12,000
(–) USED TODAY	1,580	1,400				2,980
TOTAL TO DATE	8,150	10,000				18,150

Figure 3.61 Completed daily film inventory form #3 for day 2.

may become familiar with the different styles of camera reports and inventory forms, this example uses each of the styles for each day. On an actual production you would only use one camera report style from a single lab and one daily film inventory form and not mix them.

Using the information from the preceding camera reports and inventory forms, the following section breaks down the information and shows where it comes from for each style of daily film inventory form. In examples where information is to be transferred from one day's inventory form to the next day's form, I have included the section from each form for each day.

The following section refers to daily film inventory form #1 in Figure 3.62.

- DAY #: The day number that you are shooting, based on the total number of shooting days and on how many days you have shot previous to today. In this example it is the first day of shooting.
- FILM TYPE: The type of film you are using—Kodak 7218, 7229, 5245, 5277; Fuji 8632, 8552; etc. In this example you are using Eastman Kodak Color Negative 5218.
- LOADED: The size of the roll of film loaded into the magazine. In this example it is a 1000-foot roll.
- ROLL #: The camera roll number from the camera report. In this example you have roll number 3.
- GOOD (G): The total of good or printed takes from the camera report for each roll.
- NG (NO GOOD): The total of no good takes from the camera report for each roll.
- WASTE (W): The amount of footage left over that cannot be called a short end. Less than 40 feet in 16 mm and less than 100 feet in 35 mm are considered waste.
- TOTAL: The total of GOOD plus NO GOOD plus WASTE. GOOD + NO GOOD + WASTE = TOTAL.
- SE: The amount of footage left over that is too large to be called waste. More than 40 feet in 16 mm and more than 100 feet in 35 mm are considered a short end.

DAY #1

FILM TYPE 5218

LOADED	ROLL #	GOOD	NG	WASTE	TOTAL	SE
1000	3	430	240	0	670	330

Figure 3.62 Breakdown of information for daily film inventory form #1.

The following section refers to daily film inventory form #1 in Figure 3.63.

- TOTALS: The total amount of all roll numbers combined for each category: GOOD (G), NO GOOD (NG), WASTE (W), and TOTAL.
- TODAY: The totals for all roll numbers shot today for each category: GOOD (G), NO GOOD (NG), WASTE (W), and TOTAL. In this example, for day #1, the total good for roll numbers 1 and 2 combined is 490, total no good is 260, total waste is 50, and total is 800.
- PREVIOUS (+): The totals for all roll numbers shot previous to today, obtained from the previous day's report, from the section labeled Totals—To Date. In this example, for day #1, there are no previous amounts because it is the first day of filming.
- TOTAL TO DATE: The combined total for all roll numbers shot today plus the totals for all roll numbers shot previous to today. These amounts are then written on the next day's daily inventory report, in the section labeled Totals—Previous (+).

Film on Hand

- PREVIOUS: The total amount of footage on hand at the start of the day for each film stock, obtained from the previous day's report, from the section labeled Film on Hand—Total. In this example, for day #1 you had no film on hand at the start of the day because it is the first day of filming and on day #2 you had 4400 feet on hand at the start of the day. This was the amount on hand at the end of day #1.

Day #1

TOTALS	GOOD	NG	WASTE	TOTAL
TODAY	490	260	50	800
PREVIOUS (+)	0	0	0	0
TOTAL TO DATE	490	260	50	800

Day #2

TOTALS	GOOD	NG	WASTE	TOTAL
TODAY	730	600	70	1,400
PREVIOUS (+)	490	260	50	800
TOTAL TO DATE	1,220	860	120	2,200

Day #1

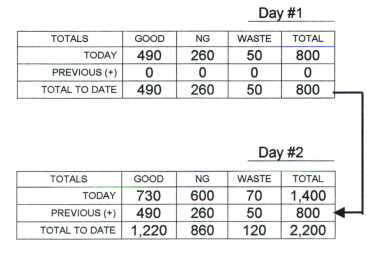

FILM ON HAND	
PREVIOUS	0
TODAY (+)	5,200
TODAY (-)	800
TOTAL	4,400

Day #2

FILM ON HAND	
PREVIOUS	4,400
TODAY (+)	7,000
TODAY (-)	1,400
TOTAL	10,000

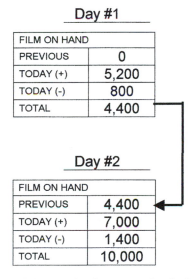

Figure 3.63 Breakdown of information for daily film inventory form #1.

- TODAY (+): The total amount of footage received today for each film stock.
- TODAY (–): The total amount of footage shot today for each film stock.
- TOTAL: The combined total of previous, plus footage received today, less footage shot today, for each film stock.

- PREVIOUS + TODAY(+) – TODAY(–) = TOTAL: This is the total amount of footage on hand at the end of the shooting day. This amount is then written on the daily inventory report for the next day in the section labeled Film on Hand—Previous.

The following section refers to daily film inventory form #1 in Figure 3.64.

Total Film Use—All Film Stocks

- TOTALS: The total amount of all roll numbers, for all film stocks combined, for each category: GOOD (G), NO GOOD (NG), WASTE (W), and TOTAL.
- TODAY: The combined total for today only, for all film stocks, for each category: GOOD (G), NO GOOD (NG), WASTE (W), and TOTAL.
- PREVIOUS (+): The combined total for all film types shot previous to today, for each category: GOOD (G), NO GOOD (NG), WASTE (W), and TOTAL. This amount is obtained from the previous day's daily report form from the section labeled Total to Date.
- TOTAL TO DATE: The combined total of all film stocks shot today plus the total of all film stocks shot previous to today. These amounts are then written on the next day's daily inventory report, in the section labeled, Totals—Previous (+).

Total Film on Hand

- PREVIOUS: The combined total amount of footage on hand at the start of today for all film stocks, obtained from the previous day's report, from the section labeled Total.
- TODAY (+): The combined total amount of footage received today for all film stocks.

Day #1

TOTALS	GOOD	NG	WASTE	TOTAL	TOTAL FILM ON HAND	
TODAY	920	500	50	1,470	PREVIOUS	0
PREVIOUS (+)	0	0	0	0	TODAY (+)	10,600
TOTAL TO DATE	920	500	50	1,470	TODAY (-)	1,470
					TOTAL	9,130

Day #2

TOTALS	GOOD	NG	WASTE	TOTAL	TOTAL FILM ON HAND	
TODAY	1,780	1,050	150	2,980	PREVIOUS	9,130
PREVIOUS (+)	920	500	50	1,470	TODAY (+)	12,000
TOTAL TO DATE	2,700	1,550	200	4,450	TODAY (-)	2,980
					TOTAL	18,150

Figure 3.64 Breakdown of information for daily film inventory form #1.

- TODAY (–): The combined total amount of footage shot today for all film stocks.
- TOTAL: The combined total of previous footage, plus footage received today, less footage shot today for all film stocks.
- PREVIOUS + TODAY(+) – TODAY(–) = TOTAL: This is the total amount of footage on hand at the end of the shooting day. This amount is then written on the daily inventory report for the next day in the section labeled Total Film on Hand—Previous. Remember, these figures are combined totals for all film stocks on hand during the production.

The following section refers to daily film inventory form #2 in Figure 3.65.

- FILM TYPE: The film stock you are using—Kodak 7218, 7229, 5245, 5277; Fuji 8632, 8552; etc. In this example you are using Eastman Kodak Color Negative 5218 and 5274.
- LOAD TYPE: The size of the roll loaded in the magazine. In this example, roll number 1 is a 400-foot roll, roll number 2 is a 400-foot roll, and roll number 3 is a 1000-foot roll.
- ROLL #: The camera roll number from the camera report. In this example, you have roll numbers 1, 2, and 3.
- GOOD (G): The total of good or printed takes from the camera report for each roll.
- NO GOOD (NG): The total of no good takes from the camera report for each roll.
- WASTE (W): The amount of footage left over that cannot be called a short end. Less than 40 feet in 16 mm and less than 100 feet in 35 mm are considered waste.
- TOTAL (T): The total of GOOD plus NO GOOD plus WASTE. GOOD + NO GOOD + WASTE = TOTAL.
- SE: The amount of footage remaining that is too large to be called waste. More than 40 feet in 16 mm and more than 100 feet in 35 mm are considered a short end. In this example there was a 330-foot short end created from roll number 3.

FILM TYPE	LOAD TYPE	ROLL #	GOOD	NO GOOD	WASTE	TOTAL	SE
5274	400	1	210	150	40	400	0
5274	400	2	280	110	10	400	0
5218	1000	3	430	240	0	670	330

Figure 3.65 Breakdown of information for daily film inventory form #2.

The following section refers to daily film inventory form #2 in Figure 3.66.

- PREVIOUS: The total for all roll numbers in each category shot previous to today: GOOD (G), NO GOOD (NG), WASTE (W), TOTAL (T), and SHORT END (SE). This information is obtained from the previous day's inventory report form, from the section labeled To Date. In this example, for day #1, there are no previous amounts because it is the first day of filming.
- TODAY (+): The total for all roll numbers shot today in each category: GOOD (G), NO GOOD (NG), WASTE (W), TOTAL (T), and SHORT END (SE). In this example, for day #1 the total good for all roll numbers shot today is 920, total no good is 500, total waste is 50, etc.
- TO DATE: The combined total for each category for all rolls shot previous to today plus all rolls shot today.
- PREVIOUS + TODAY(+) = TO DATE: These amounts are then written on the next day's daily inventory report, in the section labeled Previous.

Day #1

	GOOD	NO GOOD	WASTE	TOTAL	SE
PREVIOUS	0	0	0	0	0
TODAY (+)	920	500	50	1,470	330
TO DATE	920	500	50	1,470	330

Day #2

	GOOD	NO GOOD	WASTE	TOTAL	SE
PREVIOUS	920	500	50	1,470	330
TODAY (+)	1,780	1,050	150	2,980	420
TO DATE	2,700	1,550	200	4,450	750

Figure 3.66 Breakdown of information for daily film inventory form #2.

The following section refers to daily film inventory form #2 in Figure 3.67.

Unexposed Film on Hand

- FILM TYPE: This section is left blank so that you may fill in the type of film you are using—Kodak 7218, 7229, 5245, 5277; Fuji 8632, 8552; etc. In this example you are using Eastman Kodak Color Negative 5218 and 5274.

- 1000′ LOADS: This column is to keep totals for 1000-foot rolls received, and on hand, for each film stock you are using. In this example, on day #1, for film stock 5218, you had no film previous, you received 3000 feet in 1000-foot rolls, you used one 1000-foot roll, and you have on hand at the end of day #1 2000 feet of 5218 in 1000-foot rolls.
- 400′ LOADS: This column is to keep totals for 400-foot rolls received, and on hand, for each film stock you are using. In this example, on day #1, for film stock 5274, you had no film previous, you received 1200 feet in 400-foot rolls, you used 800 feet in 400-foot rolls, and you have on hand at the end of day #1 400 feet of film stock 5274 in 400-foot rolls.
- SE: This column is to keep totals for all short ends created, received, and on hand for each film stock you are using. In this example, on day #1, for film stock 5218, you created one short end, which is 330 feet in length.
- ON HAND: These columns are to keep combined totals on hand for each film stock and each roll size you are using. Fill in the blank space at the top of the column with the film stock that you are using: 1000′ LOADS + 400′ LOADS + SE = ON HAND.
- TOTAL ON HAND: The combined total of film stock on hand for all film stocks and roll sizes being used.
- PREVIOUS: The total amount of footage on hand at the start of each day for each film stock and each roll size, obtained from the previous day's report, from the section labeled Unexposed Film on Hand—To Date. In this example, for day #1, for film stock 5218, you had no film previous to day #1.
- TODAY (+): The total amount of footage received today for each film stock and roll size. In this example, for day #1, for film stock 5274, you received 4000 feet in 1000-foot rolls, and you received 1200 feet in 400-foot rolls.
- TODAY (–): The total amount of footage shot today for each film stock and roll size.
- TO DATE: The combined total of previous, plus footage received today, less footage shot today for each film stock, and roll size.
- PREVIOUS + TODAY(+) – TODAY(–) = TO DATE: This is the total amount of footage on hand at the end of the shooting day. This amount is then written on the daily inventory report for the next day in the section labeled Unexposed Film on Hand—Previous. Remember to separate the amounts for each film stock and roll size when transferring numbers to the next day's film inventory form.

Day #1

UN-EXPOSED FILM ON HAND											
	FILM TYPE 5218				FILM TYPE 5274				5218	5274	TOTAL
	1000' LOADS	400' LOADS	SE		1000' LOADS	400' LOADS	SE		ON HAND	ON HAND	ON HAND
PREVIOUS	0	0	0		0	0	0		0	0	0
TODAY (+)	3,000	2,400	330		4,000	1,200	0		5,730	5,200	10,930
TODAY (-)	1,000	0	0		0	800	0		1,000	800	1,800
TO DATE	2,000	2,400	330		4,000	400	0		4,730	4,400	9,130

Day #2

UN-EXPOSED FILM ON HAND											
	FILM TYPE 5218				FILM TYPE 5274				5218	5274	TOTAL
	1000' LOADS	400' LOADS	SE		1000' LOADS	400' LOADS	SE		ON HAND	ON HAND	ON HAND
PREVIOUS	2,000	2,400	330		4,000	400	0		4,730	4,400	9,130
TODAY (+)	3,000	2,000	420		5,000	2,000	0		5,420	7,000	12,420
TODAY (-)	2,000	0	0		1,000	400	0		2,000	1,400	3,400
TO DATE	3,000	4,400	750		8,000	2,000	0		8,150	10,000	18,150

Figure 3.67 Breakdown of information for daily film inventory form #2.

The following section refers to daily film inventory form #3 in Figure 3.68.

- FILM TYPE: The type of film you are using—Kodak 7218, 7229, 5245, 5277; Fuji 8632, 8552; etc. In this example you are using Eastman Kodak Color Negative 5218 and 5274.
- ROLL #: The camera roll number from the camera report. In this example you have roll numbers 1, 2, and 3.
- LOADED: The total amount of footage loaded in the magazine for that roll number. In this example, roll number 1 is a 400-foot roll, roll number 2 is a 400-foot roll, and roll number 3 is a 1000-foot roll. GOOD + NO GOOD + WASTE + SE = LOADED.
- GOOD (G): The total of good or printed takes from the camera report for each roll.
- NO GOOD (NG): The total of no good takes from the camera report for each roll.
- WASTE (W): The amount of footage left over that cannot be called a short end. Less than 40 feet in 16 mm and less than 100 feet in 35 mm are considered waste.
- TOTAL (T): The total of GOOD plus NO GOOD plus WASTE. GOOD + NO GOOD + WASTE = TOTAL.
- SE: The amount of footage left over that is too large to be called waste. More than 40 feet in 16 mm and more than 100 feet in 35 mm is considered a short end.

DAY # 1

FILM TYPE	ROLL #	LOADED	GOOD	NO GOOD	WASTE	TOTAL	SE
5274	1	400	210	150	40	400	0
5274	2	400	280	110	10	400	0
5218	3	1000	430	240	0	670	330

Figure 3.68 Breakdown of information for daily film inventory form #3.

The following section refers to daily film inventory form #3 in Figure 3.69.

- TOTALS: The total amount of all roll numbers, for all film stocks combined, for each category: LOADED, GOOD (G), NO GOOD (NG), WASTE (W), TOTAL, and SE.
- TODAY: The combined total for today only, for all film stocks, for each category: LOADED, GOOD (G), NO GOOD (NG), WASTE (W), TOTAL, and SE.
- PREVIOUS (+): The combined total for all film types shot previous to today, for each category: LOADED, GOOD (G), NO GOOD (NG), WASTE (W), TOTAL, and SE. This amount is obtained from the previous day's daily report form from the section labeled Total to Date.
- TOTAL TO DATE: The combined total of all film stocks shot today plus the total of all film stocks shot previous to today. These amounts are then written on the next day's daily inventory report, in the section labeled Totals—Previous (+).

DAY # 1

TOTALS	LOADED	GOOD	NO GOOD	WASTE	TOTAL	SE
TODAY	1,800	920	500	50	1,470	330
PREVIOUS (+)	0	0	0	0	0	0
TOTAL TO DATE	1,800	920	500	50	1,470	330

DAY # 2

TOTALS	LOADED	GOOD	NO GOOD	WASTE	TOTAL	SE
TODAY	3,400	1,780	1,050	150	2,980	420
PREVIOUS (+)	1,800	920	500	50	1,470	330
TOTAL TO DATE	5,200	2,700	1,550	200	4,450	750

Figure 3.69 Breakdown of information for daily film inventory form #3.

The following section refers to daily film inventory form #3 in Figure 3.70.

- FILM ON HAND/FILM TYPE: These columns are left blank for you to fill in with the film stock you are using. In this example you are using Eastman Kodak Color Negative 5218 and 5274.
- TOTALS: The combined totals of previous film on hand, film received today, film shot today, and film on hand at the end of today for all film stocks.
- PREVIOUS BALANCE: The total amount of film on hand at the start of today for each film stock. In this example for day #1 you had no film on hand at the start of the day because it is the first day of filming. This information is obtained from the previous day's inventory report form, from the section labeled Total to Date.
- (+) REC'D TODAY: The total amount of footage received today for each film stock. In this example, for day #1, you received 5400 feet of film stock 5218 and 5200 feet of film stock 5274.
- (–) USED TODAY: The total amount of footage shot today for each film stock.
- TOTAL TO DATE: The total of footage on hand at the end of today, which is the combined total of the previous amount of footage on hand plus the amount of footage received today less the amount of footage shot today: PREVIOUS BALANCE + REC'D TODAY – USED TODAY = TOTAL TO DATE. This amount is then written on the daily inventory report for the next day in the section labeled Previous Balance.

DAY # 1

FILM ON HAND / FILM TYPE	5218	5274				TOTALS
PREVIOUS BALANCE	0	0				0
(+) REC'D TODAY	5,400	5,200				10,600
(–) USED TODAY	670	800				1,470
TOTAL TO DATE	4,730	4,400				9,130

DAY # 2

FILM ON HAND / FILM TYPE	5218	5274				TOTALS
PREVIOUS BALANCE	4,730	4,400				9,130
(+) REC'D TODAY	5,000	7,000				12,000
(–) USED TODAY	1,580	1,400				2,980
TOTAL TO DATE	8,150	10,000				18,150

Figure 3.70 Breakdown of information for daily film inventory form #3.

Ordering Additional Film Stock

Once you have completed filling out the daily film inventory forms at the end of each shooting day, be sure you have enough film on hand to continue filming. As the film inventory gets low, notify the production office that you need additional film stock. A good rule to follow is to have at least enough film on hand for 2 or 3 days of filming. Of course, if it is the last day of filming, you probably will not need to order any additional film. Be especially aware of holidays and weekends during the shooting schedule, because you will not be able to order film on these days. Whenever you receive any additional film stock, remember to record the amounts on the daily film inventory form. If possible, obtain a copy of the packing list that came with the film so that you have proof of how much was sent.

On larger shows, the production office often keeps a reserve supply of film at the office and only sends what is needed on set for a few days at a time. Be sure that you are aware of how much and what type of film the production office has in reserve supply. You should keep an inventory, starting with the amount at the start of production and as the office sends you film from this reserve you should subtract that amount from your current inventory balance. This inventory should be separate from your daily inventory form that is filled out each day after filming. And if the office orders more film from the manufacturer for their reserve supply, this additional amount should be communicated to the 2nd A.C. so that the inventory totals can be adjusted accordingly. Keeping a separate record of film inventory from the production office often allows you to double check amounts if there is a question later on. The more detailed and accurate your records, the fewer problems you should have at the conclusion of the production.

When ordering additional film stock, be sure to double check with the D.P. regarding the type of film he or she wants. If you have been using the same film stock throughout the production, it may not be necessary to check. But if you have been using many different film stocks, checking with the D.P. will most often ensure that you have the correct film on hand. You should look at any advanced shooting schedules so that you know what scenes are coming up and plan accordingly. If there are any scenes that are quite long, you will want to have plenty of 1000-foot loads on hand. If the D.P. indicates there will be hand-held or Steadicam shots, you will want to have plenty of 400-foot loads. If upcoming scenes require multiple cameras, you must have plenty of film on hand for each camera. By keeping a constant check on the film inventory and looking at upcoming schedules or shot lists, you will eliminate a lot of problems later on. Nothing is worse than running out of film at a critical time during production because the assistant didn't look ahead and plan properly.

Many times the 2nd A.C. will make identification labels for the magazines each time a new supply of film is received. This saves time later when you are rushing to load magazines. Write the basic information on the labels and place a label on each film can. Each time a magazine is loaded, remove the label from the can and place it on the magazine, and fill in the remainder of the information. When the magazine is then placed on the camera, be sure to write in the roll number.

Storage and Care of Motion Picture Film

All motion picture films are manufactured to very high quality standards, and the proper storage and handling of these films are important. Motion picture films are sensitive to heat, moisture, and radiation. The following information is based on the recommendations of both Eastman Kodak and Fuji Film, the two manufacturers of all currently used motion picture film.

For short-term storage of less than 6 months, original cans of unopened raw stock should be kept at a temperature of 55° F or lower, and at a humidity level below 60%. For long-term storage of more than 6 months, film should be kept at a temperature of between 0° F and –10° F and at a humidity level below 60%. In addition, film should be kept away from any chemicals or fumes that could cause contamination of the emulsion layers. It should not be stored near any exhaust or heating pipes, or in direct sunlight. All film stock should also be kept away from any exposure to radiation.

When removing any film stock from cold storage, it must be allowed to properly warm up before the can is opened. Failure to allow the film to reach the proper temperature before opening the can will cause condensation to form on the film, resulting in spots in your photographic image. Never open a film can immediately after removing it from cold storage. Film should be allowed to warm up slowly, and you should never try to rush the warming up process. I once had a film student place a couple of cans of film under a 2000 watt light in an attempt to warm up the film faster. This is not recommended and I would never do it under any circumstances. After exposure, film should be unloaded as soon as possible from the magazines, placed in a black bag and film can, and properly sealed with camera tape in preparation for delivery to the lab. Table 3.4 lists the recommended warm-up times for motion picture films as recommended by Eastman Kodak.

All cans of exposed film should be sent to the lab as soon as possible. If there is any reason that exposed film cannot be sent to the lab within a reasonable amount of time, then it should be stored according to the recommendations for unexposed film.

Table 3.4 Recommended Warm-up Time for Sealed Packages of Motion Picture Film

Film Format	Warm-Up Time
16 mm	1 to 1 1/2 hours
35 mm	3 to 5 hours

Film, X-Rays, and Carrying Film on Planes

Be especially careful when transporting film on a plane. Although some of the x-ray equipment used to check baggage emits a very low-level dose of radiation, it can still cause a fogging on the film. Many airports are currently using a new type of x-ray equipment to examine luggage checked in at the ticket counter. This equipment uses a more intense x-ray beam that will cause fog damage to any exposed or unexposed film stock. It is not recommended to hand carry film when traveling by plane, but if you must do so you should request that it be inspected by hand. You must have your changing bag or changing tent available, as the security officer will want to open some of the cans to ensure that it is indeed film inside of them. Unfortunately this is very time consuming and inconvenient but it is still worth the time to avoid having fogged film. If you do plan to hand carry any film on a plane, the Producer or Production Manager should contact the security people at the airport well in advance and ask how they would like you to handle the situation. Ask if they would be willing to conduct a manual inspection of the packages containing the film.

Shipping Film (Exposed and Unexposed)

If you will be filming on a distant location that requires you to ship film to the laboratory, it is best to make arrangements with one of the professional shippers such as DHL, Federal Express, or UPS. Most of these companies use their own planes for shipping and usually do not use any type of x-ray equipment to scan packages being shipped within the United States. If you are planning to ship your film with any commercial shipping company, you should check with them before shipping to ensure that your film will not be x-rayed and will be transported safely.

Be aware that if you package your film for shipping and ship it as freight on a passenger airline, it will be subject to the same high intensity x-ray machines that checked baggage goes through. In any event, any time you ship motion picture film, you should always label all sides of the shipping carton with the following warning: "DO NOT X-RAY, MOTION PICTURE FILM."

Distribution of Reports

Once all the paperwork is completed, distribute copies to the appropriate departments. The production office should receive a copy of the daily film inventory form with copies of the day's camera reports attached. The camera department should also keep a copy of the daily film inventory form along with copies of camera reports.

Most camera reports usually consist of four copies. The top copy is always attached to the film can that is sent to the lab with the exposed film. One copy goes to the Editor, one copy to the production office, and the camera department keeps one copy. You should staple the camera reports to the daily film inventory form for each day, so that it will be easier to answer any questions later. In most cases the production office copy is given to the 2nd A.D. so that he or she may fill out the daily production report.

Record Keeping and Filing of Paperwork

As you have discovered from previous sections of this chapter, the camera department requires a lot of paperwork, most of which is filled in and prepared by the 2nd A.C. This includes shot logs, camera reports for each roll, film inventory forms, weekly time sheets, equipment records, expendables inventory, and more.

I strongly recommend that you set up some type of filing system to keep all of the paperwork organized during the production. You may choose to use a small plastic file box or cardboard box with various sections or folders for each type of form or paperwork. Set up your file box with separate, labeled file folders for each type of form, paperwork, invoice, or packing slip. An accordion-type file available at most office supply stores is also great for separating and keeping all of the various paperwork encountered during production. You may choose to use 3-ring binders to organize the paperwork. Whatever system you use, just be sure that it is organized in such a way that anybody can find a particular piece of information when necessary. Customize your filing system depending on the needs of the particular production.

In addition to the previously mentioned paperwork, other sections in your filing system include equipment received, equipment returned, film ordered and received, expendables ordered and received, short end inventory, raw stock inventory, individual and departmental time sheets, and so on. You should have copies of all packing lists for anything received by the camera department, as well as anything returned by the camera department. Each time you receive or return a piece of equipment, enter the date and description of the equipment in the record book. This way, if there are any questions later, check the book. Equipment received and equipment returned are discussed in a following section.

On many productions the 2nd A.C. is also responsible for keeping time sheets for each member of the camera department. Appendix C contains a camera department time sheet on which you keep track of the hours worked for each member of the department. The time sheet contains spaces to record the start time, start and end time of the first and second meal break, wrap time, total regular hours, total overtime hours, and overall total hours worked for each day and week. The time sheet is based on a typical time card used by many of the payroll companies in the motion picture industry.

When filling out the time cards, it is common to record the time using military time. Military time is based on a 24-hour clock instead of the 12 hour AM and 12 hour PM clock. Hours are typically broken down into tenths of an hour. Each 6-minute time period equals one tenth of an hour. For example, a call time of 8:30 AM would be written as 8.5, and a wrap time of 8:30 PM is written as 20.5. Using military time along with tenths of an hour makes the calculation of total hours each day much easier. Table 7.1 in Chapter 7, "Before, During, and After the Job," shows tenths of an hour conversion. Each day you should mark down the hours worked by each member of the department, and at the end of the week fill out the time cards. The important thing to remember is to be as complete and as organized as possible so that the production will go smoothly and problems will be minimized.

Expendables and film stock must be replenished often during a large production. You should keep accurate inventory records of both of these. I have included many different forms in Appendix C that make it easier for you to keep track of these. You may use the Expendables Inventory and Checklist not only to order your expendable supplies but also to keep track of the inventory of those items. It is important not to run out of expendables during production, especially black and white camera tape. You would be in a serious predicament if you were unloading rolls of exposed film and had no black camera tape to wrap the film cans. Appendix C contains two versions of a Daily Film Inventory Form, a Short End Inventory Form, and a Raw Stock Inventory Form. By using all of these forms, you should be able to keep a very accurate record of all film stock and be able to answer any questions during and after the shoot.

Throughout a production you may be receiving additional equipment and sending equipment back to the camera rental company. A piece of equipment may become damaged and need to be sent back for replacement. You may have some special shots requiring special equipment. There may be scenes scheduled for shooting that require additional cameras. It is important to keep track of all of this equipment. Appendix C contains an Equipment Received Log and an Equipment Returned Log that you can use to keep track of all of this information.

Whatever paperwork is required for the camera department, the 2nd A.C. should have complete and accurate records that should be easy to locate quickly if needed. It is also important to hold on to this paperwork for a brief period after production has been completed. You never know when you may have to refer back to an invoice, time sheet, or camera report. I remember receiving a telephone call from an editor a few months after a production that I worked on had wrapped. He was working on a particular scene and could not find the copy of the camera report with the scene and take number on it. By going back through my files I was able to locate my copy of the camera report, which I immediately faxed to him.

Performing the Duties of First Camera Assistant

From time to time the 2nd A.C. may be called on to act as 1st A.C. on some shots. There may be an additional camera or the 1st A.C. may have to leave for some reason. As the second assistant you should have a basic knowledge and understanding of the job requirements of a 1st A.C. in case this happens. If you someday plan on moving up from second assistant to first assistant, the more knowledge you have about the job, the better your chances are of moving up. I was once working as a second assistant on a feature film that was using multiple cameras for a series of shots. Instead of hiring an additional first assistant, I was asked to serve as the first assistant on the second camera. This was not the first time I received a bump up on a show, and because I knew and understood the job of a first assistant, the D.P. was comfortable with my pulling focus on the second camera. Shortly after this production, I made my official jump to first assistant and no longer accepted second assistant jobs. Chapter 4 discusses in detail all the responsibilities of that position.

Packing Equipment

At the end of each shooting day, all the camera equipment should be packed away in its proper case as quickly as possible and placed in a safe place until the next shooting day. Remember, the sooner you pack everything away, the sooner you go home for the day. Check all areas of the location to be sure that you have all the camera equipment and nothing is left behind. Place all equipment in the camera truck, or if you are shooting on a stage, place it in a safe area on the stage. Many stages have a separate room for the camera department for the storage of equipment. This room also may contain a darkroom for loading and unloading the film. Any camera equipment should be placed in its case and not left out where it could become damaged. This equipment is very valuable and should be handled carefully. It will be much easier to locate anything if it is put away each time instead of left lying around. I don't recommend leaving the camera set up from one day to the next. You never know what will happen overnight. But if the D.P. tells you that it is all right to leave the camera set up, be sure to remove the lens, lock the head securely, and cover the camera to protect it.

Tools and Accessories

As with many other professions, you must have some basic tools and accessories so that you may do the job properly. When first starting out, you should have a very basic tool kit or ditty bag, and as you gain more experience and work more frequently, you can add things as you feel they are needed. Some are common tools, while others are specialized pieces of equipment that are unique to the film industry. In addition to the basic tools, an assistant should also have a small inventory of expendables, film cans, cores, camera reports, etc. There will be many times when you are called for a job at the last minute and you may have no time to acquire some of these items. By having a small amount on hand, you will always be prepared for most job calls that you get. See Appendix D for a list of the common tools and equipment that should be included in an assistant cameraman's ditty bag, tool kit, or AKS case.

In addition to the PDA that is often used by the assistant cameraman, many also use a laptop computer on set. Both of these devices can save both the first and second assistant much time in the performance of their job. Having a basic understanding of word processing and spreadsheet software can save the assistant a lot of time during the course of the production. Many camera manuals are currently available in PDF format, which can be saved onto a laptop computer and referenced quickly on set if needed. In addition, all of the forms, checklists, and labels in Appendix C are available for download on the companion web site for this book. By downloading them to your laptop computer, you will have every form needed to make your job go smoothly.

I have found it important to have on set a personal bag that contains a change of clothes, extra sneakers or work shoes, along with foul weather or rain gear. You never know when you must change clothes or have additional clothing in case of extreme weather conditions. Having an extra sweatshirt, thermal underwear, and cold weather boots can make the difference between being warm and comfortable on a shoot or freezing. I bring this bag with me on any long-term jobs and keep it on one of the top shelves in the camera truck. In addition to clothing items, I also keep a small first aid kit, basic toiletry kit, and extra towels in the bag. You never know when you will find yourself away from home and in need of many of these items.

Working in Video/HD

With so many productions being shot on video these days, I thought it would be a good idea to include some basic information about the job responsibilities of the Camera Assistants when working in that format. Since all of my production experience has been working on film productions, I have had to rely on other sources for this information. I apologize if any of the information is unclear or incomplete.

Unfortunately many producers believe that you don't need a full crew when shooting in video or HD digital video. In fact you should have the same number of crew positions in the camera department as when shooting film. There should always be a separate Camera Operator so that the D.P. can be near the monitor when shooting to ensure that the image looks correct. You need a first assistant and a second assistant because of the additional equipment needed along with the many cables that must be connected to the camera. The shots still must be kept in focus, marks placed for actors, slates recorded, reports filled out, and much more.

Although there is no loading of film involved when working in video, a second assistant should still be hired. Many D.P.s feel that a second assistant is needed now more than ever because of all of the cables and equipment to move every time you move the camera to a new setup. On many video or HD digital shoots, there may be both a 2nd A.C. and a Digital Utility person, or there may be only one of these positions. Whatever name or title you give to this person, the person hired will perform many of the tasks listed later. To keep with the standard film titles that I am most familiar with, I will use the term 2nd A.C. when referring to this job classification even though the Digital Utility person may do many of these tasks.

Pre-Production

As stated earlier the second assistant works with the first assistant to prepare the list of supplies and expendables needed for the production. They may obtain a supply of tapes ahead of time and prepare the labels for these tapes with the basic production information. Anything you prepare beforehand will save you time in the long run.

Since there is no need for a darkroom for the loading and unloading of film, a camera truck equipped with a darkroom is not usually necessary on a video or HD production. A truck may still be necessary for the transportation of equipment and may be set up differently from a standard film camera truck. The second assistant may work with the Digital Utility person to clean and load the truck with all of the equipment.

Production

Camera Reports During shooting you will still need to keep track of scene and take numbers along with the time code settings from the camera or recorder. This information is recorded onto a camera report. I have designed a special camera report specifically for video that can be found in Appendix C. The video camera report is also available for download on the companion web site for this book.

Setting up the Camera The 2nd A.C. often helps the 1st A.C. in the setup of the camera at the beginning of the shoot day. The 2nd A.C. helps set up and connect the monitor to the camera and helps the Digital Imaging Technician connect the camera to the recorder and other devices. Since there are many more cables involved with a video or HD production, the second assistant should be familiar with all of the cables and their proper connection.

Marking Actors Just as in film production, actors still must be given marks for lighting and focusing purposes. The 2nd A.C. will place tape on the floor for each actor's position during a shot or scene.

Slates and Slating Procedures Again, just like in film, you need a slate to identify the tape numbers, scene, and take numbers for each shot. You never know when or if the camera, recorder, or editing system may malfunction. Using a standard film-style slate and clapping the sticks together for each shot enable you to sync up any shots when necessary.

Moving the Camera and Setting up the Video Monitor Whenever the camera needs to be moved to a new setup or camera position, the 1st A.C. should disconnect all cables from the camera, pass them to the 2nd A.C., who assists in moving the camera to its new location. Once the camera position is established, the cables can be reconnected. This would be a good time to get out the lens focus chart and reset the back focus. During the process of moving the camera, it has probably gone out of alignment.

At the start of the day, the 2nd A.C. most often will set up a monitor for the D.P. and Director and connect it to the camera or video recorder. Any additional monitors for other people to see may also be initially set up by the second assistant, but during the course of the shooting day the primary responsibility is to move and set up the monitor for the D.P. and Director. Any other monitors being used may require another crew member to move and connect them for any camera moves because the second assistant has other responsibilities to attend to.

Preparing Tapes and Reports Although you will not be downloading film and preparing it for delivery to the lab, you still must prepare the tapes, camera reports, and other paperwork for delivery to the Editor or production company. Be sure that all tapes are labeled correctly with all of the pertinent production information. Each tape should be numbered and dated and have a separate camera report with it showing all of the scene, take numbers, and time code numbers for that tape. If there is a script supervisor on the production, you should check to ensure that any takes are circled to indicate the good takes on the tape.

Ordering Additional Tapes Just as you must keep a careful watch on your film inventory for a film production, you must also keep a watch on your tape inventory when working in video or HD production. You should never run out of tapes. When in doubt, check with the D.P. and order additional tapes in advance of when you will need them. Be sure to order to proper format and length of tape.

Storage and Care of Videotapes Tapes should be stored upright, with the tape wound either to the end of the shot footage or to the beginning of the shot footage. Tapes should never be stored with the tape wound to the middle of the shot footage. They should always be kept in a cool, dry place and, unlike film, do not need to be refrigerated.

Videotape, X-Rays, and Magnetic Fields Always request that videotapes be hand inspected when traveling by air. Never expose them to x-rays or magnets of any kind, as this will erase the information on the tape.

Tools and Accessories The same complement of tools and accessories required for film is required when working in video or HD production. Although you may not use them all, I am a firm believer in the saying, "It's better to have it and not need it than to need it and not have it." Have a head cleaning tape made by the camera manufacturer, but use it sparingly (Sony recommends never more than 5 times consecutively) and only when the camera malfunctions. Some video engineers do not like cleaning tapes and prefer to clean heads manually. You should have a supply of various video connectors and cables in your ditty bag as well. You never know when you may need a specific connector or when a cable may break, and having the right replacement could save a production money and time.

Post-Production

Wrapping Equipment When wrapping equipment and packing it away at the end of the day or at the end of the shoot, you should follow the same procedures as outlined in this section dealing with film shoots. If you will be continuing to shoot on another day and the camera is being shipped to a new location, I have been told that it is a good idea to write down all of your camera settings on a piece of paper, so that if settings change during transportation, you can reset the camera to its original settings for shooting.

2nd A.C. Tips

Many of these tips apply only to the second assistant, and some of them apply to both the first and second assistants. As you read this book you will notice that some of them are repeated in Chapter 4. In the course of the day-to-day performance of your job you will often repeat orders back to someone to indicate that you heard them. I believe the repetition is important in the proper executing of your job and that is why some of these tips are repeated in the next chapter. It can only help to reinforce the importance of them.

Always arrive to work at least 15 minutes to a half hour before the call time. This shows your willingness to work and also your professionalism. If you get in this habit from the very beginning, it will stick with you throughout your career. No matter what, you should always be on set before the 1st A.C., ready to begin the workday.

Your attitude is a big part of the reason why you get hired for a job and why you keep the job. One of the first questions that may be asked about you when being considered for a job is "How does he get along with others?" Or, "Does she have a good attitude?" If you are constantly complaining or whining, nobody is going to want to work with you. Have a positive attitude every day on the set. Leave your personal problems at home. If you do, everybody will want to work with you.

Establish a relationship with the lab as soon as you are hired and know which lab will be processing the film. Be sure to have all the supplies needed for loading and unloading film. Know the name and telephone number of your lab contact and be sure to give that person your contact information.

Check the darkroom regularly to be sure that it is lightproof. This is especially important when working out of a darkroom on a camera truck. As the truck is driven from location to location, it may be traveling over varied road surfaces. This may cause the walls, ceiling, and door of the darkroom to move, creating cracks for light to leak in. I recommend checking the camera truck darkroom at the beginning of each shooting day.

Prepare a supply of camera reports beforehand with all of the basic heading information. You may also be able to include film stock information if only using one or two stocks. This saves time during production when you are in a hurry and need a new camera report. It's also a good idea to prepare magazine identification labels beforehand. You can complete all of the basic information, place a label on the side of each film can, and then when the film is loaded, write the mag number on the label and place the label on the magazine. When preparing a label for a short end of film, be sure to circle the footage amount in a contrasting color to indicate that a short end is loaded into the magazine.

If possible, color code magazine labels according to the type of film you are using. By glancing at a magazine or mag case, you will know what type of film is loaded without having to read the label. You may do this by using different color cloth camera tape for each film stock or by using a different color marker and white tape.

Prepare actor marks ahead of time and place them on an unused slate or some other surface. This saves a great deal of time when rehearsing a scene, since you only have to quickly remove a mark from the board and place it on the floor for the actor. Color code actor marks so that each actor has his or her own specific color. You may even ask the actor which color he or she would like. Keeping the actors happy makes you look good.

The 1st A.C. must stay close by the camera and the D.P. to assist the D.P. in any way necessary. The 2nd A.C. is there to assist the 1st A.C. by getting equipment when needed, moving equipment for each new setup, and anything else that may be required by the 1st A.C., Camera Operator, or D.P. This even includes getting drinks or a snack for the 1st A.C., Camera Operator, and D.P. if necessary. The camera must never be left unattended, and if the 1st A.C. must step away, the 2nd A.C. stands by until he or she returns. Unless the entire cast and crew are on a break, the camera should never be left unattended. When left unattended during meal breaks, the camera should always be covered, the camera power turned off, and the battery disconnected from the camera.

Even though things must get done as quickly as possible, never run on the set. There are too many cables, equipment, and people on the set. Someone running needlessly and then tripping and getting hurt can cause too many problems. Nothing is that important. You can get things done quickly without running.

When working around the camera, keep your talking to a minimum. If it's necessary to talk then talk in a low voice. The D.P. may be discussing the shot with the Director or the Gaffer, or the Director may be talking with the actors. Keep quiet and listen to what is going on. If it's necessary to speak with someone, either wait until the time is right or ask them to go to another area of the set where it may be quieter. And above all, there is no yelling on any film set. This is a sign of a true non-professional.

The entire camera department is a team and must work together. Things that happen within the camera department should remain within the camera department. This is especially important for the 1st A.C. and 2nd A.C. If you must leave the set for any reason, you should inform the 1st A.C. If the 1st A.C. needs you for something and doesn't know where you are, he or she may have to leave the camera unattended to take care of a particular matter like changing lenses or filters. The 1st A.C. should also inform you whenever he or she leaves the set.

If you are having personality conflicts with someone in your department or in another department on the crew, try to speak with the person directly. Work it out among yourselves so that you can at least have a good working relationship. You may not like the person, but you should at least be able to work together without any conflict.

Whenever any piece of equipment is called for, you should repeat it back to confirm that you heard the request and that you heard it correctly. If your name is called out, you should also respond so that whoever called will know that you heard him or her. As stated previously, repetition is an important element in the proper performance of your job.

When getting a piece of equipment from a case, be sure to close and lock one latch when leaving it. Even if you will be coming right back to the case, at least one latch should be locked. While you are away from the case, somebody may need to move it, and if none of the latches is locked and someone picks up the case, spilling its contents, it will be blamed on the last person using the case, not the person picking it up. Camera assistants and trainees have been fired from productions for failure to secure at least one latch of an equipment case.

When changing magazines be sure to enter the new roll number on the ID tape before handing the magazine to the 1st A.C. Never give the 1st A.C. a magazine that does not have an identification label on it and be sure that this label is completely filled in.

When breaking for lunch, always disconnect the battery. I also encourage you to remove the lens from the camera when breaking for lunch. Check that the camera is secure on the tripod head and that the pan and tilt of the head are both locked. It is also common practice to cover the camera to protect it when breaking for lunch. If working outside during the day, the camera can be covered with a space blanket with the silver side facing out. This helps to reflect the sunlight off the camera and keep it cooler.

When charging batteries, charge only those that have been used. This should prevent them from building up a memory. Always rotate batteries so that each one gets used equally. After charging, cover the cable port with a piece of white 1-inch camera tape to indicate the battery is charged. Any battery that is not working should be marked with 1-inch red camera tape. Change the battery at lunchtime so that you start the second half of the day with a fresh battery.

When preparing to shoot any scenes, be sure to obtain the proper scene and take numbers from the Script Supervisor. Place this information on the slate so that it is ready when the camera rolls. As soon as the camera cuts, change the take number to the next highest number so you are ready in case the Director decides to reshoot the shot. Be prepared to change the scene and take numbers on the slate quickly if the shot changes.

Keep your eyes and ears open at all times so that you are constantly aware of what is happening on the set. As you become familiar with a particular working style of the 1st A.C. and D.P., you should be able to anticipate their requests and be ready when they do make a certain request. The D.P. may always use a particular lens or filter for the close-up and another for the wide shot. By paying attention, you will know when a new scene is being shot, and will have the lens or filter ready when it is called for. Watch the D.P. and Director when they are blocking out the scene. If possible listen to what they are saying. They may be discussing using a particular lens for the next shot and you can have the lens ready when called for. Knowing where the next scene or setup is located will give you an idea where the camera is to be placed, and it will also be an indication of where you can move the equipment so that it is close by.

Unless you are told or asked by the 1st A.C., never go into his or her tool kit, front box, or ditty bag without permission. If something is needed from these, the 1st A.C. will either get it personally or give you permission to get it. You wouldn't like someone using your tools without permission, so treat the 1st A.C. with the same consideration.

Keep all equipment organized and in its proper place. If it is kept in the same place all of the time, it can easily be located when in a hurry. This applies to both the camera truck and equipment carts.

When on stage or location, you should have some type of four-wheel cart such as the Magliner or Rubbermaid plastic service cart for moving the equipment from place to place. You will have many equipment cases to deal with each day, and it is much easier and quicker if they can be wheeled from place to place instead of individually carried. Whenever the camera is moved to a new location, the cart should also be moved as quickly as possible.

Most important, if you make a mistake, tell someone immediately, usually the 1st A.C. This information should be communicated to the 1st A.C. quietly so as not to alarm anybody else. It may not be as bad as you think, and keeping it between the 1st A.C. and 2nd A.C. usually allows you to take care of it without anybody finding out. If you must tell the D.P. or any other production personnel, do it quickly and quietly.

As a 2nd A.C., you must be able to work very closely with the D.P., the Camera Operator, and the 1st A.C. Keep in mind that everybody does things differently. Be flexible and when working with a new crew, try to do things the way that they want. After a while you will develop a system of doing things that works best for you. But don't forget that you will always have to adjust your way of doing things when working with others who have their own system.

Always maintain a positive and professional attitude, and if you are ever unsure of something, do not be afraid to ask. Always do your job to the best of your ability, and if a mistake is made, admit it so that it can be corrected. Remember that some day you will be in their position, dealing with the same situations and problems.

POST-PRODUCTION

Post-production is the time when the shooting of the film is done. This is the time when the editing is completed and all promotional and distribution details of the production are worked out and finalized. The 2nd A.C. works only 1 or 2 days during post-production, depending on the size of the project. On very small projects there may be no post-production time for the 2nd A.C. The entire wrap-up may be completed at the end of the last day of filming.

Post-production for the camera department means that all equipment must be cleaned, checked, and packed away so that it can be returned to the rental company. A final inventory of film stock and expendables is usually done and turned in to the production office. If a camera truck was used, it should be cleaned out for the next production's use. Finally, the 2nd A.C. packs up all his or her gear and gets ready for the next job call where the entire process starts all over again.

Wrapping Equipment

At the completion of filming, the camera equipment, camera truck, and anything else relating to the camera department must be wrapped. This means that everything should be cleaned and packed away. All equipment must be cleaned, packed, and sent back to the camera rental house. The wrap can take anywhere from a few hours to an entire day, depending on the size of the camera package. Usually the 1st A.C. wraps out the camera equipment, while the 2nd A.C. wraps out the truck, darkroom, and film stock. Many times, if it is a small production, only the 1st A.C. wraps the camera equipment. All equipment should be cleaned, any tape or other markings removed, and it should be placed in the proper equipment case. If you look at the Expendables Inventory and Checklist in Appendix C, you will notice that I have listed cleaning supplies. I believe that it is important to send equipment back to the rental company in the same or better condition than when you received it. This means cleaning each piece of equipment before placing it in the equipment case. If you show the rental company that you take care of their equipment, they will be more inclined to help you in the future. You should use the original packing slip, listing all of the equipment to double check that you are sending back everything that you received. Any discrepancies should be reported to the production office immediately. The truck and darkroom should be left clean for the next job. A final inventory of the film stock should be done, and all remaining film raw stock should be packed in boxes for the production company.

RESOURCES

During your career as an assistant cameraman, you will rely on a variety of professional resources to enable you to do your job completely. This includes camera manufacturers and rental companies, grip and lighting companies, expendables companies, film laboratories, sellers of film raw stock, professional organizations, and much more. You should have all contact information for these companies readily available in case you need something at the last minute or in case of emergency. Rather than list all of the possible names, addresses, telephone numbers, e-mail addresses, and web sites for the various companies, this information is included in a section of the companion web site for the book. The web site address is www.cameraassistantmanual.com. Because companies move and change addresses, telephone numbers, and e-mail addresses quite frequently, I have chosen not to include a list in the book for fear that by the time you read the list much of the information will be inaccurate. The companion web site will be updated on a regular basis so that you should be able to have the most current information for any of the companies listed. In addition to the various companies and suppliers that you will be dealing with, the web site also includes many links to industry-related web sites for listing your résumé and searching for jobs. If you have web sites or know of any web sites of interest that you would like to see included, please feel free to contact me by e-mail.

2ND A.C. REVIEW CHECKLIST (CLAPPER/LOADER)

- Before production obtains a supply of empty cans, black bags, camera reports, and cores from the lab or asks the Production Manager to arrange this
- Prepares a list of expendables with the 1st A.C.
- Preps the camera package along with the 1st A.C.
- Cleans the camera truck and/or darkroom for use during the production, and makes sure that each is loaded with the proper supplies and equipment
- Loads and unloads film in the magazines, and places proper identification on each if there is no loader
- Checks with loader (if there is one) to be sure that all film magazines are loaded and properly labeled
- Checks darkroom to be sure that it is light proof on a daily basis if necessary
- Communicates with the Script Supervisor to obtain the scene and take number for each shot, and also which takes are to be printed
- Records all information on the slate
- Records all information on the camera reports
- Checks with Script Supervisor as to what takes are to be printed for each scene
- Helps to set up the camera at the start of each shooting day
- Marks the position of actors during the rehearsals
- Slates each scene, whether sound (sync) or silent (MOS)
- Assists in changing lenses, filters, magazines, and so on, and in moving the camera to each new position
- Sets up and moves video monitor for each new camera setup and makes sure the cable is connected to the film camera
- Prepares exposed film for delivery to the lab and delivers it to the production company representative at the end of each shooting day
- Cans and labels any film recans or short ends
- Serves as camera department contact with production office, film laboratory, and camera equipment rental house

- Maintains a record of all film received, film shot, short ends created, and film on hand at the end of each shooting day during the production
- Maintains an inventory of film stock and expendables on hand and requests additional supplies from the production office as needed
- Maintains an inventory of camera equipment on hand, additional equipment ordered, and any equipment damaged or returned
- Distributes copies of the camera reports and film inventory forms to the appropriate departments
- Keeps a file of all paperwork relating to the camera department during the production: camera reports, daily film inventory forms, processing reports from the lab, equipment packing lists, expendable requests, etc.
- Keeps a record of all hours worked by the camera department and prepares time cards at the end of each day
- Performs the job of 1st A.C. if necessary, in the absence of the 1st A.C. or when additional cameras are used
- Works with the 1st A.C. to move the camera to each new position
- Works with the 1st A.C. to be sure that all camera batteries are kept fully charged and ready for use
- At the end of each shooting day, helps the 1st A.C. pack away all camera equipment in a safe place
- At the completion of filming, helps the 1st A.C. wrap and clean all camera equipment for returning to the rental house
- At the completion of filming, cleans and wraps the camera truck
- Provides all the necessary tools and accessories associated with performing the job

4

First Camera Assistant

After 2 or 3 years, you probably will move up from Second Camera Assistant (2nd A.C.) to First Camera Assistant (1st A.C.). In Britain and Europe, the 1st A.C. may be called the Focus-Puller. During production the 1st A.C. works directly with the 2nd A.C., the Camera Operator, and especially the Director of Photography (D.P.). The position of 1st A.C. requires great attention to detail. The 1st A.C. should stay as close as possible to the D.P. during shooting and be prepared for any number of requests. Keeping your eyes and ears open at all times, and never being too far from the D.P. or the camera is a sign of a good 1st A.C. A good 1st A.C. must be able to anticipate what the D.P. wants and respond to it immediately. You should know as much as possible about a wide variety of camera equipment and accessories. The more you know, the more jobs you will get.

One of the primary responsibilities during shooting is to maintain sharp focus throughout each shot. The 1st A.C. is also responsible for the smooth running of the camera department and maintenance of all camera equipment, as well as many other duties. This chapter discusses in detail each of the 1st A.C.'s duties and responsibilities. These duties are separated into three categories: pre-production, production, and post-production.

PRE-PRODUCTION

On most productions, the 1st A.C. will usually be involved in some of the pre-production aspects. This involvement usually requires meetings with the D.P. to discuss the camera equipment and film stock that will be used for the shoot. There may also be pre-production meetings with many of the key crew members to discuss the production. The 1st A.C. may also discuss the expendables order with the 2nd A.C. before it is submitted to the production office. In addition, the 1st A.C. must perform the camera prep, which is when all of the camera equipment is checked and tested to be sure that it is in proper working order before production. The camera prep is perhaps the most important job of the 1st A.C. during the pre-production stage. Each job may be a bit different, but the camera prep is as important to a 1-day commercial shoot as it is to a 6-week or longer feature film production. The 1st A.C. wants to feel confident that when he or she walks on to the set he or she has all of the equipment needed and that everything works properly.

Choosing Camera Equipment

During pre-production, the D.P. usually prepares a list of camera equipment that will be needed on the production. Many times he prepares this list with the 1st A.C. or sometimes the D.P. prepares the list and then sends it to the 1st A.C. for additional items to be added. Because the 1st A.C. works with the equipment daily, he or she usually knows which accessories are needed to make the shooting go as smoothly as possible. The D.P. chooses the camera, lenses, and filters and the 1st A.C. usually determines which accessories are needed to complete the camera package. You should have a working knowledge of all camera systems, as well as the accessories for each, and have copies of rental catalogs from various rental houses to help in choosing the proper equipment. Camera rental houses will give you a copy of their current rental catalog at no charge and many are available online. Appendix C contains a Camera Equipment Checklist that can be used to prepare the initial camera package order.

Choosing and Ordering Expendables

During pre-production make a list of the expendables needed for the camera department. As discussed in Chapter 3, this list is prepared by both the 1st A.C. and the 2nd A.C. Each may have specialty items needed to do his or her job, which should be included along with the standard items. The standard expendables are items that will be needed in the daily performance of your job, such as camera tape, permanent felt tip markers, ballpoint pens, compressed air, lens tissue, lens cleaning solution, and so on. They are referred to as expendables because they are items that are used up or expended during the course of the production. The size and type of production determine which items and how many of each are needed. After the initial order, the 2nd A.C. is responsible for checking the supply on a regular basis to make sure that you do not run out of anything. For a complete list of the standard items on a camera department expendables list, see Figure C.3 in Appendix C.

The Rental House

Before going to the camera rental house to prep, you should contact the staff to be sure that everything is ready for you. They will tell you what time they have scheduled for the prep for your particular production. Once you arrive, all or most of your equipment should be set aside in an area where you can work. At the rental house you should first check their list against the list that you made with the D.P. to be sure that you have everything. If any item is missing, request it immediately. A technician or prep tech from the rental house will be assigned to you, and this is the person you will communicate with about any problems or questions regarding your equipment.

As a camera assistant, please be aware that the rental house prep tech's job is not simply to pull the items requested off a shelf. Before you arrived at the rental house, the tech has done the same prep, if not a more in-depth prep than the one you will be doing. Each piece of equipment has been thoroughly checked to be sure that it works. And since you will be responsible for the equipment on the production, it is to your advantage to check each item before production begins.

The camera and equipment you have requested will most often be prepared for you and be ready at the time scheduled for the prep. However, remember you are not the only production that the rental house is dealing with at that time; therefore all of your equipment may not be ready. The rental house prep tech may be working with more than one production company, so you should have a little patience when asking for anything if you do not get it right away. It is always best to schedule your prep a few days ahead and be prepared to work around the rental house's schedule. The rental house will do its best to accommodate your schedule, but sometimes you may have to prep a little earlier or later than planned.

If you need to add any items to your list, be sure that you have the approval from your production company and the rental house, because a deal may have been previously negotiated. Additional equipment may not be part of the original agreement, and the production company needs to know what add-ons you have requested, so that they can authorize it and make additional arrangements with the rental company. If it is an item that is absolutely necessary, the rental house will most often work out an arrangement that is agreeable to all concerned.

As a camera assistant, it is important to have a good working relationship with the camera rental house. If you have treated the staff and their equipment properly in the past, they will be more inclined to help you out when a production company does not have a lot of money, but you need a few additional items. I was working for a small production and prepping the camera package at one of the major camera rental houses in Hollywood. They had worked out a special price deal for the equipment with the rental house. I asked for a few items that were not included in the original camera package. Because of the excellent relationship that I had with the rental house, the few additional items that I requested were included in the camera package at no additional charge because the rental house knew me, trusted me, and knew that I would take care of their equipment.

A negative attitude will not be tolerated at the rental house. A rental house tech told me of one show that he had prepped where the production company only had a specific amount of money that they could spend for the equipment. The A.C. attempted to get more equipment than the production company was prepared to pay for and was told that he could not have the items. The A.C. then began to throw a fit, claiming these were items that were needed to do the show properly and they must be included. Needless to say, he did not get the items and was not very welcome in the rental house after that.

The rental house prep tech is there to service the needs of the A.C. and production company, but the prep techs are not your personal servants and do not jump when called. The prep tech is there to help, and if you are unfamiliar with a piece of equipment, please ask about it. The prep tech would rather spend the time answering the question and showing you how something works than fixing it after it was broken through error. But remember, you must be patient as to how quickly your questions are answered because there are other rentals going out at the same time.

Although I have worked in the industry for quite some time and have worked with most of the currently used camera systems, I sometimes forget things. I have heard it said many times, "If you don't use it, you lose it." I was doing a prep and came across a piece of equipment that I had not used for a long time. I asked the prep tech to answer some questions about the equipment. He was busy at the time but said he would come back when he could. I continued with the prep and when the prep tech finished what he was doing, he returned to me to answer the questions. If you have forgotten how something works, don't be afraid to ask. It's better to admit that you don't know or don't remember how something works than to try to figure it out and risk damaging an expensive piece of equipment. In addition, there will be times when you are prepping a piece of equipment that you have never used before. You should always ask the rental house prep tech for help on any unfamiliar piece of equipment.

The prep will usually go faster if you have a system that you follow. Sticking to your system helps to facilitate efficiency and make the prep go quickly and smoothly. However, for various reasons a rental house may not have an item ready, may need to make an exchange, or may even have to get the item from another rental house. You must be flexible and willing to adjust your prep routine if necessary. Remember, you don't have to rush through a prep if you have a scheduled prep time. The rental house will not close on you if they are the ones who cause a delay with a piece of equipment.

I remember one prep I did for a very large-scale music video for a major music star. The initial prep involved three complete 35 mm camera packages. I arrived at the rental house around 9:00 AM and proceeded to prep the cameras. At approximately 5:00 PM I received a telephone call from the Production Manager telling me that they were adding another complete camera package. After working out my additional fees for the prep, I handed the telephone to the rental house technician. I knew that they were scheduled to close at 6:00 PM. After hanging up the phone I asked the rental house technician what we were going to do. He said that he would stay with me until all the cameras were prepped and ready for shipping. At approximately 10:15 PM I finished and left the rental house. I had done many preps at the rental company, the production was a very large show for them, and they were willing to work with the Production Manager and me so that the prep could be completed.

Preparation of Camera Equipment

Before you shoot one frame of film, the camera and all related accessories must be checked to be sure that everything is in working order. Once you know when the production will begin filming and the equipment has been ordered, contact the rental house and arrange a time when you can do the camera prep. Or the Production Manager may have already made the arrangements and will let you know when to prep the camera. A camera prep can take anywhere from a couple of hours to a few days or even a week depending on the size of the production. A few years ago I was given a full week to prep the camera package for a low budget feature film. Even though I didn't need a full week, I was able to do a thorough prep to be sure that I had everything and that it worked properly. Be sure to allow enough time to complete the prep so that you are not rushed and are able to check each piece of equipment thoroughly. When you go to the rental house, take along your tools and accessories. Have some dummy loads of film to use for scratch testing the magazines. A dummy load is a small spool of film left over from previous shoots and is called waste on the camera report. Instead of throwing out the dummy load, many assistants save these short lengths of film for use during the camera prep.

The primary purpose for doing the camera prep is to ensure that you have all the necessary camera equipment and accessories, and that they are in working order. Each item, no matter how small, must be checked and tested. Starting with the spreader, tripod, and head, you will assemble the entire camera package. Each accessory is attached to the camera and tested. Lenses are checked for sharpness and accurate focus; magazines are tested for noise and to be sure that they don't scratch the film, etc. Power cables are checked to be sure that they work properly. If you find any piece of equipment that is not performing satisfactorily during the prep, send it back immediately and request a replacement. Keep in mind, the one thing you don't check during the camera prep is probably the one thing that will not work at some point during the production, and even if you check everything, something will inevitably go wrong during the production. It's just a fact of life on a film set—nothing ever goes smoothly no matter how much preparation you do.

The following list includes the many items found in a typical camera rental package and describes what you should check for during the camera prep. Remember, all items on the list may not be needed on every production. Because of the many different types of productions and the differences between D.P.s and what equipment they use, it would be impossible to come up with one checklist to cover all possible shooting situations. I have listed the most frequently used items that will be found on many productions. All camera packages may not have every item listed. Appendix C contains a Camera Prep Checklist for your use.

When you arrive at the rental house, the first thing you should do is a preliminary inventory check to see if you have most of the items on your camera equipment list. I recommend lining up the cases, opening them, and giving them a quick visual check to see if you have all of the basic items. As you spend time checking each item, you will most likely discover some items that you didn't originally catch when doing the preliminary inventory check. As stated earlier, compare your equipment list with the list that the rental house has prepared for your production.

Camera Prep Checklist

______ 1. Spreader
- Runners slide smoothly and lock in all positions.
- Tripod points fit into receptacles.

______ 2. Tripods
- Legs slide smoothly and lock in all positions.
- Wooden legs are free from cracks and splinters.
- Top casting accommodates the head base (flat or bowl).
- Always obtain standard tripod and baby tripod.

______ 3. High hat
- High hat is mounted on smooth flat piece of wood.
- High hat top casting accommodates the head base (flat or bowl).
- High hat top casting should be the same as the tripod top casting.

______ 4. Low hat
- Low hat is mounted on smooth flat piece of wood.
- Low hat top casting accommodates the head base (flat or bowl).
- Low hat top casting should be the same as the tripod top casting.

______ 5. Fluid head
- Base fits tripod top casting and locks securely (bowl shaped or Mitchell Flat Base).
- Head includes a quick release plate allowing the fast removal of the camera from the head.
- Camera lockdown screw of quick release plate fits into camera body, adapter plate, riser plate, or sliding base plate.
- Pan and tilt movement is smooth at all tension settings.
- Tension adjustments for pan or tilt engage and do not slip.
- Head balances properly with complete camera, lens, magazine setup attached.
- Pan and tilt locks securely in all positions.
- Eyepiece leveler attaches to head securely.
- Head contains a mounting bracket for the camera assistant's front box.

______ 6. Dutch head
- Base fits into quick release opening of fluid head.
- Tilt movement is smooth at all tension settings.
- Tension adjustments for tilt engage and do not slip.
- Tilt locks securely in all positions.

______ 7. Gear head
- Base fits tripod top casting and locks securely. (All gear heads have a Mitchell Flat Base.)
- Head includes a quick release plate allowing the fast removal of the camera from the head.
- Camera lockdown screw of quick release plate fits into camera body, adapter plate, riser plate, or sliding base plate.

- Pan and tilt movement is smooth at all speed settings.
- Gears shift smoothly.
- If head contains a tilt plate, it operates smoothly and locks securely in all positions.
- Pan and tilt locks securely in all positions.
- Eyepiece leveler attaches to head securely.
- Head has a mounting bracket for the camera assistant's front box.

______ 8. Sliding base plate

- Sliding base plate mounts securely on quick release plate of head, and adapter plate mounts securely on camera body.
- Camera adapter plate slides smoothly and locks in all positions (Figure 4.1).

______ 9. Camera body

- Camera body fits securely on head, adapter plate, or quick release plate.
- Interior is clean and free from emulsion buildup or film chips.
- All rollers are clean, free from any burrs, and move smoothly.
- Aperture plate, pressure plate, and gate are clean and free from any burrs.
- Inching knob works properly.
- Pull down claw and registration pin operate smoothly and are not bent.
- Aperture plate is the same aspect ratio for the production you are shooting.
- Lens port opening is clean.

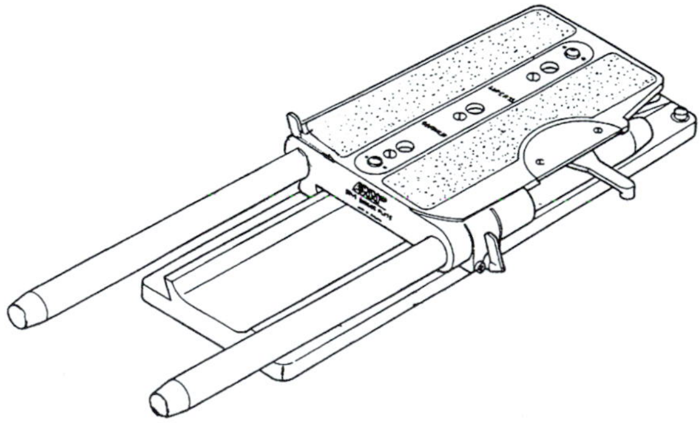

Figure 4.1 Arriflex Sliding Balance Plate. (Courtesy of ARRI Inc.)

- Mirror is clean and free from scratches. (Do not clean mirror yourself. If it is scratched or dirty, tell someone at the rental house immediately.)
- Magazine port opening is clean.
- Flange focal depth is set correctly.
- Electrical contacts in magazine port openings are clean.
- Footage counter and tachometer function properly.
- On-off switch functions properly.
- The movement of the shutter, pull-down claw, and registration pin is synchronized.
- Variable speed switch functions properly.
- Camera maintains speed at different speed settings.
- Pitch adjustment operates properly.
- Buckle trip switch operates properly. (Not all cameras have a buckle trip switch.)
- Power ports and accessory ports all function properly.
- Camera heater functions properly. (Not all cameras have an internal heater.)
- Ground glass or viewing screen is clean and is marked for the correct aspect ratio.
- Variable shutter operates smoothly through its entire range of openings.
- Long and short eyepieces mount properly and focus easily to the eye.
- Eyepiece heater functions properly.
- Eyepiece magnifier functions properly.
- Contrast viewing filter on eyepiece functions properly.
- Eyepiece leveler attaches to eyepiece securely.
- Illuminated ground glass markings function properly and are adjustable in intensity.
- Obtain rain covers for all cameras if you will be shooting in any situations where the camera may become wet (rain, snow, in or near any water—beach, pool, etc.).

______ 10. Magazines

- Magazines fit securely on camera body.
- You have high-speed magazines for high-speed cameras and regular magazines for regular cameras.
- Doors fit properly and lock securely.
- Interior is clean and free from dirt, dust, and film chips.
- Footage counter functions properly.
- Film moves smoothly through all film channels and rollers.
- Different size magazines obtained for various shooting situations: 200-foot, 400-foot, 1000-foot, etc.
- Electrical contacts on magazine are clean and free from dirt.

______ 11. Scratch test magazines

- Check all magazines on all cameras to be sure that they do not scratch film.
- Load a dummy load of film into each magazine and thread it through the camera. Be sure that the dummy load is fresh film stock that has not been previously run through a camera.
- Run approximately 10 feet to 20 feet of film through the camera.
- Remove the film from the magazine take-up side and examine it for scratches or oil spots on the base and on the emulsion side. (Turn the film from side to side while looking at it under a bright light. If there are any scratches on either side, they will be noticeable.)
- If you find any scratches, request a replacement magazine.
- On variable speed cameras, run film at various speed settings.

______ 12. Barneys

- Obtain the proper size barney for each size magazine. A barney is a padded cover used to reduce or eliminate noise from the camera or magazine.
- If necessary obtain a barney for the camera.
- On heated barneys check that the heater functions properly.

______ 13. Lenses

- Check that lens seats properly in camera body.
- Front and back glass elements are clean and free from scratches and imperfections.
- If any imperfections or scratches are found on the lenses, be sure to notify the rental house personnel immediately.
- Iris diaphragm operates smoothly.
- Focus gears of follow focus attach securely to lens.
- Focus ring operates smoothly.
- Remote focus and zoom controls fit securely and operate smoothly.
- Focus distance marks are accurate.
- When checking focus distance marks be sure that the lens is marked on both sides of the barrel. If not, wrap a thin piece of tape, such as artist's chart tape, around the lens and transfer the focus marks to the opposite side.
- On zoom lenses the zoom motor operates smoothly.
- Zoom lens tracks properly. (See step 14.)
- Zoom lens holds focus throughout the zoom range.
- Lens shade mounts securely to each lens.

- Matte box bellows fits securely around all lenses. If not, obtain various size rubber donuts to make a tight seal between lenses and matte box.

______ 14. Zoom lens tracking

- Check that the shifting of the image is minimal when zooming in or out.
- While looking through zoom lens, line up the crosshairs of the ground glass on the focus chart or on a point in the prep area where you are working.
- Lock the pan and tilt so the crosshairs remain centered on the point.
- While looking through the camera, zoom the lens in very slowly and then out very slowly, and watch to see if the crosshairs remain centered on the point throughout the length of the zoom. They may shift a small amount, and this is usually acceptable.
- If the crosshairs do not remain centered on the point or shift more than just a little, have the rental house check the lens.

______ 15. Power zoom control and zoom motor.

- Mounts securely to the lens and operates smoothly, both zooming in and zooming out.
- Variable speed adjustment is accurate.
- Camera on/off switch functions properly (if available) (Figure 4.2).

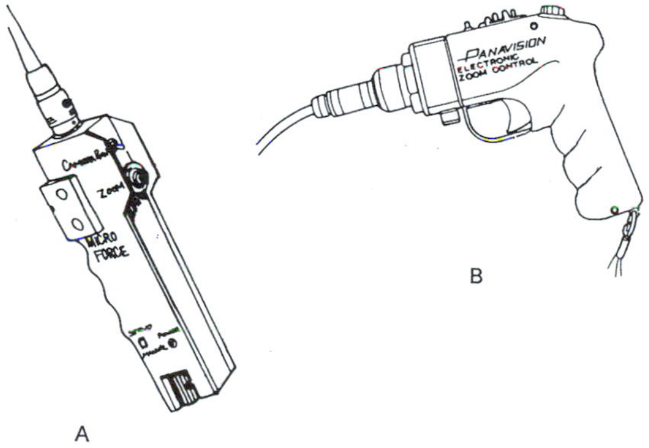

Figure 4.2 A, Microforce zoom control. (Reprinted from the *Arriflex 35 Book* by Jon Fauer with permission of the author and ARRI Inc.) **B,** Panavision zoom control. (Reprinted from the *Panaflex Users Manual,* with permission of David Samuelson and Panavision, Inc.)

_______ 16. Focus eyepiece

- With the lens removed, point the camera at a bright light source or white surface.
- While looking through the eyepiece, turn the diopter adjustment ring until the crosshairs or grains of the ground glass are sharp and in focus.
- Lock the adjustment ring and mark it so that it can be set to the proper position each time you look through the camera.
- Wrap a piece of tape around the barrel of the diopter adjustment ring and mark it so that it can be set to the proper mark for each person who looks through the camera.

_______ 17. Check focus of each lens

- Mount a lens on the camera.
- Set the aperture to its widest opening (lowest t-stop number).
- Using your tape measure, place a focus chart at specific distances from the camera. Base the distances on how the lens is marked. If the lens has focus marks at 5, 6, 7, 8, 10, 12, and 15 feet, place the focus chart at these distances and check the lens at each distance.
- If the lens does not have enough focus markings, you may need to make your own. Using the focus marks from the previous step, you may want to determine precise marks for 9, 11, 13, and 14 feet. Wrap a thin piece of tape, like artist's chart tape, around the barrel of the lens and, using a focus chart and your tape measure, determine the other marks that you may need. In many cases this will save you a great deal of time in the long run because you won't have to do it on set.
- At each distance look through the viewfinder eyepiece and focus the chart by eye.
- Compare the eye focus to the distance measured and see if they match.
- If the eye focus does not match the measured focus, have the lens checked by the rental house lens technician.
- Check each lens at various distances, including the closest focusing distance and infinity (∞). Some lenses are not marked for their closest focusing distance. You may have to wrap a thin piece of tape around the barrel of the lens and mark it for its closest focusing distance. Check it at 1-foot intervals or as stated previously at markings on the lens.
- With zoom lenses, check the focus with the lens zoomed in all the way (its longest or tightest focal length).

- Telephoto lenses must be checked at more distances than wide-angle lenses because telephoto lenses have less depth of field (Figures 4.3 and 4.4).

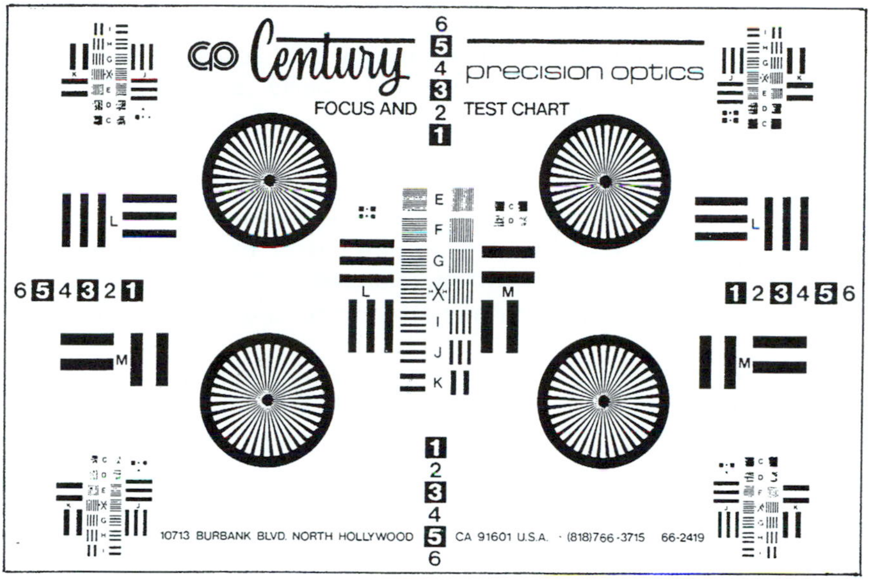

Figure 4.3 Century Precision Optics Focus Test Chart. (Courtesy of Century Precision Optics.)

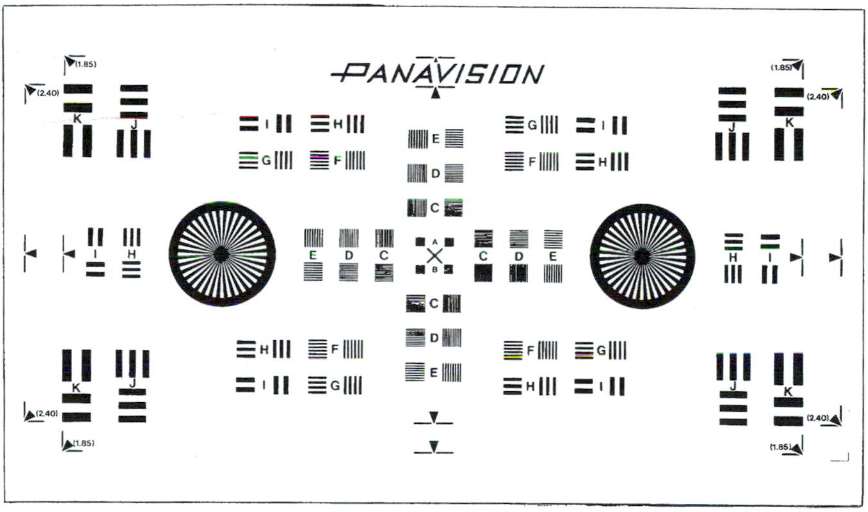

Figure 4.4 Panavision Focus Test Chart. (Courtesy of Panavision, Inc.)

______ 18. Follow focus mechanism.
- Mount follow focus mechanism securely on the camera or support rods, and be sure it operates smoothly with each lens. Check that gear fits properly to lens gear.
- If necessary obtain different focusing gears for prime lenses and zoom lenses.
- Check to be sure that you have all accessories, and that they mount and operate properly (focus whip, speed crank, right hand extension, focus marking disks, etc.) (Figures 4.5, 4.6, and 4.7).

______ 19. Matte box.
- Matte box mounts securely on the camera.
- Matte box operates properly with each lens; does not vignette with wide-angle lenses.
- Matte box has proper adapter rings and rubber donut or bellows for each lens.
- Filter trays are the correct size for filters being used.

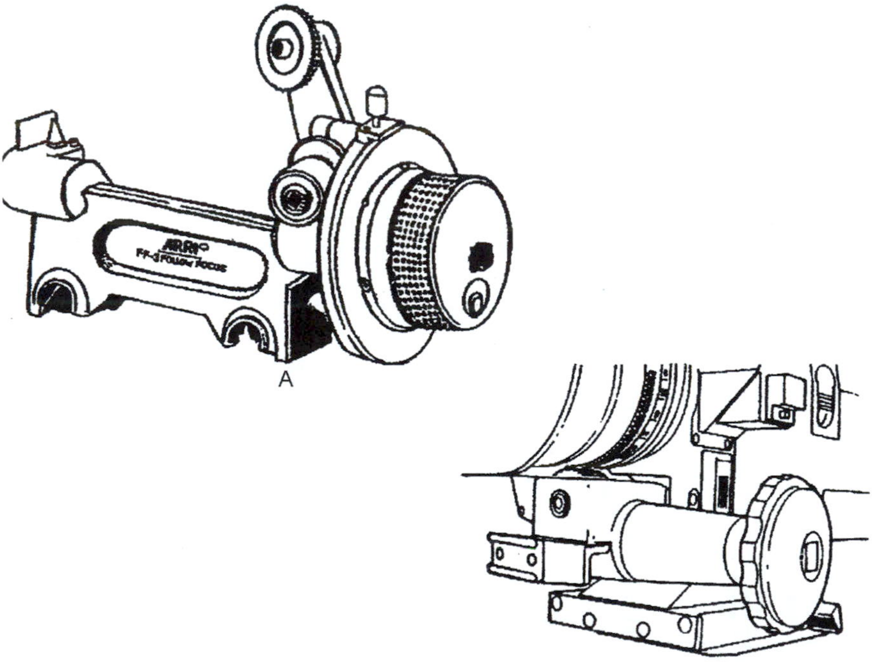

A

B

Figure 4.5 **A,** Arriflex follow focus mechanism. (Courtesy of ARRI Inc.) **B,** Panavision follow focus mechanism. (Reprinted from the *Panaflex Users Manual,* with permission of David Samuelson and Panavision, Inc.)

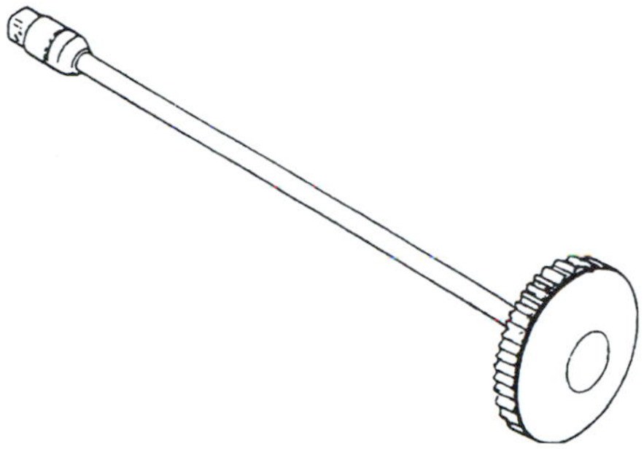

Figure 4.6
Focus whip. (Reprinted from the *Arriflex 535 Instruction Manual*, with permission of ARRI Inc.)

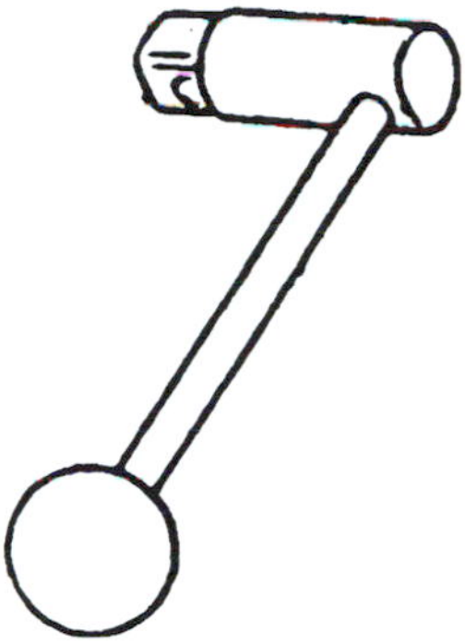

Figure 4.7
Focus speed crank. (Reprinted from the *Arriflex 535 Instruction Manual*, with permission of ARRI Inc.)

- Be sure to have the correct number of filter trays. Matte boxes are available with 2, 3, 4, or more filter trays depending on the needs of the production.
- Filter trays slide in and out smoothly and lock securely in position.
- Rotating filter trays or rings operate smoothly and lock securely in position.
- Eyebrow mounts securely and can be adjusted easily.
- Hard mattes mount securely and are the correct size for each lens (Figure 4.8).

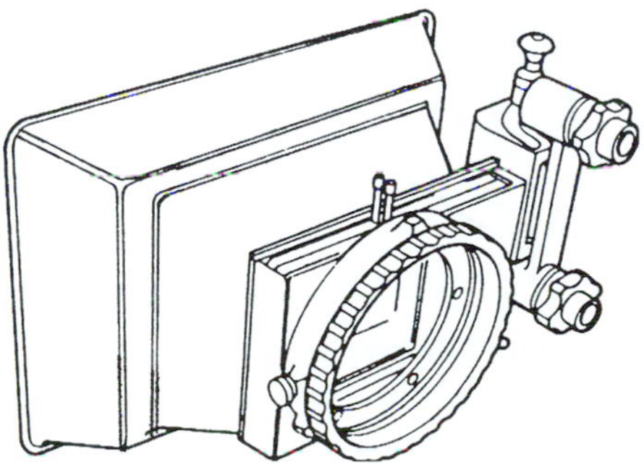

Figure 4.8
Matte box. (Reprinted from the *Panaflex Users Manual,* with permission of David Samuelson and Panavision, Inc.)

______ 20. Filters
- Each filter is clean and free from scratches.
- Filters are proper size for filter trays or retainer rings.
- Filters cover the entire front element of the lenses being used.
- Sliding filter trays for graduated filters operates smoothly and locks securely into position.
- Rotating polarizer operates smoothly.
- Always obtain optical flat or clear filter with any filter set.
- Obtain complete sets of filters for all cameras when using more than one camera.
- Are graduated filters hard edge or soft edge?

______ 21. Obie light (eye light)
- Obie light mounts securely and operates correctly at each setting.
- Be sure that you have extra bulbs for the light (Figure 4.9).

______ 22. Lens light (assistant's light)
- Lens light mounts securely and operates properly.
- Lens light is supplied with spare bulbs.

______ 23. Precision speed control
- Check that it operates correctly for both high speed and slow motion by running film through the camera at various speeds.

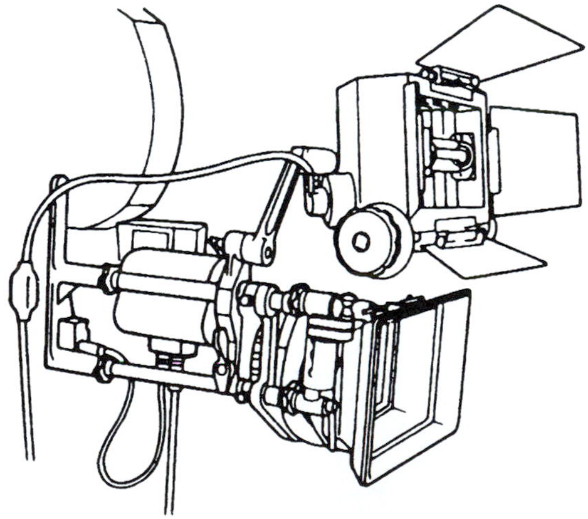

Figure 4.9 Panavision Panalite. (Reprinted from the *Panaflex Users Manual,* with permission of David Samuelson and Panavision, Inc.)

- When set to a specific speed, it holds that speed without varying.
- If using an external speed control be sure to have extra cables.

______ 24. HMI speed control

- When using HMI lights be sure that the camera has an HMI speed control so that you may adjust the speed to the correct number when filming. (HMI lights can cause the image to flicker if the camera is not run at certain speeds or shutter angles.) See Figures 4.10 through 4.13 for HMI filming speeds and shutter angles.

______ 25. Sync box

- When shooting TV screens, computer monitors, and projectors, use a sync box to eliminate the roll bar. If possible,

CINEMATOGRAPHY inc. electronics

HMI FLICKERFREE FILMING SPEEDS AT ANY SHUTTER ANGLE 60 Hz Line Frequency

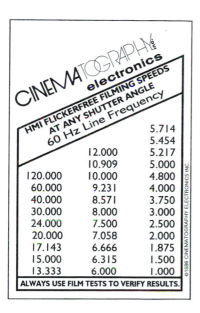

		5.714
		5.454
	12.000	5.217
	10.909	5.000
120.000	10.000	4.800
60.000	9.231	4.000
40.000	8.571	3.750
30.000	8.000	3.000
24.000	7.500	2.500
20.000	7.058	2.000
17.143	6.666	1.875
15.000	6.315	1.500
13.333	6.000	1.000

ALWAYS USE FILM TESTS TO VERIFY RESULTS.

Figure 4.10
HMI filming speeds at any shutter angle, 60 Hz line frequency—United States. (Courtesy of Cinematography Electronics, Inc., Agoura Hills, CA.)

CINEMATOGRAPHY inc. electronics

60 HZ FLICKERFREE FILMING SPEEDS WITH SPECIFIC SHUTTER ANGLES

FPS	SHUTTER ANGLES	
71.667	215	
70.000	210	
66.667	200	
65.000	195	
63.333	190	
57.600	172.8	
56.667	170	
55.000	165	
53.333	160	
50.000	150	
48.000	144	
46.667	140	
45.000	135	
43.333	130	
36.667	110	
35.000	105	210
33.333	100	200
26.667	80	160
25.000	75	150

ALWAYS USE FILM TESTS TO VERIFY RESULTS.

Figure 4.11
HMI filming speeds at specific shutter angles, 60 Hz line frequency—United States. (Courtesy of Cinematography Electronics, Inc., Agoura Hills, CA.)

CINEMATOGRAPHY inc. electronics

HMI FLICKERFREE FILMING SPEEDS AT ANY SHUTTER ANGLE 50 Hz Line Frequency

		5.000
		4.761
	10.000	4.545
100.000	9.090	4.347
50.000	8.333	4.166
33.333	7.692	4.000
25.000	7.142	3.333
20.000	6.666	3.125
16.666	6.250	2.500
14.285	5.882	2.000
12.500	5.555	1.250
11.111	5.263	1.000

ALWAYS USE FILM TESTS TO VERIFY RESULTS.

Figure 4.12
HMI filming speeds at any shutter angle, 50 Hz line frequency—Europe. (Courtesy of Cinematography Electronics, Inc., Agoura Hills, CA.)

CINEMATOGRAPHY inc. electronics

50 HZ FLICKERFREE FILMING SPEEDS WITH SPECIFIC SHUTTER ANGLES

FPS	SHUTTER ANGLES	
59.722	215	
58.333	210	
55.556	200	
54.167	195	
52.778	190	
48.000	172.8	
47.222	170	
45.833	165	
44.444	160	
41.667	150	
40.000	144	
38.889	140	
37.500	135	
36.111	130	
30.556	110	
29.167	105	
27.778	100	
24.000	86.4	172.8
22.222	80	160

ALWAYS USE FILM TESTS TO VERIFY RESULTS.

Figure 4.13
HMI filming speeds at specific shutter angles, 50 Hz line frequency—Europe. (Courtesy of Cinematography Electronics, Inc., Agoura Hills, CA.)

the camera should have a variable shutter so that you can sync the camera to the monitor or screen.
- When shooting at 30 frames per second (f.p.s.) or, more precisely, 29.97 f.p.s., the shutter angle should be set to 180 degrees.
- When shooting at 24 f.p.s. or, more precisely, 23.976 f.p.s., the shutter angle should be set to 144 degrees (Figure 4.14).

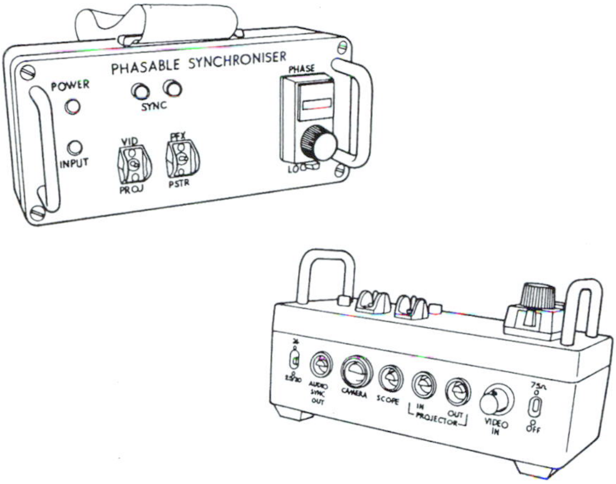

Figure 4.14 Panavision Phasable Synchroniser. (Reprinted from the *Panaflex Users Manual,* with permission of David Samuelson and Panavision, Inc.)

______ 26. Video tap and monitor
- Video tap camera mounts securely and properly to the film camera.
- Focus and gain controls operate properly.
- Iris control operates properly.
- Video tap can be adjusted so that the image is centered on the monitor and is clear and easy to view.
- Check that you have all cables and connectors necessary for the video tap and that they work properly. You should have various lengths of video cables and power cables for various shooting situations (10-foot, 25-foot, 50-foot). In addition be sure to have a supply of video connectors for connecting the cables to a television, VCR, or other device. Connect video monitor to camera and adjust video camera to obtain the best picture.

______ 27. Hand-held accessories

- If the production involves any hand-held shots, be sure you have the necessary accessories, which should attach securely and operate properly (left and right handgrips, shoulder pad, hand-held follow focus, clamp-on matte box or lens shade, 400-foot or 500-foot magazines, on-board batteries, etc.).
- Connect the handgrip with an on-off switch and be sure that it operates properly (Figure 4.15).

______ 28. Remote start switch

- Connect remote start switch to camera and ensure that it operates properly.
- Be sure to have extra cables and the proper length cables for different shooting situations (dangerous shots, car shots, stunts, etc.).

______ 29. Batteries and cables

- Be sure that all batteries are the correct voltage for the camera system being used.
- All cables should be in good condition and have no frayed or loose wires.
- At least two battery cables should be obtained for each camera being used.
- There should be no loose pins in the plugs.
- Battery cables should be of various lengths for different shooting situations.
- At least two batteries should be obtained for each camera being used.
- Extra batteries should be available for each camera in case you will be shooting high speed.
- If you will be shooting any hand-held shots, you should have at least two battery belts or on-board batteries.
- Each battery should have a charger, either built-in or separate (Figures 4.16, 4.17, and 4.18).

______ 30. Camera tests

- At the end of the camera prep, the D.P. may ask you to perform some specific tests. These tests will be shot on film so be sure to have access to some lights and have a

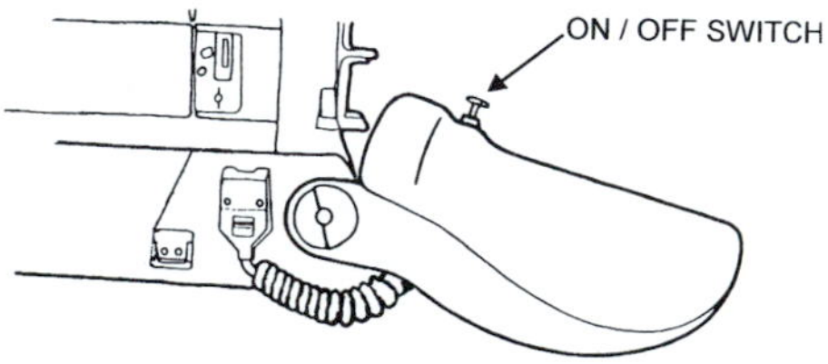

Figure 4.15
Right-hand grip with on/off switch on Arriflex 16SR camera. (Reprinted from the *Arriflex 16SR Book*, by Jon Fauer, with permission of the author and ARRI Inc.)

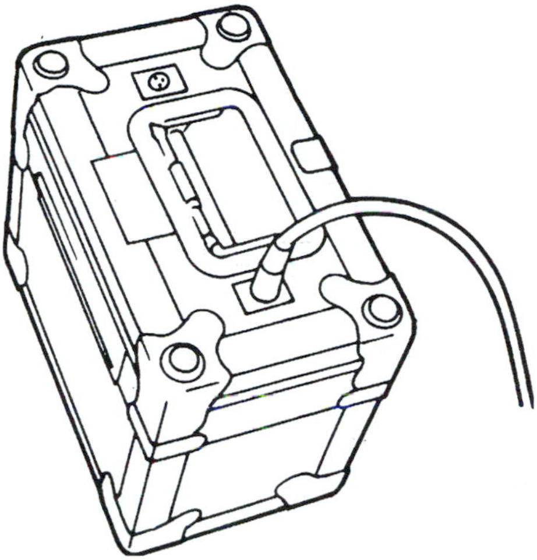

Figure 4.16
Panavision 24-volt double block battery. (Reprinted from the *Panaflex Users Manual,* with permission of David Samuelson and Panavision, Inc.)

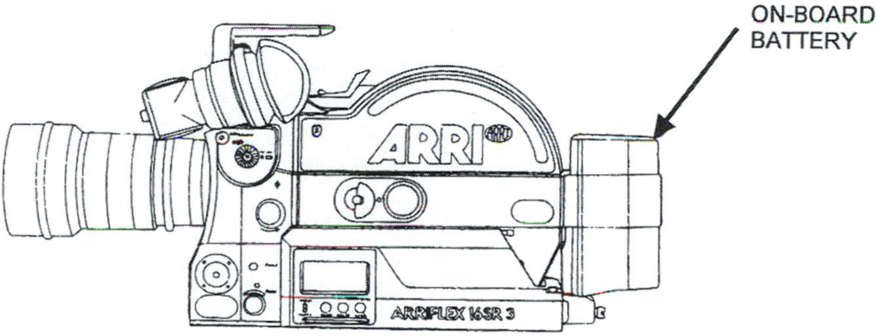

Figure 4.17 Arriflex 16SR3 camera with on-board battery. (Courtesy of ARRI Inc.)

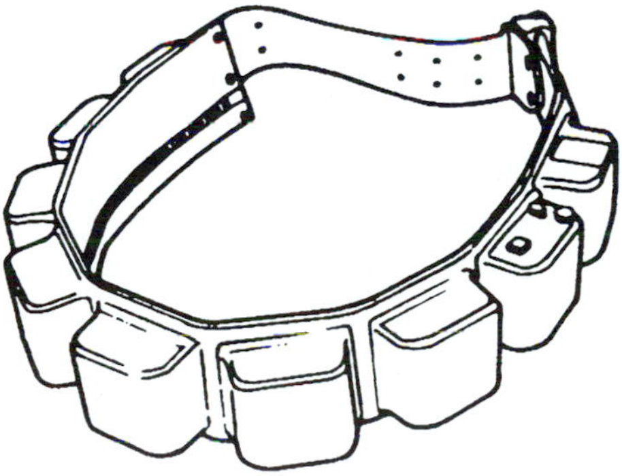

Figure 4.18
Belt battery. (Reprinted from *Motion Picture Camera and Lighting Equipment*, with permission of David Samuelson.)

light meter with you. You usually need only one 400′ roll of film for these tests, depending on how involved the tests are. If you don't have your own light meter, then borrow one from the D.P. Be sure to properly slate each shot of these tests will all information included on the slate. Keep a detailed camera report for the test as well. The slate and camera report should include the name of the test, lens focal length, focus distance, t-stop, filter name and strength, and any other pertinent information. This will be very helpful when viewing the test and better enable the D.P. to make final decisions about the equipment.

A. Film registration test
  - Check that the registration of the camera is accurate by filming a registration test chart (Figure 4.19).
  - I recommend shooting the registration test first on the roll. This test requires that you shoot a double exposure, which means that you shoot one exposure, rewind the film, and shoot another exposure. It is much easier to do at the beginning of the roll than somewhere in the middle.
  - Thread film in camera and mark the exact frame where you start, using a permanent felt tip marker (Figure 4.20).

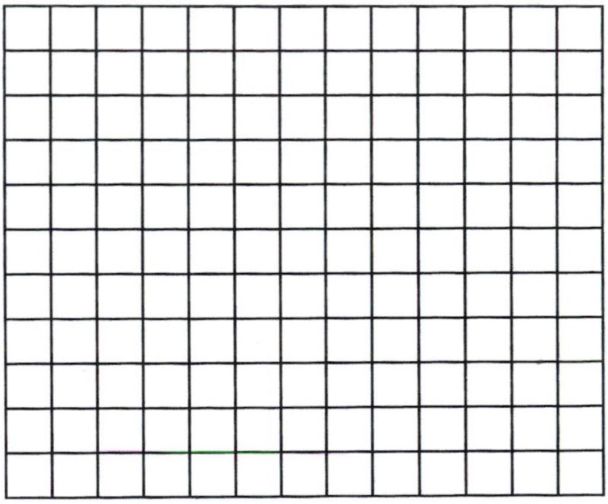

Figure 4.19
Registration test chart.

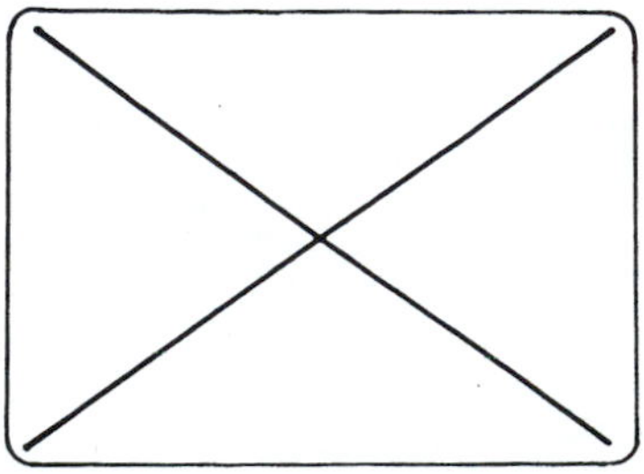

Figure 4.20
Mark the starting frame for the registration test.

- Line up the registration test chart through the eyepiece so that the crosshairs of the ground glass are centered on the lines of the chart (Figure 4.21).

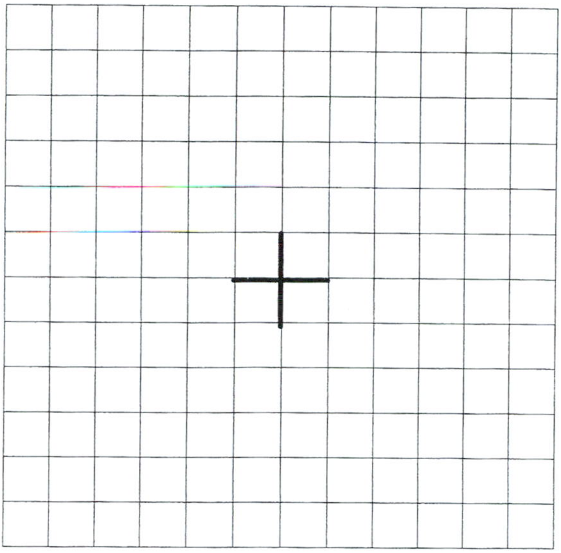

Figure 4.21 Positioning of crosshair on registration chart for shooting the first exposure.

- Lock the pan and tilt on the head.
- Shoot approximately 30 feet of the chart at one stop underexposed.
- Carefully remove the magazine, do not break the film, and go into the darkroom or use a changing bag or changing tent.
- Wind the film back to the starting frame that you marked. You may have to wind the film back to the very beginning of the roll to find the start frame. (As stated earlier, I recommend shooting the registration test first on the roll, because it is easier to wind the film back to the beginning of a roll than to a place in the middle.)
- Place the magazine back on the camera, and thread the film so that the original mark is again lined up in the gate. Release the pan and tilt of the head, and reposition the camera to line up the registration chart through the eyepiece so that the crosshairs of the ground glass are centered within one of the boxes of the chart (Figure 4.22).

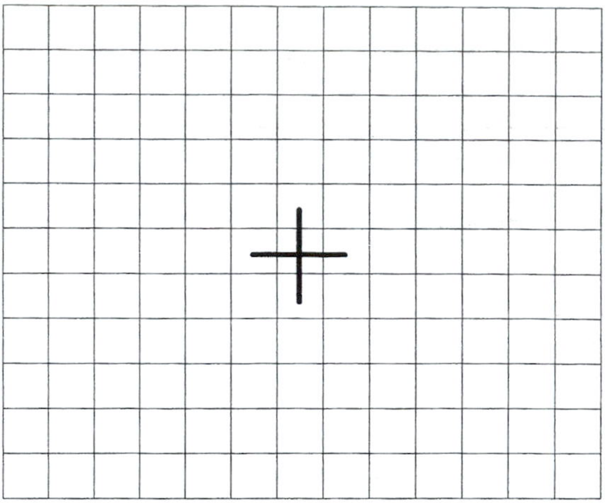

Figure 4.22 Positioning of crosshair on registration chart for shooting the second exposure.

- Lock the pan and tilt on the head.
- Shoot approximately 50 feet of the chart again at one stop underexposed.
- When the film is projected, there will be two sets of chart lines on the screen. If the registration of the camera is correct, there should be no movement of the lines.

Some important things to remember when shooting the registration test. You should never rewind the film in the camera. Some cameras have the ability to run in reverse, and you may be tempted to use this feature to quickly rewind your film back to the beginning for the second exposure. It is recommended to remove the magazine from the camera and, in a darkroom or changing bag or tent, rewind the film by hand back to the beginning of the roll. Some laboratories have told me that by rewinding the film in the camera, you are putting too much stress on the film and the perforations, possibly even stretching the film. This will have an effect on how the registration test looks and could give you false results. Although it takes a bit longer, it is better in the long run to always rewind the film by hand when doing the registration test.

B. Lens focus calibration test
   - Place each lens on the camera and frame the focus chart so that the entire chart is framed by the lens.
   - Photograph the focus test chart at various distances to be sure that the lens maintains sharp focus.

- Make sure the image is sharp in the center, as well as on the left and right sides of the frame and the top and bottom of the frame.
- Shoot the focus test with the lens open to its widest aperture whenever possible.

C. Lens color balance test

- Place each lens on the camera and photograph a color chart to check that there is consistent color balance between lenses.
- Check to see that each lens reproduces all colors the same way.
- If you do not have a color chart, cut a variety of color photographs out of magazines and paste them on a sheet of poster board and shoot this for the color balance test.

D. Filter test

- Place various filters on the camera and photograph a live subject to see the effect of each filter.

______ 31. Pack and label all equipment

- Label each case on top and sides with camera tape (just a brief description of what is in each case so that you can find things quickly: CAMERA, 1000-foot MAGS, FILTERS, PRIMES, ZOOM, HEAD, AKS, etc.).
- If you will be using more than one camera on the production, label each camera case and its corresponding accessories with the same color tape. (For example, all "A" camera and accessory cases would be labeled in red tape and all "B" camera and accessory cases would be labeled in blue tape.)
- If you will be working out of a camera truck, label the shelves for each piece of equipment the same as the cases (Figure 4.23).
- For a definition of each item on the camera prep check list, see the glossary.

Keep in mind that each prep you do will be a bit different. The rental house you are dealing with, the type of production, what equipment you are checking, along with many other factors will affect your prep. The preceding checklist is a basic guide for you to use; it is by no means a complete list. It would be impractical to try to list every possible piece of equipment you may have on your production. I have only listed the basic items that you will encounter on most camera preps that you do. It is not possible to prepare one single prep checklist that deals with every possible scenario.

When doing the camera prep, be as thorough as possible, and check every little item in each equipment case. This is important not

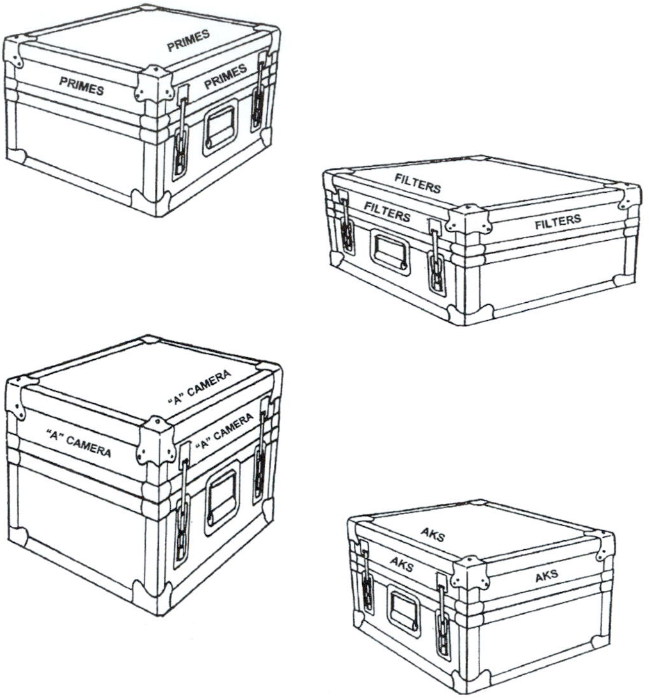

Figure 4.23 Proper labeling of equipment cases.

only for when you are shooting but also when you do the camera wrap at the end of shooting. If you have checked everything completely and it is listed on the original order, there should be no questions when the equipment is returned to the rental house.

The camera prep is not always a guarantee that nothing will go wrong with the equipment. An experience I had during one of my preps illustrates this. I was hired to work on a commercial that was to shoot for two days around Los Angeles. The camera prep took about half a day the day before we were scheduled to start shooting. The next day's call time was 5:00 AM, and the location was about a one-hour drive away. When I arrived at the location, I proceeded to set up the camera. I connected the battery and turned on the camera. Nothing happened. The camera would not run. After checking all of the batteries and power cables, I telephoned the rental house at their 24-hour number. When I explained to the camera technician what was happening, he instructed me to change one of the internal fuses in the camera. After changing the fuse, the camera still would not run, so it was decided that the production company would return to L.A., get another camera, and shoot the scenes in the studio that were scheduled for the next day. After exchanging the camera, everything went smoothly. I later found out that there was an additional fuse in the camera that could only be accessed and changed by a camera technician, and it was this fuse that had blown out, causing the camera not to run. This is an excellent example of why you should do a camera prep. It also shows that a camera prep is not always a guarantee that something won't go wrong. Without doing the camera prep, I would have had no way of knowing if the camera had been in working order when it was picked up. At least I knew the camera had been working and the problem was no fault of mine.

PRODUCTION

The prep is done, film and expendables have been ordered, the camera truck is loaded and set up for production, and it's now time for filming to start. As stated in Chapter 3, "Second Camera Assistant," the production phase of shooting is a complex operation that requires a great deal of dedication, hard work, and attention to detail on the part of all involved. This is especially important to the 1st A.C. The proper performance of the duties and responsibilities of the 1st A.C. is vital to the smooth operation of the production. You set up the camera each day, keep it clean, change lenses and filters, load film into the camera, and probably most important, keep the shot in focus during filming. You must pay close attention to detail and be ready to make quick decisions. You are one of the key people that the D.P. relies on during filming. If you let the D.P. down, you let down the entire crew.

Start of the Day Procedures

The first thing you should do each day is set up the camera. Place the camera on the head, which is either mounted to the tripod or the dolly. If the camera and head are being placed on a tripod, many assistants often use a piece of carpet in place of the spreader under the tripod. The points on the tripod legs dig into the carpet, creating a firm support for the tripod and camera. This also sometimes makes it easier when moving or repositioning the camera. This piece of carpet usually measures 3 feet × 3 feet or 4 feet × 4 feet.

If necessary, oil the camera movement and clean the gate and aperture plate to remove any dirt, dust, or emulsion buildup. Check to be sure that the interior of the camera is clean and free from any film chips or dust. Set up the camera with all the basic components except for a magazine and a lens. Attach the various accessories to it, including the follow focus, matte box, eyebrow, eyepiece leveler, lens light, and so on. While the 1st A.C. sets up the camera, the 2nd A.C. is often nearby, handing pieces of equipment to him or her. Once you have the basic camera built, it is common to warm it up. Many times the camera has been sitting in the loading room or on a camera truck all night and it may be a bit cold. A general rule to follow is to run the camera for approximately the length of the first roll of film that you will be placing on the camera. For example, if the first roll being placed on the camera is 400 feet, reset the footage counter to zero and then warm up the camera until the footage counter shows "400." After the camera has warmed up, you can then place the magazine and lens on it. You should never place a lens on the camera or remove a lens from the camera while it is running. The shutter turns while the camera is running during the warm-up, and it may hit the back of the lens if the lens is not placed on the camera properly.

If you are not sure about the proper warm-up procedure to follow with the camera you are using, check with the rental house during the camera prep. With some cameras you may cause more damage by running them without film. Certain types of cameras contain heaters that must be connected to a battery in order for the camera to warm up. This warm-up usually only takes a few minutes and the camera can then be used safely without fear of damaging the movement or any of the camera components.

Unless the D.P. requests a specific lens, place a wide or normal focal length lens on the camera. This is to allow the D.P. or Camera Operator to see as much of the scene as possible when he or she first looks through the camera. It's a good idea to establish a procedure at the beginning of the production regarding what lens to place on the camera at the beginning of each day. The D.P. may request a specific lens such as the 25-250 zoom or request the widest prime lens you have, or he or she may even tell you not to place a lens on the camera until the first shot has been decided upon. Open up the aperture to its widest opening and set the focus to the approximate distance so that the scene can be viewed clearly. Once the camera is warmed up, place the first magazine on it and finish making it ready for the first shot. Be sure to let the D.P. and Camera Operator know as soon as the camera is ready for use. This set-up procedure should take approximately 15 to 20 minutes from start to finish. It is important to get the camera set up as quickly as possible at the start of each day, but never trade safety for speed. In other words, set it up quickly but don't go so quickly that you could make mistakes.

Check that the viewfinder is clean and set to the proper position for the operator or D.P. to look through it. Nothing is more annoying to an Operator or D.P. than looking through the viewfinder that is not set for his or her eye and looking at an out of focus or soft image.

Once the camera is set up and the first camera position and angle are established, you should ensure that all needed camera equipment is nearby. The second assistant may have already done this while you were preparing the camera, but it doesn't hurt to double check. Keep any camera equipment that will be needed throughout the shooting day as close to the camera as possible, without being in the way of other people or equipment. Camera equipment includes lenses, filters, magazines, and accessories. As part of their kit, many assistants have some type of handcart or dolly to keep camera equipment cases on. These carts enable the assistant to keep all of the cases neat and organized, yet quickly movable when there is a new camera setup. The two most common types of carts or dollies used for moving camera equipment cases are the Magliner Gemini Jr. and Gemini Sr. They both collapse for shipping and storage, and can be set up quickly when needed. Many camera assistants also use a cart made by Rubbermaid. The Magliner carts can be very expensive depending on the options you choose, but you will soon discover that they are worth the price. With all of the cases on set, you will discover very quickly how time saving it is to wheel the equipment from one setup to the next rather than carry each case individually (Figures 4.24 through 4.26).

Most assistants also keep their tools and accessories near the camera during shooting. The camera assistant's ditty bag, containing basic tools and accessories, should also be kept on the cart during filming. It is also common to keep the D.P.'s meter case on one of the camera equipment carts.

Many assistants organize and set up the carts so that things on set run as efficiently as possible. It is common to have one cart designated as the lens cart, with all lens cases, lens accessory cases, and filter cases kept on this cart. Another cart would be set up with magazines, extra camera batteries, other accessories such as high hat and matte box, and anything else that may be needed. The assistant's set bag and D.P.'s meter case would usually be placed on the second cart. In addition if you are using more than one camera, it is advantageous to have a separate cart designated for each camera's accessories. Many assistants also set up their carts with drawers that can be used to store some of the most commonly used expendables such as AA, AAA, and 9-volt batteries, along with markers, pens, Velcro, lens tissue and fluid, and more. It is not uncommon to have two, three, or even more camera equipment carts on a large-scale production.

When bringing equipment to the set, keep in mind that you may not need everything from the camera truck. Bring only what will be needed for the basic shots. Use your best judgment based on the previous day's needs along with the location and types of scenes that will be shot. For example, if you will be shooting mostly interiors in a very

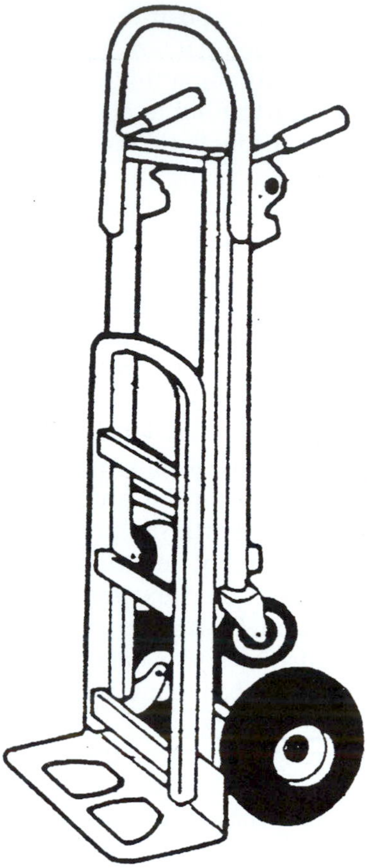

Figure 4.24
Magliner cart folded for storage and transporting.

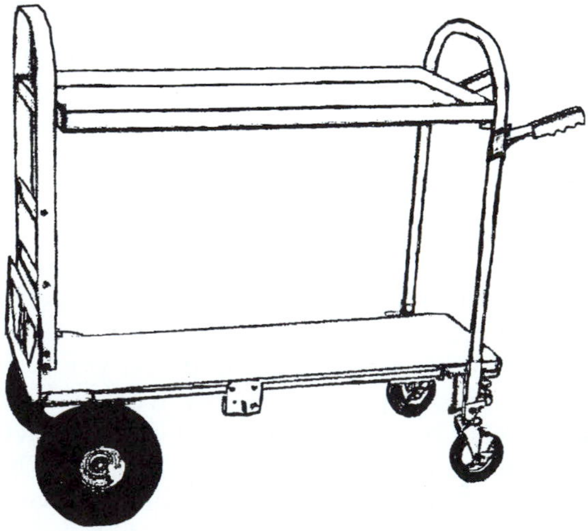

Figure 4.25
Magliner cart with top and bottom shelves, set up for use.

Figure 4.26 Rubbermaid cart.

small room, you probably won't need the 150-600 zoom lens, or if shooting night exteriors, you probably won't need the set of 85 or neutral density filters. Use your best judgment as to what equipment should be on set at any given time, but if you are unsure, bring it all so that if you do need something, the production is not held up while you or the second assistant goes to the camera truck to retrieve the item.

Another important thing to keep in mind when bringing equipment to the set is where you will put it. When filming on practical locations such as private homes or businesses, you may want to scout the location upon arrival to find a room or area close to the shooting area where you can set up a home base for the camera department. This is important so that you have everything needed in close proximity to the camera and so that you don't have to continually run back and forth to the camera truck or to another area of the location to get a piece of equipment. Find a room or area of the location that will not be used for shooting and use that area to stage your equipment. Keep in mind that the grip and electric department will also be looking for an area to stage their equipment and you all must work together. Don't block their equipment with camera carts and cases, and hope they will be equally courteous when staging their equipment.

Loading and Unloading Film in the Camera

Whenever a new magazine is placed on the camera, notify the D.P. and Camera Operator so that they know that the camera will not be available to them while you complete the reload. Reloading the camera with film should take only a minute or two depending on the camera and your level of experience. Before a new magazine is placed on the camera, clean the interior of the camera body with compressed air. Check and clean the gate and aperture plate to remove any emulsion buildup. If possible, remove the gate and aperture plate for cleaning. When cleaning the gate, never use any type of sharp tool that could scratch it and cause scratches on the film emulsion. To clean emulsion buildup use an orangewood stick, which should have been ordered with the expendables. Clean the gate and aperture plate with compressed air.

When the new magazine is placed on the camera, reset the footage counter to zero so that the dial readings and footage amounts on the camera report will be accurate. Remember to write the roll number on the identification label of the magazine if this has not already been done by the 2nd A.C. If the magazine contains a short end, place the small identification label next to the footage counter as a reminder that the magazine does not contain a full roll of film. In addition, when placing a magazine on the camera, the size and weight of the roll could affect the balance of the camera. Check and rebalance the camera if necessary so that the Camera Operator will not have difficulty in operating the shot because of an unbalanced camera. Also, when using a camera with displacement magazines, as the film travels through the camera it is displaced from the front of the camera to the back. This will also cause the camera to become unbalanced, sometimes after every shot, so you should periodically check the balance during shooting and adjust it as required. If necessary, place a barney on the magazine after it has been placed on the camera. Once you have completed loading the magazine and film on the camera, notify the 1st A.D., D.P., and Camera Operator that the camera is now ready for use.

If you will be removing a partially shot magazine and plan to finish shooting it later in the day, always mark an "X" on the frame of film in the gate. This allows you to line up the film properly when you place the magazine back on the camera later in the day. I know of a situation in which a D.P. had a magazine removed from the camera and the assistant neglected to mark the frame of film. The magazine was later placed back on the camera and they finished shooting with that roll. The D.P. took the developed film to a transfer house to have it transferred to video. During the transfer process when it came to the point in the film where the magazine had been removed, the shots were off by two perforations. The color timer had to rethread the film to continue the transfer. I had never heard of this happening before, but based on this D.P.'s description, I will now always mark the film when removing a partially shot magazine. It's a small thing but can save some confusion and headaches later on.

Keeping the Camera Clean

One of the most important things to remember during filming is to keep the camera clean. Dirt and dust on the camera not only look unprofessional, but they also can cause big problems if they get into the camera body, the magazines, on lenses or filters, in the gate, or on the shutter mirror. The smallest speck of dirt can cause emulsion scratches on the film and ruin a whole day's shooting.

Clean the camera each day when it is set up. Clean the inside with compressed air. Keep the outside of the camera body clean by using an inexpensive 2-inch-wide brush to remove the dust and dirt. If the exterior of the camera body becomes exceptionally dirty, wipe it off with a damp cloth. Never use the damp cloth to clean lenses or filters. As stated earlier, clean the gate using an orangewood stick and compressed air. When oiling the camera movement, remove any excess oil by using a cotton swab or foam-tip swab.

Each time a new lens or filter is placed on the camera, check it for dirt, dust, or smudges. If the lens or filter needs to be cleaned, don't make everybody wait while you clean it. First place it on the camera so that the D.P. can look at the shot and determine if it is the correct lens or filter. Once it has been approved for the shot, you should then have enough time to remove it and clean it before shooting. There will usually be a lighting change of some type that gives you enough time to do the cleaning. If not, you must inform the D.P or Camera Operator that the lens or filter must be cleaned before anything can be shot with it. The proper way to clean lenses and filters will be explained further in the "Lenses" section.

Oiling and Lubricating the Camera

The movement in many motion picture cameras must be oiled at regular intervals. If you are not sure whether you should oil the movement or how often to oil the camera movement, always check with the rental house when you do the camera prep. The rental house also should give you a small container of oil.

In addition to oiling the movement, it is sometimes necessary to lubricate the pull-down pins with a small drop of silicone liquid to prevent squeaking. Panavision cameras especially require a drop of the supplied silicone liquid on the felt pads at the base of the aperture plate. As the pull down claws finish their downward movement, they rub across these pads picking up just enough silicone to prevent any squeaking as they enter the film perforations at the top of their movement.

Some cameras need to be oiled every day; others only require oiling on a weekly or monthly basis. Check with the rental house, because you can do just as much damage by oiling too much as by not oiling enough. Panavision says that, as a general rule, their cameras should be oiled on a daily basis depending on how much film is being shot each day. The exception to this rule is when using the new Panavision Panaflex Millennium camera. According to the operations manual for the Millennium, the movement should be lubricated every 2 weeks or after 100,000 feet of film has run through the camera. Panavision high-speed cameras must be oiled after every 1000 feet of film has been shot, whenever you are filming at speeds greater than 60 f.p.s. Panavision cameras have anywhere from 7 to 13 oiling points in the movement, depending on which model you are using. They usually have an oiling diagram on the inside of the door to the camera body, and a small container of Panavision oil is included in the camera accessory case. Arriflex cameras use a different type of movement and do not need to be oiled nearly as often. Some Arriflex cameras require oiling only every few months or after a specified amount of film has been run through them. The oiling of Arriflex cameras is most often handled by the rental house technicians and rarely by the camera assistant in the field.

When you do oil the movement, it is necessary to place only one drop of oil on each oiling point. Be very careful not to get any oil in the gate or on the mirror. If the oil does get onto the film, it will show up as spots on the exposed negative. If you should get any excess oil in the movement, remove it by using a cotton swab or foam-tip swab from the expendables. Be very careful when using the cotton swabs so that you do not leave any of the lint from the cotton tip in the movement. If lint gets into the gate, it can cause hairs on the emulsion. If you do find it necessary to place a drop of silicone liquid on the pull down claw, or sometimes on the aperture plate, be extra careful not to get any of the silicone in the movement because it could damage it.

Another thing to remember when oiling the camera is to only use the oil supplied by the rental house or recommended for that particular camera. Never use Panavision oil on Arriflex cameras or Arriflex oil on Panavision cameras. It is a good idea to have a supply of the different oils in your kit with your tools and accessories. This way, if you do not get any oil from the rental house, you will be prepared and be able to oil the camera movement when necessary. Figures 4.27 through 4.34 show the oiling points for some of the cameras that require oiling most often.

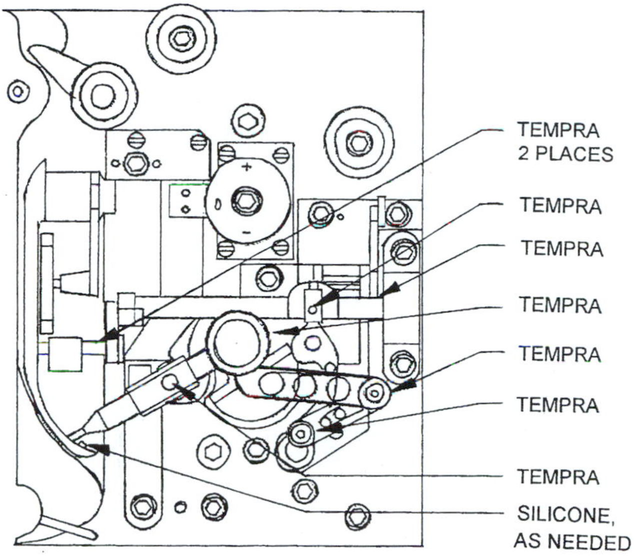

Figure 4.27 Leonetti Ultracam oiling points. (Courtesy of the Leonetti Company.)

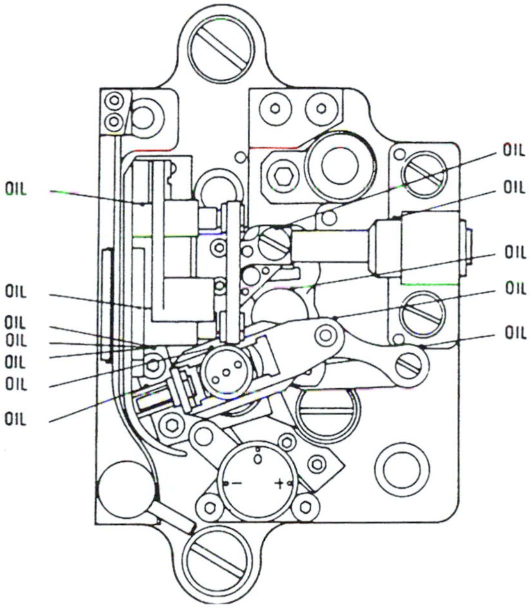

Figure 4.28
Panavision Panaflex 16 oiling points. (Reprinted from the *Hands-On Manual for Cinematographers,* with permission of David Samuelson.)

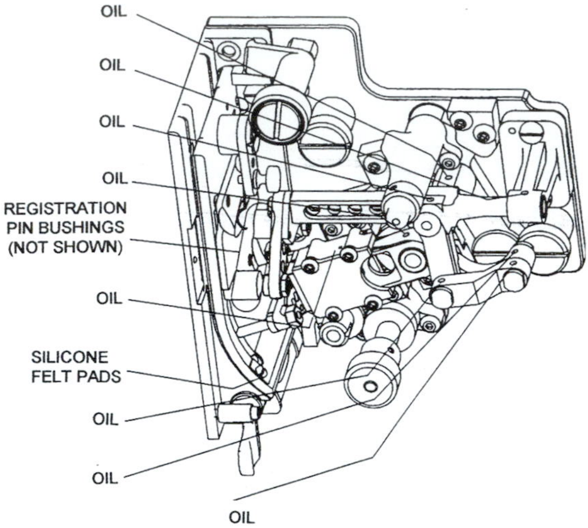

Figure 4.29
Panavision Millennium oiling points, side view. (Courtesy of Panavision, Inc.)

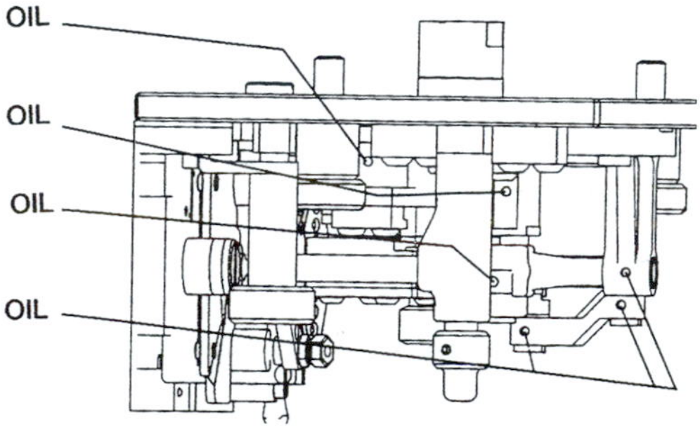

Figure 4.30
Panavision Millennium oiling points—top view. (Courtesy of Panavision, Inc.)

Remember: Never over oil the camera movement. Use only the supplied or recommended oil for a particular camera. When in doubt, check with the rental house.

Setting the Viewfinder Eyepiece

The viewfinder eyepiece must be set for each key person who looks through the camera. On most productions the key people are the Director, D.P., Producer, Camera Operator, and 1st A.C. On commercials it may also be set for the client or agency people. Because each person's vision is different, you will need different settings on the eyepiece so that the image will appear sharp and in focus to each person looking through it.

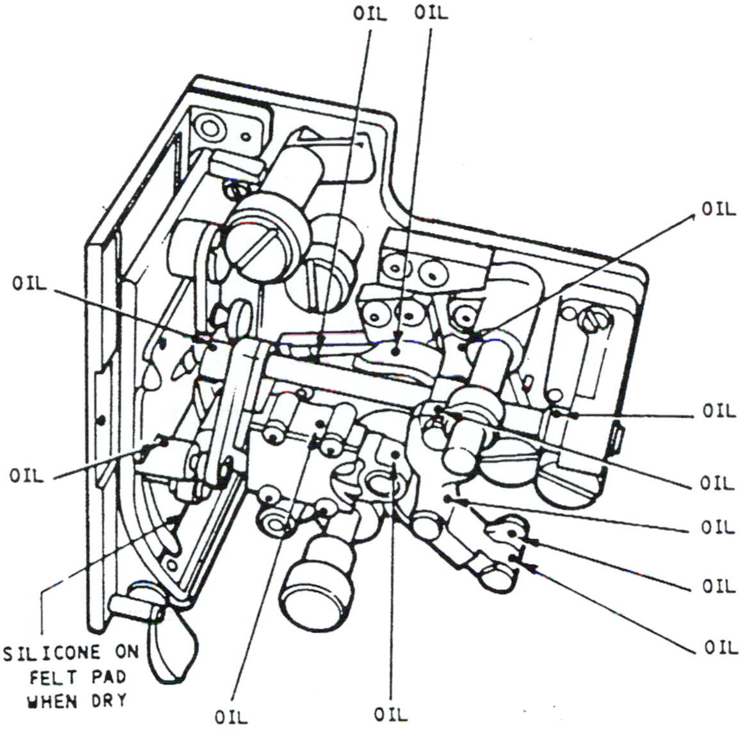

Figure 4.31 Panavision Panaflex 35 oiling points. (Reprinted from the *Hands-On Manual for Cinematographers*, with permission of David Samuelson.)

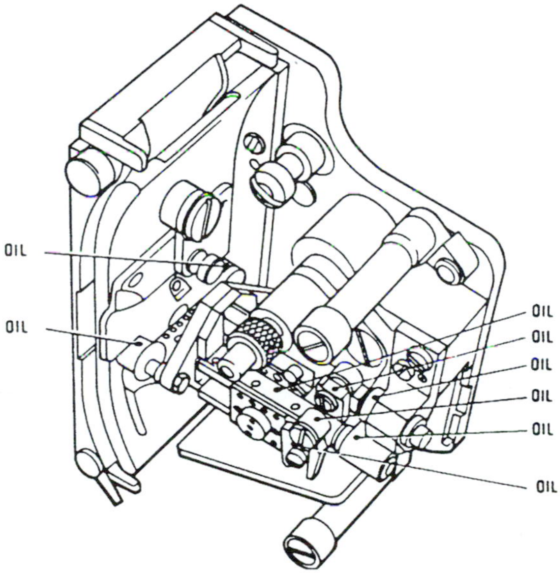

Figure 4.32 Panavision Panastar oiling points. (Reprinted from the *Hands-On Manual for Cinematographers*, with permission of David Samuelson.)

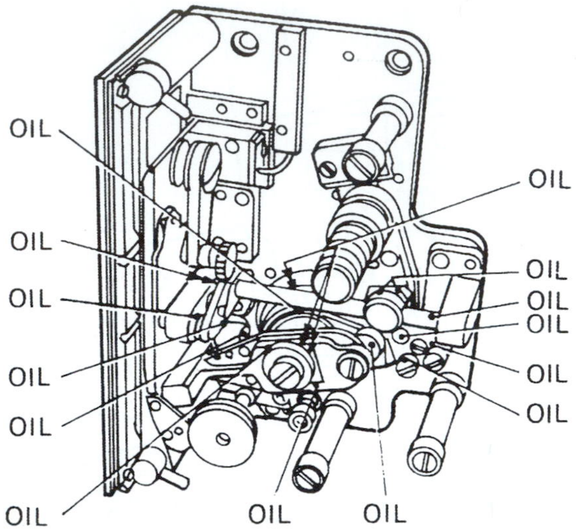

Figure 4.33 Panavision Super PSR oiling points. (Reprinted from the *Hands-On Manual for Cinematographers*, with permission of David Samuelson)

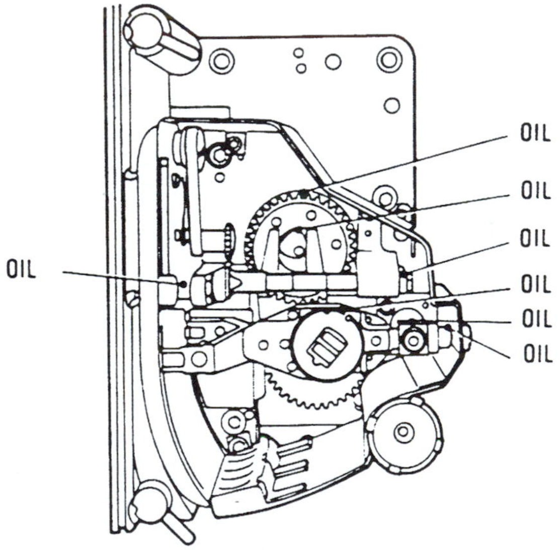

Figure 4.34 Panavision 65 mm camera oiling points. (Reprinted from the *Hands-On Manual for Cinematographers*, with permission of David Samuelson.)

To focus the eyepiece, it is best to first remove the lens. Aim the camera at a bright light source or white surface. While looking through the eyepiece, turn the diopter adjustment ring on the eyepiece until the crosshairs or the grains of the ground glass appear sharp and in focus. Figure 4.35 shows the frame lines and crosshair that is seen when looking through the viewfinder. Figures 4.36 through 4.38 show the many different ground glass configurations available for Arriflex and Panavision cameras.

Unless there is a way to mark the eyepiece, I recommend that you wrap a thin piece of white paper tape or artist's chart tape around the diopter ring so that it can be marked for each person's setting. Have the Camera Operator, D.P., and the Director set the eyepiece for their vision and mark the tape accordingly. You should also set the viewfinder for your vision. Then whenever one of these key people looks through the camera, you can set the eyepiece to their setting. Figure 4.39 shows the viewfinder marked for the key people who may look through the camera.

Note: Always remember to set the viewfinder back to the Camera Operator's mark before shooting.

To focus the eyepiece while the lens is still on the camera, first be sure that the aperture is set to its widest opening. Look through the lens and adjust the focus until everything is out of focus. If using a zoom lens, zoom in to its most telephoto focal length. Aim the camera at a bright light source or white surface. Turn the diopter adjustment ring on the eyepiece until the crosshairs or grains of the ground glass appear sharp and in focus. If you wear eyeglasses, it is recommended to remove your glasses before setting the viewfinder eyepiece for your vision.

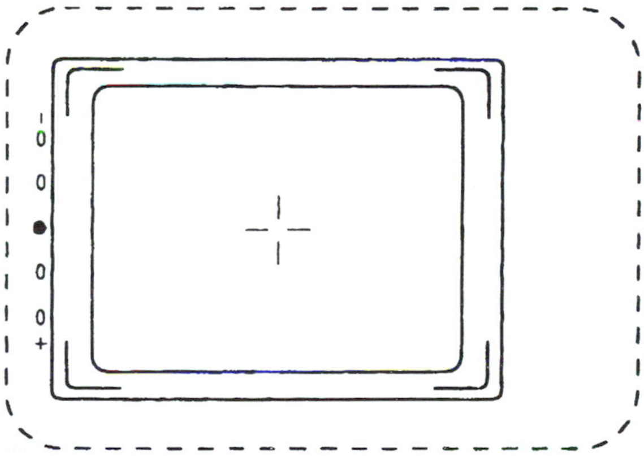

Figure 4.35 Frame lines and crosshair on the ground glass as seen through the viewfinder. (Reprinted from the *Arriflex 16SR3 Instruction Manual*, with permission of ARRI Inc.)

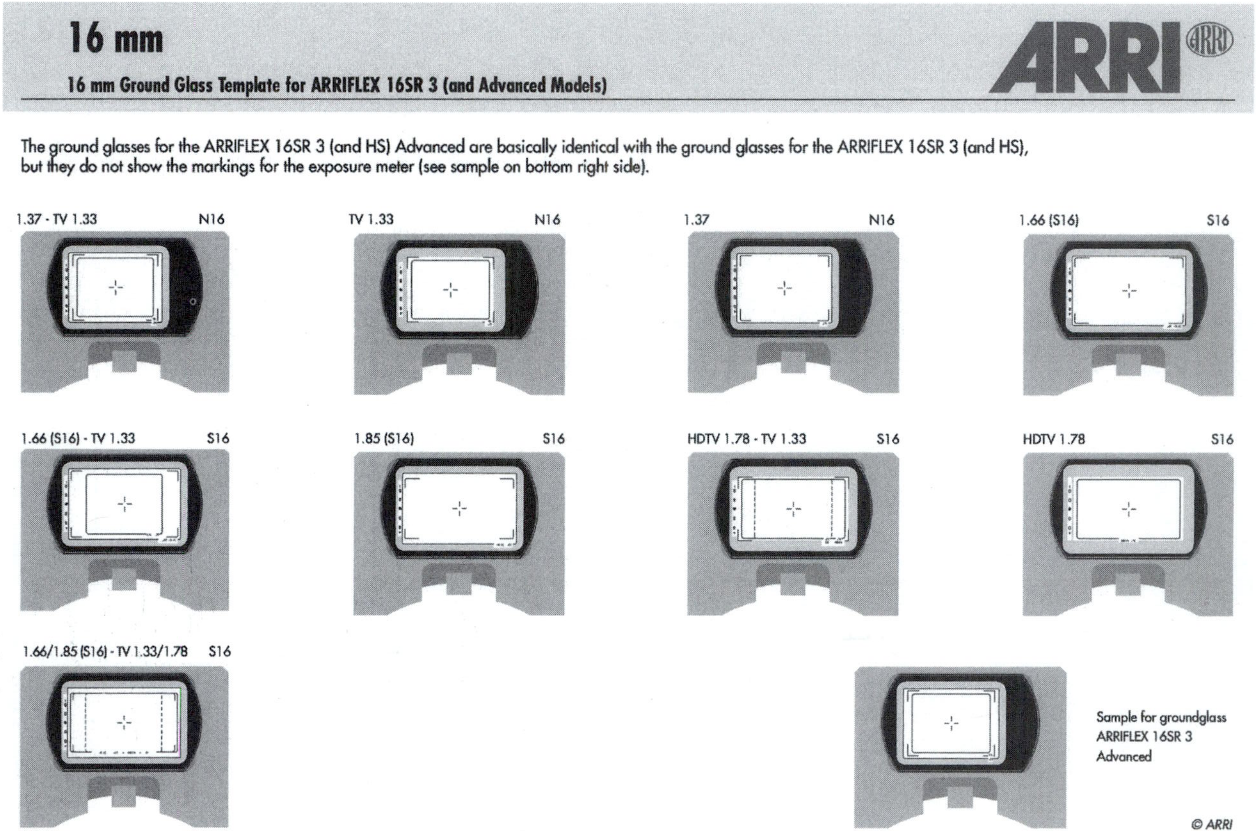

Figure 4.36 16 mm ground glass formats available for Arriflex 16SR3 cameras. (Courtesy of ARRI Inc.)

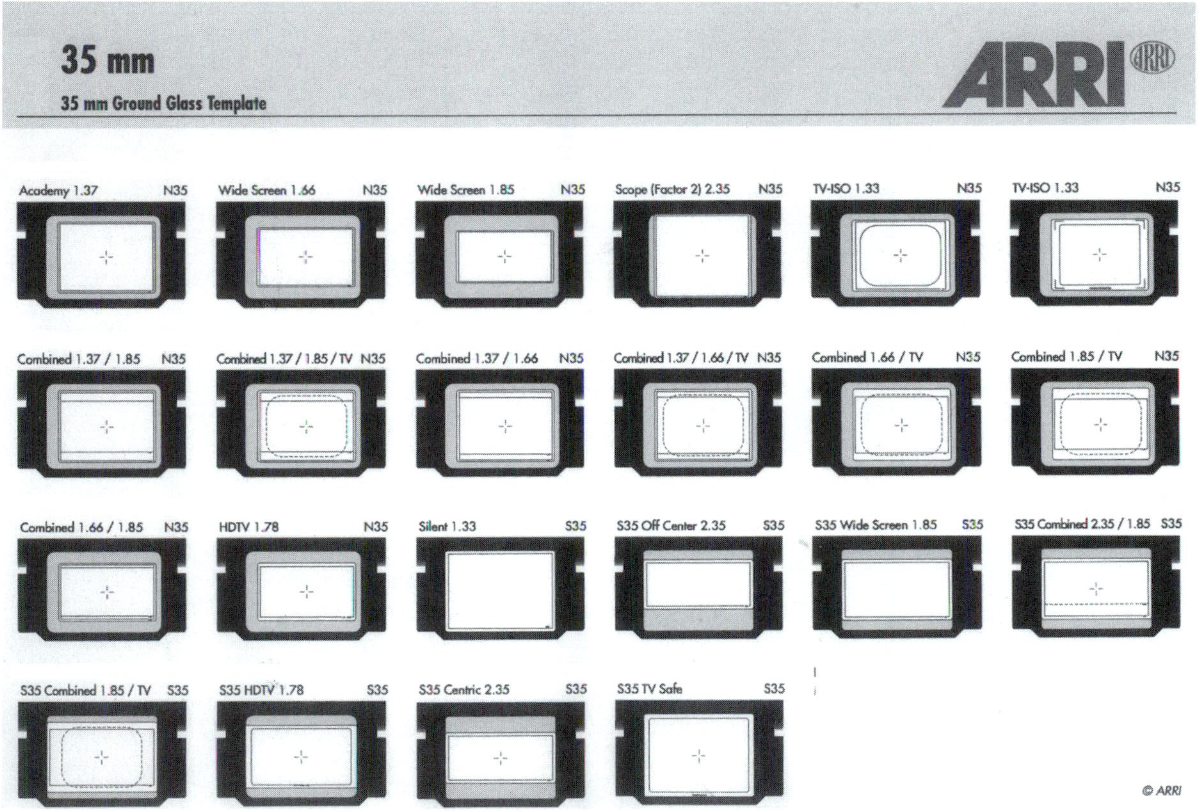

Figure 4.37 35 mm ground glass formats available for Arriflex Arricam, 435, and 535 cameras. (Courtesy of ARRI Inc.)

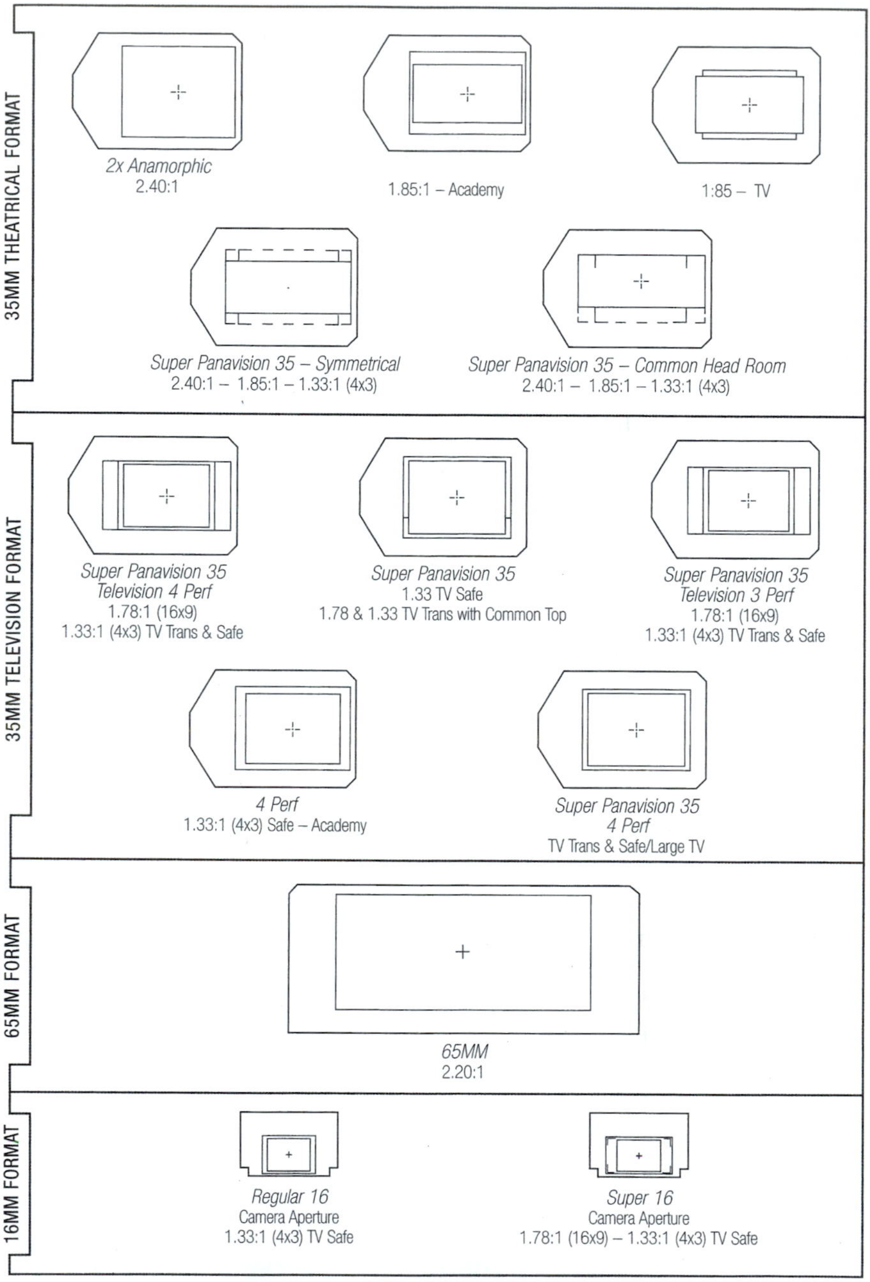

Figure 4.38 Ground glass formats available for Panavision cameras. (Courtesy of Panavision, Inc.)

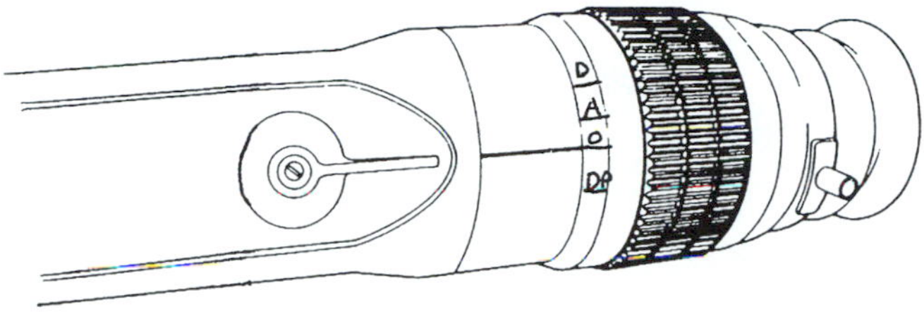

Figure 4.39 Eyepiece showing marks for each person's setting: D = Director, A = 1st A.C., O = Camera Operator, D.P. = Director of Photography.

Checking for Lens Flares

Each time the camera or lights are moved to a new position, you should check that no lights are kicking or shining directly into the lens, which will cause a flare in the photographic image. A flare causes an overall washing out of the image, so objects in the scene don't have sharp detail. If you have a French flag or eyebrow on the camera, you may be able to adjust it to eliminate the flare. The eyebrow may also be called a sunshade (Figures 4.40 and 4.41).

You also may be able to eliminate the flare by placing a hard matte on the matte box. A hard matte is snapped in place onto the front of the matte box, and it contains a cutout based on the focal length of the lens being used. This hard matte allows light to enter only the small cutout in the matte, while the rest of the matte blocks the light thus preventing a flare in the image. See Figure 4.42 for an illustration of a matte box with a hard matte in place. If the flare cannot be removed at the camera, request that a flag be set by one of the grips to keep the light from kicking into the lens.

There are a few different ways to check for lens flares. One is to place your face directly next to the lens, looking in the direction that the lens is pointed. Look around the set to see if any lights are shining directly at you, which means they are shining directly into the lens. Another way to check for flares is to stand in front of the camera, face the lens, and move your hand around the lens or matte box. If you see a shadow from your hand falling across the lens, there is probably a light flaring the lens from the angle of the shadow. A third way to check for flares is to place a convex mirror directly in front of the lens, with the mirror side facing the set. Any lights that may be causing a flare can be seen in the mirror. If you find a flare, it must be removed from the front element of the lens by either the hard matte, French flag, eyebrow, or grip flag.

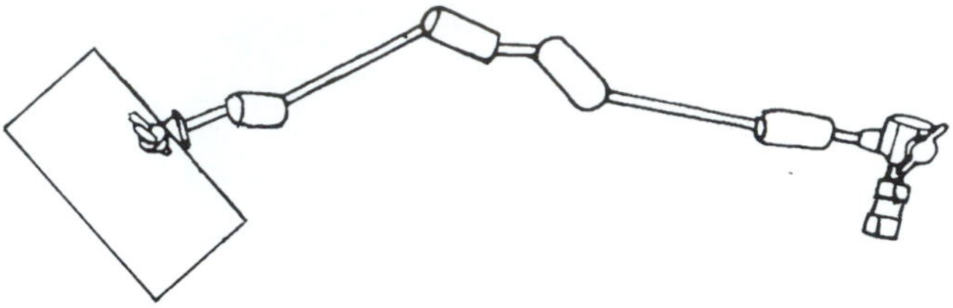

Figure 4.40 French flag attached to articulating arm.

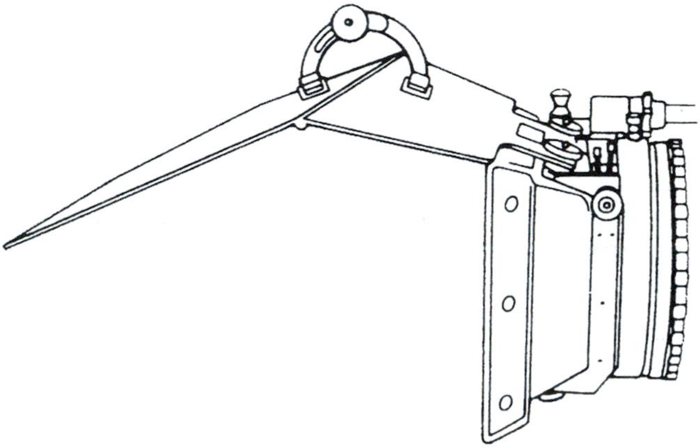

Figure 4.41 Eyebrow (sunshade) in place on matte box to eliminate lens flare. (Reprinted from the *Panaflex Users Manual,* with permission of David Samuelson and Panavision, Inc.)

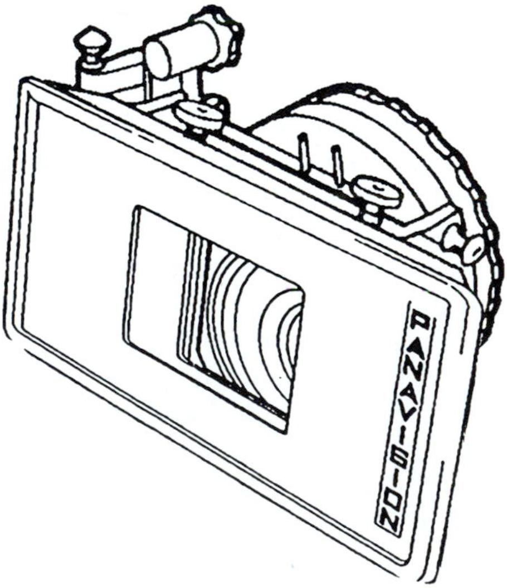

Figure 4.42
Hard matte in place on matte box. (Reprinted from the *Panaflex Users Manual,* with permission of David Samuelson and Panavision, Inc.)

Remove lens flares from the matte box and filter as well as the lens. Any light striking the matte box or filter can still reflect into the lens causing a flare in the image. Checking the lens for flares takes a certain amount of experience and cannot be fully explained or understood unless you are in an actual shooting situation. Whenever you are not sure if there is a lens flare, ask one of the grips to double-check for you.

Lenses

The basic definition of a lens is that it is an instrument that bends light waves in such a way to reproduce an image of the object from which the light was reflected. The lens directs the reflected light from an object onto the film emulsion, producing a photographic image of the object. When referring to a lens, the D.P. will call for it by its focal length. Focal length is defined as the distance from the optical center of the lens to the film plane when the lens is focused to infinity. The focal length of the lens is an indication of how much of the scene the lens will see. Focal length is always expressed in millimeters (mm). A lens with a short focal length, such as 12 mm, 18 mm, 24 mm, etc., will see a bigger area of the scene than a lens with a long focal length, such as 85 mm, 100 mm, 150 mm, etc.

Some D.P.s use a different terminology when referring to specific lenses. This terminology is not used frequently, but it is worth mentioning in case you work with someone who does refer to a lens in this manner. A 25 mm lens may be referred to as a 1-inch lens, 50 mm as 2-inch, 75 mm as 3-inch, and 100 mm as 4-inch. This is based on the fact that 25 mm is approximately equal to 1 inch.

Keep in mind that it is practically impossible to manufacture a perfect lens. All lenses will have some type of imperfection. Some anamorphic lenses give better results when filming a curved surface than when filming a flat surface. On some lenses the focus may shift when opened to their widest aperture. See the information in the section, Focusing Tips, about the yellow and blue witness marks on some Panavision lenses that discusses this further. Many zoom lenses give the appearance of zooming when shifting focus. This phenomenon is called breathing. Some zoom lenses do not track accurately throughout the range of the zoom, which often requires a slight movement (panning or tilting) of the camera to maintain proper composition. Lenses have what is often referred to as critical aperture; that is, the lens will give the best results and sharpest image when the aperture is closed down two or three stops from its widest aperture setting.

Prime Lenses and Zoom Lenses

The two main types of lenses are prime and zoom. Prime lenses have a single fixed focal length, such as 25 mm, 35 mm, 50 mm, 65 mm, and so on. Zoom lenses have variable focal lengths, which means that you can change the focal length by turning the barrel of the lens. Zoom lenses are available in many different ranges including 10–100, 20–100, 12–120, 25–250, 150–600, and so on. The 10–100, 25–250, and 12–120 ranges may be referred to as ten-to-one (10–1) zooms. The 20–100 range is called a five-to-one (5–1) zoom, and the 150–600 is called a four-to-one (4–1) zoom, and so on. These abbreviated names for the lenses are equal to the ratio of the tightest focal length of the lens to its widest focal length. The zoom lens sizes mentioned are only a small sampling of the different zoom lenses available today. Check with the rental house to see what size zooms they have. The Camera Equipment Checklist in Appendix C contains a more extensive listing of the prime and zoom lenses currently available. While prime and zoom may be specific types, the general categories of lenses may be classified as wide-angle, normal, or telephoto. This is in reference to the area of the scene that they see. A wide-angle lens sees more of the scene than a telephoto lens. A normal lens is called that because it approximates the angle of view as seen through the human eye when standing at the same position as that of the camera. Telephoto lenses are lenses that have a very large focal length such as 200 mm, 300 mm, 400 mm, 600 mm, and even 1000 mm. They allow you to photograph a close-up of an object or a subject from a great distance.

When working with lenses you should be familiar with some of the terminology used. One term, *lens perspective*, is an indication of the area that the lens sees. It may also be referred to as the lens field of view. It is an indication of how much of the scene will be visible when looking through the lens. Wide-angle lenses have a larger field of view than telephoto lenses.

Another commonly used term used regarding lenses is *lens speed*. The lens speed is an indication of the widest f-stop or t-stop setting of a particular lens. Fast lenses will have a smaller lens speed and are often used for nighttime photography. For example, a lens speed of 1.9 means that the widest aperture setting of the lens is a t 1.9.

You must be aware of the type of lens mount on the camera you will be using. Unfortunately (or fortunately) lenses are not interchangeable from one camera system to another. Currently the two most common lens mounts are the Panavision Mount, which is standard on all Panavision cameras, and the Arriflex PL Mount, which is standard on all newer Arriflex cameras. Some of the older Arriflex 16 mm cameras still use the Arriflex Standard Mount or Arriflex Bayonet Mount.

There are adapters available so that you may use these lenses on a camera with a PL Mount. The PL in the name means Positive Lock. Be sure that the lenses you are using have the same type of mount as that of the camera you will be using; if they do not, then you must have some type of adapter.

A situation that you may encounter with lenses is the possibility of using 35 mm lenses on a 16 mm camera. Although this rarely happens I still feel it is important enough to mention here briefly. There are a few things to keep in mind if you are using 35 mm lenses on a 16 mm camera. The effective focal length doubles so that it may be difficult to obtain a wide-angle shot because of the difference in the field of view. The field of view or angle of view will be the same as if you were shooting in 35 mm format. When checking your depth of field, be sure to use 35 mm tables and circles of confusion. Focus witness marks are the same but you should always check them just to be sure.

Most lenses you will be using are called spherical lenses. They are the standard types of lenses used for many filmed productions. When you are shooting for extreme wide-screen presentation you will often shoot using anamorphic lenses. An anamorphic lens is one that squeezes or compresses the image horizontally so that a wide-screen image can fit onto an almost square 35 mm film frame. During projection, the image is projected through a similar anamorphic lens creating a wide-screen image on the screen. As stated in Chapter 1, the aspect ratio for anamorphic is usually referred to as 2.40:1 but may also be called 2.35:1 or 2.36:1.

Whenever a lens is not being used it should be capped on both the front and rear elements and placed in a padded case. The padding will help to cushion the lens and protect it from shocks and vibration. The internal elements of the lens can become loosened very easily if the lens is not protected or handled properly. When you are filming in dusty conditions or any situation in which something may strike the front of the lens, it is a good idea to use an optical flat. An optical flat is simply a clear piece of optically correct glass placed in front of the lens as a means to protect it. Optical flats are available in the same standard sizes as filters. It is much less expensive to replace a filter that has become scratched than to replace the front element of the lens. This brings up a story that a D.P. colleague of mine once told me. He was shooting a scene of a plane taking off as the bad guys leapt into it. As the plane fired up, it spun around and a lot of sand and gravel was kicked up directly into the front element of the lens. The front element of the lens was severely scratched and the production company ended up paying for a new lens. If they had only placed an optical flat in front of the lens the production would have saved a great deal of money.

All professional lenses have a coating on the front element and should be cleaned only when absolutely necessary. Clean a lens first with compressed air or some type of blower bulb syringe. If there are no smudges or fingerprints, then there is nothing more that you need to do to clean the lens. If the lens has any fingerprints or smudges, clean it with lens cleaner and lens tissue. After the dirt and dust have been blown away, moisten a piece of lens tissue with lens cleaning fluid. Wipe the surface of the lens carefully, using a circular motion. While the lens is still damp from the lens solution, use another piece of tissue to remove the remaining lens cleaning fluid from the lens. I have also seen some assistants apply the lens cleaning fluid directly to the lens element. I don't recommend doing this, because of the curvature of the front element of the lens. The fluid can travel along the element of the lens, and sometimes gets between the lens housing and the glass element ending up behind the element. As a result, you have no way to remove the fluid from the back of the lens glass. The important thing to remember is that you should never use a dry piece of lens tissue on a dry lens surface. Small particles of dirt and dust may still be on the coating and will cause scratches. Also, never use any type of silicone-coated lens tissue or cloth to clean lenses.

Use the same method for cleaning lenses when cleaning filters. First clean the filter with compressed air, and then use lens cleaner and lens tissue. Another good way to clean the filter is by breathing on it and wiping off the moisture with a piece of lens tissue or a special filter cloth. Never use this method when cleaning lenses.

Remember: Clean lenses only when absolutely necessary. Never use a dry piece of lens tissue on a dry lens. Never use silicone-coated lens tissue or cloth to clean a lens.

Depth of Field

Depth of field is defined as the range of distance within which all objects will be in acceptable sharp focus, including an area in front of and behind the principal point of focus. There will always be more depth of field behind the principal point of focus than in front of it. This is generally referred to as the one-third-two-thirds rule, which says that there is approximately one-third of the depth of field in front of the subject and two-thirds behind the subject (Figure 4.43).

To determine depth of field you must know the following three factors:

1. Focal length of the lens
2. Size of the aperture (f-stop)
3. Subject distance from the camera film plane

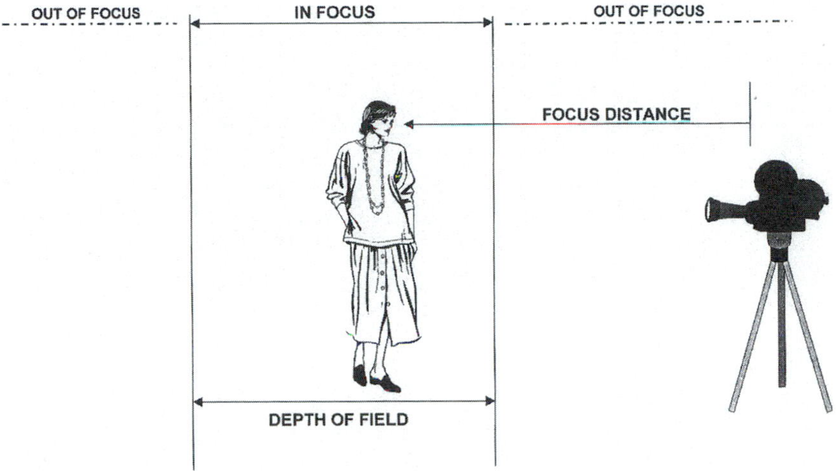

Figure 4.43 Basic principle of depth of field.

To find the depth of field for a particular situation, you may use the depth-of-field tables available in many film reference books. The problem with most of the depth-of-field tables listed is that they list only a limited number of focal length lenses. An example of a depth-of-field table is shown in Figure 4.44.

For the depth-of-field table our focal length is 50 mm. Let's use an aperture of 2.8 and a distance of 15 feet to determine our depth of field. Knowing these three things enables you to read that the depth of field is from 13 feet, 4 inches to 17 feet, 3 inches. When expressing your depth of field, it is always stated as a range from the closest point to the farthest point and not as a single number. When using depth-of-field tables, remember that the depth of field is different depending on whether you are working with 16 mm or 35 mm.

The circle of confusion chosen for the particular format you are shooting, usually 16 mm or 35 mm, will have a bearing on your depth of field. The circle of confusion for 16 mm is generally accepted to be 0.0006 inch while the circle of confusion for 35 mm is generally accepted to be 0.001 inch. The definition of circle of confusion can be quite confusing itself and depends on whom you are speaking with about the subject. I was told that circle of confusion is in reference to the closest point in front of the lens that doesn't focus as a point but focuses as a blurred circle. The diameter of this blurred circle is called the circle of confusion. Please bear in mind that depth of field is not an exact science and is based on different lens characteristics and designs. Depth of field limits should be used

LENS FOCAL LENGTH = 50mm **CIRCLE OF CONFUSION = .001"**

	f 1.4	f 2	f 2.8	f 4	f 5.6	f 8	f 11	f 16	f 22
LENS FOCUS DISTANCE	NEAR FAR	NEAR FAR	NEAR FAR	NEAR FAR	NEAR FAR	NEAR FAR	NEAR FAR	NEAR FAR	NEAR FAR
3'	3' 3' 1"	2' 11" 3' 1"	2' 11" 3' 1"	2' 11" 3' 1"	2' 10" 3' 2"	2' 10" 3' 3"	2' 9" 3' 4"	2' 8" 3' 6"	2' 6" 3' 9"
4'	3' 11" 4' 1"	3' 11" 4' 1"	3' 11" 4' 2"	3' 10" 4' 3"	3' 10" 4' 4"	3' 8" 4' 5"	3' 7" 4' 8"	3' 5" 5'	3' 2" 5' 6"
5'	4' 11" 5' 1"	4' 10" 5' 2"	4' 10" 5' 3"	4' 9" 5' 4"	4' 8" 5' 6"	4' 6" 5' 9"	4' 4" 6'	4' 1" 6" 8"	3' 9" 7' 7"
6'	5' 10" 6' 2"	5' 10" 6' 3"	5' 9" 6' 4"	5' 7" 6' 6"	5' 6" 6' 8"	5' 3" 7' 1"	5' 7' 7"	4' 8" 8' 7"	4' 3" 10' 2"
7'	6' 10" 7' 3"	6' 9" 7'4"	6' 7" 7' 5"	6' 6" 7' 8"	6' 3" 8'	6' 8' 6"	5' 9" 9' 2"	5' 3" 10' 9"	4' 10" 13' 6"
8'	7' 9" 8' 4"	7' 8" 8' 5"	7' 6" 8' 7"	7' 4" 8' 11"	7' 1" 9' 4"	6' 9" 10'	6' 4" 11'	5' 9" 13' 4"	5' 2" 17' 8"
9'	8' 8" 9' 4"	8' 7" 9' 6"	8' 4" 9' 9"	8' 2" 10' 2"	7' 10" 10' 8"	7' 5" 11' 7"	6' 11" 13'	6' 4" 16' 4"	5' 8" 23' 8"
10'	9' 7" 10' 5"	9' 5" 10' 8"	9' 3" 10'	8' 11" 11' 5"	8' 7" 12' 1"	8' 1" 13' 4"	7' 6" 15' 3"	6' 9" 20'	5' 11" 32'
12'	11' 5" 12' 8"	11' 2" 13'	10' 11"	10' 6" 14' 1"	10' 15' 2"	9' 4" 17' 1"	8' 7" 20' 5"	7' 8" 30'	6' 9" 67'
15'	14' 1" 16' 1"	13' 9" 16' 6"	13' 4" 17' 3"	12' 8" 18' 5"	12' 20' 4"	11' 23'	10' 30'	8' 9" 59'	7' 7" INF
20'	18' 5" 21'	17' 10"	17' 1" 24' 2"	16' 1" 26' 7"	14' 11"	13' 6" 39'	12' 63'	10' 2" INF	8' 7" INF
25'	22' 7" 28' 1"	21' 8" 29' 7"	20' 7" 31'11"	19' 1" 36'	17' 5" 44'	15' 5" 66'	14' 168'	11' INF	9' INF
50'	41' 1" 64'	38' 72'	35' 88'	31' 131'	27' 376'	22' INF	19' INF	14' INF	11' INF

Figure 4.44 Depth-of-field table: focal length of lens = 50 mm, film format = 35 mm.

only as a guide, and for most shooting situations the limits for near and far distances will be acceptable.

What happens if you have a lens that is not listed in the book? How do you find your depth of field? Most assistants, myself included, usually use one of the commercially available depth-of-field calculators. These devices allow you to dial in the focal length, f-stop or t-stop, and subject distance and then read the depth of field. The most commonly used depth-of-field calculators are the Guild Kelly Calculator for both 16 mm and 35 mm, and the Samuelson Mark II Calculator (Figures 4.45 and 4.46).

In Chapter 3, I mentioned software developed by assistant cameraman David Eubank for use in a PDA using the Palm operating system. In addition, there are also two applications that are very useful for assistant cameramen, pCam and pCine. These

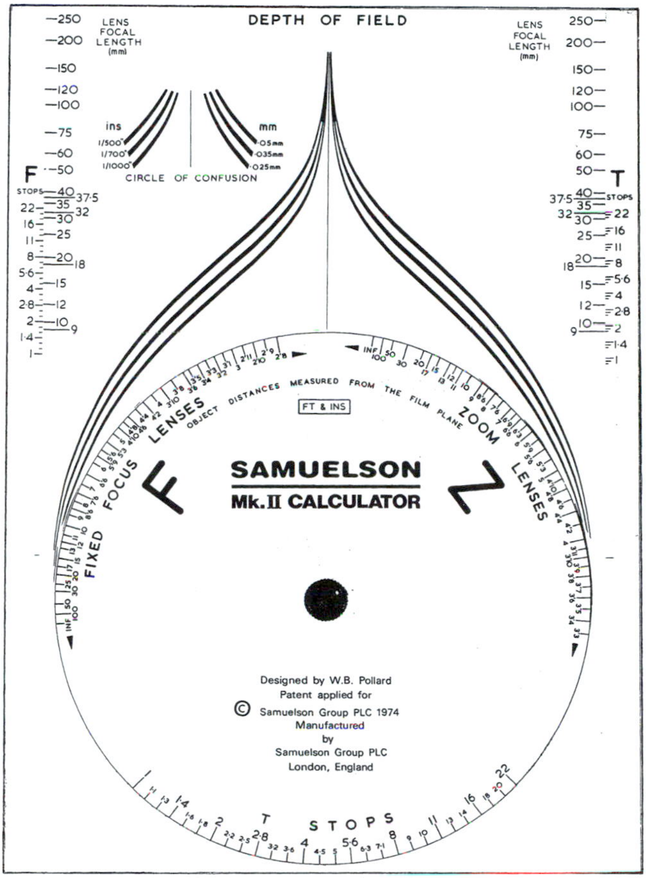

Figure 4.45 Samuelson Mark II Depth of Field Calculator.

are both available for download at David Eubank's web site at www.davideubank.com.

The pCam software is a great tool for calculating depth of field quickly. You first choose the format you are shooting. Then you enter the f-stop, focus distance, and the focal length of the lens, and the near and far limits of your depth of field are shown on the screen (Figure 4.47). Further discussion of some of the features of pCam and pCine can be found later in this chapter in the section Using Computers.

The following examples illustrate how each of the three factors affect the depth of field.

1. Size of the aperture or f-stop: You have more depth of field with larger f-stop numbers (smaller aperture openings) than with small

Figure 4.46 Guild Kelly Depth of Field Calculator.

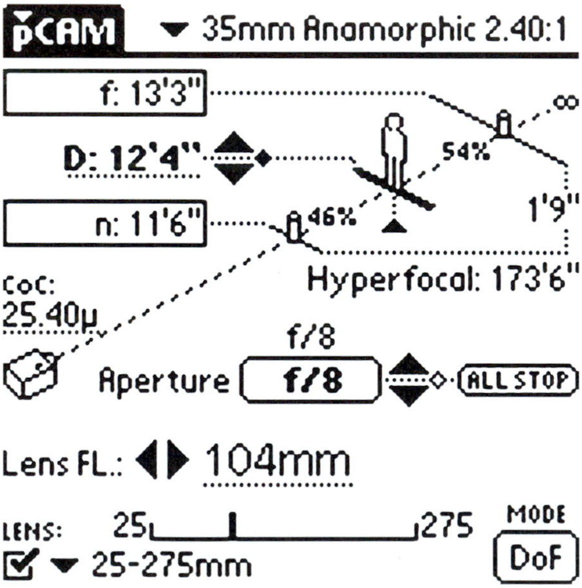

Figure 4.47 Depth of field screen shot from pCam. (Courtesy of David Eubank.)

f-stop numbers (larger aperture openings). *Example:* A large aperture, such as f 2.8, has less depth of field at a specific distance than does a small aperture, such as f 8, at the same focal length and the same distance (Figure 4.48).

2. Focal length of the lens: You have more depth of field with wide-angle lenses than with telephoto lenses at the same f-stop and

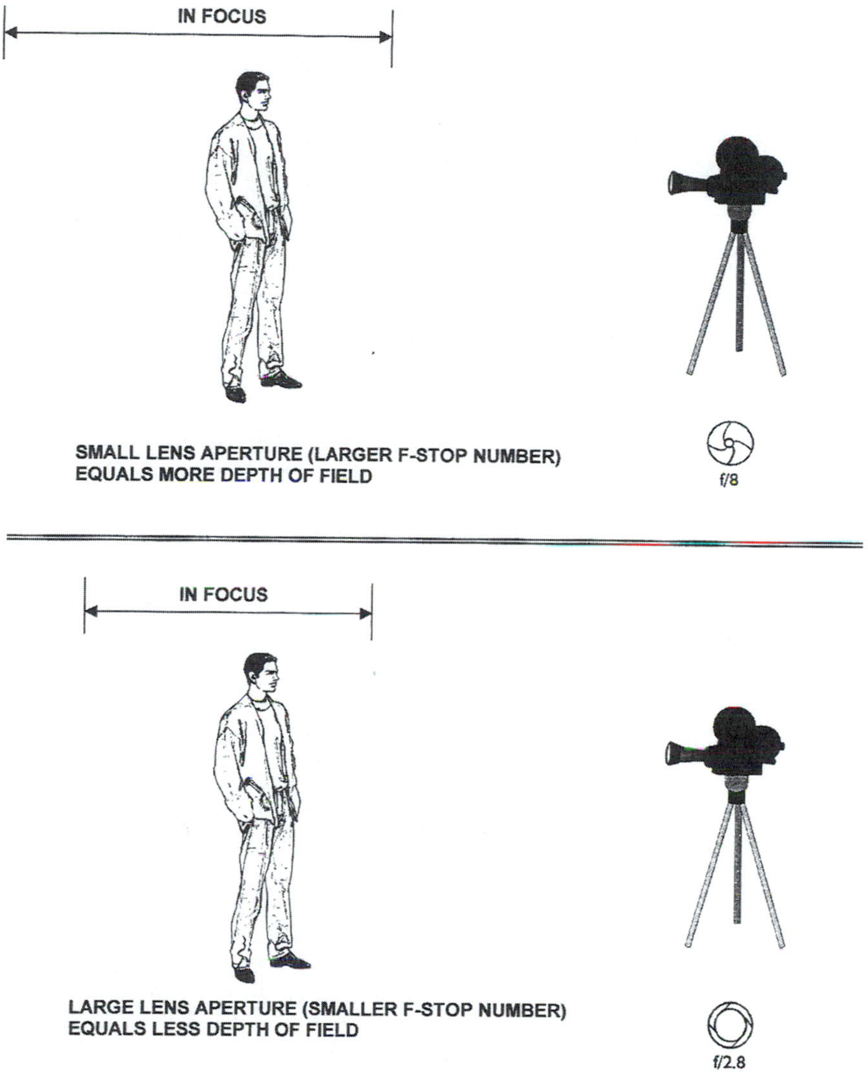
IN FOCUS
SMALL LENS APERTURE (LARGER F-STOP NUMBER)
EQUALS MORE DEPTH OF FIELD
f/8
IN FOCUS
LARGE LENS APERTURE (SMALLER F-STOP NUMBER)
EQUALS LESS DEPTH OF FIELD
f/2.8

Figure 4.48 Diagram illustrating how the size of aperture (f-stop) affects depth of field.

distance. Example: A wide-angle lens, such as 25 mm, will have more depth of field at a specific distance and f-stop than a telephoto lens, such as 100 mm, at the same distance and f-stop (Figure 4.49).

3. Subject distance from the camera: You have more depth of field with a distant subject than with a close subject at the same f-stop and focal length. Example: An object 20 feet from the camera at a

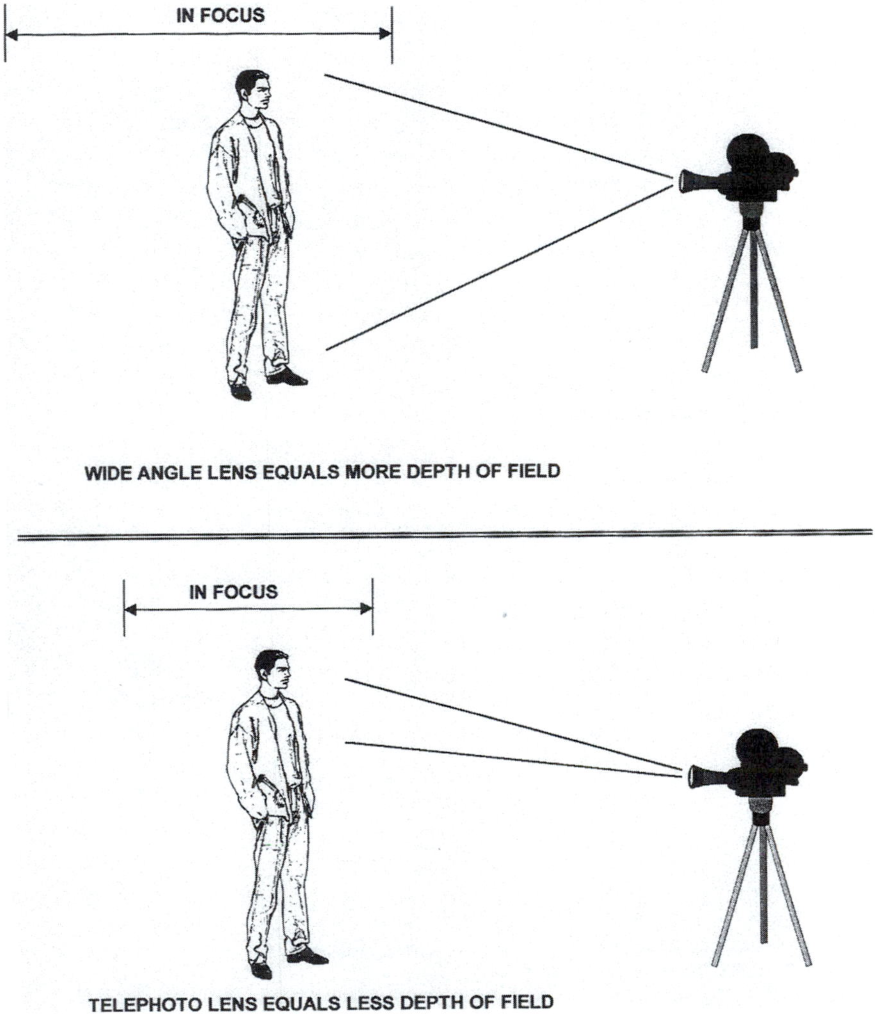

Figure 4.49 Diagram illustrating how the focal length of the lens affects depth of field.

specific f-stop and focal length has more depth of field than an object 8 feet from the camera at the same f-stop and focal length (Figure 4.50).

You will often be in a situation where there are two actors in the scene, at different distances from the camera, and the director would like to have both of them in focus for the shot. Common sense would say that if you were to focus one-half the distance between the two, they should both be in focus. But due to the principles of depth of

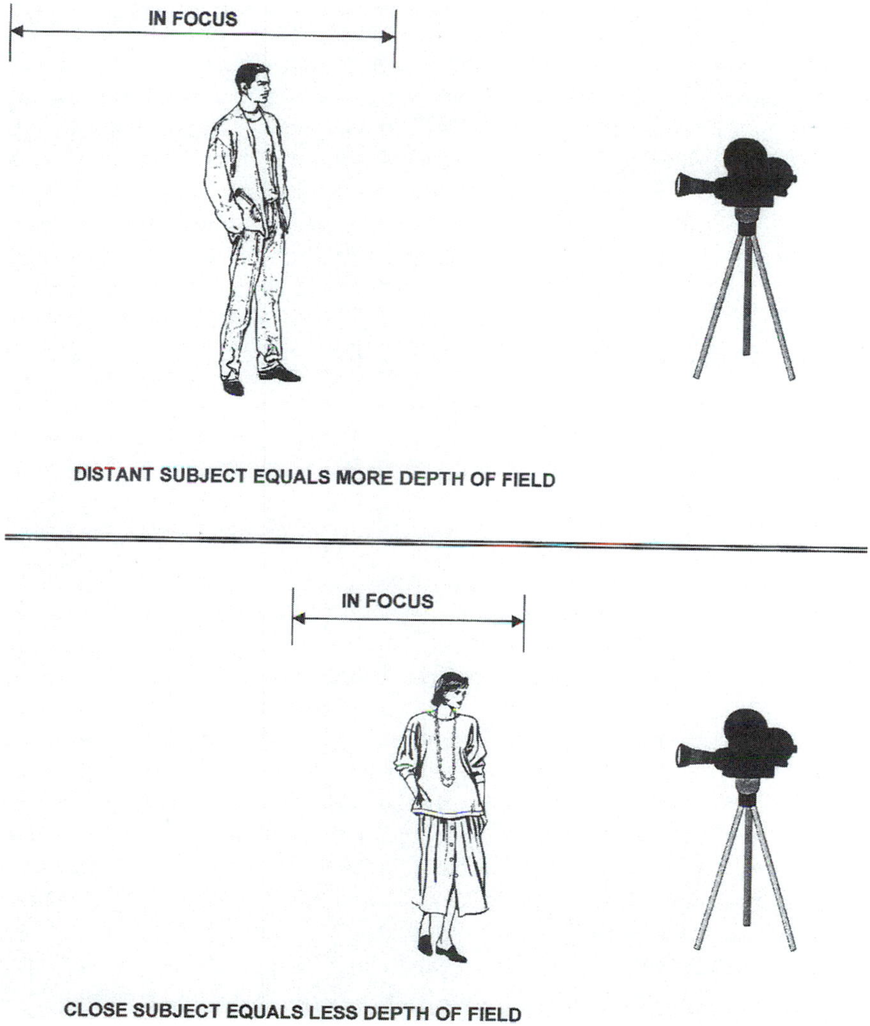
IN FOCUS
DISTANT SUBJECT EQUALS MORE DEPTH OF FIELD
IN FOCUS
CLOSE SUBJECT EQUALS LESS DEPTH OF FIELD

Figure 4.50 Diagram illustrating how the subject distance affects depth of field.

field, this is not the case. When holding focus on two different objects in the same scene, one closer to the camera than the other, you do not set the focus at a point halfway between the two. You would actually focus on a point that is one-third the distance between the two objects in order to have both of them in focus. This principle or theory is usually called the one-third rule. Remember that this is a theory that does not work in every situation. You should check the depth-of-field tables or use the depth-of-field calculators to be sure. It will depend on the depth of field for the one-third point. Check to see if the distance to each object falls within this range. If it does, then the one-third principle works. If not, you may have to move the objects, change lenses, change the lighting, or keep only one of the actors in focus at a time. Always check with the D.P. about whether you should split the focus or whether you should favor one actor over another in the scene. Splitting the focus between two subjects can be dangerous though. Each subject may be just on the edges of the depth of field and when you split the focus between them, they both end up looking a bit soft and slightly out of focus. Many D.P.s with whom I have spoken prefer to have the first assistant keep the focus on the person actually speaking and then shift the focus when the other subject is speaking. This is the method that I prefer and I feel that it looks more natural. By shifting the focus, it brings the viewer's attention to the person who is important at that particular point in the scene. The following example illustrates the one-third rule.

The first object is 6 feet from the camera, and the second is 12 feet from the camera. Using the one-third rule, set the focus at 8 feet in order to have both objects in focus. The distance between the two is 6 feet ($12 - 6 = 6$). One-third of this distance is 2 feet ($6 \div 3 = 2$). Set the focus at 8 feet ($6 + 2 = 8$). Using the depth-of-field table from Figure 4.44, we see that this example will work only for f-stop numbers of 16 or higher (Figure 4.51).

Another special case of depth of field is called the hyperfocal distance. The hyperfocal distance may be defined as the closest focus distance to the lens that will also be in focus when the lens is focused at infinity (∞). Another way to describe hyperfocal distance is to say that it is the closest point of acceptable focus when the lens is focused at infinity. You must check the depth-of-field tables to find out your hyperfocal distance for a given focal length and f-stop. In addition, if you set the focus of the lens to the hyperfocal distance, your depth of field will be from one-half the hyperfocal distance to infinity. In other words, setting the focus to the hyperfocal distance gives you the maximum depth of field. If you refer back to Figure 4.47 the screen shot from the pCam software, you will see that for that particular example the hyperfocal distance is 173 feet, 6 inches.

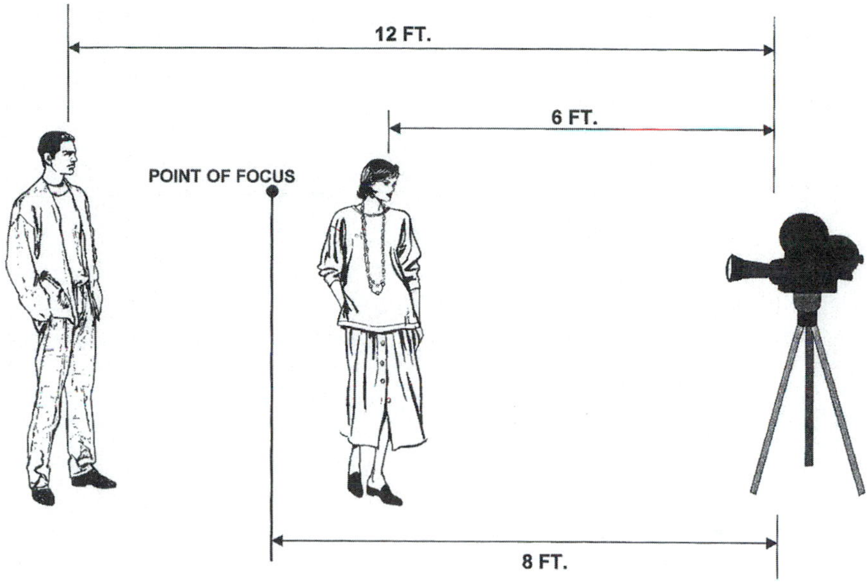

Figure 4.51 Diagram illustrating the one-third principle for splitting focus between two objects.

When calculating the depth of field, you should always use f-stops. Depth-of-field tables and calculators base all depth-of-field calculations on f-stop numbers and not t-stop settings. Use the t-stop only when setting the aperture on the lens.

Don't take the depth-of-field calculations too literally. The focus does not fall off abruptly at the near and far range of depth of field. It is more of a gradual decrease to where a point that is sharp and in focus becomes a blurred circle that is out of focus.

F-Stops and T-Stops

In professional cinematography, many lenses may be calibrated in both f-stops and t-stops. The difference between the two is that an f-stop is a mathematical calculation based on the size of the diaphragm opening, and the t-stop is a measurement of the actual amount of light transmitted through the lens at each diaphragm or aperture opening of the lens. The f-stop is a mathematical calculation determined by dividing the focal length of the lens by the diaphragm opening. This gives us an indication of how much light should get through the lens in a perfect world. The f-stop doesn't accurately represent the amount of light coming through the lens because it doesn't take into account the amount of light loss caused as the light passes through the various glass elements within the lens. But remember that all exposure meter readings are given in f-stops and all depth-of-field tables and charts are calculated using f-stops.

The t-stop is a measurement of exactly how much light is transmitted through the lens. Taking into account light loss as it passes through the various glass elements of the lens, it is much more accurate. Because the t-stop is an actual measurement and is more accurate, it should always be used when setting the exposure on the lens. In referring to the exposure readings and aperture settings, most camera people will use the terms f-stop and t-stop interchangeably.

When the D.P. gives you the exposure reading for a particular shot, repeat it back to him or her. This reminds the D.P. of what he or she told you and also enables the D.P. to change the exposure if necessary. Most D.P.s try to maintain a constant exposure, especially on interior locations, so if they forget to give you an exposure reading, you probably will be safe if you set the aperture to the setting of the previous shot. Check with the D.P. for each new setup to be sure that you set the correct exposure.

If for some reason you forget to set the exposure, or you set the wrong exposure, notify the D.P. immediately. He or she will then request another take of the shot with the exposure set correctly. It is much more professional to admit the mistake at the time it is made than to try to cover it up. We're only human and mistakes do happen. If you do not let the D.P. know about the error, it will be discovered when the dailies are viewed and the shot comes up on the screen either underexposed or overexposed.

When setting the stop on the lens, you should open the lens to its widest opening and then close down to the correct stop. This will compensate for any sticking that may occur in the leaves of the diaphragm if you just changed from one stop to another.

Example: You are using a lens that has a widest opening of 1.4. The lens is currently set at 5.6. The D.P. instructs you to change the stop to a 4. Open up the lens all the way to 1.4 and then stop down to the new setting of 4.

As mentioned in Chapter 1, the standard series of f-stop or t-stop numbers is . . . 1, 1.4, 2, 2.8, 4, 5.6, 8, 11, 16, 22, 32, 45, ... Each number represents one full f-stop, and each full stop admits one-half as much light as the one before it. For example, f 4 admits half as much light through the lens as f 2.8. Figure 4.52 shows examples of f-stop numbers and the corresponding diaphragm openings.

In the preceding example, I used the terms "open up" and "stop down" when referring to the changing of the f-stop opening. When we say stopping down or closing down the lens, it means that the diaphragm opening will get smaller and the numbers larger. Opening up the lens means that the diaphragm opening gets larger and the numbers smaller. Increasing the stop is the same as opening up the lens, and decreasing the stop is the same as stopping down the lens. When you change from one f-stop number to a larger number (smaller opening), you are closing down or stopping down the lens. When you change from one f-stop number to a smaller number (larger opening), you are opening up the lens. Opening up the lens by one stop will double the amount of light striking the film, and closing down by one stop will cut that amount of light in half.

Example: The current aperture setting is t 5.6. Stopping down or decreasing it by one stop makes the aperture become t 8. Opening up or increasing it by one stop makes the aperture become t 4 (Figure 4.52).

T-stop numbers are the same as f-stop numbers, but a t-stop is not the same as an f-stop. As mentioned earlier, f-stops are mathematical calculations based on the size of the diaphragm opening. A t-stop is an actual measurement of the light that is transmitted by the lens at a given diaphragm opening or aperture setting. Many times a lens will be calibrated for both f-stops and t-stops. When setting the exposure precisely on the lens, you should always use t-stops. When measuring the intensity of the light with a light meter or when calculating depth of field, you should always use f-stops.

When working with f-stops or t-stops on lenses, be aware of the *critical aperture*. Because of the physical limitations in the design and manufacture of lenses, it is not possible to make a lens of uniform photographic quality. This means that the image at the edges of the lens may not be as sharp as the image closer to the center of the lens. Many lens manufacturers recommend that you not use the edges of the lens by stopping down approximately two stops from the widest f-stop or t-stop setting. This is called your critical aperture, and in theory it will give you the sharpest image.

When the D.P. tells you the f-stop or t-stop to be set on the lens, he or she may say it in a number of different ways, for example,

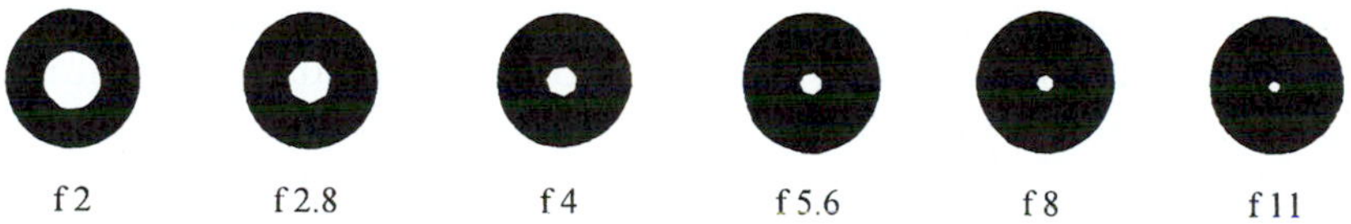

Figure 4.52 Diaphragm openings for different f-stop or t-stop settings.

halfway between 2.8 and 4, or the stop is 3 1/3, or it is a 3.4, and so on. I recommend working with the D.P. to determine how he or she describes the stops so that you understand exactly what the D.P. means. There are actual numbers for the intermediate f-stops listed previously. See Table E-3 in Appendix E for the intermediate f-stop or t-stop settings for one-fourth, one-third, one-half, two-thirds, and three-fourths of the way between full stops.

Whenever you film at a frame rate other than 24 f.p.s., you must change the stop to compensate for the new frame rate. If you film at speeds faster than 24 f.p.s., less light strikes each frame of film, so you must increase your exposure. If you film at speeds slower than 24 f.p.s., more light strikes each frame of film, so you must decrease your exposure. Table E-6 in Appendix E shows the f-stop compensation for various changes in frames per second.

It also may be necessary to adjust your exposure when you are using certain filters on the camera. Some filters decrease the amount of light passing through the lens, while others have no effect on the light. Any exposure change will always be an increase, requiring you to open up the aperture. Tables E-4 and E-5 in Appendix E lists some of the most commonly used filters and the amount of f-stop or t-stop compensation, if any, for each. There are many other filters in use that require some type of exposure compensation. Check with the camera rental house about the filters you are using.

It is also necessary to adjust your exposure when you are filming with a different shutter angle set on the camera. The standard shutter angle on a motion picture camera is 180 degrees. The maximum shutter angle you can achieve with some cameras is 200 degrees. In most cases, changing your shutter angle involves making it smaller than normal to achieve a desired effect on the film. When reducing the shutter angle, you are causing less light to strike your film as the shutter spins, so you must open your lens aperture accordingly. Table E-7 in Appendix E shows the f-stop or t-stop compensation for changes in shutter angle.

Changing Lenses and Filters

Whenever you are asked to place a new lens, filter, or any other accessory on the camera, it should be done as quickly as possible so that the D.P. or Camera Operator can line up the shot. The standard procedure for changing lenses or filters on the camera is as follows. The D.P. calls out the item and it is repeated back by the 1st A.C. The 1st A.C. then tells the 2nd A.C. what the new lens or filter is. The 2nd A.C. repeats it back and while the 2nd A.C. obtains the new item from the equipment case, the 1st A.C. removes the old item from the camera and prepares the camera to accept the new item. The 2nd A.C. brings the new item to the camera and exchanges it for the old item with the 1st A.C. Remember, when exchanging items both assistants should give some type of indication that they have a firm grip on the item so that the other person knows that it is all right to release it. I usually say, “Got it” when exchanging items with my assistant. This lets him know that I have a firm grip on it and he can let go. While the 1st A.C. places the new item on the camera, the 2nd A.C. places the old one back in the equipment case. The 1st A.C. makes the camera ready for any other accessories, while the 2nd A.C. obtains the accessory from the proper equipment case.

As stated in Chapter 3, don't leave an equipment case alone without closing the case and securing at least one of the latches on the case. I recommend always securing both latches on any case before you walk away from it, but if you are in a rush, at least one latch will be sufficient until you can get back to the case. There have been a few times when I have picked up a case that my assistant or the camera intern forgot to latch. Fortunately, I realized it in time before any of the contents spilled out. During filming, there are many different camera setups, and the equipment must be moved many times during the day. If a case is not latched and someone else picks it up to move it, there could be disastrous results. If someone did pick up an unlatched case and spill its contents, it would not be the fault of the person picking up the case, but rather the fault of the person who failed to secure one of the latches.

Before placing any lens or filter on the camera, check it for dirt, dust, or scratches. If the lens or filter requires cleaning, first place it on the camera for the D.P. or Camera Operator to approve. Once it has been approved, it may be removed and cleaned before shooting the shot. Don't waste time cleaning a lens before placing it on the camera only to find out that the D.P. wants a different lens. When a new lens is placed on the camera, set the aperture to its widest opening and the focus to an approximate distance to the subject. If using a zoom lens, unless the D.P. has specified a focal length, always set it to the widest-angle focal length. Remember to engage the follow focus gear and adjust the position of the matte box if necessary. If using a zoom motor, check that it is engaged on the gears of the lens, the power cable is connected, and it works properly. Look through the eyepiece after changing a lens to be sure that it is focused properly; that there is no vignetting; that the matte box, hard matte, or lens shade is not cutting into the shot; and that the shutter is cleared for the Camera Operator to view the scene. If you are not able to look through the eyepiece, ask the Camera Operator to check for you. Also, when changing lenses, you may have to change the lens support rods because of the physical size of the lens. When bringing the lens from the case, the 2nd A.C. should remember to bring the appropriate lens support rods and support brackets when required. When changing lenses it may also often be necessary to rebalance the camera, such as when you change from a prime lens to a zoom lens or vice versa. Remember to check the balance whenever any new piece of equipment has been added to or taken away from the camera. The camera must be balanced properly for the Camera Operator to do the job correctly.

If you are using any filters, a small identification label should be placed on the side of the matte box or camera stating which filter is in use. Without this reminder tag, the D.P., Camera Operator, or 1st A.C. may forget which filter is in place and then forget to compensate the exposure. Placing a tag on the matte box or camera reminds the 1st A.C. and the D.P. that there is a filter in front of the lens (Figures 4.53 and 4.54).

85	LLD	LC 1/8
85N3	FLAT	LC 1/4
85N6	PM 1/8	LC 1/2
85N9	PM 1/4	LC 1
POLA	PM 1/2	DF 1/8
ND3	C 1/8	DF 1/4
ND6	C 1/4	DF 1/2
ND9	C 1/2	DF 1

Figure 4.53
Filter identification tags.

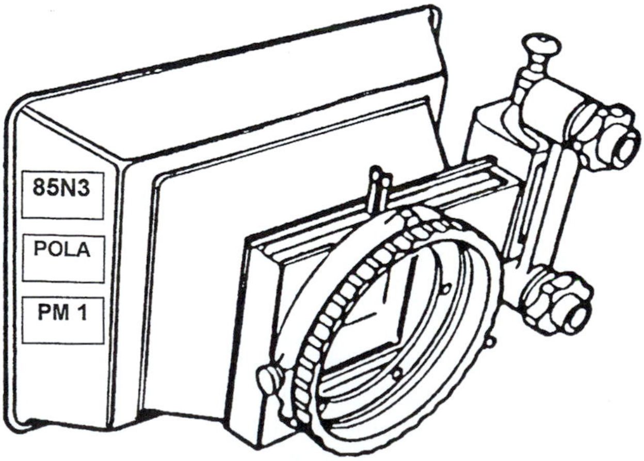

Figure 4.54 Filter identification tags in place on matte box. (Reprinted from the *Panaflex Users Manual*, with permission of David Samuelson and Panavision, Inc.)

Focus Measurements and Following Focus

During rehearsals the 2nd A.C. should place tape or some other type of mark on the floor or ground for each actor's position for the scene. During this time the 1st A.C. will measure the distance from the camera film plane to the subject for each subject position and each camera position of the shot. There are times when actors don't stop on their marks, so by knowing the distances to these marks you may be able to estimate their distance from the camera. Actor's marks were discussed in detail in Chapter 3.

Focus may also be obtained by eye through the viewfinder; this will be discussed later in this section. For beginners, it is important to remember that the focus measurement is taken from the film plane of the camera to the actor or subject. The film plane is the point in the camera where the film sits in the gate and where the image comes into focus on the film; it is from this point that all focus measurements are taken. On most professional motion picture cameras, there is a pin or hook attached to the body of the camera that is precisely in line with the film plane. The 1st A.C. will connect the tape measure to this pin or hook in order to measure the focus distance. There may also be a special symbol engraved or painted on the side of the camera to indicate the positioning of the film plane (Figure 4.55).

If it is not possible or convenient to measure to the actor during rehearsals, obtain focus marks by measuring to the positions of the stand-ins. The stand-ins will stand at the marks for each actor so that you can measure the distance. Just before you get ready to shoot the scene, you may need to double-check these focus measurements when the actors step in. This is especially important on scenes that involve critical focus marks where you have very little depth of field. After a shot has been completed, if you have any doubts about the focus, ask for a moment to check the focus of the actor on his mark to determine if the focus was good, or you may ask the Camera Operator if he or she noticed any focus problems with the shot. If you are unsure, the

Figure 4.55
Mark indicating the film plane on a motion picture camera.

Camera Operator is the best person to tell if the focus was sharp or not. The Camera Operator is the only person who sees the image through the viewfinder and he or she will be able to see any shifts or problems with the focus of the image. Since many video taps are not very accurate, it is best to not rely on the video tap image to judge the focus unless you have checked its accuracy beforehand. Many of the newer video taps and small monitors are actually very good for judging focus. The important thing is to check the accuracy of the video tap and monitor before relying on it for judging focus.

When obtaining the focus measurements, try to do it as quickly and unobtrusively as possible without interfering with the Director, actors, or other crew members. I have heard it said that a good camera assistant is one who is efficient, quick, invisible, and quiet. There are so many people on the set that any idle chatter or unnecessary noise tends to be distracting to crew members trying to work and also to the actors trying to rehearse their lines. It is important to remember to never let anyone rush you when obtaining your focus marks or distances. The most beautiful lighting, set design, costumes, makeup, and performance is not worth anything if the shot is out of focus.

When obtaining your focus mark or measuring the distance to subjects, you must be aware of a special situation that often arises. When you are filming the reflection of a subject such as in a mirror, you must measure the distance from the camera to the mirror and then to the subject. For example, if the distance from the camera to the mirror is 10 feet, and the distance from the mirror to the subject is 5 feet, then you would set the focus of the lens to 15 feet (10 + 5 = 15) in order to have the reflection of the subject sharp and in focus.

You will usually be in one of the following four situations regarding focus for a shot:

1. Stationary camera and stationary actor
2. Stationary camera and moving actor
3. Moving camera and stationary actor
4. Moving camera and moving actor

If an actor and camera are stationary, focusing is actually pretty simple. Measure the distance to the actor and set this distance on the focus barrel of the lens. When an actor or camera or both are moving, focusing during the shot becomes more challenging and sometimes for me even more fun. When the camera is stationary and the actor is moving in the scene, such as walking toward or away from the camera, the 1st A.C. will often place tape marks or chalk marks on the ground as reference points for focusing. Depending on the complexity of the shot, there may only be a beginning mark and an end mark, or there may be these two marks plus many in-between marks. The focus marks are usually placed about 1 foot apart, but the easiest and best way is to place them according to the markings on the lens.

When I am getting focus marks, I usually base my marks on how the lens is marked. For example, if the lens has focus markings at 5, 6, 7, 8, 10, 12, 15, and 20 feet, I place focus marks according to these distances. When following focus it is much easier for me to hit an exact mark on the lens rather than having to guess. As an actor passes these marks, the 1st A.C. adjusts the focus to correspond to the distance measured to each point. If the ground or floor is seen in the shot, the 1st A.C. would measure to various places on the set, such as pieces of furniture, paintings on the wall, light switches, trees, shrubs, or rocks if you are filming outside, and so on. If the actor is stationary and the camera is moving during the scene, usually toward or away from the actor, the assistant usually places marks in line with one of the dolly wheels at 1-foot intervals or according to the marks on the lens. As the dolly wheel moves past these marks, the assistant adjusts focus to correspond with each mark. When placing these marks I have found it is easier to line them up with the center of the dolly wheel. And finally if both the actor and camera are moving, focusing can become much more difficult, challenging, and even fun depending on how you look at it.

I have done many shots where the camera on the dolly is moving backward while the actor is walking toward the lens. If it is possible the actor should try to maintain the same walking speed and distance from the camera throughout the shot. The dolly grip is an important part of this in that he or she must maintain the proper dolly speed as well. One of the tools that I use to help with the focus of this type of shot is a laser pointer. I position the pointer so that the point of light hits the floor at a specific distance from the camera, for example, 8 feet. I also check that the point is out of the film frame of the shot. As the actor and camera are moving together, if the actor gets too close or too far away from this point I can usually accurately judge the distance and adjust the focus accordingly. If it is a tight enough shot you may be able to place focus marks on the floor, but too many marks can often confuse rather than help you. The laser pointer method can also be used if the actor is moving away from the camera that is following him. But when you have the camera moving on one plane and the actor on another, things can get very interesting to say the least. Since each situation is different and no two shots are alike, you need to work out the best and easiest way to focus a complicated moving shot.

Because of the principles of depth of field, focus marks are not as critical when using a wide lens, and you may not need to measure to as many points as you would if you were shooting with a long focal length or telephoto lens.

For each distance measured, the 1st A.C. will mark the lens or focus-marking disk accordingly so that he or she may rack focus or follow focus during the scene. The focus-marking disk is a white piece of plastic that is attached to the follow focus mechanism. Using a grease pencil or erasable marker, the 1st A.C. marks the disk according to the distances measured for the shot. Some assistants wrap a thin piece of tape around the barrel of the lens and place the focus marks on it for the shot. I personally don't like to use the focus marking disks on the follow focus mechanisms and usually leave them in the equipment case when setting up the camera. I prefer to mark the lens directly either by wrapping a thin piece of chart tape around the barrel or marking the lens directly with some type of erasable marking pencil (Figures 4.56 and 4.57).

In addition, the assistant may place a reminder tape near the lens with the distances listed on it for the particular shot. It is a good idea for the 1st A.C. to keep a small note pad to record the focus distances and lens sizes for each scene. This information may be written in *The Camera Log* book that was discussed in Chapter 3. Many times you may do a shot of one actor for a scene, and then later in the day you need to do a reverse angle shot of another actor or actors for the same scene. The shots should be made with the same focal length lens and

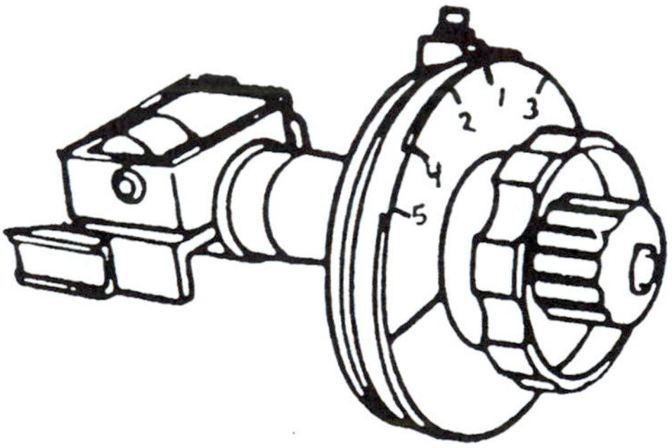

Figure 4.56
Focus marking disk on follow focus mechanism marked for following focus. (Reprinted from the *Panaflex Users Manual,* with permission of David Samuelson and Panavision, Inc.)

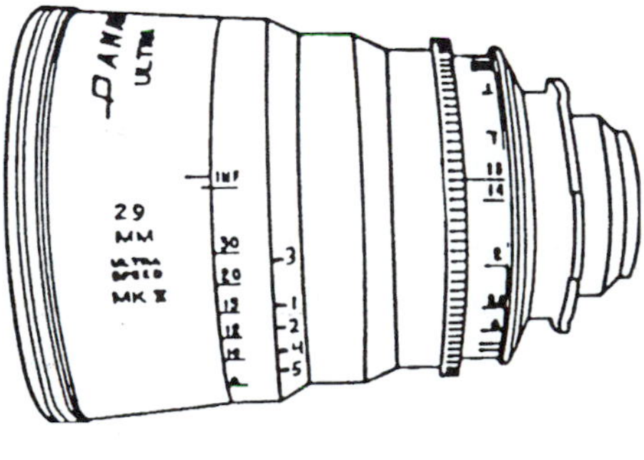

Figure 4.57
Lens marked for following focus. (Reprinted from the *Panaflex Users Manual*, with permission of David Samuelson and Panavision, Inc.)

at the same distance as the first shot so they will match when edited together. If you have the numbers written down for the previous shot, it will be no problem to match the focal length and distance for the other shots.

When you are filming on a sound stage, permanent sets, or practical locations, you often can measure the length and width of each set and record these distances on a sheet of paper or in your notepad for future use. This way if you are in a rush situation and are unable to obtain all of your focus measurements, you can estimate the distance based on where the camera is placed on the set. After a while you should become experienced at guessing the distances with some degree of accuracy. If you have a complicated focus move to do, request at least one rehearsal before shooting the scene.

You also can obtain the focus marks by looking through the eyepiece and focusing on the subject by eye. You then make a mark on the lens to indicate the focus. Always open the aperture on the lens to its widest opening when obtaining focus marks by eye. On a zoom lens, you should zoom in to the tightest focal length to obtain an eye focus. Once you have the focus mark, return the zoom to its correct focal length for shooting. On all lenses, remember to set the correct t-stop setting after obtaining eye focus marks.

Following focus or pulling focus is a very precise and exact job, and can be learned only by actually doing it. It takes much practice and experience to be able to do it well and cannot be explained fully in any book. One important thing to remember when pulling focus is to keep a very light touch on the follow focus mechanism. The Camera Operator must follow the action within a scene, and he or she does not want anything to prevent smooth pans or tilts with the camera because the 1st A.C. had a tight grip on the focus knob.

Focusing Tips

To become a better focus puller, there are some key things that you should be aware of and remember. If the lens doesn't have enough distance marks on it, make your own. Wrap a thin piece of artist's chart tape around the barrel of the lens, and using a focus test chart, determine the distances you need and mark them on the tape. This should be done during the camera prep so that you are prepared for any shot during production.

Most important, you must be able to be close to the camera, be able to see the lens, and be able to see the actor and your focus marks in order to follow focus accurately. Try not to position yourself perpendicular to the camera, which will require you to constantly turn your head from the lens to the actor to see what is happening. By the time you turn your head back to the lens, the actor is in a new position and you have missed the focus. It is best to position yourself slightly toward the back of the camera near the operator so that your line of sight is along the barrel of the lens and to the actor. Now, instead of having to turn your head constantly, you only have to move your eyes slightly from the lens to the action, and you should have no problem keeping the shot in focus.

The type of shot, the position of the camera, the position of the actor, etc., often determine which side of the camera you must be on. Be prepared to work on the right side of the camera, which many camera assistants refer to as the "dumb side" because there are usually no focus marks on the lens or controls for the camera on that side. If you are working with Arriflex cameras with a PL lens mount, you will be able to reposition the lens so that you can see the focus marks from the dumb side, but with Panavision cameras and some lenses, you may have to make your own focus marks so that you can follow focus properly. During the camera prep you should wrap a piece of tape around the barrel of the lens and transfer the distance marks to the opposite side so that you will be prepared in case you are in this situation.

Some Panavision lenses have two witness marks for aperture and focus, one blue mark and one yellow mark. The t-stop numbers on the lens are also in blue and yellow. The blue numbers are usually the first two aperture numbers on the lens; the rest are yellow. When using the blue t-stop numbers, set the aperture according to the blue witness mark. You also set your focus according to the blue witness mark for focus. When using the yellow t-stop numbers, set your aperture and your focus using the appropriate yellow witness marks. In the event your aperture setting is between one of the yellow and blue numbers, set your aperture and focus the same distance between the yellow and blue witness marks on the lens.

Determine the distance between the outstretched fingers of one hand to the outstretched fingers of the other hand when your arms are extended straight out to your side. This measurement is most often equal to your height. This will come in handy when you need to get a quick focus estimate.

When guessing or estimating the focus, keep in mind that the distance is from the film plane and not from the front of the lens or front of the matte box. Know the distance from the film plane to the front of the matte box or front of the lens.

If the operator tells you that the focus is soft on a close-up shot, you are probably focused too close. Whenever this happens you should carefully shift the focus back slightly.

As stated previously, when working in one location or set for an extended period, always try to measure the length, width, and diagonal distances of the room and jot these down in a note pad. Then if you are in a rush situation, you can usually estimate the focus based on the position of the camera and subject within the room.

There may be times when the 1st A.C. just cannot pull focus, most often on an extremely long lens such as 1000 mm. I was in this situation on a feature film and because the actors were so far away from the camera, I could not judge where they were in relation to focus reference points or landmarks in the shot. In this situation the Camera Operator did his own focus. Don't be afraid to pass off the focus to the operator if you feel you just can't do it. Some shots are simply not possible for you to do.

For most shots there will be no question as to which actor should be in focus. It will usually be whoever is facing the camera while speaking. With two or more actors in the scene, you may be in a situation where you may choose to split the focus. This means you will set the focus at a point in between the actors so that both will be in focus for the shot. Remember that you must check your depth of field for all actors' positions, along with the point of focus, to be sure that they fall within the acceptable depth of field. If one or more actors in the shot do not fall within the acceptable depth of field for your focus point, then you will most likely adjust the focus during the shot to favor whomever is talking and/or looking toward the camera. Splitting focus can be a dangerous thing, especially if the actors are on the edges of the depth of field. You may get to the dailies screening and discover that they are both soft. In most cases it is usually best to focus on the actor speaking or the lead actor in the scene. In any situation, if you are not sure who to keep in focus, you should always check with the D.P. If the D.P. does not know the answer, he or she will then check with the Director. Whenever in doubt it is best to check rather than find out in dailies that you focused on the wrong person.

When checking your depth of field, be aware of the final presentation format of the production. A production done exclusively for video may be more forgiving with regard to focus than a big budget feature film that will be projected on a big movie screen. Focus that looks acceptable in video may be out of focus and unacceptable on a large theater screen.

Get in the habit of guessing distances. Before measuring the distance for a shot, guess the distance and see how good you are at estimating. When I first started, I used to get together with another assistant friend and we used to practice guessing distances. We would set up a 35 mm SLR still camera at one of our homes. Each of us would point out an object in the room, and the other person would have to guess the focus and set it on the lens. Then we would look through the lens and focus by eye and compare our guess to the actual focus. It helped us to be better prepared when we started working steadily as first assistants.

When marking the lens or follow focus marking disks, don't put so many marks on them that you get confused during the shot. The same thing applies to placing tape marks on the ground for focus reference. Too many marks will only confuse you.

When doing a critical focus move with the camera and actor moving together, you may want to use a laser pointer to project a point on the floor that is a specific distance from the camera. As the camera and dolly move together, you will be able to use this point as a reference if the actor and dolly get too close together or too far apart.

Because the cloth or fiberglass tape measure may stretch over time, you should periodically check it against your metal tape measure for accuracy. If it has stretched, throw it out and get a new one.

Each shot will be different with regard to how fast or slow you turn the follow focus device. Because the markings on the lens follow a logarithmic progression with the closer focus marks being farther apart on the lens and the farther distances being closer together, pulling focus on a moving shot requires you to adjust your speed as the camera and subject get closer together or farther apart. For example, you must turn the focus knob faster when shifting focus for a move from 6 to 8 feet and slower when shifting focus for a move from 10 to 20 feet. The marks on the lens for 6 and 8 feet are farther apart than the marks for 10 and 20 feet.

On a dolly move, be sure to place your own marks on the ground for the dolly wheel closest to you. You should also work out a system with the Dolly Grip on signals to be used in the event the Dolly Grip misses his or her mark. Remember if the Dolly Grip misses his or her mark and you hit your mark, the shot will most likely be soft and out of focus.

Have fun with pulling or following focus, but always remember that you are only human and not perfect. Don't be afraid to ask for another take if you feel that you missed the focus. Check with the Camera Operator if you are unsure about the focus of a shot. It's better to do it again and get it right than to watch a soft shot in dailies. By speaking up at the time, you will be respected for your professionalism.

Zoom Lens Moves

In addition to pulling focus, the 1st A.C. may also be required to do a zoom lens move, which means that the assistant will be changing the focal length of the zoom lens during the shot. The focal length of the lens may change from wide to tight, or from tight to wide or anywhere in between. The important thing to remember when doing a zoom lens move is to start and end the zoom move very smoothly. Any sudden starts and stops are distracting when viewed on the screen. I compare the principle for starting or stopping a zoom move with the way you take off or stop your car at a traffic light. The proper way is to start out slowly and work up to the proper speed. Start the zoom move slowly and work up to the proper speed so that it does not look like a jerky, quick start. As you start to reach the end of the zoom move, you should slow the speed down until you stop completely.

Many zoom lens changes are done along with some type of camera move, either panning, tilting, dollying, or booming. When doing any type of zoom lens change along with a camera move, the zoom lens change should start a fraction of a second after the camera move starts and end a fraction of a second before the camera move ends. This helps to hide any sudden starts or stops in the zoom lens move and makes the zoom less noticeable to the viewer.

Most zoom controls and zoom motors have some type of switch or dial that allows you to adjust the speed of the zoom. During the rehearsal, work out the correct zoom speed with the Camera Operator. If you have a complicated zoom move to do, request at least one rehearsal before attempting to shoot the scene.

There may be some instances when you have to do a zoom lens move for a shot on a lens that does not have a zoom motor. This is often called a manual zoom move. You should keep a light touch on the lens and if possible use some type of zoom stick so that your hand is not on the actual lens that could restrict the Camera Operator's movement. A few years ago I was working with another assistant who had a device that he was using to do a zoom on a lens that did not have a zoom motor. It was actually a jar opener that is available in many specialty kitchen stores. This jar opener has a plastic handle with a rotating knob on one end and a metal strap on the other end. By turning the knob you are able to lengthen or shorten the metal strap so that it fits around the barrel of the lens. You can then position it accordingly to allow you to follow focus or zoom without having your hand actually on the lens barrel. I have used mine on many low-budget jobs where we did not have a zoom lens motor. See Figure 4.58 for an illustration of the jar opener that can be used for zooming or following focus. Just like following focus, zoom lens moves require much practice and experience to be able to do them well and cannot be explained fully in any book.

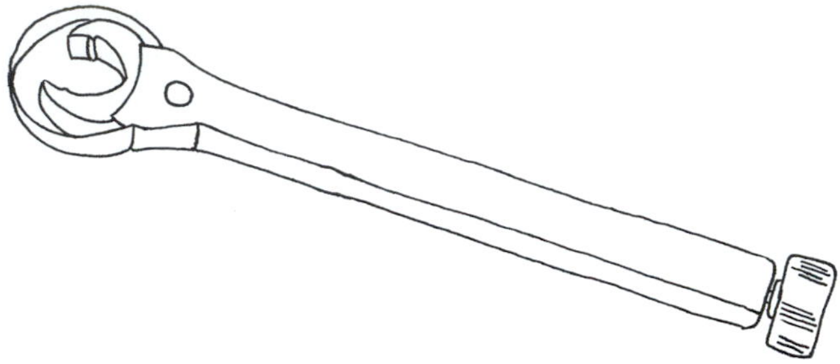

Figure 4.58 Jar opener that may be used for following focus or zooming.

Footage Readings

After each take, the 1st A.C. should call out the dial readings from the camera footage counter to the 2nd A.C. These amounts are entered in the correct space on the camera report for the particular shot. To make the mathematics easier when totaling up the figures on the camera report, round all dial readings to the nearest 10. As you probably learned in elementary school, if the number ends in 4 or less you round down, and if it ends in 5 or more you round up.

Example: The camera footage counter shows a reading of 274. Because this number ends in a 4, we round down, and it becomes 270. For this dial reading the 1st A.C. will drop the zero at the end and call out "27." The 2nd A.C. will then record "270" on the camera report for that particular shot.

Most often after a take the set becomes very noisy. The Director may be talking to the actors, the D.P. may be giving instructions to other crew members, and so on. It is a good idea to always remain as quiet as possible when working on a film set. Don't add to the noise by calling out the camera footage counter dial readings. There is a standard set of hand signals used to give dial readings. They can be used by the 1st A.C. when he or she is too far away from the 2nd A.C. Figure 4.59 shows the standard hand signals used for footage counter dial readings.

Checking the Gate

After each printed take, it is standard procedure for the 1st A.C. to check the gate for hairs, which are very fine pieces of emulsion or dust

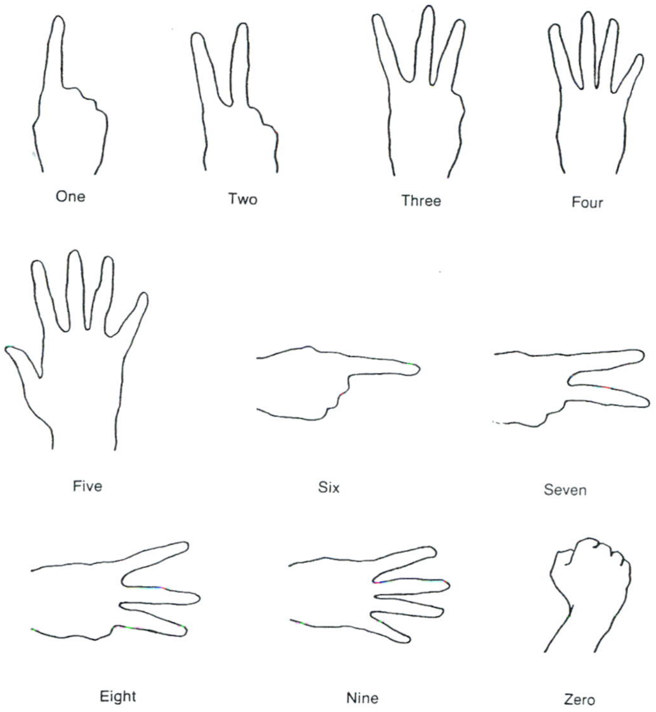

Figure 4.59 Hand signals for camera footage counter dial readings.

that may have gotten in the gate and will show up on the screen as a large rope in the frame. The gate is the opening in the aperture plate that the light passes through from the lens to the film. Most often if a hair is found, you should remove the hair and do another take to ensure that you have a clean shot. The D.P. will usually look at the gate to double-check because he or she has the final say on whether you should do another take. Many times another take is not necessary even if there is a hair. The hair may be so small that it does not reach into the frame.

There are generally three accepted ways to check the gate for hairs: remove the gate, remove the lens, and look through the lens.

- Remove the gate: This can obviously be done only on cameras that have a removable gate and aperture plate. Turn the inching knob so that the registration pin and pull down claw are away from the film. Remove the film from the gate and then remove the gate. When you hold the gate up to the light, you should be able to see any hair along the edges. This is not always an accurate way to check for hairs because when you remove the film from the gate, the hair may stick to the film and be pulled out with it. When you look at the gate, you will not see any hair and assume that the gate is clean. You are not able to remove the gate on many cameras, so this method may not be used on all cameras. Be sure to check with the rental house if you are not sure if the camera you are using has a removable gate.

- Remove the lens: Remove the lens from its mount. Then turn the inching knob to advance the shutter until you can see the emulsion in the gate while looking through the lens port opening. Using a small flashlight or magnifier with a built-in light, examine the emulsion along the top, bottom, and sides to see if there is any hair, which would be visible against the bright background of the film emulsion. I prefer to use this method whenever possible. If removing the lens is too difficult or time consuming, I use one of the other methods.
- Look through the lens: Open the aperture on the lens to its widest opening. Turn the inching knob until the emulsion is visible in the gate as you look through the lens. Place a small flashlight alongside your face and look right down the barrel of the lens. The lens will act as a magnifier for the gate, allowing you to see any hair along the top, bottom, or sides of the gate. This method works best with lenses that are 40 mm or longer in focal length. When using this method with a zoom lens, be sure to zoom the lens in to its longest focal length. Unfortunately I have never been able to master this technique, but I know quite a few camera assistants who use this method successfully.

If a hair is found, clean the gate and aperture plate with compressed air and an orangewood stick. When cleaning any emulsion from the gate, use only an orangewood stick. Once you have cleaned the gate, double-check it before shooting any additional shots.

Moving the Camera

The camera must be moved frequently throughout the day. If the camera is mounted to a dolly, it is much easier for the Dolly Grip to wheel it to each new setup. One of the camera assistants, usually the 1st A.C., should walk alongside the dolly, with one hand on the camera to steady it while the dolly is moving. The dolly may have to travel over rough terrain or over lighting cables. If the terrain is too rough, it is a good idea to remove the camera and carry it to the next setup. The bouncing of the dolly can shake loose the elements of the lens or possibly even damage the camera. If you feel it would be safer, remove the lens before transporting the camera to a new position. When the camera is mounted on a tripod, it is the sole responsibility of the camera assistants to move the camera to each new position. Many camera assistants pick up the entire tripod, with the head and camera attached, and carry it to the new position. One of the best ways to do this is as follows: Aim the lens so that it is in line with one of the legs of the tripod. Lock the pan and tilt locks on the head. Lengthen the front leg of the tripod (the one that the lens is in line with). Crouch down and place the shoulder pad of the tripod between your shoulder and the head, with the extended tripod leg in front of you. Lean into the tripod legs, and with your left and right hands grab the shorter left and right legs of the tripod and slowly push them in toward the lengthened front leg. The two shorter legs will fold up, forcing all of the weight onto the one extended leg. The camera will lean into your shoulder, making it easy to pick up. Stand up, and the camera, head, and tripod should be balanced on your shoulder. To place the entire system back on the ground first crouch down and set the long tripod leg on the ground. Grab the left and right legs, and bring them back to their normal position to form a triangle with the extended leg. Loosen the extended leg and return it to its original length. The camera is now ready for shooting at the new setup.

The previous method usually works best when the tripod is placed on a carpet. When using a spreader, the tripod legs often will not fold up with the spreader attached so that you may have to remove the spreader before moving the camera using this method. Another way to move the camera on a tripod is for the 1st A.C. to remove the camera from the head and carry it while the 2nd A.C. carries the tripod and head. And always remember to level and balance the head whenever you move the camera to a new setup.

Use whichever method is easier and safer for you. Never try to carry anything if you do not feel it is safe or you don't think that you can handle it. Before shooting be sure that the camera is level, whether it is mounted on a dolly or on a tripod. Each time the camera is moved, bring along all other needed equipment and accessories, including lenses, filters, magazines, and so on. When the D.P. requests a piece of equipment, he or she will not want to wait because you left some of the cases back at the last camera position. If the cases are on a dolly or hand cart, all you need to do is wheel it to the new position. Otherwise the cases must be hand carried to the next setup. It is the camera assistant's responsibility to make sure that the camera equipment is moved quickly and safely and is near the camera throughout the day. If you require any help in moving or carrying the equipment, do not hesitate to ask one of the Production Assistants or Grips on the set. It is much better to ask for help than to try to do it all yourself and risk getting hurt or dropping and damaging the equipment.

Performing the Duties of Second Camera Assistant

There will be times when you are working on a production that does not have a 2nd A.C. It may be a small production, such as a music video or commercial, or perhaps the production just doesn't have a big enough budget to afford an additional assistant. If this is the case, the 1st A.C. also carries out the duties of 2nd A.C. Because you are now doing two separate jobs, it is important to remember not to be rushed while working. The Director and D.P. should understand that it sometimes takes a little longer to get certain things done. If for any reason you need help, do not hesitate to ask other crew members. I have done many commercials and music videos where I was the only camera assistant on the job.

Packing Equipment

At the end of each shooting day, pack all camera equipment away in its appropriate case and store everything in a safe place until the next shooting day. If you are working out of a camera truck, place and secure all of the cases on their appropriate shelves. If you are working on a sound stage, you should have a room or special area where all of the equipment is stored at the end of each shooting day.

Tools and Accessories

As mentioned in Chapter 3, with many professions you must have some basic tools and accessories so that you may do the job properly. When first starting out, you should have a very basic tool kit or ditty bag, and as you gain more experience and work more frequently, you can add things as you feel they are needed. Some of the tools are common tools that you may need, while others are specialized pieces of equipment that are unique to the film industry. In addition to the basic tools, you should also have a small inventory of expendables—film cans, cores, camera reports, etc. There will be many times when you are called for a job at the last minute and you may have no time to acquire some of these items. By having a small amount on hand, you will always be prepared for most job calls that you get.

Many 1st A.C.s often wear some type of belt pouch or fanny pack to keep the most commonly used tools or accessories with them at all times. Instead of wearing a pouch, which can become very cumbersome when packed full of tools and accessories, some 1st A.C.s have an item called a front box, which contains all of the basic items needed each day for shooting. The front box is most often constructed of wood and has a metal bracket on the back that allows you to mount it directly on the front of the head, under the camera. It contains items such as a depth-of-field calculator, cloth and metal tape measures, permanent markers, mini flashlight, slate markers, lens tissue, and lens cleaner. The front box may also be used to hold the D.P.'s light meters. By mounting this on the head, the 1st A.C. has the basic supplies needed for shooting and does not have to be encumbered by wearing a large pouch filled with these tools and supplies. An illustration of a front box is shown in Figure 4.60. See Appendix D for a list of the common tools and equipment that should be included in an Assistant Cameraman's ditty bag or tool kit.

As discussed in Chapter 3, it is important to have a personal bag on set. This bag should contain a change of clothes, extra sneakers, or work shoes along with foul weather or rain gear. You never know when you will be in a situation where you must change clothes or have additional clothing in case of extreme weather conditions. Having an extra sweatshirt, thermal underwear, and cold weather boots can make the difference between being warm and comfortable on a shoot or freezing. I bring this bag with me on any long-term job and keep it on one of the top shelves in the camera truck. In addition to clothing items, I also keep a small first aid kit, basic toiletry kit, and extra towels in the bag. You never know when you will find yourself away from home and in need of many of these items.

Using Computers

As mentioned in Chapter 3, two common items that are being used today by many camera assistants are PDAs and laptop computers. Both

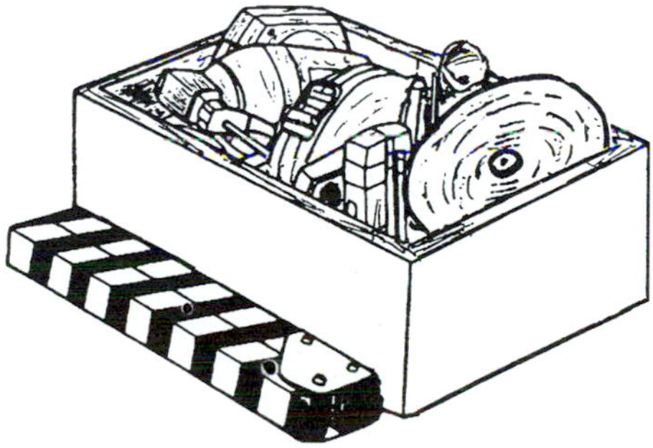

Figure 4.60
Front box used by many 1st A.C.s.

of these devices can save both the first and second assistant much time in the performance of the job.

A laptop computer can be used for much of the camera department record keeping as well as other applications. There are two software applications from Arriflex that an assistant may install on a laptop to use on productions with certain Arriflex cameras and equipment. One of these is the LCC (Laptop Camera Controller), which is used with the 435, 535, and SR3 cameras. It allows you to start and stop the camera, program speed changes, and much more. The LCC creates its own camera reports provided you enter all of the production and film stock information beforehand. The RPC (Ramp Preview Controller) is another program that some assistants may have installed in their computer. This application allows you to program a ramp in the computer, and by digitizing the image into the computer, you are able to preview the effect of the ramp before actually shooting it. Shortly after preparing the material for this section of the book, I learned that Arriflex is no longer promoting or supporting the LCC and the RPC software applications. I have chosen to leave the material in the book to provide a basic explanation of what they do, in case you ever have the opportunity to use them on a film set.

The pCam software for your Palm-operated PDA was briefly discussed in the section on depth of field and is also used for other applications. Two additional features of the pCam software are the ability to see your field of view for a particular shot and to see a basic preview of your image. See Figures 4.61 and 4.62 for screen shots of these two features of the pCam software.

Assistant Cameraman David Eubank has also developed an application called pCine, which enables you to determine the following information: exposure, running time to film length, shooting time versus screen time, time lapse, HMI safe filming speeds, diopter calculations, macro settings, color correction, scene illumination, light coverage, and underwater distances (Figures 4.63 through 4.65).

Working in Video/HD

With so many productions being shot on video these days, I thought it would be a good idea to include some basic information about the job responsibilities of the camera assistants when working in that format. Since all of my production experience has been working on film productions, I have had to rely on other sources for this information. I apologize if any of it is unclear or incomplete.

Often a camera operator may come from a background of shooting television. On many of the pedestal-mounted television cameras, there

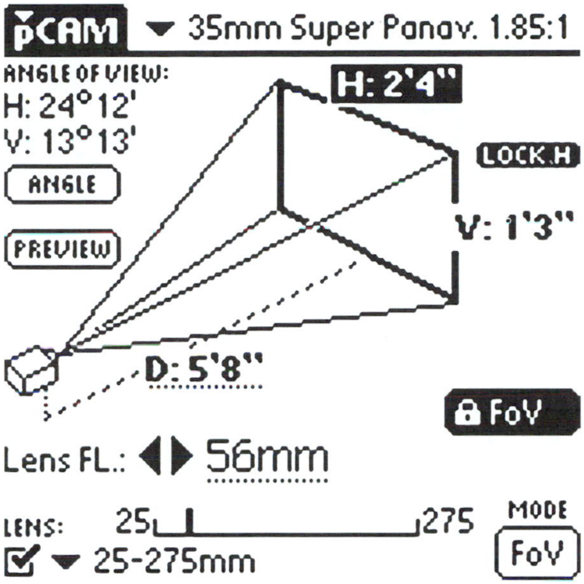

Figure 4.61 Field of view screen shot from pCam. (Courtesy of David Eubank.)

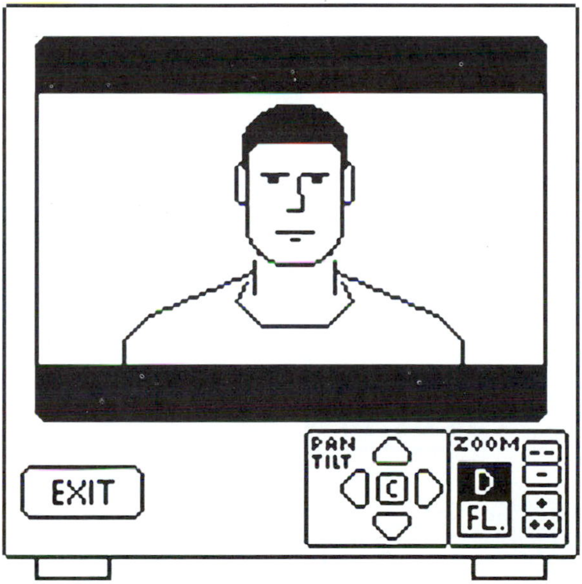

Figure 4.62 Image preview screen shot from pCam. (Courtesy of David Eubank.)

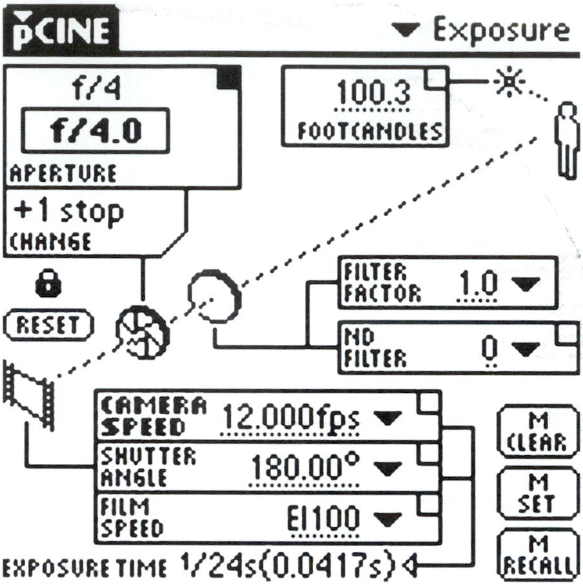

Figure 4.63 Exposure screen shot from pCine. (Courtesy of David Eubank.)

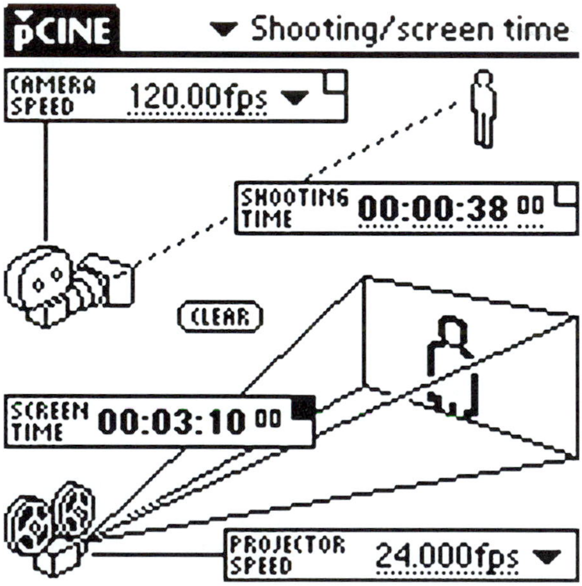

Figure 4.64 Shooting time/screen time screen shot from pCine. (Courtesy of David Eubank.)

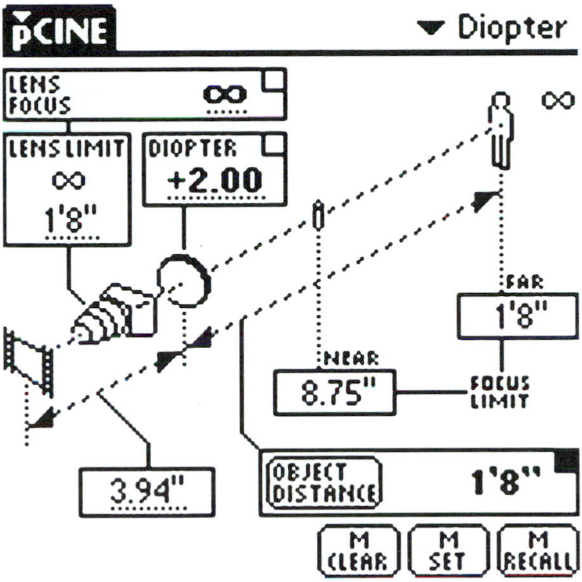

Figure 4.65 Diopter screen shot from pCine. (Courtesy of David Eubank.)

is a focusing device that is controlled by the Camera Operator. Because of this, producers often don't see the need for a first assistant when shooting video. Pulling focus on HD or video can be just as critical as when shooting 35 mm film. Because of the greater depth of field in HD, shots are often done with the aperture set wide open, giving the least depth of field. In this situation critical focus is very important and a separate focus puller is essential to quality images.

A first assistant with an ENG background will be very helpful when working in video or HD. Unfortunately many first assistants come directly from film backgrounds and must learn all of this information for the first time on the first video shoot that they do. As more and more productions move to shooting on video, there will be more qualified camera assistants to work on these types of productions.

Some of the duties of a 1st A.C. on a video or HD digital production are as follows:

Pre-Production

Choosing and Ordering Expendables Many of the expendable items needed on a film production will also be needed on a video production. The 1st A.C. will prepare this list, usually along with the 2nd A.C.

The Rental House and Preparation of Camera Equipment The 1st A.C. should contact the rental company to arrange the day and time that you will prep the camera equipment. The 1st A.C. works with the Video Controller at the prep to be sure that the system works properly and also to allow him or her to become familiar with what equipment will be used. Video and HD cameras use up much more power than film cameras so be sure you have extra batteries and chargers available for shooting.

Production

Setting up the Camera The 1st A.C. sets up the camera, often working with the Digital Utility person. At the start of each day, they should set up the camera and turn it on to let it warm up. During this time they can check back focus, white balance/black balance, and all camera settings so that the camera is ready for the first shot. User-defined switches must be properly set according to the D.P.'s request; all setup menus must be checked to be sure that the settings are correct. Newer lenses specifically designed for shooting HD have back focus adjustments that must be set. Before shooting they record bars and tone on the tape for 30 to 60 seconds. Be sure that you are connected to the sound equipment and that the sound mixer is ready before you record bars and tone. Be sure that all batteries are fully charged or being charged so that they are available throughout the day.

The first assistant must be familiar with the many menus in the video or HD cameras so that he or she has access to basic functions like battery type, shutter speed, gain settings, presets, and color settings. Many of these things are left to the Digital Imaging Technician, but it is a good idea for the first assistant to know them as well.

In addition to the many menu settings on the camera, the first assistant must also know and understand all of the external controls, switches, and connections on the camera. There are many cables that are fed from the sound department, as well as from the video recorders and monitors that must be connected to the camera. The 1st A.C. should know where all of these cables are to be connected.

Since all television monitors are different, it is a good idea to know how to set up the color bars on the monitor so that the image is seen correctly. Some HD monitors have their own setup cards and menus. Knowing how to navigate them is a good idea. Many shoots use paint boxes or external camera control units. On smaller shoots without a Digital Imaging Technician, the 1st A.C. should know how to double-check settings and control the camera using one of these units.

If possible it is a good idea for the first assistant to spend a full day with the camera, monitor, paint box, and their instruction manuals so that he or she can become familiar with their many functions and controls.

Loading and Unloading Tapes into the Video Camera The 1st A.C. will change tapes in the camera, being sure to record bars and tone on each new tape that is used. It is also important to be sure that the tape is labeled properly before putting it in the camera. Make sure that the tape has been numbered accordingly. This is often done by the 2nd A.C. but should be checked by the 1st A.C. to be sure that it is done. The 1st A.C. should also check and set proper time code, time of day, or user bits to be recorded onto each tape.

Checking for Lens Flares Whenever the camera is in position and the lights set for the shot, you should check for any lens flares using the same methods as when working with film cameras.

Lenses (Primes and Zooms) Whenever changing lenses, check the front and back elements to be sure that they are clean and free from scratches or imperfections that could affect your image. Unless there are major smudges or marks on the lens element, it should be cleaned with lens fluid or tissue only when absolutely necessary. When changing lenses, you should always check the back focus to be sure that it is set properly before shooting.

Focusing and Depth of Field Back focus on the camera must be checked quite often to ensure proper focus of the shots. It should be checked during the camera prep, each morning before shooting, anytime there is a temperature shift in the shooting environment, whenever you swap cameras and change lenses, just to name a few. Back focus can go out at any time without warning, so you should check it often. I have heard that each time you change lenses, back focus should always be checked. It's one of those things that can't be explained, but back focus will go out at the worst possible time and the first assistant will get blamed for it. A few years ago I was Camera Operator on an HD production and we had to check back focus after almost every take.

Use the following steps to check back focus:

- Place a focus chart or Siemens star chart 8 to 10 feet from the camera (Figure 4.66).
- Open the f-stop to its widest opening.
- Zoom all the way in to the tightest focal length on the lens and focus on the chart.
- Zoom out to the widest angle focal length of the lens.

Figure 4.66 Siemens star as seen on most focus test charts. (Courtesy of Century Precision Optics.)

- Loosen the back focus adjustment knob and turn the back focus ring until the chart is in focus.
- Zoom back in to the tightest focal length and check that the chart remains sharp at all points within the zoom.
- Repeat these steps until the chart is sharp at the widest angle focal length, the most telephoto focal length, and all focal lengths in between.

The depth of field for HD is slightly less than the depth of field for 16 mm film and slightly more than that of 35 mm film. There is currently available a high definition depth of field calculator, which is manufactured by the Guild of British Camera Technicians. It is very easy to use and allows you to determine your depth of field for a given shot.

Focus markings on lenses are often not very accurate and sometimes nonexistent. They are usually not as precise as motion picture camera lenses as far as image quality and focusing capabilities. Many times you are not even able to attach a follow focus device to the video lenses, which makes following focus very awkward and difficult. Because of this, focus marks are often obtained by eye, relying on the monitor image to judge if it is sharp. Some cameras have a mark on the camera to indicate the focus plane, but this is not always accurate. During an HD production I operated on a few years ago, all focus was obtained by eye. Since my assistants couldn't see the monitor, they would adjust the focus while the Digital Imaging Technician or D.P. watched on the monitor and let them know when it was sharp. This was very time consuming and frustrating for the first assistant pulling focus. Everything worked out fine, but it took much longer than getting your focus marks in film.

A D.P. friend of mine told me about a time he was shooting with a high definition camera using standard definition lenses. The camera had a witness mark on the body to indicate the focus plane (film plane for you film camerapeople). For 2 days the assistant was measuring focus from this mark on the camera body. Unfortunately they discovered that the standard definition lenses had a mark on the front of them, which you were supposed to measure from. So for 2 days the focus marks were all off by over 1 foot and the shots were out of focus. When in doubt, always check critical focus on the large monitor that you will always have on set.

Moving the Camera Moving the camera between setups can be much more time consuming than when shooting with a film camera. Even with a film camera, you will have a battery cable connecting the battery and often a video cable to the camera's video tap. But when shooting video or HD you will have many more cables to contend with. In addition, almost every time you move the HD camera you will have to recheck your back focus because it will surely be thrown off by the move.

White Balancing White balance should be done each time you move to a new set or new lighting source. The second assistant will hold up a clean white card that is lit properly while the first assistant performs the white balancing. Throughout the day, check the image for bad pixels. Sometimes individual pixels on the CCDs can malfunction and be represented by a bright dot or speck in the image. Restarting the camera and re-black balancing can sometimes eliminate the problem.

Tools and Accessories You will need your same complement of tools and accessories when working in video or HD production. Although you may not use them all, I am a firm believer in the saying, "It's better to have it and not need it than to need it and not have it." Have a head cleaning tape made by the camera manufacturer, but use them sparingly (Sony recommends never more than five times consecutively) and only when the camera malfunctions. Some engineers do not like cleaning tapes and prefer to clean heads manually.

Post-Production

Wrapping Equipment When wrapping equipment and packing it away at the end of the day or at the end of the shoot, you should follow the same procedures as outlined in this section dealing with film shoots. If you will be continuing to shoot on another day and the camera is being shipped to a new location, I have heard that it is a good idea to write down all of your camera settings on a piece of paper so in the event the settings change during transportation, you can reset the camera to its original settings for shooting.

1st A.C. Tips

Always arrive to work at least 15 minutes to one-half hour before the call time. This shows your willingness to work and also your professionalism. If you get in this habit from the very beginning, it will stick with you throughout your career. No matter what, you should always be on set before the D.P.

Your attitude is a big part of the reason why you get hired for a job and why you keep the job. One of the first questions asked about you when being considered for a job is "How does he or she get along with others?" "Does he or she have a good attitude?" If you are constantly complaining or whining, nobody is going to want to work with you. Have a positive attitude every day on the set. Leave your personal problems at home. If you do this everybody will want to work with you, and you will be getting so many job calls that you will have to start turning down jobs.

The entire camera department is a team and must work together. This is especially important for the 1st A.C. and 2nd A.C. If you must leave the set for any reason, you should inform the D.P., Camera Operator, or 2nd A.C. Never leave the camera unattended. You may also notify the Dolly Grip if you can't find any other member of the camera department. Unless the entire cast and crew are on a break, the camera should never be left unattended.

When working around the camera, keep your talking to a minimum. If you must talk then talk in a low voice. The D.P. may be discussing the shot with the Director or the Gaffer, or the Director may be talking with the actors. If it's necessary to speak with someone, either wait until the time is right or ask him or her to go to another area of the set where it may be quieter. And above all, no yelling on any film set. This is a sign of a true nonprofessional.

Whenever the D.P. calls for a piece of equipment, you should repeat it back to confirm that you heard the request and that you heard it correctly. If your name is called out, you should also respond so that whoever called will know that you heard him or her.

Get your focus marks as soon as you know what is happening in the shot. Use the stand-ins to check your focus so that you are prepared when it's time for the shot. If stand-ins are not available, then have your second assistant stand on the marks. If necessary, request a rehearsal so that you can confirm your marks. A good assistant is always prepared and doesn't have to be reminded to do his or her job.

If you are having personality conflicts with someone in your department or in another department on the crew, try to speak with him or her about it. Work it out among yourselves so that you can at least have a good working relationship. You may not like the person, but you should at least be able to work together without any conflict.

Keep your eyes and ears open at all times so that you are constantly aware of what is happening on the set. As you become familiar with a particular working style of the D.P., you should be able to anticipate requests and be ready when he or she does make a certain request. The D.P. may always use a particular lens or filter for the close-up and another for the wide shot. By paying attention, you will know when a new scene is being shot, and will have the lens or filter ready when it is called for. Also, pay close attention to what filters are used for certain shots. Watch the D.P. and Director when they are blocking out the scene. This will give you an idea where the camera is to be placed, and it will also be an indication of where you can move the equipment so that it is close by.

Keep all equipment organized and in its proper place. If it is kept in the same place all of the time, it can easily be located when in a hurry. This applies to both the camera truck and equipment cart. When on stage or location, you should have some type of four-wheel cart such as the Magliner or Rubbermaid carts for moving the equipment from place to place. You will have many equipment cases to deal with each day, and it is much easier and quicker if they can be wheeled from place to place instead of individually carried. Whenever the camera is moved to a new location, the cart should also be moved.

Most important, if you make a mistake, tell the D.P. immediately. This information should be communicated to the D.P. quietly so as not to alarm anybody else. The mistake may not be as bad as you think, and you may be able to take care of it without anybody finding out.

As a 1st A.C. you must be able to work very closely with the D.P., Camera Operator, and 2nd A.C. Keep in mind that everybody does things differently. Be flexible and when working with a new crew, try to do things the way they want. After a while you will develop a system of doing things that works best for you. But don't forget that you will always have to adjust your way of doing things when working with others who have their own system.

Don't be afraid to constantly check with your second assistant to be sure that all magazines are loaded, enough film is on hand, expendables are fully stocked, and more. As the first assistant, you are in charge of the overall running of the camera department and by checking and double-checking you will be sure that everything is running smoothly. Remind your assistant that it is in the best interest of both of you that the department looks good. Your constant checking is not an indication that you don't trust the 2nd A.C., only that you want to be sure that there are no problems. If the department is run efficiently, you both have a better chance of being hired back by the D.P. for future jobs.

If you must shoot a locked-off shot or shot where the camera may be mounted on a car mount, crane, or other device, it's important to ensure that the focus and t-stop of the lens are locked off. You may not be able to be alongside the camera during the shot, so you should secure these various components of the lens with a small piece of cloth camera tape. The movement of the car or crane could cause the f-stop or focus to shift during the shot, which would adversely affect your image. By taping them in position, you will not have to worry about problems when viewing the dailies. If using a zoom lens, you should also tape off the focal length so that it doesn't change during the shot. It's better to take the extra time and be safe than to have to shoot the shot over on another day.

When cleaning lenses, always put the lens fluid on the tissue before wiping the lens. Never place lens fluid on the lens element because it could work its way behind the glass and then you would have no way to clean it.

When threading film into the camera, be sure to check your threading with the inching knob before running the camera at speed. This will ensure that the film is traveling smoothly and will not break when you start the camera.

Be sure to use extra support when using long telephoto or zoom lenses. Failure to properly support the lens will affect the lens mount and could also affect the flange focal depth.

When using diopters on the lens, always use the lowest strength and combine it with a longer focal length lens for best results.

When filming in dusty, sandy, or windy conditions, always cover the camera and protect the lens with an optical flat. Dust and sand can work their way into the small crevices on the camera body and could cause a major problem with the motor, movement, and the film. If you don't have any type of camera barney, use a sound blanket or even a large plastic trash bag. Anything that protects the camera is better than nothing.

When attaching nets to the back of lenses, do not use rubber cement, super glue, or nail polish. Always use 1/2 inch transfer tape (also known as snot tape). Any of the other glues or adhesives could damage the coating on the lens element.

Establish a good relationship with the Dolly Grip. Your focus marks are only accurate if the Dolly Grip hits the marks as well. Work out a system of how the Dolly Grip will communicate to you during a shot if he or she misses intended marks.

Remove the lens and unplug the battery when breaking for lunch. Also cover the camera.

Always maintain a professional attitude, and if you are ever unsure of something, do not be afraid to ask. Treat people with respect and they will treat you the same. Always do your job to the best of your ability, and if a mistake is made, admit it so that it can be corrected. Remember that some day you will be in the position of Camera Operator and D.P., dealing with the same situations and problems.

POST-PRODUCTION

As stated in Chapter 3, post-production for the camera department means that all equipment must be cleaned, checked, and packed away so that it can be returned to the rental company. A final inventory of film stock and expendables is usually done and turned in to the production office. Invoices and all other paperwork must be turned in to the production office. If a camera truck was used, it will probably be cleaned out for the next production's use. Finally, the 1st A.C. packs up all of his or her gear and gets ready for that next job call where the entire process starts all over again.

Wrapping Equipment

At the completion of filming, the camera equipment, camera truck, and anything else relating to the camera department must be wrapped. This means that everything should be cleaned and packed away. All equipment must be cleaned, packed, and sent back to the camera rental house. Usually the 1st A.C. wraps out the camera equipment, while the 2nd A.C. wraps out the truck, darkroom, and film stock. Many times, if it is a small production, only the 1st A.C. does the wrap. This process usually takes a few hours, or possibly a whole day, and is usually done the same day shooting ends or the day after shooting has stopped. Clean all camera equipment and place it in the proper case. Remove any identification labels placed on the equipment during the camera prep before putting the equipment in the case. The cleaning of all cases and equipment may seem like a lot of wasted work, but it lets the rental house know that you are a professional and care about the equipment you work with. I always order some type of cleaning supplies with my expendables order so that I can keep the cases clean during a production and also so that I can thoroughly clean everything before returning it to the rental house. The rental house will also feel that the next time they send out equipment for you they do not have to worry about the equipment. You should have copies of all packing lists for all equipment received since the beginning of the production. If you find anything missing, notify the production office immediately so that they are not surprised when the rental house calls them.

RESOURCES

During your career as an assistant cameraman you will rely on a variety of professional resources to enable you to do your job completely. This includes camera manufacturers and rental companies, grip and lighting companies, expendables companies, film laboratories, sellers of film raw stock, professional organizations, and much more. You should have all contact information for these companies readily available in case you need something at the last minute or in case of emergency. Rather than list all of the possible names, addresses, telephone numbers, e-mail addresses, and web sites for the various companies, this information is included in a section of the companion web site for the book: www.cameraassistantmanual.com. Because companies change addresses, telephone numbers, and e-mail addresses quite frequently, I have chosen not to include a list in the book for fear that by the time you read the list much of the information will be inaccurate. The companion web site will be updated on a regular basis so that you should be able to have the most current information for any of the companies listed. In addition to the various companies and suppliers that you will be dealing with, the web site also includes many links to industry-related web sites for listing your resumé and searching for jobs. If you have web sites or know of any web sites of interest that you would like to see included, please feel free to contact me by e-mail.

1ST A.C. REVIEW CHECKLIST (FOCUS PULLER)

- Knows and understands all professional motion picture camera equipment and accessories currently used in the industry
- Reads the script so that he/she is aware of the story and recommends any special equipment that may be needed to carry out specific shots

- Works with the D.P. and/or Camera Operator to choose the camera equipment that will be used on the production
- Recommends the 2nd A.C. and Loader/Trainee to the D.P. and/or Production Manager
- Works with the 2nd A.C. to prepare a list of expendables, which is then given to the production office or Production Manager so that they may be purchased
- Preps the camera package alone or along with the 2nd A.C.; ensures that all equipment is in proper working order
- Responsible for the overall care and maintenance of all camera equipment during production
- Mounts the camera head onto the tripod, dolly, or other support piece and ensures that it is working properly
- Unpacks, assembles, and warms up the camera and all of its components at the start of each shooting day
- Does not leave the camera unattended
- Loads and unloads proper film into the camera for the shots and setups
- Resets the footage counter to zero after each reload
- Resets the buckle switch in the camera if necessary
- Keeps all parts of the camera, including camera body, lenses, filters, and magazines, free from dirt and dust
- Oils and lubes the camera as needed
- Sets the viewfinder eyepiece for each key person looking through the camera
- Before each shot, ensures that the camera is level and balanced
- If the camera is mounted on a tripod, ensures that it is securely positioned and leveled
- Checks to be sure that no lights are kicking into the lens, causing a flare, when the camera is in its proper position
- Places proper lens, filter, and any other accessory on the camera as instructed by the D.P. or Camera Operator
- Checks that lenses and filters are clean before filming
- Sets the t-stop on the lens before each take as instructed by the D.P.
- Measures the distances to subjects during rehearsals and marks the lens or focus marking disk
- Checks the depth of field for each shot as needed
- Follows focus and makes zoom lens moves during takes
- Adjusts the shutter angle, t-stop, or camera speed during a take, as needed and as instructed by the D.P.
- Checks that camera is running at correct speed during filming
- Gives the 2nd A.C. footage readings from the camera after each take

- After each printed take or when instructed by the D.P., checks the gate for hairs or emulsion buildup and requests another take if necessary
- Supervises the transportation and moving of all camera equipment between filming locations
- Works with the 2nd A.C. to move the camera to each new position
- Works with the 2nd A.C. to ensure that all camera batteries are kept fully charged and ready for use
- If there is no 2nd A.C. on the production, then also performs those duties
- Orders additional or special camera equipment as needed
- Checks call sheet daily to be sure any additional camera equipment and crew members are requested if needed
- Arranges for the return of any camera equipment no longer needed
- Arranges for the return and replacement of any damaged camera equipment
- Oversees all aspects of the camera department
- Disassembles the camera and its components at the completion of the shooting day and packs them away into the appropriate cases
- At the completion of filming, wraps and cleans all camera equipment for returning to the rental house
- Provides all the necessary tools and accessories associated with performing the job

5

Problems and Troubleshooting

Troubleshooting may be described as a careful system of finding the cause of a problem and correcting it. When something goes wrong, find out why, and then correct or eliminate the problem. You need common sense and logic, as well as knowledge of the equipment you are working with. If you are familiar with the equipment, you should be able to follow a step-by-step procedure to find and correct almost any problem that you encounter. Always have the instruction manual for the particular camera you are working with close at hand.

Being familiar with the equipment not only involves the ability to put the pieces together, but also feeling comfortable with the equipment. Treat the camera and its accessories gently. Do not force any pieces of equipment that will not fit together. When placing the camera on the head or base plate, slide it on gently and do not just slam it in place. Don't slam the Arriflex SR magazines onto the camera. Place them on firmly but gently. The better you take care of the equipment, the fewer problems you should have.

When you do encounter a problem, the first and most important thing is not to panic. Think about what the problem is and then decide what is the most logical cause. Try to fix it, and if it doesn't work, continue trying to correct the problem by process of elimination. Try the obvious first, eliminate what is not causing the problem, and eventually narrow down the possible choices and find out the cause.

It is important that you check only one thing at a time. For example, if the camera won't run, and you change the battery, the power cable, and the fuse at the same time, how will you know which of these was the cause of the problem? Finding the cause of most problems should usually take only a few minutes, but there will be some instances when you cannot find the cause yourself and then must telephone the rental house and ask for help. Never be afraid to contact the rental house regarding any questions you may have about the equipment.

They would rather have you ask about something than to try to do it incorrectly.

Whenever a problem occurs, it is often best to try to keep it within the camera department whenever possible. Sometimes you don't even need to tell the Director of Photography (D.P.) about it. They have enough on their mind and don't need to be worried about small camera problems. Many times you will be able to fix or correct the problem without anybody ever knowing that there even was a problem. For example, if a magazine keeps jamming, have the 2nd Assistant Cameraman (A.C.) contact the rental house and arrange to swap the magazine out for a new one. Let the Unit Production Manager or Production Coordinator know that a magazine needs to be swapped. This can be done in a short period of time without the D.P. ever knowing about it. The D.P. has enough on his or her mind and doesn't need to be bothered with something as minor as a magazine problem. Just deal with it and the D.P. never has to know there was a problem. It's all part of being a professional.

When something does go wrong, remain calm and don't freak out. There is no use causing panic on the set, especially among the Director, D.P., and Assistant Director. A few years ago I was working on a 16 mm shoot with an Arriflex SR2 that was owned by the D.P. The matte box didn't quite fit tightly on the support rods no matter what I did. While moving to a new setup I picked up the camera and the matte box fell off. One of the filter trays, holding a Tiffen Enhancer filter, fell to the floor causing the filter to shatter into many pieces. Unfortunately everybody was looking directly at me and instead of panicking I simply apologized to the D.P. and told him that I would have a new filter on set within the hour. I made a call to an expendable supply company that was just down the street from our location and arranged for a production assistant to pick up the new filter, which, by the way, I charged to my personal account. By the time the D.P. had the new setup lit and ready to shoot, the replacement filter had arrived. I didn't panic and get upset, but rather took responsibility and handled the situation in a calm and professional manner. Things will go wrong and they may or may not be your fault. If you act like a professional and handle the problem quickly, you may still get yelled at, but everybody should respect you for the professional manner in which you handled the situation.

Because it is not possible to foresee every problem, I only mention some of the typical ones that can and will happen in the course of a film production. Many of these things have actually happened to me on various shoots. Sometimes I was able to correct the problem quickly, but other times I had to call the rental house and ask for their advice, or have a technician come to the location to fix or replace the camera or accessory. These problems are listed in no particular order.

CAMERA WILL NOT RUN

When the camera will not run, first check to see if the battery is connected to the camera. This is the most logical and most common reason why the camera won't run. Also check to see if the battery contains a full charge and if it is the correct voltage for the camera being used. Be sure that you have the proper voltage battery for the camera system you are using. The battery may be dual-voltage, and the switch on the battery may be in the wrong position. If the camera has one, check the buckle trip switch inside the camera to see if it is in the proper position. The buckle trip shuts off the camera when there is a rollout or when film becomes jammed in the camera. Reset the switch if necessary, which should correct the problem. If the battery is connected and the buckle trip switch is in its proper position, try a new battery cable. If this doesn't work, try a new battery.

Often you may have to give the battery cable a closer inspection in order to locate a problem. It may even be necessary to take the plug apart to check that all the internal wires of the cable are properly connected to the connections on the end of the plug. This won't be apparent without taking the plug apart. You should have a soldering iron in your ditty bag in case you need to repair and resolder a broken cable. Many assistants have battery- or propane-powered soldering irons in their kit, which can be used anywhere. These are especially good when working in remote locations and you don't have access to electricity. If you do need to make any minor repairs to cables, it is best to take them off set and do the repair on the camera truck or out of view of the cast and crew. Producers and directors can get a little nervous if they see one of the camera assistants taking equipment apart and attempting to repair it.

Some cameras have a safety feature built into them that will not allow the camera to run if the camera body door is not closed completely. Make sure the door is closed and latched before turning on the camera. If the camera still will not run, change the fuse, if you are able to gain access to it. You can change the electronic circuit boards in some cameras including those from Panavision. I believe that it is a good idea to first check the fuse before resorting to changing the electronic circuit boards. If all of these actions still do not correct the problem, call the rental house for help. It is important to remember when this or any problem occurs to check only one thing at a time. Before changing fuses or circuit boards, always disconnect power to the camera. When trying to determine why the camera will not run, disconnect all electrical accessories from the camera and try to run it. This helps to determine if any accessories are causing the problem. Check all electrical accessories one at a time to see which one, if any, may be causing the problem. Sometimes simply disconnecting everything, including the camera from the battery, waiting a few minutes, and then reconnecting everything will solve the problem.

Many of the newer cameras have a computer processor that controls the camera functions. These can malfunction, especially when there are temperature changes in the shooting environment. Simply disconnecting power for a few minutes and then reconnecting may be enough to fix this problem. Some cameras have a thermal fuse and if this fuse trips, you need to power off the camera and leave it off for a few minutes before powering it back up again. Also, many newer cameras have a master power switch that must be turned on before you can run the camera. If the master power switch is not turned on, pushing the RUN button of the camera will have no effect.

When mounting the camera to the head or sliding base plate, you usually must screw a 3/8 inch 16 bolt into the bottom of the camera. Some cameras have circuit boards in their base. Using a mounting bolt that is too long may cause the bolt to come in contact with the circuit boards, shorting them out and causing the camera to not run. Be sure to check that you are not using a bolt that is too long before mounting the camera.

Some cameras require a minimum and maximum voltage amount in order for them to run. This is not controlled by the camera assistant but is something that is preset in the camera at the factory. In other words, if for some reason the battery voltage falls below a certain level, or rises above a certain level, the camera will automatically shut off and not run. Check your camera manual and battery voltage whenever this happens. Be sure that the battery is functioning properly so that these amounts are within the guidelines for the camera system you are using. Finally, if the camera does not run, be sure to check that the run switch is in the "on" position.

If the camera won't run, check the speed setting. You may have the camera speed set to a speed outside the range of the camera. Be sure you know the speed range of the camera you are using to ensure the proper running speed. If you are filming in extreme cold weather conditions, be sure that the camera is properly winterized for shooting in the cold. If not, it may run slowly or not at all.

BATTERY LOSES POWER

Loss of battery power is one of the most common problems you will encounter. The battery may not be fully charged or may be unable to hold a charge. Try to completely discharge the battery and then place it on charge overnight. If this does not solve the problem, then have the battery checked and replaced if necessary. You should never go out on a shoot with only one battery, just in case this does happen. By having an additional battery, you will not have to stop filming until another one can be obtained. At the very minimum you should have at least two batteries.

LENS WILL NOT FOCUS

One reason the lens may not focus is that the lens is not seated properly in the lens mount. This means that the lens is not correctly mounted on the camera. Remove the lens and check the lens mount of the camera to see if there are any obstructions. Thoroughly check and clean the lens mount and then reinsert the lens. Also check the back of the lens to see if there is anything that would prevent the lens from mounting properly. If the lens and the lens mount seem all right, reinsert the lens and check the focus again.

Another reason that the lens might not focus is that the ground glass of the camera is inserted incorrectly. Check the ground glass and reinsert it if necessary. The ground glass should be inserted into the camera with the matte or dull side facing toward the mirror of the shutter.

Another cause of lens focus problems is that the lens is damaged. Check this by using a focus chart and checking the lens as you originally did during the camera prep. Place the chart at various distances from the camera, and then check the eye focus mark on the lens to see if they match. If a problem is detected when comparing the eye focus to the measured focus, the lens should be returned to the rental house for repair and a replacement lens should be obtained.

A few years ago I was 1st A.C. on a feature film. One of the shots we did was a very long fluid master dolly move leading two characters through a large building. After the first take, the Camera Operator said the shot was soft and out of focus so we did it again. We did two more takes, but each time the operator said it was soft when we cut the camera. The D.P., Camera Operator, and I each checked the lens focus by eye and arrived at approximately 30 or 40 feet. The measured distance was approximately 7 feet, which is exactly where I had it focused for each take. I removed the lens and gave it a light shake and it sounded like a baby rattle. The elements inside the lens had all come loose. After some investigation we discovered that some of the grips had a contest during the lunch break to see who could make the boom arm of the dolly go up and down the fastest. Unfortunately they did this with the camera and lens on the dolly. This caused the lens elements to come loose, which caused our focus problem. So now when I break for lunch, I always try to remove the lens from the camera as a safety precaution.

One of the most common reasons that the lens appears out of focus when looking through the eyepiece is that the diopter adjustment of the eyepiece was changed when you were away from the camera. Each time anyone looks through the eyepiece, check that the diopter adjustment ring is set to the appropriate mark. Because each person's vision is different, the image may look sharp and in focus to one person, but blurry and out of focus to another.

A heavy fog or diffusion filter in front of the lens may prevent you from obtaining a sharp image through the viewfinder. Check the lens with the filters removed to see if you can obtain proper focus. In addition, a behind-the-lens filter may also create focus problems. This can only be seen when viewing dailies because the filter is not visible through the viewfinder. If you are planning on using any behind-the-lens filters, it is a good idea to shoot some tests beforehand to be sure that there will be no focus problems.

Many lenses have focus markings in feet and also in meters. The marks are often on opposite sides of the lens, so you must be careful when placing the lens on the camera that the proper markings are facing you. I know of an instance of a first assistant placing the lens on the camera with the meter markings facing him. He measured the distance in feet and inches, but set the focus according to the meter scale, thinking it was feet and inches. Needless to say, all of the shots were out of focus until he realized what he had done.

Finally, check to be sure that both the front and rear elements of the lens are clean. Dirty or smudged lens elements make it quite difficult to obtain proper focus of the image.

If working with video cameras the back focus adjustment of the lens may be off, which would cause the lens to not focus properly. Check and adjust the back focus; this should correct the problem. The steps for adjusting back focus are:

- Place a focus chart or Siemens star chart 8 to 10 feet from the camera.
- Open the f-stop to its widest opening.
- Zoom all the way in to the tightest focal length of the lens and focus on the chart.
- Zoom out to the widest angle focal length of the lens.
- Loosen the back focus adjustment knob and turn the back focus ring until the chart is in focus.
- Zoom back in to the tightest focal length and check that the chart remains sharp at all points within the zoom.

- Repeat these steps until the chart is sharp at the widest angle focal length, the most telephoto focal length, and all focal lengths in between.

CAMERA DOES NOT STOP WHEN SWITCHED TO “OFF”

The camera may not stop when switched to the OFF position, especially when you are using a handgrip with an ON/OFF switch or a zoom control with an ON/OFF switch. If there are any accessories plugged into the camera that contain an on/off switch, check to see that this switch is in the OFF position. If it is in the ON position, the camera will continue to run when you turn the main camera run switch off.

As stated in the section Camera Will Not Run, when mounting the camera to the head or sliding base plate, you must screw a 3/8 inch 16 bolt into the bottom of the camera. Some cameras have circuit boards in their base. Using a mounting bolt that is too long may cause the bolt to come in contact with the circuit boards, shorting them out, which may cause the camera to continue running. Be sure to check that you are not using a bolt that is too long before mounting the camera.

CAMERA STARTS AND STOPS INTERMITTENTLY

If the camera starts and stops intermittently, the battery might not be fully charged. Changing batteries should correct the problem. If the battery cable is loose, reinsert it into either the camera or the battery. A loose wire in the power cable can also be one of the causes that you might not be able to see by just looking at the cable. If you suspect this, try wiggling the cable at the point where it is connected to the camera and also where it is connected to the battery to see if this causes any change. If the camera starts and stops, it is a good indication that there is a short in it. If your ditty bag contains a voltmeter, use it to check the contacts on the cable to see if there is current flowing through the cable. Try a new cable and have the other one checked as soon as possible. If you have a soldering iron and solder available, you may be able to repair a damaged power cable without sending it back to the rental house.

On Panavision cameras you may find it necessary to change the circuit boards to correct this problem. The important thing to remember when changing circuit boards in Panavision cameras is to always change all of the circuit boards at the same time. Never replace just one or two of the boards. Send the old boards back to the rental house and request a replacement set to have on hand.

Faulty accessories or a variable speed control may be the problem as well. If you have any accessories or a variable speed control attached to the camera, try removing these items and running the camera without them attached. A faulty video sync box may also cause the camera to start and stop intermittently. If you suspect any of these external devices, have them checked as soon as possible.

As stated earlier, if the camera won't run or stops running, check the speed setting. A speed setting outside of the speed range of the camera motor may cause the camera not to run properly, to suddenly stop running, or to not run at all. Be sure you know the speed range of the camera you are using to ensure the proper running speed.

CAMERA IS NOISY

The most common reason for a noisy camera is that the film is not threaded properly in the camera. The top or bottom loop may be too large or too small, causing the movement to work harder moving the film through the camera, which results in the movement being a little noisier than usual. Rethread the camera and set the loops to the proper length. On many cameras the loop may be set when threading the magazine, so you have to either rethread the magazine or change magazines. Check that all rollers are closed and that the film perforations are engaged on the sprockets correctly. If the camera has an adjustable pitch control, adjust it so that the camera is running as quietly as possible when it is threaded correctly. Sometimes none of these solutions makes the camera any quieter, so the only thing to do is to cover the camera with a sound barney to cut down on the noise. If the sound mixer is picking up any camera noise, you may also need to place an optical flat in front of the lens to minimize the noise being picked up by the sound microphones.

I have also found that some film stocks cause the camera to run noisier than others. Because of differences in the manufacturing of the different film stocks and emulsions, some film may be slightly thicker or thinner than other film. This is also true when shooting black and white versus color film. Black and white film is slightly thinner than color film and may cause the camera to be noisier as the film is running through it.

I was once working on a small production and the camera ran noisier than usual. The Director asked me if there was anything that could be done, and I explained that it was because of the film stock we were using. It was a little thinner than the stock we had used previously. The Director was not satisfied with my explanation so he telephoned the person from whom he had rented the camera and asked that he come to the location to check the camera. When he arrived, he asked me what film stock we were using. When I told him what it was, he told the Director that the film stock was causing the noise problem and that there was nothing he could do about it.

MAGAZINE IS NOISY

The film spooling off the core and rubbing against the side of the magazine may cause magazine noise. Hold the magazine flat in your hands and give the cover of the magazine a firm slap so that the film settles back onto the spool or core. When the magazine is already placed on the camera, give both sides of the magazine a firm slap to force the film back onto the spool. If the film loop is set when threading the magazine, a loop of incorrect size will also cause the magazine to be noisy. To correct this, rethread the magazine so that the loops are the proper size. There are some newer magazines that have a timing adjustment. Check with the rental house if you are not sure how to adjust the timing on the magazines that have this feature. A film jam inside the magazine may also make it noisier than usual. If the noise gets progressively louder, you should probably stop using the magazine, remove it, and rethread the camera with a new magazine. Have the 2nd A.C. check the noisy magazine and if necessary swap it out at the rental company for a new magazine.

SHUTTER DOES NOT SPIN (NO FLICKER THROUGH THE VIEWFINDER)

While a shutter rarely fails to spin, I have heard of an instance when the Camera Operator could not see any flicker through the viewfinder when shooting. This is a good indication that the shutter is not spinning. The camera was running and film was traveling through the camera and magazine, but the shutter was not spinning. Unfortunately there is really nothing you can do in the field and if this should occur, you should contact the rental house immediately and return the camera. The one time that I know of this happening, there was a drive belt that had broken. This belt was what turned the mirror shutter when the camera was running or when you turned the inching knob. This belt could only be replaced by a camera technician at the camera rental company.

YOU ARE UNABLE TO THREAD FILM INTO THE GATE AREA

If you are unable to thread film into the gate area, be sure that you have turned the inching knob to advance the pull down claw so that it is withdrawn from the aperture plate. Also, check to see if the registration pin is withdrawn from the aperture plate. These are the two most common reasons why you cannot thread the film. If after checking these two items you still encounter the problem, check to see that there are no film chips stuck in the gate area, preventing the film from threading properly. If the camera has a removable aperture plate, be sure that it is inserted correctly. Also check that the pressure plate is in the proper position.

FILM DOES NOT TAKE UP

If the film does not take up and you are using an older camera that uses some type of belt to drive the take-up side, check that you have the right size belt and that it is connected properly to the magazine. You should always have a spare drive belt with the camera equipment. On magazines using the drive belt, the belt must be placed on the correct side of the magazine for it to take up properly. It should be either connected to the feed side or the take-up side, depending on whether the film is going forward or backward. Check the belt and adjust it as necessary. Check with the rental house so that you are sure how to connect the belt properly. Have extra belts available in case one breaks while filming.

Many camera magazines have electrical contacts built into them so that when connected to the camera, the torque motor of the magazine receives power. If these contacts are dirty, the film will not take up properly. Check the contacts and clean them if necessary.

Some cameras also have the ability to run either forward or reverse. If the switch is in one position on the camera and the opposite position on the magazine, the film will not take up properly. Make sure that the switches on the camera and magazine are in the same position. Check the take-up side of the magazine to see if the film end has come off of the take-up core. Rethread the camera; this should correct the problem.

Check to be sure that you are using the proper magazine on the camera. You may have a newer model of camera and be trying to use an older model of magazine. Also with some manufacturers, there are separate magazines for high speed and regular speed cameras. These magazines are often not interchangeable between cameras.

Incorrect magazine tension or a damaged magazine clutch may also be the cause of film not taking up in the magazine. If you suspect either of these things, it is best to swap out the magazine for a new one and let the rental company deal with it. Many assistants don't have the proper tools or qualifications to adjust the magazine tension. Plus, most rental companies would prefer that an assistant not try to repair their equipment.

If you are using film on a daylight spool and the take-up reel is also a daylight spool, be sure to check that the flanges of the spool are not bent, preventing the film from winding properly on the spool.

CAMERA DOOR DOES NOT CLOSE

On some cameras the door does not close when the sprocket guide rollers are not closed, or when the movement is pulled away from the gate for threading. Be sure that both of these are in the correct position for filming, and the door is closed properly. Also check the edges around the door where it meets the camera to be sure that there are no obstructions such as a piece of film. Clean out anything that may be blocking the door and it should close properly.

CAMERA STOPS WHILE FILMING

The most common reason that the camera stops while filming is that the film jams in either the camera or the magazine. Check that the loops are the proper size and adjust them if necessary. Again, if the loop is set in the magazine, it must be removed from the camera and rethreaded, or a new magazine placed on the camera. When the film jams it can become ripped or torn, leaving a piece of film stuck in the magazine throat or in the gate of the camera. The important thing to remember when clearing any film jam is not to force any part of the camera or magazine. Gently slide the film from side to side or up and down until it will come out cleanly. If you try to force it out, you can damage the camera movement or the gears of the magazine. After clearing any film jam, clean the camera with compressed air to remove any film chips or emulsion that may have become trapped in the gears of the movement.

Another common cause of the camera stopping is that the film has rolled out. Many cameras have a safety feature built into them that shuts off power to the camera when it runs out of film. Be aware of the footage counter when filming so this does not happen. Also, when threading the new magazine on the camera, be sure to adjust the buckle switch, if the camera has one, so that the film travels smoothly through the camera.

FILM JAMS IN CAMERA

If the film jams in the camera, the film loop could be the wrong size. Rethread the camera or the magazine and adjust the loops to the proper size. If the magazine is not threaded properly, it can cause the camera motor to work harder to move the film through the camera, which results in the film becoming jammed. Be sure that all sprocket rollers are closed and the film is moving smoothly through the gate. Before running the camera, you should always check the threading with the inching knob after placing a new magazine on the camera.

FILM RIPS OR HAS TORN PERFORATIONS

Film may rip or have torn perforations for the same reasons that cause the film to jam. Improper loop sizes can result in the film becoming ripped or torn as it goes through the camera or magazine. Check the loop size in the camera and adjust if necessary. Rethread the magazine and adjust any magazine loops accordingly. Panavision cameras have a small pin located inside the camera body that is used as a guide when setting your loop size. If the top loop is too long, it may catch on this pin and tear perforations. Be sure to check your threading and loop size by turning the inching knob before running the camera.

FILM LOSES LOOP

If the film loses the loop, check the pull down claw and registration pin to be sure that they are not bent in any way. Incorrectly threading the camera or magazine can cause loss of the loop. When threading, be sure that you set the correct loop size in the camera or magazine. Also check to be sure that the film is properly engaged on the sprocket rollers and that the sprocket roller guides are engaged correctly. You may also need to adjust the pitch control, if the camera has one, in order to quiet the camera and also ensure that the proper loop size is maintained.

THERE ARE SCRATCHES ON THE FILM

Whenever the film scratches, scratch test the entire system exactly as you did during the camera prep (see Chapter 4). The cause of the scratches could be from a problem inside the magazine throat or in the gears or rollers of the magazine. It could also be coming from inside the camera at any number of places. There may be dirt or emulsion buildup in the gate that should be cleaned out before you continue to shoot. Dirt or dust in the magazine can also cause scratches on the film. The best way to determine where the scratch is occurring is to place the magazine on the camera and thread the camera normally. Run some film through the camera. Using a permanent ink marker, place an "X" on the film at the following places: where it exits the magazine, enters the gate, exits the gate, and re-enters the magazine. Check the film at these marks to determine where the scratches occurred. An incorrect loop size may also cause scratches on the film. If necessary, you may have to send some of the magazines, or even the camera, back to the rental house for replacement or repair. In the extreme case, scratches on the film may be caused by damaged or faulty film stock or even by improper handling at the processing laboratory.

CAMERA DOES NOT RUN AT SYNC SPEED

One reason that the camera does not run at sync speed may be a problem with the battery. A weak battery could affect the speed of the camera. Replace the battery with one that is fully charged and the camera should run at sync speed. Another common cause is that the motor switch on the camera is set to the variable position instead of the sync position. Reset the switch to the sync position. On Panavision cameras, a malfunctioning circuit board could also cause this to happen. If you are able, change the circuit boards to see if this corrects the problem. Also, if the magazine or the camera is threaded incorrectly, it may have an effect on the motor, causing it to lose speed. Check the threading of both and adjust as necessary.

As I stated when discussing the problem of the camera starting and stopping intermittently, check any accessories that may be attached to the camera. Disconnect the accessories and run the camera to see if this corrects the problem.

VIEWING SYSTEM IS BLACKED OUT

When you cannot see anything when looking through the eyepiece, the viewing system is blacked out. This could be due to one of a number of problems. The shutter may be closed, which makes the eyepiece dark. Turn the camera on and off quickly, or turn the inching knob to clear the shutter. The eyepiece may be set to the closed position, which allows no light to enter the eyepiece. Check the eyepiece control lever, and set it to the open position for viewing. When the lens is stopped down to its smallest opening, it may be difficult to see anything when looking through the eyepiece. Also, if there are any neutral density filters in front of the lens, it darkens the image when viewed, making it appear totally dark. The most obvious reason for not being able to see anything through the eyepiece is that there is someone or something blocking the lens, or possibly that the lens cap is in place. Remove the lens cap or whatever is blocking the front of the lens so that you can see clearly. Many cameras also have a switch or lever that is used to switch the viewing system when filming with anamorphic lenses. Check to see if this switch or lever has been bumped and is blocking the viewing system or is not in the proper position for the lenses being used.

When doing certain special effects shots and using some older cameras, you may be using a camera that contains a rack-over viewing system. If the viewfinder is not in the correct position, you will not be able to see when looking through it. Be sure to place it in the correct position for viewing.

LENS FLARES ARE SEEN WHEN LOOKING THROUGH THE VIEWFINDER

Lens flares are usually an indication that there is a light or lights shining directly into the camera lens. Placing a hard matte on the matte box or adjusting the matte box eyebrow will most often eliminate these flares. Sometimes you may have to request that a grip set a flag between the camera and the light so that the flare is eliminated. Keep in mind that often you will not see a lens flare through the lens. You must stand in front of the camera and look at the lens from various angles to see most lens flares.

ZOOM LENS MOTOR RUNS ERRATICALLY

If the zoom lens motor runs erratically, there may be a short in the zoom control or in the power cable from the motor to the control. Replace the zoom motor power cable; if this does not correct the problem, replace the zoom control. Check the motor gear where it attaches to the lens. There may be some chips in the motor gear teeth or lens gear teeth that could cause the motor to slip. Replace the motor gear or lens gear as necessary. The zoom motor may also run without your having to touch the zoom control. Some zoom controls have an adjustment inside the control that must be set to prevent the motor from running without being engaged. Be sure to check with the rental house before attempting to take apart any piece of equipment.

ZOOM LENS DOES NOT ZOOM THROUGHOUT ITS ENTIRE RANGE OF FOCAL LENGTHS

Some zoom lenses, especially those for 16 mm cameras, have a macro setting so that you can do extreme close-up shots. To set the lens in macro, press a button on the side of the lens and move the zoom control ring into the macro range marked on the lens. This limits the range of the zoom and when looking through the lens and zooming, it appears that you are focusing. Because the lens is now in the macro setting, you are actually focusing when you turn the zoom ring of the lens. This allows you to get an extreme close-up of an object. So, if you are attempting to zoom and the lens does not move throughout its entire range, it is probably in the macro setting. Simply press the macro button on the side of the lens and move the zoom barrel until it is back in normal mode.

TRIPOD HEAD DOES NOT PAN OR TILT

The most obvious reason that the tripod head will not pan or tilt is that the pan and tilt locks are engaged. Check the locks for each and release them if necessary. Check the head to be sure that there are no obstructions that could prevent the head from panning or tilting. Remove any obstruction, and the problem should be corrected. Never force the head in either direction. You may worsen the problem, making it impossible for you to correct in the field. The head must then be sent to the rental house for repair and a replacement head sent to you. On gear heads, check that the gear adjustment lever is not in the neutral position. When in neutral, turning either the pan or tilt wheel has no effect on the head. Place the pan and tilt gear adjustment lever in one of the gear positions, which should allow you to pan and tilt with ease. On most gear heads there are usually two sets of locks for the pan and tilt. One is for the pan and tilt controls, to lock them in position, and the other is for the pan and tilt movements, to physically lock them in position, even when the gears are in the neutral position. Be sure that all locks are released before trying to pan or tilt the head.

TRIPOD LEGS DO NOT SLIDE UP AND DOWN

Quite often, when in a hurry you may forget to release the locks for the legs before attempting to adjust the height of them. By releasing the tripod leg locks, they should slide up and down smoothly. Tripod legs get dirty after much use and usually begin to stick when you try to adjust them. Clean the legs regularly and if using aluminum or metal tripods spray them with a light coating of silicone spray. This should keep them in working order and help them to last longer.

THE IMAGE ON THE VIDEO MONITOR IS OUT OF FOCUS OR TILTED TO THE SIDE

On most camera video taps there are adjustments for both the focus and the position of the image on the outside of the video tap. If the image on the monitor is out of focus or tilted, turn these adjustment knobs until the image comes into focus or the image is in the correct position. If this still does not correct the problem, remove the cover of the video tap, if you are able to, and turn the adjustment knobs located inside. Sometimes if the video tap is not firmly mounted to the film camera, the image appears tilted or out of focus. Check to be sure that it is mounted securely and correctly to the camera.

SHOOTING IN EXTREME COLD WEATHER

If you will be working in extreme cold weather situations for an extended period, leave the camera equipment in the camera truck at night so that it remains at a consistent cold temperature throughout the production. If it is necessary to bring the camera equipment inside after being in a cold camera truck overnight, try to warm it up as quickly as possible so that condensation does not form. Open all lens, filter, magazine, and accessory cases so that they can reach room temperature. You may also want to remove lens caps to help the lenses warm up.

Whenever possible, obtain the appropriate size barneys for the camera and magazines so that you can protect them as much as possible from the cold. Also be sure to let the rental house know if you will be doing any extended filming in cold weather. They may need to add a special heater element or change the lubricant in the camera to one that is better suited to the cold.

You should also keep in mind that the film stock can become very brittle in cold temperatures and should be used as soon as possible after you have removed it from the manufacturer's sealed can. You may want to keep loaded magazines in a warm, dry location until ready for filming. But sometimes it is actually better to keep loaded magazines in the same environment and temperature that you will be shooting in. I worked on a music video that was shot in Boulder, Colorado, in late November. We were filming outside using an Arriflex 16SR2 camera. At the D.P.'s request I loaded all of the magazines, placed them in their case and kept them outside with us during shooting. There were no problems with film breaking during shooting because it wasn't going from one temperature to another, which could actually cause more problems than keeping the film in the temperature at which you are filming. In any case, use your best judgment and always consult with the D.P. if you are unsure.

SHOOTING IN EXTREME HEAT

Film stock may deteriorate very quickly if subjected to very high heat for even short periods of time. When working in extreme heat, you should have coolers or some other type of container to keep the film in. Film should be kept in the cooler or container in a cool, dry location whenever possible. In addition you should process any film as soon as possible after it has been exposed. See the section in Chapter 3 on proper storage of motion picture film.

WHEN FILMING IN OR AROUND SALT WATER, THE CAMERA AND MAGAZINE FALL INTO THE WATER

Before taking any equipment from the rental house, if you know that you will be filming around salt water, ask them what you should do if any of the equipment falls into the water. The following procedure is the accepted method, but you should check with the rental house beforehand just to be safe. First, rinse the camera completely in fresh water as soon as possible. Don't worry about getting the camera wet. It's already wet from the salt water. Salt water is highly corrosive and can damage the working parts of the camera very quickly. The faster it is removed, the fewer problems you should have. Don't allow a fully loaded magazine of film to dry. Rinse off the magazine completely, with the film still inside, and ship the entire magazine, packed in fresh water, to the lab for processing. I was told a story about a 1000-foot magazine containing a full roll of exposed film that had fallen into salt water. The assistant immediately removed the magazine from the salt water, immersed it in a cooler of fresh water, and sent it to the lab packed in the fresh water. The lab was able to process the film and there was very little if any damage to the image.

A FUSE BLOWS WHEN CONNECTING ELECTRICAL ACCESSORIES

Blowing a fuse when connecting electrical accessories is a common problem that can be easily corrected. The important thing to remember when connecting any electrical accessories is always to disconnect the power to the camera before attaching the accessories. If the camera has a master power switch, be sure to turn it off before connecting or disconnecting any electrical accessory. If the camera is connected to a power source, the connection of any electrical accessory may cause a power surge to the motor, which will then cause a fuse to blow. It is often best to disconnect the battery before connecting any external electronic accessory to the camera.

SHOOTING OUTSIDE USING TUNGSTEN-BALANCED FILM WITHOUT AN 85 FILTER TO CORRECT THE EXPOSURE

If you are using negative film, the lab can usually correct the color during processing. If necessary you may use an orange color gel, which is the same color as the number 85 glass filter, in front of the lens. Eastman Kodak manufactures a gel that is called an 85 Wratten Gel. It gives the same effect as a glass 85 filter placed in front of the camera. While the Kodak Wratten Gel looks very similar to a CTO lighting gel, the Wratten Gel is optically superior to the lighting gel. I recommend requesting some of these Wratten Gels when ordering the expendables so that you have them available in case of emergencies. Many assistants carry these gels in their ditty bags just in case they encounter this situation. Be sure to properly adjust the exposure setting when using an 85 Wratten Gel or glass filter.

SHOOTING INSIDE WITH TUNGSTEN LIGHT DAYLIGHT-BALANCED FILM, AND NO 80A FILTER FOR CORRECTION

This problem is similar to the previous one. You may use a number 80A Kodak Wratten Gel in front of the lens to correct the exposure. You can also instruct the lab to make the necessary corrections during processing. A few years ago a production company that I was working for mistakenly purchased daylight-balanced film for a shoot that was being done entirely on stage using tungsten lights. I sent a Production Assistant to a local camera shop to purchase a Kodak 80A Wratten Gel filter. I taped the filter to the optical flat in the matte box, and the D.P. made the necessary lighting and exposure changes. We shot the commercial and it turned out just fine. As with the 85 filter, be sure to adjust your exposure accordingly when using the 80A Wratten Gel or glass filter.

WHEN SHOOTING A TELEVISION MONITOR OR COMPUTER SCREEN, A ROLL BAR MOVES THROUGH THE SCREEN

When shooting TV screens and computer monitors you need to use a sync box to eliminate the roll bar. The camera should also have a variable shutter so that you can sync the camera to the monitor or screen.

When shooting at 30 frames per second (f.p.s.) or, more precisely, 29.97 f.p.s., the shutter angle should be set to 180 degrees. When shooting at 24 f.p.s. or, more precisely, 23.976 f.p.s., the shutter angle should be set to 144 degrees.

PROJECTED IMAGE IS SHAKY OR UNSTEADY

A shaky or unsteady projected image will only be noticed after the film has been exposed, developed, and projected. The most common cause of this problem is improper registration of the camera movement. What this means is that the film is not positioned properly in the gate area and as a result is not moving through the mechanism smoothly. If you suspect a problem with the camera movement you should shoot some tests before sending the camera back for repair or replacement. If you don't have time to shoot tests, I recommend sending the camera back to the rental house and obtaining a new camera. Let the rental house determine what the problem is. On some cameras, there may not be a problem with the camera but rather the magazine was not placed on the camera properly or the film was simply not placed securely in the gate area during threading. You should eliminate any of these causes before sending the camera back to the rental house. Before shooting, during the camera prep, the first assistant should have shot a registration test to check the registration of the camera. Unless the camera has been mishandled, dropped, or otherwise shaken or jarred in some way, the registration should not suddenly be off if you correctly checked it during prep.

In addition to problems with the camera registration, shaky images may also be caused by film stock with irregularly punched perforations, an error in printing the film, or possibly unsteady projection. If you can shoot some tests using a different film stock batch, this will help to determine if the error is in the film's perforations. Checking with the lab and seeing if there is any problem with their machines that print the film will confirm or eliminate that cause, and double-checking the projector threading should confirm or eliminate any projector problems.

PROJECTED IMAGE IS OUT OF FOCUS

Many of the causes discussed with regard to the lens not focusing also apply to a projected image that is out of focus. A few additional causes of out-of-focus images that would most often only be noticed after the film has been shot and processed are discussed next.

If the film was not set in the gate area securely, the film may have moved slightly as it moved through the camera. This can be a registration problem requiring that the camera be serviced and a new camera be obtained to continue shooting. The flange focal depth of the camera may be off, which would cause the image to be out of focus. You may still be able to focus the image through the viewfinder, but the image on film will not be in focus. You should check the depth with a flange focal depth gauge to be sure it is set properly according to the camera manufacturer.

The lens markings may be off and unless you checked the lenses completely during the camera prep, you may not notice this. If you suspect this problem, you should thoroughly check each lens using a focus test chart.

The first assistant may have based the focus setting on incorrect depth-of-field calculations. This should be noticed when looking through the viewfinder, but depending on the shooting conditions, it may be difficult to judge until you see the projected image.

SHOOTING IN OTHER COUNTRIES

When planning on filming in another country, especially one that uses a different electrical system than that used in the United States, be sure that you have the proper electrical adapters or converters with you. This is especially important if you are taking equipment from the United States to another country. You will need to charge batteries and power a laptop computer or other electrical device. Having the proper adapters or converter can mean the difference between a smoothly running shoot and a disaster.

TROUBLESHOOTING TIPS

I have often found that the simplest solution is often the best when it comes to troubleshooting. Sometimes when you encounter a problem, it is best just to disconnect or disassemble everything and then connect or assemble it again. Surprisingly this sometimes works to correct whatever the problem was. There may have been a loose connection somewhere that is corrected simply by removing and then reattaching the item. I actually had a camera assistant telephone me from across the country to ask how to get the microforce zoom motor to work on an Arriflex 35BL camera. He explained everything he had done, and the motor just would not operate properly. I suggested that he disconnect all accessories and the battery from the camera and then reconnect them. After doing this he reported that everything was working fine. While he was not able to determine what or why there was a problem, at least he didn't have the problem any longer and shooting could continue. In any case, be sure to have the item in question checked as soon as possible.

Try the obvious solution first and then continue in a step-by-step manner until you find out what the cause of the problem is. You will most likely encounter some different problems from those listed here, but if you are familiar with the equipment, you should have no trouble finding and correcting almost any problem that you come across. If you are not sure of how to fix a particular problem, call the rental house for their help. Most rental houses will send a technician to your location if you cannot fix the problem in the field. Don't try to fix something yourself if you are not sure what to do. And as I stated earlier, remain calm; don't panic. Quite often you can solve many problems without anybody else on the crew even knowing that the problem occurred.

6

Cameras

As a camera assistant you will be working with many different camera systems throughout your career. You should be familiar with as many different cameras as possible. This section contains basic information such as format, magazine sizes, and simple line drawings of the threading diagrams of cameras and magazines for most of the cameras currently used in the film industry.

The threading diagrams included here are not meant to teach you how to load the magazines or thread the cameras. They are intended only as a reference, in case you have forgotten about a specific camera system. If you want to learn how to load magazines or thread cameras, you should contact a camera rental house that has the particular camera you are interested in. I recommend obtaining instruction manuals and reference books for all professional cameras that you will be working with. You never know when you will be working with a specific camera, and it may be many months between jobs with a particular camera. Having the instruction manuals or books about all cameras will allow you to refresh your memory for any cameras and equipment that you may have forgotten.

To learn more about any of these cameras, speak with a representative at any professional motion picture camera rental house.

Remember: These illustrations are to be used only as a reference.

AATON A-MINIMA

Format: 16 mm
Magazine sizes: 200′ Coaxial

For camera and magazine illustrations and threading diagrams, see Figures 6.1 and 6.2.

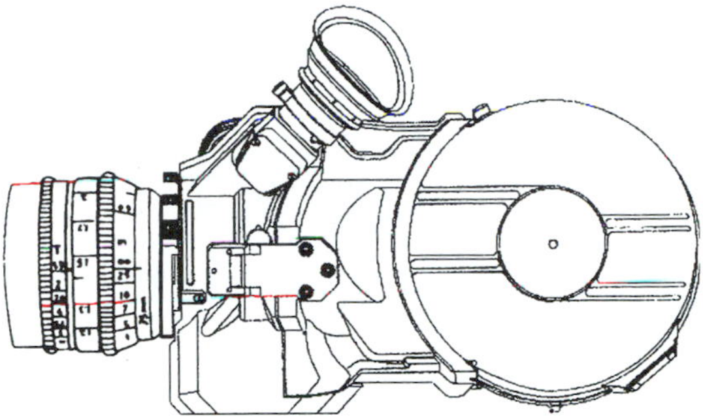

Figure 6.1
Aaton A-Minima 16 mm camera. (Courtesy of Aaton.)

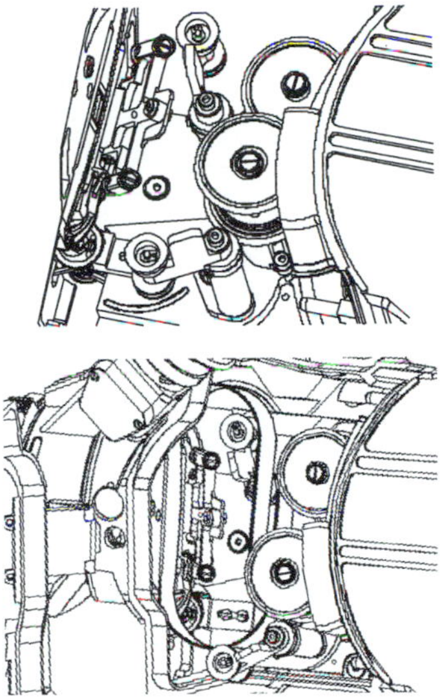

Figure 6.2
Aaton A-Minima camera threading. (Courtesy of Aaton.)

AATON XTR PROD

Format: 16 mm
Magazine sizes: 400′ and 800′ Coaxial

For camera and magazine illustrations and threading diagrams, see Figures 6.3 through 6.5.

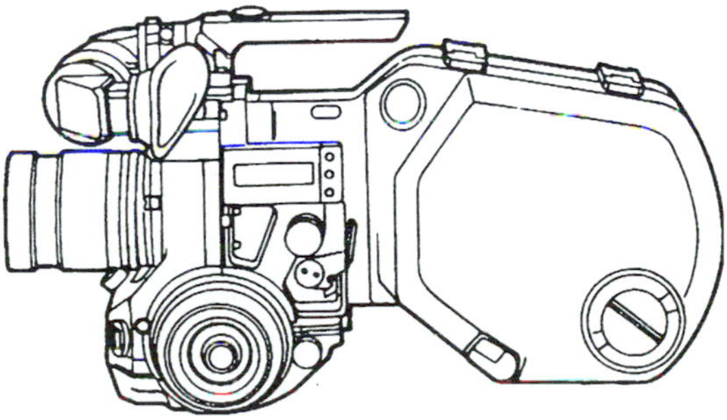

Figure 6.3
Aaton XTR Prod 16 mm camera. (Courtesy of Aaton.)

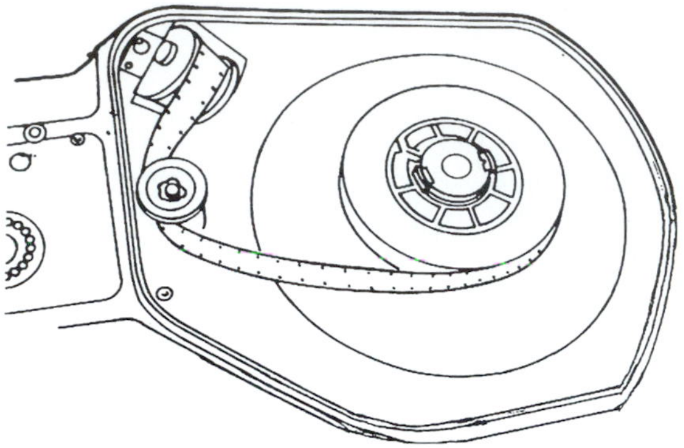

Figure 6.4
Aaton XTR magazine—feed side. (Courtesy of Aaton.)

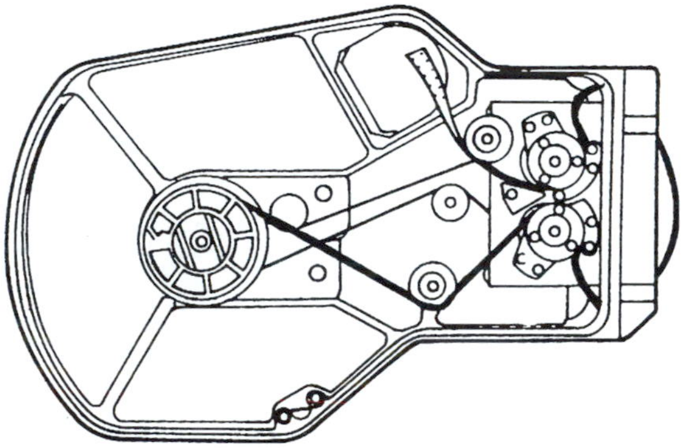

Figure 6.5
Aaton XTR magazine—take-up side. (Courtesy of Aaton.)

AATON 35

Format: 35 mm
Magazine sizes: 400′ Active Displacement

For camera and magazine illustrations and threading diagrams, see Figures 6.6 and 6.7.

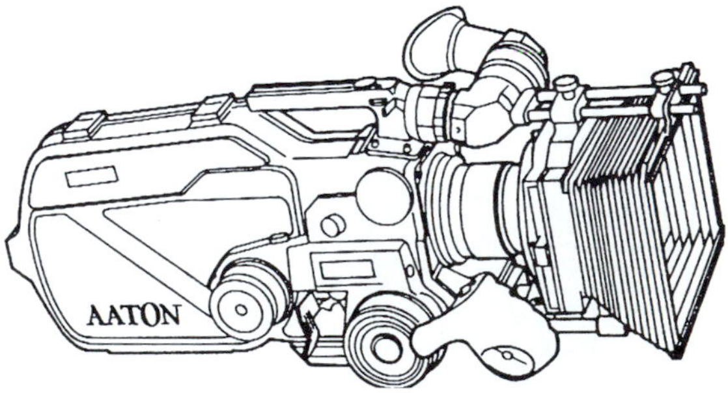

Figure 6.6
Aaton 35 camera. (Courtesy of Aaton.)

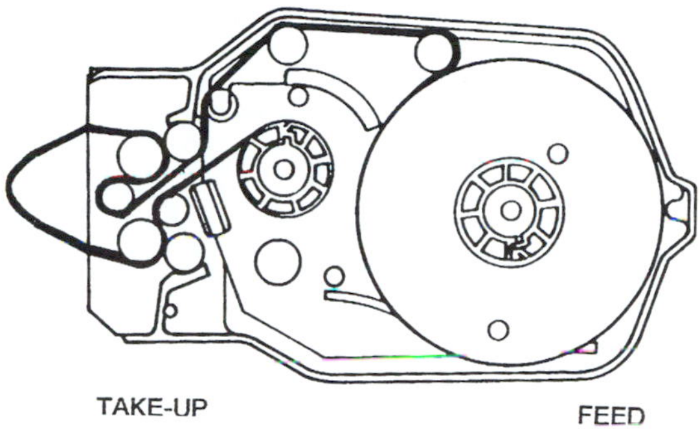

Figure 6.7
Aaton 35 magazine.
(Courtesy of Aaton.)

ARRIFLEX 16BL

Format: 16 mm
Magazine sizes: 200′ and 400′ Displacement

For camera and magazine illustrations and threading diagrams, see Figures 6.8 through 6.11.

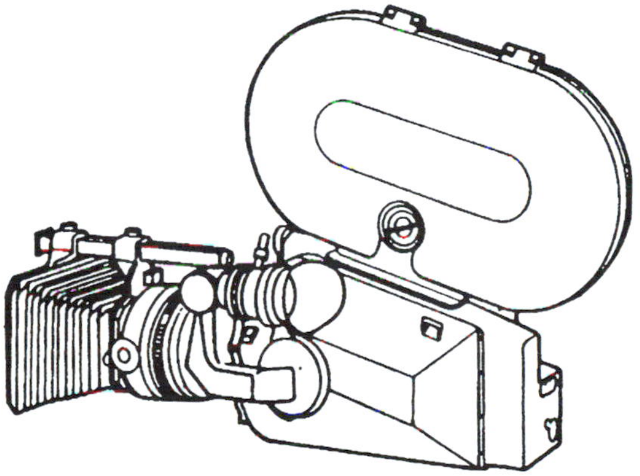

Figure 6.8
Arriflex 16BL camera.
(Courtesy of ARRI Inc.)

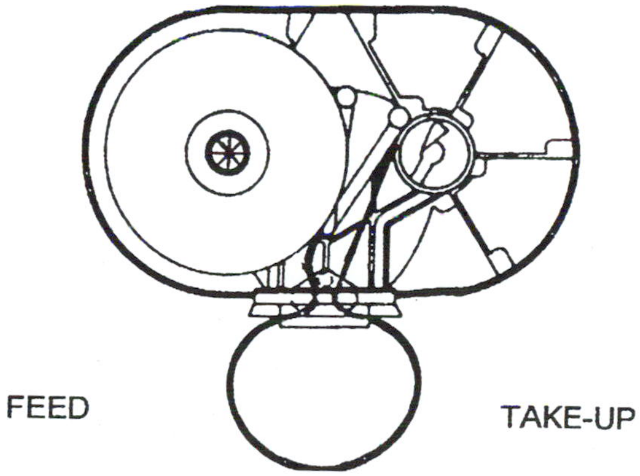

Figure 6.9
Arriflex 16BL magazine.
(Courtesy of ARRI Inc.)

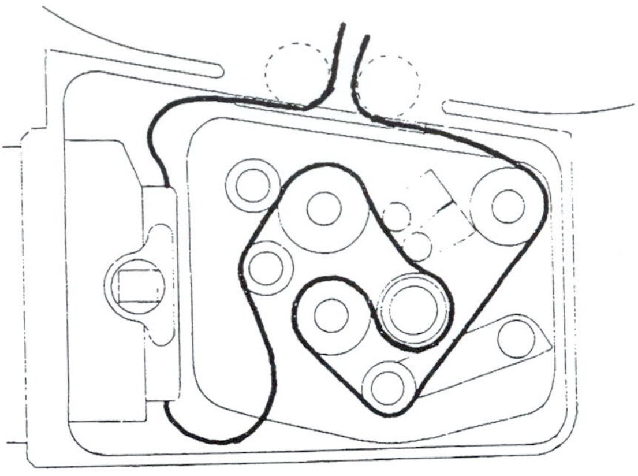

Figure 6.10 Arriflex 16BL camera threading—single system sound. (Courtesy of ARRI Inc.)

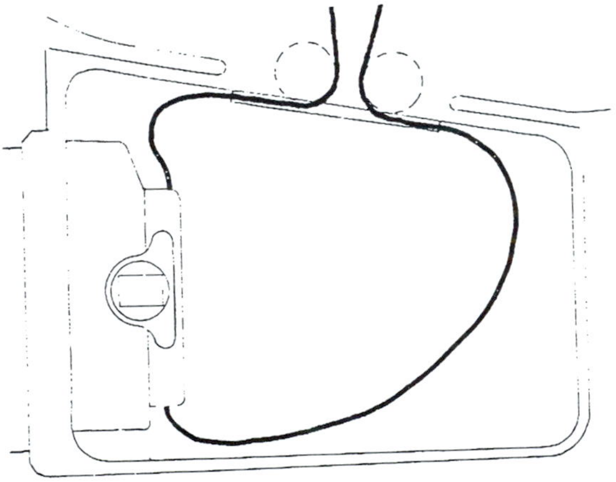

Figure 6.11 Arriflex 16BL camera threading—double system sound. (Courtesy of ARRI Inc.)

ARRIFLEX 16S/SB

Format: 16 mm
Magazine sizes: 200′ and 400′ Displacement

Note: This camera also has the ability to accept a 100′ daylight spool internal load.

For camera and magazine illustrations and threading diagrams, see Figures 6.12 through 6.14.

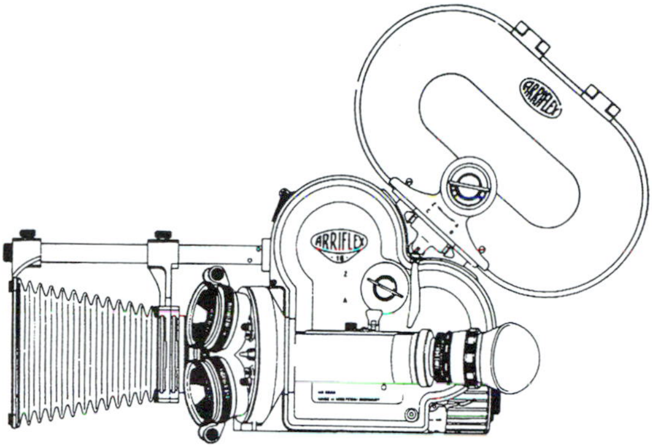

Figure 6.12
Arriflex 16S/SB camera.
(Courtesy of ARRI Inc.)

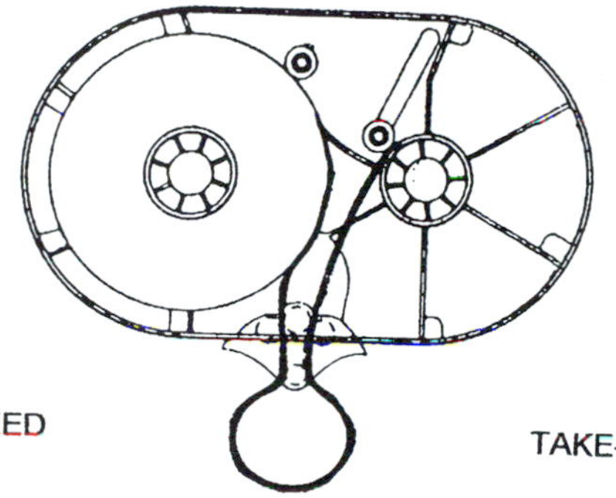

Figure 6.13
Arriflex 16S/SB magazine.
(Courtesy of ARRI Inc.)

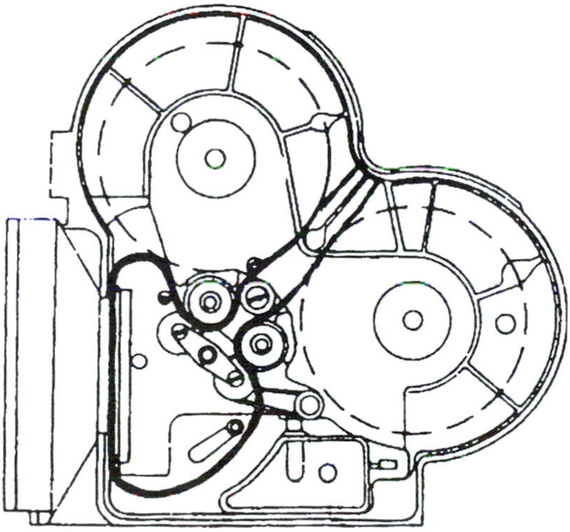

Figure 6.14
Arriflex 16S/SB camera threading. (Courtesy of ARRI Inc.)

ARRIFLEX 16 SR1, 16 SR2, AND 16 SR3

Format: 16 mm (high speed model also available)
Magazine sizes: 400′ and 800′ Coaxial

For camera and magazine illustrations and threading diagrams, see Figures 6.15 through 6.18.

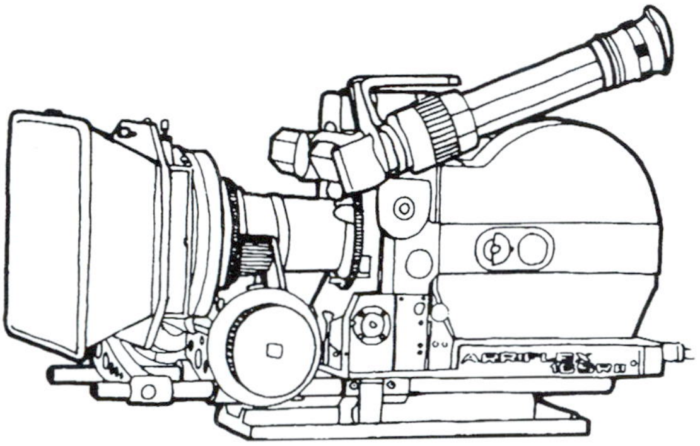

Figure 6.15 Arriflex 16 SR1 and 16 SR2 camera. (Reprinted from the *Arriflex 16SR Book* by Jon Fauer, with permission of the author and ARRI Inc.)

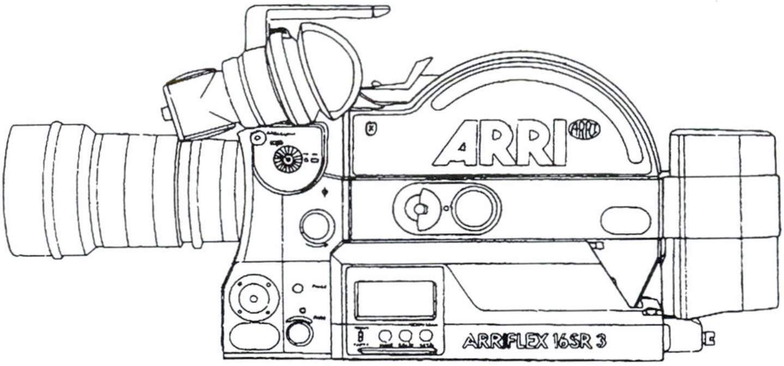

Figure 6.16 Arriflex 16 SR3 camera. (Courtesy of ARRI Inc.)

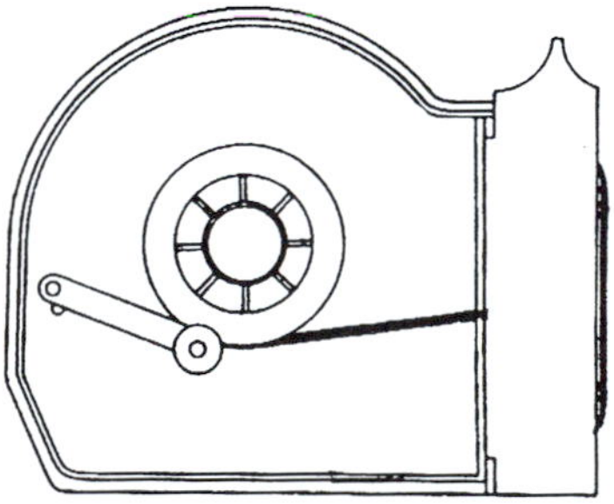

Figure 6.17 Arriflex 16 SR 400′ magazine—feed side. (Courtesy of ARRI Inc.)

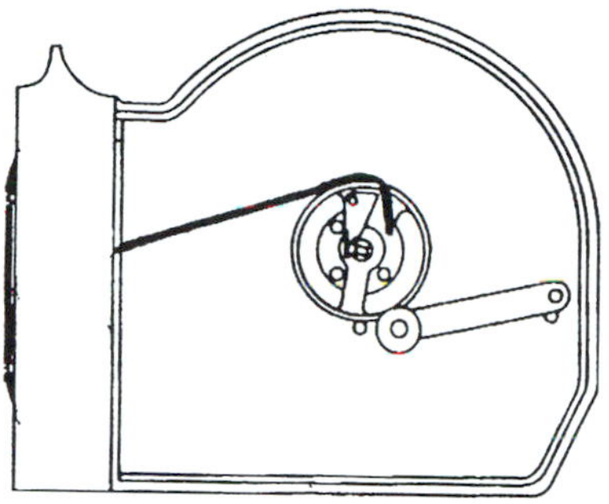

Figure 6.18
Arriflex 16 SR 400′ magazine—take-up side. (Courtesy of ARRI Inc.)

ARRIFLEX ARRICAM LITE (LT)

Format: 35 mm
Magazine sizes: 400′ and 1000′ Displacement Studio Magazines
400′ Active Displacement Lite Shoulder Magazine
400′ Active Displacement Lite Steadicam Magazine

For camera and magazine illustrations and threading diagrams, see Figures 6.19 through 6.22.

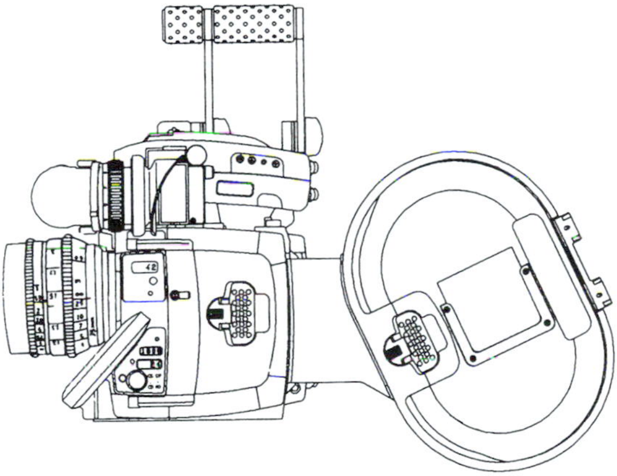

Figure 6.19 Arriflex Arricam Lite camera. (Courtesy of ARRI Inc.)

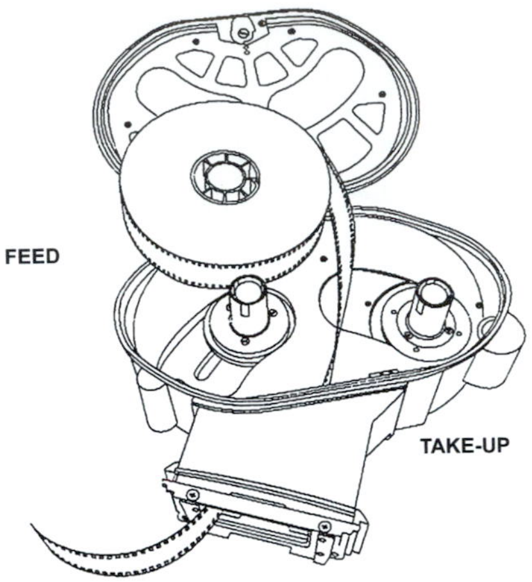

Figure 6.20
Arriflex Arricam Lite 400′ Shoulder magazine. (Courtesy of ARRI Inc.)

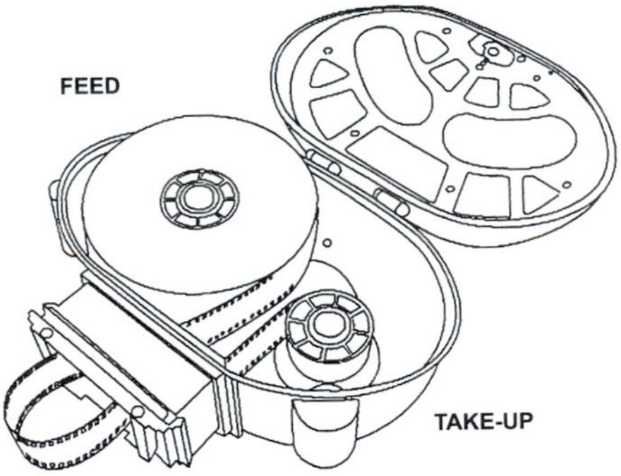

Figure 6.21
Arriflex Arricam Lite 400′ Steadicam magazine. (Courtesy of ARRI Inc.)

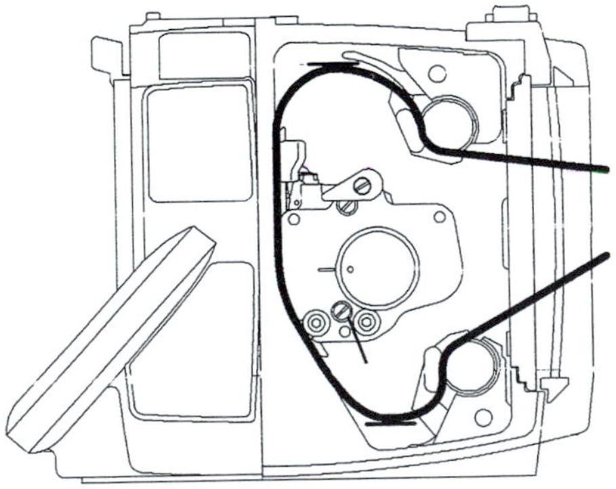

Figure 6.22
Arriflex Arricam Lite camera threading. (Courtesy of ARRI Inc.)

ARRIFLEX ARRICAM STUDIO (ST)

Format: 35 mm
Magazine sizes: 400′ and 1000′ Displacement Studio Magazines

For camera and magazine illustrations and threading diagrams, see Figures 6.23 through 6.25.

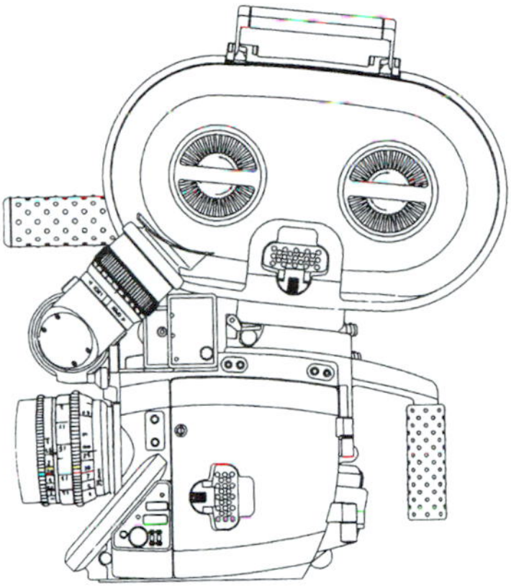

Figure 6.23
Arriflex Arricam Studio camera. (Courtesy of ARRI Inc.)

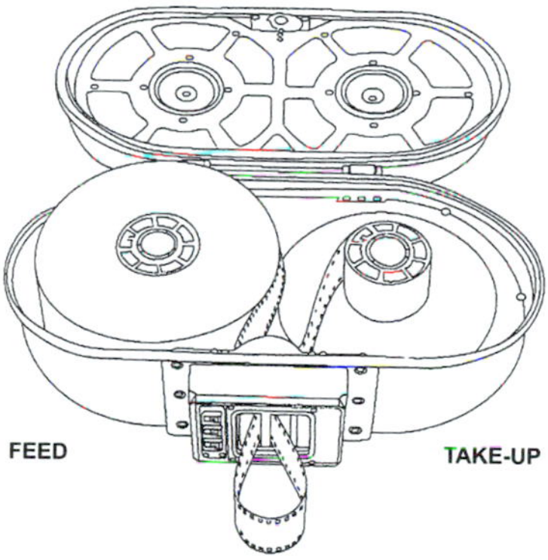

Figure 6.24
Arriflex Arricam Studio 400′ magazine. (Courtesy of ARRI Inc.)

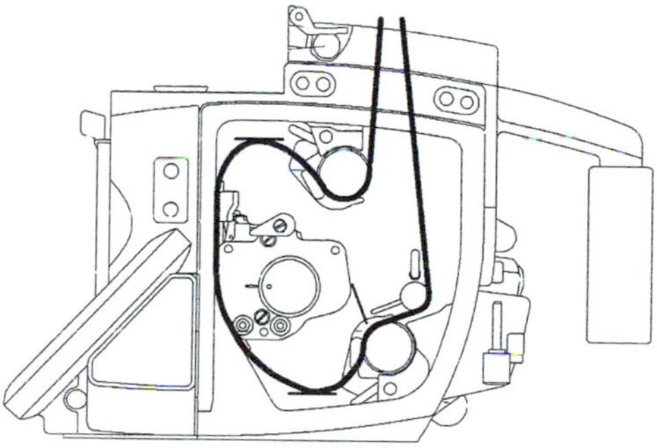

Figure 6.25
Arriflex Arricam Studio camera threading. (Courtesy of ARRI Inc.)

ARRIFLEX 535A AND 535B

Format: 35 mm
Magazine sizes: 400′ and 1000′ Coaxial

For camera and magazine illustrations and threading diagrams, see Figures 6.26 through 6.29.

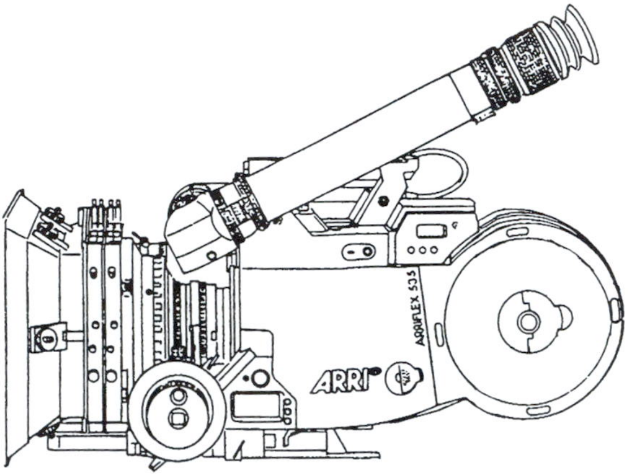

Figure 6.26 Arriflex 535 camera. (Courtesy of ARRI Inc.)

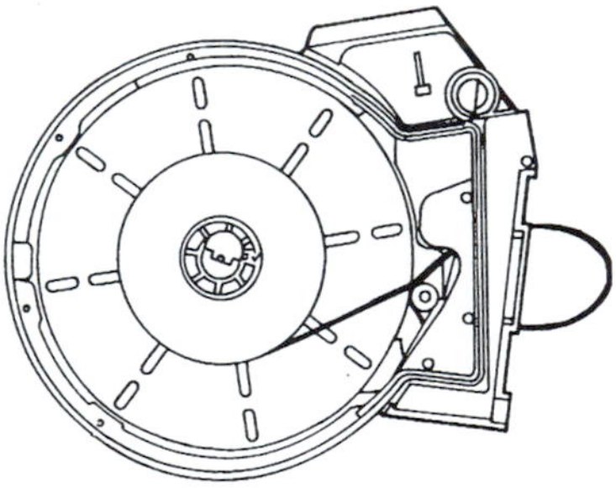

Figure 6.27 Arriflex 535 magazine—feed side. (Courtesy of ARRI Inc.)

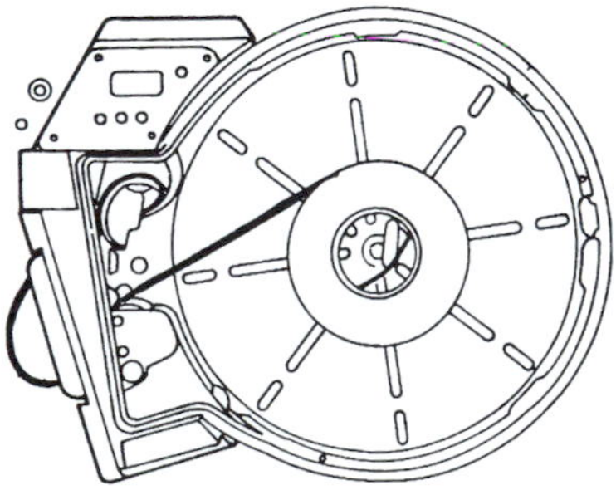

Figure 6.28 Arriflex 535 magazine—take-up side. (Courtesy of ARRI Inc.)

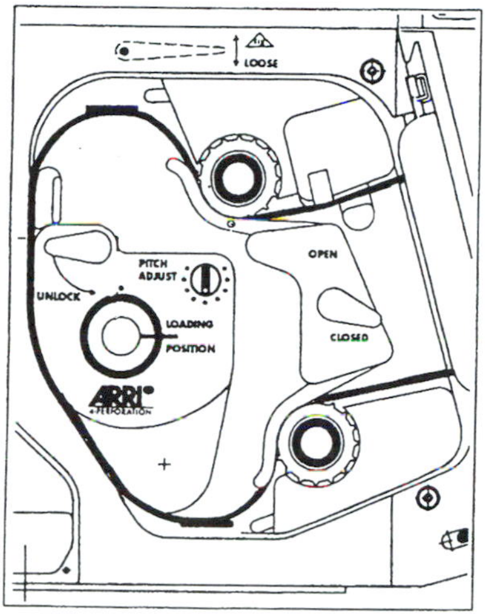

Figure 6.29
Arriflex 535 camera threading. (Courtesy of ARRI Inc.)

ARRIFLEX 435

Format: 35 mm
Magazine sizes: 400′ and 1000′ Displacement
400′ Displacement Steadicam magazine

For camera and magazine illustrations and threading diagrams, see Figures 6.30 through 6.32.

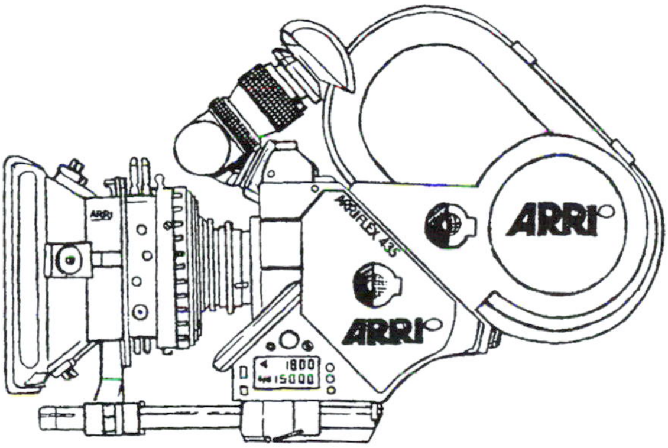

Figure 6.30
Arriflex 435 camera. (Courtesy of ARRI Inc.)

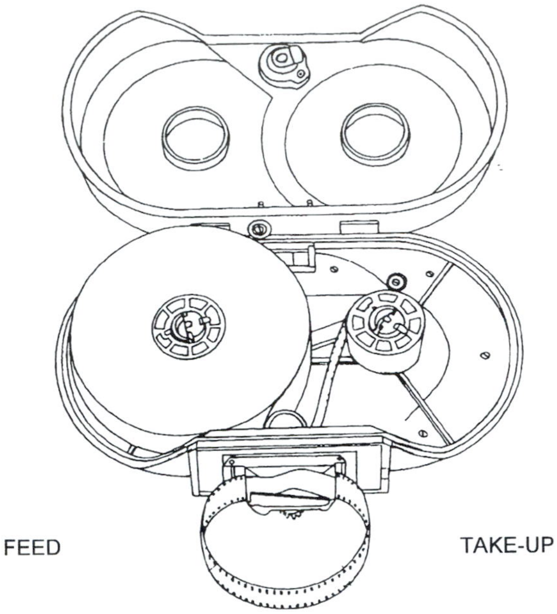

Figure 6.31
Arriflex 435 400′ magazine. (Courtesy of ARRI Inc.)

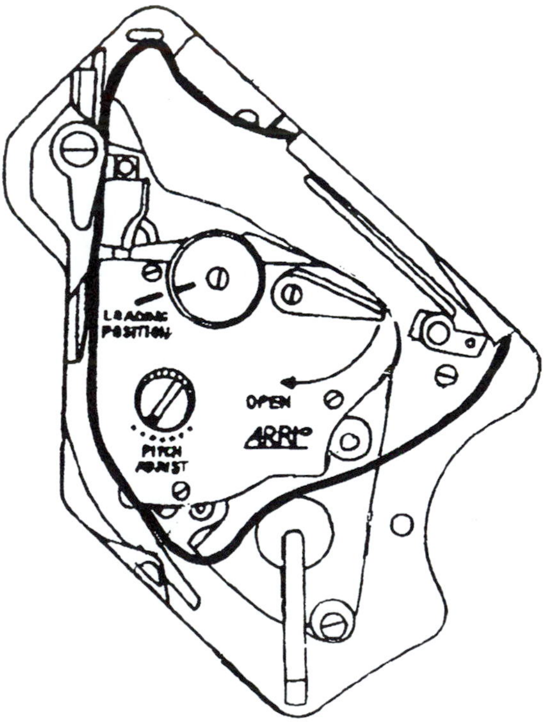

Figure 6.32
Arriflex 435 camera threading. (Courtesy of ARRI Inc.)

ARRIFLEX 35BL3 AND 35BL4

Format: 35 mm
Magazine sizes: 400′ and 1000′ Coaxial

For camera and magazine illustrations and threading diagrams, see Figures 6.33 through 6.36.

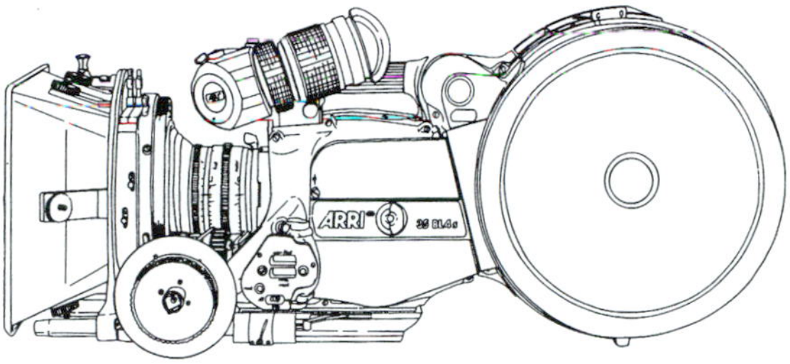

Figure 6.33
Arriflex 35BL camera. (Reprinted from the *Arriflex 35 Book* by Jon Fauer, with permission of the author and ARRI Inc.)

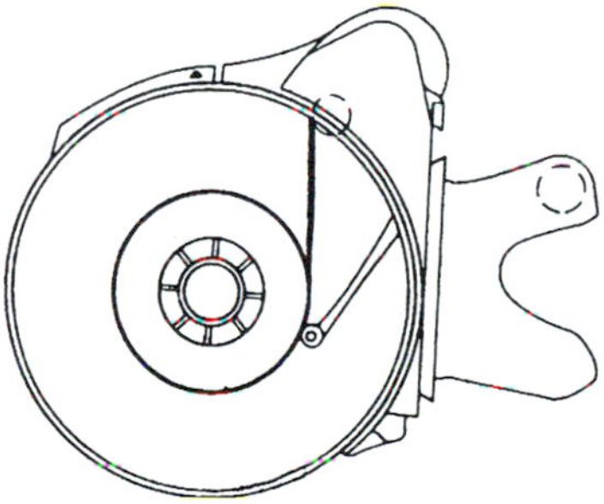

Figure 6.34
Arriflex 35BL magazine—feed side. (Courtesy of ARRI Inc.)

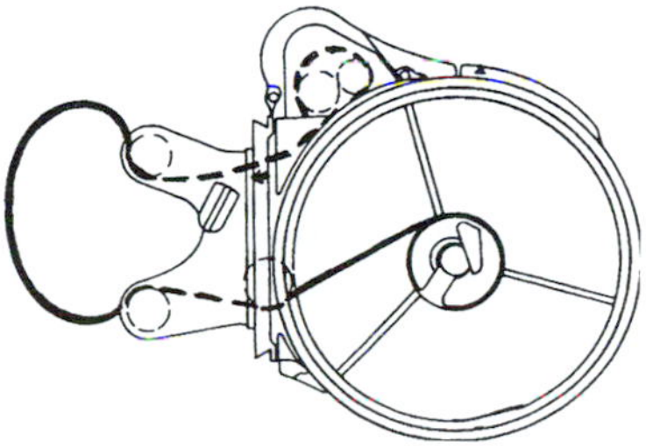

Figure 6.35
Arriflex 35BL magazine—take-up side. (Courtesy of ARRI Inc.)

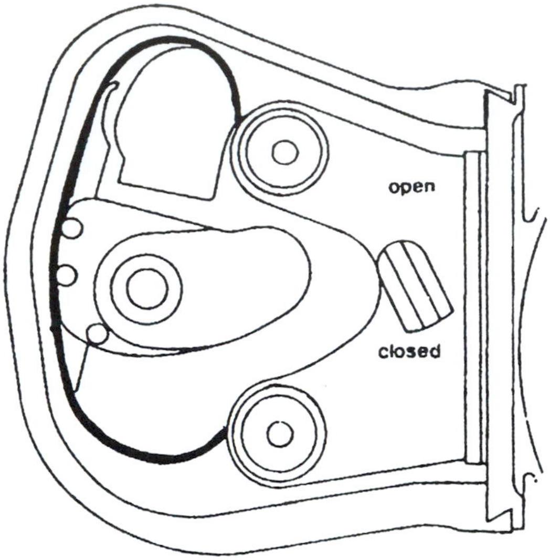

Figure 6.36
Arriflex 35BL camera threading. (Courtesy of ARRI Inc.)

ARRIFLEX 35-3

Format: 35 mm
Magazine sizes: 200′, 400′ 1000′ Displacement
400′ Coaxial hand-held shoulder magazine
400′ Displacement Steadicam magazine

For camera and magazine illustrations and threading diagrams, see Figures 6.37 through 6.43.

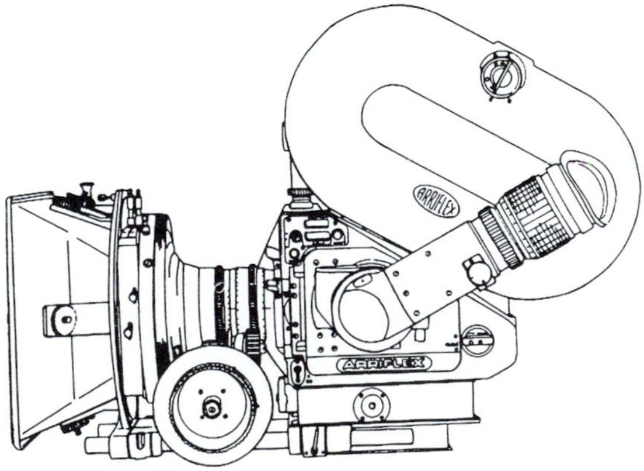

Figure 6.37
Arriflex 35-3 camera. (Reprinted from the *Arriflex 35 Book* by Jon Fauer with permission of the author and ARRI Inc.)

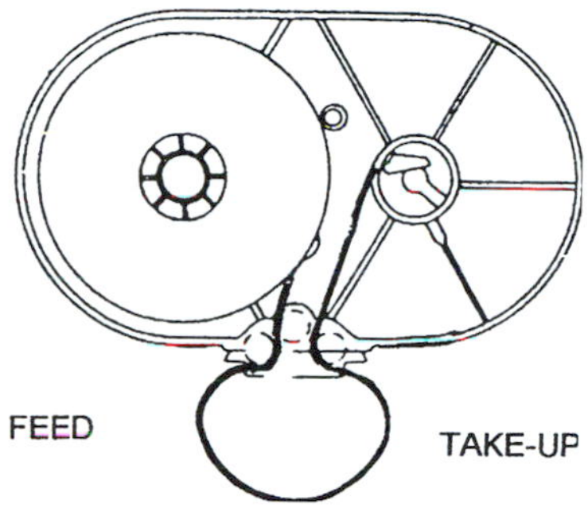

Figure 6.38
Arriflex 35-3 400′ magazine. (Courtesy of ARRI Inc.)

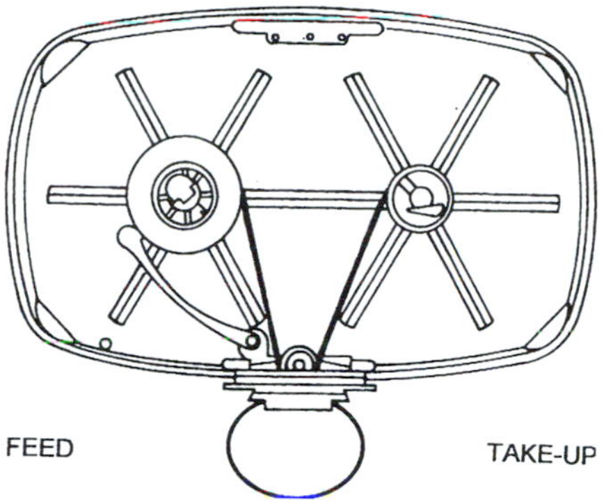

Figure 6.39
Arriflex 35-3 1000′ magazine. (Courtesy of ARRI Inc.)

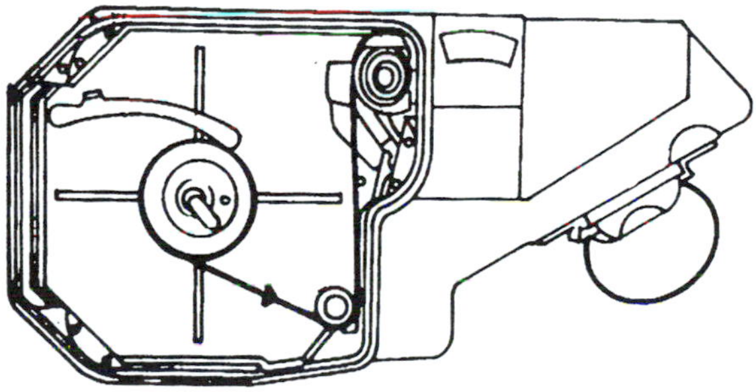

Figure 6.40
Arriflex 35-3 shoulder magazine—feed side. (Courtesy of ARRI Inc.)

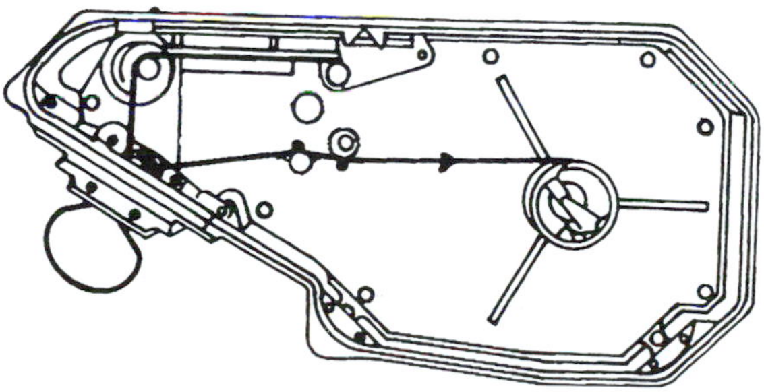

Figure 6.41
Arriflex 35-3 shoulder magazine—take-up side. (Courtesy of ARRI Inc.)

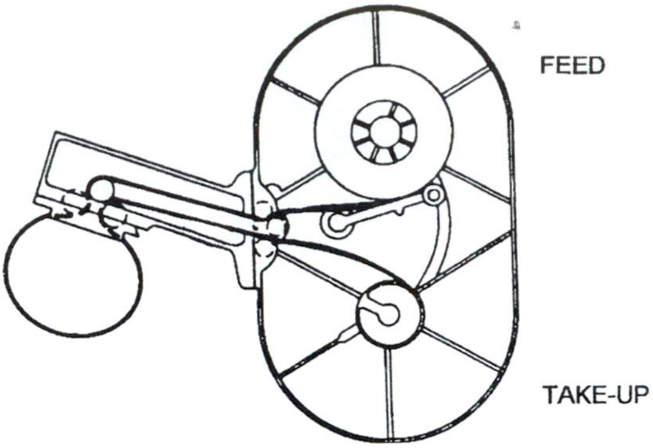

Figure 6.42
Arriflex 35-3 Steadicam magazine. (Courtesy of ARRI Inc.)

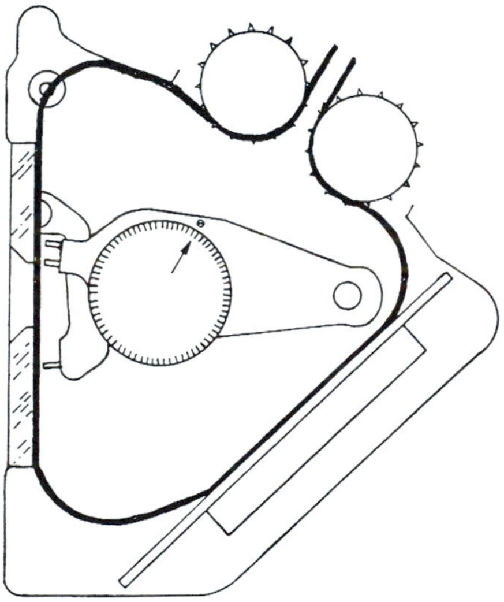

Figure 6.43
Arriflex 35-3 camera threading. (Courtesy of ARRI Inc.)

ARRIFLEX 2-C

Format: 35 mm
Magazine sizes: 200′ and 400′ Displacement

For camera and magazine illustrations and threading diagrams, see Figures 6.44 through 6.46.

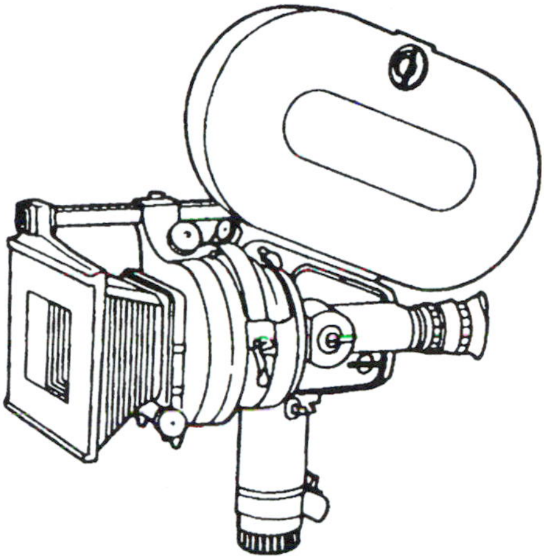

Figure 6.44
Arriflex 2-C camera. (Courtesy of ARRI Inc.)

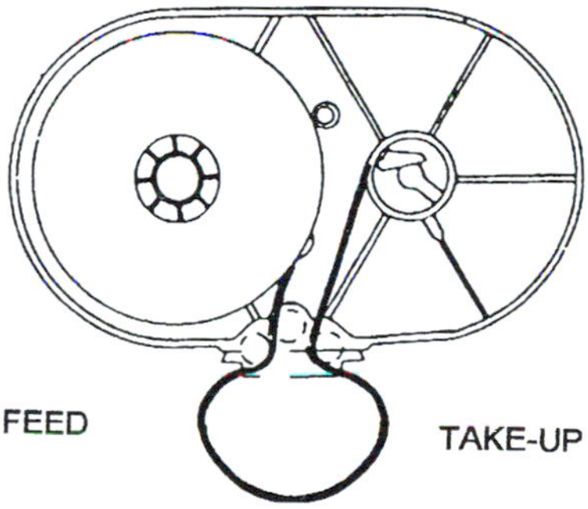

Figure 6.45
Arriflex 2-C 400′ magazine. (Courtesy of ARRI Inc.)

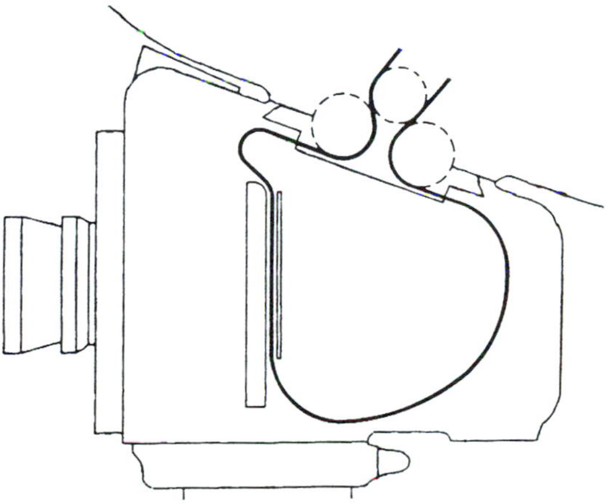

Figure 6.46
Arriflex 2-C camera threading. (Courtesy of ARRI Inc.)

ARRIFLEX 765

Format: 65 mm
Magazine sizes: 500′ and 1000′ Displacement

For camera and magazine illustrations and threading diagrams, see Figures 6.47 through 6.49.

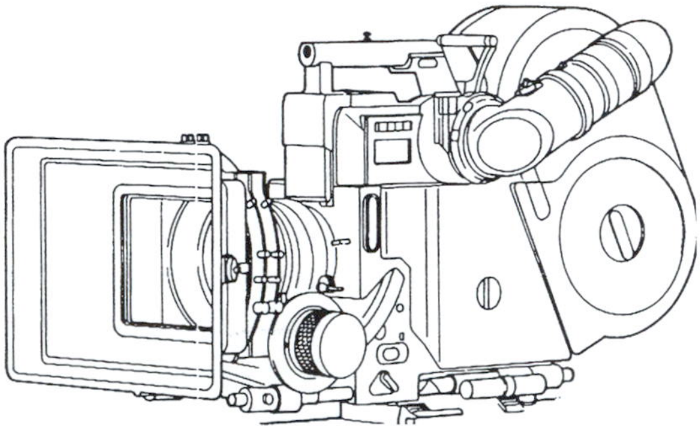

Figure 6.47
Arriflex 765 camera.
(Courtesy of ARRI Inc.)

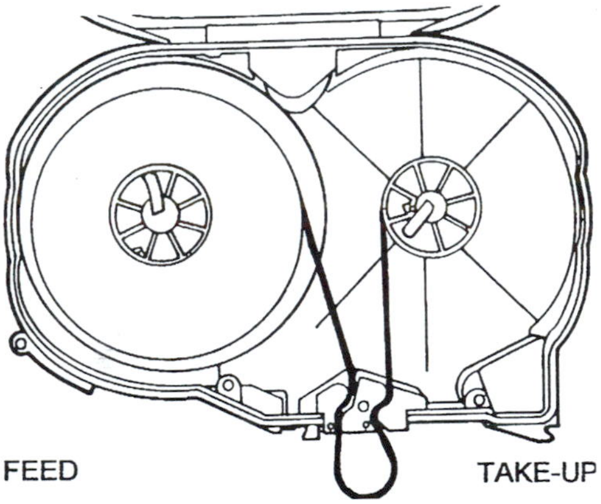

Figure 6.48
Arriflex 765 magazine.
(Courtesy of ARRI Inc.)

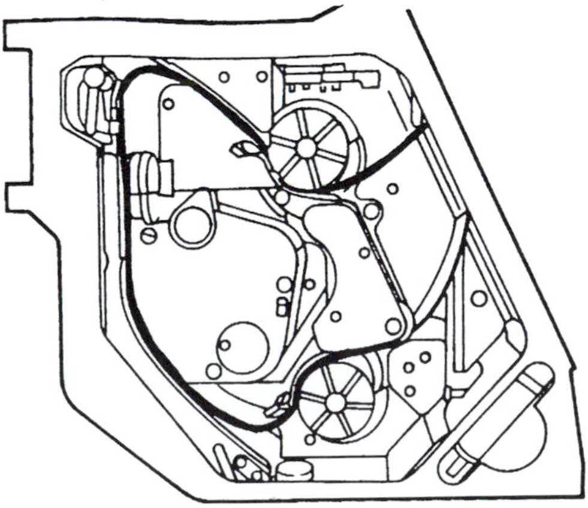

Figure 6.49
Arriflex 765 camera threading.
(Courtesy of ARRI Inc.)

BELL & HOWELL EYEMO

Format: 35 mm
Magazine sizes: 100′ daylight spool, internal load only

For camera illustration and threading diagrams, see Figures 6.50 and 6.51.

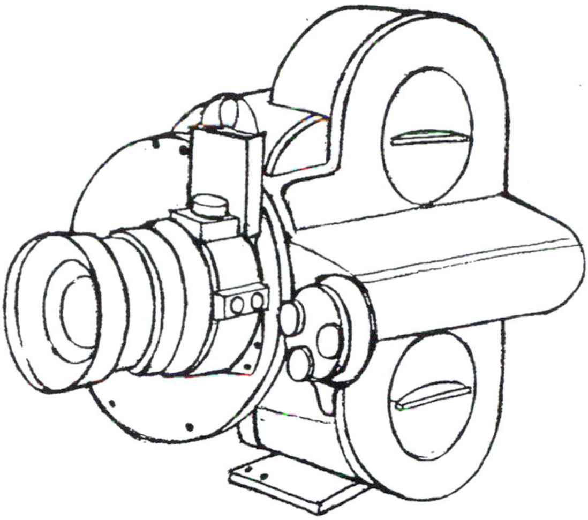

Figure 6.50
Bell and Howell Eyemo camera.

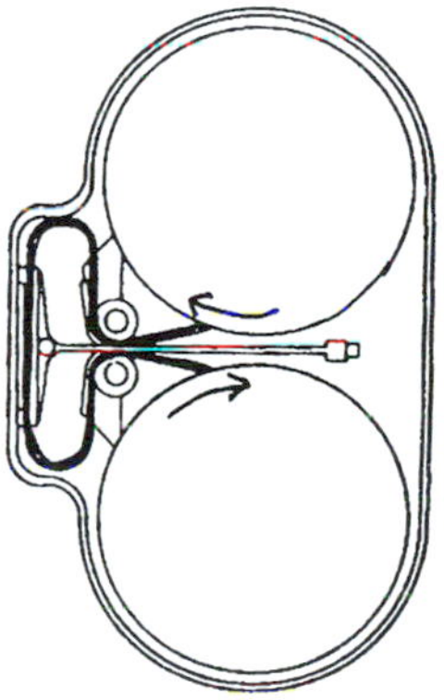

Figure 6.51
Bell and Howell Eyemo threading diagram.

CINEMA PRODUCTS CP16

Format: 16 mm
Magazine sizes: 400′ Displacement

For camera and magazine illustrations and threading diagrams, see Figures 6.52 through 6.54.

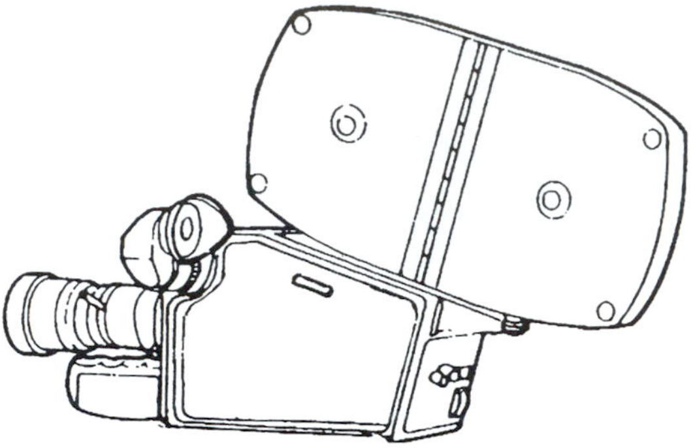

Figure 6.52
Caption: Cinema Products CP16 camera. (Reprinted from the *Hands-On Manual for Cinematographers*, with permission of David Samuelson.)

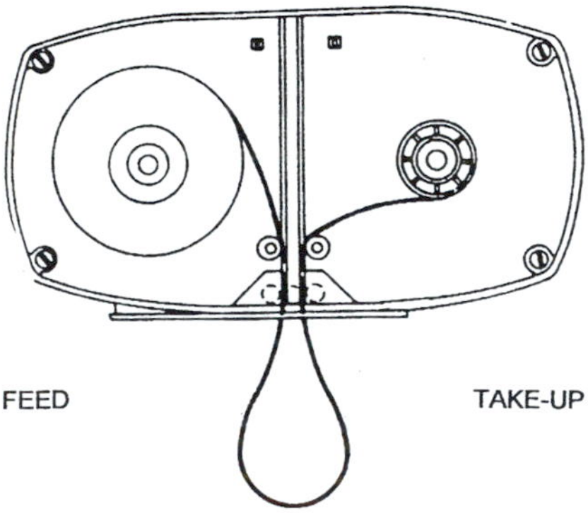

Figure 6.53
Cinema Products CP16 magazine. (Reprinted from the *Hands-On Manual for Cinematographers*, with permission of David Samuelson.)

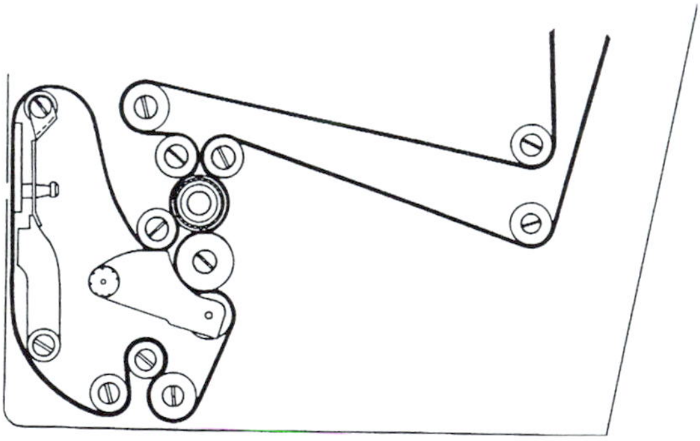

Figure 6.54
Cinema Products CP16 camera threading. (Reprinted from the *Hands-On Manual for Cinematographers*, with permission of David Samuelson.)

ECLAIR ACL

Format: 16 mm
Magazine sizes: 200′ and 400′ Coaxial

For camera and magazine illustrations and threading diagrams, see Figures 6.55 through 6.57.

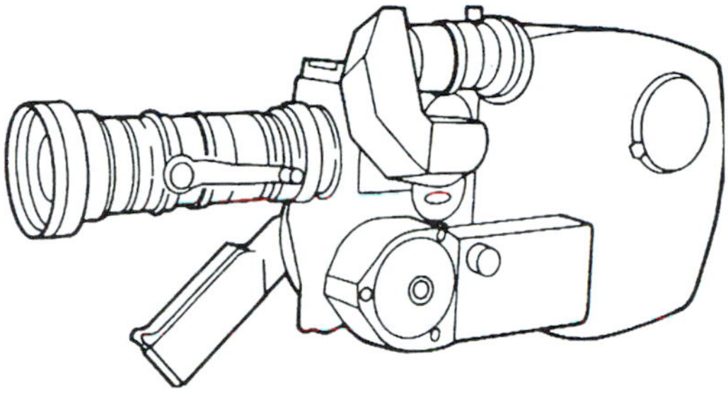

Figure 6.55
Eclair ACL camera.
(Reprinted from the *Hands-On Manual for Cinematographers*, with permission of David Samuelson.)

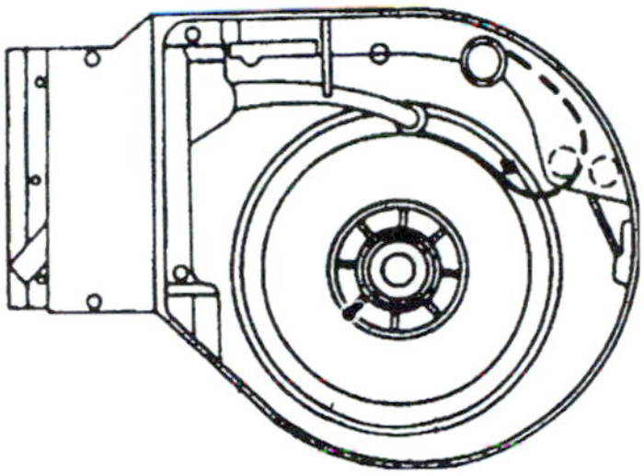

Figure 6.56
Eclair ACL 200′ magazine—feed side.
(Reprinted from the *Hands-On Manual for Cinematographers*, with permission of David Samuelson.)

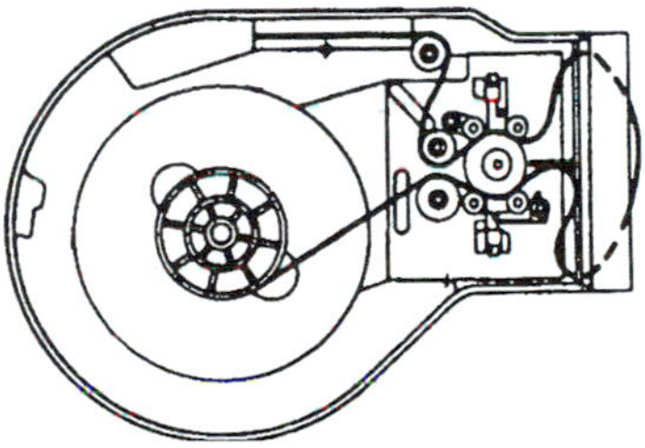

Figure 6.57
Eclair ACL 200′ magazine—take-up side.
(Reprinted from the *Hands-On Manual for Cinematographers*, with permission of David Samuelson.)

ECLAIR NPR

Format: 16 mm
Magazine sizes: 400′ Coaxial

For camera and magazine illustrations and threading diagrams, see Figures 6.58 through 6.60.

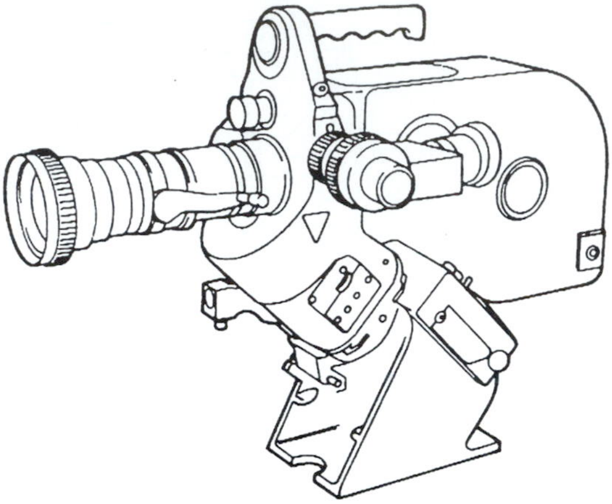

Figure 6.58
Eclair NPR camera. (Reprinted from the *Hands-On Manual for Cinematographers*, with permission of David Samuelson.)

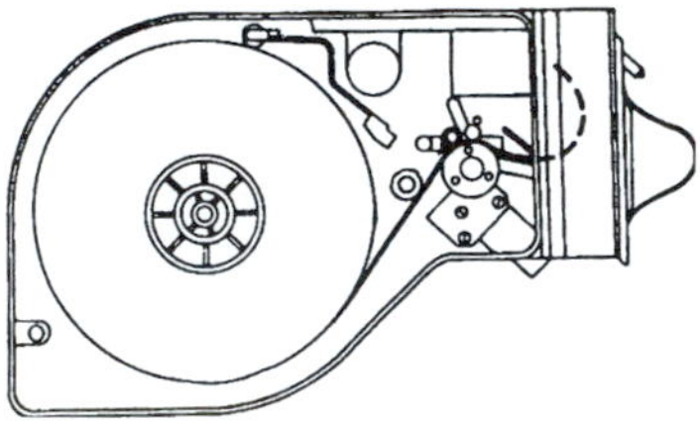

Figure 6.59
Eclair NPR magazine—feed side. (Reprinted from the *Hands-On Manual for Cinematographers*, with permission of David Samuelson.)

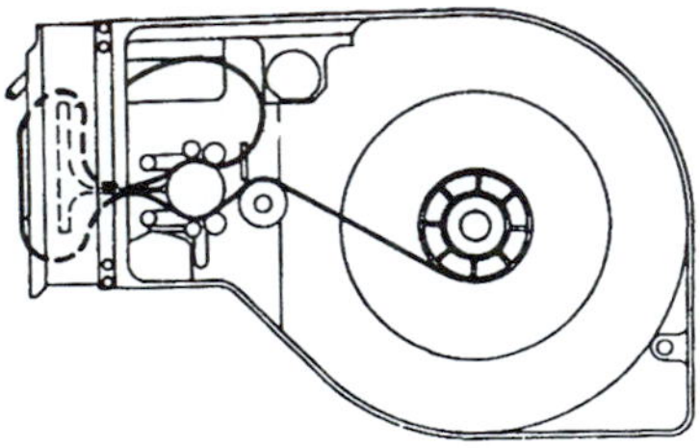

Figure 6.60
Eclair NPR magazine—take-up side. (Reprinted from the *Hands-On Manual for Cinematographers*, with permission of David Samuelson.)

IMAGE 300

Format: 35 mm High Speed
Magazine sizes: 1000′ Coaxial

For camera and magazine illustrations and threading diagrams, see Figures 6.61 through 6.63.

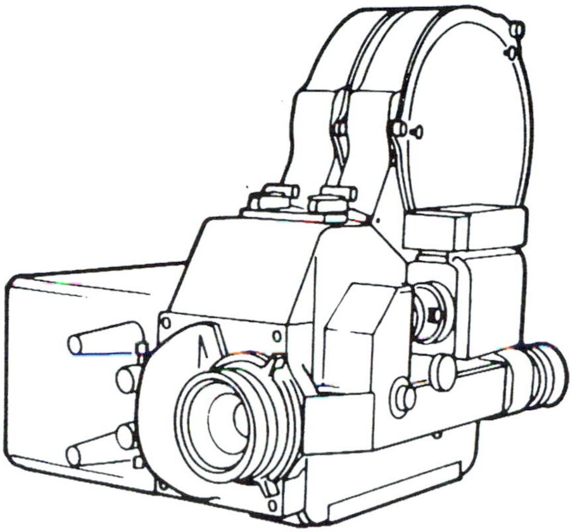

Figure 6.61
Image 300 camera. (Courtesy of Alan Gordon Enterprises.)

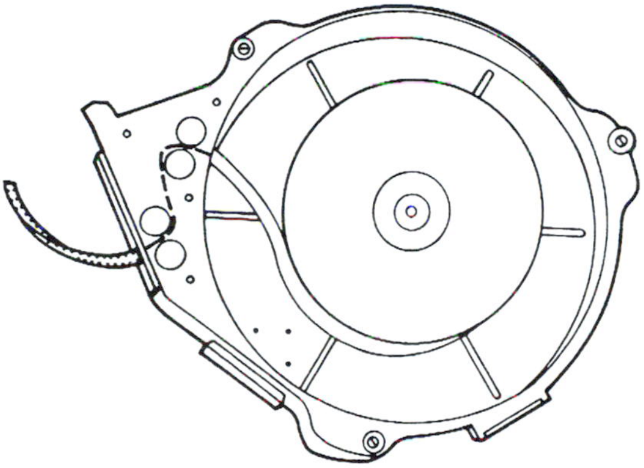

Figure 6.62
Image 300 magazine—feed side. (Courtesy of Alan Gordon Enterprises.)

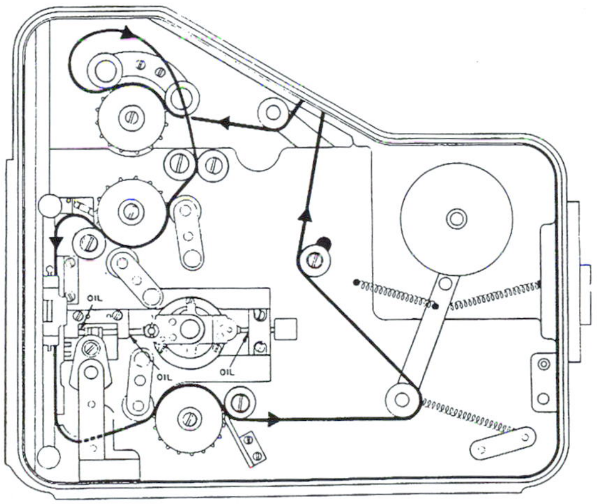

Figure 6.63
Image 300 camera threading. (Courtesy of Alan Gordon Enterprises.)

KRASNOGORSK K-3

Format: 16 mm
Magazine sizes: 100′ daylight spool, internal load only

For camera illustration and threading diagram, see Figures 6.64 and 6.65.

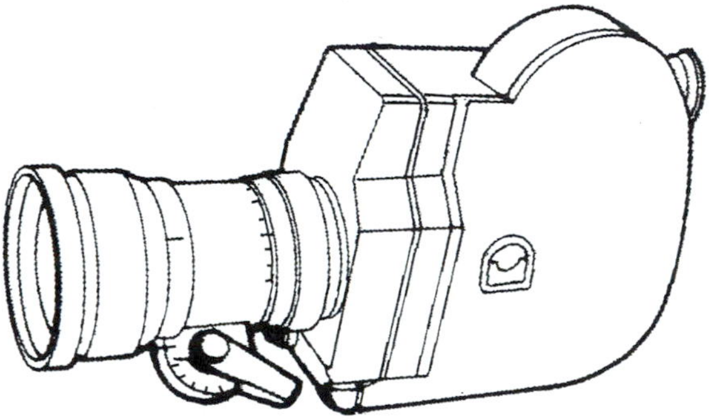

Figure 6.64
Krasnogorsk K-3 camera.

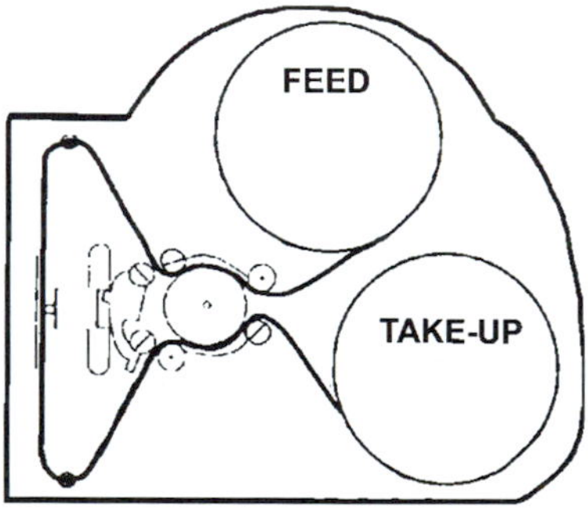

Figure 6.65
Krasnogorsk K-3 threading diagram.

LEONETTI ULTRACAM

Format: 35 mm
Magazine sizes: 500′ and 1000′ Displacement

For camera and magazine illustrations and threading diagrams, see Figures 6.66 through 6.68.

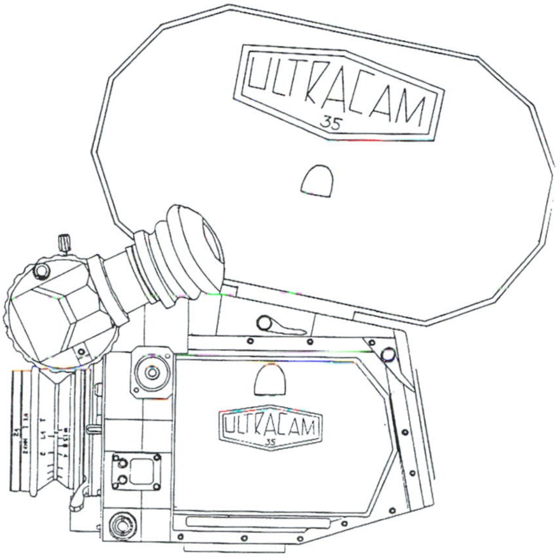

Figure 6.66
Leonetti Ultracam. (Courtesy of Leonetti Camera.)

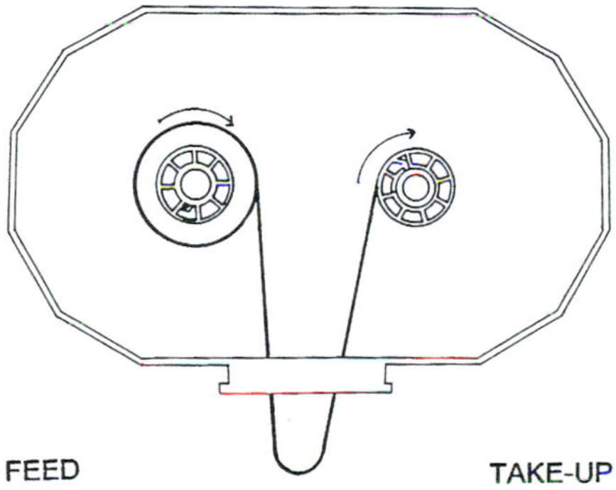

Figure 6.67
Leonetti Ultracam magazine. (Courtesy of Leonetti Camera.)

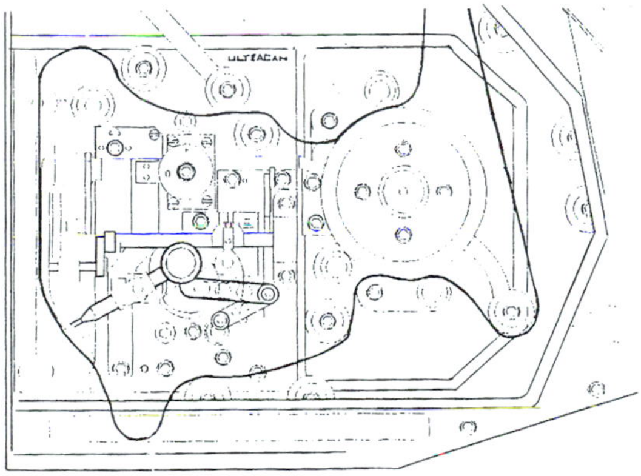

Figure 6.68
Leonetti Ultracam camera threading. (Courtesy of Leonetti Camera.)

MITCHELL BNC

Format: 35 mm
Magazine sizes: 500′ and 1000′ Displacement

For camera and magazine illustrations and threading diagrams, see Figures 6.69 through 6.71.

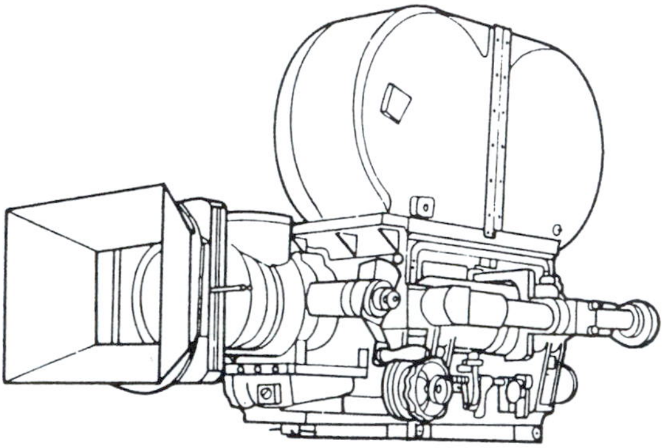

Figure 6.69
Mitchell BNC camera.

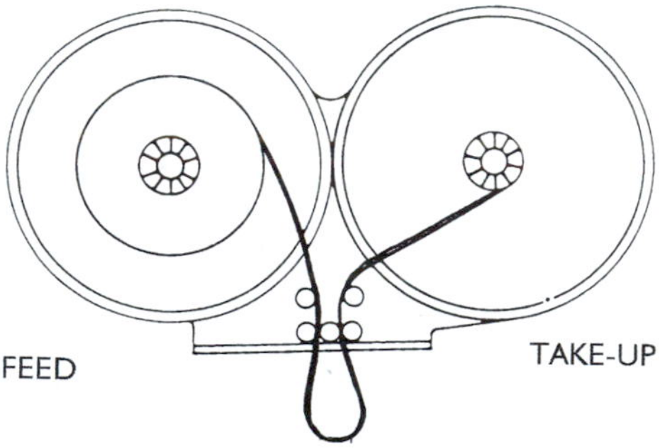

Figure 6.70
Mitchell BNC magazine. (Reprinted from the *Hands-On Manual for Cinematographers*, with permission of David Samuelson.)

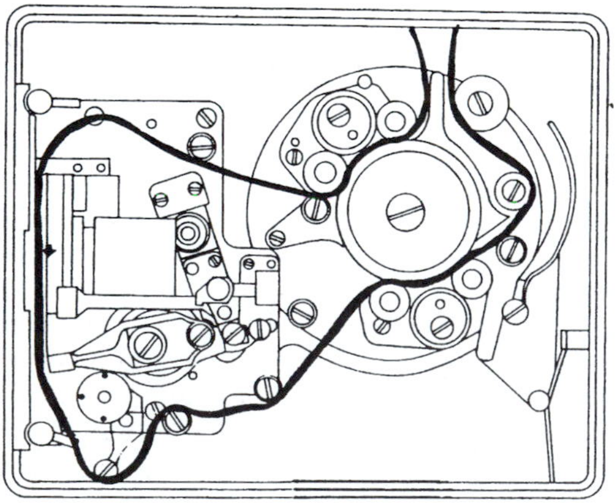

Figure 6.71
Mitchell BNC camera threading.

MOVIECAM COMPACT AND MOVIECAM SUPER AMERICA

Format: 35 mm
Magazine sizes: 500′ and 1000′ Displacement

For camera and magazine illustrations and threading diagrams, see Figures 6.72 through 6.77.

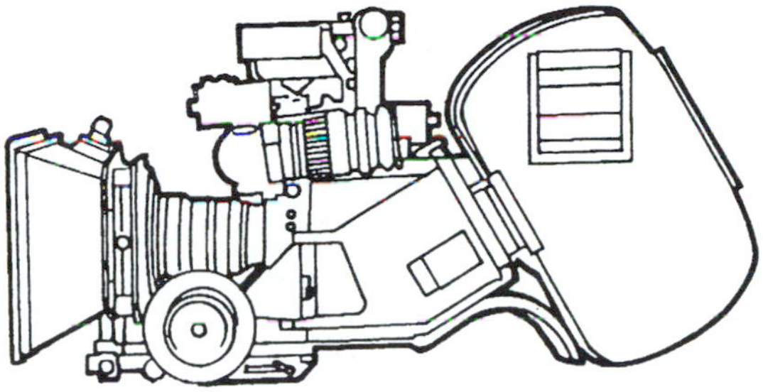

Figure 6.72
Moviecam Compact camera. (Reprinted from the *Hands-On Manual for Cinematographers*, with permission of David Samuelson.)

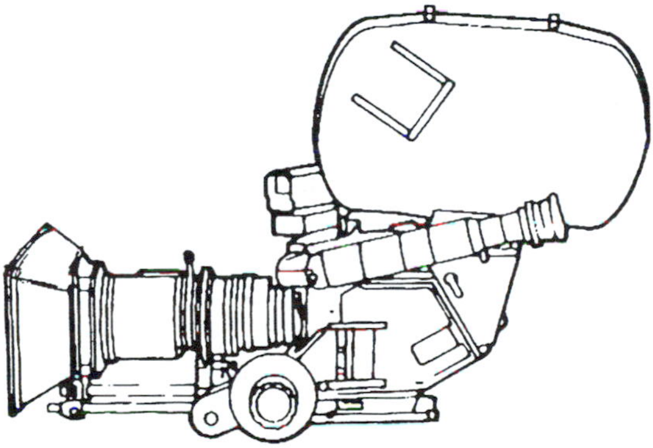

Figure 6.73
Moviecam Super America camera. (Reprinted from the *Hands-On Manual for Cinematographers*, with permission of David Samuelson.)

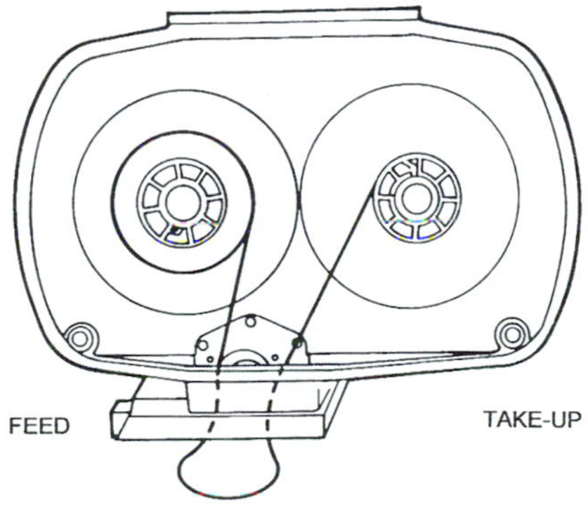

Figure 6.74
Moviecam magazine. (Reprinted from the *Hands-On Manual for Cinematographers*, with permission of David Samuelson.)

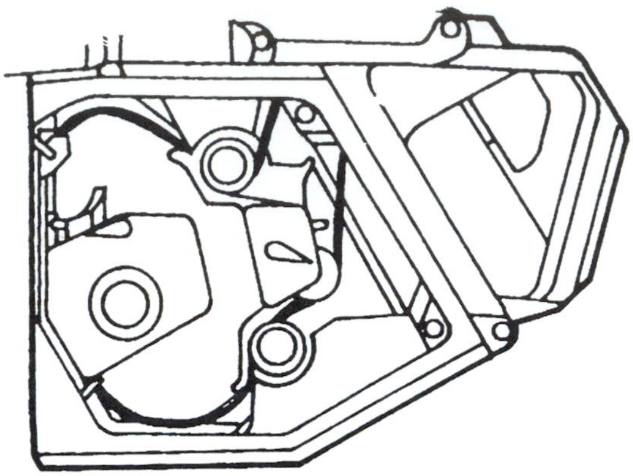

Figure 6.75
Moviecam Compact camera threading—top load. (Reprinted from the *Hands-On Manual for Cinematographers*, with permission of David Samuelson.)

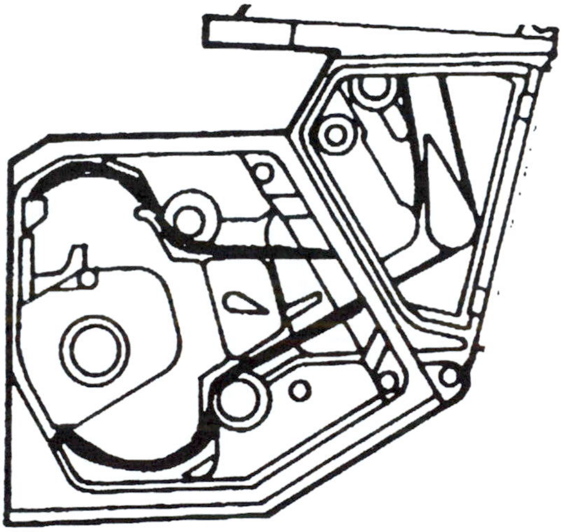

Figure 6.76
Moviecam Super America camera threading—top load. (Reprinted from the *Hands-On Manual for Cinematographers*, with permission of David Samuelson.)

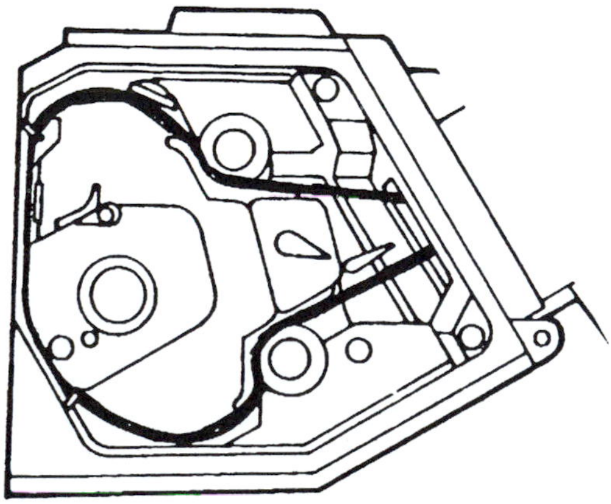

Figure 6.77
Moviecam camera threading—slant load. (Reprinted from the *Hands-On Manual for Cinematographers*, with permission of David Samuelson.)

MOVIECAM SL

Format: 35 mm
Magazine sizes: 500′ and 1000′ Active Displacement

For camera and magazine illustrations and threading diagrams, see Figures 6.78 through 6.80.

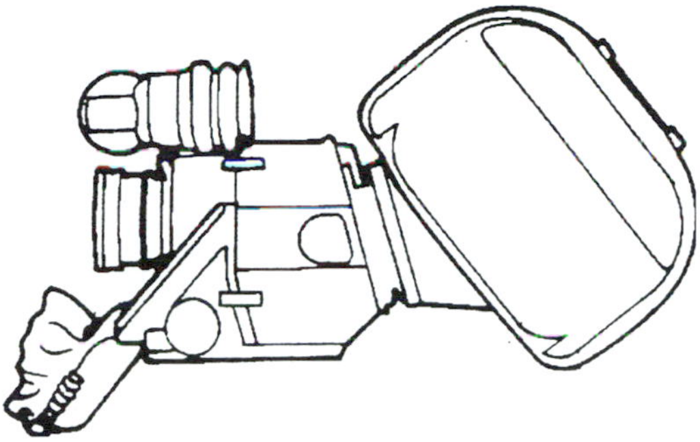

Figure 6.78
Moviecam SL camera. (Reprinted from the *Hands-On Manual for Cinematographers*, with permission of David Samuelson.)

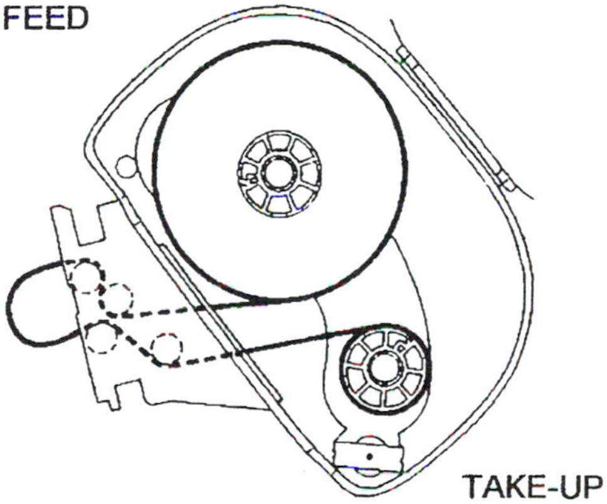

Figure 6.79
Moviecam SL magazine. (Reprinted from the *Hands-On Manual for Cinematographers*, with permission of David Samuelson.)

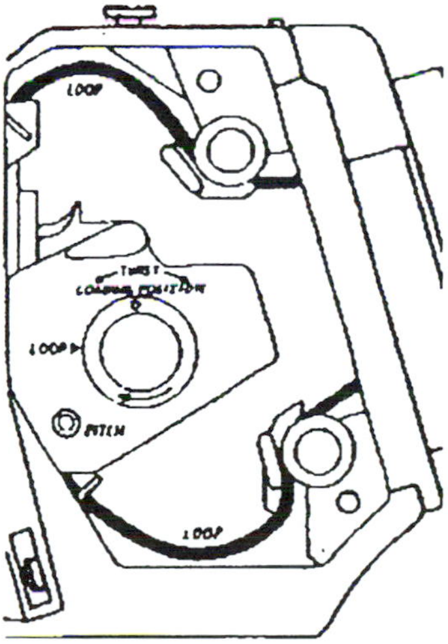

Figure 6.80
Moviecam SL camera threading. (Reprinted from the *Hands-On Manual for Cinematographers*, with permission of David Samuelson.)

PANAVISION PANAFLEX 16

Format: 16 mm
Magazine sizes: 500′ and 1200′ Displacement

For camera and magazine illustrations and threading diagrams, see Figures 6.81 through 6.83.

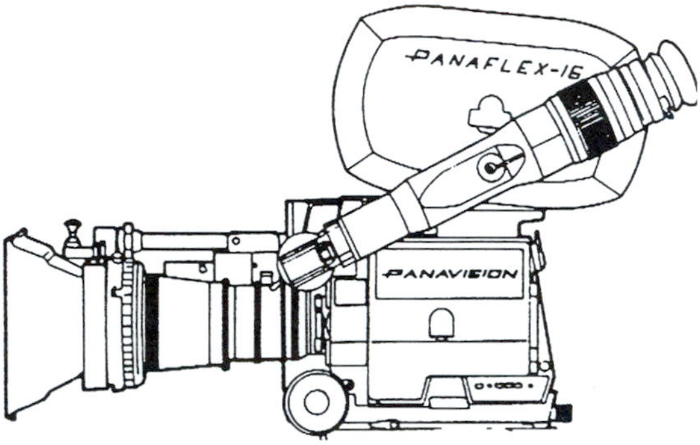

Figure 6.81
Panavision Panaflex 16 camera. (Reprinted from the *Hands-On Manual for Cinematographers*, with permission of David Samuelson.)

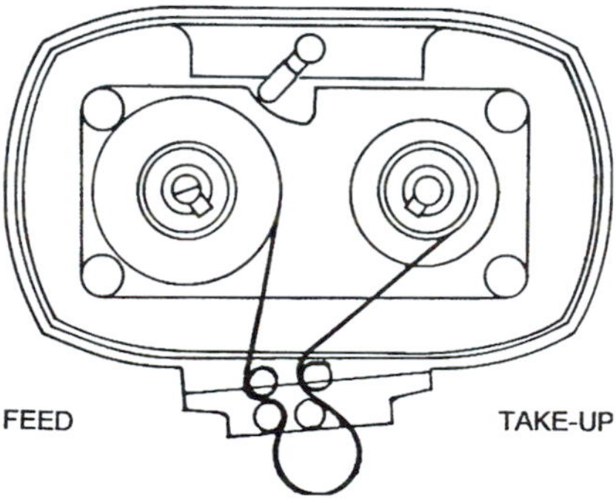

Figure 6.82
Panavision Panaflex 16 magazine. (Reprinted from the *Hands-On Manual for Cinematographers,* with permission of David Samuelson.)

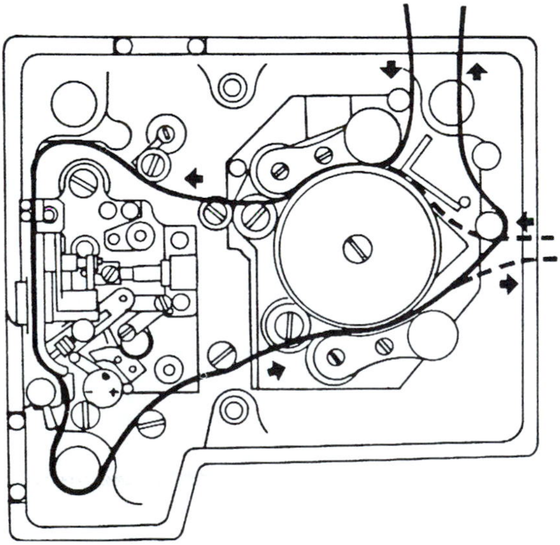

Figure 6.83
Panavision Panaflex 16 camera threading. (Reprinted from the *Hands-On Manual for Cinematographers*, with permission of David Samuelson.)

PANAVISION PANAFLEX GOLDEN AND GII

Format: 35 mm
Magazine sizes: 250′, 500′, 1000′, and 2000′ Displacement

For camera and magazine illustrations and threading diagrams, see Figures 6.84 through 6.86.

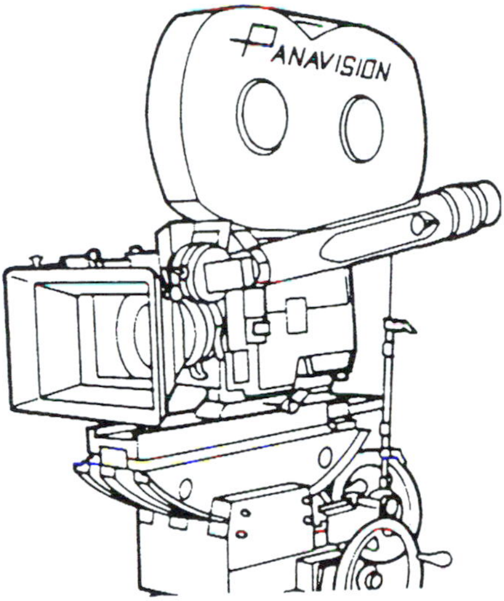

Figure 6.84
Panavision Panaflex Golden and GII camera. (Reprinted from the *Hands-On Manual for Cinematographers*, with permission of David Samuelson.)

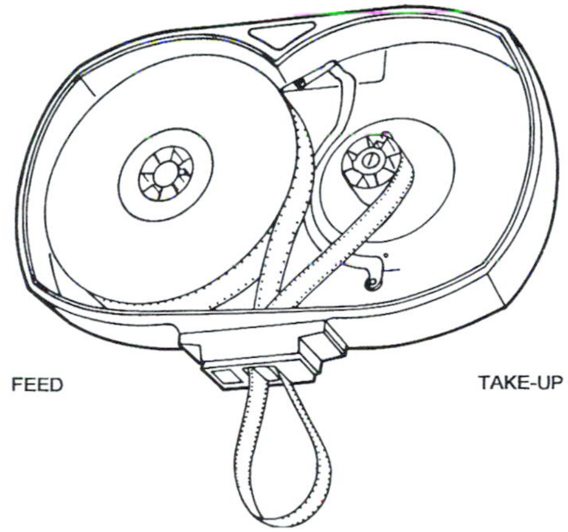

Figure 6.85
Panavision Panaflex Standard 35 mm magazine—Golden, GII, Millennium, Platinum, Panaflex X, and Panastar. (Reprinted from the *Hands-On Manual for Cinematographers*, with permission of David Samuelson.)

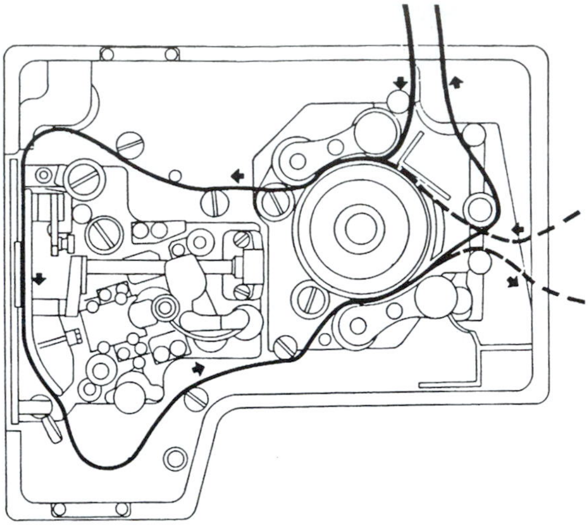

Figure 6.86
Panavision Panaflex Golden and GII camera threading. (Reprinted from the *Hands-On Manual for Cinematographers*, with permission of David Samuelson.)

PANAVISION PANAFLEX MILLENNIUM

Format: 35 mm
Magazine sizes: 250′, 500′, 1000′, and 2000′ Displacement

For camera and magazine illustrations and threading diagrams, see Figures 6.87 and 6.88. See Figure 6.85 for standard magazine threading diagram.

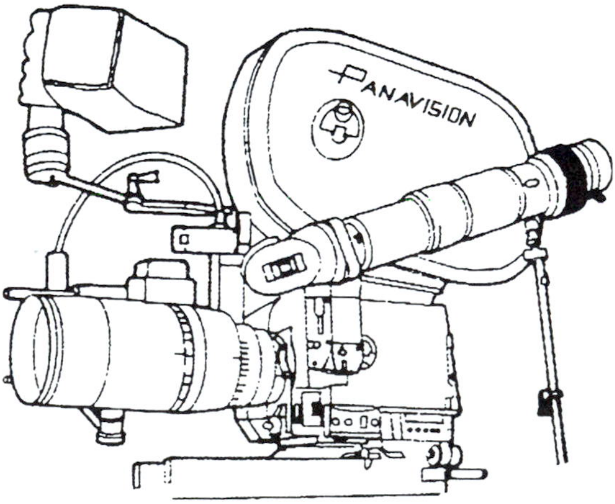

Figure 6.87
Panavision Panaflex Millennium camera. (Reprinted from the *Hands-On Manual for Cinematographers*, with permission of David Samuelson.)

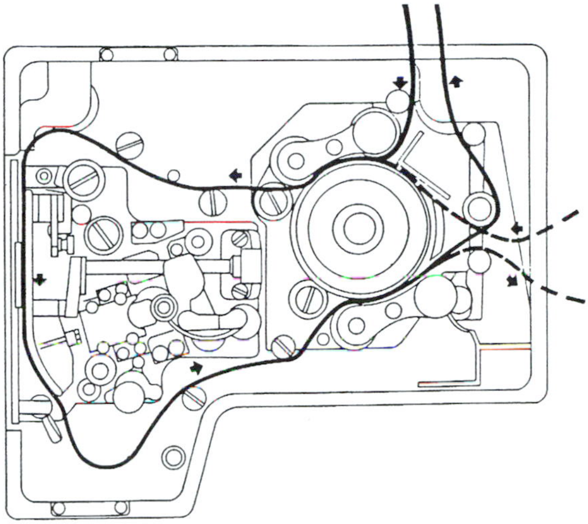

Figure 6.88 Panavision Panaflex Millennium camera threading. (Reprinted from the *Hands-On Manual for Cinematographers*, with permission of David Samuelson.)

PANAVISION PANAFLEX PLATINUM

Format: 35 mm
Magazine sizes: 250′, 500′, and 1000′ Displacement
1000′ reversing Displacement

For camera and magazine illustrations and threading diagrams, see Figures 6.89 through 6.92. See Figure 6.85 for standard magazine threading diagram.

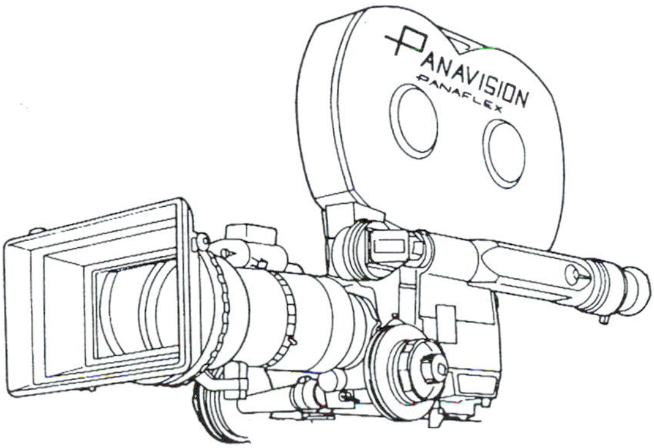

Figure 6.89 Panavision Panaflex Platinum camera. (Reprinted from the *Hands-On Manual for Cinematographers*, with permission of David Samuelson.)

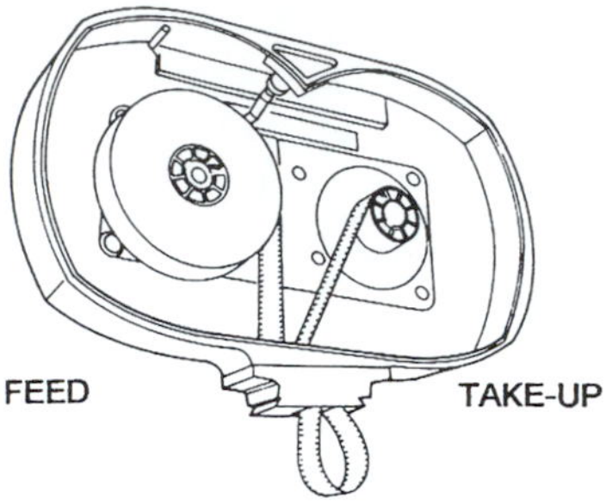

Figure 6.90
Panavision Panaflex reversing magazine—forward-running mode: Platinum and Panastar. (Reprinted from the *Hands-On Manual for Cinematographers*, with permission of David Samuelson.)

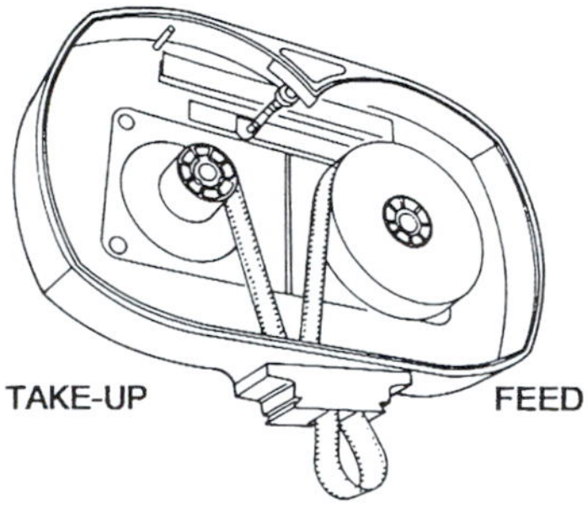

Figure 6.91
Panavision Panaflex reversing magazine—reverse-running mode: Platinum and Panastar. (Reprinted from the *Hands-On Manual for Cinematographers*, with permission of David Samuelson.)

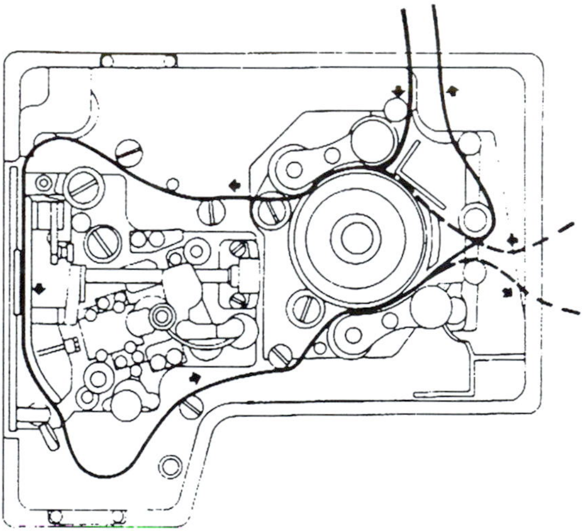

Figure 6.92
Panavision Panaflex Platinum camera threading. (Reprinted from the *Hands-On Manual for Cinematographers*, with permission of David Samuelson.)

PANAVISION PANAFLEX X

Format: 35 mm
Magazine sizes: 250′, 500′, 1000′, and 2000′ Displacement

For camera and magazine illustrations and threading diagrams, see Figures 6.93 and 6.94. See Figure 6.85 for standard magazine threading diagram.

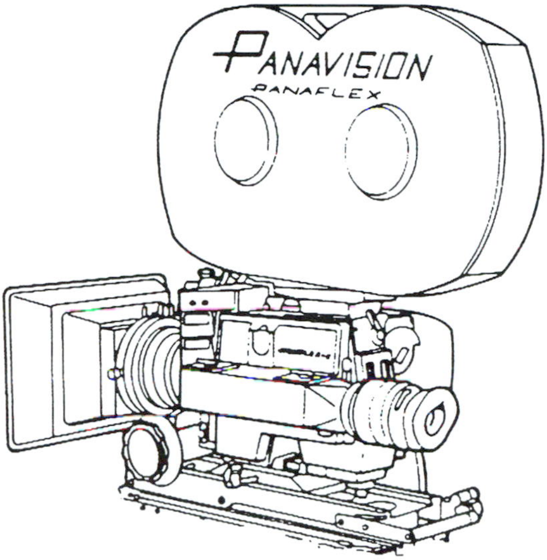

Figure 6.93
Caption: Panavision Panaflex X camera. (Reprinted from the *Hands-On Manual for Cinematographers*, with permission of David Samuelson.)

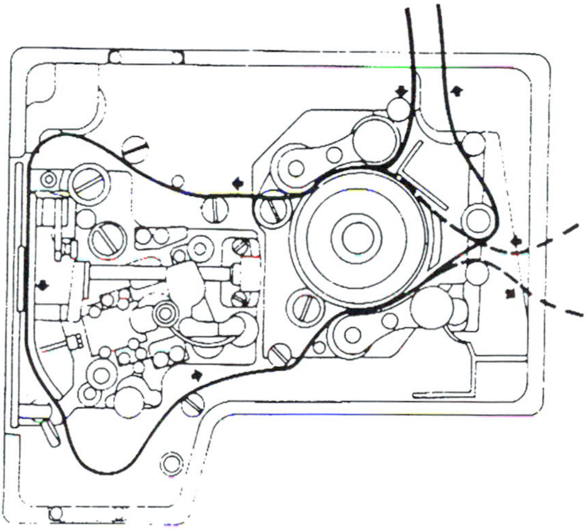

Figure 6.94
Panavision Panaflex X camera threading. (Reprinted from the *Hands-On Manual for Cinematographers*, with permission of David Samuelson.)

PANAVISION PANASTAR I AND PANASTAR II

Format: 35 mm High Speed
Magazine sizes: 500′ and 1000′ Displacement
Panastar II only: 1000′ reversing Displacement

For camera and magazine illustrations and threading diagrams, see Figures 6.95 and 6.96. See Figure 6.85 for standard magazine threading diagram. See Figures 6.90 and 6.91 for reversing magazine threading diagrams.

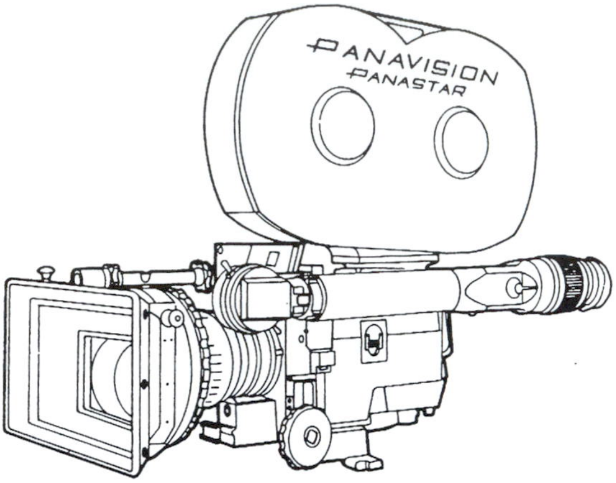

Figure 6.95
Panavision Panastar camera. (Reprinted from the *Hands-On Manual for Cinematographers*, with permission of David Samuelson.)

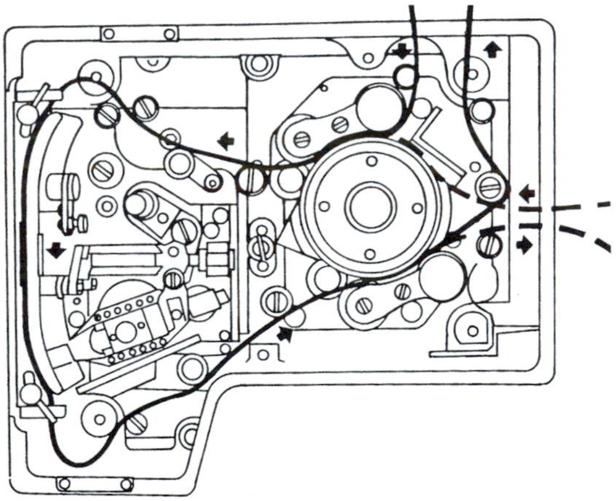

Figure 6.96
Panavision Panastar camera threading. (Reprinted from the *Hands-On Manual for Cinematographers*, with permission of David Samuelson.)

PANAVISION SUPER PSR

Format: 35 mm
Magazine sizes: 1000′ double chamber Displacement.

For camera and magazine illustrations and threading diagrams, see Figures 6.97 through 6.99.

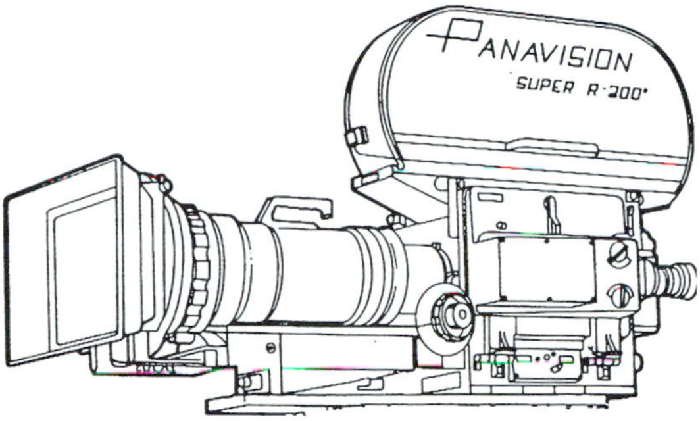

Figure 6.97
Panavision Super PSR camera. (Reprinted from the *Hands-On Manual for Cinematographers,* with permission of David Samuelson.)

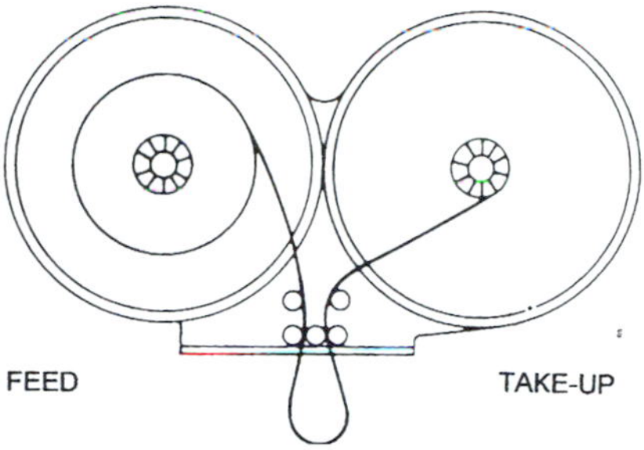

Figure 6.98
Panavision Super PSR magazine. (Reprinted from the *Hands-On Manual for Cinematographers,* with permission of David Samuelson.)

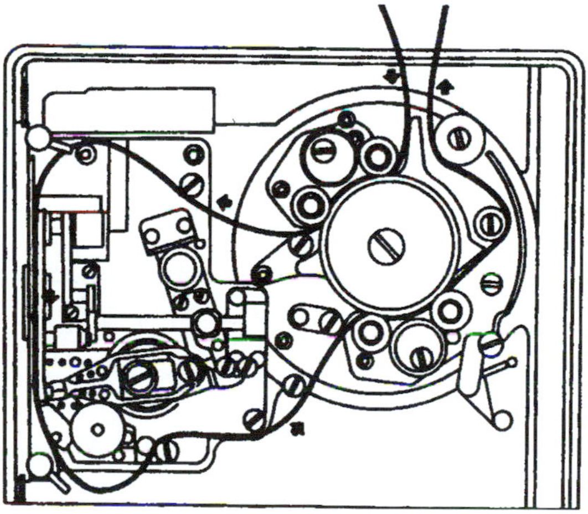

Figure 6.99
Panavision Super PSR camera threading. (Reprinted from the *Hands-On Manual for Cinematographers,* with permission of David Samuelson.)

PANAVISION PANAFLEX 65

Format: 65 mm
Magazine sizes: 500′ and 1000′ Displacement

For camera and magazine illustrations and threading diagrams, see Figures 6.100 through 6.102.

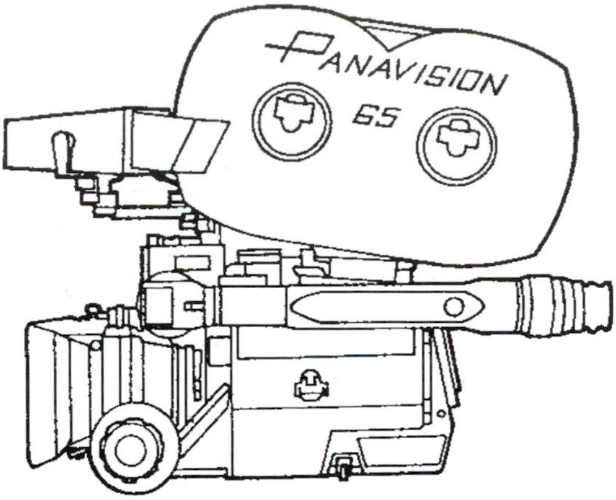

Figure 6.100
Panavision Panaflex 65 camera. (Reprinted from the *Hands-On Manual for Cinematographers*, with permission of David Samuelson.)

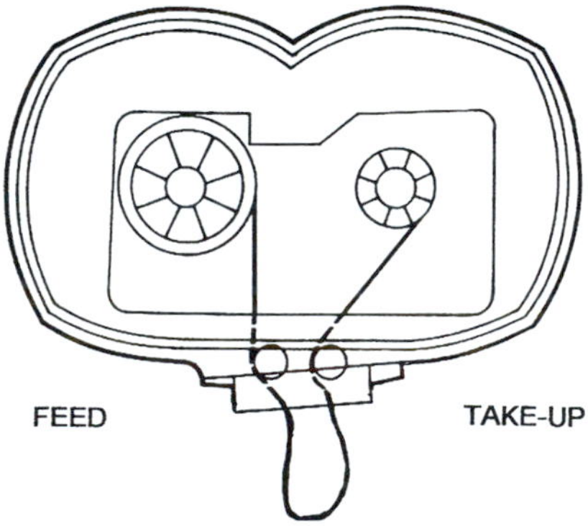

Figure 6.101
Panavision Panaflex 65 magazine. (Reprinted from the *Hands-On Manual for Cinematographers*, with permission of David Samuelson.)

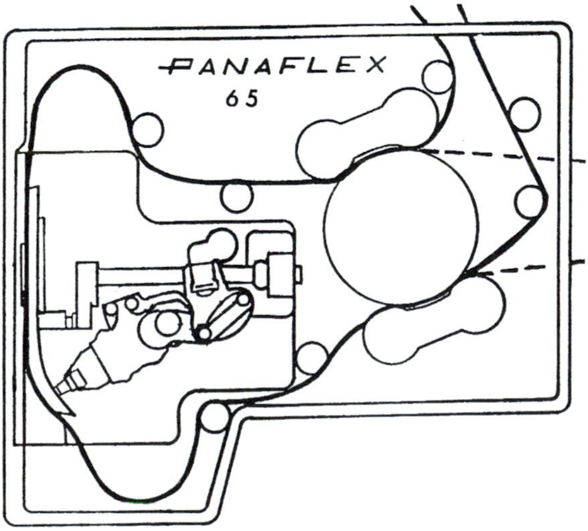

Figure 6.102
Panavision Panaflex 65 camera threading. (Courtesy of Panavision, Inc.)

PANAVISION 65 MM HIGH SPEED

Format: 65 mm
Magazine sizes: 500′ and 1000′ Displacement

For camera and magazine illustrations and threading diagrams, see Figures 6.103 through 6.105.

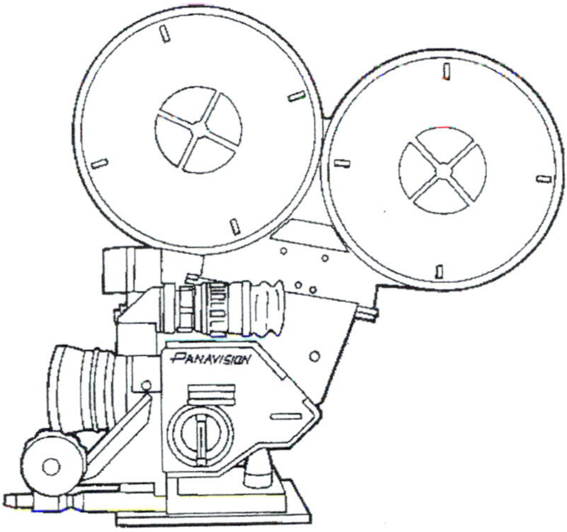

Figure 6.103
Panavision 65 mm High Speed camera. (Reprinted from the *Hands-On Manual for Cinematographers*, with permission of David Samuelson.)

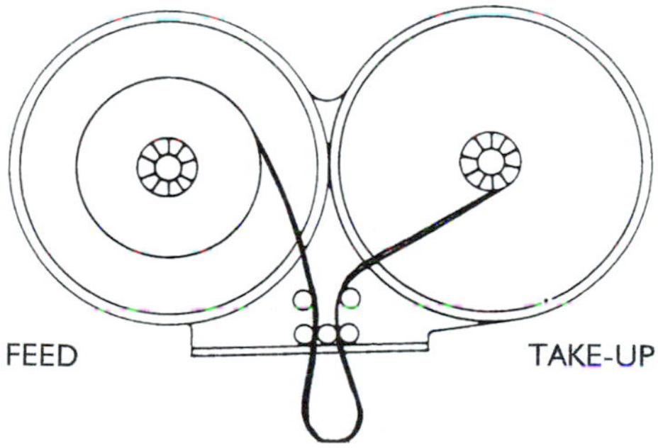

Figure 6.104
Panavision 65 mm High Speed magazine. (Reprinted from the *Hands-On Manual for Cinematographers,* with permission of David Samuelson.)

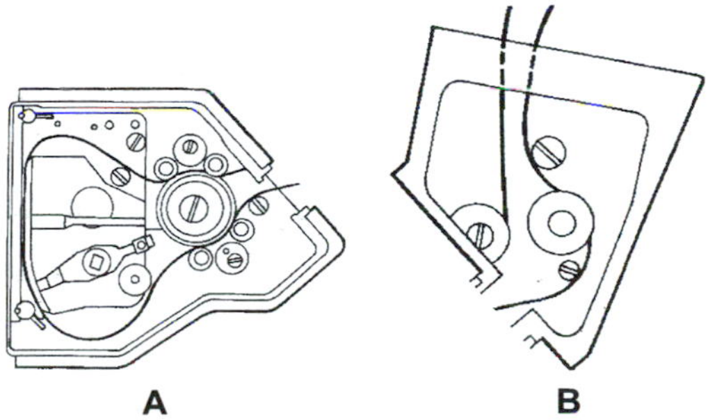

Figure 6.105
Panavision 65 mm High Speed camera threading. **A,** Camera threading, **B,** Top mount adapter. (Reprinted from the *Hands-On Manual for Cinematographers,* with permission of David Samuelson.)

PANAVISION 65 MM HAND-HELD

Format: 65 mm
Magazine sizes: 250′, 500′, and 1000′ Displacement

For camera and magazine illustrations and threading diagrams, see Figures 6.106 through 6.108.

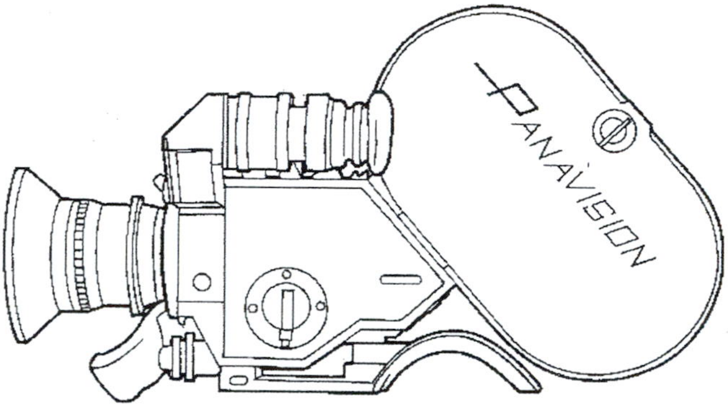

Figure 6.106 Panavision 65 mm Hand-Held camera. (Reprinted from the *Hands-On Manual for Cinematographers*, with permission of David Samuelson.)

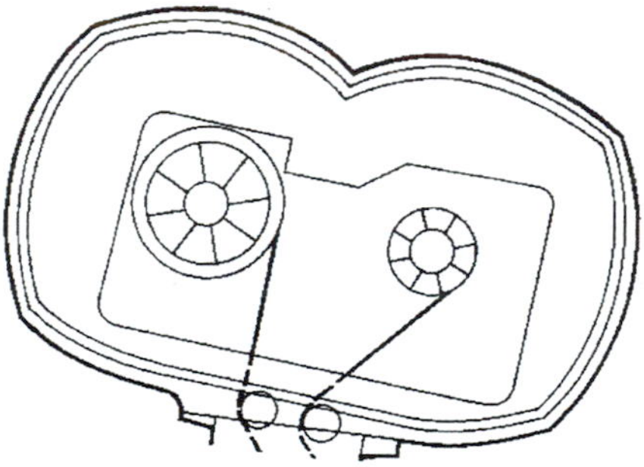

Figure 6.107 Panavision 65 mm Hand-Held magazine. (Reprinted from the *Hands-On Manual for Cinematographers*, with permission of David Samuelson.)

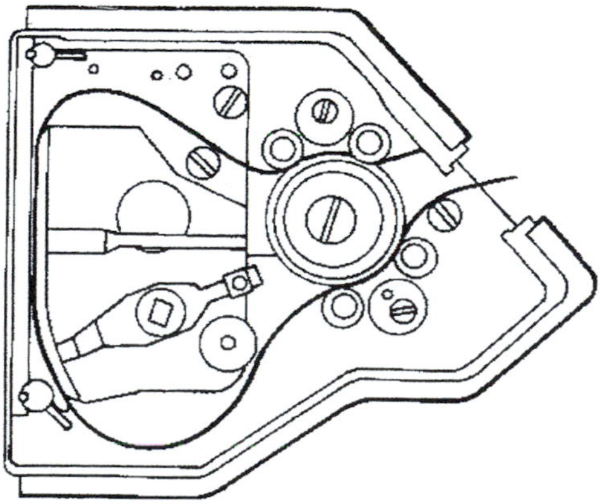

Figure 6.108 Panavision 65 mm Hand-Held camera threading. (Reprinted from the *Hands-On Manual for Cinematographers*, with permission of David Samuelson.)

PHOTO-SONICS ACTIONMASTER 500

Format: 16 mm High speed
Magazine sizes: 400′ Coaxial Daylight Spool Loading

For camera and magazine illustrations and threading diagrams, see Figures 6.109 and 6.110.

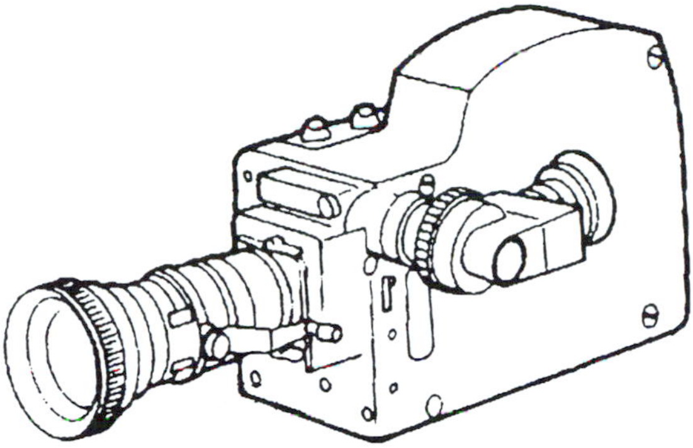

Figure 6.109
Photo-Sonics Actionmaster 500 camera with 400′ magazine. (Courtesy of Photo-Sonics, Inc.)

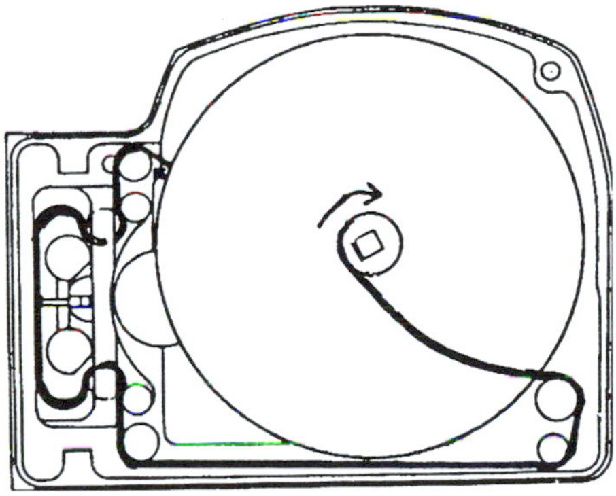

Figure 6.110
Photo-Sonics Actionmaster magazine—film path outline. (Courtesy of Photo-Sonics, Inc.)

PHOTO-SONICS 1VN

Format: 16 mm High Speed
Magazine sizes: 100′ Daylight Spool Load, 100′ and 200′ Core Load

For camera and magazine illustrations and threading diagrams, see Figures 6.111 and 6.112.

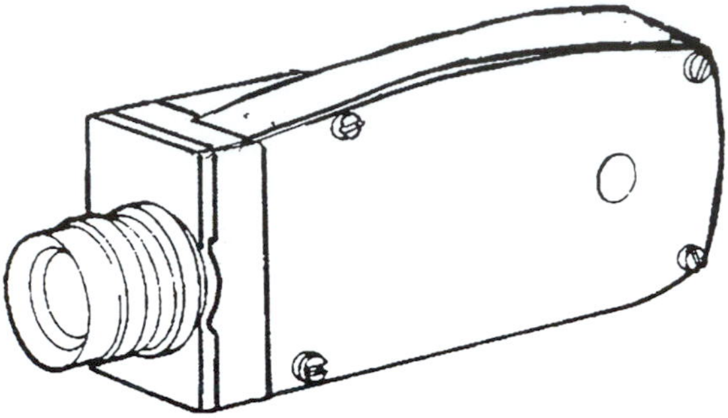

Figure 6.111
Photo-Sonics 1VN camera. (Courtesy of Photo-Sonics, Inc.)

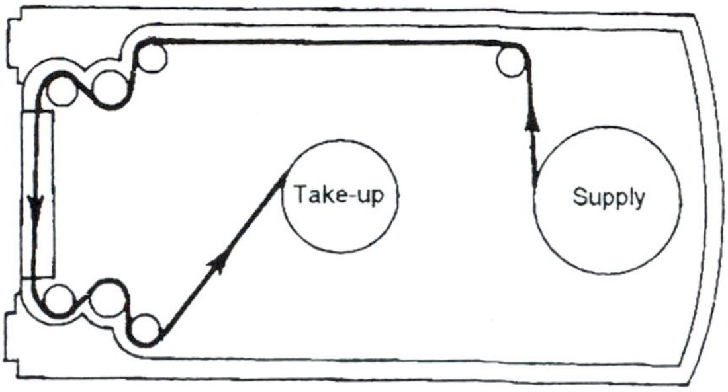

Figure 6.112
Photo-Sonics 1VN camera threading. (Courtesy of Photo-Sonics, Inc.)

PHOTO-SONICS NAC E-10

Format: 16 mm High Speed
Magazine sizes: 100′ and 400′ Daylight Spool Load

For camera and magazine illustrations and threading diagrams, see Figures 6.113 through 6.115.

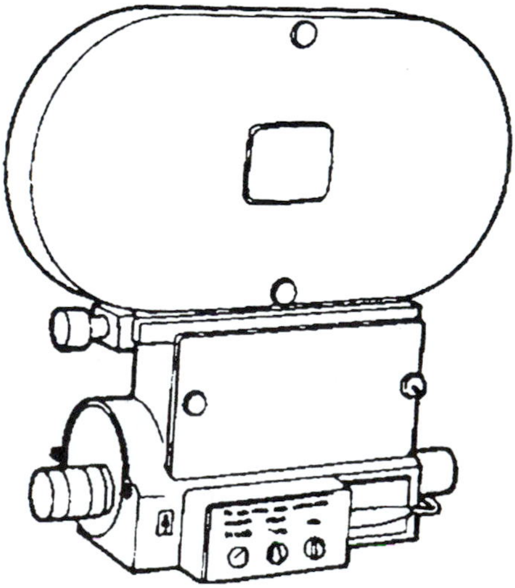

Figure 6.113
Photo-Sonics NAC E-10 camera. (Courtesy of Photo-Sonics, Inc.)

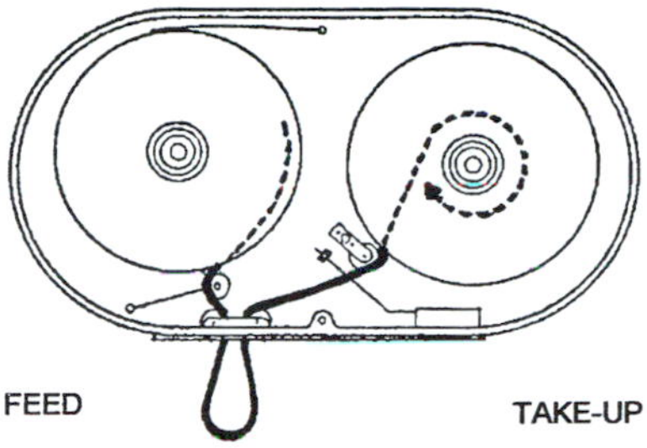

Figure 6.114
Photo-Sonics NAC E-10 magazine. (Courtesy of Photo-Sonics, Inc.)

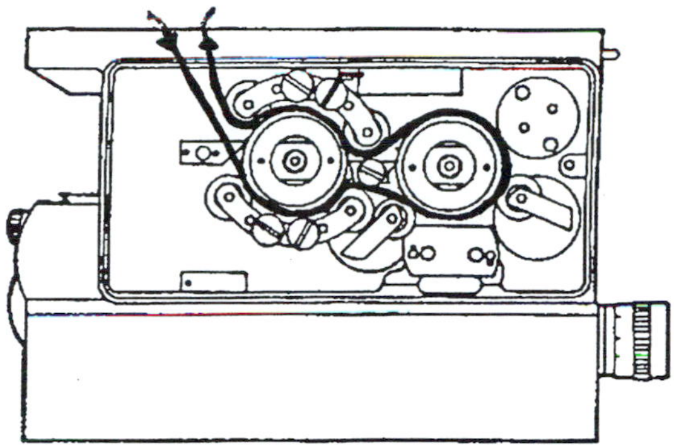

Figure 6.115
Photo-Sonics NAC E-10 camera threading. (Courtesy of Photo-Sonics, Inc.)

PHOTO-SONICS 35-4B/4C

Format: 35 mm High Speed
Magazine sizes: 1000′ Displacement

For camera and magazine illustrations and threading diagrams, see Figures 6.116 through 6.119.

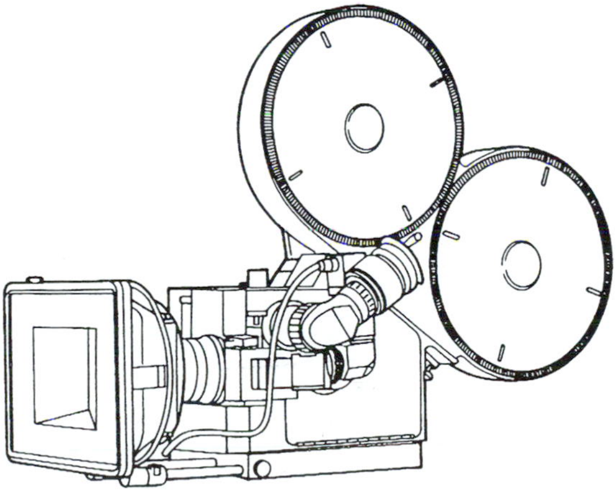

Figure 6.116
Photo-Sonics 35-4B/4C camera. (Courtesy of Photo-Sonics, Inc.)

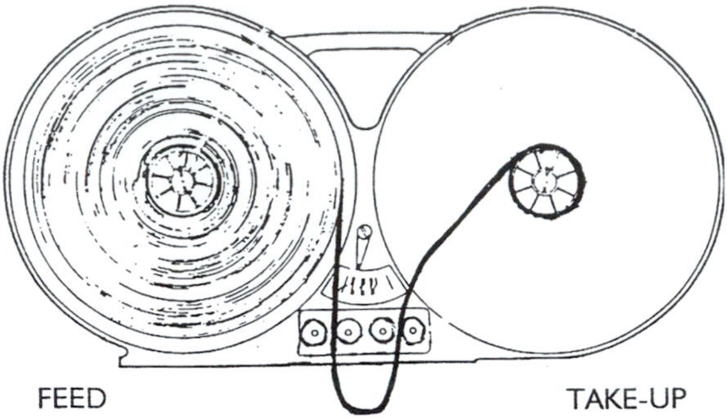

Figure 6.117 Photo-Sonics 35-4B/4C magazine. (Courtesy of Photo-Sonics, Inc.)

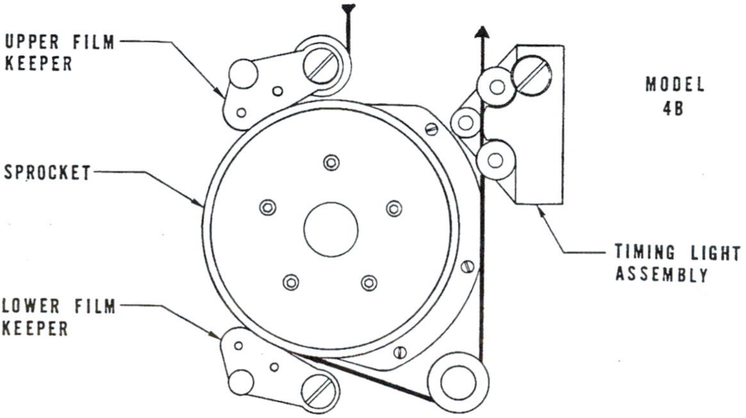

Figure 6.118 Photo-Sonics 35-4B camera threading. (Courtesy of Photo-Sonics, Inc.)

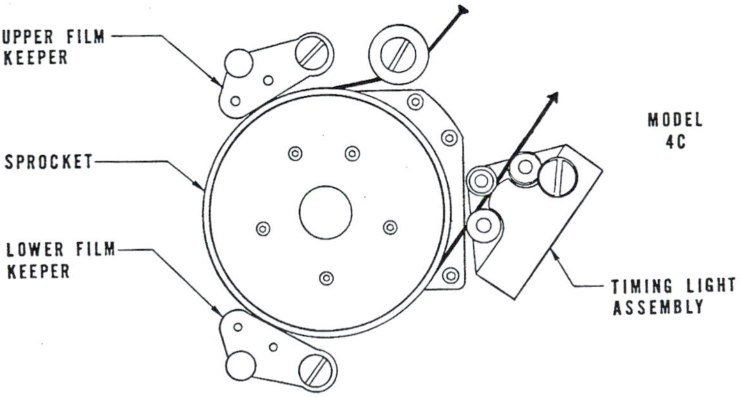

Figure 6.119 Photo-Sonics 35-4C camera threading. (Courtesy of Photo-Sonics, Inc.)

PHOTO-SONICS 35-4E/ER

Format: 35 mm High Speed
Magazine sizes: 1000′ Displacement

For camera and magazine illustrations and threading diagrams, see Figures 6.120 through 6.122.

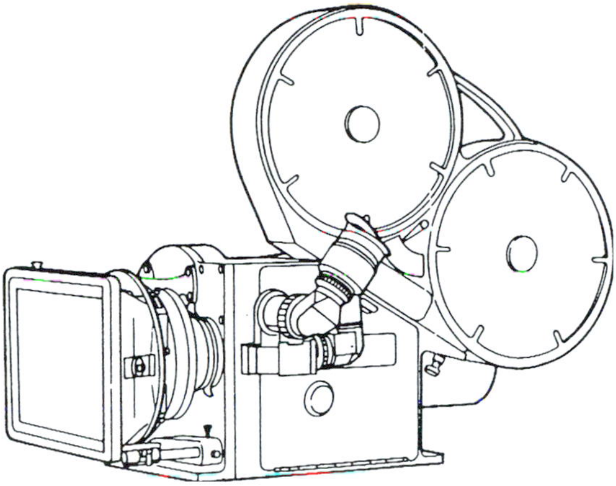

Figure 6.120
Photo-Sonics 35-4E/ER camera. (Courtesy of Photo-Sonics, Inc.)

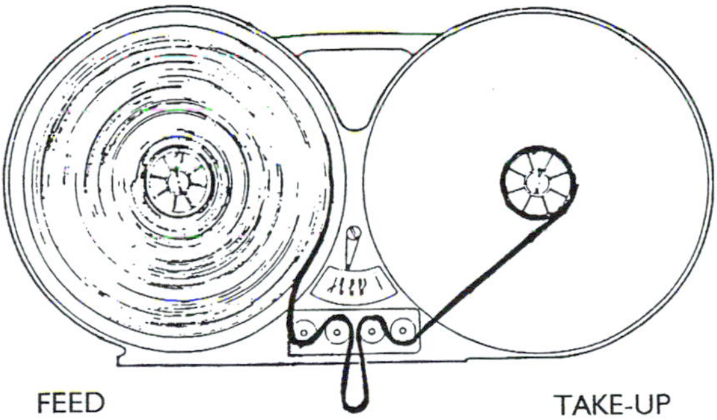

Figure 6.121
Photo-Sonics 35-4E/ER magazine. (Courtesy of Photo-Sonics, Inc.)

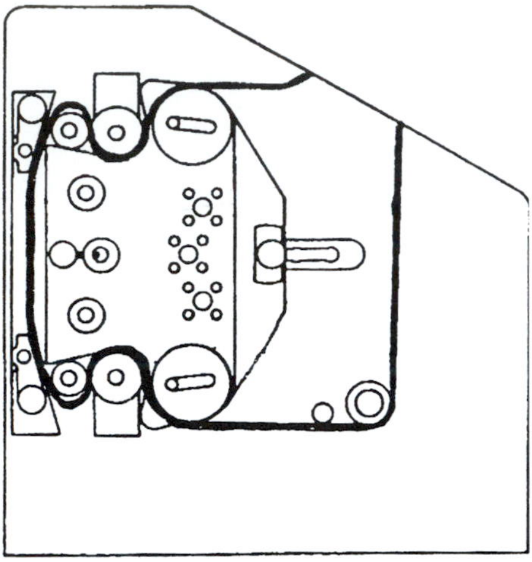

Figure 6.122
Photo-Sonics 35-4E/ER camera threading. (Courtesy of Photo-Sonics, Inc.)

PHOTO-SONICS 35-4ML

Format: 35 mm High Speed
Magazine sizes: 200′ and 400′ Displacement

For camera and magazine illustrations and threading diagrams, see Figures 6.123 and 6.124.

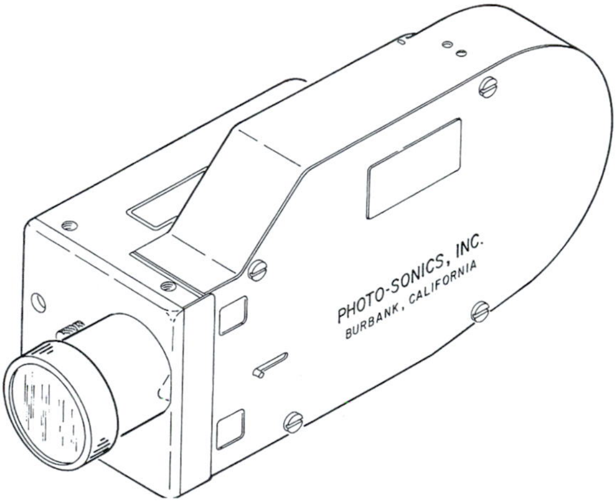

Figure 6.123
Photo-Sonics 35-4ML camera with 400′ magazine. (Courtesy of Photo-Sonics, Inc.)

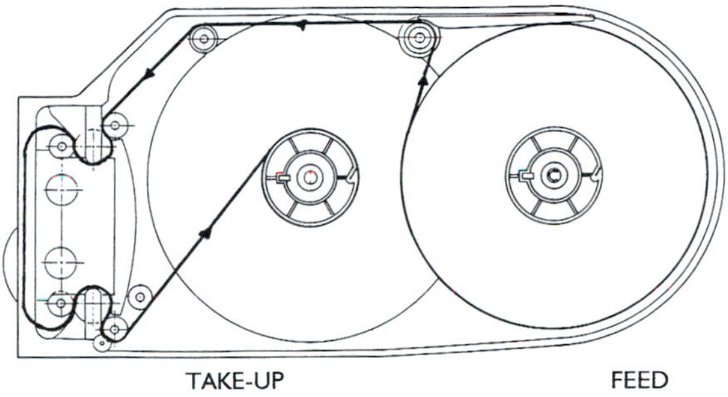

Figure 6.124
Photo-Sonics 35-4ML 400′ magazine. (Courtesy of Photo-Sonics, Inc.)

7

Before, During, and After the Job

Now that you have read the first six chapters, and, it is hoped, know how to do the job of a First and Second Assistant Cameraman, I'd like to mention some of the things you should do before you get the job, how to act once you have the job, and finally what to do when it's all over. Some of what is discussed here includes preparing a résumé, questions to ask during the interview, proper set etiquette, and how to behave while on the job, and staying in contact with crew people after the job.

First I want to discuss the differences and similarities between union and non-union work. Most likely when you start out you will work on non-union productions, but there may come a time after gaining more experience when you decide that you would like to join the union. The following information is based on my knowledge and experience of working on non-union productions and also of being a union member. If any of this information is incorrect or inaccurate, I apologize for any errors or omissions.

UNION OR NON-UNION

Many people ask me what the primary difference is between a union production and a non-union production. There can be many answers to this question, but my very simple answer is as follows. In general on a non-union production you may work long hours, with overtime, meal penalties, and short turnarounds, and not be adequately compensated for it. On a union production you may still work long hours with overtime and meal penalties but due to union regulations, you must be compensated for all of these things. Please don't misunderstand me here because many of my jobs have been on non-union productions, and I was treated fairly in every way. But union productions have minimum wage requirements, overtime, meal penalty, and turnaround rules that must be adhered to. Union productions have a specific requirement as to the crew positions that must be filled within the camera department as well.

The most typical jobs that a beginning filmmaker encounters are non-union productions. Many of these are independent, low-budget productions and are often first-time productions by a company or individual. But many non-union productions may be done by established individuals or companies that have just not signed the agreement with the various production unions. These can include feature films, television pilots, commercials, music videos, educational and industrial films, and more.

A non-union production doesn't mean that it is not a reputable production, just that they are not required to abide by the union rules and regulations with regard to the crew. But they still must abide by the basic state and federal guidelines regarding employment and fair treatment of their workers. One of the biggest problems I have encountered on non-union productions is their failure to provide a meal or a meal break 6 hours after the call time. Having worked in Los Angeles for so many years, I know that the wage, hours, and working conditions for the motion picture industry clearly state that a minimum 30-minute meal break must be given after 6 hours from the crew call. There have been a few times in my career that I had to remind a producer or production manager on a non-union shoot about this regulation. In most cases, though, the non-union productions abide by this guideline.

One of the main differences between union and non-union work is the pay scale. Often on a non-union production you will be asked to work for a flat rate per day. What this means is that no matter how many hours you work in a day, your rate of pay is a set amount. If you work 8 hours, 10 hours, 12 hours, 14 hours, or more, you are still paid the same rate of pay. I try to avoid these types of jobs whenever possible. When speaking with a producer or production manager about my daily rate I always quote a rate based on a 10- or 12-hour day, with overtime to be paid after the specific number of hours at a specific rate, usually time and a half. The producer often negotiates, but I almost never accept a flat rate deal, and whatever deal I do accept I get it in writing on a deal memo or contract for the production. It is important to get this information in writing so that you have something to refer to later on in case there is ever a question or problem.

When you first start working on non-union productions, you must determine your daily pay rate. When I started working in this industry, I worked for anything from $50 to $200 a day as a Second Assistant Cameraman, depending on how much experience I had at the time of the production, the type of production, and finally what the company was willing to pay.

Once I started working as a First Assistant Cameraman, my daily rate went up because I had much more experience and felt comfortable quoting a higher rate. Each person's situation is going to be a bit different. If and when you join the union, your pay rate will be determined by your classification and the current rate for that classification as established by the union.

JOINING THE UNION

How do you actually go about joining the International Cinematographers Guild? It is not that complicated, but it does involve a little bit of work to gather up all of the documentation as proof of your non-union work.

If you are interested in joining the union, you must first work non-union and build up a specific number of paid days or hours worked in a particular classification before applying for membership. Whether or not you ever join the union is a matter of personal preference. I know a lot of people who have had successful careers without joining the union and a lot of people who have had successful careers because they joined the union. Your decision depends on a number of factors. If you know some other camera people in the union and know that you will be able to get union jobs, then it may be a benefit to you to join. This is especially true if you are working in one of the larger film markets such as New York or Los Angeles. If you are located in an area outside of these large markets, it may not be to your advantage to join the union, both from a practical and a financial standpoint. A union job is one in which the producer or production company has signed a signatory agreement with the union agreeing to abide by its rules and regulations. Virtually all of the major studio productions, productions done by the major production companies, or major television network productions are union jobs. When in doubt just ask if a job is a union job when inquiring about the availability of work.

There are a number of ways that you can currently become a member of the International Cinematographers Guild Local 600. Since I am mostly familiar with the Western Region Guidelines, I will discuss those requirements here. If you are located in either the Central Region or the Eastern Region you should contact the local office for their membership requirements.

To work in the Western Region you must be placed on what is called the Industry Experience Roster. The industry roster is maintained by an organization called the Contract Services Administration Trust Fund. The following are some basic descriptions of how to get placed on the roster:

- When a producer cannot find qualified union personnel in a specific classification, he or she may seek them from other sources.
- If you are working on a non-union production and the company signs the union agreement, you are then eligible to be placed on the roster after you have worked 30 days in your classification with that company. The 30 days must be within 1 year of applying.
- If you have 100 days of paid non-union work within a 3-year period, in the classification that you are applying for, you may then submit an application to the union for that classification.

If you meet one of the preceding requirements for joining, you must then provide documentation as proof of your eligibility. This documentation may include letters from a producer, production manager, or other company official stating that you were employed by them in the specific classification you are applying for. This letter should include the number of days worked and the dates of employment, the name of the production, your job classification, where you were hired, and where the work was performed. You also need to submit paycheck stubs or copies of cancelled paychecks. In some cases you may also be asked to provide copies of call sheets, crew lists, or a deal memo as proof of your previous work. This documentation must be submitted along with the Contract Services application form and an I-9 form as proof of your eligibility to work in the United States. Once all of your paperwork has been received and processed, if you meet all of the requirements you will then be invited to join the International Cinematographers Guild Local 600.

Joining the union is expensive. The initiation fees range from approximately $2800 for a Film Loader to almost $10,000 for a Director of Photography (D.P.). Currently the initiation fee for an assistant cameraman is approximately $5000. These are the fees just to become a member. You must also pay quarterly dues and other fees. The quarterly dues are assessed whether you are working or not, so you should be sure that you will be able to get union work before spending a great deal of money to join. Quarterly dues range from approximately $110 to $250 depending on your classification. Please be aware that these amounts are subject to change at any time.

Once you make the decision to join, you must then decide which classification you will apply for. If all of your non-union work is as a First Assistant Cameraman then that is the classification you should apply for. Because you must provide documentation of your non-union work, you really cannot apply for a union classification for which you have little or no experience. If your work is split between 1st A.C. and 2nd A.C., you must decide which would be more beneficial to you. The union guidelines do not permit you to hold two classifications at once. But once you are a member, you have the ability to re-rate to a new classification provided you have worked in that classification and are able to pay the new initiation fees and dues.

Once you are a member of International Cinematographers Guild Local 600, you should be confident that you will be paid a fair wage and be treated fairly on all union jobs that you take. Keep in mind that the guild has different rates based on where you live and work in the country and also based on the type of production. In addition there are different rates for studio work versus location work. For example, a First Assistant Cameraman may be paid approximately $33.50 per hour for work on 1-hour episodic television productions and approximately $34.00 per hour for work on a feature film. On many productions the first assistant is classified as a technician and paid at a higher rate. For example, on a feature film the technician rate is approximately $40.75 per hour. A First Assistant Cameraman working with a specialized piece of equipment such as Panavision cameras is paid at the Technician rate instead of the 1st A.C. rate because special training and experience is required to work with specialized pieces of camera equipment. When working in HD or Video, there are specific rates for each classification as well. They range from approximately $25.00 to $47.00 per hour depending on your classification.

These amounts are subject to change at any time and if you are a member of the union, you will receive updates of any rate changes. The current rates are available to union members on the union web site. The common practice in the camera union is to pay 1 1/2 times the hourly rate after 8 hours worked up to 12 hours and two times the hourly rate after 12 hours worked.

In addition to minimum wage rates, the union also requires a minimum turnaround time between shifts. This is the time between wrap on one day and call time for the next day's shooting. The typical turnaround time for an assistant is 9 hours and for the Camera Operator and D.P. it is 11 hours.

The union also requires that you be paid a meal penalty if the meal break is not given after 6 hours from the call time or from the end of the previous meal break. The only time the meal penalty is not accessed is when you are in the middle of shooting a shot or scene and wish to finish the scene before breaking for the meal. It is quite common for the first assistant director to announce to the crew that they would like to finish the current shot or scene before breaking and in most cases the crew will agree. Once the scene or shot is finished, you may not continue shooting until after the crew has been given a meal break. Meal penalty starts at $7.50 for the first half hour or fraction of a half hour and increases for each subsequent half hour period that you don't get the meal break. The standard meal period is 1 half hour if the production company provides the meal, and the time actually starts once the last person goes through the meal line and gets food. If the production company does not provide a meal, the standard meal break is 1 hour.

No matter what decision you make about whether or not to join the union, I am sure that you will have a successful and rewarding career in the camera department. Good luck and happy shooting.

BEFORE THE JOB

Keep in mind that the film industry is unlike any other business or industry. Before starting in this business, many people have no idea what they are up against. First, this is not a 9-to-5 typical job. Most days you will work a minimum of 12 hours. Working more than 12 hours a day is not uncommon in this business. So don't make dinner plans for a particular evening because you probably won't be there on time.

Most if not all of your jobs will come from word-of-mouth and recommendations from other camera people. In most cases you will not be working for a single company or studio. The film industry is made up of freelance workers in many different job categories. Being freelance is great for some people, but others can't handle it and get out of the business quickly. As a freelance camera person you will always be working to find that next job. You must be aware of what productions are coming up and especially of the latest cameras and equipment. When looking for work it is usually more important who you know than what you know. Many of my jobs have come from recommendations from other D.P.s or camera assistants whom I have worked with.

When starting out it may be to your advantage to work at a camera rental company. You will get to know many of the cameras and accessories that an assistant uses. Plus you will have the opportunity to meet D.P.s and assistants who come into the rental company. Unfortunately working at a camera rental company takes you out of the job market for production work. If you choose to start looking for production jobs, you may need to accept jobs for no pay just to prove that you are a hard worker and know what you are doing. Don't be afraid to start out as a camera intern, carrying cases and doing other jobs within the camera department. Show that you are a hard worker and you will most likely be hired for pay on a future production.

When not working, try to learn as much as possible. Attend seminars that are often offered by camera rental companies. Obtain camera instruction books or manuals and other camera-related books. Many camera manufacturer web sites offer their manuals for downloading.

The more you can learn when first starting out, the better chances you will have of getting work.

The Résumé

One of the first things you should do is prepare a résumé. At the beginning of your career you will have minimal experience. If you have recently graduated from film school, you will most likely have some experience on student productions. A beginning résumé should list any production experience that you may have. This includes production assistant, craft service, grip, electrician, and any other jobs you may have done. At the top of the résumé you should state that your goal is to work in the camera department so that anyone reading it will know that you do have a specific goal. Once you have acquired more camera-related experience, then you may remove the other jobs not related to the camera department and also may remove the statement about your goal. It will be quite clear from your list of production credits that you are applying for a position within the camera department.

Your résumé should include your basic personal contact information: name, address, and telephone numbers. If you have a cell phone, pager, or fax machine, be sure to include these numbers. I recommend getting a cell phone as soon as possible so you don't miss out on any job calls. Also include an e-mail address if you have one. And if you don't have one, get one. As a freelance camera assistant, prospective employers need to be able to get in touch with you.

Next, your résumé should list your production credits. These are most often listed in reverse chronological order, which means that the most recent job is at the top of the listing. The exception to this is if you have any production credits from well-known, recognizable productions. In this case, those credits should be listed first. As a D.P. or Production Manager looks at your résumé, these names will jump out at them and indicate that you are qualified for the job.

The format that you use for the résumé is up to your personal preference. Most résumés that I have seen contain the same or similar basic information. This includes the title of the production, type of production—feature film, television show, commercial, and so forth; whether the job performed was that of a 1st A.C., 2nd A.C., or Loader; the name of the D.P.; and sometimes the name of the Director, Producer, or production company.

Many production managers or D.P.s who you interview with will most often ask, "What D.P.s have you worked with?" In preparing my résumé, I included the names of all D.P.s that I have worked with on the various productions. I currently work as both a Camera Operator and First Assistant, so I list all of my production credits for these positions, as well as my past experience as a Second Assistant. I have listed my credits in subcategories based on the type of production: television series, feature film, commercial, music video, and other credits.

Following your listing of credits, you may list any special skills or equipment knowledge that relates to your experience. You may also list any industry-related organizations or unions that you belong to. Next you should list your education, including the name of the school, years attended, and degree earned. At the end of the résumé, include the following statement: "References available upon request." Don't volunteer reference information unless it is asked for. When giving names of references, be sure that you have their permission. My current résumé may be viewed on the companion web site for this book. The web site address is www.cameraassistantmanual.com.

The most important thing to remember about your résumé is don't lie. If you do, it will be discovered sooner or later and will only cause you more problems than it is worth.

Your résumé is done, and now you need to get that first job. Send it out to as many production companies as possible. The best places to look for listings are the film industry-related trade papers or magazines, such as *Daily Variety* and the *Hollywood Reporter*. These publications are available on most newsstands and also by subscription. Each week they list current productions, along with productions in the pre-production or planning stages. Keep in mind that many of these listings are most likely on union productions and unless you have extensive union experience and know somebody on the show, you will most likely not receive a reply to your inquiry. In addition to the publications already mentioned, there are many other industry magazines and publications, as well as some excellent Internet web sites that contain job information. If you have friends or colleagues in the film industry, you may also ask them for any job leads. Remember, a great deal of the film industry relies on networking to learn about upcoming work. Don't be afraid to ask people you have worked with if they know of any future jobs. Also, don't be afraid to tell other crew people about jobs you know of.

When mailing your résumé, you should include a brief cover letter that introduces yourself and explains why you are writing to the company. Mail your letter to as many productions that interest you. If you are able to obtain a telephone number for the production company, wait about a week and then call them. Ask if your résumé was received, and ask if you can come in for a personal interview. Show that you are seriously interested in the job. The old saying that the squeaky wheel gets the grease does apply in the film business. Telephoning and showing that you are truly interested may be the difference between your getting the job and someone else getting it. Sometimes you may have to work for little or no money to prove yourself. Don't be discouraged by rejection, because you will send out hundreds of résumés and may get only one or two replies. Be persistent and eventually you will get that first big break. If you want that first job badly enough and are willing to work to get it, the job will come and you will be on your way to a successful career.

The Job Interview

Now that you have prepared your résumé and sent it out, you are ready to go on that first job interview. In most cases the D.P., Production Manager, or both will conduct the interview. Arrive a little early for the interview and be prepared. Have additional copies of your résumé with you in case anyone asks for one. I also recommend having business cards with all of your contact information on them. An important part of the interview is asking the right questions. There are many things that you need to know about the job before starting, and you have the right to ask these questions. The following are some key questions that you should ask when interviewing for a job on any production. They are listed in no specific order.

- What format is the film being shot in—16 mm, 35 mm, video?
- What camera system will be used?
- Is it a union or non-union crew?
- What is the daily rate for the position I am applying for? Be prepared to quote your daily rate.
- Is the daily rate based on 10 hours, 12 hours, or more?
- Is this a flat rate or is there overtime pay after a specific number of hours?
- How often will I be paid or how soon after the completion of production will I be paid?
- Does this rate include prep and wrap days?
- Do you pay a box or kit rental?
- Would you be willing to rent any equipment from me?
- Is the shooting local or on a distant location?
- If it is a distant location, do you pay travel expenses, per diem, and lodging?
- Are meals provided?
- How many weeks of shooting will there be?
- Is the workweek 5 or 6 days? (Never work a 7-day week.)
- How many hours per day do you anticipate shooting? (12 is good; anything over 12 is usually too much.)

- What are the scheduled start and end dates of the shooting schedule?
- Are any other crew positions still available? Recommend other crew members that you have worked with in the past.

These are some of the typical questions that you should ask during the interview. You may add others as you gain more experience. Once you have completed this basic part of the interview, you may be asked to sign a deal memo, which outlines the terms and conditions of your employment as well as the pay scale. Be sure to obtain a copy of all paperwork that you sign so that if there are any problems or questions later, you can refer to it.

It is important to ask how many hours your rate is based on. This will affect your overtime rate if and when you work any overtime hours. Be sure to ask this up front during your interview. The section later in this chapter, After the Job, discusses daily rate and invoicing for services in more detail.

If you have any special camera-related equipment that may be used on the production, ask if the company will rent it from you instead of from the camera rental company. Many assistants own camera batteries, filters, or other camera equipment. Give the production company a fair price to make it worth renting from you. One thing you should remember when owning and renting your equipment is that you may be taking business away from a rental house that you will be dealing with regularly in the course of your career. Don't jeopardize your reputation with a rental company just to make a few extra dollars.

DURING THE JOB

Once you have been hired for the job, you should follow some basic guidelines while on the set. There is a proper set etiquette that should be followed by all crew members on any production. How you conduct yourself is just as important as knowing how to do the job properly. You are a professional and should act accordingly.

Some people in the film industry let it go to their head and often develop an ego. Don't let this happen to you. Just because you are part of a film crew doesn't mean you are better than anybody else. And just because you have the basic knowledge to do the job doesn't mean that you know everything. I learn something new on every job I do. Be willing to learn something new. It will make you much happier. And don't forget to thank other crew members for their efforts and help. Most important, if you make a mistake, admit it. Never try to blame your errors on someone else. A friend shared a story with me that illustrates this point. An assistant on a show took the magazines home with him one night to make sure that they were all loaded for the next day's shooting. The next day the crew arrived at the designated area and boarded the crew van to travel to the location. After about 10 or 15 minutes into the trip, the assistant realized that he had left the magazines at home. For the remainder of the trip he tried to think of a way out of his predicament but did and said nothing. When they arrived at the location he made some telephone calls but couldn't get anybody. Just as he was about to inform the D.P. of his error, it started to rain and the shoot was cancelled for the day. Fortunately for him nobody ever found out about his error. But if it hadn't started raining the assistant would have been forced to admit his mistake. I think that it would have been best to admit the mistake as soon as it was discovered and take the consequences. We are only human, and we sometimes make mistakes. Trying to cover them up only causes more problems.

The first time you step onto a film set you may feel like a stranger in a foreign land. Learn the names of other crew members as quickly as possible. Also learn the names of the cast. Write them down on a notepad if necessary. If you have any questions, don't hesitate to ask. Don't attempt to do something that you may not be familiar with. It is important to stay within your own department and give help only if it is asked for, especially on union productions. This may sound selfish, but there are good reasons for doing this. On most shoots there are specific guidelines regarding each department and the job responsibilities within that department. I was on a union show as 1st A.C., and during a setup for a new scene, the D.P. asked me to move the camera dolly a few inches. I unlocked the dolly, moved it, and as I was locking it in place, the Key Grip was right in my face and said, "If you touch that dolly again I'll report you to the union." The D.P. tried to explain that he had asked me to move the dolly and the Key Grip proceeded to yell at him as well, saying that there was a specific crew member to do that job and nobody else. Although I had worked with that Key Grip many times in the past, I learned a valuable lesson that day: Don't touch a piece of equipment that is not part of your department unless specifically asked to do so by someone in that department.

Each day you will be given a call time, which is the time that you should be on the set ready to work, not the time that you are to arrive at work. I recommend arriving at work anywhere from 15 to 30 minutes before the call time. Showing up a little early shows your interest and desire to do a good job. If you will be traveling to an area that you are not familiar with, be sure to look at any maps and call sheets the night before so that you have an approximate idea where you are going and what time you should leave home so that you get there on time.

When traveling to a distant location for a job, be sure that you take certain personal items with you. You should have an extra change of clothes and various personal hygiene items on the camera truck in case of emergency. You may be away from home for an extended period, so be prepared. Even if not on a distant location you should have a change of clothes and other items with you because you never know when you may need them.

Many of your jobs will come from recommendations from other crew members, especially from people within your own department. Work hard, do a good job, and always be willing to give a little extra in the performance of your job. Whenever possible, make your superior look good. By doing this you will have more job offers than you know what to do with.

Whenever a question or problem arises, it is best to follow the chain of command. Start within your department. If you are the 2nd A.C., then go to the 1st A.C. with your question or problem. If he or she can't help, then you should both go to the D.P. Going over someone's head will only make you look bad and could risk your possible employment on future productions.

Being safety conscious is important on any film set. No shot is so important that you should jeopardize an actor or crew person's safety. I have a favorite saying that I tell students: "It's only a movie." It's not so important that you need to jeopardize somebody's safety. If you have a concern, it should be brought up immediately. I have refused to do certain shots because I felt that my personal safety was in jeopardy. In most cases you will be respected for your professionalism and willingness to speak up.

Professionalism is an important aspect of the job in many different ways. If you feel that you are being treated unfairly, you should mention it immediately. As I stated earlier, you are a professional and should act accordingly. You should also be treated as a professional. A situation that I was in a few years ago illustrates this point. I was hired on a production as the 2nd A.C. During the interview I was told that an overtime rate would be paid on hours worked past 12 hours per day. We were using two cameras, and as the 2nd A.C., the job sometimes required me to continue working 45 minutes to an hour or more after most of the crew had wrapped and gone home for the day. I had to prepare the film to be sent to the lab, complete all paperwork, and get the equipment ready for the next day's shooting. At the start of the second week of filming, the Production Manager came to me and told me that he couldn't pay me for the overtime hours that I had put on my time card. I reminded him of the agreement regarding overtime pay and he told me that overtime was based on when the official wrap time was called for the entire crew. I explained that my job required me to work longer each day to complete the extra duties. He said he was sorry but that he could only pay overtime based on the crew wrap time. I looked at him and said, very sternly, "Fine, when you call wrap tonight, I am going home. You unload the film and complete all of the paperwork." At this point I walked back onto the set. A short time later the Producer called me into his office. I explained that we had agreed on an overtime deal during the job interview, and if he wasn't going to honor his agreement then I would leave then, and he could find someone else to do the job. He then told me to put any overtime hours on the time card and promised to honor his original agreement. By standing up for what was right, I showed my professionalism. I did not let the Production Manager or Producer force me into a situation that was unfair. From that day until the end of production, the Producer showed greater respect for me because of my willingness to stand up for what I felt was right.

Another part of being professional is having the right tools and equipment for the job. Many of the tools in your ditty bag may not be used regularly, but having that one special item when it is needed may be the difference between you and someone else being hired for the next job. Be sure to have at least the basic tools and accessories to fulfill your job responsibilities.

Wrap time is the time that filming ends and the crew packs up to go home for the day. When the Assistant Director calls wrap, you should put everything away and leave as quickly as possible. Especially as the 2nd A.C., if you have kept up on the magazines and paperwork throughout the day, you should have minimal work to do at the wrap. Remember, the faster you wrap, the sooner you get home.

Being truthful on the time card is just as important as being truthful on the résumé. During the job interview you should have worked out the deal for overtime and other time-related issues. As the story I told earlier illustrates, the second assistant usually needs to stay later than most of the other crew members. Be sure that the Production Manager or producer understands that up front so that there are no questions later on when you put the additional time on your time card. By filling in your time card accurately and truthfully, you will also show your professionalism and will get more jobs.

As part of a film crew, there will be many times when you are filming on location, in offices, business establishments, and private homes, and so on. Whenever you are on a location you should respect these people's homes, businesses, and property. Being part of a film crew doesn't give you the right to act as you please. The proper attitude and behavior apply as much to location work as they do when you are working on a stage or in a studio. No matter how bad the day is going, having a positive attitude is key. How you act on the job today will affect your chances of getting jobs in the future.

When filming in any situation, whether it is on location or in a studio, there are certain commonsense guidelines that you should be aware of. Avoid any type of sexual, racial, political, or religious comments that could offend others. Avoid the use of profanity as much as possible. Don't wear any clothing that contains slogans, sayings, or images that may offend others. The use of drugs or alcohol before, during, or after work is not recommended. Avoid negative comments or opinions about other production companies, rental companies, equipment, or crew members. The production community is very small, and any bad things you may say now will come back to haunt you sooner or later. Any of these behaviors only show a non-professional attitude.

Here are some important rules to be aware of on any film set.
Always make the D.P. and your immediate superior look good.
Stay in your own department—let other crew members do their job.
Come to work early.
Be enthusiastic and work hard. Go that extra mile.
Learn the names of co-workers and actors.
Keep eyes and ears open at all times.
Don't be afraid to ask questions.
Don't have an ego and claim to know everything.

AFTER THE JOB

What you do after a job may be just as important as what you do during the job. It may often be advantageous to call the D.P. to thank him or her for the opportunity to work on the job. Express your interest to work with him or her again. Also let the production company know that you would like to work with them on any future projects. Remember that the film industry relies heavily on word-of-mouth and networking. Stay in touch with the appropriate people after a job so that you won't have to worry about where the next job is coming from.

Invoicing and Filling in the Time Card

If you have worked as an independent contractor you must submit an invoice to the production company for your equipment and/or services. Be sure to submit your invoice promptly. How long should you wait before receiving payment? I usually try to find this out during my interview or when hired for the job. Most companies pay on a 30-day basis, which means that you won't be paid until 30 days after they receive your invoice. So the sooner you submit the invoice, the sooner you get paid. If you haven't received any payment after 30 days from the end of production, you should call the production office to inquire. My invoice contains the following statement: *Payment is due 30 days from date of invoice. Payment not received is subject to interest charge of 1 1/2% per month.* If I haven't received payment in the proper amount of time, I submit a new invoice with the interest charge added. This usually gets the attention of the production company and they submit payment very quickly.

Check your deal memo because the terms of payment may be specified there. Often in this business you will be paid based on a daily rate. Be sure to find out exactly what your daily rate will be if you haven't quoted a specific rate. And don't forget to ask about how many hours the daily rate applies to. Is it based on a 10-hour workday, 12-hour workday, or longer?

Sometimes you will be asked to work with your rate based on a 14-hour day or even longer. I recommend staying away from these jobs. They are probably low paying and when you calculate it out you are often making less than minimum wage.

As stated in Chapter 3, on union productions and many non-union productions it is common to break down the hour into tenths of an hour. Each 6-minute block of time equals one-tenth of an hour. This makes it much easier to calculate the total time worked, since you will most often finish at odd times and not exactly on the hour. It is also quite common to write the time in military time on your time card. For example if you finish work at 10:25 PM, this would be rounded to the nearest tenth of an hour and written as 22.5 on the time card. Table 7.1 lists the times for tenths of an hour conversion.

Whether you invoice for your services or fill out a time card, you should know what your base hourly rate is along with overtime rates. Tables 7.2, 7.3, and 7.4 show typical daily rates and break them down into hourly rates. Table 7.2 shows the typical daily rates and breaks them down into straight hourly rates based on 8 hours, 10 hours, and 12 hours. In other words the 8-hour day hourly rate is simply the daily rate divided by 8, the 10-hour day hourly rate is the daily rate divided by 10, and so on. Table 7.3 shows the daily rate based on a 10-hour day, with the rate converted to an hourly rate based on 8 hours. Overtime is then paid at the rate of 1 1/2 times your hourly rate after 8 hours. For example, if you are being paid a daily rate of $300.00, then your hourly rate based on an 8-hour day would be $27.27 and your overtime rate would be $40.91. Then, for a 10-hour day, it calculates as follows: $(8 \times 27.27) + (2 \times 40.91) = \$299.98$, which is approximately $300.00 or your daily rate. Table 7.4 shows the daily rate based on a 12-hour day with the rate converted to an hourly rate based on 8 hours. Overtime is then paid at the rate of 1 1/2 times your hourly rate after 8 hours. For example, if you are being paid a daily rate of $300.00, then your hourly rate based on an 8-hour day would be $21.43 and your overtime rate would be $32.15. Then, for a 12-hour day, it calculates as follows: $(8 \times 21.43) + (4 \times 32.15) = \$300.04$, which is approximately $300.00, or your daily rate.

Networking

One of the main things that you should do after the job is to stay in contact with certain crew members. This industry relies heavily on networking and word of mouth. Many of your jobs will come from the recommendations of other crew people that you have worked with. By staying in touch, you will keep your name fresh in their minds, and when the next job comes up, they may call you.

It is especially important to stay in touch with the camera crew members that you have worked with. Call them periodically to let them know that you are available for any future projects. Often a camera assistant may get a job call, but because of a conflict with another job, will have to turn it down. If you stay in touch with other camera crew people, you may be recommended for a job that another assistant turned down. Also, if you must turn down a job because of a conflicting job, be sure to recommend a fellow assistant for the position. And remember, whenever you are forced to turn down a job, be sure to tell the production company that it is because of a conflict with another job. A production company will be more inclined to call you again if it knows that you work steady. Steady work is usually an indication that you are good at what you do.

Table 7.1 Tenths of an hour conversion

1–6 minutes = .1 hour
7–12 minutes = .2 hour
13–18 minutes = .3 hour
19–24 minutes = .4 hour
25–30 minutes = .5 hour
31–36 minutes = .6 hour
37–42 minutes = .7 hour
43–48 minutes = .8 hour
49–54 minutes = .9 hour
55–60 minutes = 1 hour

Table 7.2 Payroll Conversion Table for 8-, 10-, and 12- Hour Base Rate

Daily Rate	Straight Hourly Rate Based on 8 Hours (Daily Rate Divided by 8)	1.5 × 8-Hour Rate	2 × 8-Hour Rate	Straight Hourly Rate Based on 10 Hours (Daily Rate Divided by 10)	1.5 × 10-Hour Rate	2 × 10-Hour Rate	Straight Hourly Rate Based on 12 Hours (Daily Rate Divided by 12)	1.5 × 12-Hour Rate	2 × 12-Hour Rate
$ 50.00	6.25	9.38	12.50	5.00	7.50	10.00	4.17	6.26	8.34
$ 75.00	9.38	14.07	18.76	7.50	11.25	15.00	6.25	9.38	12.50
$ 100.00	12.50	18.75	25.00	10.00	15.00	20.00	8.33	12.50	16.66
$ 125.00	15.63	23.45	31.26	12.50	18.75	25.00	10.42	15.63	20.84
$ 150.00	18.75	28.13	37.50	15.00	22.50	30.00	12.50	18.75	25.00
$ 175.00	21.88	32.82	43.76	17.50	26.25	35.00	14.58	21.87	29.16
$ 200.00	25.00	37.50	50.00	20.00	30.00	40.00	16.67	25.01	33.34
$ 225.00	28.13	42.20	56.26	22.50	33.75	45.00	18.75	28.13	37.50
$ 250.00	31.25	46.88	62.50	25.00	37.50	50.00	20.83	31.25	41.66
$ 275.00	34.38	51.57	68.76	27.50	41.25	55.00	22.92	34.38	45.84
$ 300.00	37.50	56.25	75.00	30.00	45.00	60.00	25.00	37.50	50.00
$ 325.00	40.63	60.95	81.26	32.50	48.75	65.00	27.08	40.62	54.16
$ 350.00	43.75	65.63	87.50	35.00	52.50	70.00	29.17	43.76	58.34
$ 375.00	46.88	70.32	93.76	37.50	56.25	75.00	31.25	46.88	62.50
$ 400.00	50.00	75.00	100.00	40.00	60.00	80.00	33.33	50.00	66.66
$ 425.00	53.13	79.70	106.26	42.50	63.75	85.00	35.42	53.13	70.84
$ 450.00	56.25	84.38	112.50	45.00	67.50	90.00	37.50	56.25	75.00
$ 475.00	59.38	89.07	118.76	47.50	71.25	95.00	39.58	59.37	79.16
$ 500.00	62.50	93.75	125.00	50.00	75.00	100.00	41.67	62.51	83.34

Table 7.3 Payroll Conversion Table—10-Hour Day Rate Converted to 8-Hour Day

Daily Rate for 10-Hour Day	8-Hour Day Rate (10-Hour Rate Divided by 11)	1.5 × 8-Hour Rate	2 × 8-Hour Rate
$ 50.00	4.55	6.83	9.10
$ 75.00	6.82	10.23	13.64
$ 100.00	9.09	13.64	18.18
$ 125.00	11.36	17.04	22.72
$ 150.00	13.64	20.46	27.28
$ 175.00	15.91	23.87	31.82
$ 200.00	18.18	27.27	36.36
$ 225.00	20.45	30.68	40.90
$ 250.00	22.73	34.10	45.46
$ 275.00	25.00	37.50	50.00
$ 300.00	27.27	40.91	54.54
$ 325.00	29.55	44.33	59.10
$ 350.00	31.82	47.73	63.64
$ 375.00	34.09	51.14	68.18
$ 400.00	36.36	54.54	72.72
$ 425.00	38.64	57.96	77.28
$ 450.00	40.91	61.37	81.82
$ 475.00	43.18	64.77	86.36
$ 500.00	45.45	68.18	90.90

After a job, call or email the D.P. to thank him or her for having you as part of the crew. Let the D.P. know that you would like to work with him or her again, and ask if you may call from time to time to keep in touch. Sometimes the first person to be hired for a job is the most recent person with whom the D.P. talked. Let's hope that person is you.

Good luck, don't get discouraged, and I wish you all the best for a long and rewarding career in the camera department.

Table 7.4 Payroll Conversion Table—12-Hour Day Rate Converted to 8-Hour Day

Daily Rate for 12-Hour Day	8-Hour Day Rate (12-Hour Rate Divided by 14)	1.5 × 8-Hour Rate	2 × 8-Hour Rate
$ 50.00	3.57	5.36	7.14
$ 75.00	5.36	8.04	10.72
$ 100.00	7.14	10.71	14.28
$ 125.00	8.93	13.40	17.86
$ 150.00	10.71	16.07	21.42
$ 175.00	12.50	18.75	25.00
$ 200.00	14.29	21.44	28.58
$ 225.00	16.07	24.11	32.14
$ 250.00	17.86	26.79	35.72
$ 275.00	19.64	29.46	39.28
$ 300.00	21.43	32.15	42.86
$ 325.00	32.21	34.82	46.42
$ 350.00	25.00	37.50	50.00
$ 375.00	26.79	40.19	53.58
$ 400.00	28.57	42.86	57.14
$ 425.00	30.36	45.54	60.72
$ 450.00	32.14	48.21	64.28
$ 475.00	33.93	50.90	67.86
$ 500.00	35.71	53.57	71.42

Appendix A

Film Stock

Currently there are two manufacturers of professional motion picture film stock, Eastman Kodak and Fuji, and there are a large number of film stocks available for both 16 mm and 35 mm professional cinematography. These film stocks are available in color and black and white, in negative and reversal. Emulsions are available in slow-, medium-, and high-speed exposure index (EI) ratings. Some of the film stocks are balanced for shooting in tungsten light and some are balanced for shooting in daylight. Table A.1 contains a listing of all current film stocks available from Eastman Kodak and Fuji at publication time.

Rolls of film come in various lengths because of the different camera and magazine sizes in use today. Motion picture film is available on plastic cores or daylight spools, sometimes referred to as camera spools. See Figures 1.7 and 1.8 for illustrations of plastic cores and daylight spools. Table A.2 lists the standard packaging sizes for motion picture film. When choosing a film stock, check with the manufacturer or distributor to be sure that it is available in the size and type that will suit your filmmaking needs. Not all films are available in all roll sizes. Also be sure that the sizes of the rolls you order correspond to the size of the camera magazines that you will be using. If you plan to use daylight spools, be sure that the camera has the ability to accept internal loads. It is not recommended to use daylight spools in a magazine, although you can do it. When using a daylight spool in a magazine, the flanges of the spool will often rub against the cover of the magazine causing unnecessary noise. If you will be using the Aaton A-Minima 16 mm camera, be aware that it only takes 200′ daylight spools specially designed for the camera by Eastman Kodak Company.

When filming on distant locations, it is sometimes necessary to ship the film to the lab. You will often have many cans of film from each day's shooting that must be carefully packed into boxes for shipping. To help you better prepare your film stock for shipping, Table A.3 gives the individual weight of each full can of film for all sizes currently available for both 16 mm and 35 mm.

Table A.1 Professional Motion Picture Film Stock

Film Stock		16 mm or 35 mm	Color Balance	EI Tungsten	EI Daylight
EASTMAN KODAK COLOR NEGATIVE					
7212	Vision 2 100T	16 mm	Tungsten	100	64 w/85
7217	Vision 2 200T	16 mm	Tungsten	200	125 w/85
7218	Vision 2 500T	16 mm	Tungsten	500	320 w/85
7229	Vision 2 Expression 500T	16 mm	Tungsten	500	320 w/85
7245	EXR 50D	16 mm	Daylight	12 w/80A	50
7246	Vision 250D	16 mm	Daylight	64 w/80A	250
7248	EXR 100T	16 mm	Tungsten	100	64 w/85
7274	Vision 200T	16 mm	Tungsten	200	125 w/85
7277	Vision 320T	16 mm	Tungsten	320	200 w/85
7279	Vision 500T	16 mm	Tungsten	500	320 w/85
7284	Vision Expression 500T	16 mm	Tungsten	500	320 w/85
7289	Vision 800T	16 mm	Tungsten	800	500 w/85
5212	Vision 2 100T	35 mm	Tungsten	100	64 w/85
5217	Vision 2 200T	35 mm	Tungsten	200	125 w/85
5218	Vision 2 500T	35 mm	Tungsten	500	320 w/85
5229	Vision 2 Expression 500T	35 mm	Tungsten	500	320 w/85
5245	EXR 50D	35 mm	Daylight	12 w/80A	50
5246	Vision 250D	35 mm	Daylight	64 w/80A	250
5248	EXR 100T	35 mm	Tungsten	100	64 w/85
5274	Vision 200T	35 mm	Tungsten	200	125 w/85
5277	Vision 320T	35 mm	Tungsten	320	200 w/85
5279	Vision 500T	35 mm	Tungsten	500	320 w/85
5284	Vision Expression 500T	35 mm	Tungsten	500	320 w/85
5289	Vision 800T	35 mm	Tungsten	800	500 w/85

Continued

Table A.1 Professional Motion Picture Film Stock *(continued)*

Film Stock		16 mm or 35 mm	Color Balance	EI Tungsten	EI Daylight
EASTMAN KODAK COLOR REVERSAL					
7239	Ektachrome	16 mm	Daylight	40 w/80A	160
7240	Ektachrome	16 mm	Tungsten	125	80 w/85B
7250	Ektachrome	16 mm	Tungsten	400	250 w/85B
7251	Ektachrome	16 mm	Daylight	100 w/80A	400
5285	Ektachrome	35 mm	Daylight	25 w/80A	100
EASTMAN KODAK BLACK & WHITE NEGATIVE					
7222	Double-X	16 mm	B & W	200	250
7231	Plus-X	16 mm	B & W	64	80
5222	Double-X	35 mm	B & W	200	250
5231	Plus-X	35 mm	B & W	64	80
EASTMAN KODAK BLACK & WHITE REVERSAL					
7265	Plus-X	16 mm	B & W	100	125
7266	Tri-X	16 mm	B & W	160	200
7276	Plus-X	16 mm	B & W	40	50
7278	Tri-X	16 mm	B & W	160	200
FUJI COLOR NEGATIVE					
8622	F-64D	16 mm	Daylight	16 w/80A	64
8632	F-125	16 mm	Tungsten	125	80 w/85
8652	F-250	16 mm	Tungsten	250	160 w/85
8662	F-250D	16 mm	Daylight	64 w/80A	250
8672	F-500	16 mm	Tungsten	500	320 w/85
8682	F-400	16 mm	Tungsten	400	250 w/85
8692	F-500D	16 mm	Daylight	125 w 80A	500
8522	F-64D	35 mm	Daylight	16 w/80A	64
8532	F-125	35 mm	Tungsten	125	80 w/85
8552	F-250	35 mm	Tungsten	250	160 w/85
8562	F-250D	35 mm	Daylight	64 w/80A	250
8572	F-500	35 mm	Tungsten	500	320 w/85
8582	F-400	35 mm	Tungsten	400	250 w/85
8592	F-500D	35 mm	Daylight	125 w 80A	500

Table A.2 Film Stock Packaging Sizes

16 mm	35 mm
100 ft. Daylight Spool	100 ft. Daylight Spool
200 ft. Daylight Spool	200 ft. Plastic Core
400 ft. Daylight Spool	400 ft. Plastic Core
400 ft. Plastic Core	1000 ft. Plastic Core
800 ft. Plastic Core	2000 ft. Plastic Core
1200 ft. Plastic Core	

Table A.3 Individual Film Can Weights

16 mm		35 mm	
100 ft. Daylight Spool	6.5 oz.	100 ft. Daylight Spool	13 oz.
200 ft. Daylight Spool	9.6 oz.	200 ft. Core	1 lb. 3 oz.
400 ft. Daylight Spool	1 lb. 10 oz.	400 ft. Core	2 lb. 7 oz.
400 ft. Core	1 lb. 11 oz.	1000 ft. Core	5 lb. 13 oz.
800 ft. Core	2 lb. 7 oz.	2000 ft. Core	11 lb. 10 oz.
1200 ft. Core	3 lb. 13 oz.		

Appendix B

Equipment

As a Camera Assistant you need to have a working knowledge of all of the equipment that you will use on a daily basis. This section contains listings of the various cameras, accessories, filters, heads, and tripods that you should be familiar with. These lists are by no means complete and include only the most commonly used equipment that you may be working with. Equipment is being added, updated, or even discontinued on a regular basis, so it is not possible or practical to try to list every piece of equipment that you may or may not be working with.

There are a few different ways to become familiar with a new piece of equipment. One is to learn at an industry-related seminar that is usually offered by a vendor, one of the unions, or some other organization. Another is to contact a rental house and ask if they would show you the item at their convenience. And finally you can be hired on a film and obtain on-the-job training and experience with a particular piece of equipment. Whenever a new piece of equipment is introduced into the industry, you should make every effort to learn about it as quickly as possible. You never know if that next job call may be using the new item, and, if you are familiar with it, your chances of landing the job are much greater. The more you know, the more jobs you will get.

Often when a new piece of equipment is introduced, the manufacturer may offer a seminar to industry professionals so that they can get introduced to the new item and become familiar with it. The International Cinematographers Guild and the Society of Camera Operators periodically conduct seminars to introduce their members to specific pieces of equipment. Many manufacturers offer an instruction or operations manual for specific equipment. This manual may be free or may be available for purchase. In any case, you should have manuals for any equipment that you will be working with. You cannot be expected to know everything about a specific piece of equipment, and if you have the manual, you may be able to troubleshoot any problems without having to contact the rental house (see Chapter 5).

When working with a piece of equipment for the first time it is a good idea to check it out with the rental house so that you are familiar with how it works. Most rental houses are willing to help and show you any piece of equipment that you are not familiar with. Don't just walk into a rental house and expect them to drop everything to show you a particular piece of equipment. Call them ahead of time. Ask them when it would be convenient for you to come in so that they can show it to you. This is especially important if the equipment is being rented from that rental house. If you establish a good relationship with them, they will be more willing to help you out in the future (see Chapter 4).

CAMERAS

The following is a basic list of the most commonly used 16 mm and 35 mm cameras in use today. I have also included 65 mm cameras along with some of the currently available video or HD cameras. Remember that equipment is changing every day and by the time you read this, one or more of these pieces of equipment may no longer exist. If you are not familiar with a specific camera, ask the rental house personnel to show it to you and explain how it works. Chapter 6 contains simple illustrations and threading diagrams of most of the film cameras and their magazines listed here. The illustrations in Chapter 6 are not meant to teach you how to thread cameras or magazines. They are intended only as a guide for you to refer to in case you have forgotten how to thread a particular camera or magazine.

16 mm Cameras

Aaton A-Minima
Aaton XTR-Plus
Aaton XTR-Prod
Arriflex 16BL
Arriflex 16M
Arriflex 16S/SB
Arriflex 16SR1
Arriflex 16SR2 (regular and high speed)
Arriflex 16SR3 (regular and high speed)
Arriflex 16SR3 Advanced (regular and high speed)
Bolex H-16
Canon Scoopic 16MS
Cinema Products CP16R
Eclair ACL
Eclair NPR
Krasnogorsk K-3

Mitchell Professional
Panavision Panaflex 16
Photo-Sonics Actionmaster 500 (high speed)
Photo-Sonics 1VN (high speed)
Photo-Sonics NAC (high speed)

35 mm Cameras

Aaton 35-III
Arriflex Arricam Lite
Arriflex Arricam Studio
Arriflex 535A
Arriflex 535B
Arriflex 435
Arriflex 435 Advanced
Arriflex 35BL3
Arriflex 35BL4
Arriflex 35-3
Arriflex 2-C
Bell & Howell Eyemo
Cinema Products XR 35
Image 300 (high speed)
Leonetti Ultracam
Mitchell/Fries 35 R
Mitchell/Fries 35 R3
Mitchell NC, NCR
Mitchell BNC, BNCR
Mitchell S 35 R/MKII, S 35 RB
Mitchell Standard
Mitchell High Speed
Moviecam Compact
Moviecam Super America
Moviecam SL
Panavision Panaflex Platinum
Panavision Panaflex Golden
Panavision Panaflex Golden G-II
Panavision Panaflex Millennium
Panavision Panaflex Millennium XL
Panavision Panaflex-X
Panavision Panaflex Panastar I & II (high speed)
Panavision PSR
Panavision Super PSR
Photo-Sonics 4B/4C (high speed)

Photo-Sonics 4E/ER (high speed)
Photo-Sonics 4ML (high speed)
Wilcam W-12

65 mm Cameras

Arriflex 765
Panavision Panaflex 65 Studio Camera
Panavision 65 Hand Held Camera
Panavision 65 High Speed Camera

Video Cameras

Canon XL-1
Panasonic DVC Pro AJ-SDX900
Panasonic DVC Pro HDC20A
Panasonic DVC Pro HDC27V
Panasonic DVX 100
Panasonic DVX 100A
Panavision HDW 900F
Sony HDW F750
Sony HDW F900
Sony MSW 900
Thomson Viper HD

CAMERA LENSES AND ACCESSORIES

In addition to becoming familiar with the cameras you will be working with, you must also have a thorough understanding of the basic accessories that are used with virtually all professional motion picture cameras. The camera is only one part of the entire package. The more you know about the lenses and basic accessories, as well as the more advanced accessories, the more jobs you will have.

Lenses and Lens Accessories

Rather than list each individual lens, I am listing only some of the specialty lenses along with lens accessories that you should become familiar with. Refer to the Camera Equipment Checklist in Appendix C for a more complete listing of lenses and lens accessories currently in use.

1.4X Extender
2X Extender
Arriflex Variable Primes
Arriflex Shift and Tilt Lenses
Aspheron Attachment for 9.5 mm and 12 mm Zeiss Lenses
Century Precision Optics Periscope
Innovision Probe
Low Angle Prism
Mesmerizer
Mutar Attachment for Zeiss 10 mm–100 mm Zoom Lens
Panavision Lightweight Zooms
Panavision Frazier Lens System
Revolution Lens System
Shift and Tilt Bellows Lens System
Snorkle Lens

Camera Accessories

Arriflex 35-3 Hand Held Door
Arriflex 35-3 Video Door
Arriflex 435 Single Frame Shutter
Arriflex Iris Control Unit (ICU)
Arriflex Integrated Video System (IVS)
Arriflex Laptop Camera Controller (LCC)
Arriflex Lens Control System (LCS)
Arriflex Ramp Preview Controller (RPC)
Arriflex Steadicam Magazines (Arricam, 35-3, 435, and 535)
Arriflex Shoulder Magazines (Arricam, 35-3 and 435)
Arriflex Remote Control Unit (RCU)
Arriflex Wireless Remote Control (WRC)
Auxiliary Carry Handle
Camera Barney
Camera Hand Grip
Capping Shutter
Clamp-on Matte Box
Clamp-On Shade
Coaxial Cable
Director's Finder
Eyebrow
Eyepiece Extension
Eyepiece Heater
Eyepiece Leveler

Film/Video Synchronizer
Focus Whip
Follow Focus
Hard Mattes
HMI Speed Control
Intervalometer
Iris Rods
Junction Box
Lens Light
Lens Shade
Magazine Barney
Matte Box
Medium Iris Rods
Microforce Handle for Sachtler
Microforce Motor
Microforce Zoom Control
Obie Light
Panavision Focus, T-Stop, Zoom, Speed/Aperture Controller (FTZSAC)
Panavision LAC
Panavision Remote Digital Control (RDC)
Panavision Zoom Control
Panavision Zoom Holder
Precision Speed Control
Preston F I + Z
Rain Cover
Rain Deflector
Remote Switch
Rubber Donuts
Sliding Balance Plate
Speed Crank
Utility Base Plate
Video Monitors
Video Tap
Zoom Bridge Support

SPECIALIZED CAMERA ACCESSORIES

There are so many specialized accessories available to the camera department that it would be difficult to describe all of them here. I have chosen to give a brief description of some of the most common camera accessories including some that I have used and am familiar with. Remember, if there is any piece of equipment that you are not familiar with, you should check with the rental house when renting and prepping the camera package.

Arriflex Remote Control Unit (RCU)

The Arriflex Remote Control Unit or RCU is a hand-held controller that allows you to operate the camera from a remote head, with the RCU displaying all camera information. The RCU allows you to perform speed changes and should be used along with the Iris Control Unit so that you may also compensate the f-stop. You may dial in a speed change by hand during the shot or you may preprogram a speed ramp to occur over a period of time. The display of the RCU is similar to the display on the camera. The RCU works with most of the current generation of Arriflex cameras.

Arriflex Wireless Remote Control (WRC)

The Arriflex Wireless Remote Control Unit or WRC is similar to the RCU, but you are not restricted by the use of cables to connect the unit to the camera. The WRC allows you to perform speed changes, shutter angle changes, and t-stop changes, all from a small hand-held unit. The WRC works with most of the current generation of Arriflex cameras.

Arriflex Iris Control Unit (ICU)

Any speed changes that you may do with the RCU will require you to also compensate your t-stop accordingly. This is accomplished by using the Arriflex Iris Control Unit or ICU. Whenever using the RCU, you should also use the ICU. The motor unit of the ICU attaches to the iris rods of the camera and then engages the gears of the aperture ring. After careful calibration, the ICU works along with the RCU so that whenever a speed change is performed, the proper aperture exposure change is done along with it. The ICU works with most of the current generation of Arriflex cameras.

Arriflex Lens Control System (LCS)

The Arriflex LCS allows you to have remote control of the aperture, zoom, and focus. This is especially useful when doing precise shots that must be repeated. The LCS contains three motor units similar to those of the ICU. They are attached respectively to the aperture, focus, and zoom rings of the lens. Once they are connected and properly calibrated, you have remote control capabilities of the t-stop, the focus, and the zoom range of the lens. The LCS works with most of the current generation of Arriflex cameras.

Arriflex Wireless Lens Control System

Like the Wireless Remote Control, the Arriflex Wireless Lens Control System allows you to have remote control of the aperture, zoom, and focus but without the restrictions of a cable. The LCS contains three motor units similar to those of the ICU. They are attached respectively to the aperture, focus, and zoom rings of the lens. Once they are connected and properly calibrated, you have remote control capabilities of the t-stop, the focus, and the zoom range of the lens.

Arriflex Laptop Camera Controller (LCC)

The LCC allows you to control many of the features of the camera from a notebook computer. Although Arriflex no longer distributes or supports the software, many assistants have it installed on their laptop computers. It was available for both Macintosh- and Windows-based computer systems and came with the proper cables for connecting the computer to the camera. Although it is no longer sold or supported by Arriflex, I discuss it here in case you have the opportunity to use it.

One of the great features of the program is virtual camera. By selecting this option in one of the menus, you are making the computer think it is connected to a camera even though it is not. This allows you to practice and become familiar with the software without having a camera connected to the computer. The Arriflex LCC can be used with the Arriflex 16SR3, 535, and 435 camera systems. Some of the important features of the LCC are as follows:

- Remote control of all camera functions—Start/Stop, Fps, Shutter Angle, Arriglow, and Timecode. The LCC has the ability to fast forward or rewind the camera to a specific frame, as well as to run the 535 and 16SR3 at 1 fps.
- Speed and exposure ramps. You can program many different speed/exposure changes into the computer for specific types of shots. The display screen of the program shows exactly how long the speed ramp will take to get from one speed to the next.

- The ability to keep track of all scene and take numbers along with footage amounts, timecode settings, and any other information that the assistant programs into the computer. At the beginning of the production, you enter all pertinent information regarding the shoot including all film stocks and sizes of rolls. The program will generate its own camera reports, raw stock inventory, and much more. This simplifies the end of the day paperwork that must be prepared and given to the production office.
- With the new IVS—Integrated Video System—available for the Arriflex 435, 535, and 16SR3 cameras, you can now insert up to 52 characters of text on the video screen by using the LCC program. It can also insert camera report information or camera warnings on the screen.

Arriflex Ramp Preview Controller (RPC)

All of the current Arriflex cameras have the ability to change speed while running. Any time you change speeds from one to another during a shot, this is called a speed ramp or simply a ramp. The RPC allows you to preview the speed change before actually shooting the shot. As with the LCC, Arriflex no longer distributes the software, and I mention it here only because some assistants may have it installed on a laptop computer.

During a rehearsal, you digitize the image from the video tap into a laptop computer. Using the software, you enter your settings for the speed ramp, and it can then be viewed on the computer without actually having to shoot it. If the shot doesn't work, simply try different settings until you get the effect you are looking for. Once you decide on the exact settings for the speed ramp, connect the computer to the camera and shoot the shot.

The Arriflex Ramp Preview Controller can be used with the Arriflex 16SR3, 535, and 435 camera systems.

Panavision Focus, T-Stop, Zoom, Speed-Aperture Controller—FTZSAC

The Panavision FTZSAC system is a specially designed modular unit that gives you control over the three lens variables: focus, t-stop, and zoom. By using this device along with the Smart Shutter accessory, you can now control five different camera variables. The FTZSAC system can be used on any Panavision Panaflex camera system, including the high speed Panastar Cameras and the 16 mm Panaflex 16.

Panavision Remote Digital Control (RDC)

The Panavision RDC is a specially designed control for use by the camera assistant. It can be used as a wireless control or it may be hardwired to the camera. The RDC can be used with most of the Panavision film cameras and controls the focus, t-stop, camera speed, shutter angle, and speed ramps. It contains an LCD screen that displays much of the camera information and can also display a video image.

CAMERA FILTERS

A wide variety of filters are available for motion picture cameras. Each filter has its own specific effect and is chosen based on the D.P.'s preference. They may be used to adjust the color balance or to give a certain look to the image such as softening the image or adding a foglike effect. Filters are available in many different sizes, as well as varying densities, with the lower numbers being lighter density and the higher numbers being heavier density.

The most common camera filters for motion picture photography are manufactured by Tiffen, Harrison & Harrison; Mitchell; Schneider Optics; Formatt Filters, Ltd.; Wilson Film Services; and Fries Engineering. The following are the various sizes that most of the filters are available in and also the most commonly used filters in motion picture photography. The numbers following some of the filters indicate their available densities. The smaller numbers indicate a very light effect and the larger numbers indicate a heavier effect. For example, a Diffusion 1/8 would have a lesser effect on the image than a Diffusion 2.

Filter Sizes

40.5 mm round
48 mm round
Series 9—3 1/2″ round
4 1/2″ round
138 mm—5 1/2″ round
3″ × 3″ square
4″ × 4″ square
4″ × 5.65″ Panavision
5″ × 6″
6.6″ × 6.6″ square

Filters

85, 85N3, 85N6, 85N9, 85B, 85C, 85 Pola
85B, 85BN3, 85BN6, 85BN9, 85B Pola
ND3, ND6, ND9, ND12
80A, 80B, 80C
81A, 81B, 81C, 81EF
82, 82A, 82B, 82C
812 Warming
Black Diffusion/FX—1/2, 1, 2, 3, 4, 5
Black Dot Texture Screens—1, 2, 3, 4, 5
Black Frost—1/8, 1/4, 1/2, 1, 2
Black Net—1, 2, 3, 4, 5
Black Pro Mist—1/8, 1/4, 1/2, 1, 2, 3, 4, 5
Black Supafrost—00, 00+, 0, 0+, 1, 1+
Classic Soft—1/8, 1/4, 1/2, 1, 2
Clear (Optical Flat)
Color Compensating—Blue, Cyan, Green, Magenta, Red, Yellow
Color Grads—Cool Blue, Red, Green, Blue, Cyan, Yellow, Magenta, Pink, Sunset, Chocolate, Sepia, Tobacco, Cranberry, Plum, Tangerine, Straw, Grape, Skyfire, Tropic Blue, Twilight, Amber, Gold, Paradise Blue, Sapphire Blue, Storm Blue, Absorptive ND3, Absorptive ND6, Absorptive ND9
Cool Day for Night
Coral—1/8, 1/4, 1/2, 1, 2, 3, 4, 5, 6, 7, 8
Coral Grad—1/8, 1/4, 1/2, 1, 2, 3, 4, 5
Day for Night
Diffusion—1/2, 1, 1 1/2, 2, 2 1/2, 3
Diopters—+1/2, +1, +1 1/2, + 2, +3
Double Fog—1/8, 1/4, 1/2, 1, 2, 3, 4, 5
Enhancer
Fluorescent Light Correction—FLD (daylight), FLB (tungsten)
Fog—1/8, 1/4, 1/2, 1, 2, 3, 4, 5
Gold Diffusion/FX—1/2, 1, 2, 3, 4, 5
Haze 1
Haze 2
LLD
Low Contrast—1/8, 1/4, 1/2, 1, 2, 3, 4, 5
Low Light Ultra Contrast—1, 2, 3, 4
Mitchell Diffusion—A, B, C, D, E
Monochrome Day for Night
Neutral Blended Ratio Attenuator—1, 1 1/2, 2, 2 1/2, 3

ND3 Grad, ND6 Grad, ND9 Grad, ND12 Grad (Hard Edge and Soft Edge)
Polarizing
Sky 1A
Soft Centric—1/4, 1/3, 1/2, 1, 2
Soft Contrast—1, 2, 3, 4, 5
Soft FX—1, 2, 3, 4, 5
Softnet—Black, White, Red, Skintone—1, 2, 3, 4, 5
Solid Color—Red, Green, Blue, Cyan, Yellow, Magenta, Sepia, Chocolate, Tobacco, Grape, Tangerine, Cranberry, Tropic Blue, Plum, Straw, Antique Suede, Gold, Storm Blue
Split Diopters—+1/2, +1, +1 1/2, +2, +3
Star—4 pt., 6 pt., 8 pt. (available in 1 mm, 2 mm, 3 mm, or 4 mm grid pattern.)
Supafrost—00, 00+, 0, 0+, 1, 1+,
Ultra Contrast—1/8, 1/4, 1/2, 1, 2, 3, 4, 5
Ultra Pol
UV
UV Haze
UV 410
Warm Black Frost—1/8, 1/4, 1/2, 1, 2
Warm Black Pro Mist—1/8, 1/4, 1/2, 1, 2
Warm Classic Soft—1/8, 1/4, 1/2, 1, 2
Warm Pro Mist—1/8, 1/4, 1/2, 1, 2
Warm Soft FX—1/2, 1, 2, 3, 4, 5
Warm White Frost—1/8, 1/4, 1/2, 1, 2
White Frost—1/8, 1/4, 1/2, 1, 2
White Net—1, 2, 3, 4, 5
White Pro Mist—1/8, 1/4, 1/2, 1, 2, 3, 4, 5

Filters for Black and White Cinematography

#6 Yellow
#8 Yellow
#9 Yellow
#11 Green
#12 Yellow
#13 Green
#15 Deep Yellow
#16 Orange
#21 Orange
#23A Light Red

#25 Red
#25A Red
#29 Dark Red
#47 Blue
#47B Dark Blue
#56 Light Green
#58 Green
#61 Dark Green

HEADS AND TRIPODS

In addition to having a working knowledge of the cameras, accessories, and filters in use today, a Camera Assistant should know the various heads and tripods on which the cameras may be mounted. The following are the most commonly used heads and tripods.

Fluid Heads

Cartoni C-20
Cartoni C-40
Cartoni Dutch Head
Cartoni Lambda
Cartoni Omega
Cartoni Sigma
O'Connor 1030
O'Connor 2060
O'Connor 2575
O'Connor 100
O'Connor 100 C
O'Connor 50 D
O'Connor 50-200
Ronford Baker Fluid 7
Ronford Baker Fluid 2015
Ronford Baker Fluid 2003
Ronford Baker Fluid 2004
Sachtler Studio 7 + 7
Sachtler 9 + 9
Sachtler Horizon
Sachtler Video 90
Sachtler Dutch Head
Tango Swing Head
Vinten

Weaver-Steadman 2-Axis
Weaver-Steadman 3-Axis
Weaver-Steadman Multi-Axis

Gear Heads

Arriflex Arrihead
Cinema Products Mini-Worrall
Cinema Products Worrall
Mitchell Lightweight
NCE/Ultrascope MK III
Panavision Panahead
Panavision Super Panahead
Technovision Technohead MK III

Miscellaneous Heads or Camera Mounts

Dutch Head
Rocker Plate
Tilt Plate

Tripods

Bazooka
O'Connor Wooden Tripod with Mitchell Flat Top Casting—standard and baby
O'Conner Wooden Tripod with Ball Top Casting—standard and baby
Panavision Panapod with Mitchell Flat Top Casting—standard and baby
Ronford Aluminum Tripod with Mitchell Flat Top Casting—standard and baby
Ronford Aluminum Tripod with Ball Top Casting—standard and baby
Sachtler Aluminum Tripod with Ball Top Casting—standard and baby

Miscellaneous Mounting Platforms

Hi-Hat
Low-Hat

Appendix C

Camera Department Checklists, Production Forms, and Labels

As a Camera Assistant, you will be preparing equipment lists, completing camera reports and inventory forms, keeping shooting logs, and completing many other types of forms and labels in the day-to-day performance of your job. Included in this section are a variety of forms, checklists, and labels that you may use during the course of your work as a Camera Assistant. Using these forms, checklists, and labels will make your job go much smoother each day and also help you and the camera department be a bit more organized.

All of these forms and labels are available for download on the companion web site for this book at www.cameraassistantmanual.com. They are available in Microsoft Word Document Template form and also as PDF Forms. The PDF forms may be opened and filled out using the Adobe Reader free software. You may print the filled out PDF forms but in order to fill out and save a PDF form, you must have the full version of Adobe Acrobat software.

FORMS AND CHECKLISTS

The various equipment checklists are provided to help you in the ordering and preparation of camera equipment and expendables. By using them, you will be sure that you have all equipment and supplies needed for your shoot. Figure C.1 is a camera equipment checklist; Figure C.2 is a filter checklist. These will help when you are working with the D.P. to prepare the listing of camera equipment that will be needed for the shoot. Figure C.3 is the expendables inventory and checklist, which will ensure that you have all the expendables needed to complete the job. You may also use this form to keep track of your expendables inventory during the course of the production. Figure C.4 is a camera prep checklist that will be helpful during the pre-production camera prep that is completed at the camera rental house. This list will help you to be sure that you have all the necessary equipment and that it functions properly. Figures C.5, C.6, and C.7 are equipment forms that you may need in the day-to-day performance of your job. Figure C.5 is the equipment received log that allows you to keep a record of all equipment received during the course of the production. You will soon learn that you often will need additional equipment as shooting progresses. You may need an additional camera for one or more days of shooting, and you can use this form to keep track of the new equipment received for the days. Figure C.6, the equipment returned log, allows you to keep a record of all equipment returned to the rental house during the course of the production. Often when you have an additional camera, it may only be needed for 1 or 2 days of shooting. When you are finished with the additional camera and all related equipment, you should return them to the rental house so that the production company does not incur any additional rental fees. When you return the equipment, list each piece on the equipment returned log. Figure C.7 is the missing or damaged equipment log that allows you to keep a record of all equipment lost or damaged during the course of the production. Let's hope you don't have any lost or damaged equipment during any of your productions.

PRODUCTION TITLE ______________________________

CAMERAS		***MAGAZINES***		***PRIME LENSES***	
Aaton 35		200	800	3.5mm	30mm
Aaton A-Minima		250	1000	4mm	32mm
Aaton XTR Plus		400	1200	5.9mm	35mm
Aaton XTR Prod		500	2000	6mm	40mm
Arriflex Arricam Studio		Reverse	High Speed	8mm	50mm
Arriflex Arricam Lite				9.5mm	55mm
Arriflex 535				9.8mm	60mm
Arriflex 435		Arricam Shoulder		10mm	65mm
Arriflex 35 BL3		Arricam Steadicam		12mm	75mm
Arriflex 35 BL4		Arri 35-3 Shoulder		14mm	85mm
Arriflex 35-3		Arri 35-3 Steadicam		14.5mm	100mm
Arriflex 2C		Arri 535 Steadicam		16mm	125mm
Arriflex 16 SR3		Arri 435 Shoulder		17mm	135mm
Arriflex 16 SR3 High Speed		Arri 435 Steadicam		17.5mm	150mm
Arriflex 16 SR2				18mm	180mm
Arriflex 16 SR2 High Speed				20mm	210mm
Bell & Howell Eyemo		***VIDEO ASSIST***		21mm	
Leonetti Ultracam		Arri 35-3 Video Door		24mm	
Moviecam Super America		B & W Video Tap		25mm	
Moviecam Compact		Color Video Tap		27mm	
Moviecam SL		Wireless Transmitter		28mm	
Panavision Millennium XL				29mm	
Panavision Millennium					
Panavision Panaflex Platinum		Transvideo Monitor			
Panavision Panaflex Gold II		4" Monitor	Watchman	***ZOOM LENSES***	
Panavision Panaflex Gold		5" Monitor	Video 8	7 – 56	18 – 100
Panavision Panaflex–X		6" Monitor	VHS Deck	7– 63	18.5 – 55.5
Panavision Panastar I		6.5" Monitor	DVD Deck	7 – 81	20 – 60
Panavision Panastar II		8.4" Monitor	DV Deck	8 – 64	20 – 100
Panavision Panaflex–16		9" Monitor		9 – 50	20 – 120
Photo Sonics 4ER		10.4" Monitor	25' Coaxial	9.5 – 57	20 – 125
Photo Sonics 4C		12" Monitor	50' Coaxial	10.4 – 52	23 – 460
Photo Sonics 4 ML		15" Monitor		10 – 30	24 – 275
Photo Sonics Actionmaster 500		19" Monitor		10 – 100	24 – 290
Photo Sonics 1VN				10 – 150	25 – 80
Photo Sonics NAC		Adapters, Connectors		10.5 – 210	25 – 250
Wilcam W-12				11 – 110	25 – 625
				11 – 165	27 – 68
				11.5 – 138	28 – 70
		HAND HELD		12 – 120	35 – 140
		Right-Hand Grip		12 – 240	40 – 200
GROUND GLASS		Left-Hand Grip		14 – 70	48 – 550
1.33	2.35/2.40	Shoulder Pad		14.5 – 50	50 – 500
1.33/1.78	TV	Shoulder Brace		16 – 44	85 – 200
1.33/1.85/2.40	TV/1.85	Follow Focus		17 – 35	135 – 420
1.66	Super TV	Clamp-on Matte Box		17 – 75	150 – 450
1.78	Super 16	Arri 35-3 Handheld Door		17 – 102	150 – 600
1.85	Super 35	Lens Shade		17.5 – 34	190 – 595
1.85/Academy		Handheld Microforce Handle		17.5 – 75	270 – 840
1.33/1.78/Super 35				18 – 90	

Figure C.1 Camera equipment checklist.

PRODUCTION TITLE ____________________

	TELEPHOTO LENSES		
	200mm		800mm
	300mm		1000mm
	400mm		1200mm
	500mm		2000mm
	600mm		

	MACRO LENSES		
	16mm		75mm
	24mm		90mm
	32mm		100mm
	40mm		140mm
	50mm		200mm
	60mm		280mm

	SLANT FOCUS LENSES		
	24mm		
	34mm		
	45mm		
	63mm		
	90mm		

	ARRIFLEX SHIFT & TILT		
	18mm		60mm
	20mm		80mm
	24mm		90mm
	28mm		110mm
	35mm		150mm
	45mm		

	ARRIFLEX VARIABLE PRIMES
	VP1 16 – 30
	VP2 29 – 60
	VP3 55 – 105

	PANAVISION LIGHTWEIGHT ZOOMS		
	17.5 – 34		
	27 – 68		
	85 – 200		

	EYEMO LENSES		
	14mm		24mm
	15mm		35mm
	17mm		50mm
	18mm		
	20mm		

	OPTICAL ACCESSORIES
	Eyepiece Extension
	Medium Eyepiece
	Eyepiece Leveler
	Super Wide Eyepiece

	LENS ACCESSORIES
	Microforce Motor
	Microforce Zoom Control
	Panavision Zoom Control
	Panavision Zoom Holder
	Zoom Power Cables
	Microforce Extension Cable
	1.4X Extender
	2X Extender
	Aspheron for 9.5 & 12
	Mutar for 10-100
	Mesmerizer
	PL to Bayonet Mount
	Revolution Lens System
	Low-Angle Prism
	Century Periscope
	Snorkel
	Innovision Probe

	ELECTRONIC ACCESSORIES
	Eyepiece Heater
	Eyepiece Heater Cable
	Remote Switch
	Lens Light
	HMI Speed Control
	Precision Speed Control
	Intervalometer
	Capping Shutter
	Film/Video Synchronizer
	Oble Light
	CE Crystal Speed Control
	Remote Follow-Focus
	Wireless Follow-Focus
	Junction Box
	Moviecam Sync Box
	Preston FI + Z

	MISCELLANEOUS ACCESSORIES
	Short Iris Rods
	Medium Iris Rods
	Long Iris Rods
	Lens Bridge Support
	Bridge Plate
	Sliding Balance Plate
	Studio Follow-Focus
	Mini Follow-Focus
	Follow Focus Right Hand Knob
	Focus Gears
	Focus Whip – 6", 12"
	Speed Crank
	4 x 4 Studio Matte Box
	4 x 5 Studio Matte Box
	4 x 5.65 Studio Matte Box
	5 x 6 Studio Matte Box
	6.6 x 6.6 Studio Matte Box
	9 x 9 Studio Matte Box
	4 x 4 Filter Trays
	4 x 5.65 Filter Trays
	6.6 x 6.6 Filter Trays
	6.6 x 6.6 Step Down to 4 x 5.65
	4 x 4 Clamp–on Matte Box
	4 x 5.65 Clamp–on Matte Box
	Matte Box Adapter Rings
	Matte Box Bellows
	Rubber Donuts
	Lens Shade
	4 1/2" Clamp-on Shade
	138mm Clamp-on Shade
	Hard Mattes
	Extra Filter Retaining Rings
	Eyebrow
	French Flag
	Utility Base Plate
	Auto Base
	Auxiliary Carry Handle
	Camera Barney
	Magazine Barney
	Rain Cover/Weather Protector
	Rain Deflector
	Director's Finder
	Microforce Handle
	Oppenheimer Handle
	Filters—See Filters Checklist

Figure C.1 Camera equipment checklist. *(continued)*

PRODUCTION TITLE ______________________________

	ARRIFLEX ACCESSORIES		***PANAVISION ACCESSORIES***		***BATTERIES & CABLES***
	On-Board Video Monitor		On-Board Video Monitor		12-Volt Block
	RCU—Remote Control Unit		Telescoping Eyepiece Extension		24-Volt Block
	WRC-1—Wireless Remote Control		FTZSAC		12/24 Blocks
	ICU—Iris Control Unit		Remote Focus & T–Stop		12-Volt Belt
	LCS—Lens Control System		Modular Follow-Focus		24-Volt Belt
	IVS—Integrated Video System		Modular Follow-Focus Remote		12/24 Belt
	LCC—Laptop Camera Controller		Flange Focal Depth Set		Chargers
	RPC —Ramp Preview Controller		Filter Frame Gel Punch		12-Volt On–Board
	Director's Viewfinder		Smart Shutter Control II		24-Volt On–Board
	Wireless LCS		Digital Remote Switch		On–Board Chargers
	Single-Frame Shutter for 435		LAC		Arriflex SR2 On–Board Adapter
	Controlled Focus Motor		Phaseable Synchronizer		Arriflex SR3 On–Board Adapter
	Wireless Remote Focus		Panafinder Director's Finder		Power Cables
			Panavision/Frazier Lens System		Power Cable Extension
			Panavision/Century Swing Shift		Junction Box
			Panaclear Auxiliary Handle		
	HEADS		Panavision Universal Autobase		
	Arrihead		Panatate 360-Degree Mount		
	Arrihead 2		Panaflasher		
	Panahead		Panatape II		
	Super Panahead				***MISCELLANEOUS***
	Mitchell Gear Head				400' Film Cans
	Mini Worral				800' Film Cans
	Worral Gear Head				1000' Film Cans
	Cartoni C 20 S		***SUPPORT***		1200' Film Cans
	Cartoni C 40 S		Standard Tripod		2000' Film Cans
	Cartoni Dutch		Baby Tripod		400' Black Bags
	Cartoni Lambda		Bazooka		800' Black Bags
	Cartoni Omega		Spreader		1000' Black Bags
	Cartoni Sigma		High Hat		1200' Black Bags
	O'Connor 1030		Low Hat		2000' Black Bags
	O'Connor 2060		Rocker Plate		2" Film Cores
	O'Connor 2575		Tilt Plate		3" Film Cores
	O'Connor 100		Cardelini Head Lock		Camera Reports
	O'Connor 50-200				Inventory Forms
	Ronford Fluid 7				Film Can Labels
	Ronford Fluid 2015				Changing Bag
	Ronford Fluid 2003				Changing Tent
	Ronford Fluid 2004				Slate
	Sachtler 7 + 7				Expendables — See Checklist
	Sachtler 9 + 9				
	Sachtler Horizon				
	Sachtler Video 90				
	Sachtler Dutch				
	Tango Swing Head				
	Vinten				
	Weaver Steadman 2-Axis				
	Weaver Steadman 3-Axis				
	Weaver Steadman Multi-Axis				

Figure C.1 Camera equipment checklist. *(continued)*

PRODUCTION TITLE ________________________________

TIFFEN

	40.5	48	4 ½	138	4 X 4	4 X 5.65	6.6 X 6.6
Clear							
85, 85N3, 85N6, 85N9							
85B, 85BN3, 85BN6, 85BN9							
ND3, ND6, ND9							
Polarizer							
Warm Polarizer							
80A							
80B							
80C							
80D							
81A							
81B							
81C							
81D							
81EF							
82							
82A							
82B							
82C							
LLD							
85/Polarizer							
85B/Polarizer							
Enhancer							
UV							
UV Haze							
Sky 1A							
Haze 1							
Haze 2							
812 Warming							

	40.5	48	4 ½	138	4 X 4	4 X 5.65	6.6 X 6.6
Diffusion 1/8, ¼. ½, 1, 2, 3							
Black Diffusion/FX ½, 1, 2, 3, 4, 5							
Gold Diffusion/FX ½, 1, 2, 3, 4, 5							
Black Pro-Mist 1/8, ¼. ½, 1, 2, 3, 4, 5							
Pro-Mist 1/8, ¼. ½, 1, 2, 3, 4, 5							
Warm Pro-Mist1/8, ¼. ½, 1, 2, 3, 4, 5							
Warm Black Pro-Mist 1/8, ¼. ½, 1, 2, 3, 4, 5							
Black Net 1, 2, 3, 4, 5							
White Net 1, 2, 3, 4, 5							
Black Soft Net 1, 2, 3, 4							
White Soft Net 1, 2, 3, 4							
Red Soft Net 1, 2, 3, 4							
Skintone Soft Net 1, 2, 3, 4							
Soft F/X ½, 1, 2, 3, 4, 5							
Wrm Soft F/X ½, 1, 2, 3, 4, 5							
Fog 1/8, ¼. ½, 1, 2, 3, 4, 5							
Double Fog 1/8, ¼. ½, 1, 2, 3, 4, 5							
Low Con 1/8, ¼. ½, 1, 2, 3, 4, 5							
Soft Con 1, 2, 3, 4, 5							
Ultra Con 1/8, ¼. ½, 1, 2, 3, 4, 5							
Low Light Ultra Con 1, 2, 3, 4							
Diopter +½, +1, +2, +3, +4							
Split Diopter +½, +1, +2, +3							
Fluorescent FLB (TUNGSTEN)							
Fluorescent FLD (DAYLIGHT)							
Star 1, 2, 3, 4 ☐ 4 pt. ☐ 6 pt. ☐ 8 pt. ☐ 12 pt.							
Cool Day for Night							
Monochrome Day for Night							
Smoque							

Figure C.2 Filters checklist.

PRODUCTION TITLE ________________________________

TIFFEN

COLOR FILTERS

[redacted]	40.5	48	4 ½	138	4 X 4	4 X 5.65	6.6 X 6.6
Red 1, 2, 3, 4, 5							
Green 1, 2, 3, 4, 5							
Blue 1, 2, 3, 4, 5							
Yellow 1, 2, 3, 4, 5							
Cyan 1, 2, 3, 4, 5							
Magenta 1, 2, 3, 4, 5							
Coral 1/8, ¼. ½, 1, 2, 3							
Antique Suede 1, 2, 3							
Chocolate 1, 2, 3							
Cranberry 1, 2, 3							
Grape 1, 2, 3							
Plum 1, 2, 3							
Sepia 1, 2, 3							
Straw 1, 2, 3							
Tobacco 1, 2, 3							
Tangerine 1, 2, 3							
Tropic Blue 1, 2, 3							

COLOR GRAD

	40.5	48	4 ½	138	4 X 4	4 X 5.65	6.6 X 6.6
Red 1, 2, 3, 4, 5							
Green 1, 2, 3, 4, 5							
Blue 1, 2, 3, 4, 5							
Yellow 1, 2, 3, 4, 5							
Cyan 1, 2, 3, 4, 5							
Magenta 1, 2, 3, 4, 5							
Coral 1/8, ¼. ½, 1, 2, 3							
ND3, ND6, ND9 Soft Edge							
ND3, ND6, ND9 Hard Edge							
Chocolate 1, 2, 3							
Cool Blue 1, 2, 3, 4, 5,							
Cranberry 1, 2, 3							
Grape 1, 2, 3							
Pink 1, 2, 3, 4, 5							
Plum 1, 2, 3							
Sunset 1, 2, 3							
Skyfire 1, 2, 3							
Straw 1, 2, 3							
Tangerine 1, 2, 3							
Tobacco 1, 2, 3							
Tropic Blue 1, 2, 3							
Twilight 1, 2, 3							

SCHNEIDER

	40.5	48	4 ½	138	4 X 4	4 X 5.65	6.6 X 6.6
Clear							
85, 85N3, 85N6, 85N9							
ND3, ND6, ND9							
Linear True Pol							
Circular True Pol							
85/True Pol							
81EF/True Pol							
Coral 1/8, ¼, ½, 1, 2							
Enhancer							
Absorptive ND3, ND6, ND9							
Reflective ND3, ND6, ND9							

	40.5	48	4 ½	138	4 X 4	4 X 5.65	6.6 X 6.6
Classic Soft 1/8, ¼, ½, 1, 2							
Warm Classic Soft 1/8, ¼, ½, 1, 2							
Black Frost 1/8, ¼, ½, 1, 2							
Warm Black Frost 1/8, ¼, ½, 1, 2							
White Frost 1/8, ¼, ½, 1, 2							
Warm White Frost 1/8, ¼, ½, 1, 2							
Low Con 2000 1/8, ¼, ½, 1, 2							
Soft Centric 1/4, 1/3, ½, 1, 2							
UV 410							
Diopter +½, +1, +2, +3, +4							
Split Diopter +½, +1, +2, +3							
Achromat Diopter +1, +2, +3							

Figure C.2 Filters checklist. *(continued)*

PRODUCTION TITLE ______________________________

	40.5	48	4½	138	4 X 4	4 X 5.65	6.6 X 6.6
SCHNEIDER COLOR GRADS							
Amber 1, 2, 3							
Attenuator ND 1.2							
Coral 1/2, 1, 2, 3							
Gold 1, 2, 3							
ND3, ND6, ND9							
Paradise Blue 1, 2, 3							
Sapphire Blue 1, 2, 3							
Storm Blue 1, 2, 3							
SCHNEIDER SOLID COLOR							
Gold 1, 2, 3							
Storm Blue 1, 2, 3							
FILTERS FOR BLACK & WHITE							
#6 Yellow							
#8 Yellow							
#9 Yellow							
#11 Green							
#12 Yellow							
#13 Green							
#15 Deep Yellow							
#16 Orange							
#21 Orange							
#23A Light Red							
#25 Red							
#25A Red							
#29 Dark Red							
#47 Blue							
#47B Dark Blue							
#56 Light Blue							
#58 Green							
#61 Dark Green							

	40.5	48	4½	138	4 X 4	4 X 5.65	6.6 X 6.6
HARRISON & HARRISON							
Red 1, 2, 3, 4, 5							
Green 1, 2, 3, 4, 5							
Blue 1, 2, 3, 4, 5							
Yellow 1, 2, 3, 4, 5							
Cyan 1, 2, 3, 4, 5							
Magenta 1, 2, 3, 4, 5							
Coral 1/8, ¼, ½, 1, 2, 3							
85, 85N3, 85N6, 85N9							
ND3, ND6, ND9							
Polarizer							
Diffusion ⅛, 1, 2, 3, 4, 5							
Black Dot Texture 1, 2, 3, 4, 5							
Fog ¼, ½, 1, 2, 3, 4, 5							
Double Fog ¼, ½, 1, 2, 3, 4, 5							
Scenic Fog 1, 2, 3, 4, 5							
Low Con ¼, ½, 1, 2, 3, 4, 5							
Day for Night							
Neu. Blend. Ratio Att. 1, 1½, 2, 2½, 3							
HARRISON & HARRISON GRADS							
Red 1, 2, 3, 4, 5							
Green 1, 2, 3, 4, 5							
Blue 1, 2, 3, 4, 5							
Yellow 1, 2, 3, 4, 5							
Cyan 1, 2, 3, 4, 5							
Magenta 1, 2, 3, 4, 5							
ND3, ND6, ND9 Grads							
OTHER FILTERS							
Mitchell A, B, C, D, E							

Figure C.2 Filters checklist. *(continued)*

PRODUCTION TITLE ______________________________

	1" CAMERA TAPE – CLOTH		**1" PAPER TAPE**
	White		Red
	Black		Green
	Red		Light Blue
	Yellow		Dark Blue
	Blue		Orange
	Grey		Yellow
	Green		White
	Teal		Black
	Purple		Purple
	Fluorescent Pink		
	Fluorescent Green		
	Fluorescent Orange		
	Fluorescent Yellow		**½" PAPER TAPE**
			Red
			Green
			Light Blue
	½" CAMERA TAPE – CLOTH		Dark Blue
	White		Orange
	Black		Yellow
	Red		White
			Black
			Pink
			Fluorescent Orange
	2" GAFFER TAPE – CLOTH		Fluorescent Pink
	Gray		
	Black		
	White		
	Bright Blue		**2" PAPER TAPE**
	Dark Blue		Black
	Yellow		White
	Red		Blue
	Green		Red
	Brown		Green
	Fluorescent Orange		Yellow
	Fluorescent Yellow		Orange
	Fluorescent Pink		Fluorescent Orange
	MISCELLANEOUS TAPE		**CHART TAPE**
	"Warning Exposed Film" – 1" Tape		1/8" Chart Tape ☐ White ☐ Yellow
	"Do Not X-Ray" – 1" Tape		3/16" Chart Tape ☐ White ☐ Yellow
	Magazine & Film Can – 2" White Cloth Tape		1/4" Chart Tape ☐ White ☐ Yellow
	Transfer Tape (Snot Tape)		

Figure C.3 Expendables inventory and checklist.

PRODUCTION TITLE ______________________

	CANNED AIR		**CABLE TIES, RIP-TIES, VELCRO**
	Dust-Off		Plastic Cable Ties
	Dust-Off Nozzle		Rip Tie Velcro Cable Wrap
	Dust-Off Plus		Bongo Tie Cable Ties
	Dust-Off Plus Nozzle		Velcro ☐ 1" ☐ 2"
	MARKERS – PERMANENT		**STICK-ON LETTERS**
	Fine-Point Sharpies – Black		1/2" Stick-on Letters & Numbers – Black
	Fine-Point Sharpies – Red		1/2" Stick-on Letters & Numbers – Red
	Fine-Point Sharpies – Blue		1/2" Stick-on Letters & Numbers – Blue
			3/4" Stick-on Letters & Numbers – Black
	Extra Fine-Point Sharpies – Black		3/4" Stick-on Letters & Numbers – Red
	Extra Fine-Point Sharpies – Red		3/4" Stick-on Letters & Numbers – Blue
	Extra Fine-Point Sharpies – Blue		1" Stick-on Letters & Numbers – Black
			1" Stick-on Letters & Numbers – Red
	Double Tip Sharpies – Black		1" Stick-on Letters & Numbers – Blue
	Double Tip Sharpies – Red		
	Double Tip Sharpies – Blue		**P-TOUCH LABEL TAPE**
			½" Black on White
	Super Sharpie – Black		½" Black on Clear
	Super Sharpie – Red		¾" Black on White
	Super Sharpie – Blue		¾" Black on Clear
			1" Black on White
	MARKERS - ERASABLE		1" Black on Clear
	Staedtler Marking Pen 311 Black		1" White on Black
	Staedtler Marking Pen 311 Red		
	Staedtler Marking Pen 311 Blue		
	Staedtler Marking Pen 311 Green		**LENS/FILTER CLEANING SUPPLIES**
			Rosco Lens Tissue
	Vis–A–Vis Felt Marker – Black		Rosco Lens Fluid
	Vis–A–Vis Felt Marker – Red		Pancro Lens Fluid
	Vis–A–Vis Felt Marker – Blue		Ultra Clarity Lens Cleaner
	Vis–A–Vis Felt Marker – Green		Regular Mikros Cloth
			Jumbo Mikros Cloth
	Stabilo Grease Pencil – White		Small Kimwipes
	Stabilo Grease Pencil – Red		Large Kimwipes
	Stabilo Grease Pencil – Yellow		
	Erasable Slate Marker – Black		**EYEPIECE COVERS**
	Erasable Slate Marker – Blue		Chamois Eyepiece Covers – Large
	Erasable Slate Marker – Red		Chamois Eyepiece Covers – Small

Figure C.3 Expendables inventory and checklist. *(continued)*

PRODUCTION TITLE ____________________

	WRATTEN GELS		**BATTERIES**
	Kodak Wratten Gel – 85		AAA Alkaline
	Kodak Wratten Gel – 85 N3		AA Alkaline
	Kodak Wratten Gel – 85 N6		C Alkaline
	Kodak Wratten Gel – 85 N9		D Alkaline
	Kodak Wratten Gel – 81EF		9-Volt Alkaline
	Kodak Wratten Gel – 80 A		PX-28L
	Kodak Wratten Gel – 82 B		DL-123
	Kodak Wratten Gel – 85 B		CR-2
	Kodak Wratten Gel – ND 3		
	Kodak Wratten Gel – ND 6		
	Kodak Wratten Gel – ND 9		
			CLEANING SUPPLIES, LUBRICANTS
			Paper Towels
	GRAY CARDS, COLOR CHARTS, SLATES		Box of Rags
	Kodak Gray Card Plus		Spray Cleaner (409, Simple Green)
	Gray Card		Goo Gone
	Macbeth Color Checker		Lighter Fluid
			WD-40 or Silicone Spray
	Insert Slate		
	Sync Slate		
			MISCELLANEOUS
			Chalk – Box
	OFFICE SUPPLIES		Orangewood Sticks
	Medium Point Ballpoint Pens – Black		Camera Wedges
	Medium Point Ballpoint Pens – Blue		Powder Puffs for Slate
	Fine Point Ballpoint Pens – Black		Cotton Swabs (Q-Tips)
	Fine Point Ballpoint Pens – Blue		Foam-Tip Swabs
	Lined Legal Pad – 8 1/2" x 11"		Mag Lite Replacement Bulbs
			Large Plastic Trash Bags
			Small Plastic Storage Bags
	ALTOIDS		
	Peppermint		
	Cinnamon		
	Wintergreen		
	Spearmint		

Figure C.3 Expendables inventory and checklist. *(continued)*

PRODUCTION TITLE ______________________

	FORMS		CANS, BAGS, CORES
	Box Rental		100' Daylight Spools & Cans
	Camera Equipment Checklist		200' Daylight Spools & Cans
	Camera Prep Checklist		400' Daylight Spools & Cans
	Camera Department Contact List		200' Film Cans
	Camera Department Log Sheet		400' Film Cans
	Camera Department Time Sheet		800' Film Cans
	Daily Film Inventory		1000' Film Cans
	Damaged Equipment Log		1200' Film Cans
	Deal Memo		2000' Film Cans
	Equipment Received Log		200' Black Bags
	Expendables Inventory & Checklist		400' Black Bags
	Film Camera Reports		800' Black Bags
	Filter Checklist		1000' Black Bags
	Film Developing Purchase Order		1200' Black Bags
	Job Information Form		2000' Black Bags
	Personal Time Sheet and Invoice		2" Film Cores
	Rawstock Inventory		3" Film Cores
	Returned Equipment Log		
	Short End Inventory		
	Video Camera Report		**OTHER**
	I-9 Employment Eligibility		
	LABELS		
	Develop Normal		
	Do Not X-Ray		
	Film Can		
	One Light Workprint		
	Prep for Video Transfer		
	Recan		
	Short End		

Figure C.3 Expendables inventory and checklist. *(continued)*

PRODUCTION TITLE ______________________

CAMERA RENTAL COMPANY ______________________

	SPREADER
	Runners slide smoothly and lock in all positions.
	Tripod points fit into spreader receptacles.
	TRIPODS – BABY & STANDARD
	Legs slide smoothly and lock in all positions.
	Top casting accommodates the head base (flat or bowl).
	Wooden legs are free from cracks and splinters.
	HIGH HAT OR LOW HAT
	Mounted on smooth flat piece of wood or other suitable material.
	Top casting accommodates the head base (flat or bowl).
	FLUID HEAD
	Base fits top casting of tripod and locks securely (Mitchell flat base or bowl shape).
	Camera lock down screw fits into camera body, adapter plate or sliding base plate.
	Pan and tilt movement is smooth at all tension settings.
	Tension adjustments for pan or tilt engage and do not slip.
	Pan and tilt locks securely at all settings
	Eyepiece leveler attaches to head securely.
	Head contains a mounting bracket for the front box.
	DUTCH HEAD
	Easily mounted to main fluid head.
	Tilt movement is smooth at all tension settings.
	Tension adjustments for tilt engage securely and do not slip.
	Tilt locks securely at all settings.
	GEAR HEAD
	Base fits tripod top casting and locks securely. (All gear heads should have a Mitchell flat base).
	Camera lock down screw fits into camera body, adapter plate or sliding base plate.
	Pan and tilt movement is smooth at all speed settings. Pan and tilt locks securely at all settings.
	Gears shift smoothly.
	Tilt plate operates smoothly and locks securely in all positions.
	Eyepiece leveler attaches to head securely
	Head contains a mounting bracket for the front box.
	SLIDING BASE PLATE
	Mounts securely onto head and adapter plate mounts securely onto camera.
	Slides smoothly and locks in all positions.
	VIEWFINDER
	Long and short eyepieces mount properly and focus easily to the eye.
	Eyepiece heater and magazine heater functions properly.
	Eyepiece magnifier functions properly.
	Diopter adjustment functions properly.
	Contrast viewing filters work correctly.

Figure C.4 Camera prep checklist.

PRODUCTION TITLE ______________________

CAMERA RENTAL COMPANY ______________________

	CAMERA BODY
	Fits securely on head or adapter plate.
	Interior and exterior is clean and free of dirt and dust. Interior is free of emulsion buildup and film chips.
	Aperture plate, pressure plate and gate areas are clean and free of any burrs.
	Pressure plate is easily removable.
	Lens port opening is clean.
	Mirror is clean and free from scratches. (Do not clean mirror yourself)
	Magazine port opening is clean.
	On certain cameras, especially Panavision, electrical contacts in the magazine port opening are clean.
	Footage counter and tachometer function properly.
	On-off switch functions properly.
	The movement of the shutter, pull-down claw, and registration pin is synchronized.
	The mirror shutter stops in the viewing position when the camera is switched off.
	Pitch control functions properly to quiet camera.
	The variable speed switch functions properly.
	Ground glass is clean and is marked for the correct aspect ratio.
	Variable shutter operates smoothly through its entire range of openings.
	Doors close tightly and latches lock securely to protect from light leaks.
	Contrast viewing filter on eyepiece functions properly.
	Behind the lens filter slot is clear and free of any obstruction.
	Illuminated ground glass markings function properly and are adjustable in intensity.
	Rain covers are available and fit properly for all lens and magazine configurations.
	MAGAZINES
	Fit securely on camera body.
	Doors fit properly and lock securely
	Interior is clean and free of dirt, dust and film chips.
	Footage counter functions properly.
	Have different size magazines for various shooting situations.
	Magazine torque motor functions to properly to take-up film.
	Magazine heater (if available) functions properly.
	Electrical contacts on magazine are clean and function properly.
	BARNEYS
	Obtain proper size barneys for cameras and magazines.
	Check heated barneys to be sure that they function properly.
	SCRATCH TEST MAGAZINES
	Check all magazines on all cameras.
	Load a dummy load (approximately 20-30 feet) into each magazine.
	Place magazine on camera and thread film in camera.
	Run approximately 10-20 feet of film through the magazine.
	Remove film from take-up side and examine under bright light for any scratches. Check emulsion side and base side for scratches.
	When using high speed or variable speed cameras check magazines at various speeds.
	FOCUS EYEPIECE
	Set eyepiece diopter for your vision.
	With lens removed, point camera at a bright light source.
	While looking through eyepiece, turn the diopter adjustment ring until the crosshairs or grains of the
	If possible, lock the adjustment ring and mark it so that it can be returned to your setting if it should get moved.

Figure C.4 Camera prep checklist. *(continued)*

PRODUCTION TITLE ______________________
CAMERA RENTAL COMPANY ______________________

	LENSES
	Contains the proper mount for the camera being used.
	Lens seats properly in camera body.
	Mirror shutter does not strike rear element of lens when spinning.
	Front and rear glass elements are clean and free from scratches.
	Front element coating is not scratched or worn away.
	Iris (t-stop) diaphragm operates smoothly.
	Focus gear threads properly.
	Focus distance marks are accurate.
	On zoom lenses the zoom motor operates smoothly.
	Zoom lens tracks properly. (See below)
	Lens shade mounts securely to each lens.
	Zoom lens holds focus throughout the zoom range.
	Matte box bellows fits securely around all lenses.
	Obtain various size rubber donuts to insure a tight seal with matte box.
	Support rods are proper size for the lens being used.
	ZOOM LENS – TRACKING
	Place zoom lens on camera body.
	Look through lens and line up the cross hair of the ground glass on a point in your prep area.
	Lock the head so that the camera cannot pan or tilt.
	Look through lens and slowly zoom lens all the way in to telephoto and all the way out to wide angle.
	Look to see that the cross hair does not shift too noticeably from the original point. A small amount of shifting is acceptable.
	If there is too much shifting (up/down or left/right) have the lens checked before taking it.
	POWER ZOOM CONTROL & MOTOR
	Check that zoom motor is mounted securely to lens.
	Connect zoom control and motor and check that they function properly.
	Check all power cables to be sure that they are in working order.
	ALL LENSES – CHECK FOCUS
	Mount lens to camera.
	Set aperture (t-stop) to its widest setting.
	Using your tape measure, place a focus chart at a specific distance as marked on lens.
	Look through viewfinder and focus chart to your eye.
	Check that measured distance matches the eye focused distance.
	Check each lens at various distances including closest focusing point and infinity.
	When checking a zoom lens, set it to its most telephoto focal length for checking focus.
	MATTE BOX
	Mounts properly and securely to iris rods, camera body or lens.
	Operates smoothly with each lens.
	Does not vignette with wide angle lenses.
	Contains the proper adapter rings and rubber donut or bellows for each lens.
	Filter trays are the correct size and slide in and out smoothly.
	Rotating filter rings operate smoothly and lock securely in position.
	Geared filter trays operate smoothly.
	Swing away matte box operates smoothly.
	Eyebrow or shade mounts securely and can be adjusted easily.
	Hard mattes mount securely and are the correct size for each lens.

Figure C.4 Camera prep checklist. *(continued)*

PRODUCTION TITLE ______________________

CAMERA RENTAL COMPANY ______________________

	FOLLOW FOCUS MECHANISM
	Check that follow focus mounts securely to iris rods or camera body.
	Engage follow focus gear to lens gear.
	Check that it operates smoothly with each lens.
	Have correct focusing gears for zooms and primes.
	FOLLOW FOCUS ACCESSORIES
	Check all accessories to be sure that they fit and operate smoothly – focus whip, speed crank, right hand extension, marking disks, etc.
	FILTERS
	All filters are correct size for matte box and lens shades being used.
	All filters are clean and free from scratches.
	Rotating polarizer operates smoothly.
	Filter set contains an optical flat.
	When using more than one camera, have enough filters for all cameras.
	Check graduated filters for hard or soft edge.
	OBIE LIGHT OR EYE LIGHT
	Mounts securely to camera and operates correctly at each setting.
	Spare bulb is included with light.
	LENS LIGHT (ASSISTANT'S LIGHT)
	Mounts securely to camera and is easily adjustable.
	Spare bulb and power cable is provided.
	PRECISION SPEED CONTROL
	Mounts easily to camera and operates correctly for both high speed and slow motion.
	Spare power cable is provided.
	HMI SPEED CONTROL
	Mounts easily to camera and operates correctly for both high speed and slow motion.
	Spare power cable is provided.
	SYNC BOX
	Connect sync box and test to be sure that you can sync to computer screen or video monitor if necessary.
	Camera must have an adjustable shutter in order to properly use the sync box.
	VIDEO TAP & MONITOR
	Connect video tap and monitor to be sure that you have proper image on screen.
	Obtain extra cables and connectors.
	Be sure that monitor can be powered from AC as well as battery power.
	Check On-Board Video Monitor if one is being used. Be sure that it mounts securely to the camera.
	HAND HELD ACCESSORIES
	Obtain proper accessories and magazines if shooting any hand held shots – left and right hand grips, shoulder pad, light weight matte box, mini follow focus, on board or belt batteries, small magazines.
	Mount all accessories and check for proper fit and comfort of operator.
	Check hand grip with on/off switch to be sure that it functions properly.

Figure C.4 Camera prep checklist. *(continued)*

PRODUCTION TITLE ______________________________

CAMERA RENTAL COMPANY ______________________________

	REMOTE START SWITCH
	Connect to camera and be sure that it functions properly.
	Obtain extension cable for switch if necessary.
	BATTERIES & CABLES
	Have enough batteries for all cameras and accessories.
	Check all cables for any frayed or loose wires.
	Check that there are no loose pins in the plugs or connectors.
	Check that all cables connect properly to camera body and batteries
	Obtain extra batteries if shooting in cold weather or when doing high speed work.
	Obtain proper charges for all batteries being used.
	Obtain extra power cables – each camera should have at least two power cables.
	ADDITIONAL ITEMS

Figure C.4 Camera prep checklist. *(continued)*

EQUIPMENT RECEIVED LOG

PRODUCTION TITLE ______________________________

DATE RECEIVED	DESCRIPTION (ITEM NAME & SERIAL NUMBER)	RENTAL COMPANY NAME	NOTES

Figure C.5 Equipment received log.

RETURNED EQUIPMENT LOG

PRODUCTION TITLE ______________________________

DATE RETURNED	DESCRIPTION (ITEM NAME & SERIAL NUMBER)	RENTAL COMPANY NAME	NOTES

Figure C.6 Returned equipment log.

MISSING OR DAMAGED EQUIPMENT LOG

PRODUCTION TITLE ______________________________

DATE MISSING OR DAMAGED	DESCRIPTION (ITEM NAME & SERIAL NUMBER)	RENTAL COMPANY NAME	NOTES

Figure C.7 Missing or damaged equipment log.

Figures C.8 through C.21 are additional forms that I have created for use by the camera department. Most of these are based on industry standard forms that I have used in the course of my career and have been created using the best information from these forms and then modifying or adding to them. I have specially created other forms that I have used successfully for many years. These include a film camera report, video camera report, a daily film inventory form, a camera department log sheet, a weekly time sheet, an invoice that can be used when providing services as an independent contractor, an example of a simple deal memo, and an equipment rental agreement, just to name a few.

The first form is a job information form (Figure C.8). I found that whenever I received a telephone call regarding work, I usually scribbled down the information on a piece of scrap paper. I created this form so that when I now get job calls, I can fill in all of the pertinent information regarding the job, and it also helps me to remember to ask the right questions regarding the job.

Chapter 3 contains three different types of industry standard camera reports. Figure C.9 shows a film camera report that could be used any time you are shooting film, no matter what laboratory you are working with. It contains all of the pertinent information, as well as a space to write in the name of the lab that will be processing the film. While most labs provide copies of their camera reports, there may be instances when you don't have time to get them or you simply run out of the lab reports. This custom camera report will serve the purpose until you can obtain additional reports from the lab. The companion web site contains a full-page version of the film camera report along with a smaller version with two camera reports on a single 8 1/2 × 11 sheet of paper. You may want to print these out and have them printed on 3-part or 4-part carbonless paper for use on your individual productions.

Figure C.10 shows a film developing purchase order. Many labs and production companies require the use of a purchase order when submitting rolls of film for developing. If the lab or production company doesn't have its own purchase order form, you may use this one when submitting film. Unlike a standard purchase order form, this form is specifically designed for use when submitting film for processing. Figure C.11 is a special camera report designed specifically for shooting video or HD. It contains specific spaces to record the time-code from the camera along with much of the same information that is recorded on a film camera report. As with the film camera report, the companion web site also contains a full-page version of the video camera report along with a smaller version containing two camera reports on a single 8 1/2 × 11 sheet of paper. These may also be

JOB INFORMATION

DATE ____________________

PROD. TITLE ____________________ PROD #

FORMAT FILM ☐ 16 mm ☐ 35 mm ☐ VIDEO ☐ VIDEO FORMAT __________

PROD. COMPANY ____________________

ADDRESS ____________________

CITY ____________________ STATE ______ ZIP ______

PHONE __________ FAX E-MAIL

CONTACT PERSON ____________________ TITLE __________

SHOOTING DATE(S) ____________________

POSITION DP ☐ OPERATOR ☐ 1ST AC ☐ 2ND AC ☐ LOADER ☐

UNION ☐ NON-UNION ☐ RATE __________

DAILY - 10 HOURS ☐ DAILY - 12 HOURS ☐ WEEKLY ☐ OTHER __________

INVOICE ☐ TIME CARD ☐ BOX OR KIT RENTAL ☐ Y ☐ N AMOUNT __________

ADDITIONAL INFORMATION ____________________

LOCAL ☐ DISTANT ☐ TRAVEL DATES (IF APPLICABLE) __________

PER DIEM __________

DIRECTOR OF PHOTOGRAPHY ____________________

CAMERA RENTAL COMPANY ____________________

ADDRESS ____________________

CITY ____________________ STATE ______ ZIP ______

PHONE __________ FAX __________ E-MAIL __________

CONTACT PERSON ____________________

CAMERA (SEE EQUIPMENT CHECKLIST) ____________________

PREP DATE(S) ____________________

LABORATORY ____________________

ADDRESS ____________________

CITY ____________________ STATE ______ ZIP ______

PHONE __________ FAX __________ E-MAIL __________

CONTACT PERSON ____________________

ADDITIONAL INFORMATION ____________________

Figure C.8 Job information form.

FILM CAMERA REPORT

LABORATORY		PAGE		OF	

PROD. CO.			
PROD. TITLE			
DIRECTOR		D.P.	
1st AC		2nd AC	

DATE		PROD. #		CAMERA	
MAG #		ROLL #		FOOTAGE	
FILM TYPE		EMULSION #			

SCENE	TAKE	DIAL	FEET	LENS	F-STOP	REMARKS

☐ 16mm	☐ Super 16mm	☐ 35mm	☐ COLOR	☐ B & W	**GOOD**	
☐ PROCESS NORMAL	☐ ONE LIGHT PRINT	☐ BEST LIGHT PRINT			**NO GOOD**	
☐ PREP FOR TRANSFER	☐ TIME TO GRAY SCALE	☐ TIMED WORK PRINT			**WASTE**	
☐ PRINT ALL	☐ TIME TO THESE LIGHTS	____ — ____ — ____			**SE**	
☐ OTHER					**TOTAL**	

COMMENTS	

Figure C.9 Film camera report.

CAMERA DEPARTMENT
FILM DEVELOPING PURCHASE ORDER

PURCHASE ORDER # ____________

LABORATORY			DATE		
ADDRESS					
CITY		STATE		ZIP	
PHONE		FAX			

PROD. TITLE			PROD. NO.		
PROD. CO.					
CONTACT NAME					
ADDRESS					
CITY		STATE		ZIP	
PHONE		FAX			

FILM TYPE AND FORMAT	☐ 16mm	☐ Super 16mm	☐ 35mm	☐ Super 35mm	☐ Color	☐ B & W

NUMBER OF 400-ft ROLLS/CANS		FOOTAGE		ROLL NUMBERS
NUMBER OF 1000-ft ROLLS/CANS		FOOTAGE		
NUMBER OF OTHER ROLLS/CANS		FOOTAGE		
TOTAL NUMBER OF ROLLS/CANS		TOTAL FOOTAGE		

☐ PROCESS NORMAL	☐ ONE LIGHT PRINT	☐ BEST LIGHT PRINT
☐ PREP FOR VIDEO TRANSFER	☐ TIME TO GRAY SCALE	☐ TIMED WORK PRINT
☐ PRINT ALL	☐ TIME TO THESE LIGHTS	____ – ____ – ____
☐ OTHER		

TRANSFER TO	☐ MINI DV	☐ DVC-PRO	☐ DV-CAM	☐ HD CAM	☐ BETA
	☐ DIGI BETA	☐ 8MM	☐ HI 8	☐ DIGITAL 8MM	
	☐ VHS	☐ S-VHS	☐ VHS-C	☐ S-VHS-C	
	☐ OTHER				

☐ PRINT ALL	☐ PRINT CIRCLE TAKES ONLY

SPECIAL INSTRUCTIONS

☐ VAULT ORIGINAL ☐ RETURN ORIGINAL WITH ORDER

SIGNATURE ______________________________

Figure C.10 Film developing purchase order.

VIDEO CAMERA REPORT	TAPE #	

PROD. CO.		PAGE		OF	
PROD. TITLE		PROD. #			
DIRECTOR		D.P.			
1st AC		2nd AC			
D.I.T.					

DATE		CAMERA	

TAPE FORMAT					
	☐ MINI DV	☐ DVC-PRO	☐ DV-CAM	☐ HD CAM	☐ DIGI BETA
	☐ BETA	☐ VHS	☐ VHS-C	☐ S-VHS	☐ S-VHS-C
	☐ 8MM	☐ HI 8	☐ DIGITAL 8MM	☐ OTHER	

SCENE	TAKE	TIME CODE				LENS	F-STOP	REMARKS
		H	M	S	F			

COMMENTS:	

Figure C.11 Video camera report.

printed out on 3-part or 4-part carbonless paper for use on your individual productions.

The daily film inventory forms shown in Figures C.12 and C.13 are used to keep a daily record of film stock used for each roll shot during the day. I have included two different versions so that you can choose the one that is better suited to your production. The daily film inventory forms are also included on the web site in a full-page version along with two forms per 8 1/2 × 11 sheet of paper. Figure C.14, the short end inventory form, was designed to allow me to better keep track of short ends created and used during the course of a production. Figure C.15 allows you to keep track of all raw stock on hand for every size roll of film including short ends. I realize that the daily film inventory and short end inventory forms each indicate how much raw stock is on hand, but they are not specific enough. The raw stock inventory form breaks available stock down more precisely into each size roll. The Production Manager or even the Director of Photography often want a precise count of how much film and what size rolls are available for each film stock.

Figure C.16, the camera department log sheet, can be used by the camera department to keep track of specific information for each shot or only for particular shots. This form contains much more information than is included on the camera report and is useful if it becomes necessary to reshoot a scene after principal photography is completed. It can also be helpful when shooting coverage or reverse angles of a scene later in the day or even later in the production schedule. Having all of the information regarding lens focal length, distance to subject, filters, etc., will make it easier to match a shot later on in production. The log sheet is also available in a full-page version along with two sheets per 8 1/2 × 11 sheet of paper. As indicated in Chapter 3, there is a small pocket-size book called *The Camera Log* that many camera assistants use on set. This form contains much of the same information that is in that book.

As mentioned in Chapter 3, the 2nd A.C. often is responsible for keeping track of hours worked by each member of the camera department. Figure C.17 is a weekly time sheet that allows the assistant to write in the hours for all key members of the department along with any day-players who may come on the production. Figure C.18 is a combination individual time sheet and invoice. It can be used to keep track of hours worked and also may be submitted at the conclusion of production for payment when working as an independent contractor.

Because of the nature of the film business, you will often be asked to work as an independent contractor. This means that you will most likely not fill out a time card or time sheet, but rather submit an invoice for your services. In addition, you may be asked to fill out a deal memo

DAILY FILM INVENTORY	SHEET #		OF	

PROD. CO. ______________________ DAY # ____ DATE ____________

PROD. TITLE ______________________ PROD. NO. ____________

LABORATORY ______________________

FILM TYPE

LOADED	ROLL #	GOOD	NG	WASTE	TOTAL	SE	FILM ON HAND	
							PREVIOUS	
							TODAY (+)	
							TODAY (-)	
							TOTAL	
							400' ROLLS	
							1000' ROLLS	
							SHORT ENDS	
							OTHER	
							COMMENTS:	
TOTALS		GOOD	NG	WASTE	TOTAL			
	TODAY							
	PREVIOUS (+)							
	TOTAL TO DATE							

FILM TYPE

LOADED	ROLL #	GOOD	NG	WASTE	TOTAL	SE	FILM ON HAND	
							PREVIOUS	
							TODAY (+)	
							TODAY (-)	
							TOTAL	
							400' ROLLS	
							1000' ROLLS	
							SHORT ENDS	
							OTHER	
							COMMENTS:	
TOTALS		GOOD	NG	WASTE	TOTAL			
	TODAY							
	PREVIOUS (+)							
	TOTAL TO DATE							

TOTAL FILM USE	GOOD	NG	WASTE	TOTAL	SE	TOTAL FILM ON HAND	
TODAY						PREVIOUS	
PREVIOUS (+)						TODAY (+)	
TOTAL TO DATE						TODAY (-)	
						TOTAL	

Figure C.12 Daily film inventory form #1.

DAILY FILM INVENTORY	SHEET #		OF	

PROD. CO. ____________________ DAY # ____ DATE __________

PROD. TITLE ____________________ PROD. NO. __________

LABORATORY ____________________

FILM TYPE	ROLL #	LOADED	GOOD	NO GOOD	WASTE	TOTAL	SE

TOTALS	LOADED	GOOD	NO GOOD	WASTE	TOTAL	SE
TODAY						
PREVIOUS (+)						
TOTAL TO DATE						

FILM ON HAND / FILM TYP						TOTALS
PREVIOUS BALANCE						
(+) REC'D TODAY						
(–) USED TODAY						
TOTAL TO DATE						

Figure C.13 Daily film inventory form #2.

SHORT END INVENTORY

PROD. CO. ____

PROD. TITLE ________________________________ PROD. NO. __________

DATE CREATED	FILM STOCK	SHORT END	DATE USED	AMOUNT USED	AMOUNT REMAINING

Figure C.14 Short end inventory form.

RAW STOCK INVENTORY

PROD. CO. ______________________ DAY # ______ DATE ____________

PROD. TITLE ______________________ PROD. NO. ____________

FILM STOCK								
	100'	200'	400'	800'	1000'	1200'	2000'	SHORT ENDS
PREVIOUS								
TODAY (+)								
TODAY (–)								
TO DATE								
				TOTAL ON HAND TO DATE				

FILM STOCK								
	100'	200'	400'	800'	1000'	1200'	2000'	SHORT ENDS
PREVIOUS								
TODAY (+)								
TODAY (–)								
TO DATE								
				TOTAL ON HAND TO DATE				

FILM STOCK								
	100'	200'	400'	800'	1000'	1200'	2000'	SHORT ENDS
PREVIOUS								
TODAY (+)								
TODAY (–)								
TO DATE								
				TOTAL ON HAND TO DATE				

FILM STOCK								
	100'	200'	400'	800'	1000'	1200'	2000'	SHORT ENDS
PREVIOUS								
TODAY (+)								
TODAY (–)								
TO DATE								
				TOTAL ON HAND TO DATE				

FILM STOCK								
	100'	200'	400'	800'	1000'	1200'	2000'	SHORT ENDS
PREVIOUS								
TODAY (+)								
TODAY (–)								
TO DATE								
				TOTAL ON HAND TO DATE				

Figure C.15 Raw stock inventory form.

CAMERA DEPARTMENT LOG SHEET

PROD. COMPANY ______________________ DAY # ______ DATE ______________

PROD. TITLE ______________________ PROD. NO. ______________

SCENE #	SCENE DESCRIPTION	LENS	STOP	F.P.S.	FOCUS	FILTER	LENS HEIGHT	REMARKS

Figure C.16 Camera department log sheet.

CAMERA DEPARTMENT WEEKLY TIME SHEET

PROD. CO. ______________________________

PROD. TITLE ______________________________ PROD. NO. __________

WEEK ENDING ____________________

D.P. NAME ______________________________ SS # __________

DAY	DATE	CALL	1ST MEAL		2ND MEAL		WRAP	TOTAL HOURS			
			OUT	IN	OUT	IN		1x	1.5x	2x	TOTAL
Sunday											
Monday											
Tuesday											
Wednesday											
Thursday											
Friday											
Saturday											
								WEEK TOTAL			

Operator NAME ______________________________ SS # __________

DAY	DATE	CALL	1ST MEAL		2ND MEAL		WRAP	TOTAL HOURS			
			OUT	IN	OUT	IN		1x	1.5x	2x	TOTAL
Sunday											
Monday											
Tuesday											
Wednesday											
Thursday											
Friday											
Saturday											
								WEEK TOTAL			

1st AC NAME ______________________________ SS # __________

DAY	DATE	CALL	1ST MEAL		2ND MEAL		WRAP	TOTAL HOURS			
			OUT	IN	OUT	IN		1x	1.5x	2x	TOTAL
Sunday											
Monday											
Tuesday											
Wednesday											
Thursday											
Friday											
Saturday											
								WEEK TOTAL			

2nd AC NAME ______________________________ SS # __________

DAY	DATE	CALL	1ST MEAL		2ND MEAL		WRAP	TOTAL HOURS			
			OUT	IN	OUT	IN		1x	1.5x	2x	TOTAL
Sunday											
Monday											
Tuesday											
Wednesday											
Thursday											
Friday											
Saturday											
								WEEK TOTAL			

Figure C.17 Camera department weekly time sheet.

CAMERA DEPARTMENT WEEKLY TIME SHEET

PROD. CO. ____________________

PROD. TITLE ____________________ PROD. NO. __________

WEEK ENDING ____________________

NAME ____________________ SS # __________

DAY	DATE	CALL	1ST MEAL		2ND MEAL		WRAP	TOTAL HOURS			
			OUT	IN	OUT	IN		1x	1.5x	2x	TOTAL
Sunday											
Monday											
Tuesday											
Wednesday											
Thursday											
Friday											
Saturday											
								WEEK TOTAL			

NAME ____________________ SS # __________

DAY	DATE	CALL	1ST MEAL		2ND MEAL		WRAP	TOTAL HOURS			
			OUT	IN	OUT	IN		1x	1.5x	2x	TOTAL
Sunday											
Monday											
Tuesday											
Wednesday											
Thursday											
Friday											
Saturday											
								WEEK TOTAL			

NAME ____________________ SS # __________

DAY	DATE	CALL	1ST MEAL		2ND MEAL		WRAP	TOTAL HOURS			
			OUT	IN	OUT	IN		1x	1.5x	2x	TOTAL
Sunday											
Monday											
Tuesday											
Wednesday											
Thursday											
Friday											
Saturday											
								WEEK TOTAL			

NAME ____________________ SS # __________

DAY	DATE	CALL	1ST MEAL		2ND MEAL		WRAP	TOTAL HOURS			
			OUT	IN	OUT	IN		1x	1.5x	2x	TOTAL
Sunday											
Monday											
Tuesday											
Wednesday											
Thursday											
Friday											
Saturday											
								WEEK TOTAL			

Figure C.17 Camera department weekly time sheet. *(continued)*

PERSONAL TIME SHEET AND INVOICE

NAME ______________________________ DATE ______________

ADDRESS ______________________________

CITY ______________________________ STATE ________ ZIP ____________

HOME PHONE ______________ SS# or FED ID # ______________

CELL PHONE ______________ EMAIL ______________________________

PROD. TITLE ______________________________ PROD. NO. ____________

PROD. CO. ______________________________

ADDRESS ______________________________

CITY ______________________________ STATE ________ ZIP ____________

PHONE ______________________

FOR SERVICES RENDERED AS: ☐ DP ☐ Camera Operator ☐ 1st AC ☐ 2nd AC ☐ Loader

☐ Other ______________________________

RATE: ____________ ☐ Weekly ☐ Hourly ☐ Daily ____ Hours FOR WEEK ENDING: ____________

DATE	DAY	CALL	1ST MEAL		2ND MEAL		WRAP	TOTAL
			Out	In	Out	In		
	MONDAY							
	TUESDAY							
	WEDNESDAY							
	THURSDAY							
	FRIDAY							
	SATURDAY							
	SUNDAY							

MINUTES TO TENTH OF AN HOUR CONVERSION

1-6 minutes = .1 hour	31-36 minutes = .6 hour
7-12 minutes = .2 hour	37-42 minutes = .7 hour
13-18 minutes = .3 hour	43-48 minutes = .8 hour
19-24 minutes = .4 hour	49-54 minutes = .9 hour
25-30 minutes = .5 hour	55-60 minutes = 1 hour

ADDITIONAL CHARGES OR SERVICES ______________________________ AMOUNT DUE ____________

______________________________ ____________

______________________________ ____________

______________________________ ____________

______________________________ ____________

______________________________ ____________

TOTAL AMOUNT DUE ____________

PAYMENT IS DUE 30 DAYS FROM DATE OF INVOICE
PAYMENT NOT RECEIVED IS SUBJECT TO INTEREST CHARGE OF 1 ½% PER MONTH

SIGNATURE ______________________________

APPROVED BY ______________________________

PAID BY CHECK # ______________ DATE ______________

Figure C.18 Personal time sheet and invoice.

before the production. The deal memo is a type of contract between you and the production company. It will detail the terms of your employment for the duration of the production and is to be signed by you and a representative of the production company. Most production companies have their own form of deal memo, but, if not, you may use the generic deal memo created for the camera department. Figure C.19 shows a form of deal memo specifically designed for use by the camera crew.

As a freelance camera assistant you may also have some equipment that you will be renting to the production company during the course of the production. Figure C.20 is an example of an equipment rental agreement that can be used between you and the production company.

So that you can keep in touch with the members of your camera crew, Figure C.21 is a camera crew contact list form so that you can enter in name, address, phone numbers, e-mail address, etc., of all members of the camera department.

CAMERA DEPARTMENT – DEAL MEMO

PROD. TITLE ______________________ PROD. NO. __________
PROD. CO. ______________________
ADDRESS ______________________
CITY ______________ STATE ____ ZIP ________
PHONE ______________

START DATE: ______________ END DATE: ______________

NAME ______________________ DATE __________
ADDRESS ______________________
CITY ______________ STATE ____ ZIP ________
PHONE ______________ CELL PHONE ______________
E-MAIL ______________________
SS# or FED ID # ______________

POSITION: ☐ DP ☐ CAMERA OPERATOR ☐ 1st AC ☐ 2nd AC ☐ LOADER
☐ OTHER: ______________________
UNION/GUILD: ______________________

SHOOT RATE __________ ☐ WEEKLY ☐ HOURLY ☐ DAILY ______ HOURS

PREP RATE __________ ☐ WEEKLY ☐ HOURLY ☐ DAILY ______ HOURS

OVERTIME RATE __________ AFTER ______ HOURS ☐ SEE TERMS ON PAGE 2

BOX / EQUIPMENT RENTAL __________ PER ☐ DAY ☐ WEEK

(SEE EQUIPMENT RENTAL AGREEMENT)

TRAVEL / ACCOMMODATIONS ______________________

EXPENSES / PER DIEM ______________________

OTHER ______________________

EMPLOYER OF RECORD ______________________
ADDRESS ______________________
CITY ______________ STATE ____ ZIP ________
PHONE ______________

SCREEN CREDIT WILL BE AWARDED AT PRODUCER'S DISCRETION.
IF AWARDED SCREEN CREDIT, INDICATE HOW YOU WOULD LIKE YOUR NAME TO READ

____

Figure C.19 Camera department deal memo.

TERMS AND CONDITIONS

1. If an hourly rate is stated, Employee will be paid straight time for the first eight hours worked and _____ times the straight time rate after eight hours worked and _____ times after twelve hours worked. Deals are for ANY five consecutive days out of seven, including weekends.
2. Weekend and holiday work must be authorized, in advance, by the Production Manager.
3. Any sixth day worked will be paid at _____ times the straight time rate for the first _____ hours worked and double time thereafter. Any seventh day worked is paid at _____ times the straight time rate for the first _____ hours worked and double time thereafter.
4. Holidays not worked are not paid. Holidays worked are paid at _____ times straight time only for hours actually worked.
5. Payment for services is due 30 days after date of invoice or 30 days from the last date worked.
6. Petty cash expenses not accompanied by original receipts will not be reimbursed.
7. Timecards must reflect hours worked and must be turned in on time. Timecards turned in late will result in late payment.
8. Employee acknowledges that personal property rented to the Production Company as part of the Box/Equipment Rental must be insured by the Employee.
9. Box/Equipment Rentals will be prorated for any partial week worked.
10. Production Company reserves the right to suspend work without compensation, if a force majeure or labor dispute occurs.
11. Director of Photographer and Camera Operator will be provided a reel of the finished product on a master format when made available to the Producer.

ADDITIONAL TERMS: ____

____

____

____

____

APPROVED BY ______________________________ ____________________

PROD. CO. REPRESENTATIVE SIGNATURE TITLE

ACCEPTED ______________________________ ____________________

EMPLOYEE SIGNATURE DATE

Figure C.19 Camera department deal memo. *(continued)*

BOX / EQUIPMENT RENTAL AGREEMENT

NAME ______________________________ DATE ______________
ADDRESS ______________________________
CITY ______________________________ STATE ______ ZIP ______________
PHONE ________________ SS# or FED ID # ______________________

PROD. TITLE ______________________________ PROD. NO. ______________
PROD. CO. ______________________________
ADDRESS ______________________________
CITY ______________________________ STATE ______ ZIP ______________
PHONE ________________

The above named production company agrees to rent the equipment listed below from employee beginning on ______________ and ending on ______________ The rental rate shall be ________ per ☐ day ☐ week.

Company agrees to take full responsibility for the safety of equipment and agrees to replace or repair any equipment lost or damaged while being rented by the company. Total value for equipment listed below and/or on additional sheets is $ ______________

Any extensions beyond the above listed dates will be charged at the daily rate for rental of equipment unless other arrangements have previously been made.

Employee acknowledges that personal property rented to the Production Company as part of this Box/Equipment Rental Agreement must be insured by the Employee.

☐ INVOICE WILL BE SUBMITTED WEEKLY ☐ CHARGES WILL BE LISTED ON WEEKLY TIME CARD

EQUIPMENT INVENTORY (Attach additional pages if necessary)

ITEM	SERIAL #	VALUE

- *Box and equipment rentals are subject to 1099 reporting.*
- *The Production Company is not responsible for any claims of loss or damage to box/equipment rental items that are not listed on the inventory.*

APPROVED BY ______________________________ ______________________________
PROD. CO. REPRESENTATIVE SIGNATURE TITLE

ACCEPTED ______________________________ ______________________________
EMPLOYEE SIGNATURE DATE

Figure C.20 Box/equipment rental agreement.

BOX / EQUIPMENT RENTAL AGREEMENT **PAGE ____ OF ____**

NAME ______________________________ DATE ________________

PROD. TITLE ______________________________ PROD. NO. ____________

EQUIPMENT INVENTORY

ITEM	SERIAL #	VALUE

Figure C.20 Box/equipment rental agreement. *(continued)*

PROD. CO. ______________________________

PROD. TITLE ______________________ **PROD. NO.** __________

DP
NAME ______________________ HOME PHONE __________
ADDRESS ______________________ CELL PHONE __________
CITY ______________________ STATE ______ ZIP __________
E-MAIL ______________________________

CAMERA OPERATOR
NAME ______________________ HOME PHONE __________
ADDRESS ______________________ CELL PHONE __________
CITY ______________________ STATE ______ ZIP __________
E-MAIL ______________________________

1ST AC
NAME ______________________ HOME PHONE __________
ADDRESS ______________________ CELL PHONE __________
CITY ______________________ STATE ______ ZIP __________
E-MAIL ______________________________

2ND AC
NAME ______________________ HOME PHONE __________
ADDRESS ______________________ CELL PHONE __________
CITY ______________________ STATE ______ ZIP __________
E-MAIL ______________________________

LOADER
NAME ______________________ HOME PHONE __________
ADDRESS ______________________ CELL PHONE __________
CITY ______________________ STATE ______ ZIP __________
E-MAIL ______________________________

POSITION ______________________
NAME ______________________ HOME PHONE __________
ADDRESS ______________________ CELL PHONE __________
CITY ______________________ STATE ______ ZIP __________
E-MAIL ______________________________

POSITION ______________________
NAME ______________________ HOME PHONE __________
ADDRESS ______________________ CELL PHONE __________
CITY ______________________ STATE ______ ZIP __________
E-MAIL ______________________________

POSITION ______________________
NAME ______________________ HOME PHONE __________
ADDRESS ______________________ CELL PHONE __________
CITY ______________________ STATE ______ ZIP __________
E-MAIL ______________________________

Figure C.21 Camera department contact list.

PROD. CO. ______________________________

PROD. TITLE ______________________ PROD. NO. __________

POSITION ______________________
NAME ______________________ HOME PHONE __________
ADDRESS ______________________ CELL PHONE __________
CITY ______________________ STATE ______ ZIP __________
E-MAIL ______________________________

POSITION ______________________
NAME ______________________ HOME PHONE __________
ADDRESS ______________________ CELL PHONE __________
CITY ______________________ STATE ______ ZIP __________
E-MAIL ______________________________

POSITION ______________________
NAME ______________________ HOME PHONE __________
ADDRESS ______________________ CELL PHONE __________
CITY ______________________ STATE ______ ZIP __________
E-MAIL ______________________________

POSITION ______________________
NAME ______________________ HOME PHONE __________
ADDRESS ______________________ CELL PHONE __________
CITY ______________________ STATE ______ ZIP __________
E-MAIL ______________________________

POSITION ______________________
NAME ______________________ HOME PHONE __________
ADDRESS ______________________ CELL PHONE __________
CITY ______________________ STATE ______ ZIP __________
E-MAIL ______________________________

POSITION ______________________
NAME ______________________ HOME PHONE __________
ADDRESS ______________________ CELL PHONE __________
CITY ______________________ STATE ______ ZIP __________
E-MAIL ______________________________

POSITION ______________________
NAME ______________________ HOME PHONE __________
ADDRESS ______________________ CELL PHONE __________
CITY ______________________ STATE ______ ZIP __________
E-MAIL ______________________________

POSITION ______________________
NAME ______________________ HOME PHONE __________
ADDRESS ______________________ CELL PHONE __________
CITY ______________________ STATE ______ ZIP __________
E-MAIL ______________________________

Figure C.21 Camera department contact list. *(continued)*

LABELS

As indicated in Chapter 3, when preparing film for delivery to the lab, each can must be labeled. To ensure that all of the proper information is included on the film can, Figure C.22 is a film can label that you can use when sending film to the lab for developing. If you would like to print these from the companion web site, I recommend using one of the following Avery brand labels that are available at any office supply store: #5164, #5264, or #8164. You may also use any 3.33-inch × 4-inch label similar to the Avery labels listed previously.

At the end of the shooting day or at the end of production, you may have film left over that has not yet been shot. There may be short ends or even full rolls that were loaded into a magazine but not used. These rolls must be unloaded from the magazines, placed in a black bag and film can, sealed, and labeled so that they can either be sold or used on a future production. Figures C.23 and C.24 are short end and recan labels that you may use for labeling these cans of unexposed film stock. If you would like to print these from the companion web site, I recommend using one of the following Avery brand labels that are available at any office supply store: #5163, #5263, or #8163. You may also use any 2-inch × 4-inch label similar to the Avery labels listed previously.

If you plan to ship the film from a distant location, it is important to label the shipping carton properly so that the film does not get exposed to harmful x-rays. Figure C.25 is a label that you should place on all sides of the carton when shipping film. If you would like to print these from the companion web site, I recommend using one of the following Avery brand labels that are available at any office supply store: #5163, #5263, or #8163. You may also use any 2-inch × 4-inch label similar to the Avery labels listed previously.

Laboratory ______________________________

Date ______________ Prod # ______________

Prod. Co. ______________________________

Prod. Title ______________________________

Exposed Footage ______________________________

Film Type ______________________________

Camera __________ Mag # __________ Roll # __________

☐ Process Normal ☐ One Light Print ☐ Best Light Print

☐ Prep for Transfer ☐ Time to Gray Scale ☐ Timed Work Print

☐ Time to These Lights _____—_____—_____

☐ Other ______________________________

Figure C.22 Film can developing label.

SHORT END

Date ______________________________

Loader ______________________________

Footage ______________________________

Film Type ______________________________

Emulsion Number ______________________________

Comments ______________________________

Figure C.23 Short end label.

RECAN

Date ______________________________

Loader ______________________________

Footage ______________________________

Film Type ______________________________

Emulsion Number ______________________________

Comments ______________________________

Figure C.24 Recan label.

MOTION PICTURE
FILM
DO NOT X-RAY

Figure C.25 X-ray warning label.

Appendix D

Tools and Accessories

Many professions require that you have your own tools and equipment necessary to do the job. This is the case with a professional Camera Assistant. Without some basic tools, accessories, and expendables, you will not be able to perform your job properly and most likely will not be hired for future jobs. Some of the tools are basic everyday items that you may need to mount the camera onto a particular platform or to perform minor repairs on the camera. Others are specialized pieces of equipment that are unique to the film industry. Some of the items in your tool kit or ditty bag should also include many of the items on the camera department expendables list. In addition, many assistants also have certain specialty items in their ditty bag based on personal preference. As you work more and more, your ditty bag or kit will go through many changes as you improve upon it and make it as complete as possible.

Since you will be investing a lot of money into the various tools and accessories needed to do your job, I recommend having some type of case or cases to keep them in. Most assistants have one or more cases or bags that contain all of the tools, accessories, and supplies needed to do the job. The type of bag or case you choose is up to you. The important thing to remember is that this is your career, and you will be using these tools and supplies for a long time. Keep them safe, protected, and organized in some type of case or bag so that they are always available when needed and you can carry them with you without too much difficulty. Some assistants have soft-side bags containing various size compartments, while others choose to keep their equipment in hard-side cases for more protection. The type of bag or case you use should be based on whatever works best for you.

In addition to having bags or cases for your tools and equipment, many camera assistants have some type of rolling four-wheel cart to assist them in moving all of the camera equipment from place to place in the course of a shooting day. Two of the most common types of carts are the Magliner Gemini Junior and Gemini Senior. There are also a few companies that have modified or made their own version of the Magliner carts. In addition to the Magliner, many camera assistants have a rolling cart manufactured by Rubbermaid. Both of these carts are illustrated in Chapter 4. Choose the type and style of cart based on shooting needs as well as cost.

The following list contains a basic set of tools and accessories, and a brief description of what each is used for. Also listed are the expendables along with a brief description of what each is used for.

TOOLS AND ACCESSORIES

Ditty bag or case: to keep and protect all of your tools and accessories

Belt pouch or fanny pack: to keep small items handy such as pens, pencils, flashlight, etc.

Sync slate: to slate sync sound shots. See Figure 3.38 for an illustration of a sync slate.

Small sync slate: for slating close-up sync sound shots

Insert slate: to slate silent or insert shots. See Figure 3.40 for an illustration of an insert slate.

Large clapper sticks: for slating multiple camera shots

50′ cloth tape measure: to measure focus distances to the actors

25′ metal tape measure: for measuring to points on the set, and for placing marks along the floor (not recommended for measuring to actors because of danger of injury from the metal edge)

Changing bag or changing tent: for loading and unloading film when no darkroom is available. See Figure 3.31 for illustration of the changing bag and changing tent.

Scissors: for cutting film along the perforations so that it has a smooth edge for threading

Magnifier with light: for checking the gate

Small flashlight: for checking the gate

Large flashlight: useful on dark sets or locations to see your way

French flag with arm: to flag lights that are flaring the lens. See Figure 4.40 for an illustration of a French flag.

6″ focus whip: an extension for the follow focus mechanism to allow the first assistant to better follow focus during shooting. See Figure 4.6 for an illustration of a focus whip.

Color chart and gray scale: to photograph at the head of the first roll of film for the lab to use in timing the print

Tweezers: for removing pieces of film from inside the camera body

Blower bulb syringe: to clean dirt and dust off the lens and filters

Bubble level: to ensure that the camera is level on uneven surfaces

Small pocket level: to ensure that the camera is level on uneven surfaces

Ground glass puller: to aid in removing the ground glass, especially in some Arriflex cameras (also referred to as Hirschmann forceps)

Camera oil (Mitchell, Panavision, Arriflex): to be used to oil the camera at proper intervals

Camera silicone lubricant: for lubricating camera pull down claw when necessary

Electrical adapters: for use when plugging in camera batteries for charging or any other electrical accessory

Cube taps: same as electrical adapters; allows you to plug three items into a single electrical outlet

Multiple outlet strips: same as cube taps but allows you to plug in five or six items at once

Electrical extension cords: for use when plugging in camera batteries or other items that need electricity such as video monitors, etc.

Depth-of-field charts or calculator: to determine your depth of field for a particular shot

Set of jeweler's screwdrivers: for minor camera repairs

Soldering iron: for repairing damaged power cable connections

4-in-1 screwdriver: combination slotted and Phillips for minor camera repairs

Slotted screwdriver: 1/8″, 3/16″, 1/4″, 5/16″ for minor camera repairs

Phillips screwdrivers: #1, #2 for minor camera repairs

Magnetic screwdriver: for making basic repairs on the camera

Allen wrenches—metric and American: for minor camera repairs

Adjustable wrenches: for minor camera repairs

Vise grips: for minor camera repairs

Pliers: for minor camera repairs

Needlenose pliers: for minor camera repairs

Razor knife: used for cutting gels or anything else that needs cutting

Wire cutters: for minor camera and power cable repairs

Leatherman, Gerber, other multipurpose tools: for minor repairs on the camera

Swiss Army knife or similar pocket knife: various uses, including repairs to camera

16 3/8″ bolts—short and long: used for mounting camera body to various surfaces

Rubber T-marks: for marking actors, especially outside where tape will not stick

Space blanket: for covering the camera to protect it from weather or heat

Velcro cable ties: to keep power cables coiled up

Engraved filter tags: for identifying filters placed on the camera or in the matte box

Assorted video connectors and cables: for connecting the video tap to monitors or video recorders

Empty filter pouches (various sizes): for storing and protecting filters or other small items

1″ brush: for dusting off the camera and equipment

Camera fuses: for use in case the fuse in the camera blows

Oil dropper or syringe: used for oiling the camera

Duvetyne (black cloth): various uses, including covering the camera if it is reflected in glass or a mirror

Convex mirror: placed in front of the lens to check for lens flares

Extra power cables: used as spare in case power cables become worn, frayed, or damaged

Dental mirror: used when adjusting the shutter and synching the camera to a video monitor or projector screen

Small C-clamps: used to secure the camera when mounting it to unsteady surfaces

Small grip clamps: used for securing space blanket or duvetyne to the camera

Front box: for storage of basic accessories used daily by the 1st A.C., and mounted on the head so that these accessories are readily available. See Figure 4.60 for an illustration of a front box.

ASC Manual: used as a reference

Professional Cameraman's Handbook: used as a reference

The Camera Assistant's Manual: used as a reference

Camera Terms and Concepts: used as a reference

Various camera instruction manuals: used as a reference

SPECIAL TOOLS

Some companies such as Arriflex sell special tools that are needed when working with their camera equipment. If you know or think you may be working with Arriflex cameras on a regular basis, you may want to pick up the tool set for your ditty bag. This set consists of the following items that are needed when making any minor repairs or adjustments on the Arriflex 16SR2, 16SR3, 435, 535 or Arricam cameras.

ARRI TOOLS

1.3 mm hex driver
1.5 mm hex driver
2 mm hex driver
2 mm hex key
Small Phillips screwdriver
Large Phillips screwdriver
Slotted screwdriver
Special bushing tool

EXPENDABLES

1″ camera tape—black, white, red, yellow, blue, gray, green, teal, purple, fluorescent pink, fluorescent green, fluorescent orange, fluorescent yellow: for wrapping cans and making labels and marks

2″ gaffer tape—black, gray, white, yellow, red, green, brown, dark blue, fluorescent orange, fluorescent yellow, fluorescent pink: for labeling equipment and securing various items during production

1/2″ or 1″ paper tape—red, green, yellow, white, orange, light blue, dark blue, purple, black: for marking actors

1/8″ or 1/4″ chart tape—white, yellow: for marking focus distances on the lens

Transfer tape (also called snot tape): tape that is sticky on both sides and is easily removable. It is often used for attaching nets to the back of lenses.

Lens tissue: to clean lenses and filters along with lens cleaner

Lens cleaner: to clean lenses and filters along with lens tissue

Pancro lens cleaner: used to clean Pancro filters

Orangewood sticks: to clean emulsion buildup from the gate

Eyepiece covers: for the camera operator's comfort when looking through eyepiece

Permanent felt tip markers (Sharpies)—red, black, blue: for making labels

Wide tip permanent felt tip markers (Magic Marker)—red, black, blue: for labeling equipment cases

Ballpoint pens: to fill out camera reports, inventory forms, time sheets, etc.

Grease pencils (Stabilo)—white, yellow, red: for marking the film and making focus marks on the lens

Vis-A-Vis erasable felt tip markers—black, red, green, blue: for marking focus distances on follow focus marking disk or with chart tape when making marks directly on lens

Slate marker: for writing information on the slate

Makeup-type powder puff: for erasing information written on slate with slate markers

Chalk: to mark the position of the camera, dolly, or actors

Camera wedges: to aid in leveling the camera when it is placed on a high hat or any uneven surface

Stick-on letters—black, red, blue: for placing production information on the slate

Compressed air with nozzle (Dust Off): same as blower bulb syringe and also to clean the inside of the camera body

Cotton swabs or foam-tip swabs (Q-Tips): used for removing excess oil from camera movement

Kimwipes—large and small: used for small cleaning jobs on camera and equipment (not to be used on camera lenses, but may be used on filters along with cleaning solution)

Silicone spray: to lubricate parts that may be sticking (not to be used on the interior of the camera body)

Lighter fluid: to remove glue or sticky residue from tape or stick-on letters

Kodak Wratten gels (85, 85N3, 85N6, 85N9, ND3, ND6, ND9, 80A): for placing filters behind the lens, as in the Panavision cameras, or when a glass filter in front of the lens is not available

Spare batteries (AAA, AA, C, D, 9-volt): for powering mini mag lights or magnifiers

Spare Mini Mag Lite bulbs: replacement bulbs for the small Mini Mag Lite flashlight used by most assistants

Small plastic storage bags: for keeping small parts from becoming lost or misplaced

Trash bags: for disposing of any trash and also for covering the camera and equipment in the rain

Spray cleaner: for cleaning camera equipment and cases during production and also at wrap

Rags, paper towels: used along with spray cleaner to clean equipment and cases

MISCELLANEOUS ITEMS

Spare cores and daylight spools: for threading film in the magazines. See Figures 1.7 and 1.8 for illustrations of cores and daylight spools.

Extra film cans and black bags (400′ and 1000′): for canning out exposed film and short ends

Camera reports: for keeping a record of all scenes shot for each roll of film

Film inventory forms: for keeping a record of all film shot and received each day

The camera log: for keeping a record of all shot information. See Figures 3.12 and 3.13 for illustrations of pages from the camera log.

Rental catalogs: used as a reference when ordering additional equipment

As mentioned in the opening paragraph, along with the preceding items, you should have some type of hard-side or soft-side case or cases to store and transport all of these items. These tools and accessories are important for the performance of your job, so it is a good idea to protect them and keep them in good condition when not being used. The type of case you use is a matter of personal preference. This listing is subject to change depending on the individual needs of each Camera Assistant. You may find a particular item that helps you to perform the job better. The basic items in the Camera Assistant ditty bag are essentially standard throughout the industry. Additional specialty items are based on individual needs and what is required for you to do your job completely. No two Camera Assistant ditty bags or kits are identical.

As listed in the Tools and Equipment section, many assistants have a belt pouch or fanny pack that they wear on their belt to keep specific items available at all times. These are items that are needed regularly during shooting and may include the following: permanent felt tip markers, ballpoint pens, grease pencil, lens tissue, lens cleaner, slate marker with powder puff attached, small flashlight, magnifier with light, and depth-of-field calculator. Many assistants also make a small loop of rope on which to keep a roll of black and white camera tape with them in case they need to make marks or labels of any kind. As mentioned earlier, since you will be working with a great number of equipment cases, not including your own equipment, you should have some type of four-wheel dolly or cart to assist in moving and transporting the equipment cases on the set.

As stated in Chapters 3 and 4, you should also have a personal bag with extra clothing, towels, and toiletry items with you as well. You may need an extra shirt, shoes, or coat and it's best to be prepared. Having an extra sweatshirt, thermal underwear, and cold weather boots can make the difference between being comfortable and enjoying the job or being miserable because you are cold, wet, and uncomfortable.

The following is a list of items that I keep in my personal bag. You may modify this list to suit your individual needs.

- Pants, shirt, sweatshirt, underwear (regular and thermal), socks
- Sneakers or work shoes/boots
- Rain gear
- Towels and washcloths
- Disposable moist towelettes
- Small blanket
- First aid kit, aspirin, prescription medication
- Toothbrush, toothpaste, razors, shave cream, deodorant
- Comb, brush, mirror, soap, shampoo
- Insect repellent, skin cream
- Sunglasses and sunscreen
- Travel radio/alarm clock

As you gain more experience as an assistant, you will probably find other tools and accessories that you will keep in the ditty bag or AKS case. An AKS case is any case that contains a wide variety of tools, equipment, and supplies. Its literal translation is "All Kinds of Stuff" or "All Kinds of S--t." This list is meant only as a guide for people starting out who want to acquire the basics for doing the job.

And finally, because you will have a great deal of money invested in your tools and equipment, I strongly urge you to obtain an insurance policy to cover your tools and equipment in the event that they get lost, stolen, or damaged. Many homeowner's or renter's policies do not cover specialized tools for your profession so you may have to obtain a separate insurance policy. You may have to contact a company that deals specifically with insurance for the motion picture industry. Check with your insurance agent regarding this.

Appendix E

Tables and Formulas

Included in this section are many tables and formulas that a Camera Assistant may refer to for a variety of information. The tables include footage tables, hyperfocal distances, f-stop compensation for changes in frames per second, f-stop compensation for various filters used, footage to time conversions, time to footage conversions, and many more. The formulas include feet per minute, exposure time, hyperfocal distance, depth of field, feet to meters, and more.

If you have a Palm Pilot or other similar device, much of this information is available to you in the programs pCam and pCine, which are available online at www.davideubank.com. These are two excellent programs developed by assistant cameraman David Eubank. I have used them successfully for many years and strongly recommend them to anyone working in the industry.

TABLES

Film Speed Comparisons

The film speed is most often expressed as an EI (exposure index) number. ASA numbers are not used as often, but some people may still use this term when referring to the film's speed. The German numbering system uses DIN numbers to indicate the film speed. Table E.1 shows the comparison between EI/ASA numbers and DIN numbers.

Standard Feet per Minute and Frames per Foot at 24 Frames per Second

Since most cinematography is done at the filming speed of 24 frames per second to give the illusion of normal motion, many calculations are based on the standard information for each film format at that fps. Table E.2 lists the standard feet per minute and frames per foot for the

Table E.1 Comparison of EI/ASA and DIN Numbers

EI/ASA	DIN
12	12
16	13
20	14
25	15
32	16
40	17
50	18
64	19
80	20
100	21
125	22
160	23
200	24
250	25
320	26
400	27
500	28
640	29
800	30

Table E.2 Feet per Minute and Frames per Foot at 24 Frames per Second

Film Format	Feet per Minute at 24 f.p.s.	Frames per Foot
Super 8	20	72
16 mm	36	40
35 mm, 3-perf format	67.5	21.33
35 mm, 4-perf format	90	16
65 mm, 5-perf format	112.5	12.8

most commonly used film formats of 16 mm and 35 mm along with information for Super 8 mm and 65 mm formats.

Intermediate F-Stop Values

When the Director of Photography (D.P.) measures the light, the f-stop reading that he or she gets will not always be exactly on one of the f-stop values mentioned in Chapter 1. The value of the light measurement often falls between two f-stop numbers. Table E.3 gives the intermediate f-stop values between each successive pair of f-stop numbers. For example, the f-stop value that is halfway between f 4 and f 5.6 is f 4.8.

F-Stop Compensation When Using Filters

During the course of shooting, the D.P. will ask that various filters be placed on the camera to achieve a specific effect or to correct for the color temperature. Many of the filters used reduce the amount of light that reaches the film. Remember that if a filter requires an f-stop compensation, the amount of compensation listed refers to how much you should open up the lens aperture. Table E.4 lists the f-stop compensation for various filters that you may be using. For example, when using an 85 filter, you must open up your f-stop 2/3 of a stop from the exposure

Table E.3 Intermediate F-Stop Values for 1/4, 1/3, 1/2, 2/3, and 3/4 Stops

FULL STOP	1/4 STOP	1/3 STOP	1/2 STOP	2/3 STOP	3/4 STOP	FULL STOP
1	1.1	1.1	1.2	1.3	1.3	**1.4**
1.4	1.5	1.6	1.7	1.8	1.9	**2**
2	2.1	2.2	2.4	2.5	2.6	**2.8**
2.8	3.1	3.2	3.3	3.5	3.7	**4**
4	4.4	4.5	4.8	5	5.2	**5.6**
5.6	6.2	6.3	6.7	7	7.3	**8**
8	8.7	9	9.5	10	10.5	**11**
11	12.3	12.7	13.5	14	14.6	**16**
16	17.4	18	19	20	21	**22**
22	24.6	25.5	27	28.6	29.2	**32**
32	34.9	35.9	38	40.3	41.5	**45**

Table E.4 F-Stop Compensation for Various Filters

Filter	F-Stop/T-Stop Compensation (Open Aperture)
UV	0
Sky 1-A	0
Haze 1	0
Haze 2	0
Warm UV	1/3
85	2/3
85 N3	1 2/3
85 N6	2 2/3
85 N9	3 2/3
LLD	0
ND 3	1
ND 6	2
ND 9	3
80A	2
80B	1 2/3
80C	1
81A	1/3
81B	1/3
81C	1/3
81EF	2/3
812	1/3
82A	1/3
82B	2/3
85B	2/3
85C	1/3

Filter	F-Stop/T-Stop Compensation (Open Aperture)
Optical Flat	0
Polarizer	2 STOPS
Enhancer	1 STOP
FLB	1 STOP
FLD	1 STOP
Soft Net	1/3–2/3 STOP
Coral	Based on Density
Sepia	Based on Density
Antique Suede	Based on Density
Chocolate	Based on Density
Tobacco	Based on Density
Fog	0
Double Fog	0
Low Contrast	0
Soft Contrast	0
Ultra Contrast	0
Black Dot	1
Pro Mist	0
Warm Pro Mist	1/3
Soft F/X	0
Diopter	0

without the filter. If you are not sure about the exposure compensation of a particular filter, you can check with the company where you rented the camera equipment. A quick way to determine the exposure compensation for a particular filter is to take a light reading with your exposure meter in the light you are shooting under. Then hold the filter over the photosphere of the light meter and take another reading.

Compare the difference and you will have determined your exposure compensation for that filter.

F-Stop Compensation When Using Filters for Black and White

When shooting black and white film, the D.P. uses specific filters to change the way that specific colors appear in black and white. On black and white film, all colors are reproduced as a certain shade of gray. By using a filter, the D.P. can alter or change how light or dark the shade of gray is for a particular color. Table E.5 lists the f-stop compensation for the most common filters used in black and white photography. For example, when using a #12 yellow filter, you must open up your f-stop 1 stop when shooting in daylight, and 2/3 of a stop when shooting in tungsten light.

Table E.5 F-Stop Compensation When Using Filters for Black and White

Filter	F-Stop/T-Stop Compensation (Open Aperture)	
	DAYLIGHT	TUNGSTEN
#6 YELLOW	2/3	2/3
#8 YELLOW	1	2/3
#9 YELLOW	1	2/3
#11 GREEN	2	1 2/3
#12 YELLOW	1	2/3
#13 GREEN	2 1/3	2
#15 DEEP YELLOW	1 2/3	1
#16 ORANGE	1 2/3	1 2/3
#21 ORANGE	2 1/3	2
#23A LIGHT RED	2 2/3	1 2/3
#25 RED	3	2 2/3
#29 DARK RED	4 1/3	2
#47 DARK BLUE	2 1/3	3
#47B DARK BLUE	3	4
#56 LIGHT GREEN	2 2/3	2 2/3
#58 DARK GREEN	3	3
#61 DARK GREEN	3 1/3	3 1/3

F-Stop Compensation for Changes in Frames per Second

When you change the speed that the film travels through the camera (i.e., the f.p.s.), you are changing how long each frame is exposed to light. If you run the camera at a higher speed, each frame is exposed to light for less time, and if you run the camera at a slower speed, each frame is exposed to light for a longer time. Table E.6 lists the f-stop compensation for various changes in frames per second. For example, if you change the camera speed to 60 f.p.s., you must open your f-stop 1 1/3 stops.

F-Stop Compensation for Changes in Shutter Angle

Similar to changing camera speed, if you change the shutter angle, you affect how much light strikes the film. Increasing the shutter angle allows more light to reach the film, and decreasing the shutter angle allows less light to reach the film. Table E.7 lists the f-stop compensation for various changes in shutter angle. For example, when you change the shutter angle to 90 degrees, you must open the f-stop 1 stop.

Table E.6 F-Stop Compensation for Changes in Frames per Second

Frames per Second	F-Stop/T-Stop Compensation	Frames per Second	F-Stop/T-Stop Compensation
5	Close 2 1/4	32–35	Open 1/2
6	Close 2	36–38	Open 2/3
7	Close 1 3/4	39–43	Open 3/4
8	Close 1 1/2	44–51	Open 1
9	Close 1 1/3	52–57	Open 1 1/4
10	Close 1 1/4	58–62	Open 1 1/3
11–12	Close 1	63–70	Open 1 1/2
13–14	Close 3/4	71–76	Open 1 2/3
15	Close 2/3	77–87	Open 1 3/4
16–17	Close 1/2	88–104	Open 2
18–19	Close 1/3	105–115	Open 2 1/4
20–21	Close 1/4	116–125	Open 2 1/3
22–25	0	126–141	Open 2 1/2
26–28	Open 1/4	142–150	Open 2 2/3
29–31	Open 1/3		

Table E.7 F-Stop Compensation for Changes in Shutter Angle

Shutter Angle	F-Stop/T-Stop Compensation
199–200	Close 1/4
167–198	Full Exposure
150–166	Open 1/4
138–149	Open 1/3
124–137	Open 1/2
113–123	Open 2/3
101–112	Open 3/4
85–100	Open 1
75–84	Open1 1/4
69–74	Open 1 1/3
62–68	Open 1 1/2
57–61	Open 1 2/3
50–56	Open 1 3/4
42–49	Open 2
38–41	Open 2 1/4
35–37	Open 2 1/3
31–34	Open 2 1/2
29–30	Open 2 2/3
26–28	Open 2 3/4
22.5–25	Open 3

Hyperfocal Distances

Hyperfocal distance is a special case of depth of field. It is sometimes defined as the closest point in front of the lens that will be in acceptable focus when the lens is focused to infinity. In other words, it is the closest focus distance at which objects at infinity and close to the lens are in focus. It is this focus point that gives the maximum depth of field for a given shooting situation. At certain times during filming, you need to know the hyperfocal distance for a particular shot. Tables E.8 and E.9 list the hyperfocal distances for various focal length lenses for both 16 mm and 35 mm formats. All amounts are rounded to the nearest inch. For example, from Table E.9, when shooting in 35 mm with

Table E.8 16 mm Hyperfocal Distances—Circle of Confusion = .0006″

F-Stop/T-Stop

Focal Length	1	1.4	2	2.8	4	5.6	8	11	16	22
5.9	7′ 6″	5′ 5″	3′ 8″	2′ 8″	1′ 11″	1′ 4″	11″	8″	6″	4″
8	13′ 10″	9′ 10″	6′ 11″	4′ 11″	3′ 5″	2′ 6″	1′ 8″	1′ 2″	11″	7″
9.5	19′ 5″	13′ 11″	9′ 8″	6′ 11″	4′ 11″	3′ 6″	2′ 5″	1′ 10″	1′ 2″	11″
10	21′ 6″	15′ 5″	10′ 10″	7′ 8″	5′ 5″	3′ 10″	2′ 8″	2′	1′ 4″	1′
12	31′	22′ 1″	15′ 6″	11′ 1″	7′ 8″	5′ 6″	3′ 11″	2′ 10″	1′ 11″	1′ 5″
14	42′ 2″	30′ 1″	21′ 1″	15′ 1″	10′ 6″	7′ 6″	5′ 4″	3′ 10″	2′ 7″	1′ 11″
16	55′ 1″	39′ 5″	27′ 6″	19′ 8″	13′ 10″	9′ 10″	6′ 11″	5′	3′ 5″	2′ 6″
17	62′ 2″	44′ 5″	31′ 1″	22′ 2″	15′ 7″	11′ 1″	7′ 10″	5′ 8″	3′ 11″	2′ 10″
18	69′ 8″	49′ 10″	34′ 11″	24′ 11″	17′ 5″	12′ 6″	8′ 10″	6′ 4″	4′ 5″	3′ 2″
20	86′ 1″	61′ 6″	43′ 1″	30′ 10″	21′ 6″	15′ 5″	10′ 10″	7′ 10″	5′ 5″	3′ 11″
21	94′ 11″	67′ 10″	47′ 6″	33′ 11″	23′ 8″	16′ 11″	11′ 11″	8′ 7″	5′ 11″	4′ 4″
24	124′	88′ 7″	62′	44′ 4″	31′	22′ 1″	15′ 6″	11′ 4″	7′ 8″	5′ 7″
25	134′ 6″	96′ 1″	67′ 4″	48′ 1″	33′ 7″	24′	16′ 10″	12′ 2″	8′ 5″	6′ 1″
27	156′ 11″	112′ 1″	78′ 6″	56′	39′ 2″	28′	19′ 7″	14′ 4″	9′ 10″	7′ 1″
28	168′ 7″	120′ 6″	84′ 5″	60′ 4″	42′ 2″	30′ 1″	21′ 1″	15′ 3″	10′ 5″	7′ 7″
29	181′	129′ 4″	90′ 6″	64′ 8″	45′ 4″	32′ 4″	22′ 7″	16′ 6″	11′ 4″	8′ 2″
32	220′ 5″	157′ 6″	110′ 2″	78′ 8″	55′ 1″	39′ 4″	27′ 6″	20′	13′ 10″	10′
35	263′ 8″	188′ 5″	131′ 11″	94′ 2″	65′ 11″	47′ 1″	33′	24′	16′ 6″	12′
40	344′ 5″	246′	172′ 2″	123′	86′ 1″	61′ 6″	43′ 1″	31′ 3″	21′ 5″	15′ 8″
50	538′ 2″	384′ 5″	269′ 1″	192′ 2″	134′ 6″	96′ 1″	67′ 3″	48′ 9″	33′ 6″	24′ 5″
60	775′	553′ 7″	387′ 6″	276′ 10″	193′ 8″	138′ 5″	96′ 11″	70′ 6″	48′ 5″	35′ 2″
65	909′ 6″	649′ 8″	454′ 8″	324′ 10″	227′ 5″	162′ 5″	113′ 8″	82′ 8″	56′ 10″	41′ 4″
75	1211′	865′	605′ 6″	432′ 6″	302′ 8″	216′ 2″	151′ 5″	110′ 1″	75′ 8″	55′
85	1555′	1111′	777′ 8″	555′ 6″	388′ 10″	277′ 8″	194′ 5″	141′ 5″	97′ 2″	70′ 8″
100	2153′	1538′	1076′	768′ 11″	538′ 2″	384′ 5″	269′ 1″	195′ 8″	134′ 6″	97′ 11″
125	3364′	2403′	1682′	1201′	840′ 11″	600′ 8″	420′ 5″	305′ 8″	210′ 2″	152′ 11″
135	3923′	2802′	1962′	1401′	980′ 11″	700′ 8″	490′ 4″	356′ 7″	245′ 2″	178′ 4″
150	4844′	3460′	2422′	1730′	1211′	865′	605′ 6″	440′ 4″	302′ 8″	220′ 2″
180	6975′	4982′	3487′	2491′	1744′	1246′	871′ 11″	634′ 1″	435′ 11″	317′

Table E.9 35 mm Hyperfocal Distances—Circle of Confusion = .001″

F-Stop/T-Stop

Focal Length	1	1.4	2	2.8	4	5.6	8	11	16	22
5.9	4′ 6″	3′ 2″	2′ 2″	1′ 7″	1′ 1″	10″	7″	5″	4″	2″
8	8′ 4″	5′ 11″	4′ 1″	2′ 11″	2′ 1″	1′ 6″	1′	10″	6″	5″
9.5	11′ 8″	8′ 4″	5′ 10″	4′ 2″	2′ 11″	2′ 1″	1′ 6″	1′ 1″	9″	6″
10	12′ 11″	9′ 2″	6′ 6″	4′ 7″	3′ 2″	2′ 4″	1′ 6″	1′ 2″	10″	7″
12	18′ 7″	13′ 4″	9′ 4″	6′ 7″	4′ 7″	3′ 4″	2′ 4″	1′ 8″	1′ 2″	10″
14	25′ 4″	18′ 1″	12′ 8″	9′	6′ 4″	4′ 6″	3′ 2″	2′ 4″	1′ 7″	1′ 2″
16	33′ 1″	23′ 7″	16′ 6″	11′ 10″	8′ 4″	5′ 11″	4′ 1″	3′	2′ 1″	1′ 6″
17	37′ 4″	26′ 8″	18′ 8″	13′ 4″	9′ 4″	6′ 8″	4′ 8″	3′ 5″	2′ 4″	1′ 8″
18	41′ 10″	29′ 11″	20′ 11″	14′ 11″	10′ 6″	7′ 6″	5′ 2″	3′ 10″	2′ 7″	1′ 11″
20	51′ 8″	36′ 11″	25′ 10″	18′ 6″	12′ 11″	9′ 2″	6′ 6″	4′ 8″	3′ 2″	2′ 4″
21	57′	40′ 8″	28′ 6″	20′ 4″	14′ 2″	10′ 2″	7′ 1″	5′ 2″	3′ 7″	2′ 7″
24	74′ 5″	53′ 1″	37′ 2″	26′ 7″	18′ 7″	13′ 4″	9′ 4″	6′ 10″	4′ 7″	3′ 5″
25	80′ 8″	57′ 8″	40′ 5″	28′ 10″	20′ 2″	14′ 5″	10′ 1″	7′ 4″	5′	3′ 8″
27	94′ 2″	67′ 4″	47′ 1″	33′ 7″	23′ 6″	16′ 10″	11′ 10″	8′ 7″	5′ 11″	4′ 4″
28	101′ 4″	72′ 4″	50′ 7″	36′ 2″	20′ 10″	18′ 1″	12′ 8″	9′ 2″	6′ 4″	4′ 7″
29	108′ 8″	77′ 7″	54′ 4″	38′ 10″	27′ 2″	19′ 5″	13′ 7″	9′ 11″	6′ 10″	4′ 11″
32	132′ 4″	94′ 6″	66′ 1″	47′ 2″	33′ 1″	23′ 7″	16′ 6″	12′	8′ 4″	6′
35	158′ 2″	113′	79′ 1″	56′ 6″	39′ 7″	28′ 4″	19′ 10″	14′ 5″	9′ 11″	7′ 2″
40	206′ 8″	147′ 7″	103′ 4″	73′ 10″	51′ 8″	36′ 11″	25′ 10″	18′ 10″	12′ 11″	9′ 5″
50	322′ 11″	230′ 8″	161′ 6″	115′ 4″	80′ 8″	57′ 8″	40′ 5″	29′ 4″	20′ 2″	14′ 7″
60	465′	332′ 1″	232′ 6″	166′ 1″	116′ 2″	83′	58′ 1″	42′ 4″	29′ 1″	21′ 1″
65	545′ 8″	389′ 10″	272′ 11″	194′ 11″	136′ 5″	97′ 6″	68′ 2″	49′ 7″	34′ 1″	24′ 10″
75	726′ 7″	518′ 11″	363′ 4″	259′ 6″	181′ 7″	129′ 8″	90′ 10″	66′ 1″	45′ 5″	33′
85	933′ 2″	666′ 7″	466′ 7″	333′ 4″	233′ 4″	166′ 7″	116′ 8″	84′ 10″	58′ 4″	42′ 5″
100	1292′	922′ 7″	645′ 10″	461′ 4″	322′ 11″	230′ 8″	161′ 6″	117′ 5″	80′ 8″	58′ 8″
125	2018′	1442′	1009′	720′ 10″	504′ 7″	360′ 5″	252′ 4″	183′ 6″	126′ 1″	91′ 8″
135	2354′	1682′	1177′	840′ 8″	588′ 6″	420′ ″	294′ 4″	214′	147′ 1″	107′
150	2906′	2076′	1453′	1038′	726′ 7″	519′	363′ 4″	264′ 4″	181′ 7″	132′ 1″
180	4185′	2989′	2092′	1495′	1046′	747′ 4″	523′ 1″	380′ 6″	261′ 7″	190′ 2″

a 29 mm lens and an f-stop of 5.6, the hyperfocal distance is 19 feet 5 inches. You may also determine the hyperfocal distance for a given situation if you use the pCam and pCine software mentioned in Chapter 4.

Feet per Second and Feet per Minute

Remember that at 24 f.p.s., for 16 mm format the film travels through the camera at the rate of 36 feet per minute, for 35 mm 3-perf format the film travels through the camera at the rate of 67.5 feet per minute, and for 35 mm 4-perf format, the film travels through the camera at the rate of 90 feet per minute. Since you will not always be filming at sync speed, Table E.10 lists feet per second and feet per minute for various frames per second for each format. For example, when shooting 16 mm film at 18 f.p.s., the film travels through the camera at the rate of 27 feet per minute.

Running Time to Film Length and Film Length to Running Time

You will often need to determine if you have enough film to complete a certain shot. Tables E.11 to E.13 list the approximate running times for full rolls of film at various frames per second. All amounts are

Table E.10 Feet per Second and Feet per Minute.

	16 mm		35 mm 3-perf		35 mm 4-perf	
F.P.S.	Feet per Second	Feet per Minute	Feet per Second	Feet per Minute	Feet per Second	Feet per Minute
6	.15	9	.28	16.9	.375	22.5
12	.3	18	.56	33.8	.75	45
18	.45	27	.85	50.7	1.125	67.5
24	.6	36	1.13	67.5	1.5	90
30	.75	45	1.41	84.5	1.875	112.5
36	.9	54	1.69	101.4	2.25	135
48	1.2	72	2.25	135.2	3	180
60	1.5	90	2.82	169	3.75	225
72	1.8	108	3.38	202.8	4.5	270
96	2.4	144	4.5	270.4	6	360
120	3	180	5.63	338	7.5	450

Table E.11 Running Times for 16 mm

16 mm Running Time					
F.P.S.	**100 feet**	**200 feet**	**400 feet**	**800 feet**	**1200 feet**
6	11 min 7 sec	22 min 13 sec	44 min 26 sec	88 min 53 sec	133 min 20 sec
12	5 min 33 sec	11 min 7 sec	22 min 13 sec	44 min 26 sec	66 min 40 sec
18	3 min 42 sec	7 min 24 sec	14 min 49 sec	29 min 38 sec	44 min 26 sec
24	2 min 46 sec	5 min 33 sec	11 min 7 sec	22 min 13 sec	33 min 20 sec
30	2 min 13 sec	4 min 26 sec	8 min 53 sec	17 min 46 sec	26 min 40 sec
36	1 min 51 sec	3 min 42 sec	7 min 25 sec	14 min 49 sec	22 min 13 sec
48	1 min 23 sec	2 min 46 sec	5 min 33 sec	11 min 7 sec	16 min 40 sec
60	1 min 7 sec	2 min 13 sec	4 min 26 sec	8 min 53 sec	13 min 20 sec
72	55 sec	1 min 51 sec	3 min 42 sec	7 min 25 sec	11 min 7 sec
96	41 sec	1 min 23 sec	2 min 46 sec	5 min 33 sec	8 min 20 sec
120	33 sec	1 min 7 sec	2 min 13 sec	4 min 26 sec	6 min 40 sec

Table E.12 Running Times for 35 mm 3-Perf Format

35 mm 3-perf Running Time					
F.P.S.	**100 feet**	**200 feet**	**400 feet**	**1000 feet**	**2000 feet**
6	5 min 55 sec	11 min 50 sec	23 min 40 sec	59 min 10 sec	118 min 18 sec
12	2 min 58 sec	5 min 55 sec	11 min 50 sec	29 min 35 sec	59 min 10 sec
18	1 min 58 sec	3 min 56 sec	7 min 53 sec	19 min 43 sec	39 min 27 sec
24	1 min 29 sec	2 min 58 sec	5 min 56 sec	14 min 49 sec	29 min 38 sec
30	1 min 11 sec	2 min 22 sec	4 min 44 sec	11 min 50 sec	23 min 40 sec
36	59 sec	1 min 58 sec	3 min 56 sec	9 min 52 sec	19 min 43 sec
48	44 sec	1 min 29 sec	2 min 58 sec	7 min 24 sec	14 min 47 sec
60	35 sec	1 min 11 sec	2 min 22 sec	5 min 55 sec	11 min 50 sec
72	29 sec	59 sec	1 min 58 sec	4 min 56 sec	9 min 52 sec
96	22 sec	44 sec	1 min 29 sec	3 min 42 sec	7 min 24 sec
120	18 sec	35 sec	1 min 11 sec	2 min 58 sec	5 min 55 sec

Table E.13 Running Times for 35 mm 4-Perf Format

35 mm 4-perf Running Time					
F.P.S.	**100 feet**	**200 feet**	**400 feet**	**1000 feet**	**2000 feet**
6	4 min 26 sec	8 min 53 sec	17 min 47 sec	44 min 26 sec	88 min 53 sec
12	2 min 13 sec	4 min 26 sec	8 min 53 sec	22 min 13 sec	44 min 26 sec
18	1 min 29 sec	2 min 58 sec	5 min 56 sec	14 min 49 sec	29 min 37 sec
24	1 min 7 sec	2 min 13 sec	4 min 26 sec	11 min 7 sec	22 min 13 sec
30	53 sec	1 min 46 sec	3 min 33 sec	8 min 53 sec	17 min 46 sec
36	44 sec	1 min 29 sec	2 min 58 sec	7 min 24 sec	14 min 48 sec
48	33 sec	1 min 7 sec	2 min 13 sec	5 min 33 sec	11 min 7 sec
60	26 sec	53 sec	1 min 46 sec	4 min 26 sec	8 min 53 sec
72	22 sec	44 sec	1 min 29 sec	3 min 42 sec	7 min 24 sec
96	16 sec	33 sec	1 min 7 sec	2 min 46 sec	5 min 33 sec
120	13 sec	26 sec	53 sec	2 min 13 sec	4 min 26 sec

rounded to the nearest minute and second. For example, from Table E.12, you can determine that when shooting 35 mm 3-perf format and using a 400 foot roll, at a speed of 36 f.p.s., the roll will last approximately 3 minutes and 56 seconds.

Tables E.14 to E.16 show the amount of film used for different times at various frames per second. All lengths are rounded to the nearest foot and inch. For example, from Table E.16, you can determine that when shooting the 35 mm 4-perf format, at 24 f.p.s., a shot that lasts 14 seconds is approximately 21 feet in length.

Tables E.17 to E.19 show the amount of time for different film lengths at various frames per second. All amounts are rounded to the

Table E.14 Running Time to Film Length—16 mm

Frames per Second

Seconds	6	12	18	24	30	36	48	60	72	96	120
1	2″	4″	6″	7″	9″	11″	1′ 2″	1′ 6″	1′ 10″	2′ 5″	3′
2	4″	7″	11″	1′ 2″	1′ 6″	1′ 10″	2′ 5″	3′	3′ 7″	4′ 10″	6′
3	6″	11″	1′ 5″	1′ 10″	2′ 3″	2′ 8″	3′ 7″	4′ 6″	5′ 5″	7′ 2″	9′
4	7″	1′ 2″	1′ 10″	2′ 5″	3′	3′ 7″	4′ 10″	6′	7′ 2″	9′ 7″	12′
5	9″	1′ 6″	2′ 3″	3′	3′ 9″	4′ 6″	6′	7′ 6″	9′	12′	15′
6	11″	1′ 10″	2′ 8″	3′ 7″	4′ 6″	5′ 5″	7′ 2″	9′	10′ 10″	14′ 5″	18′
7	1′ 1″	2′ 1″	3′ 2″	4′ 2″	5′ 3″	6′ 4″	8′ 5″	10′ 6″	12′ 7″	16′ 10″	21′
8	1′ 2″	2′ 5″	3′ 7″	4′ 10″	6′	7′ 2″	9′ 7″	12′	14′ 5″	19′ 2″	24′
9	1′ 4″	2′ 8″	4′ 1″	5′ 5″	6′ 9″	8′ 1″	10′ 10″	13′ 6″	16′ 2″	21′ 7″	27′
10	1′ 6″	3′	4′ 6″	6′	7′ 6″	9′	12′	15′	18′	24′	30′
11	1′ 8″	3′ 4″	5′	6′ 7″	8′ 3″	9′ 11″	13′ 2″	16′ 6″	19′ 10″	26′ 5″	33′
12	1′ 10″	3′ 7″	5′ 5″	7′ 2″	9′	10′ 10″	14′ 5″	18′	21′ 7″	28′ 10″	36′
13	2′	3′ 11″	5′ 10″	7′ 10″	9′ 9″	11′ 8″	15′ 7″	19′ 6″	23′ 4″	31′ 2″	39′
14	2′ 1″	4′ 2″	6′ 4″	8′ 5″	10′ 6″	12′ 7″	16′ 10″	21′	25′ 2″	33′ 7″	42′
15	2′ 3″	4′ 6″	6′ 9″	9′	11′ 3″	13′ 6″	18′	22′ 6″	27′	35′	45′
16	2′ 5″	4′ 10″	7′ 2″	9′ 7″	12′	14′ 5″	19′ 2″	24′	28′ 10″	38′ 5″	48′
17	2′ 7″	5′ 1″	7′ 8″	10′ 2″	12′ 9″	15′ 4″	20′ 5″	25′ 6″	30′ 7″	40′ 10″	51′
18	2′ 8″	5′ 5″	8′ 1″	10′ 10″	13′ 6″	16′ 2″	21′ 6″	27′	32′ 5″	43′ 2″	54′
19	2′ 11″	5′ 8″	8′ 7″	11′ 5″	14′ 3″	17′ 1″	22′ 10″	28′ 6″	34′ 2″	45′ 7″	57′
20	3′	6′	9′	12′	15′	18′	24′	30′	36′	48′	60′
21	3′ 2″	6′ 4″	9′ 6″	12′ 7″	15′ 9″	18′ 11″	25′ 2″	31′ 6″	37′ 8″	50′ 5″	63′
22	3′ 4″	6′ 4″	9′ 6″	12′ 7″	15′ 9″	18′ 11″	25′ 2″	31′ 6″	37′ 10″	50′ 5″	63′
23	3′ 6″	6′ 11″	10′ 4″	13′ 10″	17′ 3″	20′ 8″	27′ 7″	34′ 6″	41′ 5″	55′ 2″	69′
24	3′ 7″	7′ 2″	10′ 10″	14′ 5″	18′	21′ 7″	28′ 10″	36′	43′ 2″	57′ 7″	72′
25	3′ 9″	7′ 6″	11′ 3″	15′	18′ 9″	22′ 6″	30′	37′ 6″	45′	60′	75′
26	3′ 11″	7′ 10″	11′ 8″	15′ 7″	19′ 6″	23′ 5″	31′ 2″	39′	46′ 7″	62′ 4″	78′
27	4′ 1″	8′ 1″	12′ 2″	16′ 2″	20′ 3″	24′ 4″	32′ 5″	40′ 6″	48′ 7″	64′ 10″	81′
28	4′ 2″	8′ 5″	12′ 7″	16′ 10″	21′	25′ 2″	33′ 7″	42′	50′ 5″	67′ 2″	84′
29	4′ 4″	8′ 8″	13′ 1″	17′ 5″	21′ 9″	26′ 1″	34′ 10″	43′ 6″	52′ 2″	69′ 7″	87′
30	4′ 6″	9′	13′ 6″	18′	22′ 6″	27′	36′	45′	54′	72′	90′

Table E.14 *(continued)*

Frames per Second

Seconds	6	12	18	24	30	36	48	60	72	96	120
31	4′ 8″	9′ 4″	13′ 11″	18′ 7″	23′ 3″	27′ 11″	37′ 2″	46′ 6″	55′ 10″	74′ 5″	93′
32	4′ 10″	9′ 7″	14′ 5″	19′ 2″	24′	28′ 10″	38′ 5″	48′	57′ 7″	76′ 10″	96′
33	4′ 11″	9′ 11″	14′ 11″	19′ 10″	24′ 9″	29′ 8″	39′ 7″	49′ 6″	59′ 5″	79′ 2″	99′
34	5′ 1″	10′ 2″	15′ 4″	20′ 5″	25′ 6″	30′ 7″	40′ 10″	51′	61′ 2″	81′ 7″	102′
35	5′ 3″	10′ 6″	15′ 9″	21′	26′ 3″	31′ 6″	42′	52′ 6″	63′	84′	105′
36	5′ 5″	10′ 10″	16′ 2″	21′ 7″	27′	32′ 5″	43′ 2″	54′	64′ 10″	86′ 5″	108′
37	5′ 7″	11′ 1″	16′ 7″	22′ 2″	27′ 9″	33′ 4″	44′ 5″	55′ 6″	66′ 7″	88′ 10″	111′
38	5′ 8″	11′ 5″	17′ 1″	22′ 10″	28′ 6″	34′ 2″	45′ 7″	57′	68′ 5″	91′ 2″	114′
39	5′ 11″	11′ 8″	17′ 7″	23′ 5″	29′ 3″	35′ 1″	46′ 10″	58′ 6″	70′ 2″	93′ 7″	117′
40	6′	12′	18′	24′	30′	36′	48′	60′	72′	96′	120′
41	6′ 2″	12′ 4″	18′ 6″	24′ 7″	30′ 9″	36′ 11″	49′ 2″	61′ 6″	73′ 10″	98′ 5″	123′
42	6′ 4″	12′ 7″	18′ 11″	25′ 2″	31′ 6″	37′ 10″	50′ 5″	63′	75′ 6″	100′ 10″	126′
43	6′ 6″	12′ 11″	19′ 4″	25′ 10″	32′ 3″	38′ 8″	51′ 7″	64′ 6″	77′ 5″	103′ 2″	129′
44	6′ 7″	13′ 2″	19′ 10″	26′ 5″	33′	39′ 7″	52′ 10″	66′	79′ 2″	105′ 7″	132′
45	6′ 9″	13′ 6″	20′ 3″	27′	33′ 9″	40′ 6″	54′	67′ 6″	81′	108′	135′
46	6′ 11″	13′ 10″	20′ 8″	27′ 7″	34′ 6″	41′ 5″	55′ 2″	69′	82′ 10″	110′ 5″	138′
47	7′ 1″	14′ 1″	21′ 2″	28′ 2″	35′ 3″	42′ 4″	56′ 5″	70′ 6″	84′ 7″	112′ 10″	141′
48	7′ 2″	14′ 5″	21′ 7″	28′ 10″	36′	43′ 2″	57′ 6″	72′	86′ 5″	115′ 2″	144′
49	7′ 4″	14′ 8″	22′ 1″	29′ 5″	36′ 9″	44′ 1″	58′ 10″	73′ 6″	88′ 2″	117′ 7″	147′
50	7′ 6″	15′	22′ 6″	30′	37′ 6″	45′	60′	75′	90′	120′	150′
51	7′ 8″	15′ 4″	22′ 11″	30′ 7″	38′ 3″	45′ 11″	61′ 2″	76′ 6″	91′ 10″	122′ 5″	153′
52	7′ 10″	15′ 7″	23′ 5″	31′ 2″	39′	46′ 10″	62′ 5″	78′	93′ 7″	124′ 10″	156′
53	7′ 11″	15′ 11″	23′ 11″	31′ 10″	39′ 9″	47′ 8″	63′ 7″	79′ 6″	95′ 5″	127′ 2″	159′
54	8′ 1″	16′ 2″	24′ 4″	32′ 5″	40′ 6″	48′ 7″	64′ 10″	81′	97′ 2″	129′ 7″	162′
55	8′ 3″	16′ 6″	24′ 9″	33′	41′ 3″	49′ 6″	66′	82′ 6″	99′	132′	165′
56	8′ 5″	16′ 10″	25′ 2″	33′ 7″	42′	50′ 5″	67′ 2″	84′	100′ 10″	134′ 5″	168′
57	8′ 7″	17′ 1″	25′ 8″	34′ 2″	42′ 9″	51′ 4″	68′ 5″	85′ 6″	102′ 7″	136′ 10″	171′
58	8′ 8″	17′ 5″	26′ 1″	34′ 10″	43′ 6″	52′ 2″	69′ 7″	87′	104′ 5″	139′ 2″	174′
59	8′ 11″	17′ 8″	26′ 7″	35′ 5″	44′ 3″	53′ 1″	70′ 10″	88′ 6″	106′ 2″	141′ 7″	177′
60	9′	18′	27′	36′	45′	54′	72′	90′	108′	144′	180′

Table E.15 Running Time to Film Length—35 mm 3 Perf.

Frames per Second

Seconds	6	12	18	24	30	36	48	60	72	96	120
1	3″	7″	10″	1′ 2″	1′ 5″	1′ 8″	2′ 3″	2′ 10″	3′ 5″	4′ 6″	5′ 7″
2	7″	1′ 2″	1′ 8″	2′ 3″	2′ 10″	3′ 5″	4′ 6″	5′ 7″	6′ 9″	9′	11′ 3″
3	10″	1′ 8″	2′ 7″	3′ 5″	4′ 3″	5′ 1″	6′ 9″	8′ 6″	10′ 2″	13′ 6″	16′ 11″
4	1′ 1″	2′ 2″	3′ 5″	4′ 6″	5′ 7″	6′ 9″	9′	11′ 3″	13′ 6″	18′	22′ 6″
5	1′ 5″	2′ 10″	4′ 4″	5′ 7″	7′ 1″	8′ 6″	11′ 3″	14′ 1″	16′ 11″	22′ 6″	28′ 2″
6	1′ 8″	3′ 5″	5′ 1″	6′ 10″	8′ 6″	10′ 2″	13′ 6″	16′ 11″	20′ 3″	27′	33′ 10″
7	2′	3′ 11″	6′	7′ 11″	9′ 11″	11′ 10″	15′ 9″	19′ 9″	23′ 8″	31′ 6″	39′ 5″
8	2′ 2″	4′ 6″	6′ 10″	9′	11′ 3″	13′ 6″	18′	22′ 7″	27′ 1″	36′	45′ 1″
9	2′ 6″	5′	7′ 8″	10′ 1″	12′ 8″	15′ 3″	20′ 3″	25′ 5″	30′ 5″	40′ 6″	50′ 8″
10	2′ 10″	5′ 7″	8′ 6″	11′ 4″	14′ 1″	16′ 11″	22′ 6″	28′ 2″	33′ 10″	45′	56′ 4″
11	3′ 1″	6′ 2″	9′ 5″	12′ 5″	15′ 6″	18′ 7″	24′ 9″	31′ 1″	37′ 2″	49′ 6″	61′ 11″
12	3′ 5″	6′ 8″	10′ 2″	13′ 6″	16′ 11″	20′ 3″	27′	33′ 10″	40′ 7″	54′	67′ 7″
13	3′ 7″	7′ 4″	11′ 1″	14′ 7″	18′ 4″	21′ 11″	29′ 3″	36′ 7″	43′ 11″	58′ 6″	73′ 2″
14	3′ 11″	7′ 10″	11′ 11″	15′ 10″	19′ 9″	23′ 7″	31′ 6″	39′ 6″	47′ 4″	63′	78′ 10″
15	4′ 2″	8′ 5″	12′ 10″	16′ 11″	21′ 2″	25′ 4″	33′ 9″	42′ 4″	50′ 8″	67′ 6″	84′ 6″
16	4′ 6″	9′	13′ 7″	18′	22′ 6″	27′ 1″	36′	45′ 2″	54′ 1″	72′	90′ 1″
17	4′ 10″	9′ 6″	14′ 6″	19′ 1″	23′ 11″	28′ 9″	38′ 3″	47′ 11″	57′ 6″	76′ 6″	95′ 8″
18	5′	10′ 1″	15′ 4″	20′ 4″	25′ 4″	30′ 5″	40′ 6″	50′ 9″	60′ 10″	81′	101′ 4″
19	5′ 4″	10′ 7″	16′ 2″	21′ 5″	26′ 9″	32′ 11″	42′ 9″	53′ 7″	64′ 2″	85′ 6″	106′ 11″
20	5′ 7″	11′ 2″	17′	22′ 5″	28′ 2″	33′ 10″	45′	56′ 5″	67′ 7″	90′	112′ 7″
21	5′ 11″	11′ 10″	17′ 11″	23′ 7″	29′ 7″	35′ 6″	47′ 3″	59′ 2″	71′	94′ 6″	118′ 3″
22	6′ 2″	12′ 4″	18′ 8″	24′ 10″	31′ 1″	37′ 2″	49′ 6″	62′ 1″	74′ 4″	99′	123′ 11″
23	6′ 5″	12′ 11″	19′ 7″	25′ 11″	32′ 5″	38′ 11″	51′ 9″	64′ 11″	77′ 9″	103′ 6″	129′ 6″
24	6′ 8″	13′ 5″	20′ 5″	27′	33′ 10″	40′ 7″	54′	67′ 7″	81′ 2″	108′	135′ 2″
25	7′	14′	21′ 4″	28′ 1″	35′ 3″	42′ 3″	56′ 3″	70′ 6″	84′ 6″	112′ 6″	140′ 9″
26	7′ 4″	14′ 7″	22′ 1″	29′ 4″	36′ 8″	43′ 11″	58′ 6″	73′ 4″	87′ 11″	117′	146′ 5″
27	7′ 7″	15′ 1″	23′	30′ 5″	38′ 1″	45′ 7″	60′ 9″	76′ 2″	91′ 3″	121′ 6″	152′
28	7′ 10″	15′ 8″	23′ 10″	31′ 6″	39′ 6″	47′ 4″	63′	78′ 11″	94′ 7″	130′ 6″	163′ 3″
29	8′ 1″	16′ 2″	24′ 8″	32′ 7″	40′ 11″	49′	65′ 3″	81′ 9″	98′	130′ 6″	163′ 3″
30	8′ 5″	16′ 10″	26′ 6″	33′ 9″	42′ 4″	50′ 8″	67′ 6″	84′ 7″	101′ 5″	135′	168′ 11″

Table E.15 *(continued)*

Frames per Second

Seconds	6	12	18	24	30	36	48	60	72	96	120
31	8′ 8″	17′ 5″	26′ 5″	34′ 11″	43′ 8″	52′ 5″	69′ 9″	87′ 5″	104′ 10″	139′ 6″	174′ 6″
32	9′	17′ 11″	27′ 2″	36′	45′ 1″	54′ 1″	72′	90′ 3″	108′ 2″	144′	180′ 2″
33	9′ 2″	18′ 6″	28′ 1″	37′ 1″	46′ 6″	55′ 8″	74′ 3″	93′ 1″	111′ 6″	148′ 6″	185′ 10″
34	9′ 6″	19′	28′ 11″	38′ 4″	47′ 11″	57′ 6″	76′ 6″	95′ 11″	114′ 11″	153′	191′ 5″
35	9′ 10″	19′ 7″	29′ 10″	39′ 5″	49′ 4″	59′ 2″	78′ 9″	98′ 8″	118′ 4″	157′ 6″	197′ 1″
36	10′ 1″	20′ 2″	30′ 7″	40′ 6″	50′ 9″	60′ 9″	81′	101′ 6″	121′ 7″	162′	202′ 7″
37	10′ 5″	20′ 8″	31′ 6″	41′ 7″	52′ 2″	62′ 6″	83′ 3″	104′ 4″	125′ 1″	166′ 6″	208′ 4″
38	10′ 7″	21′ 4″	32′ 4″	42′ 10″	53′ 7″	64′ 3″	85′ 6″	107′ 2″	128′ 6″	171′	213′ 11″
39	10′ 11″	21′ 11″	33′ 2″	43′ 11″	55′	65′ 11″	87′ 9″	110′	131′ 10″	175′ 6″	219′ 7″
40	11′ 2″	22′ 5″	34′	45′	56′ 5″	67′ 7″	90′	112′ 10″	135′ 2″	180′	225′ 2″
41	11′ 6″	23′	34′ 11″	46′ 1″	57′ 10″	69′ 4″	92′ 3″	115′ 7″	138′ 7″	184′ 6″	230′ 10″
42	11′ 10″	23′ 6″	35′ 8″	47′ 4″	59′ 3″	71′	94′ 6″	118′ 6″	142′	189′	236′ 6″
43	12′	24′ 1″	36′ 7″	48′ 5″	60′ 7″	72′ 7″	96′ 9″	121′ 3″	145′ 4″	193′ 6″	242′ 1″
44	12′ 4″	24′ 7″	37′ 5″	49′ 6″	62′	74′ 4″	99′	124′ 1″	148′ 8″	198′	247′ 9″
45	12′ 7″	25′ 2″	38′ 4″	50′ 7″	63′ 6″	76′ 1″	101′ 3″	126′ 11″	152′ 1″	202′ 6″	253′ 4″
46	12′ 11″	25′ 10″	39′ 1″	51′ 10″	64′ 11″	77′ 9″	103′ 6″	129′ 9″	155′ 6″	207′	259′
47	13′ 2″	26′ 4″	40′	52′ 11″	66′ 3″	79′ 5″	105′ 9″	132′ 6″	158′ 11″	211′ 6″	264′ 7″
48	13′ 5″	26′ 11″	40′ 10″	54′	67′ 8″	81′ 2″	108′	135′ 4″	162′ 3″	216′	270′ 3″
49	13′ 8″	27′ 5″	41′ 8″	55′ 1″	69′ 1″	82′ 10″	110′ 3″	138′ 2″	165′ 7″	220′ 6″	275′ 11″
50	14′	28′	42′ 6″	56′ 4″	70′ 6″	84′ 6″	112′ 6″	141′	169′	225′	281′ 6″
51	14′ 4″	28′ 7″	43′ 5″	57′ 5″	71′ 11″	86′ 2″	114′ 9″	143′ 10″	172′ 5″	229′ 6″	287′ 2″
52	14′ 7″	29′ 1″	44′ 2″	58′ 6″	73′ 4″	87′ 11″	117′	146′ 7″	175′ 9″	234′	292′ 9″
53	14′ 10″	29′ 8″	45′ 1″	59′ 7″	74′ 9″	89′ 7″	119′ 3″	149′ 6″	179′ 2″	238′ 6″	298′ 5″
54	15′ 1″	30′ 2″	45′ 11″	60′ 10″	76′ 2″	91′ 3″	121′ 6″	152′ 3″	182′ 6″	243′	304′
55	15′ 5″	30′ 10″	46′ 10″	61′ 11″	77′ 6″	93′	123′ 9″	155′ 1″	185′ 11″	247′ 6″	309′ 8″
56	15′ 8″	31′ 5″	47′ 7″	63′	79′	94′ 7″	126′	158′	189′ 3″	252′	315′ 3″
57	16′	31′ 11″	48′ 6″	64′ 1″	80′ 4″	96′ 4″	128′ 3″	160′ 9″	192′ 8″	256′ 6″	320′ 11″
58	16′ 2″	32′ 6″	49′ 4″	65′ 4″	81′ 9″	98′	130′ 6″	163′ 7″	196′	261′	326′ 6″
59	16′ 6″	33′	50′ 2″	66′ 5″	83′ 2″	99′ 8″	132′ 9″	166′ 5″	199′ 5″	265′ 6″	332′ 2″
60	16′ 10″	33′ 7″	51′	67′ 6″	84′ 7″	101′ 5″	135′	169′ 2″	202′ 10″	270′	337′ 10″

Table E.16 Running Time to Film Length—35 mm 4-Perf.

Frames per Second

Seconds	6	12	18	24	30	36	48	60	72	96	120
1	5″	9″	1′ 1″	1′ 6″	1′ 11″	2′ 3″	3′	3′ 9″	4′ 6″	6′	7′ 6″
2	9″	1′ 6″	2′ 3″	3′	3′ 9″	4′ 6″	6′	7′ 6″	9′	12′	15′
3	1′ 2″	2′ 3″	3′ 5″	4′ 6″	5′ 8″	6′ 9″	9′	11′ 3″	13′ 6″	18′	22′ 6″
4	1′ 6″	3′	4′ 6″	6′	7′ 6″	9′	12′	15′	18′	24′	30′
5	1′ 11″	3′ 9″	5′ 8″	7′ 6″	9′ 5″	11′ 3″	15′	18′ 9″	22′ 6″	30′	37′ 6″
6	2′ 3″	4′ 6″	6′ 9″	9′	11′ 3″	13′ 6″	18′	22′ 6″	27′	36′	45′
7	2′ 8″	5′ 3″	7′ 11″	10′ 6″	13′ 2″	15′ 9″	21′	26′ 3″	31′ 6″	42′	52′ 6″
8	3′	6′	9′	12′	15′	18′	24′	30′	36′	48′	60′
9	3′ 5″	6′ 9″	10′ 2″	13′ 6″	16′ 11″	20′ 3″	27′	33′ 9″	40′ 6″	54′	67′ 6″
10	3′ 9″	7′ 6″	11′ 3″	15′	18′ 9″	22′ 6″	30′	37′ 6″	45′	60′	75′
11	4′ 2″	8′ 3″	12′ 5″	16′ 6″	20′ 7″	24′ 9″	33′	41′ 3″	49′ 6″	66′	82′ 6″
12	4′ 6″	9′	13′ 6″	18′	22′ 6″	27′	36′	45′	54′	72′	90′
13	4′ 11″	9′ 9″	14′ 7″	19′ 6″	24′ 5″	29′ 3″	39′	48′ 9″	58′ 6″	78′	97′ 6″
14	5′ 3″	10′ 6″	15′ 9″	21′	26′ 3″	31′ 6″	42′	52′ 6″	63′	84′	105′
15	5′ 8″	11′ 3″	16′ 11″	22′ 6″	28′ 2″	33′ 9″	45′	56′ 3″	67′ 6″	90′	112′ 6″
16	6′	12′	18′	24′	30′	36′	48′	60′	72′	96′	120′
17	6′ 5″	12′ 9″	19′ 2″	25′ 6″	31′ 11″	38′ 3″	51′	63′ 9″	76′ 6″	102′	127′ 6″
18	6′ 9″	13′ 6″	20′ 3″	27′	33′ 9″	40′ 6″	54′	67′ 6″	81′	108′	135′
19	7′ 2″	14′ 3″	21′ 5″	28′ 6″	35′ 7″	42′ 9″	57′	71′ 3″	85′ 6″	114′	142′ 6″
20	7′ 6″	15′	22′ 6″	30′	37′ 6″	45′	60′	75′	90′	120′	150′
21	7′ 11″	15′ 9″	23′ 7″	31′ 6″	39′ 5″	47′ 3″	63′	78′ 9″	94′ 6″	126′	157′ 6″
22	8′ 3″	16′ 6″	24′ 9″	33′	41′ 3″	49′ 6″	66′	82′ 6″	99′	132′	165′
23	8′ 8″	17′ 3″	25′ 11″	34′ 6″	43′ 2″	51′ 9″	69′	86′ 3″	103′ 6″	138′	172′ 6″
24	9′	18′	27′	36′	45′	54′	72′	90′	108′	144′	180′
25	9′ 5″	18′ 9″	28′ 2″	37′ 6″	46′ 11″	56′ 3″	75′	93′ 9″	112′ 6″	150′	187′ 6″
26	9′ 9″	19′ 6″	29′ 3″	39′	48′ 9″	58′ 6″	78′	97′ 6″	117′	156′	195′
27	10′ 2″	20′ 3″	30′ 5″	40′ 6″	50′ 7″	60′ 9″	81′	101′ 4″	121′ 6″	162′	202′ 6″
28	10′ 6″	21′	31′ 6″	42′	52′ 6″	63′	84′	105′	126′	168′	210′
29	10′ 11″	21′ 9″	32′ 7″	43′ 6″	54′ 5″	65′ 3″	87′	108′ 10″	130′ 6″	174′	217′ 6″
30	11′ 3″	22′ 6″	33′ 9″	45′	56′ 3″	67′ 6″	90′	112′ 6″	135′	180′	225′

Table E.16 *(continued)*

Frames per Second

Seconds	6	12	18	24	30	36	48	60	72	96	120
31	11′ 8″	23′ 3″	34′ 11″	46′ 6″	58′ 2″	69′ 9″	93′	116′ 4″	139′ 6″	186′	232′ 6″
32	12′	24′	36′	48′	60′	72′	96′	120′	144′	192′	240′
33	12′ 5″	24′ 9″	37′ 2″	49′ 6″	61′ 11″	74′ 3″	99′	123′ 10″	148′ 6″	198′	247′ 6″
34	12′ 9″	25′ 6″	38′ 3″	51′	63′ 9″	76′ 6″	102′	127′ 5″	153′	204′	255′
35	13′ 2″	26′ 3″	39′ 5″	52′ 6″	65′ 8″	78′ 9″	105′	131′ 4″	157′ 6″	210′	262′ 6″
36	13′ 6″	27′	40′ 6″	54′	67′ 6″	81′	108′	135′	162′	216′	270′
37	13′ 11″	27′ 9″	41′ 8″	55′ 6″	69′ 5″	83′ 3″	111′	138′ 10″	166′ 6″	222′	277′ 6″
38	14′ 3″	28′ 6″	42′ 9″	57′	71′ 3″	85′ 6″	114′	142′ 6″	171′	228′	285′
39	14′ 8″	29′ 3″	43′ 11″	58′ 6″	73′ 2″	87′ 9″	117′	146′ 4″	175′ 6″	234′	292′ 6″
40	15′	30′	45′	60′	75′	90′	120′	150′	180′	240′	300′
41	15′ 5″	30′ 9″	46′ 2″	61′ 6″	76′ 11″	92′ 3″	123′	153′ 10″	184′ 6″	246′	307′ 6″
42	15′ 9″	31′ 6″	47′ 3″	63′	78′ 9″	94′ 6″	126′	157′ 6″	189′	252′	315′
43	16′ 2″	32′ 3″	48′ 5″	64′ 6″	80′ 8″	96′ 9″	129′	161′ 4″	193′ 6″	258′	322′ 6″
44	16′ 6″	33′	49′ 6″	66′	82′ 6″	99′	132′	165′	198′	264′	330′
45	16′ 11″	33′ 9″	50′ 8″	67′ 6″	84′ 5″	101′ 4″	135′	168′ 10″	202′ 6″	270′	337′ 6″
46	17′ 3″	34′ 6″	51′ 9″	69′	86′ 3″	103′ 6″	138′	172′ 6″	207′	276′	345′
47	17′ 8″	35′ 3″	52′ 11″	70′ 6″	88′ 2″	105′ 10″	141′	176′ 4″	211′ 6″	282′	352′ 5″
48	18′	36′	54′	72′	90′	108′	144′	180′	216′	288′	360′
49	18′ 5″	36′ 9″	55′ 2″	73′ 6″	91′ 11″	110′ 4″	147′	183′ 10″	225′	300′	375′
50	18′ 9″	37′ 6″	56′ 3″	75′	93′ 9″	112′ 6″	150′	187′ 6″	225′	300′	375′
51	19′ 2″	38′ 3″	57′ 5″	76′ 6″	95′ 8″	114′ 10″	153′	191′ 4″	229′ 6″	306′	382′ 6″
52	19′ 6″	39′	58′ 6″	78′	97′ 6″	117′	156′	195′	234′	312′	390′
53	19′ 11″	39′ 9″	59′ 8″	79′ 6″	99′ 5″	119′ 4″	159′	198′ 10″	238′ 6″	318′	397′ 6″
54	20′ 3″	40′ 6″	60′ 9″	81′	101′ 4″	121′ 6″	162′	202′ 6″	243′	324′	405′
55	20′ 8″	41′ 3″	61′ 11″	82′ 6″	103′ 1″	123′ 10″	165′	206′ 3″	247′ 6″	330′	412′ 6″
56	21′	42′	63′	84′	105′	126′	168′	210′	252′	336′	420′
57	21′ 5″	42′ 9″	64′ 2″	85′ 6″	106′ 11″	128′ 4″	171′	213′ 10″	256′ 6″	342′	427′ 6″
58	21′ 9″	43′ 6″	65′ 3″	87′	108′ 10″	130′ 6″	174′	217′ 6″	261′	348′	435′
59	22′ 2″	44′ 3″	66′ 5″	88′ 6″	110′ 7″	132′ 10″	177′	221′ 4″	265′ 6″	354′	442′ 6″
60	22′ 6″	45′	67′ 6″	90′	112′ 6″	135′	180′	225′	270′	360′	450′

Table E.17 Film Length to Running Time—16 mm

Frames per Second

Feet	6	12	18	24	30	36	48	60	72	96	120
1	7 sec	3 sec	2 sec	2 sec	1 sec	1 sec	1 sec	.7 sec	.6 sec	.4 sec	.3 sec
2	13 sec	7 sec	4 sec	3 sec	3 sec	2 sec	2 sec	1 sec	1 sec	1 sec	.7 sec
3	20 sec	10 sec	7 sec	5 sec	4 sec	3 sec	3 sec	2 sec	2 sec	1 sec	1 sec
4	27 sec	13 sec	9 sec	7 sec	5 sec	4 sec	3 sec	3 sec	2 sec	2 sec	1 sec
5	33 sec	17 sec	11 sec	8 sec	7 sec	6 sec	4 sec	3 sec	3 sec	2 sec	2 sec
6	40 sec	20 sec	13 sec	10 sec	8 sec	7 sec	5 sec	4 sec	3 sec	3 sec	2 sec
7	47 sec	23 sec	16 sec	12 sec	9 sec	8 sec	6 sec	5 sec	4 sec	3 sec	2 sec
8	53 sec	27 sec	18 sec	13 sec	11 sec	9 sec	7 sec	5 sec	4 sec	3 sec	3 sec
9	1 min	30 sec	20 sec	15 sec	12 sec	10 sec	7 sec	6 sec	5 sec	4 sec	3 sec
10	1 min 7 sec	33 sec	22 sec	17 sec	13 sec	11 sec	8 sec	7 sec	6 sec	4 sec	3 sec
20	2 min 13 sec	1 min 7 sec	44 sec	33 sec	27 sec	22 sec	17 sec	13 sec	11 sec	8 sec	7 sec
30	3 min 20 sec	1 min 40 sec	1 min 7 sec	50 sec	40 sec	33 sec	25 sec	20 sec	17 sec	13 sec	10 sec
40	4 min 26 sec	2 min 13 sec	1 min 29 sec	1 min 7 sec	53 sec	44 sec	33 sec	27 sec	22 sec	17 sec	13 sec
50	5 min 33 sec	2 min 47 sec	1 min 51 sec	1 min 23 sec	1 min 6 sec	56 sec	42 sec	34 sec	28 sec	21 sec	17 sec
60	6 min 40 sec	3 min 20 sec	2 min 13 sec	1 min 40 sec	1 min 20 sec	1 min 7 sec	50 sec	40 sec	33 sec	25 sec	20 sec
70	7 min 47 sec	3 min 53 sec	2 min 35 sec	1 min 57 sec	1 min 33 sec	1 min 18 sec	58 sec	47 sec	39 sec	29 sec	23 sec
80	8 min 54 sec	4 min 26 sec	2 min 58 sec	2 min 14 sec	1 min 46 sec	1 min 29 sec	1 min 6 sec	54 sec	44 sec	33 sec	26 sec
90	10 min	5 min	3 min 20 sec	2 min 30 sec	2 min	1 min 40 sec	1 min 15 sec	1 min	50 sec	38 sec	30 sec
100	11 min 7 sec	5 min 33 sec	3 min 42 sec	2 min 47 sec	2 min 13 sec	1 min 51 sec	1 min 23 sec	1 min 7 sec	55 sec	41 sec	33 sec
200	22 min 14 sec	11 min 6 sec	7 min 24 sec	5 min 34 sec	4 min 26 sec	3 min 42 sec	2 min 46 sec	2 min 13 sec	1 min 51 sec	1 min 23 sec	1 min 7 sec
400	44 min 28 sec	22 min 12 sec	14 min 48 sec	11 min 7 sec	8 min 53 sec	7 min 25 sec	5 min 33 sec	4 min 26 sec	3 min 42 sec	2 min 46 sec	2 min 13 sec
800	88 min 53 sec	44 min 26 sec	29 min 38 sec	22 min 13 sec	17 min 46 sec	14 min 49 sec	11 min 7 sec	8 min 53 sec	7 min 25 sec	5 min 33 sec	4 min 26 sec
1200	133 min 24 sec	66 min 36 sec	44 min 24 sec	33 min 20 sec	26 min 40 sec	22 min 13 sec	16 min 40 sec	13 min 20 sec	11 min 7 sec	8 min 20 sec	6 min 40 sec

Table E.18 Film Length to Running Time—35 mm, 3-Perf.

Frames per Second

Feet	6	12	18	24	30	36	48	60	72	96	120
1	4 sec	2 sec	1 sec	.9 sec	.7 sec	.6 sec	.4 sec	.4 sec	.3 sec	.2 sec	.2 sec
2	7 sec	4 sec	2 sec	2 sec	1 sec	1 sec	.9 sec	.7 sec	.6 sec	.4 sec	.4 sec
3	11 sec	5 sec	4 sec	4 sec	2 sec	2 sec	1 sec	1 sec	.9 sec	.7 sec	.5 sec
4	14 sec	7 sec	5 sec	4 sec	3 sec	2 sec	2 sec	1 sec	1 sec	.9 sec	.7 sec
5	18 sec	9 sec	6 sec	4 sec	4 sec	3 sec	2 sec	2 sec	1 sec	1 sec	.9 sec
6	21 sec	11 sec	7 sec	5 sec	4 sec	4 sec	3 sec	2 sec	2 sec	1 sec	1 sec
7	25 sec	12 sec	8 sec	6 sec	5 sec	4 sec	3 sec	3 sec	2 sec	2 sec	1 sec
8	28 sec	14 sec	9 sec	7 sec	6 sec	5 sec	4 sec	3 sec	2 sec	2 sec	1 sec
9	32 sec	16 sec	11 sec	8 sec	6 sec	5 sec	4 sec	3 sec	2 sec	2 sec	2 sec
10	36 sec	18 sec	12 sec	9 sec	7 sec	6 sec	4 sec	4 sec	3 sec	2 sec	2 sec
20	1 min 11 sec	36 sec	24 sec	18 sec	14 sec	12 sec	9 sec	7 sec	6 sec	4 sec	4 sec
30	1 min 47 sec	53 sec	35 sec	26 sec	21 sec	18 sec	13 sec	11 sec	9 sec	7 sec	5 sec
40	2 min 22 sec	1 min 11 sec	47 sec	35 sec	28 sec	24 sec	18 sec	14 sec	12 sec	9 sec	7 sec
50	2 min 57 sec	1 min 29 sec	59 sec	44 sec	36 sec	30 sec	22 sec	18 sec	15 sec	11 sec	9 sec
60	3 min 33 sec	1 min 47 sec	1 min 11 sec	53 sec	43 sec	35 sec	26 sec	22 sec	18 sec	13 sec	11 sec
70	4 min 12 sec	2 min 5 sec	1 min 23 sec	1 min 2 sec	50 sec	41 sec	31 sec	25 sec	21 sec	15 sec	13 sec
80	4 min 44 sec	2 min 22 sec	1 min 34 sec	1 min 10 sec	57 sec	47 sec	35 sec	29 sec	24 sec	18 sec	14 sec
90	5 min 20 sec	2 min 40 sec	1 min 46 sec	1 min 19 sec	1 min 4 sec	53 sec	40 sec	32 sec	27 sec	20 sec	16 sec
100	5 min 55 sec	2 min 58 sec	1 min 58 sec	1 min 29 sec	1 min 11 sec	59 sec	44 sec	35 sec	30 sec	22 sec	18 sec
200	11 min 50 sec	5 min 55 sec	3 min 56 sec	2 min 58 sec	2 min 22 sec	1 min 58 sec	1 min 29 sec	1 min 11 sec	59 sec	44 sec	35 sec
400	23 min 40 sec	11 min 50 sec	7 min 53 sec	5 min 56 sec	4 min 44 sec	3 min 56 sec	2 min 58 sec	2 min 22 sec	1 min 58 sec	1 min 29 sec	1 min 11 sec
1000	59 min 10 sec	29 min 35 sec	19 min 43 sec	14 min 49 sec	11 min 50 sec	9 min 52 sec	7 min 24 sec	5 min 55 sec	4 min 56 sec	3 min 42 sec	2 min 58 sec
2000	118 min 18 sec	59 min 10 sec	39 min 27 sec	29 min 38 sec	23 min 40 sec	19 min 43 sec	14 min 47 sec	11 min 50 sec	9 min 52 sec	7 min 24 sec	5 min 55 sec

Table E.19 Film Length to Running Time—35 mm, 4-Perf.

Frames per Second

Feet	6	12	18	24	30	36	48	60	72	96	120
1	3 sec	1 sec	.9 sec	.7 sec	.5 sec	.4 sec	.3 sec	.3 sec	.2 sec	.2 sec	.1 sec
2	5 sec	3 sec	2 sec	1 sec	1 sec	.9 sec	.7 sec	.5 sec	.4 sec	.3 sec	.3 sec
3	8 sec	4 sec	3 sec	2 sec	2 sec	1 sec	1 sec	.8 sec	.7 sec	.5 sec	.4 sec
4	11 sec	5 sec	4 sec	3 sec	2 sec	2 sec	1 sec	1 sec	.9 sec	.7 sec	.5 sec
5	13 sec	7 sec	4 sec	3 sec	3 sec	2 sec	2 sec	1 sec	1 sec	.9 sec	.7 sec
6	16 sec	8 sec	5 sec	4 sec	3 sec	3 sec	2 sec	2 sec	1 sec	1 sec	.8 sec
7	19 sec	9 sec	6 sec	5 sec	4 sec	3 sec	2 sec	2 sec	2 sec	1 sec	.9 sec
8	21 sec	11 sec	7 sec	5 sec	4 sec	4 sec	3 sec	2 sec	2 sec	1 sec	1 sec
9	24 sec	12 sec	8 sec	6 sec	5 sec	4 sec	3 sec	2 sec	2 sec	2 sec	1 sec
10	27 sec	13 sec	9 sec	7 sec	5 sec	4 sec	3 sec	3 sec	2 sec	2 sec	1 sec
20	53 sec	27 sec	18 sec	13 sec	11 sec	9 sec	7 sec	5 sec	4 sec	3 sec	3 sec
30	1 min 20 sec	40 sec	26 sec	20 sec	16 sec	13 sec	10 sec	8 sec	7 sec	5 sec	4 sec
40	1 min 47 sec	53 sec	35 sec	27 sec	21 sec	18 sec	13 sec	11 sec	9 sec	7 sec	5 sec
50	2 min 14 sec	1 min 6 sec	44 sec	34 sec	27 sec	22 sec	17 sec	14 sec	11 sec	9 sec	7 sec
60	2 min 40 sec	1 min 20 sec	53 sec	40 sec	32 sec	26 sec	20 sec	16 sec	13 sec	10 sec	8 sec
70	3 min 7 sec	1 min 33 sec	1 min 2 sec	47 sec	37 sec	31 sec	23 sec	19 sec	15 sec	12 sec	9 sec
80	3 min 34 sec	1 min 46 sec	1 min 10 sec	54 sec	42 sec	35 sec	26 sec	22 sec	18 sec	14 sec	10 sec
90	4 min	2 min	1 min 19 sec	1 min	48 sec	40 sec	30 sec	24 sec	20 sec	15 sec	12 sec
100	4 min 26 sec	2 min 13 sec	1 min 29 sec	1 min 7 sec	53 sec	44 sec	33 sec	26 sec	22 sec	16 sec	13 sec
200	8 min 53 sec	4 min 26 sec	2 min 58 sec	2 min 13 sec	1 min 46 sec	1 min 29 sec	1 min 7 sec	53 sec	44 sec	33 sec	26 sec
400	17 min 47 sec	8 min 53 sec	5 min 56 sec	4 min 26 sec	3 min 33 sec	2 min 58 sec	2 min 13 sec	1 min 46 sec	1 min 29 sec	1 min 7 sec	53 sec
1000	44 min 26 sec	22 min 13 sec	14 min 49 sec	11 min 7 sec	8 min 53 sec	7 min 24 sec	5 min 33 sec	4 min 26 sec	3 min 42 sec	2 min 46 sec	2 min 13 sec
2000	88 min 53 sec	44 min 26 sec	29 min 37 sec	22 min 13 sec	17 min 46 sec	14 min 48 sec	11 min 7 sec	8 min 53 sec	7 min 24 sec	5 min 33 sec	4 min 26 sec

nearest minute and second. For example, from Table E.17, you can determine when shooting 16 mm at 48 f.p.s., 60 feet of film will last approximately 50 seconds.

Feet to Meters and Meters to Feet

Because of the many different camera lenses that are available for shooting, you may sometimes use lenses that are calibrated only in feet or only in meters, and you need to convert this information to the other format. Tables E.20 and E.21 are conversion tables for converting feet and inches to meters or meters to feet and inches.

Table E.20 Meters to Feet Conversion Table

Meters	Feet / Inches
.1 meter	3.9 inches
.2 meter	7.9 inches
.3 meter	11.8 inches
.4 meter	15.7 inches
.5 meter	19.7 inches
.6 meter	23.6 inches
.7 meter	27.6 inches
.8 meter	31.5 inches
.9 meter	35.4 inches
1 meter	3 feet 3.4 inches
2 meters	6 feet 6.7 inches
3 meters	9 feet 10.1 inches
4 meters	13 feet 1.5 inches
5 meters	16 feet 4.8 inches
6 meters	19 feet 8.2 inches
7 meters	22 feet 11.6 inches
8 meters	26 feet 3 inches
9 meters	29 feet 6.3 inches
10 meters	32 feet 9.7 inches

Table E.21 Feet to Meters Conversion Table

Feet	Meters
1 foot	.30 meter
2 feet	.61 meter
3 feet	.91 meter
4 feet	1.22 meters
5 feet	1.52 meters
6 feet	1.83 meters
7 feet	2.13 meters
8 feet	2.44 meters
9 feet	2.74 meters
10 feet	3.05 meters
15 feet	4.57 meters
20 feet	6.10 meters
30 feet	9.14 meters
40 feet	12.19 meters
50 feet	15.24 meters

FORMULAS

You may often not be able to find specific information needed to calculate depth of field, exposure time, feet per minute, etc. The following formulas may be useful to calculate these and some other values.

Depth of Field—Near

$$\text{depth of field (near)} = \frac{\text{hyperfocal distance} \times \text{focus distance}}{\text{hyperfocal distance} + \text{focus distance}}$$

Depth of Field—Far

$$\text{depth of field (near)} = \frac{\text{hyperfocal distance} \times \text{focus distance}}{\text{hyperfocal distance} - \text{focus distance}}$$

Hyperfocal Distance

$$\text{Hyperfocal distance} = \frac{\text{focal length}^2}{\text{circle of confusion} \times \text{f-stop}}$$

Electrical

$$\text{amps} = \frac{\text{watts}}{\text{volts}}$$

OR

$$\text{watts} = \text{volts} \times \text{amps}$$

Exposure Time

$$\text{exposure time} = \frac{\text{shutter angle}}{360 \times \text{frames per second}}$$

F-Stop

$$\text{f-stop} = \frac{\text{focal length of lens}}{\text{diameter of lens opening}}$$

Feet per Minute for 16 mm

$$\text{feet per minute (16 mm)} = \frac{\text{frames per second} \times 60}{40}$$

Feet per Minute for 35 mm 3-Perf Format

$$\text{feet per minute (35 mm 3-perf format)} = \frac{\text{frames per second} \times 60}{21.33}$$

Feet per Minute for 35 mm 4-Perf Format

$$\text{feet per minute (35 mm 4-perf format)} = \frac{\text{frames per second} \times 60}{16}$$

Feet and Inches to Meters

$$\text{Meters} = \frac{(\text{feet} \times 12) + \text{inches}}{39.37}$$

Meters to Feet and Inches

$$\text{feet} = \text{meters} \times 3.2808$$

Screen Time

$$\text{Screen time} = \frac{\text{camera running time} \times \text{frames per second}}{24}$$

Recommended Reading

Alton, John. *Painting with Light.* Berkeley and Los Angeles, CA: University of California Press, 1995.

Barclay, Steven. *The Motion Picture Image: From Film to Digital.* Boston, MA: Focal Press. 2000.

Bergery, Benjamin. *Reflections: Twenty-One Cinematographers at Work.* Hollywood, CA: ASC Press, 2002.

Bernstein, Steven. *The Technique of Film Production.* Boston, MA: Focal Press, 1988.

Bloedow, Jerry. *Filmmaking Foundations.* Boston, MA: Focal Press, 1991.

Bognar, Desi K. *International Dictionary of Broadcasting and Film,* 2nd ed. Boston, MA: Focal Press, 1999.

Box, Harry C. *Set Lighting Technician's Handbook,* 3rd ed. Boston, MA: Focal Press, 2003.

Brown, Blain. *The Filmmaker's Pocket Reference.* Boston, MA: Focal Press, 1994.

Brown, Blain. *Cinematography Theory and Practice.* Boston, MA: Focal Press, 2002.

Brown, Blain. *Motion Picture and Video Lighting.* Boston, MA: Focal Press, 1995.

Browne, Steven E. *Film-Video Terms and Concepts.* Boston, MA: Focal Press, 1992.

Cardiff, Jack. *Magic Hour.* London: Faber & Faber, 1996.

Carlson, Verne, and Sylvia Carlson. *Professional Cameraman's Handbook,* 4th ed. Boston, MA: Focal Press, 1994.

Carlson, Verne, and Sylvia Carlson. *Professional Lighting Handbook,* 2nd ed. Boston, MA: Focal Press, 1991.

Case, Dominic. *Film Technology in Post Production.* Boston, MA: Focal Press. 2001.

Cheshire, David. *The Book of Movie Photography.* New York, NY: Alfred A. Knopf, 1979.

Clarke, Charles. *Charles Clarke's Professional Cinematography.* Hollywood, CA: ASC Press, 1994.

Coe, Brian. *The History of Movie Photography.* New York, NY: Zoetrope, 1982.

Courter, Philip R. *The Filmmakers Craft: 16mm Cinematography.* New York, NY: Van Nostrand Reinhold, 1982.

Daley, Ken. *Basic Film Technique.* Boston, MA: Focal Press, 1980.

Dancyger, Ken. *The Technique of Film and Video Editing.* Boston, MA: Focal Press, 1993.

Dancyger, Ken. *The World of Film and Video Production: Aesthetics and Practices.* Belmont, CA: Wadsworth Publishing, 1999.

De Leeuw, Ben. *Digital Cinematography.* San Diego, CA: Academic Press/Morgan Kaufmann, 1997.

Dmytryk, Edward. *Cinema: Concept & Practice.* Boston, MA: Focal Press, 1988.

Eastman Kodak Co. *The Book of Film Care.* Rochester, NY: Eastman Kodak Co., 1983.

Eastman Kodak Co. *Cinematographer's Field Guide* 8th ed., Rochester, NY: Eastman Kodak Co., 2002.

Eastman Kodak Co. *Eastman Professional Motion Picture Films.* Rochester, NY: Eastman Kodak Co., 1992.

Eastman Kodak Co. *Exploring the Color Image.* Rochester, NY: Eastman Kodak Co., 1996.

Eastman Kodak Co. *Handbook of Kodak Photographic Filters.* Rochester, NY: Eastman Kodak Co., 1990.

Eastman Kodak Co. *Kodak Motion Picture Film.* Rochester, NY: Eastman Kodak Co., 1983.

Eastman Kodak Co. *Student Filmmakers Handbook.* Rochester, NY: Eastman Kodak Co., 1999.

Ettedgui, Peter. *Cinematography—Screencraft Series.* Boston, MA: Focal Press, 1999

Fauer, Jon. *Arriflex 16SR Book,* 3rd ed. Boston, MA: Focal Press, 1999.

Fauer, Jon. *Arriflex 16SR3—The Book.* Blauvelt, NY: Arriflex, 1996.

Fauer, Jon. *Arriflex 35 Book,* 3rd ed. Boston, MA: Focal Press, 1999.

Fauer, Jon. *Arriflex 435 Book*, 3rd ed. Blauvelt, NY: Arriflex, 1999.

Fauer, Jon. *Arricam Book.* Hollywood, CA: ASC Press, 2002.

Fauer, Jon. *Shooting Digital Video: DVCAM, MiniDV and DVC Pro.* Boston, MA: Focal Press, 2001.

Ferncase, Richard K. *Film and Video Lighting Terms and Concepts.* Boston, MA: Focal Press, 1994.

Ferncase, Richard K. *Basic Lighting Worktext for Film and Video.* Boston, MA: Focal Press, 1992.

Ferrara, Serena. *Steadicam: Techniques and Aesthetics.* Boston, MA: Focal Press, 2000.

Fielding, Raymond. *The Technique of Special Effects Cinematography.* Boston, MA: Focal Press, 1985.

Fielding, Raymond. *A Technological History of Motion Pictures and Television.* Berkeley, CA: University of California Press, 1967.

Galer, Mark and John Child. *Photographic Lighting: Essentials,* 2nd ed. Boston, MA: Focal Press, 2003.

Garvey, Helen. *Before You Shoot.* Santa Cruz, CA: Shire Press, 1985.

Gloman, Chuck B., and Tom Letourneau. *Placing Shadows: Lighting Techniques for Video Production.* Boston, MA: Focal Press, 2002.

Gross, Lynne S., and Larry W. Ward. *Digital Moviemaking,* 5th ed. Belmont, CA: Wadsworth Publishing, 2004.

Grotticelli, Michael. *American Cinematographer Video Manual*—3rd ed. Hollywood, CA: ASC Press, 2001.

Happe, L. Bernard. *Basic Motion Picture Technology.* Boston, MA: Focal Press, 1971.

Harrison, H. K. *Mystery of Filters II.* Porterville, CA: Harrison and Harrison, 1981.

Hart, Douglas C. *The Camera Assistant: A Complete Professional Handbook.* Boston, MA: Focal Press, 1995.

Hershey, Fritz Lynn. *Optics and Focus for Camera Assistants.* Boston, MA: Focal Press, 1996.

Hines, William. *Operating Cinematography for Film and Video.* Los Angeles, CA: Ed-Venture Films/Books, 1997.

Hines, William. *Job Descriptions for Film, Video and CGI.* Los Angeles, CA: Ed-Venture Films/Books, 1999.

Hirschfeld, Gerald, A.S.C. *Image Control.* Boston, MA: Focal Press, 1993.

Hummel, Rob, ed. *American Cinematographer Manual,* 8th ed. Hollywood, CA: ASC Press, 2002.

Kindem, Gorham. *The Moving Image: Production Principles and Practice.* Glenview, IL: Scott, Foresman, 1987.

Krasilovsky, Alexis. *Women Behind the Camera.* Westport, CT: Praeger Publishing, 1997.

Lazslo, Andrew. *Every Frame a Rembrandt: Art and Practice of Cinematography.* Boston, MA: Focal Press, 1999.

Lowell, Ross. *Matters of Light & Depth.* Philadelphia, PA: Broad Street Books, 1992.

Lyver, Des, and Graham Swainson. *Basics of Video Production,* 2nd ed. Boston, MA: Focal Press, 1999.

Lyver, Des, and Graham Swainson. *Basics of Video Lighting,* 2nd ed. Boston, MA: Focal Press, 1999.

Macdonald, Scott. *A Critical Cinema.* Berkeley, CA: University of California Press, 1988.

Malkiewicz, Kris, and Robert E. Rogers. *Cinematography.* New York: Prentice-Hall, 1988.

Malkiewicz, Kris, and Robert E. Rogers. *Film Lighting.* New York: Prentice-Hall, 1986.

Maltin, Leonard. *The Art of the Cinematographer: A Survey and Interview with Five Masters.* New York: Dover, 1978.

Mamer, Bruce. *Film Production Technique: Creating the Accomplished Image*, 3rd ed. Belmont, CA: Wadsworth Publishing, 1999.

Mascelli, Joseph V. *The Five C's of Cinematography.* Los Angeles, CA: Silman-James Press, 1998.

Miller, Pat P. *Script Supervising and Film Continuity,* 3rd ed. Boston, MA: Focal Press, 1999.

Millerson, Gerald. *Video Camera Techniques.* Boston, MA: Focal Press, 1994.

Millerson, Gerald. *Lighting for Television and Film,* 3rd ed. Boston, MA: Focal Press, 1999.

Millerson, Gerald. *Lighting for Video,* 3rd ed. Boston, MA: Focal Press, 1991.

Ohanian, Thomas A., and Michael E. Phillips. *Digital Filmmaking: The Changing Art and Craft of Making Motion Pictures.* Boston, MA: Focal Press, 1996.

Penney, Edmund F. *The Facts on File Dictionary of Film and Broadcast Terms.* New York: Facts on File, 1991.

Perisic, Zoran. *Visual Effects Cinematography.* Boston, MA: Focal Press, 1999.

Petrie, Duncan. *The British Cinematographer.* London, England: British Film Institute, 1996.

Pincus, Edward, and Steven Ascher. *The Filmmaker's Handbook.* New York: New American Library, 1984.

Rahmel, Dan. *Nuts and Bolts Filmmaking.* Boston, MA: Focal Press, 2004.

Ratcliff, John. *Timecode: A User's Guide.* Boston, MA: Focal Press, 1999.

Ray, Sidney F. *Applied Photographic Optics,* 3rd ed. Boston, MA: Focal Press, 2003.

Ray, Sidney F. *The Photographic Lens,* 2nd ed. Boston, MA: Focal Press, 1992.

Roberts, Kenneth H., and Win Sharples, Jr. *A Primer for Filmmaking: A Complete Guide to 16 and 35mm Film Production.* New York: Bobbs-Merrill, 1971.

Rogers, Pauline B. *Art of Visual Effects—Interviews on the Tools of the Trade.* Boston, MA: Focal Press, 1999.

Rogers, Pauline B. *Contemporary Cinematographers on Their Art.* Boston, MA: Focal Press, 1998.

Rogers, Pauline B. *More Contemporary Cinematographers on Their Art.* Boston, MA: Focal Press, 1999.

Samuelson, David W. *"Hands-On" Manual for Cinematographers.* Boston, MA: Focal Press, 1994.

Samuelson, David W. *Motion Picture Camera and Lighting Equipment.* Boston, MA: Focal Press, 1987.

Samuelson, David W. *Motion Picture Camera Data.* Boston, MA: Focal Press, 1979.

Samuelson, David W. *Motion Picture Camera Techniques.* Boston, MA: Focal Press, 1984.

Samuelson, David W. *Panaflex Users' Manual.* Boston, MA: Focal Press, 1990.

Schaefer, Dennis, and Larry Salvato. *Masters of Light: Conversations with Contemporary Cinematographers.* Berkeley, CA: University of California Press, 1985.

Schroeppel, Tom. *The Bare Bones Camera Course for Film and Video,* 2nd rev. ed. Tampa, FL: Tom Schroeppel, 1982.

Schroeppel, Tom. *Video Goals: Getting Results with Pictures and Sound.* Tampa, FL: Tom Schroeppel, 1998.

Singleton, Ralph S. *Filmmaker's Dictionary.* Beverly Hills, CA: Lone Eagle Publishing Co., 1990.

Souto, Mario Raimondo. *The Technique of the Motion Picture Camera.* Boston, MA: Focal Press, 1969.

Stone, Judy. *Eye on the World: Conversations with International Filmmakers.* Los Angeles, CA: Silman-James Press, 1997.

Taub, Eric. *Gaffers, Grips and Best Boys.* New York, NY: St. Martin's Press, 1987.

Thompson, Roy. *Grammar of the Shot.* Boston, MA: Focal Press, 1998.

Underdahl, Douglas. *The 16 mm Camera Book.* New York, NY: Media Logic, 1993.

Uva, Michael G., and Sabrina Uva. *Uva's Basic Grip Book.* Boston, MA: Focal Press, 2001.

Uva, Michael G., and Sabrina Uva. *Uva's Guide to Cranes, Dollies and Remote Heads.* Boston, MA: Focal Press, 2001.

Viera, Dave, and Maria Viera. *Lighting for Film and Digital Cinematography,* 2nd ed. Belmont, CA: Wadsworth Publishing, 2004.

Ward, Peter. *Studio and Outside Broadcast Camerawork.* Boston, MA: Focal Press, 2001.

Ward, Peter. *Picture Composition,* 2nd ed. Boston, MA: Focal Press, 2002.

Wheeler, Leslie J. *Principles of Cinematography.* Indianola, IN: Fountain Press, 1953.

Wheeler, Paul. *Digital Cinematography.* Boston, MA: Focal Press, 2001.

Wheeler, Paul. *High Definition and 24P Cinematography.* Boston, MA: Focal Press, 2003.

Wheeler, Paul. *Practical Cinematography*. Boston, MA: Focal Press, 1999.

Wilson, Anton. *Anton Wilson's Cinema Workshop,* 4th ed. Hollywood, CA: ASC Press, 1994.

Zone, Ray, ed. *New Wave King: The Cinematography of Laszlo Kovacs, ASC.* Hollywood, CA: ASC Press, 2002.

Glossary

Aaton: Trade name of a brand of professional 16 mm and 35 mm cameras.

Abby Singer Shot: During production this shot is used to refer to the next-to-the-last shot of the day. The term is named for Abby Singer. According to Mr. Singer, the term was started during the mid-1950s while he was an Assistant Director at Universal Studios. To keep ahead of things, he would always inform the crew that they would shoot the current shot plus one more shot, before moving to a different area of the studio, either a different stage or the back lot. Through the years other Assistant Directors used the term; today the term is always used to indicate the next-to-the-last shot of the day.

A.C.: Abbreviation for Assistant Cameraman.

Academy Aperture: The image size of a frame of 35 mm motion picture film. It is the ratio of the width to height and is written as 1.33:1. Feature films are no longer shot in academy format, but it is still used for most of the television series and movies made for television. May also be referred to as 1.37:1.

Acetate Base: A film base made up of a slow burning chemical substance that is much more durable than the older nitrate film base, which was highly flammable. Film that is coated onto an acetate base is sometimes referred to as safety film.

Aerial Shot: Any filmed shot that is done from high above the ground, often from a plane or helicopter.

A.K.S.: A slang term used to refer to an assortment of equipment, tools, and accessories. Its literal translation is "All Kinds of Stuff" or "All Kinds of S**t." Any case that contains many different pieces of equipment or accessories is called an A.K.S. case.

American Cinematographer's Manual: See *A.S.C. Manual.*

American Society of Cinematographers (A.S.C.): An honorary organization of Cinematographers. It is not a labor guild or union. To become a member you must be invited by the current membership.

Anamorphic Lens: A film lens that allows you to film wide-screen format when using standard 35 mm film. It produces an image that is squeezed or compressed to fit the film frame. The developed print of the film is projected through a special projector using a similar type lens, which unsqueezes the image and makes it appear normal on the screen.

Angle of View: The angle covered by the camera lens. It may also be called field of view. A wide-angle lens shows more of the scene and therefore has a wider angle of view than a telephoto lens.

Answer Print: The first combined sound and picture print done by the laboratory.

Anti-Halation Backing: The dark coating on the back of the unexposed film stock that prevents light from passing through the film, striking the back of the aperture, and then going back through the film causing a flare or fogging of the film image.

Aperture (Camera): The opening in the film gate or aperture plate that determines the precise area of exposure of the frame of film. During exposure, the film is held in place in the gate by the registration pin, and during this brief period of time, light passes through the camera aperture striking the film and causing an exposure.

Aperture (Lens): The opening in the lens, formed by an adjustable iris, through which light passes in order to expose the film. The size of this opening is expressed as an f-stop number.

Aperture Plate: A metal plate within the camera that contains an opening, in front of the film, which determines the size of the frame. It determines the frame size by allowing light to strike only a portion of the frame and preventing light from striking the edges of the film.

Arriflex: Trade name for a brand of professional 16 mm, 35 mm, and 65 mm camera.

A.S.A.: Abbreviation for the American Standards Association. The A.S.A. value assigned to a particular film stock is an indication of the speed of the film or the sensitivity of the film to light. The higher the number, the more sensitive the film is to light. A film stock with a low rating may be referred to as a slow film and one with a high rating may be referred to as fast film or high-speed film. Today, the film speed is indicated by an exposure index (EI) number. The A.S.A. or EI number is used by the Director of Photography to determine the exposure. *See Exposure Index.*

A.S.C.: Abbreviation for American Society of Cinematographers.

***A.S.C. Manual*:** A technical manual published by the American Society of Cinematographers. It contains useful information needed by Directors of Photography and Camera Assistants during shooting. This includes information on cameras, lighting, filters, depth of field, exposure compensation, film speed tables, etc. Most D.P.s and Assistants keep a copy of this book in their meter case or ditty bag.

Aspect Ratio: The relationship between the width of the frame to the height of the frame. For television and 16 mm films, the standard aspect ratio is 1.33:1, for standard theatrical 35 mm feature films it is 1.85:1, and for anamorphic 35 mm films it is 2.35:1 or 2.40:1.

Aspheron: A 16 mm lens attachment designed for the 9.5 mm and the 12 mm Zeiss prime lenses. It is used to increase the angle of view of these wide-angle lenses.

Assistant Cameraman (A.C.): A member of the camera crew who works closely with the Director of Photography and Camera Operator during the shooting day. Some of the job responsibilities include maintaining and setting up the camera, changing lenses, loading film, measuring focus distances, focusing and zooming during the shot, clapping the slate, placing tape marks for actors, keeping camera reports and other paperwork, etc. The camera department usually consists of the First Assistant Cameraman (1st A.C.) and the Second Assistant Cameraman (2nd A.C.). *See First Assistant Cameraman and Second Assistant Cameraman.*

B & W: Abbreviation for Black and White.

Baby Legs, Baby Tripod, Babies: A short tripod used for low-angle shots or any shots where the standard size tripod is not appropriate.

Barney: A flexible, padded, and insulated cover used to reduce noise coming from the camera or magazine. A heated version is used to keep the camera and magazine warm in extremely cold shooting situations.

Barrel Connector: A metal connector that allows two BNC video cables to be interconnected to make a longer cable.

Base: The smooth transparent surface on which the film emulsion is attached. In the earlier days of filmmaking, a nitrate base was used, which was highly flammable. Today a safer acetate type base is used for all film stocks.

Batteries: Rechargeable power supply used to power the camera. Belt batteries and on-board batteries are usually used when doing hand-held shots. Block batteries are used when working on a dolly or tripod. Most camera batteries are either 12 volts or 24 volts depending on the camera system you are using. Some older 16 mm cameras use an 8-volt battery. Check with the rental house to be sure that you have the correct voltage battery.

Battery Belt: A belt containing the cells of the battery that may be worn by the Operator or the Assistant when doing hand-held shots. It may also be used when a block battery is impractical.

Battery Cables: Power cables that are used to connect the camera or any other accessory to the battery and that supply the power from the battery to the camera or accessory being used.

Battery Chargers: Electrical device used to keep the batteries fully charged when not being used. When charging, the battery is connected to the charger, and the charger is plugged into a standard 110-volt electrical outlet. Never connect the battery to the camera while it is being charged.

Belt Battery: *See Battery Belt.*

Black and White (B & W): Any film shot without using color film. Sometimes a film is shot using color film and during the developing and printing process, the color is taken away to give a black-and-white image.

Black Bag: A small plastic or paper bag that contains the raw film stock when it is inside the film can. After the film has been exposed, it is placed back in the black bag, and then in the film can and sealed for delivery to the lab. Some Camera Assistants also refer to the changing bag as the black bag.

Black Dot Texture Screen: A diffusion filter that looks like a clear piece of glass containing small black dots in a random pattern. These black dots cause the light striking them to become spread out over a large area, which causes the image to appear diffused and out of focus. These filters come in a set ranging from number 1, the lightest, to number 5, the heaviest. These filters require an exposure compensation of one stop.

Block Battery: A large camera battery that is enclosed in some type of case containing the cells of the battery and often a built-in charger. Block batteries may come in single blocks containing only one battery or dual blocks containing two batteries.

Breathing: The characteristic of some lenses that gives the illusion of zooming when you are adjusting the focus of the lens.

Buckle Switch: A switch within the camera that acts as a safety shut-off device in the event of a film jam or rollout within the camera. Also called buckle trip switch.

Camera: The basic piece of equipment used to photograph the images. Most cameras consist of a lens that projects the image onto the film stock, a shutter to regulate the light striking the film, a viewfinder that enables the Camera Operator to view the image during filming, some type of mechanism to transport the film through the camera, a motor that drives the film through the camera, and a lightproof container, called a magazine, which holds the film before and after exposure.

Camera Angle: The position of the camera in relation to the subject being filmed (high, low, left, right, etc.).

Camera, Hand-Held: A camera that has been set up so that the Camera Operator may hold it on his or her shoulder during filming. It may be used to film moving shots or point-of-view shots of an actor walking or moving through the scene.

Camera Jam: A malfunction that occurs when the film backs up in the camera and becomes piled up in the camera movement. The film usually becomes caught between the sprocket wheels and the guide rollers. Torn perforations or improper threading in the camera or magazine may cause this.

Camera Left: The area to the left side of camera as seen from the Camera Operator's point of view. As the actor faces the camera, camera left is to the actor's right.

Camera Mount: Any type of device that the camera is mounted on for support. It may be mounted on a head and placed on a dolly, tripod, high hat, camera car, etc.

Cameraman: *See Director of Photography.*
Camera Oil: A special type of oil used for lubricating the movement in the camera. The camera rental house or camera manufacturer usually supplies it. You should use only the recommended oil for the particular camera.
Camera Operator: The member of the camera crew who looks through and operates the camera during filming. He or she maintains the composition of the shot, as instructed by the Director and Director of Photography, by making smooth pan and tilt moves.
Camera Package: Umbrella term used for the camera, lenses, magazines, batteries, head, tripod, and all other camera equipment needed for shooting.
Camera Rental House: A company that specializes in the rental and maintenance of motion picture camera equipment.
Camera Report: A form that is filled in with the pertinent information for each roll of film shot. It includes all production information such as Company, Title, Director's name, and the Cameraman's name. It should also have spaces for the magazine number, roll number, amount of film in the magazine, emulsion number, date shot, and scene and take numbers. The report also lists the length of each shot, how much film is used, which takes are good or no good, and any instructions to the lab regarding developing instructions.
Camera Right: The area to the right side of camera as seen from the Camera Operator's point of view. As the actor faces the camera, camera right is to the actor's left.
Camera Speed: The rate at which the film is transported through the camera during filming. It is expressed in frames per second, abbreviated f.p.s. Normal sync camera speed is 24 f.p.s.
Camera Tape (1 Inch): Cloth tape, usually 1 inch wide, which is used for making labels on cases, film cans, magazines, and any other labels that may be required. It is also for wrapping cans of exposed film and unexposed film and short ends. It may be used by the First Assistant for focus marks on the ground. The most commonly used colors of camera tape are white and black, but it is also available in red, yellow, orange, blue, gray, green, teal, purple, fluorescent pink, fluorescent green, fluorescent orange, and fluorescent yellow.
Camera Truck: A large enclosed truck used to transport and store all camera equipment when filming on location. It is usually set up with a workbench, shelves for storage of equipment, and a darkroom for loading and unloading film.
Camera Wedge: A small wooden wedge that may be used to help level the camera when it is placed on uneven surfaces.
CC Filters: *See Color Compensating Filters.*
Chamois: Cloth used for cleaning camera and magazines.

Changing Bag: A lightproof cloth bag used to load and unload film when a darkroom is not available. It is actually two bags sewn together, one inside the other. The top of each bag contains a zipper giving access to the inside of the bag, and two sleeves containing elastic cuffs, on the opposite side of the bag from the zippers. The magazine is placed inside the inner bag and both zippers are then closed. With the zippers closed and the assistant's arms placed inside the sleeves, it forms a light tight compartment for loading and unloading the film stock.
Changing Tent: Very similar in design to a changing bag except that it forms a dome-shaped tent over the working surface. It is constructed of two layers, similar to the construction of the changing bag, and contains a double-zippered door, with one sleeve on each side of the door.
Cinematographer: *See Director of Photography.*
Cinematography: The art and craft of recording images on motion picture film.
Clap Sticks: Wooden sticks attached to the slate, which are clapped together at the beginning of a sync sound take. *See Slate.*
Clapper Board: *See Slate.*
Clapper/Loader: A member of the camera crew who is responsible for clapping the slate for the shot and also for loading and unloading the film in the magazines along with other duties. This term is used primarily in Britain and Europe. In the United States this crew member is the Second Assistant Cameraman.
Closing Down the Lens: Turning the diaphragm adjustment ring on the lens to a higher f-stop number, which results in a smaller diaphragm opening. Also referred to as stopping down the lens.
Coaxial Cable: *See Video Cables.*
Coaxial Magazine: A magazine that contains two distinct compartments, one for the feed side and another for the take-up side. Coaxial refers to the fact that these two distinct compartments share the same axis of rotation.
Collapsible Core: A permanent core in the take-up side of the film magazine, onto which the film is wound after if has been exposed. It has a slot cut into it, into which the end of the film slips. The film is held in place by a small locking lever that pinches the end of the film against the inside of the core.
Combination Meter: A light meter that is a combination of an incident meter and spot meter in one device.
Color Chart: A card or chart containing strips of colors corresponding to the colors of the spectrum that is used by the lab to assist in developing and processing the film.
Color Compensating Filter (CC Filter): A filter that is one of the primary or complementary colors. It comes in varying densities and is

used to make very small adjustments in the color temperature of the light as it strikes the film. They require an exposure compensation depending on the color and density of the filter.

Color Grad Filter: A filter that is half color and half clear. Used when a specific color effect is desired.

Color Temperature: A measurement or scale in degrees Kelvin that measures the specific color of a light source.

Combination Filter: Two different filter types that are combined into one filter, for example, an 85 combined with a neutral density (85N3, 85N6, 85N9) or an 85 combined with a polarizer (85Pola). The most commonly used combination filters are the 85 combined with a neutral density. The exposure compensation for the combination filter is the total of the exposure compensation for each individual filter added together. For example, when using an 85N3, the exposure compensation would be 1 2/3 stop—1 stop for the ND3 and 2/3 stop for the 85.

"Common Marker" or "Common Slate": What the Second Camera Assistant calls out when slating a shot for two or more cameras by using only one slate. When using only one slate, all cameras point toward the slate at the beginning of the shot.

Compressed Air: Canned air used for blowing out the magazine and camera body. Also used to clean dust off lenses and filters.

Conversion Filter: A filter used to convert one color temperature to another. The two most common conversion filters are the 85 and the 80A. The 85 converts tungsten-balanced film for use in daylight and the 80A filter converts daylight-balanced film for use in tungsten light. *See 85 Filter* and *80A Filter.*

Coral Filter: Filter that is used to warm up the overall scene and to enhance skin tones. It is also used to make slight adjustments in Kelvin temperature for different times of day. It requires an exposure compensation depending on the density of the filter.

Core: Plastic disks around which the raw stock film is wound. They can be either 2 or 3 inches in diameter.

Cotton Swabs: Long wooden sticks with a small piece of cotton wrapped around one end, which can be used to remove excess oil when oiling the camera.

Crosshairs: A cross shape that is located on the ground glass of the camera's viewing system. The cross is positioned in the exact center of the film frame to assist the Camera Operator in framing the shot.

Crystal Motor: The most common type of camera motor for motion picture cameras. A built-in crystal allows the motor to run at precise speeds, especially when filming with sound, without the use of a cable running from the camera to the sound recorder.

CTB: A blue colored gel that is placed on tungsten lights to covert the color temperature to the color temperature of daylight. It stands for

Color Temperature Blue and comes in varying densities ranging from 1/8 CTB to Full CTB.

CTO: An orange colored gel that is used to convert the color temperature of daylight to the color temperature of tungsten light. It stands for Color Temperature Orange and comes in varying densities ranging from 1/8 CTO to Full CTO.

Dailies: The developed and printed scenes from the previous day's filming, which are viewed by the key production personnel each day. They are usually viewed by the Director, Director of Photography, Camera Operator, First Camera Assistant, Editor, etc. Also called rushes.

Daily Film Inventory: A form filled in with information relating to how much film is shot each day. It lists all film stocks and roll numbers used for the day, with a breakdown of good and no-good takes, waste footage, and any short ends made. It also shows how much film is on hand at the end of each day's shooting. Each Camera Assistant usually uses his or her own style of inventory form.

Darkroom: A small, lightproof room, usually 4 × 4 feet. in size, on a stage or in a camera truck, which is used for the loading and unloading of film. The unexposed raw stock film is usually stored in the darkroom during production.

Daylight: A light source with a color temperature of approximately 5600° Kelvin.

Daylight Spool: A special reel, usually made of metal or plastic, containing opaque edges, onto which the raw stock is tightly wound. It allows the film to be loaded into the camera in daylight, so that only the outer layers of the film will become exposed to the light. Daylight spools are most commonly used in 16 mm cinematography, but they are also available for 35 mm filming. Also referred to as a camera spool.

Depth of Field: The range of distance within which all objects will be in acceptable sharp focus. It is an area in front of and behind the principal point of focus that will also be in acceptable focus. In general, there is more depth of field behind the point of focus than there is in front of it.

Diaphragm: The adjustable metal blades within the lens that controls the size of the opening through which the light enters the lens. It may also be called an iris. The size of the opening is expressed by an f-stop number. By turning the barrel of the lens to set the f-stop, you are adjusting the diaphragm within the lens.

Diffusion Filter: A filter that is used to slightly decrease the sharpness of the image. It is good for smoothing out facial blemishes or wrinkles. It can also be used for dreamlike effects. When used, this filter may give the appearance that the image is out of focus. Diffusion filters are available in various densities from very light to very heavy. Most diffusion filters require no exposure compensation.

DIN: An abbreviation meaning Deutsche Industrie Norm. It is the German system for rating the film stock's sensitivity to light or film speed.

Diopter: A filter that allows you to focus on something much closer than the lens would normally allow. They are available in various strengths; the higher the number of the diopter, the closer you can focus. A diopter requires no exposure compensation.

Director of Photography (D.P.): The person in charge of lighting the set and photographing a film. He or she works closely with the director to transform the written words of the script to the screen, based on the director's vision. The D.P. oversees all aspects of the camera department and the camera crew. The D.P. supervises all technical crews on a production during filming. He or she is also called the Cinematographer or Cameraman.

Displacement Magazine: A magazine that usually contains the feed and take-up sides in the same compartment of the magazine. When the magazine is placed on the camera, the feed side is toward the front and the take-up side is toward the rear. As the film runs through the camera, it is displaced from the feed side to the take-up side. A displacement magazine may be of the single-chamber type that contains both the feed and take-up in the same compartment or a double-chamber displacement magazine that has separate compartments for the feed and take-up sides.

Ditty Bag: A canvas bag usually containing many compartments of different sizes, which is used by the Camera Assistant to hold tools and supplies needed for filming. Some of the items kept in the ditty bag include basic tools, the slate, tape measure, pens, Sharpies, and camera tape.

Dolly: A four-wheeled platform on which a camera is mounted for moving shots. It may also have a boom arm, which allows the camera to be raised or lowered for a shot. The dolly allows the camera to be moved in any direction during the shot. It usually contains seats for the Camera Operator and Camera Assistant to sit on during filming. A member of the crew known as the Dolly Grip operates it.

Donut: A circular piece of rubber of various sizes, approximately 1/4 or 1/2 inch thick with a circle cut out of the center. It is placed on the front of the lens and is used to seal the opening between the lens and the matte box. The donut prevents any light from entering the matte box from behind the lens, and reflecting off the filters and into the lens.

Double Perf: Film stock that contains perforations on both sides of the film frame.

Downloading: The act of unloading the film from the camera and magazine.
D.P.: Abbreviation for Director of Photography.
Dummy Load: A short roll of raw stock film that is too small to be used for photographing any shots. It may be used to test the magazines for scratches during the camera prep.
Dutch Angle: Framing a shot with the camera tilted either left or right so that the image will appear diagonally within the frame.
Dutch Head: A special type of head that is usually attached to the standard fluid head and that allows you to shoot "Dutch angle" shots. It is set up so that the tilt action is opposite from the tilt of the regular head, producing the Dutch angle.
Eastman Kodak: Trade name of a brand of professional motion picture film stock. Sometimes shortened and referred to as Kodak.
80A Filter: Conversion filter used to convert daylight-balanced film for filming with tungsten light sources. When using this filter you must adjust your exposure by 2 stops. The 80A filter is blue.
85 Filter: Conversion filter used to convert tungsten-balanced film for filming under daylight conditions. When using this filter you must adjust your exposure by 2/3 stop. The 85 filter is orange.
EI: Abbreviation for Exposure Index. *See Exposure Index.*
Emulsion: The part of the film stock that is sensitive to light. The emulsion is where the photographic image is recorded. It is made up of particles of silver halide embedded in a gelatin compound. Exposure to light causes a change in the silver halide crystals and forms what is called a latent image on the film. When the film is treated with certain chemicals in the developing and print process at the lab, a visual image is formed.
End Slate: *See Tail Slate.*
Enhancing Filter: A filter used to improve the color saturation of red and orange objects in the scene while having little effect on other colors. It usually requires an exposure compensation between 1 and 1 1/2 stops depending on the manufacturer of the filter.
Expendables: Items such as tape, pens, markers, batteries, etc., that are used by the camera department in the daily performance of the job. They are called expendables because they are usually used up during the course of a production.
Exposed Film: Any film that has been run through the camera and contains a photographed image. Exposed film must be kept in a cool, dark place and opened in a darkroom only.
Exposure: The f-stop or t-stop that has been set on the lens for a particular shot. It can also be used to refer to the act of subjecting the film to light. The degree of exposure is determined by how much light strikes the film, and for how much time the light is allowed to strike the film.

Exposure Index (EI): A numeric value assigned to a film stock that is a measurement of the film's speed or sensitivity to light. The higher the number, the faster the film and the more sensitive it is to light. It may be used in the same way as the ASA number or DIN number.

Exposure Meter: A measuring device used to determine the amount or intensity of light that is illuminating a scene. The two main types of exposure meters are incident and reflected. A spot meter is one type of reflected light meter. A reflected or spot meter measures the amount of light reflected from a subject and an incident meter measures the amount of light falling on a subject. *See Incident Meter; Light Meter; and Spot Meter.*

Exposure Time: The amount of time that each frame of film is exposed to light. For normal motion picture photography, the standard exposure time is 1/48 of a second with a film speed of 24 frames per second. This number is usually rounded and expressed as 1/50 of a second at 24 frames per second.

EXT: Abbreviation for exterior. It is an indication of a scene that takes place outdoors. An exterior scene may be shot on an exterior location, or it may be shot in a sound stage that has been set up to look like an exterior.

Eyebrow: A small flag that mounts directly to the matte box and is used to block any light from hitting the lens. It may also be called a sunshade or French flag.

Eyepiece: The attachment on the camera that allows the Camera Operator to view the scene as it is being filmed. On most modern film cameras, a mirror shutter directs the image entering the lens to the eyepiece for the operator to view. The eyepiece usually contains an adjustable diopter to compensate for the differences in each person's vision and some type of rubber eyecup for comfort and to protect the operator's eye.

Eyepiece Covers: A small round cover, with a hole in the center, usually made of foam or chamois material and placed on the eyepiece so that it is more comfortable for the Camera Operator.

Eyepiece Extension: A long version of the camera eyepiece used when a short eyepiece is not convenient or comfortable for the Camera Operator. It is used most often when the camera is mounted to a gear head.

Eyepiece Heater: A heater element used to keep the eyepiece warm when shooting in cold weather situations. It prevents the eyepiece from fogging. It may also be called an eyepiece warmer.

Eyepiece Leveler: A long adjustable rod that is used to keep the eyepiece level while the camera is panning and tilting. The eyepiece leveler allows the eyepiece to remain at a comfortable position for the Camera Operator when doing extreme tilt moves with the fluid or gear head.

Feed Side: The side of the magazine or camera that contains the fresh, unexposed film. On some magazines the feed side is separate from the take-up side, while on other magazines the feed and take-up rolls of film may be contained in the same compartment.
Field of View: The angle covered by the camera lens. It may also be called angle of view.
Film Can: A metal or plastic container that the fresh raw stock is packaged in. It is also used along with the black bag to wrap any exposed film or short ends created during shooting. A roll of film should never be placed in a film can without first being placed in a black bag.
Film Plane: The point located behind the lens where the film is held in place during exposure. It is the plane where the rays of light entering the lens come together in sharp focus.
Film Speed: The rating assigned to the film based on its sensitivity to light. Slow-speed film is not very sensitive to light and high-speed film is very sensitive to light. The film speed is expressed as ASA, DIN, EI, or ISO.
Film to Video Synchronizer: A device used when filming a video monitor or computer screen image with a film camera. Because the standard frame rate of video is different from that of film, the synchronizer must be used between the camera and the video source. By using the film to video synchronizer you are able to eliminate the moving bars on the screen, which are common when filming a video image or computer screen without using any kind of synchronizer.
Filter: A piece of optically correct glass or gel that is placed in front of a lens or light source to cause a change in the image or a change in the light. The filter may be a special color or have a particular texture that gives the desired effect.
Filter Trays: Compartments used to hold a filter in the matte box. They usually slide in and out of the matte box and come in various sizes to accommodate different matte box and filter sizes.
First Camera Assistant, First Assistant Cameraman (1st A.C.): A member of the camera crew whose duties include overseeing all aspects of the camera department during filming, setting up and maintaining the camera, changing lenses and filters, loading film into the camera, keeping the camera in working order, and maintaining focus during shooting. The 1st A.C. works closely with the Director of Photography and the Camera Operator during filming. The 1st A.C. also coordinates any additional camera crew needed during the course of production.
Fish Eye Lens: A wide-angle lens that distorts the image to great effect.
Flare: A bright spot or flash of light in the photographic image that may be caused by lights shining directly into the lens or by reflections from shiny surfaces.

FLB Filter: Filter used when shooting under fluorescent lights with indoor type B films. It requires an exposure compensation of 1 stop.
FLD Filter: Filter used when filming under fluorescent lights with daylight-type film. It requires an exposure compensation of 1 stop.
Fluid Head: A mounting platform for the camera that allows the Camera Operator to do smooth pan and tilt moves during shooting. Its internal elements contain a highly viscous fluid that controls the amount of tension on the pan and tilt components of the head. It is attached to a high hat, tripod, or dolly and is usually operated by using one or two handles that are mounted to the sides of the head.
Foam-Tip Swab: A foam-tip swab is a long wooden or plastic stick that contains a small piece of foam on one end. It may be used to remove any excess oil when oiling the camera. *See Cotton Swabs.*
Focal Length: The distance between the optical center of the lens to the film plane when the lens is focused at infinity. Lenses are always referred to by their focal length. It is usually expressed in millimeters, such as 25 mm, 32 mm, 50 mm, etc. A short focal length lens has a wide angle of view, and a long focal length or telephoto lens has a narrow angle of view. A specific focal length lens determines the image size based on the distance from the camera to the subject.
Focal Plane: The specific point behind the lens where the image is focused onto the piece of film. As the film travels through the camera it is held between the pressure plate and the aperture plate in the film gate. This area where it is held while the image is being recorded is the focal plane. Also referred to as the film plane.
Focal Plane Shutter: A rotating shutter located at the focal plane that alternately blocks light from striking the film and then allows the light to strike the film. It works along with the mirror shutter of the camera. When the shutter is open, light strikes the film, forming an image. When the shutter is closed, no light strikes the film, and the film is being transported through the camera bringing the next frame into position.
Focus: The point in the scene that appears sharp and clear when viewed through the camera eyepiece. It may also refer to the act of adjusting the lens to produce a sharp image. Focus may be determined by looking through the eyepiece and turning the focus barrel of the lens until the image appears sharp. It also may be determined by measuring the distance from the film plane to the object being photographed.
Focus Chart: A special chart that is used when testing photographic lenses. It is used to help determine if the lens focus is accurate.
Focus Extension: An accessory for the follow focus mechanism that makes the job of focusing easier. The focus extension attaches to the right side of the follow focus so you can pull focus from either side of the camera. A flexible focus accessory may be attached to either

side of the follow focus mechanism. This flexible piece is sometimes called a focus whip or a whip.

Focus Puller: A member of the camera crew who is responsible for maintaining focus during a shot. During the rehearsal, measurements are taken to various points on the set. During shooting he or she adjusts the focus barrel of the lens so that the image will remain in focus throughout the shot. In the United States, the Focus Puller is usually the same as the First Camera Assistant.

Focus Whip: An extension that allows the assistant to step back from the camera and still be able to follow focus for a shot. It is a flexible extension 6 or 12 inches long. Also referred to as a whip.

Fog Filter: Filter that simulates the effect of natural fog. A fog filter causes any light in the shot to have a flare. No exposure compensation is required.

Follow Focus, Following Focus: The act of turning the focus barrel of the lens during the shot, so that the actors stay in focus as they move through the scene. When following focus it is important to know the depth of field for the shot. It may also be referred to as pulling focus.

Follow Focus Mechanism: A geared attachment that mounts to the camera and contains gears that are engaged to gears on the lens. It enables the First Assistant to follow focus or pull focus during the shot.

Footage Counter: A digital or dial type of gauge on the camera that shows the amount of film that has been run through the camera. Each time the camera is loaded with a fresh roll of film, the First Camera Assistant should reset the footage counter to zero.

Format: The shape of the photographed image when it is projected on a movie screen or television. It is the ratio of the width to the height and may also be referred to as the aspect ratio. *See Aspect Ratio.* The term *format* may also be used to refer to what film gauge you are shooting—16 mm, 35 mm, or 65 mm.

Four-Inch Lens (4-Inch Lens): A slang term used in the early days of filmmaking to indicate a 100 mm lens. The term is still used today by some cameramen.

F.P.S.: Abbreviation for Frames per Second. *See Frames per Second.*

Frame: An individual photographic image. A motion picture is made up of thousands of individual frames.

Frames per Second: The standard measurement for film speed as it runs through the camera or projector; In the United States, 24 f.p.s. is the standard film speed; in Britain, Europe, and Australia, 25 f.p.s. is the standard film speed when filming with synchronous sound recording.

Frame Rate: The speed that the film runs through the camera. It is expressed in terms of frames per second (f.p.s.).

French Flag: A small flag that is mounted onto the camera and used to help keep any lights from causing a flare in the lens. It consists of a flexible arm onto which the flag is attached. The arm is positioned so that the flag keeps the flare from striking the front element of the lens.

Friction Head: A mounting platform for the camera that allows the Camera Operator to perform smooth pan and tilt moves when composing the scene. Its internal elements create friction by rubbing against each other, creating the tension for the pan and tilt portions of the head. It may be mounted to a high hat, tripod, or dolly for use during filming. Friction heads are not used very much today, but were used quite often in the earlier days of filmmaking.

Front Box: A wooden storage box that attaches to the front of the camera head and is used to hold a variety of tools and accessories. It is mainly used by the First Camera Assistant for storing the tape measure, mini flashlight, depth of field charts, pens, markers, compressed air, lens cleaner, gum, mints, etc. The Director of Photography may also use it as a place to keep meters during filming.

F-Stop: The setting on the lens that indicates the size of the aperture. It is an indication of the amount of light entering the lens and does not take into account any light loss due to absorption. The f-stop of a lens is a mathematical calculation and is determined by dividing the focal length of the lens by the diameter of the aperture opening. The smaller the number, the larger the opening. The standard series of f-stop numbers is 1, 1.4, 2, 2.8, 4, 5.6, 8, 11, 16, 22, 32, etc. Each f-stop opening admits half the amount of light as the stop before it. It is important to remember that the f-stop numbers go infinitely in both directions.

Fuji: Trade name for a brand of professional motion picture film stock.

Full Aperture: The entire area of the film frame that extends out to the perforations on the film. When looking through the eyepiece, it extends beyond the frame lines inscribed on the ground glass.

Gaffer: The chief lighting technician and head of the lighting/electrical crew on a film set. The Gaffer works closely with the Director of Photography to light the set according to the D.P.'s instructions.

Gaffer Tape (2 Inch): Cloth tape, usually 2 inches wide, that is used to tape up any holes or cracks in the darkroom and for any taping job that requires tape wider than the 1 Inch camera tape. The standard colors are gray, black, and white. Gaffer tape is also available in bright blue, dark blue, red, green, brown, yellow, fluorescent orange, fluorescent pink, and fluorescent yellow.

Gate: The part of the camera where the film is held while it is being exposed. When speaking of the gate we sometimes mean the opening that is cut into the aperture plate, which allows light to pass through so that it strikes the film and creates an exposure on the film. Sometimes when referring to the gate, we include the aperture plate, pressure plate, pull down claw, and registration pin.

Gear Head: A mounting platform for the camera that allows the Camera Operator to do smooth pan and tilt moves during shooting. It may be mounted to a high hat, tripod, or dolly and is operated by turning two control wheels that are connected to gears in the head. One control wheel, mounted on the left side is used for panning the camera. The other control wheel is mounted toward the back of the head and is used for making any tilt moves.
Gel: Transparent cellophane material used for changing the color of a light either for visual effect or for correction of color temperature or exposure. It is available in many colors and densities so that you may achieve just the effect you are looking for.
Good (G): Any takes on the camera report that the Director chooses as his or her preference for each scene. The take number and footage amount are usually circled on the camera report. It may also refer to the total amount of footage for all takes on the camera report that are circled and are to be printed or transferred by the lab.
Graduated Filter, Grad Filter: A filter that is of variable density so that half of it is clear and the other half contains the filter. Some of the most common graduated filters are the graduated neutral density filters and color graduated filters. Graduated filters are available in both hard edge and soft edge grads.
Gray Scale, Gray Card: A standard series of tonal shades ranging from white to gray to black. The card or scale may be photographed at the beginning of each film roll and is used by the lab when processing the film to check for the correct tonal values in the film.
Grease Pencils: Erasable pencils used for making focus marks directly on the lens or focus-marking disk. Some of the colors that they are available in are white, yellow, red, and black. One popular brand of grease pencils is the Stabilo brand.
Grip: Film crew member responsible for laying dolly track, setting c-stands, and flags, moving large set pieces, and much more. A jack-of-all-trades on the set. A film set will have many different Grips on set including the Key Grip, Dolly Grip, and Best Boy Grip.
Ground Glass: A small piece of optical material, onto which a portion of the light from the lens is focused, to allow the Camera Operator to see the image that the lens is seeing. It is usually inscribed with lines that indicate the aspect ratio being used for filming, which assists the operator in composing the shot.
Guild Kelly Calculator: Trade name for a brand of depth of field calculator used by many First Camera Assistants. There are currently three types in use today: 16 mm, 35 mm, and HD Kelly Calculators.
Hair: A very fine piece of emulsion that appears in the gate and can look like an actual hair. If not removed from the gate it will appear as a large rope on a big movie screen. It may be caused by the emulsion

being scraped off of the film as it travels through the gate. There may be a small burr in the metal of the aperture plate that would cause the emulsion to be removed as it travels through the camera. It is common practice to check for hairs after each completed setup and/or printed take.

Hand-Held: Any shot that is done by the Camera Operator physically holding the camera on his or her shoulder while filming. It is often used for point-of-view shots of an actor walking or moving through the scene. When filming hand-held shots it is customary to have a wide-angle lens on the camera, which helps to minimize the shakiness associated with any hand-held camera shots. *See Camera, Hand-Held.*

Hand-Held Accessories: Any item needed to make hand-held shots easier. These items may include left- and right-hand grips, shoulder pad, smaller clamp-on-style matte box, and smaller film magazines.

Hard Mattes: Covers placed in front of the matte box to block any unwanted light from striking the lens. These covers have the center portion cut out in various sizes depending on the focal length of the lens being used.

Harrison & Harrison: Trade name of a brand of motion picture camera filters.

HD: Abbreviation for high definition.

Head: A platform for mounting the camera that allows the Camera Operator to make smooth pan and tilt moves during the shot. A head may be one of three types: fluid, friction, or gear. The two most commonly used heads are fluid heads and gear heads.

Head Slate: A slate that is photographed at the beginning of a shot. When doing a head slate, the slate is held right side up.

High Angle: A shot that is done with the camera placed high above the action and pointed down toward the subject or action. When doing a high-angle shot the camera may be placed on the tripod, on a ladder, or even on a crane boom arm.

High Definition: A video format that captures images at a much higher quality than VHS, Beta, or any other previous video format. HD is said to have an image quality as good as 35 mm motion picture film. More and more productions are converting from shooting on film to shooting in HD format.

High Hat (Hi Hat): A very low camera mount used when filming low-angle shots. The head is mounted to the high hat and then the camera is mounted onto the head.

High Speed: Any filmed shot that is done at a speed greater than the normal sync speed of 24 or 25 frames per second. There are many specialized cameras that allow you to film at high speeds, anywhere from 300 to 1000 or 2000 frames per seconds. When filming at high speed, the final projected film image will have the illusion of moving at a much slower rate of speed. It is very useful for slowing down fast action.

HMI Lights (Hydrargyum Medium Arc-Length Iodide): Lighting devices that produce a color temperature that is equivalent to the color temperature of natural daylight. They are often used when filming daylight interior scenes to help supplement the existing daylight coming through the windows. Because of the design of the lights they will sometimes cause a flicker in the photographic image if the camera is not run at the proper speed. A company called Cinematography Electronics has published tables that list the correct speeds to use when filming with HMI lights.

HMI Speed Control: A camera speed control used when filming with HMI lights.

Hyperfocal Distance: A special case of depth of field. It is sometimes defined as the closest point in front of the lens that will be in acceptable focus when the lens is focused to infinity. In other words it is the closest focus distance at which objects at infinity and close to the lens are both in focus. It is the focus point that gives you the maximum depth of field for a given shooting situation. This distance is determined by the focal length of the lens and the f-stop set on the lens. If you set the focus of the lens to the hyperfocal distance, everything from half the distance to infinity will be in focus. Tables listing the hyperfocal distance for various lenses and f-stops are published in many film books.

I.A.T.S.E.: Abbreviation for International Alliance of Theatrical and Stage Employees.

Inching Knob: A small knob that may be located either inside or outside the camera body that allows you to slowly advance the film through the movement. It is most often used at the time of threading to check that the film is traveling smoothly and not binding or catching anywhere.

Incident Light: The light from all sources that falls on the subject being filmed. To measure the amount of incident light falling on a subject, use an incident light meter.

Incident Meter: A light meter used to measure the amount of incident light that is falling on the subject.

Insert Slate: A small scene slate used to identify any MOS or insert shots being filmed. The information written on it includes the production title, roll number, scene and take numbers, date, Director's name, and Director of Photography's name. The insert slate is different from the sync slate because it usually does not contain the clapper sticks, but there are some small insert slates that do contain the clapper sticks.

INT: Abbreviation for interior. It is an indication of a scene that takes place indoors.

Intermittent Movement: The starting and stopping movement of the film transport mechanism as it advances the film through the camera. To the human eye, it appears that the film going through a motion picture camera is moving continuously. In reality each frame stops long enough in the film gate so that it may be exposed and it is then moved out of the way so the next frame may be exposed.

Iris: An adjustable diaphragm that is used to control the amount of light transmitted through the lens. The iris of the lens consists of overlapping leaves that form a circular opening to vary the amount of light coming through the lens. By changing the f-stop or t-stop setting of the lens, you are changing the iris opening of the lens.

Iris Rods: Metal rods of varying lengths that are used to support the matte box, follow focus, or other accessory on the camera. Each time a different lens is placed on the camera, the rods may need to be changed or adjusted so that the matte box will fit properly against the lens.

ISO: Abbreviation for International Standards Organization. It is a rating of the film stock based on its sensitivity to light. It is sometimes used in place of ASA or EI.

Kelvin: The temperature scale used for measuring the color temperature of a light source.

Kimwipes: Soft tissue-like material similar to lens tissue. They can be use for cleaning filters or any other small cleaning job, but should not be used to clean lenses.

Kodak: Trade name for a brand of professional motion picture film stock. Also known by its full name, Eastman Kodak.

Lab or Laboratory: The facility where the film is sent to be processed, developed, and printed.

Latitude: The ability of the film emulsion to be underexposed or overexposed and still produce an acceptable image. Many of the newer, faster speed films have greater latitude than the earlier slow-speed film stocks.

Left-Hand Grip: An attachment for the camera used when shooting hand-held shots. It is placed on the left side of the camera and allows the Camera Operator to hold the camera steady in a comfortable position for shooting.

Legs: A slang term used to refer to the tripod for the camera. Baby legs refer to the smaller tripod and standard legs refer to the larger tripod.

Lens: An optical device through which light rays pass to form a focused image on the film. Lenses are usually referred to by their focal length. There are basically two main types of lenses used for motion picture photography. Prime lenses are lenses of a single fixed focal length such as 25 mm, 35 mm, 50 mm, etc. Zoom lenses allow you to vary the focal length by turning the barrel of the lens. The zoom is usually referred to by its range of focal lengths such as 10 to 100, 20 to 100,

25 to 250, etc. A type of prime lens that is also available is the telephoto lens. It is a lens of an extremely long focal length such as 200 mm, 300 mm, 400 mm, 600 mm, etc. Telephoto lenses allow you to film close-up shots of objects that are very far away.

Lens Cleaner: Liquid that is used to clean lenses and filters along with lens tissue. Lens cleaner should be used to clean lenses only when absolutely necessary. Professional motion picture lenses have a coating on the front element and too much cleaning with the lens cleaner can wear down this coating, which can cause a degradation in the film image.

Lens Extender: An attachment that is mounted between the lens and the camera that increases the focal length of the lens being used. The most common lens extenders are the 1.4×, which increases the focal length by 1.4 times the actual focal length and the 2×, which doubles the actual focal length. When using a lens extender, you must adjust your exposure by the strength of the extender. For example, when using a 2× extender, you must adjust your exposure by 2 stops.

Lens Light: A small light, mounted to a flexible arm that is attached to the camera, and allows the First Assistant to see the lens focus and zoom markings when filming in a dark set. It is sometimes called a Little Light or Niner Light.

Lens Shade: A rubber or metal device that either screws on or is clamped onto the front of the lens. It is used to hold round filters and to keep any stray light from striking the front element of the lens. It may also be called a Sunshade.

Lens Speed: The lens speed refers to the widest f-stop to which the lens opens up. The smaller the f-number, which means the larger the opening of the lens aperture, then the faster the lens. Fast lenses allow you to film in very low light situations.

Lens Tissue: Small tissues used to clean lenses and filters along with lens cleaner. It is recommended that you never use a dry piece of lens tissue on a lens because it may scratch the coating or front element of the lens. Lens tissue should always be used with some type of commercial lens cleaning solution when cleaning lenses or filters.

L-Handle: *See Speed Crank.*

Light Meter: A measuring device that is used to measure the amount of light illuminating the scene. *See Combination Meter; Exposure Meter; Incident Meter; Reflected Meter; and Spot Meter.*

LLD Filter: A filter used when filming with tungsten-balanced film in low light daylight situations. It is usually used in early morning or late afternoon and requires no exposure compensation.

Loader: The member of the camera crew who is responsible for loading and unloading the film into the magazines. A loader is usually used on larger productions when two or more cameras are being used.

Lock Off: Any shot that is done with the pan and tilt mechanisms of the camera head locked so that the camera is not moved during filming. Many times it is used for a stunt or special effects shot.

Long Eyepiece (Eyepiece Extension): An extended version of the camera eyepiece or viewfinder that is used when a short eyepiece is not convenient or comfortable for the Camera Operator. It is used most often when the camera is mounted to a gear head.

Long Lens: Term used to refer to a telephoto lens or a lens that has a focal length that is longer than that of a normal lens.

Loop: A slack length of film between sprocket wheels and camera or projector gate that is designed to absorb the tension caused by intermittent movement, thus avoiding the tearing of film as it travels through the camera. If the loop is not set correctly, the film may become jammed in the camera or magazine, and the camera will not run properly or it may run loudly.

Low Angle: A shot that is done with the camera placed very close to the ground and pointed up toward the subject or action. When doing a low-angle shot the camera may be placed directly on the ground, placed on a high hat, or on a rocker plate.

Low Contrast Filter: A filter that lowers the contrast by causing light to spread from highlight areas to shadow areas. It will mute colors and make blacks appear lighter, and it also allows more detail in dense shadow areas. Also referred to as lo-con filter. No exposure compensation is required.

Low Hat: A very low camera mount used when filming low-angle shots. It is similar to the high hat, but it enables you to get the camera lower. The head is mounted to the low hat and then the camera is mounted onto the head.

Mag: Abbreviation for magazine.

Magazine: A removable, lightproof container that contains the film before and after exposure. The two main types of film magazines are the displacement magazine and the coaxial magazine. There are two distinct areas in each film magazine: the feed side, which contains the fresh unexposed film, and the take-up side, which contains the exposed film. Each time the camera is started, the film travels from the feed side, through the camera and into the take-up side. *See Coaxial Magazine and Displacement Magazine.*

Magliner: The trade name of a four-wheel folding hand truck used by many Camera Assistants to expedite the moving of the many equipment cases on a film set. Throughout the shooting day, equipment must be moved many times for each different camera setup. By having the cases on the cart, it saves the assistant from having to hand carry each case each time it must be moved. The two most common types of Magliner carts are the Gemini Junior and the Gemini Senior.

Mini Mag Lite: Small pocket-type flashlight used by most crew people. It has a very bright and powerful bulb and, by turning the head of the light, you are able to adjust the beam from spotlight to flood light.

Mag Lite Bulbs: Replacement bulbs for the small flashlight usually used by most Camera Assistants.

Marks: Small pieces of colored tape, chalk marks, or any other item placed on the ground and used to identify various positions. They may indicate where the actor is to stand for the shot, where the dolly starts and stops its move, or as a reference for focus used by the First Camera Assistant. The most common type of actor's mark is the T-mark.

Matte Box: An accessory that mounts to the front of the camera to shield the lens against unwanted light and also used to hold any filters. It is usually referred to by the size of filters that it normally holds. For example, a matte box that holds 4 × 4-inch filters is called a 4 × 4 matte box. In addition to holding two or three square or rectangle filters, most matte boxes have a snap- in piece that holds one round filter, either 4 1/2 inches in diameter or 138 mm in diameter. The matte box usually comes with a set of hard mattes for each prime lens being used. Each time a different lens is placed on the camera, the matte box should be adjusted for a proper fit with the lens.

Mirrored Shutter: A shutter that incorporates a mirror into its design so that the image may be reflected to the viewfinder when the shutter is closed to the film. When the shutter is open, the light goes to the film and the image is recorded on film. When the shutter is closed, the light strikes the mirror and the image is directed to the viewfinder for the Camera Operator to view the shot.

Mitchell: A trade name of one of the earlier models of motion picture cameras. It was mainly used for studio work because of its large size. Some of the models of the Mitchell camera include BNC and BNCR. It is also the name of a type of diffusion filter used in front of the camera lens. *See Mitchell Diffusion.*

Mitchell Diffusion: The trade name of a brand of motion picture camera diffusion filters. As with other diffusion, they are used to soften and decrease the sharpness of the image. Mitchell Diffusion filters are available in various densities from very light to very heavy. They require no exposure compensation. *See Diffusion Filters.*

Mitchell Flat Base: A type of top casting of the high hat, low hat, tripod, or dolly onto which the head is mounted.

Monitor: A television or video screen used by the Director during filming to check the framing of the shot and the quality of the performance. It is used in conjunction with a video camera that is attached to the film camera viewing system. The video camera sees the same image that the film camera is photographing, so that the director can watch the shot during shooting.

MOS: Any shot that is done without recording synchronous sound. It is an abbreviation for "minus optical sound." When doing this type of shot, the word MOS is written on the slate along with the other standard information. When slating an MOS shot, the clapper sticks of the slate are usually kept in a closed position.

Multicamera: The use of two or more cameras simultaneously to shoot a scene from more than one angle. Scenes must be carefully planned and cameras placed so that one camera does not appear in the viewing field of another during filming. Many times, any scenes that contain a great deal of action or dangerous stunts are filmed with multicamera setups. These shots are usually very dangerous or costly, and there is only one chance to photograph them. Many of the television situation comedies (sitcoms) that are filmed in front of a live audience use multiple cameras.

Mutar: A 16 mm lens attachment that is designed for use on a Zeiss 10 mm to 100 mm zoom lens. It is used to increase the angle of view of the lens and make it more wide angle than it already is. The lens is placed in its macro setting before the mutar is attached. Focus is then adjusted by turning the zoom barrel of the lens instead of the focus barrel.

N.D.: Abbreviation for neutral density filter.

Negative Film Stock: Film that, when processed, produces a negative image of the scene. In other words it is a film stock that renders all lights, darks, and colors as their opposite on the developed original. A positive print must be made of this negative for viewing purposes. This term is sometimes used to refer to unexposed raw stock used for most film productions.

Neutral Density Filter (N.D.): A filter used to reduce the amount of light that strikes the film. It has no effect on colors. Neutral density filters are gray and come in varying densities. They require an exposure compensation depending on the number and density of the filter: ND 3, 1 stop; ND 6, 2 stops; ND 9, 3 stops.

Nitrate Base Film: A highly flammable film stock used in the early days of filmmaking. It was made up of cellulose nitrate that was capable of self-igniting under certain circumstances. It is no longer used for the manufacture of motion picture film. The newer film stocks are composed of a triacetate base.

No Good (N.G.): Any take that is not printed or circled on the camera report. There may have been a technical problem during shooting or possibly the performance was not acceptable to the Director. On the daily film inventory report form it refers to the total amount of footage for all takes on the camera report that are not to be printed or transferred by the lab.

Normal Lens: A lens that essentially gives an approximate image size as that seen by the human eye if viewed from the position of the camera.

The accepted focal length of a normal lens for 35 mm cinematography is 50 mm and for 16 mm cinematography it is 25 mm.

N.T.S.C.: An abbreviation for National Television Standards Committee.

Obie Light: A light that is mounted on the camera directly over the matte box. Its common use is to highlight the actor's eyes.

O'Connor: Trade name for a brand of professional motion picture fluid head.

1.85 (One-Eight-Five): The standard aspect ratio for most of today's theatrical motion pictures. It may also be written as 1.85:1, which means that the picture area is 1.85 times as wide as it is high. When filming in 1.85 format, standard spherical lenses and equipment may be used.

One-Inch Lens (1-Inch Lens): A slang term used in the early days of filmmaking to indicate a 25 mm lens. The term is still used today by some cameramen.

One-Light Print: A print made from the negative with no color correction. It is made by using one printer light setting for all shots within the roll of film.

1/3-2/3 Rule: The rule that states that one third of the depth of field is in front of the focus point and two thirds is behind the focus point.

Opening up the Lens: Turning the diaphragm adjustment ring on the lens to a smaller f-stop number, which results in a larger diaphragm opening. Opening up allows more light to strike the film.

Operator: *See Camera Operator.*

Optical Flat: A clear piece of optically corrected glass that is placed in front of the lens to protect the lens. During many types of filming, there may be some kind of object or substance that is projected toward the lens. To protect the front of the lens, the optical flat would be placed in the matte box. Because of the special coating on the front of most lenses, it is much easier and less expensive to replace the optical flat than to replace a lens. The optical flat may also be used to help reduce the sound coming from the camera. Most of the sound from a camera comes out from the lens port opening, so an optical flat in front of the lens helps to cut down this sound, making the Sound Mixer's job a little easier. It is available in the same sizes as most filters and should be included in the filter order on any film production.

Orangewood Sticks: Wooden sticks that are used to remove emulsion buildup in the gate or aperture plate. The aperture plate or gate should only be cleaned with these sticks. You should never use any type of metal or sharp instrument when cleaning the gate.

Overcrank: Running the camera at a speed that is higher than normal sync speed. This causes the action to appear in slow motion when it is projected at sync speed of 24 frames per second. The term was originated in the early days of filmmaking when all cameras were cranked by hand.

Overexpose: Allowing too much light to strike the film as it is being exposed. This results in the photographic image having a washed-out look or being much lighter than normal. The Director of Photography may overexpose the film to achieve a desired effect. If you accidentally overexpose the film stock, it is much easier to correct it in the lab because you have more latitude when overexposing.

Pan or Panning: The horizontal or left and right movement of the camera. The camera is usually mounted to either a gear head or fluid head, which is on the tripod or dolly. The gear head contains a wheel that is turned to move the camera either left or right. The fluid head contains a handle that enables the operator to make the pan moves, by moving the handle either left or right. By panning the camera during the shot, the camera operator is able to follow the action within the scene.

Panavision: Trade name of a brand of professional 16 mm, 35 mm, and 65 mm film cameras and HD video cameras.

Paper Tape (1/8 Inch or 1/4 Inch): Tape that is most often used to make focus marks on the lens. It is wrapped around the barrel of the lens so that you may mark it for following focus.

Paper Tape (1/2 Inch or 1 Inch): Tape that may be used for making actor's marks, labeling equipment, or any other taping job during production. It is available in many colors including red, green, dark blue, light blue, orange, yellow, white, black, pink, purple, fluorescent orange, and fluorescent pink.

Paper Tape (2 Inch): Tape that is used for the same types of things as gaffer tape. Used for hanging items on painted walls because the glue is not as strong as that on gaffer tape, so that it will not remove paint when taken down. It may also be used to seal any cracks or holes in the darkroom. It is available in many colors including black, white, red, blue, green, yellow, orange, and fluorescent orange.

Perforations, Perfs: Equally spaced holes, punched into the edges of the film along the entire length of the roll. These holes are engaged by the teeth of the sprockets, in the film magazines and camera movements, allowing the film to accurately travel through the camera before and after exposure. In 35 mm film there are four perforations per film frame, on each side, and in 16 mm there are two per frame on each side.

Persistence of Vision: The phenomenon that allows the human eye to retain an image for a brief moment after it has been viewed. This allows the illusion of movement when a series of still pictures are projected on a screen at a specified rate of speed. At normal sync speed of 24 frames per second, a series of still frames projected on the screen appear to be moving continuously to the human eye.

Pitch: The distance between the bottom edge of one perforation to the bottom edge of the next perforation. This distance is measured along the length of the film.

Polarizing Filter: A filter that is used to reduce glare and reflections from non-metallic reflective surfaces. It may be used when filming into or through a window. It is also used to enhance or darken a blue sky or water. It is mounted so that it can be rotated until the desired effect is achieved. While looking through the lens, the Director of Photography or Camera Operator rotates the filter until the correct or desired effect is achieved. An exposure compensation of 2 stops is required.

Powder Puffs: Soft make-up-type pads that are used to erase information placed on an acrylic slate with erasable slate markers. The puffs are usually attached to the slate marker to make it easier for use.

Precision Speed Control: A speed control attachment that allows you to vary the speed of the camera. It enables you to vary the speed to a precise degree, sometimes to three decimal places. It may be used when filming high speed or slow motion. It can also be used when filming a television screen or computer monitor in order to synchronize the camera with the monitor image.

Prep: The time during pre-production when the equipment is checked to ensure that it is in working order. During the camera prep, the First Camera Assistant goes to the camera rental house and sets up and tests all of the camera equipment to ensure that he or she has everything needed for filming and that everything is in proper working order.

Pressure Plate: A flat, smoothly polished piece of metal that puts pressure on the film, keeping it flat against the aperture plate, and steady as it travels through the gate. It is usually spring loaded and is located behind the aperture plate inside the camera. Many times the pressure plate is a part of the film magazine. Without this plate keeping the film flat and steady as it travels through the camera, the photographic image would be unsteady or blurred and out of focus.

Primary Colors: For the purposes of cinematography, the three primary colors of light are red, blue, and green. When equal amounts of these three colors of light are combined, they form what is known as white light. All colors of light are made up of varying combinations of these primary colors. The corresponding complementary colors to these are cyan, yellow, and magenta, respectively.

Prime Lens: A lens of a single, fixed focal length that cannot be changed. Examples of prime lenses are 25 mm, 35 mm, 50 mm, 75 mm, 100 mm, etc.

Print All: The instructions given to the lab that tells them to print all of the takes on a given roll of exposed film.

Print Circle Takes Only: The instructions given to the lab that tell them to print only the takes that have been circled on the camera report for a specific roll of film.
Production Company: The name of the company that is producing the film. It may be a small independent company or a major Hollywood studio.
Production Number: The number of the film or television episode as assigned by the production company. If a production company is filming more than one project at a time, each project is assigned a different number so that the company can keep track of the various expenses and things needed for each project. When filming a weekly television series, each weekly episode is given a new production number.
Production Title: The working title of the film as assigned by the production company.
Professional Cameraman's Handbook: An indispensable manual used by both Camera Assistants and Directors of Photography. It contains illustrations and descriptions of the many different cameras and related pieces of equipment in use today. The handbook describes how to load the magazine with film and how to thread it in the camera.
Pro-Mist Filter: A diffusion filter that is used to soften harsh lines in an actor's face. It may sometimes give the illusion of the image being out of focus. Pro-Mist filters come in varying densities and are available in White, Black, and Warm Pro-Mist. No exposure compensation is required.
Pull Down Claws: These are the small hooks or pins, located in the camera movement, that engage into the perforations of the film and pull the film down into position in the gate so that it may be photographed.
Pulling Focus: *See Following Focus.*
Quick Release Plate: A detachable plate that is used to secure the camera to the tripod head. It allows for quick and easy removal and attachment of the camera.
Raincover: A waterproof cover used to protect the camera and magazine in extreme weather conditions, including snow and rain. It has an opening for the viewfinder eyepiece and contains clear panels for the assistant to view the lens markings. The front of the cover is open so that the lens is not obstructed.
Raw Stock: Fresh unexposed and unprocessed film stock.
Reflected Light: Any light that is bouncing off, or being reflected by, an object. Reflected light is usually measured with a reflected light meter or spot meter.
Reflex Camera: Any camera that allows viewing through the lens during filming. The camera contains a mirrored shutter that directs the image to the viewfinder for the camera operator to see the shot.

Reflex Viewing System: A viewing system that allows the camera operator to view the image as it is being filmed. The image coming through the lens is reflected to the viewfinder, usually by a mirror shutter, allowing the camera operator to see the image. Because the image is sent to the viewfinder intermittently, there is a slight flicker in the viewfinder while the camera is running and the shutter is spinning.

Registration: The accurate positioning of the film in the film gate as it is running through the camera. Any variation causes a jump or blur in the photographic image. During the camera prep, the registration may be checked by filming a registration chart and then viewing the results.

Registration Chart: A chart containing a series of crossed lines that is used during the camera prep to check the registration of the camera. By shooting a double-exposed image of the chart and then viewing the results, you can tell if the registration of the camera is accurate.

Registration Pins: Part of the camera movement consisting of a small metal spike or pin that holds the film securely in the gate while it is being exposed. Some cameras contain a single registration pin, while many professional cameras contain two registration pins. These cameras are often referred to as dual pin registered cameras.

Remote Switch: A camera switch that is used to turn the camera on and off in situations when it is not possible to be right next to the camera during the shot. This may occur when filming dangerous shots or when filming car shots. It is usually connected to a long cable running from the camera that allows starting and stopping the camera from a distance.

Reversal: Film that, when processed, produces a positive image of the scene. It may also be called positive film and it may be viewed directly.

Right-Hand Grip: A camera accessory item used when filming handheld shots. As the name implies, it attaches to the right-hand side of the camera and is used to hold the camera steady during shooting. Most right-hand grips contain an on/off switch for the camera operator to start and stop the camera.

Rocker Plate: A low-angle camera mount usually consisting of two separate pieces. The camera mounts to the top section, which has a curved base allowing it to rock back and forth. This top section fits into the bottom cradle, which swivels left and right. The combined movement of rocking the camera back and forth and swiveling the base left and right allows the camera operator to make smooth pans and tilts from very low angles without using a fluid head or geared head.

Roll Number: The number assigned to a roll of film when it is placed on the camera. Each time a new roll of film is placed on the camera, the next higher number is assigned to that roll.

Ronford: Trade name of a brand of professional motion picture fluid heads and tripods.
Rubber Donut: *See Donut.*
Rushes: *See Dailies.*
Sachtler: Trade name of a brand of professional motion picture camera fluid heads and tripods.
Samuelson MKII Calculator: Trade name of a brand of depth of field calculator used by most 1st A.C.s.
Scene: The basic unit of a script with action occurring in a single setting.
Scene Number: The number assigned to a scene based on its place in the script. A scene is a section of the film as it takes place in a particular location or time in the story. Normally each time the location or the time changes, a new scene number is assigned to the action. When filming a small portion of a scene that has already been shot, the scene number is a combination of the scene number and a letter of the alphabet. The first time a portion of a scene is shot it is assigned the letter A, then B, then C, and so on. For slating purposes, the scene number is written on the slate and on the camera report as a reference to which scenes have been filmed on which roll of film.
Scratches: Grooves or lines on the surface of the film that can distort the image. In most instances, any film scratches detected indicate that those shots containing the scratch must be shot again. Many different things, including film chips or metal burrs in the magazine or gate area of the camera, can cause a film scratch. A small imperfection in the aperture plate may cause a fine piece of emulsion to scrape off the film, creating a scratch on the film emulsion. It is standard practice to check the gate of the camera and the film on a regular basis to ensure that there are no scratches. Most First Camera Assistants check the gate after each printed take.
Script Supervisor: The person on the film crew who keeps track of the action for each scene. He or she keeps notes for each shot regarding actor movement, placement of props, and dialogue spoken. The Script Supervisor tells the Second Camera Assistant what the scene and take number are for each shot.
Second Camera: An additional camera used for filming shots or scenes at the same time as the primary or main camera. Most productions are filmed using only one camera, moving it for each new shot or setup. By using a second camera you are able to film two different shots at the same time. For example, one camera may be shooting a master shot while the second camera is shooting a close-up of one of the actors. The second camera may also be used when filming shots or scenes that can only be staged once such as car stunts, fire shots, explosions, etc.
Second Camera Assistant, Second Assistant Cameraman (2nd A.C.): The member of the camera crew whose duties include assisting the

First Assistant Camera (1st A.C.), clapping the slate for the shot, keeping camera reports, placing marks for actors and loading and unloading film into the magazines. The 2nd A.C. reports directly to the 1st A.C. during production.

"Second Marker," "Second Slate," or "Second Sticks": What the 2nd A.C. calls out when slating a shot if the first slate was missed by the Camera Operator or Sound Mixer.

Setup: The basic component of a film's production, referring to each camera position or angle.

Short End (SE): A roll of unexposed raw stock which is less than a full size roll but larger than a waste roll or dummy load. In 16 mm, a short end is usually any roll larger than 40 feet; in 35 mm it is usually any roll larger than 100 feet.

Short Eyepiece: A smaller version of the camera eyepiece that is used especially when filming hand-held shots. It may also be used on the camera in certain filming situations where the long eyepiece is too uncomfortable or in an awkward position.

Shoulder Pad: A small pad that attaches to the underside of the camera when doing hand-held shots. It is used to make the Camera Operator more comfortable by allowing him or her to hold the camera on the shoulder for longer periods of time without becoming fatigued. If a shoulder pad is not available, you may use a rolled up jacket or towel, or anything else that can be used as padding.

Shutter: The mechanical device in a camera that rotates during filming to alternately block light from the film and then allow it to strike the film. Most shutters contain a mirror that reflects some of the light so that it enters the eyepiece, allowing the Camera Operator to view the shot during filming. As the shutter spins, it alternately blocks the light from the eyepiece, allowing it to strike the film, and then blocks the light from hitting the film, allowing it to go to the eyepiece. This causes a slight flicker in the eyepiece when viewing the shot during filming.

Shutter Angle: A measurement in degrees of the open part of the camera shutter that allows light to strike the film. For most professional cinematography, the standard shutter angle is 180 degrees. Many cameras contain fixed shutters that cannot be changed or adjusted. Some cameras have an adjustable shutter angle to allow for special types of filming. Some of the cameras that have adjustable shutters include the Arriflex Arricam, Arriflex 535, Arriflex 435, Panavision Millennium, Panavision Platinum, and the Panavision Golden.

Shutter Speed: The exposure time of the shutter while the camera runs at a specific speed. The standard shutter speed or exposure time for motion pictures is 1/48 of a second, which is usually rounded to 1/50 of a second at sync speed of 24 frames per second.

Silicone: A type of lubricant that is available in a spray or liquid form. The spray is used to lubricate various components including the sliding base plate or tripod legs if they begin to stick. It should never be used on any of the moving parts of the camera motor or movement. The liquid type is usually used to lubricate the pull down claws of some cameras including Panavision and Ultracam. When using silicone on the camera pull down claw, you should only use the type recommended for the particular camera you are using and it should be provided by the camera rental company.
16 mm: A film gauge, introduced in 1923, that was used mainly for nontheatrical or amateur productions. It is most commonly used today for music videos, commercials, and many television series. Because of the lower price of the film stock, the lower price of renting the camera equipment, and lower developing costs, it provides a less expensive filming alternative to using 35 mm film. For television broadcast or videocassette release, it can provide very good results. 16 mm film contains 40 frames per foot and contains two perforations per frame on each side of the film. At normal sync speed of 24 frames per second, it travels through the camera at the rate of 36 feet per minute.
65 mm/70 mm: Film gauge that is most often used for release prints of theatrical films. It is very rarely used for actual productions. There are some 65 mm cameras available for filming for any production company that would like to shoot with 65 mm. Arriflex and Panavision are two companies that still manufacture 65 mm cameras for filming.
Slate: A board marked with the pertinent identifying information for each scene photographed. It should contain the film's title, Director's name, Cameraman's name, date, camera roll number, scene number, and take number. The two main types of slates are sync and insert. *See Insert Slate; Sync Slate.*
Slate Markers: Erasable markers that are used to mark information on acrylic slates. It is usually some type of dry erase marker. The most common brands of slate markers are Expo, Write On/Wipe Off, and Marks-A-Lot.
Sliding Base Plate: An attachment used for mounting the camera to the head. It is usually a two-part plate, with the bottom piece mounted to the tripod head and the top piece mounted to the camera. It allows you to slide the camera forward or backward on the head to achieve proper balance. By achieving proper balance, the Camera Operator does not have to struggle to make smooth pan and tilt moves.
S.O.C.: Abbreviation for the Society of Camera Operators.
Society of Camera Operators: An honorary organization composed of several hundred men and women who make their living operating film and/or video cameras.

Soft Contrast Filter: A filter that lowers the contrast by darkening the highlight areas. Also referred to as Soft-Con filter. No exposure compensation is required.

Soft Focus: Indicates a shot or scene that appears to be out of focus to the viewer's eye. It may be caused by not setting the focus on the lens properly, so that the image is fuzzy and lacks any sharp detail around the edges. It may also refer to a shot that contains some type of a diffusion filter in front of the lens to create a specific soft or dreamlike effect. If a soft focus shot is noticed during shooting, it is usually standard practice to check the focus by eye and also to measure the distance, and then shoot the shot over again correctly. A soft focus shot that is not noticed until the next day's screening of dailies may create many problems for the production company, including rescheduling actors and locations, transportation of cast and crew, rebuilding sets, etc.

Space Blanket: A large cover used to protect the camera and equipment from the sun and weather. It is usually a bright silver color on one side and may be red, green, blue, or another color on the opposite side. In bright sunlight, the cover is used with the silver side facing towards the sun. This silver coating reflects the sun off the cover and helps to keep the camera cool. When placing the cover on the camera with the silver side toward the camera, the heat from the sun is absorbed which keeps the camera warm in cooler situations.

Speed (Camera): The rate at which the film travels through the camera. Standard sync speed in the United States is 24 frames per second and in Britain, Europe, and Australia it is 25 frames per second. At 24 frames per second, for 16 mm film this translates to 36 feet per minute and for 35 mm film it is 90 feet per minute.

Speed Crank: An L-shaped handle that attaches to the follow focus mechanism. It is used when the First Camera Assistant or Focus Puller has a very long focus change to do during a shot. By turning the handle of the crank, it is much easier for the assistant to perform a long focus shift than to try to repeatedly turn the knob of the follow focus mechanism.

Speed (Film): An indication of the film's sensitivity to light. The film speed may be referred to as ASA, DIN, or EI number. A fast film has a higher number while a slow film has a smaller number. The higher the number, the more sensitive the film is to light.

Speed (Lens): The f-stop or t-stop setting of the lens at its widest opening. The smaller this number, the faster the lens. Fast lenses are used many times for filming in extreme low light situations.

Split Diopter: A filter that may be used to maintain focus on two objects, one in the foreground and one in the background. The split diopter is round and only half of it contains the diopter. The remaining half of the filter is clear. No exposure compensation is required.

Split Focus: The technique of setting the focus so that a foreground object and a background object are both in focus for a shot or scene. It is used in place of a split diopter or when the split diopter may not work for the particular situation. By setting the focus to a point in between the two objects, you may be able to keep them both in focus. Split focus is not possible in every shooting situation. It depends on the distance of the subjects, the lens used, the t-stop set on the lens, and the depth of field for the particular situation. It is usually a good idea to check with the Director of Photography to see if he or she wants you to try to do a split focus for a shot.

Spot Meter: An exposure meter that takes a light reading by measuring the light that is reflected by an object. It is called a spot meter because it takes its measurement from a very small area of the object. This small area is called the angle of acceptance and in most cases it is around 1 degree. When using a spot meter it is standard practice to stand at the position of the camera and point the meter toward the object.

Spreader: A metal or rubber device that has three arms and opens up to form a horizontal Y-shape to support the legs of the tripod. It prevents the legs of the tripod from slipping out from under the camera. It may also be called a spider or a triangle. In place of a spreader, many Camera Assistants use a piece of carpet approximately 4 × 4 feet.

Sprocket Holes: Equally spaced holes punched into the edges of film stock so that it may be advanced through the camera or projector. *See Perforations.*

Sprockets: Small teeth or gears inside the camera or projector that advances the film. The wheels that contain the sprockets turn and engage with the perforations of the film, moving it through the camera.

Stabilo Grease Pencil: The brand name of an erasable marker used by many First Camera Assistants. It is used to make focus marks on lenses or on the white focus-marking disk of the follow focus mechanism. They are available in red, black, white, and yellow.

Standard Legs, Standards: The slang term to indicate the tripod on which the camera and head are mounted. They are called standards because it is the tripod that is most commonly used when not mounting the camera on a dolly. Most standard tripods can be adjusted in height from approximately 4 feet to 6 or 7 feet.

Star Filter: A filter placed in front of the lens to give highlights to any lights that appear in the scene. The star filter produces lines coming from bright lights in the scene, depending on the texture of the star filter. Star filters have a tendency to soften the shot similar to a diffusion filter. When using any star filter, no exposure compensation is required.

Stick-on Letters (1/2 Inch or 3/4 Inch): Plastic or vinyl adhesive-backed letters and numbers that are used to label the slate with production title, Director's name, Cameraman's name, and date. They are available in many colors including red, blue, green, black, white, and yellow.

Sticks: Slang term used to refer to the tripod. Also slang for the sync slate or clap sticks.

Stop: An abbreviation meaning the f-stop or t-stop.

Stop Pull: The technique of changing the f-stop or t-stop setting of the lens during a shot. The actor may be moving from a brightly lit area to a shady area, requiring a change in the f-stop because of the change in the amount of light that is illuminating the actor.

Stopping Down the Lens: *See Closing Down the Lens.*

Sunshade: A small flag or hood that attaches directly to the matte box or the lens to help eliminate any light from striking the lens or the filter. It may also be called an eyebrow, French flag, or lens shade. *See Eyebrow; French Flag; Lens Shade.*

Supa-Frost Filter: Trade name of a brand of motion picture camera diffusion filter. It is a type of diffusion filter used to soften the overall image. Great care must be taken when using these filters because they are constructed from plastic and scratch very easily. As with most other diffusion filters, they come in varying densities and require no exposure compensation.

Sync: Abbreviation for synchronization or synchronized. It is usually used to indicate a film or scene that is shot with sound being recorded simultaneously.

Sync Slate: Slate used for identifying all shots done with sound. It contains two hinged pieces of wood that are clapped together at the beginning of each sound take.

Sync Speed: The speed that gives motion pictures the appearance of normal motion to the viewer. In the United States, sync speed is 24 frames per second and in Britain, Europe, and Australia it is 25 frames per second.

Tachometer: A dial or meter located on the camera that shows the speed while the camera is running. The First Camera Assistant watches the tachometer during filming to be sure that it maintains the correct speed.

Tail Slate: A slate that is photographed at the end of a shot. A tail slate may be needed for a variety of reasons: the Camera Operator or Sound Mixer may not have recorded the head slate properly, or it may be a very emotional scene and in order to not distract the actors, a tail slate is done. When doing a tail slate, the slate is held upside down.

Take, Take Number: The number assigned to a scene each time it is photographed. It refers to a single, uninterrupted shot filmed by the camera. Each time a scene or portion of a scene is shot, it is given a new take number. The Director may request many takes of a particular action until he or she is satisfied with the performance or the action.

When the film is developed and processed, selected takes are printed to be used when editing the film.

Take-up Side: The side of the magazine that contains the exposed film. The unexposed film travels from the feed side of the magazine, through the camera, and then into the take-up side of the magazine.

Tape Measure: A device used by the First Camera Assistant to measure the distance from the film plane of the camera to the subject. This measurement allows the first assistant to maintain focus during filming. During each shooting day, the assistant takes many measurements for each scene and each position that the actor may be in during the shot. The typical tape measure is 50 feet long and is made of cloth or fiberglass material. It should not be made of metal for safety reasons.

Telephoto Lens: A lens of long focal length that allows you to photograph close shots of far away objects. It has a small angle of view. A telephoto lens has a tendency to flatten images and reduce perspective. It can make objects appear closer together than they actually are. Also, when using telephoto lenses, depth of field is greatly reduced.

35 mm: The standard film gauge, introduced in 1889, that is used for most professional theatrical and television productions. It is used primarily for larger productions because of its excellent image quality. It may also be used for commercials, music videos, and smaller productions in order to have the highest quality image. 35 mm film stock contains 16 frames per foot and 4 perforations per frame on each side of the film. At normal sync speed of 24 frames per second it travels through the camera at the rate of 90 feet per minute.

Three-Inch Lens (3-Inch Lens): A slang term used in the early days of filmmaking to indicate a 75 mm lens. The term is still used today by some cameramen.

Tiffen: Trade name of a brand of motion picture camera filter.

Tilt: The vertical or up and down movement of the camera. By turning the tilt wheel of the gear head or moving the handle of the fluid head up or down, the camera operator is able to follow any vertical movement of the actor in the scene.

Tilt Plate: An accessory that is attached between the camera and the head and is used when doing extreme tilt angles with the camera. It allows the Camera Operator to tilt the camera at a much steeper angle than is possible with the standard gear head or fluid head. Many gear heads contain a built-in tilt plate for these types of shots.

Total (T): A section on the camera report and also on the film inventory form that indicates the combined total of all Good, No Good, and Waste footage.

Tracking (Lens): The ability of a zoom lens to stay centered on a particular point throughout the range of its zoom.

Triangle: *See Spreader.*

Tripod: A three-legged camera support that can be adjusted in height. Tripods are usually made of wood or metal. When choosing a tripod, be sure that its top-casting piece is the same as the head that will be used for filming. For example, a tripod with a flat base will not accept a head with a bowl base, without some type of adapter piece. *See Baby Legs; Standard Legs.*

T-Stop: A number that is similar to the f-stop, but it is much more precise. It indicates the exact amount of light transmitted through the lens. The f-stop indicates the size of the iris diaphragm opening, and does not take into account light loss due to absorption. The standard series of t-stop numbers is 1, 1.4, 2, 2.8, 4, 5.6, 8, 11, 16, 22, 32, 45, 64, etc. As with f-stop numbers, the t-stop numbers theoretically go infinitely in both directions.

Tungsten: Any light source with a color temperature of approximately 3200° Kelvin.

Two-Inch Lens (2-Inch Lens): A slang term used in the early days of filmmaking to indicate a 50 mm lens. The term is still used today by some cameramen.

Ultracam: Trade name for a brand of professional 35 mm camera.

Undercrank: To operate the camera at any speed that is slower than normal sync-sound speed of 24 or 25 frames per second. When the final film is projected, it gives the illusion of faster speed on the screen. It is often used in comedy films for a specific effect. As with the term overcrank, it originated in the early days of filmmaking when all cameras were cranked by hand.

Underexpose: Exposing the film to less light than you would for a normal exposure. By allowing too little light to expose the shot, you end up with a very dark image. For example, when shooting a night scene, the actor in the scene may have the correct amount of light shining on him or her, but you want the background to appear slightly darker. To achieve this you would underexpose the shot. In general it is not a good idea to underexpose any shot because it is much harder to correct it in the lab during processing.

Variable Shutter: A camera shutter that allows you to change the angle for specific filming situations. It allows you to make longer or shorter exposures while the speed of the camera remains constant. It may be used to make fades and dissolves within the camera. It may also be used by the director of photography to control the exposure and change the depth of field of a shot without changing the exposure setting on the lens. On some cameras containing variable shutters, you are able to adjust the shutter angle while the camera is running.

Variable Speed Camera Motor: A motor that allows you to change the speed of the camera for certain types of shots. It enables you to film at very slow speeds or very fast speeds, depending on the effect that you want. Many variable speed camera motors are not crystal sync, and when shooting at any speed other than normal 24 frames per second, the shot is usually done without sound.

Video Assist: A system that incorporates a video camera onto the film camera. The image striking the mirror shutter of the camera is split so that part of it goes to the viewfinder and part goes to the video camera. This allows the director to see the shot on a video monitor as it is being filmed. The shot may also be recorded by connecting a video recorder to the video assist. It is helpful for the director to determine if the performance and action were acceptable before moving on to the next shot.

Video Cables: Any cables needed to connect the video tap to the video monitor or recorder. They may connect the video tap to the monitor or the monitor to the video recorder. They may also be called coaxial cables or BNC cables.

Video Monitor: A television monitor that is used along with the video tap to allow the Director to view the shot during filming. *See Video Assist.*

Video Tap: This is a video camera that is attached to the film camera during shooting. It is used by the Director to view the shot on the video monitor as it is being filmed. The image entering the lens is split so that part of it goes to the video camera and is sent by cable to the video monitor. *See Video Assist.*

Viewfinder: The attachment on the camera that allows the Camera Operator to view the action. Today's modern film cameras all contain a reflex viewfinder system. This allows the Camera Operator to line up the shot and view it during filming exactly as it will appear on film. The image coming through the lens is reflected onto a mirror shutter and is formed on a ground glass, which is seen through the viewfinder by the Camera Operator. The ground glass allows the operator to focus the image properly. *See Eyepiece.*

Vignetting: Term used to indicate that a portion of the matte box or lens shade is visible or blocking the frame when viewing through the lens. It usually occurs on a very wide-angle lens. When looking through the viewfinder, the operator should look around all of the edges of the frame to be sure that nothing is creeping in or blocking any of the frame. In most cases all that is needed to correct this problem is to slide the matte box back or remove the lens shade, so that it no longer is seen through the viewfinder.

Vinten: Trade name of a brand of professional fluid camera head.

Vitesse: Trade name of a brand of professional motion picture gear head.

Waste (W): The amount of footage remaining on a roll, which is left over after the Good and No Good footage have been totaled. It is too small to be called a short end and may be used as a dummy load. In 16 mm, waste is usually any roll that is less than 40 feet and in 35 mm it is any roll that is less than 100 feet. It is written in a section of the camera report and also on the film inventory report form.

Weaver Steadman: The trade name of a brand of professional motion picture fluid head.

Whip: A slang term used for a type of follow focus extension. It usually consists of a small round knob attached to a long flexible cable, which connects to the follow focus mechanism on the camera. It may also be called a focus whip.

Wide-Angle Lens: A lens that has a very short focal length or a focal length less than that of a normal lens. It may exaggerate perspective and covers a large angle of view. A wide-angle lens is most often used for establishing or long shots, but may be used for a close-up if the intent is to have a distorted image. When using a wide-angle lens, depth of field is greatly increased.

Wrap: The period at the end of a day's shooting or at the completion of the film or production, when all of the equipment is packed away. At the conclusion of filming entirely, the wrap usually consists of cleaning and packing the equipment and returning it to the rental house.

Wratten Filter: An optically correct gel filter that is used on a camera lens in place of or in addition to a glass filter. In many cases the gel filter is placed behind the lens in a special gel filter holder. These gels are different from the gels used on lights because they are manufactured to very high standards for use on photographic lenses. They are manufactured by Eastman Kodak and the common size of Wratten gels is 3 × 3 inches square.

Zeiss: Trade name of a brand of professional motion picture camera lens.

Zoom: The effect achieved by turning the barrel of the zoom lens, to change the focal length of the lens, so that the object in the frame appears to move either closer or farther away from the camera. Doing a zoom move with the lens is not the same as dollying with the camera without changing the lens focal length. When doing a zoom move, the relationship between objects in the frame remains the same.

Zoom In: The act of changing the focal length of the lens so that the angle of view decreases and the focal length of the lens increases. By doing this, the subject becomes larger in the frame. Zooming in decreases depth of field.

Zoom Lens: A lens that has varying focal lengths. It allows you to change the focal length by turning an adjustment ring on the barrel of the lens. An object can be held in focus while the angle of view and size of the object are changed during the shot. One advantage of the zoom lens is that it eliminates the need to put a new lens on the camera each time a new focal length is needed. By turning the barrel of the lens you are able to change the focal length. A disadvantage of using a zoom lens instead of a prime lens is that the image quality will not be as good. Because of the many different glass elements contained in a zoom lens, the amount of light reaching the film is reduced a small amount, which affects the depth of field.

Zoom Motor: A motor that attaches to the zoom lens to allow you to do a smooth zoom move during a shot. It may be built into the lens or it may be an additional item that you must attach to the lens.

Zoom Out: The act of changing the focal length of the lens so that the angle of view increases and the focal length of the lens decreases. By doing this, the subject becomes smaller in the frame. Zooming out increases depth of field.

Index